THE WORLD ALMANAC®
ATLAS
of the WORLD

Maps created by

MapQuest.com, Inc.

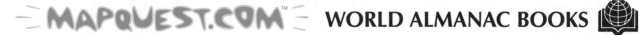 WORLD ALMANAC BOOKS

World Almanac Education Group Staff

Editorial Director
William A. McGeveran, Jr.

Director–Purchasing and Production
Edward A. Thomas

Managing Editor
Lori Wiesenfeld

Associate Editors
Mette Bahde, David M. Faris, Kevin Seabrooke

Desktop Production Manager
Lisa Lazzara

Publisher
Ken Park

Cover Design
Eileen Svajger

MapQuest.com/Digital Mapping Services Staff

Project Managers
Keith Winters, Robert Woolley

Project Coordinators
Matt DiBerardino, Andrew Green, Matt Tharp

Research & Compilation
Marley Amstutz, Laura Hartwig, Bill Truninger

Research Librarian
Craig Haggit

GIS
Dave Folk, Mark Leitzell

Cartographers
Brian Goudreau, Kendall Marten, Jeff Martz, Hylon Plumb

Editors
Robert Harding, Dana Wolf

Production Support
Shawna Roberts

TABLE OF CONTENTS

PORTRAIT OF THE U.S., CENSUS 2000

THE WORLD IN THE 21ST CENTURY

4 WORLD

6 ASIA and OCEANIA

8 Japan
9 North Korea, South Korea, Taiwan
10 China
11 Vietnam, Laos, Cambodia, Mongolia
12 Thailand, Myanmar (Burma), Philippines
13 Indonesia, Brunei, Singapore, Malaysia
14 Australia
15 Papua New Guinea, New Zealand, Federated States of Micronesia
16 Marshall Is., Nauru, Solomon Is., Tuvalu
17 Kiribati, Fiji, Palau, Tonga
18 Vanuatu, New Caledonia & Dependencies, Samoa, American Samoa
19 Nepal, Maldives, Bhutan, Sri Lanka
20 India
21 Bangladesh, Pakistan
22 Afghanistan, Iran, Turkmenistan
23 Kazakhstan, Uzbekistan, Kyrgyzstan, Tajikistan
24 Iraq, Kuwait, Saudi Arabia
25 Bahrain, Qatar, United Arab Emirates, Yemen, Oman
26 Lebanon, Israel, Jordan
27 Turkey, Cyprus, Syria

28 EUROPE

30 Great Britain & Northern Ireland
31 Republic of Ireland
32 Denmark, Netherlands
33 Belgium, Liechtenstein, Luxembourg
34 France
35 Monaco, Switzerland
36 Portugal, Malta, Gibraltar, Andorra
37 Spain
38 Italy
39 Austria, Vatican City, San Marino
40 Germany
41 Poland
42 Czech Republic, Slovakia
43 Hungary, Romania
44 Russia
45 Armenia, Georgia, Azerbaijan
46 Estonia, Latvia, Lithuania
47 Belarus, Ukraine
48 Slovenia, Croatia, Bosnia & Herzegovina, F.Y.R. Macedonia
49 Albania, Yugoslavia
50 Moldova, Bulgaria
51 Greece
52 Iceland, Norway
53 Sweden, Finland

54 AFRICA

56 Egypt, Libya
57 Algeria, Tunisia, Morocco
58 Western Sahara, Cape Verde, Mali, Mauritania
59 Chad, Niger, Sudan
60 Eritrea, Djibouti, Ethiopia, Somalia
61 Kenya, Uganda, Rwanda, Burundi
62 Senegal, The Gambia, Guinea, Guinea-Bissau
63 Sierra Leone, Côte d'Ivoire, São Tomé & Príncipe, Liberia
64 Ghana, Burkina Faso, Benin, Togo
65 Nigeria, Cameroon
66 Equatorial Guinea, Republic of the Congo, Gabon, Central African Republic
67 Comoros, Democratic Republic of the Congo, Zambia
68 Tanzania, Malawi, Mozambique
69 Mauritius, Zimbabwe, Botswana, Madagascar
70 Angola, Namibia, Seychelles
71 South Africa, Swaziland, Lesotho

72 SOUTH AMERICA

74 Argentina
75 Paraguay, Uruguay
76 Chile
77 Peru, Bolivia
78 Colombia
79 Ecuador, Venezuela
80 Guyana, Suriname, French Guiana
81 Brazil

82 NORTH AMERICA

84 Mexico
85 Belize, Guatemala
86 Honduras, El Salvador, Costa Rica
87 Nicaragua, Panama
88 Cuba, Jamaica
89 Dominican Republic, Haiti, Bahamas, Turks & Caicos Is.
90 Puerto Rico, Antigua & Barbuda, St. Kitts & Nevis, Dominica
91 St. Lucia, Barbados, St. Vincent & the Grenadines, Grenada, Trinidad & Tobago
92 Canada
93 Canadian Provincial & Territorial Flags
94 Alberta
95 British Columbia
96 Manitoba
97 New Brunswick
98 Newfoundland
99 Northwest Territories, Nunavut
100 Nova Scotia, Prince Edward Island
101 Ontario, Québec
102 Southern Ontario
103 Southern Québec
104 Saskatchewan
105 Yukon Territory

POLAR REGIONS

106 Arctic Regions, Greenland
107 Antarctica

108 WORLD INDEX

UNITED STATES

126 U.S. Political
127 U.S. Physical
128 Alabama
129 Alaska
130 Arizona
131 Arkansas
132 California
133 Colorado
134 Connecticut
135 Delaware
136 Florida
137 Georgia
138 Hawaii
139 Idaho
140 Illinois
141 Indiana
142 Iowa
143 Kansas
144 Kentucky
145 Louisiana
146 Maine
147 Maryland
148 Massachusetts
149 Michigan
150 Minnesota
151 Mississippi
152 Missouri
153 Montana
154 Nebraska
155 Nevada
156 New Hampshire
157 New Jersey
158 New Mexico
159 New York
160 North Carolina
161 North Dakota
162 Ohio
163 Oklahoma
164 Oregon
165 Pennsylvania
166 Rhode Island
167 South Carolina
168 South Dakota
169 Tennessee
170 Texas
171 Utah
172 Vermont
173 Virginia
174 Washington
175 West Virginia
176 Wisconsin
177 Wyoming

178 STATE INDEXES

General

⊛ National Capital

★ Territorial Capital

• Other City

International Boundary (subject area)

International Boundary (non-subject)

Internal Boundary (state, province, etc.)

----- Disputed Boundary

Perennial River

Intermittent River

Canal

Dam

U.S. States, Canadian Provinces & Territories
(additions and changes to general legend)

★ State Capital

◉ County Seat

Built Up Area

State Boundary

County Boundary

National Park

Other Park, Forest, Grassland

Indian, Other Reservation

■ Point of Interest

▲ Mountain Peak

·········· Continental Divide

········· Time Zone Boundary

Limited Access Highway

Other Major Road

(90) Highway Shield

PROJECTION

The only true representation of the Earth, free of distortion, is a globe. Maps are flat, and the process by which the geographic locations (latitude and longitude) are transformed from a three-dimensional sphere to a two-dimensional flat map is called a Projection.

For a detailed explanation of Projections, see *MapScope* in Volume 2 of *Funk & Wagnalls New Encyclopedia.*

TYPES OF SCALE

VISUAL SCALE

Every map has a bar scale, or a Visual Scale, that can be used for measuring. It shows graphically the relationship between map distance and ground distance.

Miles

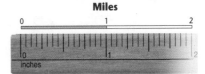

One inch represents 1 mile

Kilometers

One centimeter represents 10 kilometers

REPRESENTATIVE FRACTION

The scale of a map, expressed as a numerical ratio of map distance to ground distance, is called a Representative Fraction (or RF). It is usually written as 1/50,000 or 1:50,000, meaning that one unit of measurement on the map represents 50,000 of the same units on the ground.

This example is used on pages 20, 21 for India, Bangladesh, and Pakistan.

— The Globe is centered on the continent of Asia, as shown on pages 6, 7.

— The subject countries are shown in a stronger red/brown color.

LOCATOR

U.S. CENSUS 2000

The following four pages look at results from Census 2000. Some highlights:
- The U.S. population increased a remarkable 13.2% over 1990.
- Most growth was in the South and West. California had the largest increase (4,111,627) and Nevada had the largest percentage increase (66.3%).
- The Hispanic population grew 57.9% since 1990, reaching 35.3 million, or 12.5% of the total population.

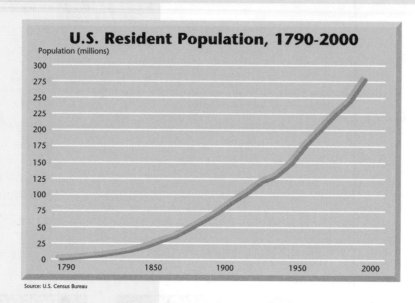

U.S. Resident Population, 1790-2000

Population (millions)

Source: U.S. Census Bureau

United States Resident Population per Census

2000	281,421,906
1990	248,709,873
1980	226,542,199
1970	203,302,031
1960	179,323,175
1950	151,325,798
1940	132,164,569
1930	123,202,624
1920	106,021,537
1910	92,228,496
1900	76,212,168
1890	62,979,766
1880	50,189,209
1870	38,558,371
1860	31,443,321
1850	23,191,876
1840	17,063,353
1830	12,860,702
1820	9,638,453
1810	7,239,881
1800	5,308,483
1790	3,929,214

Source: U.S. Census Bureau

Population Density, 2000
(persons per sq. mi., land area only)

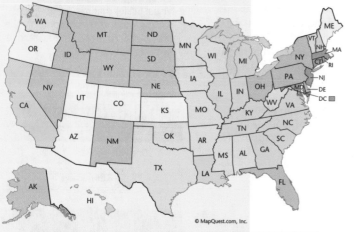

© MapQuest.com, Inc.

Most People per Sq. Mi.

Washington, D.C.	9,378.0
New Jersey	1,134.5
Rhode Island	1,003.2
Massachusetts	809.8
Connecticut	702.9

Fewest People per Sq. Mi.

Alaska	1.1
Wyoming	5.1
Montana	6.2
North Dakota	9.3
South Dakota	9.9

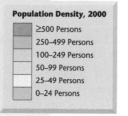

Population Density, 2000

- ≥500 Persons
- 250–499 Persons
- 100–249 Persons
- 50–99 Persons
- 25–49 Persons
- 0–24 Persons

New Apportionment in U.S. House of Representatives

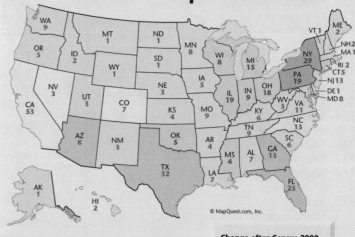

© MapQuest.com, Inc.

Apportionment is the process of dividing the 435 seats in the U.S. House of Representatives among the states. The apportionment calculation is based upon the total resident population of each state as determined by the latest U.S. Census.

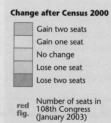

Change after Census 2000

- Gain two seats
- Gain one seat
- No change
- Lose one seat
- Lose two seats

red fig. Number of seats in 108th Congress (January 2003)

ercent Change in State
Population, 1990-2000

Percent Change, 1990–2000

- ≥30.0% increase
- 25.0–29.9% increase
- 20.0–24.9% increase
- 15.0–19.9% increase
- 10.0–14.9% increase
- 5.0–9.9% increase
- 0–4.9% increase
- decrease

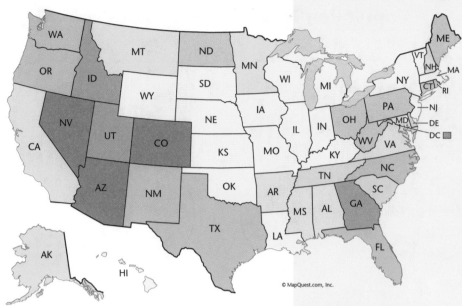

© MapQuest.com, Inc.

Population by State, 1990-2000

Source: U.S. Census Bureau

	2000 Pop.	1990 Pop.	Percent Change
ma	4,447,100	4,040,587	10.1
a	626,932	550,043	14.0
na	5,130,632	3,665,228	40.0
sas	2,673,400	2,350,725	13.7
rnia	33,871,648	29,760,021	13.8
ado	4,301,261	3,294,394	30.6
ecticut	3,405,565	3,287,116	3.6
vare	783,600	666,168	17.6
t of Columbia	572,059	606,900	-5.7
a	15,982,378	12,937,926	23.5
gia	8,186,453	6,478,216	26.4
ii	1,211,537	1,108,229	9.3
	1,293,953	1,006,749	28.5
s	12,419,293	11,430,602	8.6
na	6,080,485	5,544,159	9.7
s	2,926,324	2,776,755	5.4
s	2,688,418	2,477,574	8.5
cky	4,041,769	3,685,296	9.7
ana	4,468,976	4,219,973	5.9
e	1,274,923	1,227,928	3.8
and	5,296,486	4,781,468	10.8
achusetts	6,349,097	6,016,425	5.5
gan	9,938,444	9,295,297	6.9
esota	4,919,479	4,375,099	12.4
ssippi	2,844,658	2,573,216	10.5
uri	5,595,211	5,117,073	9.3
ana	902,195	799,065	12.9
aska	1,711,263	1,578,385	8.4
da	1,998,257	1,201,833	66.3
Hampshire	1,235,786	1,109,252	11.4
Jersey	8,414,350	7,730,188	8.9
Mexico	1,819,046	1,515,069	20.1
York	18,976,457	17,990,455	5.5
Carolina	8,049,313	6,628,637	21.4
Dakota	642,200	638,800	0.5
	11,353,140	10,847,115	4.7
oma	3,450,654	3,145,585	9.7
on	3,421,399	2,842,321	20.4
sylvania	12,281,054	11,881,643	3.4
e Island	1,048,319	1,003,464	4.5
Carolina	4,012,012	3,486,703	15.1
Dakota	754,844	696,004	8.5
essee	5,689,283	4,877,185	16.7
	20,851,820	16,986,510	22.8
	2,233,169	1,722,850	29.6
ont	608,827	562,758	8.2
ia	7,078,515	6,187,358	14.4
ington	5,894,121	4,866,692	21.1
Virginia	1,808,344	1,793,477	0.8
nsin	5,363,675	4,891,769	9.7
ing	493,782	453,588	8.9

Distribution of Population by Region, 1900, 1950, 2000

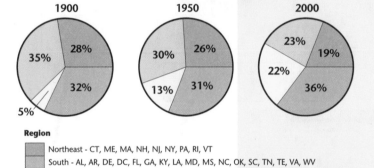

1900
- 35%
- 28%
- 32%
- 5%

1950
- 30%
- 26%
- 13%
- 31%

2000
- 23%
- 19%
- 22%
- 36%

Region
- Northeast - CT, ME, MA, NH, NJ, NY, PA, RI, VT
- South - AL, AR, DE, DC, FL, GA, KY, LA, MD, MS, NC, OK, SC, TN, TE, VA, WV
- Midwest - IL, IN, IA, KS, MI, MN, MO, NE, ND, OH, SD, WI
- West - AK, AZ, CA, CO, HI, ID, MT, NV, NM, OR, UT, WA, WY

Source: U.S. Census Bureau

U.S. Center of Population

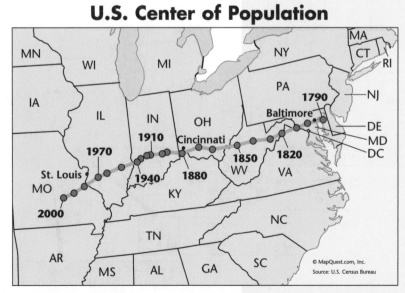

© MapQuest.com, Inc.
Source: U.S. Census Bureau

U.S. Center of Population = center of population gravity, or the point on which the U.S. would balance if it were a rigid plane, assuming all individuals weigh the same and exert influence proportional to their distance from a central point

Population Breakdown by Race and Hispanic or Latino Origin

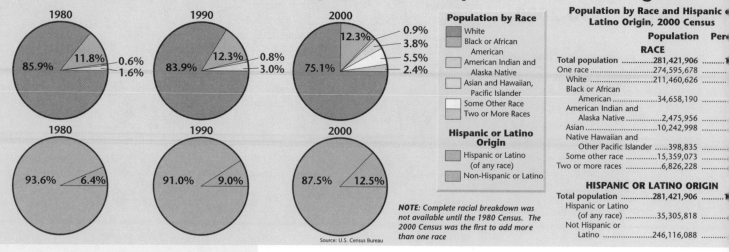

1980
85.9% · 11.8% · 0.6% · 1.6%

1990
83.9% · 12.3% · 0.8% · 3.0%

2000
75.1% · 12.3% · 0.9% · 3.8% · 5.5% · 2.4%

Population by Race
- White
- Black or African American
- American Indian and Alaska Native
- Asian and Hawaiian, Pacific Islander
- Some Other Race
- Two or More Races

Hispanic or Latino Origin
- Hispanic or Latino (of any race)
- Non-Hispanic or Latino

1980
93.6% · 6.4%

1990
91.0% · 9.0%

2000
87.5% · 12.5%

Source: U.S. Census Bureau

NOTE: *Complete racial breakdown was not available until the 1980 Census. The 2000 Census was the first to add more than one race*

Population by Race and Hispanic or Latino Origin, 2000 Census

	Population	Per
RACE		
Total population	281,421,906	
One race	274,595,678	
White	211,460,626	
Black or African American	34,658,190	
American Indian and Alaska Native	2,475,956	
Asian	10,242,998	
Native Hawaiian and Other Pacific Islander	398,835	
Some other race	15,359,073	
Two or more races	6,826,228	
HISPANIC OR LATINO ORIGIN		
Total population	281,421,906	
Hispanic or Latino (of any race)	35,305,818	
Not Hispanic or Latino	246,116,088	

20 Largest Metropolitan Areas, 2000 Census

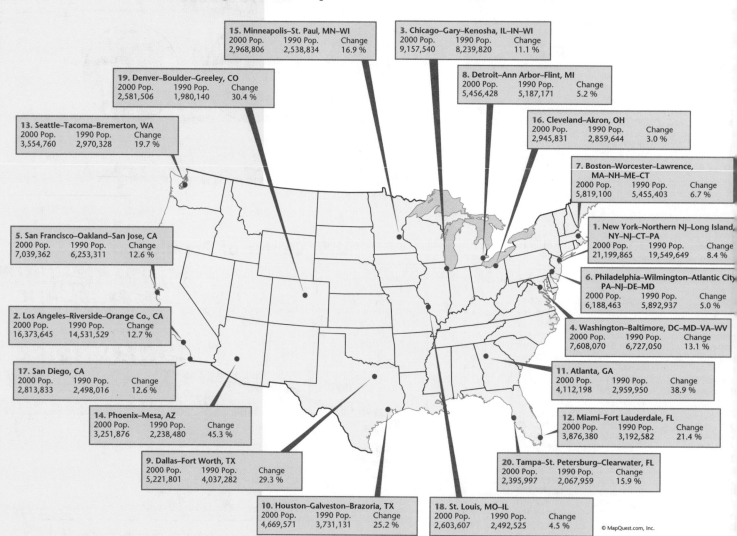

15. Minneapolis–St. Paul, MN–WI
2000 Pop.	1990 Pop.	Change
2,968,806	2,538,834	16.9 %

3. Chicago–Gary–Kenosha, IL–IN–WI
2000 Pop.	1990 Pop.	Change
9,157,540	8,239,820	11.1 %

19. Denver–Boulder–Greeley, CO
2000 Pop.	1990 Pop.	Change
2,581,506	1,980,140	30.4 %

8. Detroit–Ann Arbor–Flint, MI
2000 Pop.	1990 Pop.	Change
5,456,428	5,187,171	5.2 %

13. Seattle–Tacoma–Bremerton, WA
2000 Pop.	1990 Pop.	Change
3,554,760	2,970,328	19.7 %

16. Cleveland–Akron, OH
2000 Pop.	1990 Pop.	Change
2,945,831	2,859,644	3.0 %

7. Boston–Worcester–Lawrence, MA–NH–ME–CT
2000 Pop.	1990 Pop.	Change
5,819,100	5,455,403	6.7 %

5. San Francisco–Oakland–San Jose, CA
2000 Pop.	1990 Pop.	Change
7,039,362	6,253,311	12.6 %

1. New York–Northern NJ–Long Island, NY–NJ–CT–PA
2000 Pop.	1990 Pop.	Change
21,199,865	19,549,649	8.4 %

6. Philadelphia–Wilmington–Atlantic City, PA–NJ–DE–MD
2000 Pop.	1990 Pop.	Change
6,188,463	5,892,937	5.0 %

2. Los Angeles–Riverside–Orange Co., CA
2000 Pop.	1990 Pop.	Change
16,373,645	14,531,529	12.7 %

4. Washington–Baltimore, DC–MD–VA–WV
2000 Pop.	1990 Pop.	Change
7,608,070	6,727,050	13.1 %

17. San Diego, CA
2000 Pop.	1990 Pop.	Change
2,813,833	2,498,016	12.6 %

11. Atlanta, GA
2000 Pop.	1990 Pop.	Change
4,112,198	2,959,950	38.9 %

14. Phoenix–Mesa, AZ
2000 Pop.	1990 Pop.	Change
3,251,876	2,238,480	45.3 %

12. Miami–Fort Lauderdale, FL
2000 Pop.	1990 Pop.	Change
3,876,380	3,192,582	21.4 %

9. Dallas–Fort Worth, TX
2000 Pop.	1990 Pop.	Change
5,221,801	4,037,282	29.3 %

20. Tampa–St. Petersburg–Clearwater, FL
2000 Pop.	1990 Pop.	Change
2,395,997	2,067,959	15.9 %

10. Houston–Galveston–Brazoria, TX
2000 Pop.	1990 Pop.	Change
4,669,571	3,731,131	25.2 %

18. St. Louis, MO–IL
2000 Pop.	1990 Pop.	Change
2,603,607	2,492,525	4.5 %

© MapQuest.com, Inc.

20 Largest Cities, 2000 Census

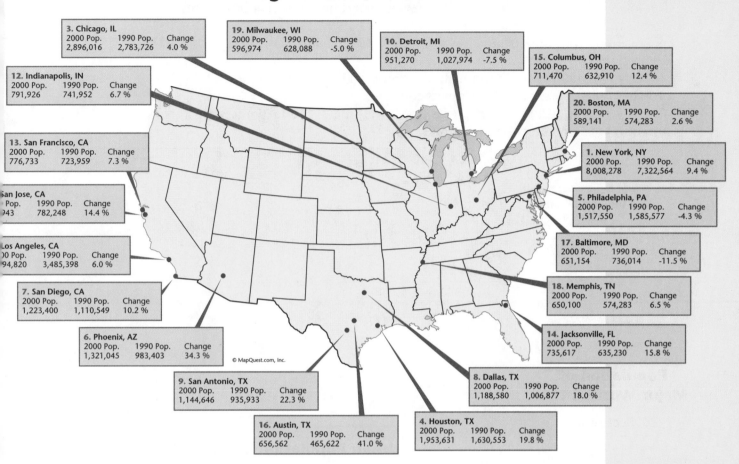

3. Chicago, IL
2000 Pop.	1990 Pop.	Change
2,896,016	2,783,726	4.0 %

19. Milwaukee, WI
2000 Pop.	1990 Pop.	Change
596,974	628,088	-5.0 %

10. Detroit, MI
2000 Pop.	1990 Pop.	Change
951,270	1,027,974	-7.5 %

15. Columbus, OH
2000 Pop.	1990 Pop.	Change
711,470	632,910	12.4 %

12. Indianapolis, IN
2000 Pop.	1990 Pop.	Change
791,926	741,952	6.7 %

20. Boston, MA
2000 Pop.	1990 Pop.	Change
589,141	574,283	2.6 %

13. San Francisco, CA
2000 Pop.	1990 Pop.	Change
776,733	723,959	7.3 %

1. New York, NY
2000 Pop.	1990 Pop.	Change
8,008,278	7,322,564	9.4 %

San Jose, CA
Pop.	1990 Pop.	Change
943	782,248	14.4 %

5. Philadelphia, PA
2000 Pop.	1990 Pop.	Change
1,517,550	1,585,577	-4.3 %

Los Angeles, CA
0 Pop.	1990 Pop.	Change
94,820	3,485,398	6.0 %

17. Baltimore, MD
2000 Pop.	1990 Pop.	Change
651,154	736,014	-11.5 %

7. San Diego, CA
2000 Pop.	1990 Pop.	Change
1,223,400	1,110,549	10.2 %

18. Memphis, TN
2000 Pop.	1990 Pop.	Change
650,100	574,283	6.5 %

6. Phoenix, AZ
2000 Pop.	1990 Pop.	Change
1,321,045	983,403	34.3 %

© MapQuest.com, Inc.

14. Jacksonville, FL
2000 Pop.	1990 Pop.	Change
735,617	635,230	15.8 %

9. San Antonio, TX
2000 Pop.	1990 Pop.	Change
1,144,646	935,933	22.3 %

8. Dallas, TX
2000 Pop.	1990 Pop.	Change
1,188,580	1,006,877	18.0 %

16. Austin, TX
2000 Pop.	1990 Pop.	Change
656,562	465,622	41.0 %

4. Houston, TX
2000 Pop.	1990 Pop.	Change
1,953,631	1,630,553	19.8 %

Percent of Population by Race and Hispanic or Latino Origin for the 20 Largest Cities

City		2000 Population	White	Black or African American	American Indian, Alaska Native	Asian	Hawaiian & Other Pacific Islander	Some Other Race	Two or More Races	Hispanic or Latino (of any race)
New York	NY	8,008,278	44.7	26.6	0.5	9.8	0.1	13.4	4.9	27.0
Los Angeles	CA	3,694,820	46.9	11.2	0.8	10.0	0.2	25.7	5.2	46.5
Chicago	IL	2,896,016	42.0	36.8	0.4	4.3	0.1	13.6	2.9	26.0
Houston	TX	1,953,631	49.3	25.3	0.4	5.3	0.1	16.5	3.1	37.4
Philadelphia	PA	1,517,550	45.0	43.2	0.3	4.5	0.0	4.8	2.2	8.5
Phoenix	AZ	1,321,045	71.1	5.1	2.0	2.0	0.1	16.4	3.3	34.1
San Diego	CA	1,223,400	60.2	7.9	0.6	13.6	0.5	12.4	4.8	25.4
Dallas	TX	1,188,580	50.8	25.9	0.5	2.7	0.0	17.2	2.7	35.6
San Antonio	TX	1,144,646	67.7	6.8	0.8	1.6	0.1	19.3	3.7	58.7
Detroit	MI	951,270	12.3	81.6	0.3	1.0	0.0	2.5	2.3	5.0
San Jose	CA	894,943	47.5	3.5	0.8	26.9	0.4	15.9	5.0	30.2
Indianapolis	IN	791,926	69.3	25.3	0.3	1.4	0.0	2.0	1.6	3.9
San Francisco	CA	776,733	49.7	7.8	0.4	30.8	0.5	6.5	4.3	14.1
Jacksonville	FL	735,617	64.5	29.0	0.3	2.8	0.1	1.3	2.0	4.2
Columbus	OH	711,470	67.9	24.5	0.3	3.4	0.1	1.2	2.6	2.5
Austin	TX	656,562	65.4	10.0	0.6	4.7	0.1	16.2	3.0	30.5
Baltimore	MD	651,154	31.6	64.3	0.3	1.5	0.0	0.7	1.5	1.7
Memphis	TN	650,100	34.4	61.4	0.2	1.5	0.0	1.5	1.0	3.0
Milwaukee	WI	596,974	50.0	37.3	0.9	2.9	0.0	6.1	2.7	12.0
Boston	MA	589,141	54.5	25.3	0.4	7.5	0.1	7.8	4.4	14.4

Source: U.S. Census Bureau

THE WORLD IN THE 21ST CENTURY

The following four pages look at the growing world population and the latest trends in health and mortality. Some highlights:

• The world population has passed 6.1 billion, with 1.3 billion people in China alone.

• By 2050 the world population may pass 11 billion, with most of the growth in urban areas and developing countries.

• The highest life expectancies and lowest infant mortality rates are in North America, Western Europe, and Australia.

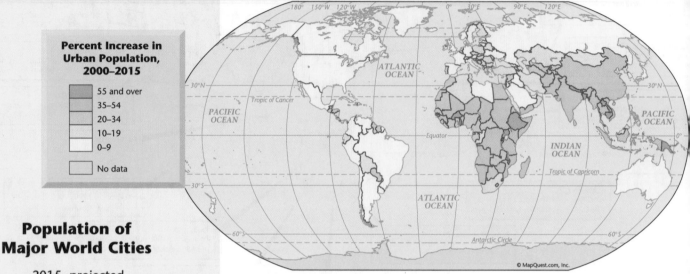

Percent Increase in Urban Population, 2000–2015

- 55 and over
- 35–54
- 20–34
- 10–19
- 0–9
- No data

Source: *UN World Resources*, pp. 274–275.

Urban Population Growth, 2000–2015

The world population will become increasingly urbanized in the early 21st century. It is predicted that the largest increases in urban population will occur in Africa and southern and eastern Asia.

Population of Major World Cities

2015, projected

1	Tokyo	28,887,000
2	Mumbai	26,218,000
3	Lagos	24,640,000
4	São Paulo	20,320,000
5	Mexico City	19,180,000
6	Shanghai	17,969,000
7	New York	17,602,000
8	Kolkata	17,305,000
9	Delhi	16,860,000
10	Beijing	15,572,000
11	Los Angeles	14,217,000
12	Buenos Aires	13,856,000
13	Seoul	12,980,000
14	Rio de Janeiro	11,860,000
15	Osaka	10,609,000

These figures are for "urban agglomerations," which are densely populated urban areas, larger than the cities by themselves.

Source: UN, Dept. for Economic and Social Information and Policy Analysis

© MapQuest.com, Inc.

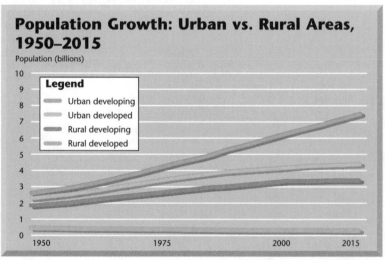

Population Growth: Urban vs. Rural Areas, 1950–2015

Population (billions)

Legend
- Urban developing
- Urban developed
- Rural developing
- Rural developed

Source: *UN World Resources*, p. 146.

Population growth in rural areas will taper off where it has not already. But urban growth will increase, especially in the developing nations.

Developed regions include United States, Canada, Japan, Europe, and Australia and New Zealand.

Developing regions include Africa, Asia (excluding Japan), South America and Central America, Mexico, and Oceania (excluding Australia and New Zealand). The European successor states of the former Soviet Union are classified as developed regions, while the Asian successor states are classified as developing regions.

Population Density, 2000

Population

Persons per sq. mi.		Persons per sq. km.
and over		200 and over
260–519		100–199
130–259		50–99
25–129		10–49
1–24		1–9
under 1		under 1

© MapQuest.com, Inc.

World population total (May 1, 2001): 6,144,488,802

Source: International Programs Center, U.S. Census Bureau

Population Density, Largest Countries

2000

	People per square mile
China	330
India	800
United States	70
Indonesia	290
Brazil	50
Russia	20

2050

	People per square mile
China	360
India	1,400
United States	100
Indonesia	450
Brazil	70
Russia	20

The world is becoming more crowded in the 21st century. In mid-2000, China already had the highest population in the world, with an estimated 1.3 billion inhabitants, more than one-fifth of the total population. India had passed 1 billion, while the United States had the world's third-largest population, with about 281 million, followed by Indonesia, Brazil, and Pakistan.

Source: U.S. Census Bureau

Anticipated World Population Growth

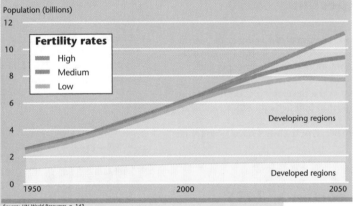

Population (billions)

Fertility rates
- High
- Medium
- Low

Developing regions

Developed regions

1950   2000   2050

Source: *UN World Resources*, p. 143.

The world population has grown from about 2 billion in 1950 to more than 6 billion today, and could almost double by 2050. Most of the growth will continue to occur in developing regions, where fertility rates (number of children born per woman of childbearing age) are relatively high.

Where the fertility rate is around 2 children per woman of childbearing age, the population will tend to stabilize. This figure indicates roughly that couples, over a lifetime, are replacing themselves without adding to the population.

Population experts at the United Nations actually give three different projections for future population growth. Under a **high** fertility-rate projection, which assumes rates would stabilize at an average of 2.6 in high-fertility regions and 2.1 in low-fertility regions, the global population would reach 11.2 billion by 2050. Under a **medium** projection, which assumes rates would ultimately stabilize at around replacement levels, the population would rise to 9.4 billion by 2050. Under a **low** fertility-rate projection, which assumes rates would eventually stabilize at lower-than-replacement levels, the world population would still reach about 7.7 billion by 2050.

Population Projections by Continent

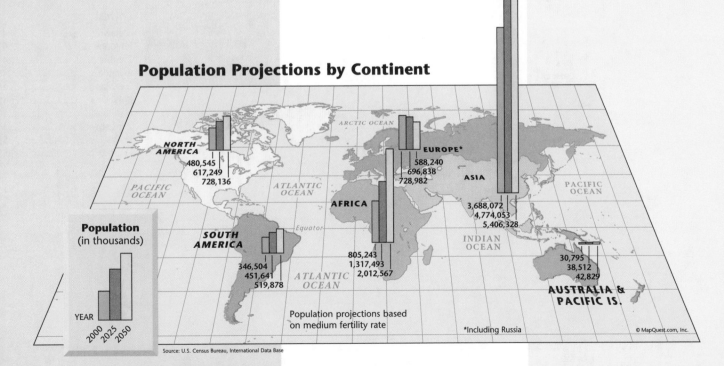

NORTH AMERICA
480,545
617,249
728,136

EUROPE*
588,240
696,838
728,982

ASIA
3,688,072
4,774,053
5,406,328

AFRICA
805,243
1,317,493
2,012,567

SOUTH AMERICA
346,504
451,641
519,878

AUSTRALIA & PACIFIC IS.
30,795
38,512
42,829

Population (in thousands)

YEAR
2000 2025 2050

Population projections based on medium fertility rate

*Including Russia

© MapQuest.com, Inc.

Source: U.S. Census Bureau, International Data Base

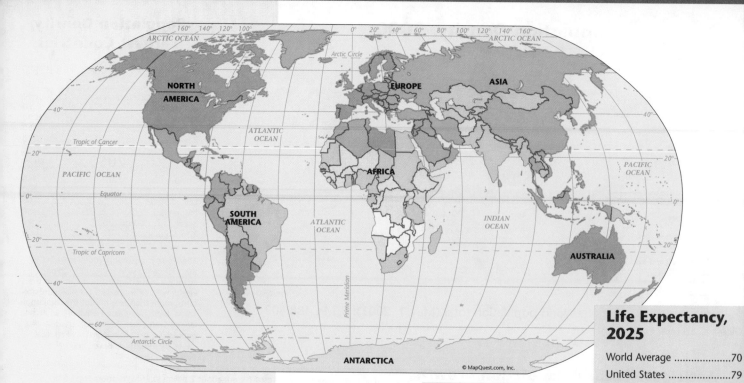

World Life Expectancy, 2000

Life Expectancy (in years)

- 75–84
- 65–74
- 50–64
- 40–49
- Less than 40
- No data

Life expectancy at birth is a common measure of the number of years a person may expect to live. There are many factors, such as nutrition, sanitation, health and medical services, that contribute to helping people live longer.

As some of the above factors improve in the developing countries, life expectancy there should increase. But most of Sub-Saharan Africa will have less than average life expectancies.

Although it is not indicated here, females almost always have a longer life expectancy than males.

World Life Expectancy, 2025

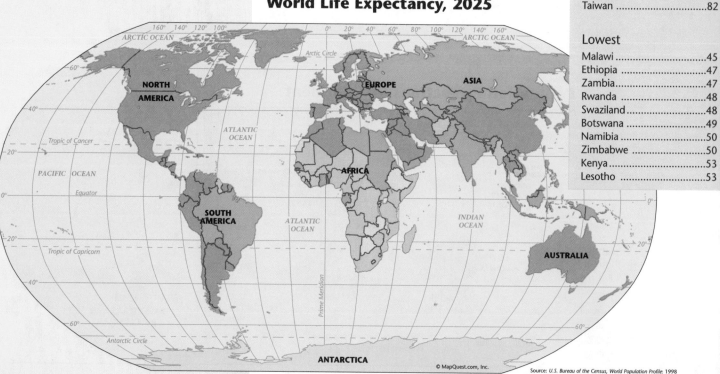

Life Expectancy, 2025

World Average	70
United States	79

Highest

Andorra	84
Austria	84
Australia	83
Canada	82
Cyprus	82
Dominica	82
Israel	82
Japan	82
Kuwait	82
Monaco	82
San Marino	82
Singapore	82
Taiwan	82

Lowest

Malawi	45
Ethiopia	47
Zambia	47
Rwanda	48
Swaziland	48
Botswana	49
Namibia	50
Zimbabwe	50
Kenya	53
Lesotho	53

Source: U.S. Bureau of the Census, World Population Profile: 1998

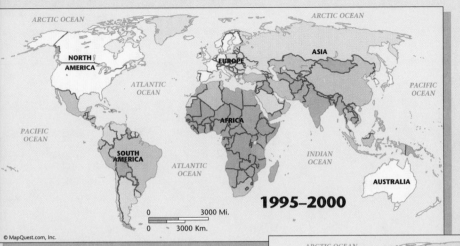

1995–2000

© MapQuest.com, Inc.

Infant Mortality Averages, 2015–2020
by continent with highest and lowest country

World Average 35

Africa 55	Europe 8
Sierra Leone 114	Albania 20
Mauritius 8	Austria
	& 14 others..........5
Asia 32	
Afghanistan 118	North America 22
Japan 4	Haiti 82
	Canada...................5
Australia & Oceania ..15	U.S. 5
Papua	
New Guinea 37	South America 23
Australia 5	Guyana.................37
	Chile.......................9

Infant Mortality

Infant mortality means the number of deaths before the age of one per 1,000 live births. It is a fairly common way of judging how healthy a country is. Presently there are about 14 countries with infant mortality rates lower than that of the United States.

With improvements in sanitation and health care, it is expected that infant mortality will decline substantially in the 21st century. However, it will continue to be a serious problem especially in Sub-Saharan Africa and other developing regions

Infant Mortality Rate
(per 1,000 live births)

- 85–169
- 50–85
- 25–49
- 10–24
- Less than 10
- No data

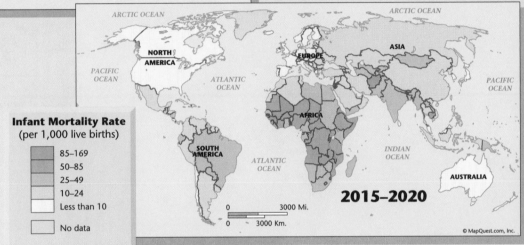

2015–2020

© MapQuest.com, Inc.

Source: UN Population Division and UN Children's Fund

Food & Nutrition

There has been a general trend towards better nutrition, but Sub-Saharan Africa remains a problem area: increasing numbers of people will be suffering from undernutrition.

On a worldwide basis, the food supply seems adequate. Unfortunately the availability of food and the distribution of people don't always match up.

Undernutrition in Developing Countries, 1969-2010

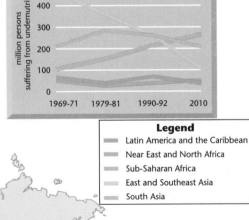

Legend
- Latin America and the Caribbean
- Near East and North Africa
- Sub-Saharan Africa
- East and Southeast Asia
- South Asia

Fertility

This rate is the number of births related to the number of women of childbearing age. Currently the rate for developed nations is about 1.6, but it is about 2.9 in developing nations.

Africa shows the slowest reduction in the fertility rate. With improvements in infant mortality and the implementation of family planning programs, the rate should stabilize.

Average Daily per Capita Calorie Supply, 1999
by continent with highest and lowest country

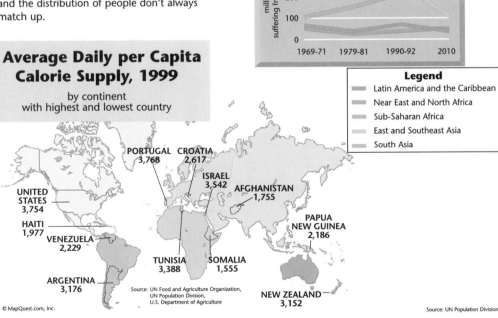

PORTUGAL 3,768
CROATIA 2,617
ISRAEL 3,542
AFGHANISTAN 1,755
UNITED STATES 3,754
HAITI 1,977
VENEZUELA 2,229
PAPUA NEW GUINEA 2,186
TUNISIA 3,388
SOMALIA 1,555
ARGENTINA 3,176
NEW ZEALAND 3,152

Source: UN Food and Agriculture Organization, UN Population Division, U.S. Department of Agriculture

© MapQuest.com, Inc.

Trends in Fertility Rates

Legend
- Africa
- Asia
- South and Central America
- Developed
- Developing

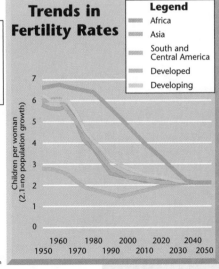

Source: UN Population Division

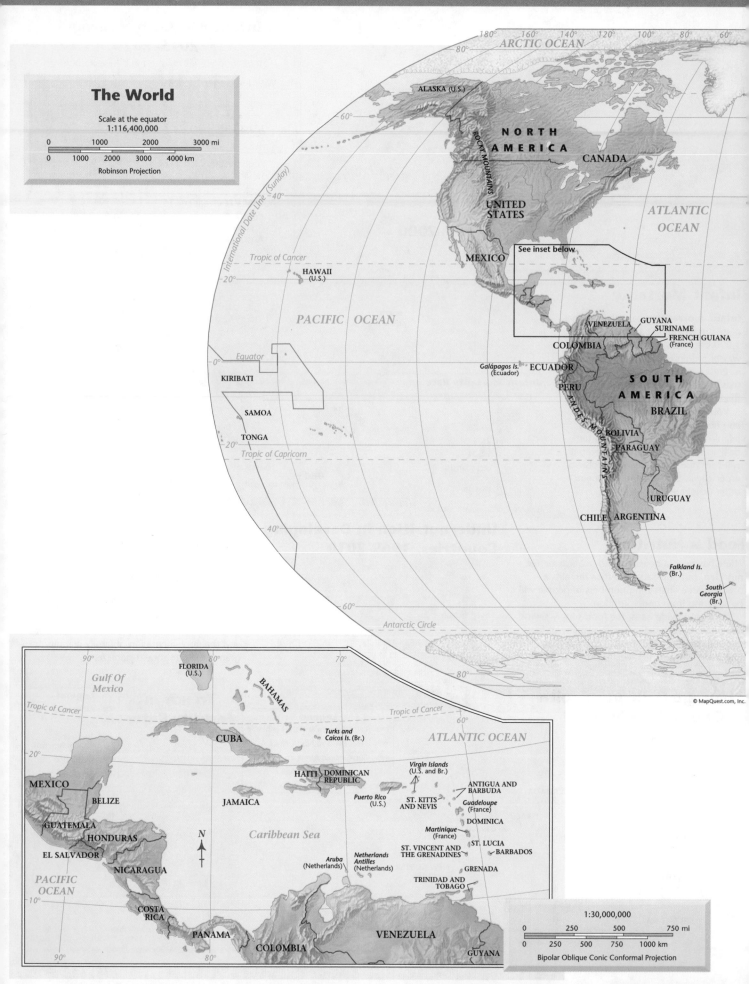

The World

Scale at the equator
1:116,400,000

0   1000   2000   3000 mi
0   1000   2000   3000   4000 km

Robinson Projection

ARCTIC OCEAN

180° 160° 140° 120° 100° 80° 60°
80°

ALASKA (U.S.)

60°

NORTH AMERICA

CANADA

ROCKY MOUNTAINS

40°

UNITED STATES

ATLANTIC OCEAN

MEXICO

See inset below

International Date Line (Sunday)

Tropic of Cancer

20°

HAWAII (U.S.)

VENEZUELA   GUYANA
SURINAME
FRENCH GUIANA
(France)

COLOMBIA

PACIFIC OCEAN

Galápagos Is.
(Ecuador)   ECUADOR

Equator   0°

KIRIBATI

PERU

SOUTH AMERICA

BRAZIL

ANDES MOUNTAINS

BOLIVIA

SAMOA

PARAGUAY

TONGA

20°

Tropic of Capricorn

URUGUAY

40°

CHILE   ARGENTINA

Falkland Is.
(Br.)

60°

South
Georgia
(Br.)

Antarctic Circle

80°

© MapQuest.com, Inc.

90°   80°   FLORIDA
(U.S.)   70°

Gulf Of
Mexico

BAHAMAS

Tropic of Cancer   Tropic of Cancer

60°

Turks and
Caicos Is. (Br.)   ATLANTIC OCEAN

20°

CUBA

MEXICO

HAITI   DOMINICAN
REPUBLIC

Virgin Islands
(U.S. and Br.)

ANTIGUA AND
BARBUDA

BELIZE

JAMAICA

Puerto Rico
(U.S.)

ST. KITTS
AND NEVIS

Guadeloupe
(France)

GUATEMALA

N

DOMINICA

HONDURAS

Caribbean Sea

Martinique
(France)

ST. LUCIA

EL SALVADOR

ST. VINCENT AND
THE GRENADINES

BARBADOS

NICARAGUA

Aruba
(Netherlands)

Netherlands
Antilles
(Netherlands)

GRENADA

PACIFIC
OCEAN

10°

COSTA
RICA

TRINIDAD AND
TOBAGO

PANAMA   VENEZUELA

COLOMBIA

GUYANA

90°   80°

1:30,000,000

0   250   500   750 mi
0   250   500   750   1000 km

Bipolar Oblique Conic Conformal Projection

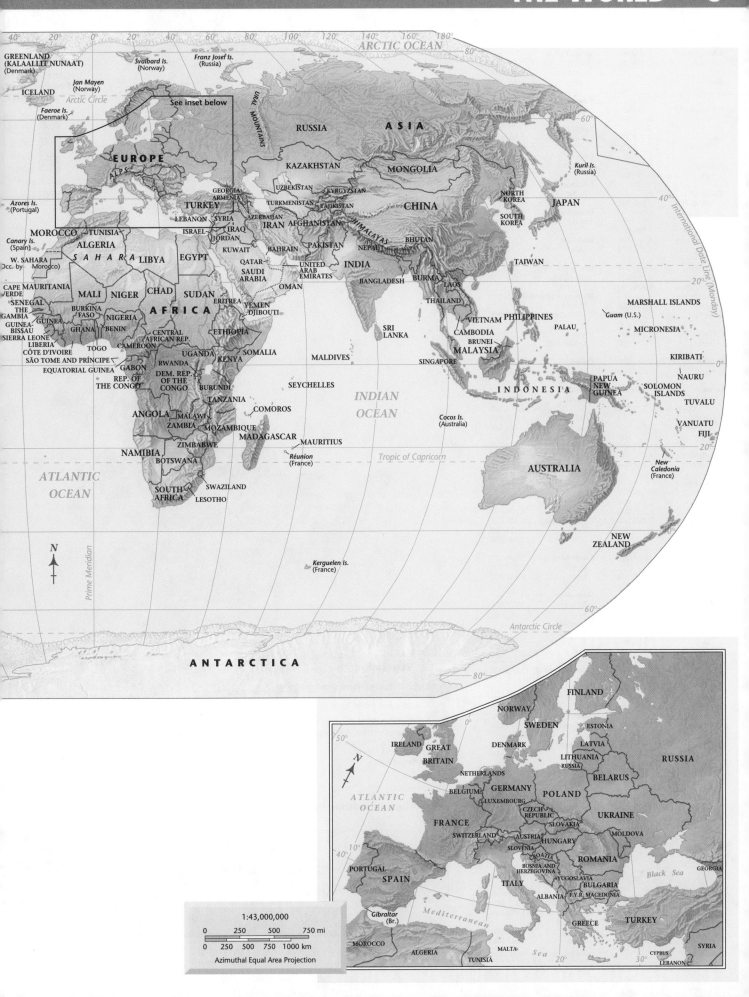

ARCTIC OCEAN

GREENLAND
(KALAALLIT NUNAAT)
(Denmark)

Svalbard Is.
(Norway)

Franz Josef Is.
(Russia)

ICELAND

Jan Mayen
(Norway)

Arctic Circle

ASIA

RUSSIA

See inset below

URAL MOUNTAINS

Faeroe Is.
(Denmark)

EUROPE

KAZAKHSTAN

MONGOLIA

Kuril Is.
(Russia)

ALPS

Azores Is.
(Portugal)

GEORGIA
ARMENIA

UZBEKISTAN
KYRGYZSTAN

CHINA

NORTH
KOREA

JAPAN

TURKEY

TURKMENISTAN
TAJIKISTAN

SOUTH
KOREA

International Date Line (Monday)

MOROCCO TUNISIA

LEBANON SYRIA
ISRAEL
JORDAN

AZERBAIJAN
IRAN AFGHANISTAN

HIMALAYAS

BHUTAN

Canary Is.
(Spain)

IRAQ

KUWAIT

BAHRAIN

PAKISTAN

NEPAL

TAIWAN

ALGERIA

SAHARA

LIBYA

EGYPT

QATAR
SAUDI
ARABIA

UNITED
ARAB
EMIRATES

INDIA

W. SAHARA
Occ. by
Morocco)

OMAN

BANGLADESH

BURMA

LAOS

MARSHALL ISLANDS

CAPE MAURITANIA
VERDE

MALI NIGER CHAD SUDAN

ERITREA

YEMEN
DJIBOUTI

THAILAND

VIETNAM PHILIPPINES

Guam (U.S.)

MICRONESIA

SENEGAL
THE
GAMBIA

AFRICA

SRI
LANKA

CAMBODIA

PALAU

GUINEA-
BISSAU
GUINEA

BURKINA
FASO

NIGERIA

BENIN

ETHIOPIA

MALDIVES

BRUNEI
MALAYSIA

KIRIBATI

SIERRA LEONE
LIBERIA
CÔTE D'IVOIRE

GHANA

CENTRAL
AFRICAN REP.

SINGAPORE

NAURU

SÃO TOME AND PRÍNCIPE

TOGO

CAMEROON

UGANDA
KENYA

SOMALIA

INDONESIA

PAPUA
NEW
GUINEA

SOLOMON
ISLANDS

EQUATORIAL GUINEA

GABON
REP. OF
THE CONGO

RWANDA
DEM. REP.
OF THE
CONGO

BURUNDI

SEYCHELLES

Cocos Is.
(Australia)

TUVALU

TANZANIA

INDIAN
OCEAN

VANUATU
FIJI

ANGOLA

MALAWI

ZAMBIA

COMOROS

New
Caledonia
(France)

ZIMBABWE

MOZAMBIQUE

MADAGASCAR

MAURITIUS

NAMIBIA

BOTSWANA

Réunion
(France)

Tropic of Capricorn

AUSTRALIA

ATLANTIC
OCEAN

SOUTH
AFRICA

SWAZILAND

LESOTHO

N

Prime Meridian

NEW
ZEALAND

Kerguelen Is.
(France)

Antarctic Circle

ANTARCTICA

1:43,000,000

0   250   500   750 mi

0   250 500 750 1000 km

Azimuthal Equal Area Projection

FINLAND

NORWAY

SWEDEN

ESTONIA

IRELAND GREAT
BRITAIN

DENMARK

LATVIA

RUSSIA

NETHERLANDS

LITHUANIA
RUSSIA

BELARUS

ATLANTIC
OCEAN

BELGIUM

GERMANY

POLAND

LUXEMBOURG

UKRAINE

FRANCE

CZECH
REPUBLIC

SLOVAKIA

SWITZERLAND

AUSTRIA

MOLDOVA

HUNGARY

SLOVENIA
CROATIA

ROMANIA

PORTUGAL

BOSNIA AND
HERZEGOVINA

YUGOSLAVIA

Black Sea

GEORGIA

SPAIN

ITALY

BULGARIA

ALBANIA

F.Y.R. MACEDONIA

Gibraltar
(Br.)

GREECE

TURKEY

Mediterranean

MOROCCO

ALGERIA

MALTA

Sea

CYPRUS
LEBANON

TUNISIA

SYRIA

MAJOR CITIES

Afghanistan	(metro)
Kabul	2,029,000
Bahrain	
Manama	151,000
Bangladesh	(metro)
Dhaka	8,545,000
Bhutan	
Thimphu	8,900
Brunei	
Band. Seri Begawan	51,000
Cambodia	
Phnom Penh	800,000
China	
Shanghai	7,500,000
Hong Kong	6,502,000
Beijing	5,700,000
Tianjin	4,500,000
Shenyang	3,600,000
Wuhan	3,200,000
Guangzhou	2,900,000
Chongqing	2,700,000
Harbin	2,500,000
Chengdu	2,500,000
Zibo	2,200,000
Xi'an	2,200,000
Nanjing	2,091,000
Cyprus	
Nicosia	193,000
India	(metro)
Mumbai	
(Bombay)	12,572,000
Kolkata	
(Calcutta)	10,916,000
Delhi	8,375,000
Madras	5,361,000
Hyderabad	4,280,000
Bangalore	4,087,000
Indonesia	
Jakarta	9,113,000
Surabaya	2,664,000
Bandung	2,356,000
Medan	1,844,000
Iran	
Tehran	6,750,000
Mashhad	1,964,000
Iraq	(metro)
Baghdad	4,336,000
Israel	
Jerusalem	585,000
Japan	
Tokyo	7,968,000
Yokohama	3,320,000
Osaka	2,600,000
Nagoya	2,151,000
Sapporo	1,774,000
Kyoto	1,464,000
Kobe	1,420,000
Fukuoka	1,296,000
Kawasaki	1,209,000
Hiroshima	1,115,000
Jordan	(metro)
Amman	1,183,000
Kazakhstan	
Almaty	
(Alma-Ata)	1,064,000
North Korea	
P'yŏngyang	2,741,000

South Korea	
Seoul	10,231,000
Pusan	3,814,000
Taegu	2,449,000
Kuwait	
Kuwait	29,000
Kyrgyzstan	
Bishkek	589,000
Laos	
Vientiane	377,000
Lebanon	(metro)
Beirut	1,826,000
Malaysia	(metro)
Kuala Lumpur	1,236,000
Maldives	
Male	55,000
Mongolia	
Ulaanbaatar	536,000
Myanmar (Burma)	(metro)
Yangon	
(Rangoon)	3,873,000
Nepal	
Kathmandu	419,000
Oman	
Muscat	85,000
Pakistan	(metro)
Karachi	5,181,000
Lahore	2,953,000
Faisalabad	1,104,000
Islamabad	204,000
Philippines	
Manila	1,655,000
Qatar	
Doha	236,000
Russia (Asian)	
Novosibirsk	1,368,000
Yekaterinburg	1,277,000
Omsk	1,161,000
Chelyabinsk	1,084,000
Saudi Arabia	(metro)
Riyadh	2,619,000
Jeddah	1,492,000
Singapore	
Singapore	3,737,000
Sri Lanka	
Colombo	615,000
Syria	
Damascus	1,549,000
Halab (Aleppo)	1,542,000
Taiwan	
Taipei	1,770,000
Tajikistan	
Dushanbe	529,000
Thailand	(metro)
Bangkok	6,547,000
Turkey (Asian)	
Ankara	2,938,000
İzmir	2,130,000
Turkmenistan	
Ashgabat	407,000
United Arab Emirates	
Abu Dhabi (metro)	799,000
Uzbekistan	(metro)
Tashkent	2,282,000
Vietnam	(metro)
Ho Chi Minh City	3,521,000
Hanoi	1,236,000
Yemen	(metro)
Sanaa	927,000

International comparability of city population
data is limited by various data inconsistencies.

© MapQuest.com, Inc.

Gross National Product (GNP) per capita

- $36,410
- $21,500
- $8625
- $2785
- $695
- $0
- No data

Vegetation

- Unclassified Highlands and Ice Cap
- Tundra and Alpine Tundra
- Coniferous Forest
- Midlatitude Deciduous Forest
- Subtropical Broadleaf Evergreen Forest
- Mixed Forest
- Midlatitude Scrub
- Midlatitude Grassland
- Desert
- Tropical Seasonal and Scrub
- Tropical Rain Forest
- Tropical Savanna

Asia: Population, by nation (in millions)*

CHINA	INDIA	INDON.	PAKIS.	BANGL.	JAPAN	PHILIP.	All other Asian countries
1254.2	1000.8	216.1	138.1	127.1	126.2	79.4	699.5*

*Excluding Russia

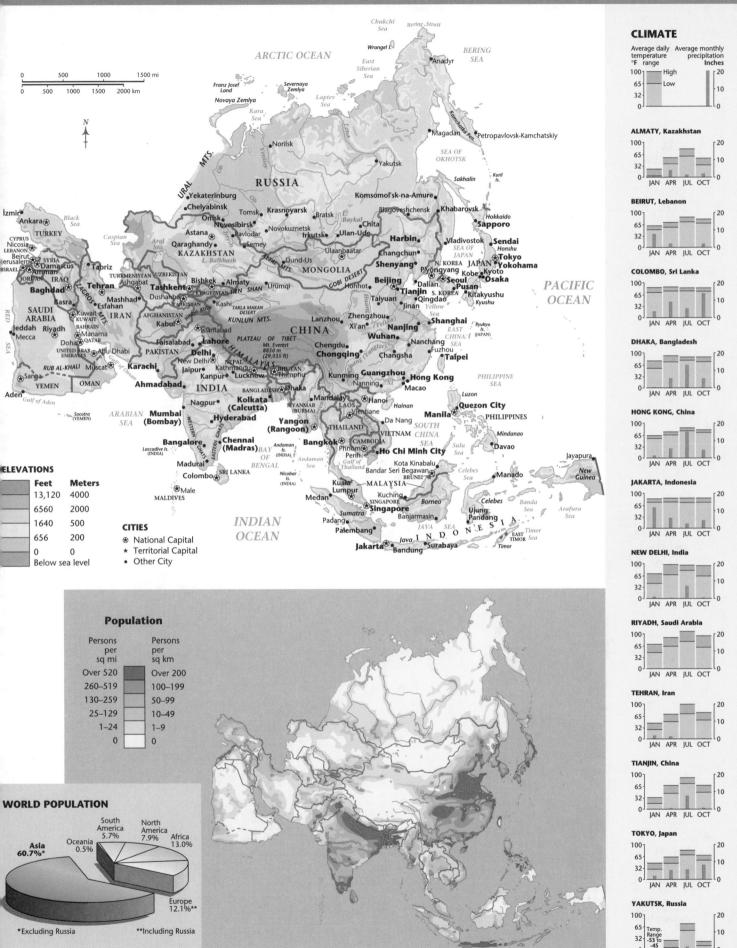

Map labels

Inset I (Hokkaido)
La Pérouse Strait • Point Soya • Rebun • Wakkanai • Rishiri • Sea of Okhotsk • Mombetsu • Cape Shiretoko • Haboro • Kitami Mts. • Kunashir (Russia) • Asahi Dake 2290 m (7513 ft) • Kitami • Nemuro Strait • Cape Kamui • Asahikawa • HOKKAIDO • Otaru • Yubari • Obihiro • Tokachi • Nemuro • Sapporo • Chitose • Kushiro • Tomakomai • HIDAKA MTS. • Okushiri • Uchiura Bay • Muroran • Cape Erimo • Oshima Pen. • Hakodate • Matsumae • Tsugaru Strait

Main map
SOUTH KOREA • P'ohang • Pusan • Korea Strait • Tsu • Iki • Izuhara • Shimonoseki • Kitakyushu • Fukuoka • FUKUOKA • Sasebo • SAGA • Kurume • OITA • Nakadori • Omuta • Saga • Oita • Fukue • Kumamoto • Yatsushiro • KYUSHU • KUMAMOTO • Amakusa Is. • MIYAZAKI • Koshiki Is. • KAGOSHIMA • Miyazaki • Satsuma Peninsula • Osumi Pen. • Kagoshima • Miyakonojo • Cape Sata • Osumi Strait • East China Sea • Tokara Islands • Yaku • Kuchino • Nakano • Suwanose • Akuseki • Takara • Tanega

HOKKAIDO (see inset) • Oshima Pen. • Hakodate • Matsumae • Tsugaru Strait • Muroran • Cape Henashi • Mutsu • Aomori • AOMORI • Hirosake • Miyako • Akita • Morioka • AKITA • IWATE • Ou Mts. • Kitakami • Towada • L. Hachinohe • Tsuruoka • YAMAGATA • Sendai • MIYAGI • Ishinomaki • Yamagata • Zao 1841 m (6040 ft) • Ishinomaki Bay • Ryotsu • Niigata • Fukushima • Sado • NIIGATA • Aizuwakamatsu • Koriyama • FUKUSHIMA • HONSHU • Noto Peninsula • Nagaoka • Iwaki • Joetsu • Nikko • TOCHIGI • IBARAKI • Hitachi • Toyama Bay • ISHIKAWA • Toyama • Nagano • GUMMA • Utsunomiya • Mito • Kanazawa • TOYAMA • Ashikaga • Koshigaya • Kawaguchi • Komatsu • Japanese Alps • Asama 2542 m (8340 ft) • Maebashi • Urawa • Omiya • Matsudo • Fukui • Matsumoto • NAGANO • SAITAMA • Kawagoe • Ichikawa • FUKUI • Tsuruga • GIFU • Kofu • Tokorozawa • TOKYO • Funabashi • Chiba • Shirane 3192 m (10,472 ft) • YAMANASHI • Machida • Sagamihara • Ichihara • Tokyo • Gifu • AICHI • KANAGAWA • Yokosuka • CHIBA • Fuji 3776 m (12,388 ft) • Fujisawa • Yokohama • Boso Pen. • Nagoya • Okazaki • Toyota • SHIZUOKA • Kawasaki • Maizuru • KYOTO • Takatsuki • Hirakata • Yokkaichi • Numazu • Izu Pen. • Kyoto • Otsu • Shizuoka • Cape Nojima • Matsue • Tottori • HYOGO • Ibaraki • SHIGA • Ichinomiya • Shimizu • Cape Hino • Yonago • TOTTORI • Toyonaka • Nara • Hamamatsu • Izu Islands • SHIMANE • Gotsu • OKAYAMA • Amagasaki • Nishinomiya • Kobe • Neyagawa • MIE • Toyohashi • Nii • Kozu • Dogo • Oki Is. • Chugoku • Himeji • Akashi • Suita • Yao • Ise • Miyake • Dozen • Masuda • HIROSHIMA • Okayama • Kurashiki • Awaji • Sakai • Higashiosaka • Ise Bay • Mikura • HIROSHIMA • Fukuyama • Takamatsu • Osaka • NARA • Sagami Bay • Yamaguchi • Kure • KAGAWA • Wakayama • Tokushima • WAKAYAMA • Kii Peninsula • YAMAGUCHI • Ube • Iwakuni • Inland Sea • Niihama • TOKUSHIMA • Tanabe • KOCHI • EHIME • Matsuyama • Ishizuchi 1981 m (6499 ft) • Cape Shiono • SHIKOKU • Uwajima • Kochi • Tosa Bay • Cape Muroto • Bungo Channel • Cape Ashizuri • PACIFIC OCEAN • Hachijo • Bonin Is. (see inset) • Aso 1592 m (5223 ft) • Nobeoka

Inset II (Ryukyu Islands / Okinawa)
Amami Islands • Amami • Naze • Nishino • Kakeroma • Tokuno • Okino Erabu • Yoron • Okinawa Islands • Okinawa • Gushikawa • Kume • Naha • OKINAWA • Senkaku Islands • RYUKYU ISLANDS • Miyako • Hirara • Ishigaki • Yonaguni • Iriomote • Sakishima Islands

Inset III (Bonin / Volcano Islands)
Muko • Nishino • Chichi • Haha • Bonin Islands • Kita • Iwo Jima • Volcano Islands • Minami

Map legend

Japan
- ⊛ National Capital
- • Other City

1:7,500,000

0 50 100 150 mi
0 50 100 150 km

Lambert Conformal Conic Projection

same scale as main map

RYUKYU ISLANDS (see inset)

N

Flag box

Japan
Capital: Tokyo
Area: 145,850 sq. mi.
377,850 sq. km.
Population: 126,182,000
Largest City: Tokyo
Language: Japanese
Monetary Unit: Yen

Cities and Towns

Aizuwakamatsu	C2
Akashi	B3
Akita	D2
Amagasaki	B3
Aomori	D1
Asahikawa	Inset I
Ashikaga	C2
Awaji	B3
Chiba	D3
Chitose	Inset I
Fujisawa	C3
Fukue	A3
Fukui	C2
Fukuoka	A3
Fukushima	D2
Fukuyama	B3
Funabashi	D3
Gifu	C3
Gotsu	B3
Gushikawa	Inset II
Haboro	Inset I
Hachinohe	D1
Hachioji	C3
Hakodate	D1, Inset I
Hamamatsu	C3
Higashiosaka	B3
Himeji	B3
Hirakata	B3
Hirara	Inset II
Hirosake	D1
Hiroshima	B3
Hitachi	D2
Ibaraki	B3
Ichihara	D3
Ichikawa	D3
Ichinomiya	C3
Ise	C3
Ishinomaki	D2
Iwaki	D2
Iwakuni	B3
Izuhara	A3
Joetsu	C2
Kagoshima	A4
Kanazawa	C2
Kashiwa	D3
Kasugai	C3
Kawagoe	C3
Kawaguchi	C3
Kawasaki	C3
Kitakyushu	A3
Kitami	Inset I
Kobe	B3
Kochi	B3
Kofu	C3
Komatsu	C2
Koriyama	C2
Koshigaya	C3
Kumamoto	A3
Kurashiki	B3
Kure	B3
Kurume	A3
Kushiro	Inset I
Kyoto	B3
Machida	C3
Maebashi	C2
Maizuru	B3
Masuda	A3
Matsudo	D3
Matsue	B3
Matsumae	D1, Inset I
Matsumoto	C2
Matsuyama	B3
Mito	D2
Miyako	D2
Miyakonojo	A4
Miyazaki	A4
Mombetsu	Inset I
Morioka	D1
Muroran	D1, Inset I
Mutsu	D1
Nagano	C2
Nagaoka	C2
Nagasaki	A3
Nagoya	C3
Naha	Inset II
Nara	B3
Naze	Inset II
Nemuro	Inset I
Neyagawa	B3
Niigata	C2
Niihama	B3
Nikko	C2
Nishinomiya	B3
Nobeoka	A3
Numazu	C3
Obihiro	Inset I
Oita	A3
Okayama	B3
Okazaki	C3
Omiya	C3
Omuta	A3
Osaka	B3
Otaru	Inset I
Otsu	B3
Ryotsu	C2
Saga	A3
Sagamihara	C3
Sakai	B3
Sapporo	Inset I
Sasebo	A3
Sendai	D2
Shimizu	C3
Shimonoseki	A3
Shizuoka	C3
Suita	B3
Takamatsu	B3
Takatsuki	B3
Tanabe	B3
Tokorozawa	C3
Tokushima	B3
Tokuyama	A3
Tokyo, capital	C3
Tomakomai	Inset I
Tottori	B3
Toyama	C2
Toyohashi	C3
Toyonaka	B3
Toyota	C3
Tsuruga	C3
Tsuruoka	C2
Ube	A3
Urawa	C3
Utsunomiya	C2
Uwajima	B3
Wakayama	B3
Wakkanai	D2
Yamagata	D2
Yamaguchi	A3
Yao	B3
Yatsushiro	A3

Japan: Map Index

Prefectures

Aichi	C3	Gumma	C2	Mie	C3
Akita	D2	Hiroshima	B3	Miyagi	D2
Aomori	D1	Hokkaido	D1, Inset I	Miyazaki	A3
Chiba	D3	Hyogo	B3	Nagano	C2
Ehime	B3	Ibaraki	D2	Nagasaki	A3
Fukui	C2	Ishikawa	C2	Nara	B3
Fukuoka	A3	Iwate	D2	Niigata	C2
Fukushima	C2	Kagawa	B3	Oita	A3
Gifu	C3	Kagoshima	A4	Okayama	B3
		Kanagawa	C3	Okinawa	Inset II
		Kochi	B3	Osaka	B3
		Kumamoto	A3	Saga	A3
		Kyoto	B3	Saitama	C2

Shiga	C3	Tochigi	C2
Shimane	B3	Tokushima	B3
Shizuoka	C3	Tokyo	C3
Tokushima	B3	Tottori	B3
		Toyama	C2
		Wakayama	B3
		Yamagata	C2
		Yamaguchi	A3
		Yamanashi	C3

© MapQuest.com, Inc.

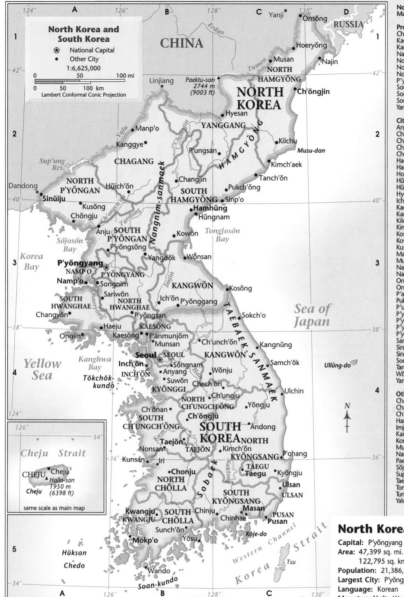

North Korea and South Korea

⊛ National Capital
• Other City
1:6,625,000

0   50   100 mi
0   50 100 km
Lambert Conformal Conic Projection

© MapQuest.com, Inc.

Cheju Strait

CHEJU Cheju
Halla-san
1950 m
(6398 ft)
Cheju

same scale as main map

Taiwan

⊛ National Capital
• Other City
1:10,292,000

0   30   60 mi
0   30   60 km
Lambert Conformal Conic Projection

© MapQuest.com, Inc.

Japan: Map Index

...okkaichi C3
...okohama C3
...okosuka C3
...onago B3
...ubari ....Inset I

Other Features

...kuseki, island A4
...makusa, island A3
...mami, island ....Inset II
...mami, islands ....Inset III
...sahi Dake, mt. ....Inset I
...sama, mt. C2
...so, mt. A3
...shizuri, cape B3
...waji, island A3
...iwa, lake A3
...onin, islands ....Inset III
...oso, peninsula D3
...ungo, channel B3
...hichi, island ....Inset III
...hugoku, mts. B3
...ogo, island B2
...ozen, island B2
...ast China, sea A4
...rimo, cape ....Inset I
...uji, mt. C3
...ukue, island A3
...achijo, island C3
...aha, island ....Inset III
...enashi, cape C1
...idaka, mts. ....Inset I
...ino, cape B3
...okkaido, island ...D1, Inset I
...onshu, island C2
...ki, island A3
...nland, sea B3
...riomote, island .....Inset II
...se, bay B3
...shigaki, island .....Inset II
...shikari, river ....Inset I
...shizuchi, mt. B3
...wo Jima, island ....Inset III
...zu, islands C3
...zu, peninsula C3
...apan, sea B2
...apanese Alps, mts. ...C3
...akeroma, island ....Inset II
...amui, cape ....Inset I
...ii, channel B3
...ii, peninsula C3
...ita, island ....Inset III
...itakami, river D2
...itami, mts. ....Inset I
...orea, strait A3
...oshiki, islands A4
...ozu, island C3
...uchino, island ......Inset II
...ume, island ....Inset II
...yushu, island A4
...a Pérouse, strait ...Inset I
...ikura, island C3
...inami, island ....Inset III
...iyake, island C3
...iyako, island ......Inset II
...ogami, river D2
...uko, island ....Inset III
...uroto, cape B3
...akadori, island A3
...akano, island A4
...emuro, strait D1
...ii, island C3
...ojima, cape D3
...oto, peninsula C2
...khotsk, sea ....Inset I
...ki, islands C2
...kinawa, island .....Inset II
...kinawa, islands .....Inset II
...kino Erabu, island ..Inset II
...kushiri, island .....C1, Inset I
...shima, peninsula ...D1, Inset I
...sumi, islands A4
...sumi, peninsula A4
...sumi, strait A4
...u, mts. D2
...ebun, island ....Inset I
...ishiri, island ....Inset I
...yukyu, islands .....A4, Inset II
...ado, island C2
...agami, bay C3
...akishima, islands ...Inset II
...ata, cape A4
...atsuma, peninsula ...A4
...enkaku, islands .....Inset II
...hikoku, island B3
...himonoseki, strait ...A3
...hinano, river C2
...hiono, cape C3
...hirane, mt. C3
...hiretoko, cape ......Inset I
...oya, point ....Inset I
...uwanose, island A4
...akara, island A4
...anega, island A4
...enryu, river C3
...eshio, river ....Inset I
...okachi, river ....Inset I
...okara, islands A4
...okuno, island ......Inset II
...one, river C2
...osa, bay B3
...owada, lake D1
...oyama, bay C2
...su, island B2
...suguru, strait .....D1, Inset I
...chiura, bay C2
...olcano, islands .....Inset III
...akasa, bay B3
...aku, island A4
...ariga, mt. C3
...onaguni, island .....Inset II
...oron, island ....Inset II
...oshino, river B3
...ao, mt. D2

North Korea:
Map Index

Provinces

Chagang B2
Kaesŏng B3
Kangwŏn B3
Namp'o A3
North Hamgyŏng C1
North Hwanghae A3
North P'yŏngan A2
P'yŏngyang A2
South Hamgyŏng B2
South Hwanghae A3
South P'yŏngan B3
Yanggang B2

Cities and Towns

Anju A3
Changjin B2
Changyŏn A3
Ch'ŏngjin C2
Chŏngju A3
Haeju A3
Hamhŭng B3
Hoeryŏng C1
Hüich'ŏn B2
Hŭngnam B3
Hyesan C2
Ich'ŏn B3
Kaesŏng B4
Kanggye B2
Kilchu C2
Kimch'aek C2
Kosŏng B3
Kowŏn B3
Kusŏng B2
Manp'o B2
Musan C1
Najin D1
Namp'o A3
Ongjin A4
Onsŏng C1
P'anmunjŏm B4
Pukch'ŏng C2
P'ungsan B2
P'yŏngsan B3
P'yŏngyang, capital ...A2
P'yŏngyang B3
P'yŏngyang, capital ...A2
Sariwŏn A3
Sinp'o B3
Sinŭiju A2
Songnim A3
Tanch'ŏn C2
Wŏnsan B3
Yangdŏk B3

Other Features

Chaeryŏng, river A3
Changjin, river B2
Ch'ŏngch'ŏn, river ...A3
Hamgyŏng, mts. C2
Imjin, river B3
Kanghwa, bay A4
Korea, bay A3
Musu-dan, point C2
Nangnim-sanmaek, mts. ..B3
Paektu-san, mt. B2
Sŏjosŏn, bay A3
Sup'ung, reservoir ...A2
Taedong, river B3
Tongjosŏn, bay B3
Tumen, river C1
Yalu, river A2

South Korea:
Map Index

Provinces

Cheju ....Inset
Inch'ŏn B4
Kangwŏn B4
Kwangju B5
Kyŏnggi B4
North Chŏlla B5
North Ch'ungch'ŏng ...B4
North Kyŏngsang C4
Pusan C5
Seoul B4
South Chŏlla B5
South Ch'ungch'ŏng ...B4
South Kyŏngsang C5
Taegu C5
Taejŏn B4
Ulsan C5

Cities and Towns

Andong C4
Anyang B4
Chech'ŏn C4
Cheju ....Inset
Chinhae C5
Chinju C5
Chŏnju B5
Ch'ŏnan B4
Ch'ŏngju B4
Ch'ŏngju B4
Ch'unch'ŏn B4
Ch'ungju B4
Inch'ŏn B4
Iri B5
Kangnŭng C4
Kimch'ŏn C4
Kunsan B5
Kwangju B5
Kyŏngju C5
Masan C5
Mokp'o B5
Munsan B4
Nonsan B4
P'ohang C4
Pusan C5
Samch'ŏk C4
Seoul, capital B4
Sokch'o C3
Sŏngnam B5
Sunch'ŏn B5
Suwŏn B4
Taegu C5
Taejŏn B4
Ulchin C4
Ulsan C5
Wŏnju B4
Yŏngju C4
Yŏsu B5

Other Features

Cheju, island ......Inset
Cheju, strait ......Inset
Halla-san, mt. .....Inset
Han, river B4
Hŭksan Chedo, islands ..A5
Kanghwa, bay A4
Koje-do, island C5
Korea, strait C5
Kum, river B4
Naktong, river C5
Soan-kundo, islands ..B5
Sobaek, mts. B5
Taebaek-Sanmaek, mts. ..C3
Tŏkchŏk-kundo, islands ..A4
Ullŭng-do, island ...D4
Western, channel ...C5

North Korea

Capital: P'yŏngyang
Area: 47,399 sq. mi.
      122,795 sq. km.
Population: 21,386,000
Largest City: P'yŏngyang
Language: Korean
Monetary Unit: Won

South Korea

Capital: Seoul
Area: 38,330 sq. mi.
      99,301 sq. km.
Population: 46,885,000
Largest City: Seoul
Language: Korean
Monetary Unit: Won

Taiwan

Capital: Taipei
Area: 13,969 sq. mi.
      36,189 sq. km.
Population: 22,113,000
Largest City: Taipei
Language: Mandarin Chinese
Monetary Unit: New Taiwan dollar

Taiwan:
Map Index

Cities and Towns

Changhua B1
Chiai B2
Chilung B1
Chunan B1
Chungho B1
Chungli B1
Fangliao B2
Fengshan B2
Fengyüan B1
Hengch'un B2
Hsinchu B1
Hsinchuang B1
Hsintien B1
Hsinying B2
Hualien B1
Ilan B1
Kangshan B2
Kaohsiung B2
Makung B1
Miaoli B1
Nant'ou B1
Panch'iao B1
P'ingtung B2

Shanchung B1
T'aichung B1
T'ainan B2
Taipei, capital B1
T'aitung B2
Tanshui B1
T'aoyüan B1
Touliu B2
Yungho B1

Other Features

Choshui, river B2
Chungyang, range B2
East China, sea B1
Kaop'ing, river B2
Lan, island B2
Lü, island B2
Luzon, strait B3
P'enghu (Pescadores),
   islands A2
Pescadores, channel ..A2
Philippine, sea B2
South China, sea A2
Taiwan, strait A1
Tanshui, river B1
Tsengwen, river B2
Yü Shan, mt. B2

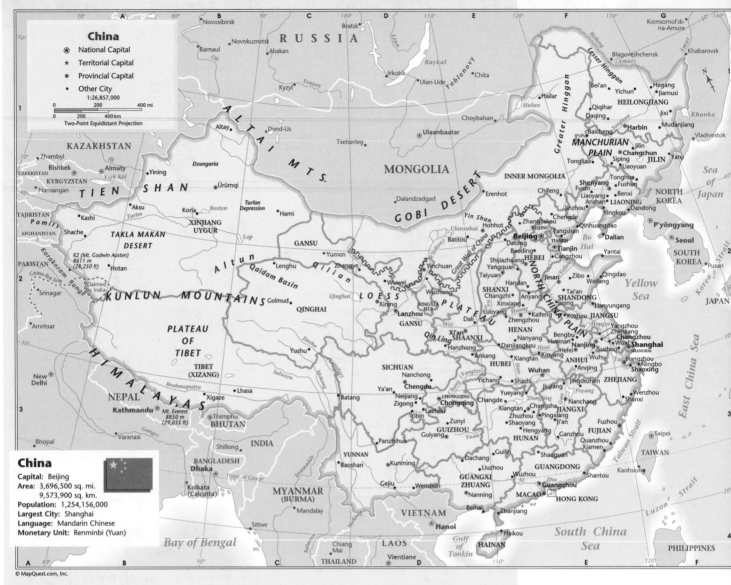

China
- ⊛ National Capital
- ★ Territorial Capital
- ◉ Provincial Capital
- • Other City

1:26,857,000

0   200   400 mi
0   200   400 km
Two-Point Equidistant Projection

China

Capital: Beijing
Area: 3,696,500 sq. mi.
    9,573,900 sq. km.
Population: 1,254,156,000
Largest City: Shanghai
Language: Mandarin Chinese
Monetary Unit: Renminbi (Yuan)

© MapQuest.com, Inc.

China:
Map Index

Internal Divisions
Provinces
Anhui E2
Fujian E3
Gansu C1, D2
Guangdong E3
Guizhou D3
Hainan D4
Hebei E2
Heilongjiang F1
Henan E2
Hubei E2
Hunan E3
Jiangsu E2
Jiangxi E3
Jilin F1
Liaoning F1
Qinghai C2
Shaanxi D2
Shandong E2
Shanxi E2
Sichuan D2
Yunnan C3
Zhejiang E3

Autonomous Regions
Guangxi Zhuang D3
Inner Mongolia E1
Ningxia Hui D2
Tibet (Xizang) B2
Xinjiang Uygur B1

Independent Municipalities
Beijing E1
Chongqing D3
Shanghai E2
Tianjin E2

**Special Administrative
Regions (S.A.R.)**
Hong Kong .... E3, Inset
Macao E3

Cities and Towns
Aberdeen .... Inset
Aksu B1
Altay B1
Ankang D2
Anqing E2
Anshan F1

Anyang E2
Baicheng F1
Baoding E2
Baoshan C3
Baotou E1
Batang C3
Bei'an F1
Beihai D3
Beijing, capital E2
Bengbu E2
Benxi F1
Cangzhou E2
Changchun F1
Changde E3
Changsha E3
Changzhi E2
Changzhou E2
Chek Keng .... Inset
Chengde E1
Chengdu D2
Chifeng E1
Chongqing D3
Chung Hau .... Inset
Dachang D3
Dali D2
Dalian F2
Dandong F1
Daqing F1
Datong E1
Danjiangkou E2
Erenhot E1
Fushun F1
Fuxin F1
Fuzhou E3
Ganzhou E3
Gejiu D3
Golmud C2
Guangzhou E3
Guilin D3
Guiyang D3
Haikou E4
Hailar E1
Hami C1
Handan E2
Hangzhou F2
Hanzhong D2
Harbin F1
Hefei E2
Hegang G1
Hengyang E3
Hohhot E1
Hotan A2

Huainan E2
Jiamusi G1
Ji'an E3
Jilin F1
Jinan E2
Jingdezhen E2
Jining E2
Jinzhou F1
Jiujiang E3
Jixi G1
Kaifeng E2
Kashi A2
Korla B1
Kowloon .... Inset
Kunming D3
Lanzhou D2
Lenghu C2
Lhasa C3
Lianyungang E2
Liaoyang F1
Liaoyuan F1
Liuzhou D3
Lo Wu .... Inset
Luoyang E2
Luzhou D3
Mudanjiang F1
Nanchang E3
Nanchong D2
Nanjing E2
Nanning D3
Nanyang E2
Neijiang D3
New Kowloon .... Inset
Ningbo F3
Panzhihua D3
Pingxiang E3
Qingdao F2
Qinhuangdao E2
Qiqihar F1
Quanzhou E3
Sai Kung .... Inset
Shache A2
Shanghai E2
Shantou E3
Shanxi E3
Shaoguan E3
Shaoxing E3
Shaoyang E3
Shashi E2
Sha Tin .... Inset
Shek Pik .... Inset
Shenyang F1

Shijiazhuang E2
Siping F1
Suzhou E2
Tai'an E2
Taiyuan E2
Tangshan E2
Tianjin E2
Tonghua F1
Tongliao F1
Tsuen Wan .... Inset
Tuen Mun .... Inset
Ürümqi B1
Weifang E2
Wenshan D3
Wenzhou F3
Wuhan E2
Wuhu E2
Wuwei D2
Wuxi F2
Wuzhong D2
Wuzhou E3
Xiamen E3
Xi'an D2
Xiangfan E2
Xiangtan E3
Xigaze B3
Xining D2
Xinxiang E2
Xinyang E2
Xuzhou E2
Ya'an D2
Yangquan E2
Yangzhou E2
Yanji F1
Yantai F2
Yibin D3
Yichang E2
Yichun F1
Yinchuan D2
Yingkou F1
Yining B1
Yuen Long .... Inset
Yueyang E3
Yumen C2
Yushu C2
Zhangjiakou E2
Zhangye D2
Zhanjiang D3
Zhengzhou E2
Zhenjiang E2
Zhuzhou E3
Zibo E2

Zigong D3
Zunyi D3

Other Features
Altai, mts. B1
Altun, range B2
Bayan Har, range C2
Bo Hai, gulf E2
Bosten, lake B1
Brahmaputra, river ... B3
Chang (Yangtze), river .D2, E2
Deep, bay .... Inset
Dongting, lake E3
Dzungaria, desert basin .B1
East China, sea F3
Fen, river E2
Gan, river E3
Gobi, desert D1
Greater Hinggan, range .E1
Great Wall of China .. D2
Han, river D2
Heilong (Amur), river .F1
Himalayas, mts. B3
Hong Kong, island ... Inset
Hongze, lake E2
Huai, river E2
Huang (Yellow), river .D2, E2
Hulun, lake E1
Indus, river A2
Jinsha (Yangtze), river .C2
Khanka, lake G1
Kunlun, mts. B2
K2 (Godwin Austen), mt. .A2
Lantau, island .... Inset
Lesser Hinggan, range .F1
Liao, river F1
Loess, plateau D2
Lop, lake C1
Manchurian, plain F1
Mekong, river D3
Nan Ling, mts. E3
New Territories, island .Inset
North China, plain E2
Pamirs, region A2
Poyang, lake E3
Qaidam, basin C2
Qilian, range D2
Qinghai, lake D2
Qin Ling, mts. D2
Salween, river C3
Songhua, river F1
South China, sea .... E4, Inset

Stonecutters (S.I.), island ..Inset
Tai, lake F2
Taiwan, strait E3
Takla Makan, desert .. B2
Tanggula, range C2
Tarim, river B1
Tibet, plateau B2
Tien Shan, range A1
Tonkin, gulf D4
Turfan, depression C1
Ulansuhai, lake D1
Wei, river D2
Xi, river D3
Yalu, river F1
Yangtze, river C2, D2
Yellow, sea F2
Yin Shan, mts. E2
Yuan, river D3
Zhu, river E3

© MapQuest.com, Inc.

Hong Kong S.A.R.

- • City

1:1,800,000

0   10   20 mi
0   10   20 km
Transverse Mercator Projection

© MapQuest.com, Inc.

Vietnam:
Map Index

Cities and Towns
Bac Lieu A5
Bien Hoa B4
Buon Me Thuot B4
Ca Mau A5
Cam Ranh B4
Can Tho A4
Cao Bang B1
Chau Doc A4
Da Lat B4
Da Nang B3
Dien Bien Phu A2
Dong Hoi B3
Ha Giang A1
Haiphong B2
Hanoi, capital A2
Hoa Binh A2
Ho Chi Minh City...............B4
Hon Gai B2
Hue B3
Khe Sanh B3
Kontum B3
Lang Son B2
Lao Cai A1
Long Xuyen A4
My Tho B4
Nam Dinh B2
Nha Trang B4
Phan Rang B4
Phan Thiet B4
Pleiku B3
Quang Ngai B3
Quang Tri B3
Qui Nhon B4
Rach Gia A5
Soc Trang A5
Son La A2
Tay Ninh B4
Thai Nguyen A2

Thanh Hoa........................A2
Tuy Hoa B4
Viet Tri A2
Vinh A2
Vung Tau- Con Dao B4
Yen Bai A2

Other Features
Annam, mts. A2
Ba, river B3
Black (Da), river A2
Ca, river A2
Central, highlands B4
Con Son, islands B5
Cu Lao Thu, island B4
Dao Phu Quoc, island A4
Dong Nai, river B4
Fan Si Pan, mt. A1
Gam, river A1
Lo, river A1
Ma, river A2
Mekong, delta B5
Mekong, river A4
Mui Bai Bung, point A5
Ngoc Linh, mt. B3
Red (Hong), river A2
Tonkin, gulf B2

Vietnam
Capital: Hanoi
Area: 127,246 sq. mi.
329,653 sq. km.
Population: 77,311,000
Largest City: Ho Chi Minh City
Language: Vietnamese
Monetary Unit: Dong

© MapQuest.com, Inc.

Vietnam
⊛ National Capital
• Other City
1:14,333,000
0   50   100   150   200 mi
0 50 100 150 200 km
Lambert Conformal Conic Projection

Laos:
Map Index

Cities and Towns
Attapu D4
Ban Houayxay....................A1
Champasak.........................C4
Louang Namtha...................A1
Luang Prabang....................B2
Muang Khammouan............C3
Muang Không......................C4
Muang Khôngxédôn............C4
Muang Paklay.....................A2
Muang Pakxan....................B2
Muang Vangviang................B2
Muang Xaignabouri.............A2
Muang Xay.........................A1
Muang Xépôn......................D3
Muang Xon.........................B1
Pakse.................................C4
Phôngsali...........................B1
Saravan..............................D4
Savannakhet.......................C3
Vientiane, capital................B3
Xam Nua............................C1
Xiangkhoang......................B2

Other Features
Annam, range.....................C3
Banghiang, river.................C3
Bolovens, plateau...............D4
Kong, river.........................D4
Luang Prabang, range.........A3
Mekong, river.............A1, C3
Nam Ngum, reservoir..........B2
Ou, river.............................B1
Phou Bia, mt.......................B2
Xiangkhoang, plateau..........B2

Laos
Capital: Vientiane
Area: 91,429 sq. mi.
236,085 sq. km.
Population: 5,407,000
Largest City: Vientiane
Language: Lao
Monetary Unit: New kip

Laos
⊛ National Capital
• Other City
1:14,533,000
0   50   100 mi
0 50 100 km
Lambert Conformal Conic Projection

© MapQuest.com, Inc.

Cambodia
Capital: Phnom Penh
Area: 70,238 sq. mi.
181,964 sq. km.
Population: 11,627,000
Largest City: Phnom Penh
Language: Khmer
Monetary Unit: New riel

Cambodia
⊛ National Capital
• Other City
▪ Ruins
1:8,573,000
0   50   100 mi
0 50 100 km
Conic Projection

© MapQuest.com, Inc.

Cambodia:
Map Index

Cities and Towns
Batdambang B2
Kampong Cham D4
Kampong Chhnang..............C3
Kampong Saom...................B5
Kampong Thum...................C5
Kampot...............................C5
Kracheh..............................D3
Krong Kaoh Kong A4
Lumphat.............................F2
Phnom Penh, capital C4
Phnum Tbeng Meanchey C2
Phumi Samraong.................B1
Pouthisat............................B3

Prey Veng...........................D4
Senmonorom.......................F3
Siempang............................E1
Siemreab.............................B2
Sisophon.............................B2
Snuol..................................E3
Sre Ambel...........................B4
Stoeng Treng.......................D2
Svay Rieng.........................D4
Takev.................................C5

Other Features
Angkor Thom, ruins B2
Angkor Wat, ruins B2
Aoral, mt.............................C3
Cardamom, mts. A3
Dangrek, mts. B1
Mekong, river D3
San, river............................E2
Sen, river............................D2
Sreng, river.........................B2
Thailand, gulf A4
Tonle Sap, lake B2, C3
Tonle Sap, river B2

Mongolia
Capital: Ulaanbaatar
Area: 604,800 sq. mi.
1,566,839 sq. km.
Population: 2,617,000
Largest City: Ulaanbaatar
Language: Mongolian
Monetary Unit: Tughrik

Mongolia:
Map Index

Cities and Towns
Altay C2
Arvayheer C2
Baruun-Urt D2
Bayanhongor.......................C2
Bulgan C2
Buyant-Uhaa D3
Choybalsan D2
Dalandzadgad C3
Darhan C2
Dund-Us.............................B2

Erdenet...............................C2
Mandalgovĭ.........................C2
Mörön................................C2
Ölgiy..................................A2
Öndörhaan..........................D2
Sühbaatar...........................C2
Tamsagbulag.......................D2
Tsetserleg...........................C2
Ulaangom............................B2
Ulaan-Uul...........................C2
Ulaanbaatar, capital............C2
Uliastay..............................B2

Other Features
Altai, mts...........................B2
Bööntsagaan, lake B2
Dörgön, lake.......................B2
Dzavhan, river....................B2
Gobi, desert........................C3
Hangayn, mts......................B2
Har Us, lake........................B2
Hovd, river..........................B2
Hövsgöl, lake......................C1
Hyargas, lake......................B2
Ih Bogd Uul, mt...................C3
Kerulen, river......................D2
Mongolian, plateau..............C2
Onon, river..........................D2
Orhon, river.........................C2
Selenge Mörön, river...........C2
Tavan Bogd Uul, mt. A2
Tesiyn, river........................B2
Tuul, river...........................C2
Uvs, lake............................B1

Mongolia
⊛ National Capital
• Other City
1:2,857,000
0   125   250 mi
0 125 250 km
Lambert Conformal Conic Projection

© MapQuest.com, Inc.

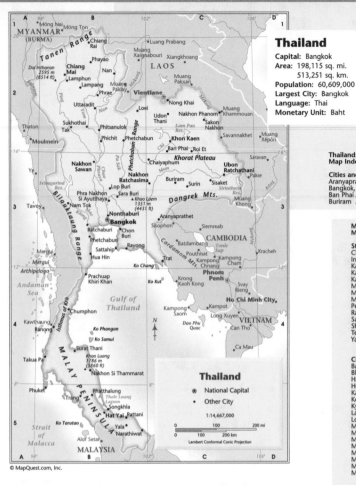

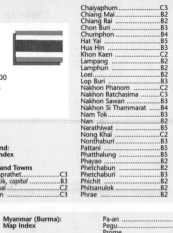

Thailand

Capital: Bangkok
Area: 198,115 sq. mi.
513,251 sq. km.
Population: 60,609,000
Largest City: Bangkok
Language: Thai
Monetary Unit: Baht

Thailand

⊛ National Capital
• Other City

1:14,667,000

0   100   200 mi
0   100   200 km
Lambert Conformal Conic Projection

© MapQuest.com, Inc.

Thailand:
Map Index

Cities and Towns
Aranyaprathet	C3
Bangkok, *capital*	B3
Ban Phai	C2
Buriram	C3
Chaiyaphum	C3
Chiang Mai	B2
Chiang Rai	B2
Chon Buri	B3
Chumphon	B4
Hat Yai	B5
Hua Hin	B3
Khon Kaen	C2
Lampang	B2
Lamphun	B2
Loei	B2
Lop Buri	B3
Nakhon Phanom	C2
Nakhon Ratchasima	C3
Nakhon Sawan	B3
Nakhon Si Thammarat	B4
Nam Tok	B3
Nan	B2
Narathiwat	B5
Nong Khai	C2
Nonthaburi	B3
Pattani	B5
Phatthalung	B5
Phayao	B2
Phetchabun	B3
Phetchaburi	B3
Phichit	B2
Phitsanulok	B2
Phrae	B2
Phra Nakhon Si Ayutthaya	B3
Phuket	B5
Prachuap Khiri Khan	B4
Ranong	B4
Ratchaburi	B3
Rayong	B3
Roi Et	C2
Sakon Nakhon	C2
Sara Buri	B3
Sattahip	B3
Sisaket	C3
Songkhla	B5
Sukhothai	B2
Surat Thani	B4
Surin	C3
Tak	B2
Takua Pa	B4
Trang	B5
Trat	C3
Ubon Ratchathani	C3
Udon Thani	C2
Uttaradit	B2
Yala	B5

Other Features
Bilauktaung, *range*	B3
Chao Phraya, *river*	B3
Chi, *river*	C3
Dangrek, *mts.*	C3
Dawna, *range*	B2
Inthanon, *mt.*	B2
Khorat, *plateau*	C3
Ko Chang, *island*	C3
Ko Kut, *island*	C4
Ko Phangan, *island*	B4
Ko Samui, *island*	B4
Ko Tarutao, *island*	B5
Kra, *isthmus*	B4
Laem, *mt.*	B3
Lam Pao, *reservoir*	C2
Luang, *mt.*	B4
Mae Klong, *river*	B3
Malacca, *strait*	B5
Malay, *peninsula*	B4
Mekong, *river*	C2
Mun, *river*	C3
Nan, *river*	B2
Pa Sak, *river*	B3
Phetchabun, *range*	B3
Ping, *river*	B3
Salween, *river*	A2
Sirinthorn, *reservoir*	C3
Srinagarind, *reservoir*	B3
Tanen, *range*	B2
Thailand, *gulf*	B4
Thale Luang, *lagoon*	B5
Yom, *river*	B2

Myanmar (Burma)

Capital: Yangon (Rangoon)
Area: 261,228 sq. mi.
676,756 sq. km.
Population: 48,081,000
Largest City: Yangon (Rangoon)
Language: Burmese
Monetary Unit: Kyat

Myanmar (Burma)

⊛ National Capital
• Other City

1:24,054,000

0   100   200 mi
0   100   200 km
Lambert Conformal Conic Projection

© MapQuest.com, Inc.

Myanmar (Burma):
Map Index

States and Divisions
Chin, *state*	B2
Irrawaddy, *division*	B3
Kachin, *state*	C1
Karen, *state*	C3
Kayah, *state*	C2
Magwe, *division*	B2
Mandalay, *division*	B2
Mon, *state*	C3
Pegu, *division*	B3
Rakhine, *state*	B2
Sagaing, *division*	B2
Shan, *state*	C2
Tenasserim, *division*	C3
Yangon (Rangoon), *division*	C3

Cities and Towns
Bassein	B3
Bhamo	C1
Haka	B2
Henzada	B3
Kawthaung	C4
Keng Tung	C2
Kyaukpyu	B2
Lashio	C2
Loi-kaw	C2
Mandalay	C2
Maymyo	C2
Meiktila	B2
Mergui	C3
Monywa	B2
Moulmein	C3
Myingyan	B2
Myitkyina	C1
Pa-an	C3
Pegu	C3
Prome	B2
Putao	C1
Sagaing	B2
Shwebo	B2
Sittwe	B2
Tamu	B1
Taunggyi	C2
Tavoy	C3
Toungoo	C3
Yangon (Rangoon), *capital*	C3
Ye	C3

Other Features
Andaman, *sea*	B3
Arakan Yoma, *mts.*	B2
Bengal, *bay*	B3
Bilauktaung, *range*	C3
Cheduba, *island*	B3
Chin, *hills*	B2
Chindwin, *river*	B1
Coco, *islands*	B3
Hkakabo Razi, *mt.*	C1
Irrawaddy, *river*	B2
Martaban, *gulf*	C3
Mekong, *river*	C2
Mergui, *archipelago*	C4
Mouths of the Irrawaddy, *delta*	B3
Preparis, *island*	B3
Ramree, *island*	B2
Salween, *river*	C2
Shan, *plateau*	C2
Sittang, *river*	C3
Tavoy, *point*	C3
Thailand, *gulf*	C4

Philippines

⊛ National Capital
• Other City

1:16,000,000

0   100   200 mi
0   100   200 km
Lambert Conformal Conic Projection

Philippines

Capital: Manila
Area: 115,860 sq. mi.
300,155 sq. km.
Population: 79,346,000
Largest City: Manila
Languages: Pilipino, English
Monetary Unit: Philippine peso

Philippines:
Map Index

Regions
Bicol	B3
Cagayan Valley	B2
Central Luzon	B3
Central Mindanao	C5
Central Visayas	B4
*Cordillera Autonomous Region	A3
Eastern Visayas	C4
Ilocos	B2
*Moslem Mindanao Autonomous Region	C5
National Capital Region	B3
Northern Mindanao	C4
Southern Mindanao	C5
Southern Tagalog	B3
Western Mindanao	B5
Western Visayas	B4

Cities and Towns
Angeles	B3
Bacolod	B4
Baguio	B2
Basilan	B5
Batangas	B3
Bislig	C4
Butuan	C4
Cabanatuan	B3
Cadiz	B3
Cagayan de Oro	C4
Calapan	B3
Calbayog	C3
Cebu	B4
Cotabato	C5
Dagupan	B2
Davao	C5
Dipolog	C4
Dumaguete	B4
General Santos	C5
Iligan	C4
Iloilo	B4
Jolo	B5
Laoag	B2
Laoang	C3
Legazpi	B3
Lipa	B3
Lucena	B3
Mamburao	B3
Mandaue	B4
Manila, *capital*	B3
Masbate	B3
Naga	B3
Olongapo	B3
Ormoc	C4
Pagadian	C4
Puerto Princesa	A4
Quezon City	B3
Roxas	B4
San Carlos	B4
San Fernando	B2
San Pablo	B3
Silay	B4
Surigao	C4
Tacloban	C4
Tuguegarao	B2
Vigan	B2
Zamboanga	B5

Other Features
Agusan, *river*	C4
Apo, *volcano*	C5
Babuyan, *channel*	B2
Babuyan, *islands*	B1
Balabac, *island*	A5
Balabac, *strait*	A5
Bashi, *channel*	B1
Basilan, *island*	B5
Bataan, *peninsula*	B3
Batan, *islands*	B1
Bohol, *island*	C4
Bohol, *sea*	C4
Cagayan, *islands*	B4
Cagayan, *river*	B2
Cagayan Sulu, *island*	A5
Calamian, *islands*	A3
Caramoan, *peninsula*	B3
Catanduanes, *island*	C3
Cebu, *island*	B4
Celebes, *sea*	C5
Cordillera Central, *mts.*	B2
Corregidor, *island*	B3
Cuyo, *islands*	B4
Davao, *gulf*	C5
Dinagat, *island*	C4
Diuata, *mts.*	C4
Jolo, *island*	B5
Laguna de Bay, *lake*	B3
Lamon, *bay*	B3
Leyte, *island*	C4
Lingayen, *gulf*	B2
Luzon, *island*	B3
Luzon, *strait*	B2
Manila, *bay*	B3
Marinduque, *island*	B3
Masbate, *island*	B3
Mayon, *volcano*	B3
Mindanao, *island*	C5
Mindoro, *island*	B3
Mindoro, *strait*	B3
Moro, *gulf*	B5
Negros, *island*	B4
Palawan, *island*	A4
Panay, *gulf*	B4
Panay, *island*	B4
Philippine, *sea*	C3
Pulangi, *river*	C5
Samar, *island*	C4
Samar, *sea*	C3
Siargao, *island*	C4
Sibuyan, *island*	B3
Sibuyan, *sea*	B3
Sierra Madre, *mts.*	B2
South China, *sea*	A3
Sulu, *archipelago*	B5
Sulu, *sea*	B4
Tablas, *island*	B3
Tawi Tawi, *island*	A5
Visayan, *islands*	B4
Visayan, *sea*	B3
Zambales, *mts.*	B3
Zamboanga, *peninsula*	B5
*Not on map	

© MapQuest.com, Inc.

Indonesia: Map Index

Cities and Towns

Amahai	D2
Ambon	D2
Balikpapan	C2
Banda Aceh	A1
Bandar Lampung	B2
Bandung	B2
Banjarmasin	C2
Baubau	D2
Bengkulu	B2
Bogor	B2
Cilacap	B2
Cirebon	C2
Denpasar	C2
Ende	D2
Fakfak	E2
Gorontalo	D1
Jakarta, *capital*	B2
Jambi	B2
Jayapura	F2
Kediri	C2
Kendari	D2
Kupang	D3
Madiun	C2
Magelang	C2
Malang	C2
Manado	D1
Manokwari	E2
Mataram	C2
Medan	A1
Merauke	F2
Padang	B2
Palangkaraya	C2
Palembang	B2
Palu	C2
Pangkalpinang	B2
Parepare	C2
Pekalongan	B2
Pekanbaru	B1
Pematangsiantar	A1

Pontianak	B2
Raba	C2
Samarinda	C2
Semarang	C2
Sorong	E2
Sukabumi	B2
Surabaya	C2
Surakarta	C2
Tanjungpinang	C1
Tarakan	C1
Tasikmalaya	B2
Tegal	B2
Ternate	D1
Ujung Pandang	C2
Waingapu	D2
Yogyakarta	C2

Other Features

Agung, *mt.*	C2
Alor, *island*	D2

Arafura, *sea*	E2
Aru, *islands*	E2
Babar, *island*	D2
Bali, *island*	C2
Banda, *sea*	D2
Bangka, *island*	B2
Belitung, *island*	B2
Biak, *island*	E2
Borneo, *island*	C1
Buru, *island*	D2
Celebes (Sulawesi), *island*	D2
Celebes, *sea*	D1
Ceram, *island*	D2
Ceram, *sea*	D2
Digul, *river*	E2
Enggano, *island*	B2
Flores, *island*	C2
Flores, *sea*	C2
Greater Sunda, *islands*	B2
Halmahera, *island*	D1

Irian Jaya, *region*	E2
Java, *island*	C2
Java, *sea*	C2
Jaya, *mt.*	E2
Kahayan, *river*	C2
Kai, *islands*	E2
Kalimantan, *region*	C2
Kerinci, *mt.*	B2
Krakatau, *island*	B2
Lesser Sunda, *islands*	C2
Lingga, *island*	B2
Lombok, *island*	C2
Madura, *island*	C2
Makassar, *strait*	C2
Malacca, *strait*	A1
Mentawai, *islands*	A2
Misool, *island*	E2
Moa, *island*	D2
Molucca, *sea*	D2
Moluccas, *islands*	D2

Morotai, *island*	D1
Muna, *island*	D2
Natuna Besar, *island*	B1
New Guinea, *island*	E2
Nias, *island*	A1
Obi, *island*	D2
Peleng, *island*	D2
Savu, *sea*	D2
Semeru, *mt.*	C2
Siberut, *island*	A2
Simeulue, *island*	A1
South China, *sea*	C1
Sudirman, *range*	E2
Sula, *islands*	D2
Sulu, *sea*	D1
Sumatra, *island*	B2
Sumba, *island*	D2
Sumbawa, *island*	C2
Talaud, *islands*	D1
Tanimbar, *islands*	E2

Timor, *island*	D2
Timor, *sea*	D3
Waigeo, *island*	E2
Wetar, *island*	D2
Yapen, *island*	E2

Indonesia

Capital: Jakarta
Area: 741,052 sq. mi.
  1,919,824 sq. km.
Population: 216,108,000
Largest City: Jakarta
Language: Bahasa Indonesian
Monetary Unit: New rupiah

Brunei

Capital: Bandar Seri Begawan
Area: 2,226 sq. mi.
  5,767 sq. km.
Population: 323,000
Largest City: Bandar Seri Begawan
Language: Malay
Monetary Unit: Brunei dollar

Brunei: Map Index

Cities and Towns

Badas	A2
Bandar Seri Begawan, *capital*	B2
Bangar	C2
Batang Duri	B2
Jerudong	B2
Kerangan Nyatan	B3
Kuala Abang	B2
Kuala Belait	A2
Labi	A3
Labu	C2
Lumut	A2
Medit	B2
Muara	C1
Seria	A2
Sukang	B3
Tutong	B2

Other Features

Belait, *river*	B3
Brunei, *bay*	C1
Brunei, *river*	B2
Bukit Pagon, *mt.*	C3
Pandaruan, *river*	C2
South China, *sea*	A2
Temburong, *river*	C2
Tutong, *river*	B2

Singapore: Map Index

Cities and Towns

Bedok	B1
Bukit Panjang	B1
Bukit Timah	B1
Changi	B1
Choa Chu Kang	A1
Jurong	A1
Kranji	B1
Nee Soon	B1
Punggol	B1
Queenstown	B1
Sembawang	B1
Serangoon	B1
Singapore, *capital*	B1
Tampines	B1
Thong Hoe	A1
Toa Payoh	A1
Tuas	A1
Woodlands	B1

Other Features

Ayer Chawan, *island*	A1
Bukum, *island*	B2
Johor, *strait*	B1

Keppel, *harbor*	B2
Pandan, *strait*	A2
Semakau, *island*	B2
Senang, *island*	A2
Sentosa, *island*	B2
Singapore, *island*	B1
Singapore, *strait*	B2
Tekong, *island*	C1
Timah, *hill*	B1
Ubin, *island*	B1

Singapore

Capital: Singapore
Area: 247 sq. mi.
  640 sq. km.
Population: 3,532,000
Largest City: Singapore
Languages: Mandarin Chinese, English, Malay, Tamil
Monetary Unit: Singapore dollar

Malaysia

Capital: Kuala Lumpur
Area: 127,584 sq. mi.
  330,529 sq. km.
Population: 21,376,000
Largest City: Kuala Lumpur
Language: Malay
Monetary Unit: Ringgit

Malaysia: Map Index

Cities and Towns

Alor Setar	A1
Batu Pahat	B2
George Town	A1
Ipoh	A2
Johor Baharu	A2
Kelang	A2
Keluang	B2
Kota Baharu	B1
Kota Kinabalu	C1
Kuala Lumpur, *capital*	A2
Kuala Terengganu	B1

Kuantan	B2
Kuching	C2
Melaka	B2
Miri	D1
Muar	B2
Sandakan	D1
Seremban	A2
Sibu	C2
Tawau	D2
Telok Anson	A2

Other Features

Banggi, *island*	D1
Baram, *river*	D2
Crocker, *range*	C2
Kinabalu, *mt.*	D1
Kinabatangan, *river*	D2
Labuan, *island*	D2
Langkawi, *island*	A1
Malacca, *strait*	A2
Malay, *peninsula*	A1
Pahang, *river*	B2
Peninsular Malaysia, *region*	B2
Perak, *river*	A2
Pinang, *island*	A2
Rajang, *river*	C2
Sabah, *state*	C2
Sarawak, *state*	C2
Tahan, *mt.*	B2

AUSTRALIA

Australia: Map Index

States and Territories
Australian Capital Territory ... D3
New South Wales ... D3
Northern Territory ... C2
Queensland ... D2
South Australia ... C2
Tasmania ... D4
Victoria ... D3
Western Australia ... B2

Aboriginal Lands
Alawa-Ngandji ... C1
Balwina ... B2
Central Australia ... B2
Central Desert ... C2
Daly River ... B1
Haasts Bluff ... C2
Lake Mackay ... B2
Nganyatjara ... B2
Petermann ... B2
Pitjantjatjara ... C2
Waani/Garawa ... C1
Yandeyarra ... A2
Unnamed ... B2
Unnamed ... C1
Unnamed ... D1

Cities and Towns
Adelaide, S.A., *capital* .. C3, Inset II
Albany, W.A. ... A3
Albury, N.S.W. ... D3
Alice Springs, N.T. ... C2
Altona, Vic. ... Inset V
Armadale, W.A. ... Inset I
Armidale, N.S.W. ... E3
Asquith, N.S.W. ... Inset IV
Auburn, N.S.W. ... Inset IV
Balcatta, W.A. ... Inset I
Bald Hills, Qld. ... Inset III
Ballarat, Vic. ... D3
Bankstown, N.S.W. ... Inset IV
Bayswater, W.A. ... Inset I
Beenleigh, Qld. ... Inset III
Belmont, W.A. ... Inset I
Bendigo, Vic. ... D3
Berwick, Vic. ... Inset V
Blacktown, N.S.W. ... Inset IV
Botany, N.S.W. ... Inset IV
Bourke, N.S.W. ... D3
Bowen, Qld. ... D2
Box Hill, Vic. ... Inset V
Brighton, S.A. ... Inset II
Brighton, Qld. ... Inset III
Brighton, Vic. ... Inset V
Brisbane, Qld., *capital* ... E2, Inset III
Broadmeadows, Vic. ... Inset V
Broken Hill, N.S.W. ... D3
Broome, W.A. ... B1
Brown Plains, Qld. ... Inset III
Bunbury, W.A. ... A3
Bundaberg, Qld. ... E2
Burnside, S.A. ... Inset II
Byford, W.A. ... Inset I
Cairns, Qld. ... D1
Campbelltown, S.A. ... Inset II
Campbelltown, N.S.W. ... Inset IV
Canberra, A.C.T., *national capital* ... D3
Cannington, W.A. ... Inset I
Canterbury, N.S.W. ... Inset IV
Carnarvon, W.A. ... A2
Castle Hill, N.S.W. ... Inset IV
Caulfield, Vic. ... Inset V
Ceduna, S.A. ... C3
Charleville, Qld. ... D2
Charters Towers, Qld. ... D2
Chelsea, Vic. ... Inset V
Chermside, Qld. ... Inset III
City Beach, W.A. ... Inset I
Cleveland, Qld. ... Inset III
Cloncurry, Qld. ... D2
Coburg, Vic. ... Inset V
Coober Pedy, S.A. ... C2
Coopers Plains, Qld. ... Inset III
Cranbourne, Vic. ... Inset V
Cronulla, N.S.W. ... Inset IV
Dampier, W.A. ... A2
Dandenong, Vic. ... Inset V
Darwin, N.T., *capital* ... C1
Dee Why, N.S.W. ... Inset IV
Devonport, Tas. ... D4
Doncaster, Vic. ... Inset V
Dubbo, N.S.W. ... D3
Elizabeth, S.A. ... Inset II
Eltham, Vic. ... Inset V
Emerald, Qld. ... D2
Enfield, S.A. ... Inset II
Epping, N.S.W. ... Inset IV
Esperance, W.A. ... B3
Essendon, Vic. ... Inset V
Fairfield, N.S.W. ... Inset IV
Ferntree Gully, Vic. ... Inset V
Ferny Grove, Qld. ... Inset III
Frankston, Vic. ... Inset V
Fremantle, W.A. ... A3, Inset I
Geelong, Vic. ... D3
Geraldton, W.A. ... A2
Gladstone, Qld. ... E2
Glenelg, S.A. ... Inset II
Glen Forrest, W.A. ... Inset I
Gold Coast, Qld. ... E2
Goodna, Qld. ... Inset III
Gosford, N.S.W. ... E3
Gosnells, W.A. ... Inset I
Grafton, N.S.W. ... E2
Grange, S.A. ... Inset II
Greenslopes, Qld. ... Inset III
Griffith, N.S.W. ... D3
Gympie, Qld. ... E2
Heidelberg, Vic. ... Inset V
Hobart, Tas., *capital* ... D4
Holland Park, Qld. ... Inset III
Holroyd, N.S.W. ... Inset IV
Hornsby, N.S.W. ... Inset IV
Hurstville, N.S.W. ... Inset IV
Inala, Qld. ... Inset III
Ipswich, Qld. ... Inset III
Kalamunda, W.A. ... Inset I
Kalgoorlie-Boulder, W.A. ... B3
Katherine, N.T. ... C1
Keilor, Vic. ... Inset V
Kelmscott, W.A. ... Inset I
Kersbrook, S.A. ... Inset II
Kwinana, W.A. ... Inset I
Kwinana Beach, W.A. ... Inset I
La Perouse, N.S.W. ... Inset IV
Launceston, Tas. ... D4
Leichhardt, N.S.W. ... Inset IV
Lilydale, Vic. ... Inset V
Lismore, N.S.W. ... E2
Liverpool, N.S.W. ... Inset IV
Lobethal, S.A. ... Inset II
Logan, Qld. ... Inset III
Longreach, Qld. ... D2
Mackay, Qld. ... D2
Mandurah, W.A. ... A3
Manly, Qld. ... Inset III
Manly, N.S.W. ... Inset IV
Marion, S.A. ... Inset II
Maryborough, Qld. ... E2
Melbourne, Vic., *capital* ... D3, Inset V
Melville, W.A. ... Inset I
Merredin, W.A. ... A3
Midland, W.A. ... Inset I
Mildura, Vic. ... D3
Mitcham, S.A. ... Inset II
Mona Vale, N.S.W. ... Inset IV
Moorabbin, Vic. ... Inset V
Mordialloc, Vic. ... Inset V
Moree, N.S.W. ... D2
Morningside, Qld. ... Inset III
Mosman Park, W.A. ... Inset I
Mount Barker, S.A. ... Inset II
Mount Gambier, S.A. ... D3
Mount Gravatt, Qld. ... Inset III
Mount Isa, Qld. ... C2
Mount Nebo, Qld. ... Inset III
Mullaloo, W.A. ... Inset I
Narrogin, W.A. ... A3
Nedlands, W.A. ... Inset I
Newcastle, N.S.W. ... E3
Newman, W.A. ... A2
Newmarket, Qld. ... Inset III
Noarlunga, S.A. ... Inset II
North Adelaide, S.A. ... Inset II
Northcote, Vic. ... Inset V
North Sydney, N.S.W. ... Inset IV
Nunawading, Vic. ... Inset V
Oakleigh, Vic. ... Inset V
Orange, N.S.W. ... D3
Parramatta, N.S.W. ... Inset IV
Perth, W.A., *capital* ... A3, Inset I
Petrie, Qld. ... Inset III
Pickering Brook, W.A. ... Inset I
Port Adelaide, S.A. ... Inset II
Port Augusta, S.A. ... C3
Port Hedland, W.A. ... A2
Port Lincoln, S.A. ... C3
Port Macquarie, N.S.W. ... E3
Port Pirie, S.A. ... C3
Prahran, Vic. ... Inset V
Preston, Vic. ... Inset V
Queenstown, Tas. ... D4
Randwick, N.S.W. ... Inset IV
Redcliffe, Qld. ... Inset III
Redland Bay, Qld. ... Inset III
Reynella, S.A. ... Inset II
Ringwood, Vic. ... Inset V
Rockdale, N.S.W. ... Inset IV
Rockhampton, Qld. ... E2
Roma, Qld. ... D2
Ryde, N.S.W. ... Inset IV
St. Ives, N.S.W. ... Inset IV
St. Kilda, S.A. ... Inset II
St. Kilda, Vic. ... Inset V
Salisbury, S.A. ... Inset II
Samford, Qld. ... Inset III
Sandgate, Qld. ... Inset III
Scarborough, W.A. ... Inset I
Spearwood, W.A. ... Inset I
Springvale, Vic. ... Inset V
Stirling, W.A. ... Inset I
Stirling, S.A. ... Inset II
Sunshine, Vic. ... Inset V
Sutherland, N.S.W. ... Inset IV
Sydney, N.S.W., *capital* ... E3, Inset IV
Tamworth, N.S.W. ... E3
Taree, N.S.W. ... E3
Tea Tree Gully, S.A. ... Inset II
Tennant Creek, N.T. ... C1
Tom Price, W.A. ... A2
Toowoomba, Qld. ... E2
Townsville, Qld. ... D1
Unley, S.A. ... Inset II
Victoria Park, W.A. ... Inset I
Victoria Point, Qld. ... Inset III
Wagga Wagga, N.S.W. ... D3
Wanneroo, W.A. ... Inset I
Warrnambool, Vic. ... D3
Waverley, Vic. ... Inset V
Weipa, Qld. ... D1
Whyalla, S.A. ... C3
Willoughby, N.S.W. ... Inset IV
Wollongong, N.S.W. ... E3
Woodside, S.A. ... Inset II
Woodville, S.A. ... Inset II
Woomera, S.A. ... C3
Wyndham, W.A. ... B1
Wynnum, Qld. ... Inset III

Other Features
Arafura, *sea* ... C1
Arnhem, *cape* ... C1
Arnhem Land, *region* ... C1
Ashburton, *river* ... A2
Ashmore and Cartier, *islands* ... B1
Australian Alps, *mts.* ... D3
Barkly, *tableland* ... C1
Bass, *strait* ... D3
Bate, *bay* ... Inset IV
Blue, *mts.* ... E3
Botany, *bay* ... Inset IV
Brisbane, *river* ... Inset III
Burdekin, *river* ... D1
Canning, *river* ... Inset I
Cape York, *peninsula* ... D1
Carpentaria, *gulf* ... C1
Coral, *sea* ... E1
Daly, *river* ... C1
Darling, *range* ... A3
Darling, *river* ... D3
Drysdale River Natl. Park ... B1
Eyre, *lake* ... C2
Eyre, *peninsula* ... C3
Fitzroy, *river* ... B1
Flinders, *range* ... C3
Flinders, *river* ... D1
Frome, *lake* ... D2
Gairdner, *lake* ... C3
Garden, *island* ... Inset
Gascoyne, *river* ... A2
Gibson, *desert* ... B2
Gilbert, *river* ... D1
Great Artesian, *basin* ... D2
Great Australian, *bight* ... B3
Great Barrier, *reef* ... D1
Great Dividing, *range* ... D1, D3
Great Sandy, *desert* ... B2
Great Victoria, *desert* ... B2
Gregory Natl. Park ... C1
Grey, *range* ... D2
Groote Eylandt, *island* ... C1
Hamersley, *range* ... A2
Hobsons, *bay* ... Inset V
Jackson, *port* ... Inset IV
Kakadu Natl. Park ... C1
Kangaroo, *island* ... C3
Kimberley, *plateau* ... B1
King Leopold, *range* ... B1
Kosciusko, *mt.* ... D3
Lakefield Natl. Park ... D1
Leeuwin, *cape* ... A3
Leichhardt, *river* ... D1
Leveque, *cape* ... B1
Logan, *river* ... Inset III
Macdonnell, *ranges* ... C2
Melville, *island* ... C1
Mitchell, *river* ... D1
Moreton, *bay* ... Inset III
Murchison, *river* ... A2
Murray, *river* ... D3
Murrumbidgee, *river* ... D3
Musgrave, *ranges* ... C2
New England, *range* ... E3
North West, *cape* ... A2
Nullarbor, *plain* ... B3
Port Phillip, *bay* ... Inset V
Roper, *river* ... C1
Rudall River Natl. Park ... B2
St. Vincent, *gulf* ... Inset II
Samsonvale, *lake* ... Inset III
Simpson, *desert* ... C2
Simpson Desert Natl. Park ... C2
Spencer, *gulf* ... C3
Swan, *river* ... Inset I
Tasman, *sea* ... E3
Timor, *sea* ... B1
Torrens, *lake* ... C2
Torrens, *river* ... Inset II
Torres, *strait* ... D1
Uluru (Ayers Rock) ... C2
Victoria, *river* ... C1
Witjira Natl. Park ... C2
Yampi, *sound* ... B1
York, *cape* ... D1

Australia

Capital: Canberra
Area: 2,966,200 sq. mi.
7,684,456 sq. km.
Population: 18,784,000
Largest City: Sydney
Language: English
Monetary Unit: Australian dollar

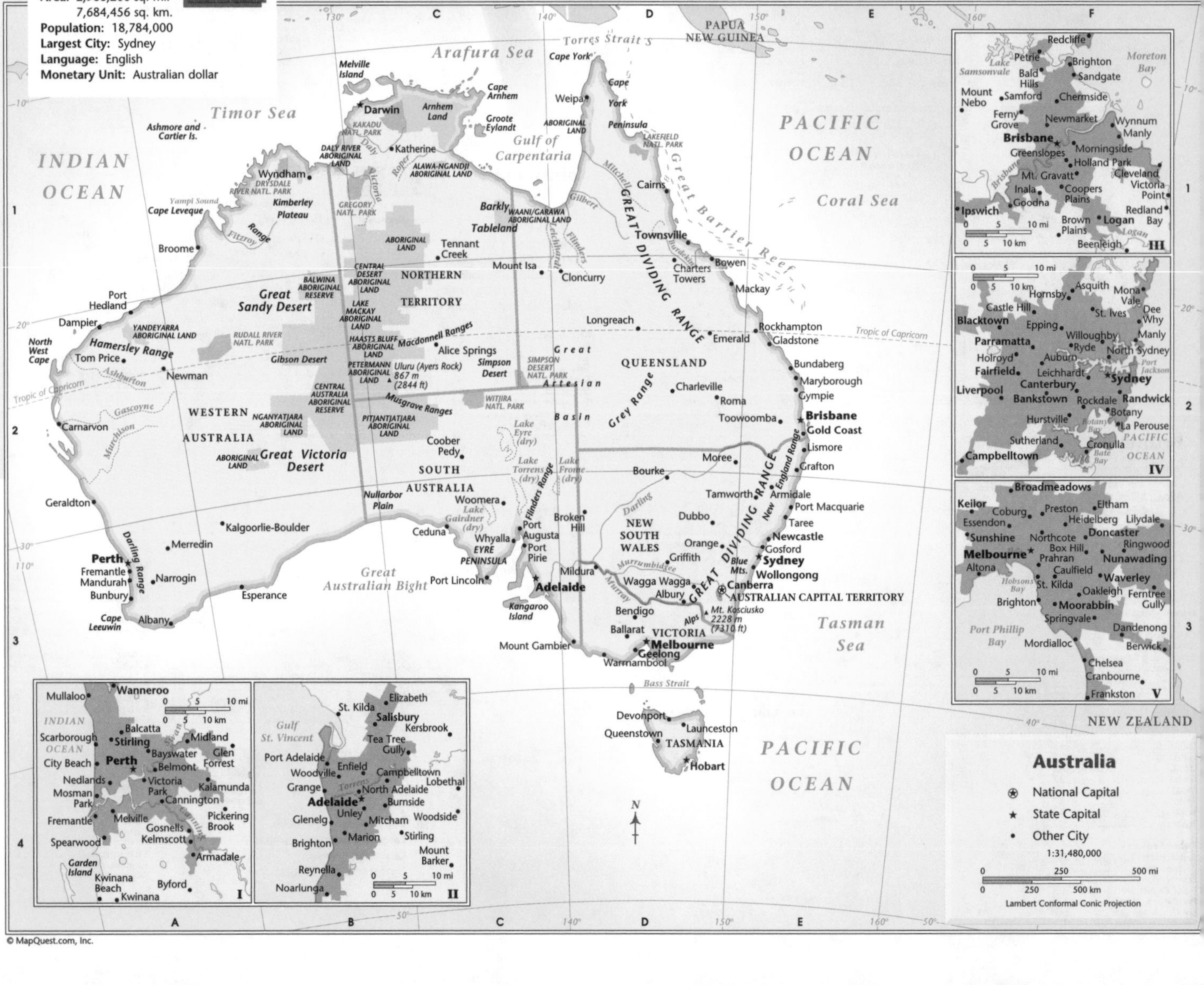

PAPUA NEW GUINEA
Arafura Sea
Torres Strait
Cape York
Timor Sea
INDIAN OCEAN
PACIFIC OCEAN
Coral Sea
Tasman Sea
Melville Island
Darwin
Arnhem Land
Cape Arnhem
Groote Eylandt
Gulf of Carpentaria
Weipa
Cape York Peninsula
Ashmore and Cartier Is.
Katherine
Wyndham
Kimberley Plateau
Cape Leveque
Broome
Port Hedland
Dampier
North West Cape
Hamersley Range
Tom Price
Newman
Great Sandy Desert
Gibson Desert
NORTHERN TERRITORY
Tennant Creek
Barkly Tableland
Mount Isa
Cloncurry
Cairns
Townsville
Charters Towers
Bowen
Mackay
GREAT DIVIDING RANGE
Great Barrier Reef
Longreach
Emerald
Rockhampton
Gladstone
Tropic of Capricorn
Alice Springs
Macdonnell Ranges
Uluru (Ayers Rock) 867 m (2844 ft)
Simpson Desert
Great Artesian Basin
QUEENSLAND
Grey Range
Charleville
Roma
Bundaberg
Maryborough
Gympie
Toowoomba
Brisbane
Gold Coast
Lismore
Grafton
Carnarvon
WESTERN AUSTRALIA
Musgrave Ranges
Great Victoria Desert
Coober Pedy
SOUTH AUSTRALIA
Lake Eyre (dry)
Lake Torrens (dry)
Lake Frome (dry)
Moree
Bourke
Geraldton
Nullarbor Plain
Woomera
Lake Gairdner (dry)
Flinders Range
Broken Hill
Tamworth
Armidale
Port Macquarie
Dubbo
NEW SOUTH WALES
Taree
Newcastle
Gosford
Sydney
Wollongong
Orange
Griffith
Blue Mts.
Kalgoorlie-Boulder
Merredin
Perth
Fremantle
Mandurah
Darling Range
Narrogin
Bunbury
Esperance
Cape Leeuwin
Albany
Great Australian Bight
Ceduna
Whyalla
Port Augusta
Port Pirie
Eyre Peninsula
Port Lincoln
Adelaide
Kangaroo Island
Mildura
Wagga Wagga
Albury
Canberra
AUSTRALIAN CAPITAL TERRITORY
Mt. Kosciusko 2228 m (7310 ft)
Bendigo
Ballarat
VICTORIA
Melbourne
Geelong
Mount Gambier
Warrnambool
Bass Strait
Devonport
Launceston
Queenstown
TASMANIA
Hobart
NEW ZEALAND
Redcliffe
Petrie
Lake Samsonvale
Brighton
Moreton Bay
Bald Hills
Sandgate
Mount Nebo
Samford
Chermside
Ferny Grove
Newmarket
Wynnum
Manly
Brisbane
Morningside
Greenslopes
Holland Park
Mt. Gravatt
Cleveland
Inala
Coopers Plains
Victoria Point
Ipswich
Goodna
Redland Bay
Brown Plains
Logan
Beenleigh
III
Hornsby
Asquith
Mona Vale
Castle Hill
St. Ives
Dee Why
Blacktown
Epping
Willoughby
Manly
Parramatta
Ryde
North Sydney
Holroyd
Auburn
Fairfield
Leichhardt
Sydney
Canterbury
Liverpool
Bankstown
Rockdale
Randwick
Hurstville
Botany
La Perouse
Sutherland
Cronulla
Campbelltown
IV
Broadmeadows
Keilor
Coburg
Preston
Eltham
Essendon
Heidelberg
Lilydale
Sunshine
Northcote
Doncaster
Melbourne
Box Hill
Ringwood
Prahran
Nunawading
Altona
Caulfield
St. Kilda
Waverley
Oakleigh
Ferntree Gully
Brighton
Moorabbin
Springvale
Port Phillip Bay
Dandenong
Mordialloc
Berwick
Chelsea
Cranbourne
Frankston
V
Mullaloo
Wanneroo
Balcatta
Scarborough
Stirling
Midland
Bayswater
Glen Forrest
City Beach
Perth
Belmont
Nedlands
Victoria Park
Kalamunda
Mosman Park
Fremantle
Melville
Cannington
Pickering Brook
Gosnells
Kelmscott
Spearwood
Armadale
Garden Island
Kwinana Beach
Kwinana
Byford
I
Gulf St. Vincent
St. Kilda
Elizabeth
Salisbury
Kersbrook
Tea Tree Gully
Port Adelaide
Enfield
Woodville
Campbelltown
Grange
North Adelaide
Lobethal
Adelaide
Burnside
Glenelg
Unley
Woodside
Mitcham
Stirling
Brighton
Marion
Mount Barker
Reynella
Noarlunga
II
Australia
National Capital
State Capital
Other City
1:31,480,000
Lambert Conformal Conic Projection

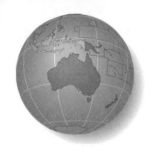

New Zealand

Capital: Wellington
Area: 104,454 sq. mi.
270,606 sq. km.
Population: 3,662,000
Largest City: Auckland
Language: English
Monetary Unit: New Zealand dollar

New Zealand: Map Index

Cities and Towns

Alexandra A4
Ashburton B3
Auckland B2
Blenheim B3
Christchurch B3
Collingwood B3
Dunedin B4
East Coast Bays...........B2
Gisborne C2
Greymouth B3
Hamilton C2
Hastings C2
Hicks Bay C2
Invercargill A4
Kaeo B2
Kaikoura B3
Kaitaia B2
Kawhia B2
Lower Hutt B3
Manukau B2
Milford Sound A3
Napier C2
Nelson B3
New Plymouth B2
Oamaru B4
Palmerston North C3
Queenstown A3
Rotorua C2
Taumaruni C2
Taupo C2
Tauranga C2
Timaru B3
Waimamaku B2
Wanganui C2
Wellington, capital B3
Westport B3
Whakatane C2
Whangarei B2

Other Features

Aspiring, mt. A3
Banks, peninsula B3
Canterbury, bight B3
Canterbury, plains B3
Clutha, river A4
Cook, mt. B3
Cook, strait B3
Coromandel, peninsula...........C2
East, cape C2
Egmont, cape B2
Egmont, mt. B2
Farewell, cape B3
Foveaux, strait A4
Great Barrier, island...........C2
Hawea, lake A3
Hawke, bay C2
Ngauruhoe, mt. C2
North, cape B1
North, island B2
North Taranaki, bight.........B2
Palliser, cape B3
Pegasus, bay B3
Plenty, bay C2
Puysegur, point A4
Rangitikei, river C2
Raukumara, range C2
Ruahine, range C2
Ruapehu, mt. C2
South, island A3
Southern Alps, mts. A3
Southland, plains A4
South Taranaki, bight.........B2
South West, cape A4
Stewart, island A4
Tararua, range C3
Tasman, bay B3
Tasman, sea A3
Taupo, lake C2
Te Anau, lake A4
Tekapo, lake B3
Three Kings, islands B1
Tongariro, mt. C2
Waikato, river C2
Wairau, river B3
Waitaki, river B3
Wanaka, lake A3

Papua New Guinea: Map Index

Cities and Towns

Alotau B3
Arawa B2
Daru A2
Goroka A2
Kavieng B2
Kerema A2
Kimbe B2
Lae A2
Lorengau A2
Madang A2
Morehead A2
Mount Hagen A2
Popondetta A2
Port Moresby, capital.........A2
Rabaul B2
Vanimo A2
Wabag A2
Wau A2
Wewak A1

Other Features

Admiralty, islands A2
Bismarck, archipelago A2
Bismarck, range A2
Bismarck, sea A2
Bougainville, island...........B2
Buka, island B2
Central, range A2
Coral, sea A3
D'Entrecasteaux, islands A2
Feni, islands B2
Fly, river A2
Gazelle, peninsula...........B2
Green, islands B2
Huon, peninsula A2
Karkar, island A2
Lihir, group B2
Louisiade, archipelago B3
Manus, island A2
Markham, river A2
Milne, bay B3
Murray, lake A2
Mussau, island A2
New Britain, island A2
New Guinea, island A2
New Hanover, island B2
New Ireland, island...........B2
Ninigo, group A2
Nuguria, islands B2
Owen Stanley, range A2
Papua, gulf A2
Purari, river A2
Ramu, river A2
Rossel, island B3
St. George's, channel B2
Sepik, river A2
Solomon, sea B2
Tabar, islands B2
Tagula, island B3
Tanga, islands B2
Tauu, islands B2
Torres, strait A2
Trobriand, islands B2
Umboi, island A2
Whiteman, range A2
Wilhelm, mt. A2
Witu, islands A2
Woodlark (Muyua), island.........B2

Papua New Guinea

Capital: Port Moresby
Area: 178,704 sq. mi.
462,964 sq. km.
Population: 4,705,000
Largest City: Port Moresby
Language: English
Monetary Unit: Kina

MAJOR CITIES

Australia		Papua New Guinea	
Sydney	3,935,000		(metro)
Melbourne	3,322,000	Morobe	439,725
Brisbane	1,548,000	Western	398,376
Perth	1,319,000	Highlands	
Adelaide	1,083,000	Southern	390,240
		Highlands	
New Zealand		Eastern	316,802
Auckland	998,000	Highlands	
Wellington	335,000	Madang	288,317
Christchurch	331,000	Port Moresby	271,813
Hamilton	159,000		
Dunedin	112,000		

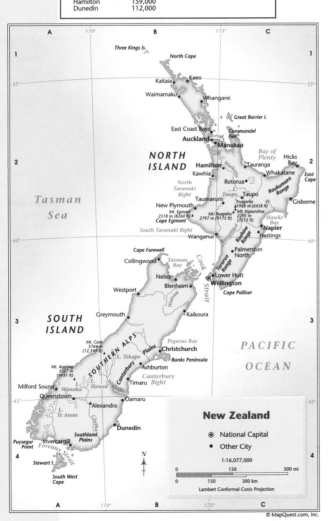

New Zealand

⊛ National Capital
• Other City

1:16,077,000

0   150   300 mi
0   150   300 km

Lambert Conformal Conic Projection

© MapQuest.com, Inc.

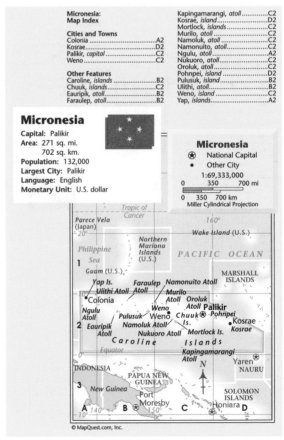

Micronesia: Map Index

Cities and Towns

Colonia A2
Kosrae D2
Palikir, capital C2
Weno C2

Other Features

Caroline, islands B2
Chuuk, islands C2
Eauripik, atoll...................B2
Faraulep, atoll...................B2
Kapingamarangi, atoll...........C2
Kosrae, island D2
Mortlock, islands C2
Murilo, atoll...................C2
Namoluk, atoll...................C2
Namonuito, atoll...................C2
Ngulu, atoll...................A2
Nukuoro, atoll...................C2
Oroluk, atoll...................C2
Pohnpei, island D2
Pulusuk, island B2
Ulithi, atoll...................B2
Weno, island C2
Yap, islands...................A2

Micronesia

Capital: Palikir
Area: 271 sq. mi.
702 sq. km.
Population: 132,000
Largest City: Palikir
Language: English
Monetary Unit: U.S. dollar

Papua New Guinea

⊛ National Capital
• Other City

1:23,692,000

0   150   300 mi
0   150   300 km

Mercator Projection

© MapQuest.com, Inc.

Micronesia

⊛ National Capital
• Other City

1:69,333,000

0   350   700 mi
0   350   700 km

Miller Cylindrical Projection

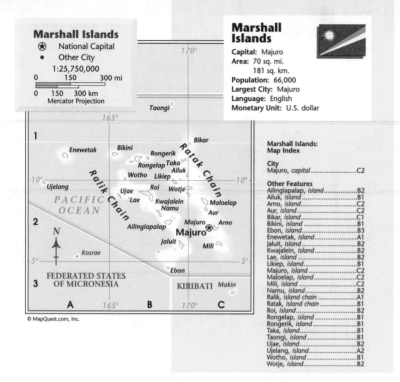

Marshall Islands

⊛ National Capital
• Other City

1:25,750,000

0   150   300 mi
0   150   300 km
Mercator Projection

Marshall Islands

Capital: Majuro
Area: 70 sq. mi.
181 sq. km.
Population: 66,000
Largest City: Majuro
Language: English
Monetary Unit: U.S. dollar

**Marshall Islands:
Map Index**

City
Majuro, *capital*......................C2

Other Features
Ailinglapalap, *island*..............B2
Ailuk, *island*........................B1
Arno, *island*........................C2
Aur, *island*.........................C2
Bikar, *island*.......................C1
Bikini, *island*......................B1
Ebon, *island*.......................B3
Enewetak, *island*..................A1
Jaluit, *island*......................B2
Kwajalein, *island*.................B2
Lae, *island*........................B2
Likiep, *island*.....................B1
Majuro, *island*....................C2
Maloelap, *island*..................C2
Mili, *island*........................C2
Namu, *island*......................B2
Ralik, *island chain*................A1
Ratak, *island chain*...............B1
Roi, *island*........................B2
Rongelap, *island*..................B1
Rongerik, *island*..................B1
Taka, *island*......................B1
Taongi, *island*.....................B1
Ujae, *island*.......................B2
Ujelang, *island*....................A2
Wotho, *island*.....................B1
Wotje, *island*......................B2

© MapQuest.com, Inc.

Nauru

⊛ National Capital
• Other City

1:135,000

0   1   2 mi
0   1   2 km
Lambert Conformal Conic Projection

Nauru

Capital: Yaren
Area: 8.2 sq. mi.
21 sq. km.
Population: 11,000
Largest City: Yaren
Languages: Nauruan, English
Monetary Unit: Australian dollar

**Nauru:
Map Index**

Cities and Towns
Aiwo.................................A2
Anabar..............................C1
Anetan.............................B1
Anibare.............................B2
Baiti.................................B1
Buada...............................B2
Denigomodu.......................A2
Ewa.................................B1
Ijuw.................................C2

Meneng..............................B3
Nibok...............................B2
Uaboe...............................B1
Yaren, *capital*....................B3

Other Features
Anibare, *bay*......................C2
Anna, *point*......................B1
Buada, *lagoon*....................B2
Central, *plateau*..................B2
Meneng, *point*...................C2
Moqua, *well*.......................B2

© MapQuest.com, Inc.

Solomon Islands

⊛ National Capital
• Other City

1:24,100,000

0   150   300 mi
0   150   300 km
Mercator Projection

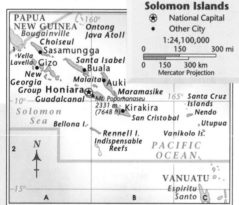

**Solomon Islands:
Map Index**

Cities and Towns
Auki.................................B1
Buala A1
Gizo................................A1
Honiara, *capital*..................A1
Kirakira.............................B2
Sasamungga........................A1

Other Features
Bellona, *island*...................A2
Choiseul, *island*..................A1
Guadalcanal, *island*..............A1
Indispensable, *reefs*..............B2
Malaita, *island*...................B1
Maramasike, *island*..............B1
Nendo, *island*....................C2
New Georgia Group,
islands........................A1
Ontong Java, *island*..............A1
Popomanaseu, *mt.*................B1
Rennell, *island*...................B2
San Cristobal, *island*.............B2
Santa Cruz, *islands*..............C2
Santa Isabel, *island*..............A1
Solomon, *sea*....................A2
Utupua, *island*...................C2
Vanikolo, *islands*.................C2
Vella Lavella, *island*.............A1

Solomon Islands

Capital: Honiara
Area: 10,954 sq. mi.
28,378 sq. km.
Population: 455,000
Largest City: Honiara
Language: English
Monetary Unit: Dollar

Tuvalu

Capital: Funafuti
Area: 9.4 sq. mi.
24.4 sq. km.
Population: 11,000
Largest City: Funafuti
Languages: Tuvaluan, English
Monetary Unit: Tuvalu dollar,
Australian dollar

**Tuvalu:
Map Index**

City
Funafuti, *capital* C3

Other Features
Funafuti, *island*...................C3
Nanumanga, *island* B2
Nanumea, *island* B1
Niulakita, *island*..................C4
Niutao, *island*....................B2
Nui, *island*.......................B2
Nukufetau, *island*................C2
Nukulaelae, *island*...............C3
Vaitupu, *island* C2

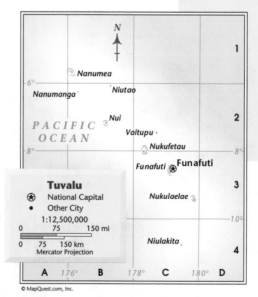

Tuvalu

⊛ National Capital
• Other City

1:12,500,000

0   75   150 mi
0   75   150 km
Mercator Projection

© MapQuest.com, Inc.

Fiji:
Map Index

Cities and Towns
Galoa B3
Labasa B2
Lami B3
Lautoka A2
Lomawai A3
Nabouwalu A2
Nadi A2
Naduri B2
Nakodu B2
Navua B3
Suva, *capital* B3
Vunisea B3

Other Features
Beqa, *island* B3
Bligh Water, *sound* B2
Cicia, *island* C2
Cikobia, *island* C1
Gau, *island* B3
Great Sea, *reef* B1
Kadavu, *island* B3
Kadavu, *passage* A3
Kioa, *island* C2

Koro, *island* B2
Koro, *sea* B2
Lakeba, *island* C3
Lakeba, *passage* C3
Lau, *island group* C2
Laucala, *island* C2
Moala, *island group* B3
Nadi, *bay* A2
Navua, *river* A3
Ono, *island* B3
Ovalau, *island* B2
Qamea, *island* C2
Qelelevu, *island* C2
Rabi, *island* C2
Soso, *bay* B3
Taveuni, *island* C2
Tomanivi, *mt.* B2
Udu, *point* C2
Vanua Balavu, *island* C2
Vanua Levu, *island* B2
Vatu Lele, *island* A3
Vetauua, *island* C1
Viti Levu, *island* A2
Vunaniu, *bay* A3
Washington, *cape* A3
Yasawa, *island group* A2

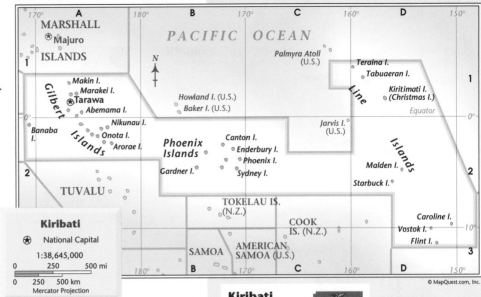

Kiribati

Capital: Tarawa
Area: 313 sq. mi.
    811 sq. km.
Population: 86,000
Largest City: Tarawa
Languages: I-Kiribati (Gilbertese), English
Monetary Unit: Australian dollar

Kiribati:
Map Index

City
Tarawa, *capital* A1

Other Features
Abemama, *island* A1
Arorae, *island* A2

Banaba, *island* A2
Canton, *island* B2
Caroline, *island* D2
Enderbury, *island* B2
Flint, *island* D3
Gardner, *island* B2
Gilbert, *islands* A1
Kiritimati (Christmas), *island* D1
Line, *islands* D1
Makin, *island* A1
Malden, *island* D2
Marakei, *island* A1
Nikunau, *island* A2
Onota, *island* A2
Phoenix, *island* B2
Phoenix, *islands* B2
Starbuck, *island* D2
Sydney, *island* B2
Tabuaeran, *island* D1
Teraina, *island* D1
Vostok, *island* D3

Kiribati

Fiji

Capital: Suva
Area: 7,056 sq. mi.
    18,280 sq. km.
Population: 813,000
Largest City: Suva
Languages: Fijian, Hindi, English
Monetary Unit: Fiji dollar

Fiji

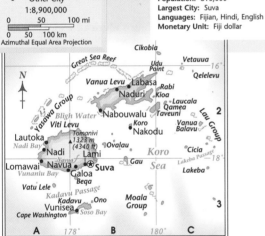

© MapQuest.com, Inc.

Tonga

(National Capital / Other City)
1:11,000,000
0   75   150 mi
0   75   150 km
Mercator Projection

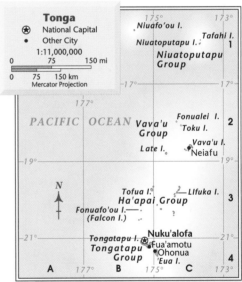

© MapQuest.com, Inc.

Palau:
Map Index

Cities and Towns
Kloulklubed B3
Koror, *capital* C3
Melekeok B3
Meyungs B3
Ngaramasch B4
Ngerkeel B3
Ngermechau C2
Ngetbong C2
Ollei C2

Other Features
Angaur, *island* B4
Arakabesan, *island* B3
Arekalong, *peninsula* C2

Babelthuap, *island* C3
Cormoran, *reef* B3
Eli Malk, *island* B3
Helen, *reef* ....Inset
Kayangel, *islands* C1
Koror, *island* C3
Kossol, *passage* C2
Kossol, *reef* C2
Merir, *island* ....Inset
Ngemelis, *islands* B3
Peleliu, *island* B4
Philippine, *sea* B2
Pulo Anna, *island* ....Inset
Sar, *passage* B3
Sonsoral, *island* ....Inset
Tobi, *island* ....Inset
Urukthapel, *island* B3

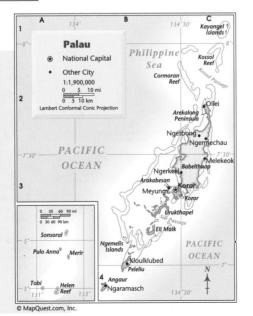

© MapQuest.com, Inc.

Palau

Capital: Koror
Area: 177 sq. mi.
    458 sq. km.
Population: 18,000
Largest City: Koror
Languages: English, Sonsorolese, Angaur, Japanese, Tobi, Palauan
Monetary Unit: U.S. dollar

Tonga

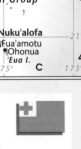

Capital: Nuku'alofa
Area: 301 sq. mi.
    780 sq. km.
Population: 109,000
Largest City: Nuku'alofa
Languages: Tongan, English
Monetary Unit: Pa'anga

Tonga:
Map Index

Cities and Towns
Fua'amotu B4
Neiafu C2
Nuku'alofa, *capital* B4
Ohonua C4

Other Features
'Eua, *island* C4
Fonuafo'ou (Falcon), *island* B3
Fonualei, *island* C2

Ha'apai, *island group* B3
Late, *island* C2
Lifuka, *island* C3
Niuafo'ou, *island* B1
Niuatoputapu, *island* C1
Niuatoputapu, *island group* C1
Tafahi, *island* C1
Tofua, *island* B3
Toku, *island* C2
Tongatapu, *island* B4
Tongatapu, *island group* B4
Vava'u, *island* C2
Vava'u, *island group* C2

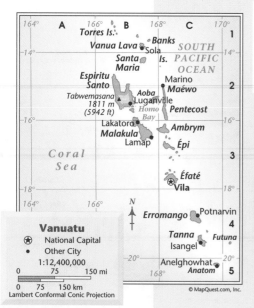

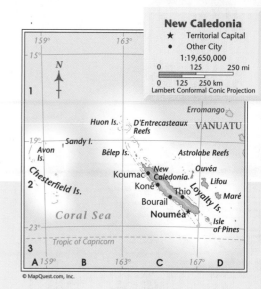

Vanuatu

Capital: Vila
Area: 4,707 sq. mi.
  12,194 sq. km.
Population: 189,000
Largest City: Vila
Languages: French, English, Bislama
Monetary Unit: Vatu

Vanuatu: Map Index

Cities and Towns
Anelghowhat	C5
Isangel	C4
Lakatoro	B3
Lamap	B3
Luganville	B2
Marino	C2
Potnarvin	C4
Sola	B1
Vila, capital	C3

Other Features
Ambrym, island	C3
Anatom, island	C5
Aoba, island	B2
Banks, islands	B1
Coral, sea	C3
Éfaté, island	C3
Épi, island	C3
Erromango, island	C4
Espiritu Santo, island	B2
Futuna, island	C4
Homo, bay	B2
Maéwo, island	C2
Malakula, island	B3
Pentecost, island	C2
Santa Maria, island	B2
Tabwemasana, mt.	B2
Tanna, island	C4
Torres, islands	B1
Vanua Lava, island	B1

New Caledonia

Capital: Nouméa
Area: 8,548 sq. mi.
  21,912 sq. km.
Population: 197,000
Largest City: Nouméa
Language: French
Monetary Unit: CFA Franc

New Caledonia: Map Index

Cities and Towns
Bourail	C2
Koné	C2
Koumac	C2
Nouméa, capital	C2
Thio	C2

Other Features
Astrolabe, reefs	C2
Avon, islands	A2
Bélep, islands	C2
Chesterfield, islands	A2
Coral, sea	B2
D'Entrecasteaux, reefs	C1
Huon, islands	B1
Lifou, island	D2
Loyalty, islands	C2
Maré, island	D2
New Caledonia, island	C2
Ouvéa, island	D2
Pines, island	D2
Sandy, island	B2

Samoa

Capital: Apia
Area: 1,093 sq. mi.
  2,832 sq. km.
Population: 230,000
Largest City: Apia
Languages: Samoan, English
Monetary Unit: Tala

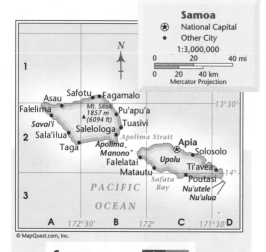

Samoa: Map Index

Cities and Towns
Apia, capital	C2
Asau	A2
Fagamalo	B1
Falelatai	B2
Falelima	A2
Matautu	C2
Poutasi	C3
Pu'apu'a	B2
Safotu	B1
Sala'ilua	A2
Salelologa	B2
Solosolo	C2
Taga	A2
Ti'avea	D2
Tuasivi	B2

Other Features
Apolima, island	B2
Apolima, strait	B2
Manono, island	B2
Nu'ulua, island	D3
Nu'utele, island	D3
Safata, bay	C3
Savai'i, island	A2
Silisili, mt.	B2
Upolu, island	C2

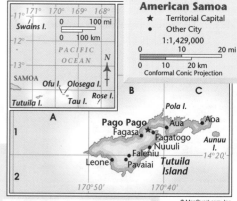

American Samoa: Map Index

Cities and Towns
Aoa	C1
Aua	C1
Fagasa	B1
Fagatogo	C1
Faleniu	B1
Leone	B2
Nuuuli	B1
Pago Pago, capital	B1
Pavaiai	B2

Other Features
Aunuu, island	C1
Ofu, island	A1
Olosega, island	A1
Pola, island	C1
Rose, island	B1
Swains, island	A1
Tau, island	A1
Tutuila, island	A1, C2

American Samoa

Capital: Pago Pago
Area: 77 sq. mi.
  199 sq. km.
Population: 64,000
Largest City: Pago Pago
Language: Samoan, English
Monetary Unit: U.S. dollar

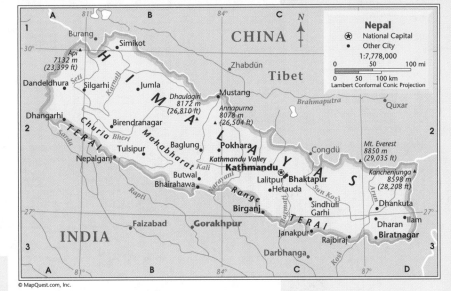

Nepal

* ⊛ National Capital
* • Other City

1:7,778,000

Lambert Conformal Conic Projection

© MapQuest.com, Inc.

Nepal:
Map Index

Cities and Towns
Baglung B2
Bhairahawa B2
Bhaktapur C2
Biratnagar D3
Birendranagar B2
Birganj C2
Butwal B2
Dandeldhura A2
Dhangarhi A2
Dhankuta D2
Dharan D3
Hetauda C2
Ilam D3
Janakpur C3
Jumla B2
Kathmandu, capital C2
Lalitpur C2
Mustang B2
Nepalganj B2
Pokhara B2
Rajbiraj C3
Silgarhi B2
Simikot B1
Sindhuli Garhi C2
Tulsipur B2

Other Features
Annapurna, mt. B2
Api, mt. A2
Arun, river D2
Bagmati, river B2
Bheri, river B2
Churia, mts. B2
Dhaulagiri, mt. B2
Everest, mt. C2
Himalayas, mts. B2
Kali, river B2
Kanchenjunga, mt. D2
Karnali, river B2
Kathmandu, valley C2
Mahabharat, range B2
Narayani, river B2
Rapti, river B2
Sarda, river A2
Seti, river A2
Sun Kosi, river C2
Terai, region A2, C3

Maldives

Capital: Male
Area: 115 sq. mi.
          298 sq. km.
Population: 300,000
Largest City: Male
Language: Divehi
Monetary Unit: Rufiyaa

Nepal

Capital: Kathmandu
Area: 56,827 sq. mi.
          147,220 sq. km.
Population: 24,303,000
Largest City: Kathmandu
Language: Nepali
Monetary Unit: Rupee

© MapQuest.com, Inc.

Maldives:
Map Index

City
Male, capital A2

Other Features
Addu, atoll A5
Ari, atoll A3
Equatorial, channel A5
Fadiffolu, atoll A2
Felidu, atoll A3
Haddummati, atoll A4
Horsburgh, atoll A2
Ihavandiffulu, atoll A1
Kardiva, channel A2
Kolumadulu, atoll A3
Malcolm, atoll A1
Male, atoll A2
Miladummadulu, atoll A1
Mulaku, atoll A3
Nilandu, atoll A3
North Malosmadulu, atoll A2
One and Half Degree, channel ...A4
South Male, atoll A3
South Malosmadulu, atoll A4
Suvadiva, atoll A4
Tiladummati, atoll A1
Veimandu, channel A3

Maldives

* ⊛ National Capital

1:11,579,000

Lambert Conformal Conic Projection

Sri Lanka:
Map Index

Provinces
Central B4
Eastern C4
North Central B3
Northern B2
North Western B4
Sabaragamuwa B5
Southern B5
Uva C5
Western A4

Cities and Towns
Amparai C4
Anuradhapura B3
Batticaloa C4
Colombo, capital A5
Dehiwala-Mt. Lavinia A5
Galle B5

Hambantota C5
Jaffna B2
Kalutara A5
Kandy B4
Kilinochchi B2
Kurunegala B4
Mankulam B2
Mannar A3
Matale B4
Matara B6
Moratuwa A5
Mullaittivu B2
Negombo B4
Nuwara Eliya B5
Point Pedro B2
Polonnaruwa C4
Pottuvil C5
Puttalam A3
Ratnapura B5
Sri Jayawardenepura, capital A5

Trincomalee C3
Vavuniya B3

Other Features
Adam's, peak B4
Adam's Bridge, shoal A3
Aruvi, river B3
Bengal, bay C3
Delft, island A2
Dondra Head, cape B6
Jaffna, lagoon B2
Kalu, river B5
Kelani, river B4
Mahaweli Ganga, river C4
Mannar, gulf A3
Mannar, island A2
Palk, strait A2
Pidurutalagala, mt. B4
Trincomalee, harbor C3
Yan, river B3

Sri Lanka

Capital: Colombo,
          Sri Jayawardenepura
Area: 25,332 sq. mi.
          65,627 sq. km.
Population: 19,145,000
Largest City: Colombo
Language: Sinhalese
Monetary Unit: Rupee

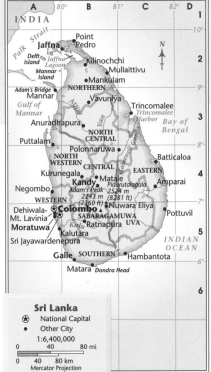

© MapQuest.com, Inc.

Bhutan

Capital: Thimphu
Area: 18,147 sq. mi.
          47,013 sq. km.
Population: 1,952,000
Largest City: Thimphu
Language: Dzongkha
Monetary Unit: Ngultrum

Bhutan

* ⊛ National Capital
* • Other City

1:6,053,000

Lambert Conformal Conic Projection

© MapQuest.com, Inc.

Bhutan:
Map Index

Cities and Towns
Chhuka A2
Geylegphug B3
Lhuntshi C2
Lingshi A2
Louri C2
Paro A2
Phuntsholing A3
Punakha A2
Sarbhang B3
Shamgong B2
Tashigang C2

Thimphu, capital A2
Tongsa B2

Other Features
Chomo Lhari, mt. A1
Dangme, river C2
Duars, plain A3
Himalayas, mts. B1
Kula Kangri, mt. B1
Kuru, river C2
Lhobrak, river B2
Sankosh, river A2
Tongsa, river B2
Wong, river A2

Sri Lanka

* ⊛ National Capital
* • Other City

1:6,400,000

Mercator Projection

© MapQuest.com, Inc.

India: Map Index

Internal Divisions
Andaman and Nicobar
  Islands (territory) F6
Andhra Pradesh (state) C5
Arunachal Pradesh (state) F3
Assam (state) F3
Bihar (state) E3
Chandigarh (territory) C2
Chhattisgarh (state) D4
Dadra and Nagar
  Haveli (territory) B4
Daman and Diu (territory) B4
Delhi (territory) C3
Goa (state) B5
Gujarat (state) B4
Haryana (state) C3
Himachal Pradesh (state) C2
Jammu and Kashmir (state) ...C2

Jharkhand (state) E4
Karnataka (state) C6
Kerala (state) C6
Lakshadweep (territory) B6
Madhya Pradesh (state) C4
Maharashtra (state) B5
Manipur (state) F4
Meghalaya (state) F3
Mizoram (state) F4
Nagaland (state) F3
Orissa (state) D4
Pondicherry (territory) C6
Punjab (state) C2
Rajasthan (state) B3
Sikkim (state) E3
Tamil Nadu (state) C6
Tripura (state) F4
Uttar Pradesh (state) C3
Uttaranchal (state) C3
West Bengal (state) E4

Cities and Towns
Agartala F4
Agra C3
Ahmadabad B4
Aizawl F4
Ajmer B3
Akola C4
Alampur ....Inset II
Aligarh C3
Allahabad D3
Alleppey (Alappuzah) C7
Amdanga ....Inset II
Amravati C4
Amritsar B2
Andheri ....Inset I
Ara D3
Asansol E4
Aurangabad C5
Babu Bheri ....Inset II
Baidyabati ....Inset II
Bally ....Inset II

Bamangachi ....Inset II
Bananga F7
Bandra ....Inset I
Bangalore C6
Bansbaria ....Inset II
Barakpur ....Inset II
Baranagar ....Inset II
Barasat ....Inset II
Bareilly C3
Bargachia ....Inset II
Bauria ....Inset II
Behala ....Inset II
Belapurpada ....Inset I
Belgaum B5
Bellary C5
Bhadrakh E4
Bhadreswar ....Inset II
Bhagalpur E3
Bhamapur D5
Bhandup ....Inset I
Bharatpur C3

Bhatapara D4
Bhatpara ....Inset II
Bhavnagar B4
Bhayandar ....Inset I
Bhimpur ....Inset II
Bhiwandi ....Inset I
Bhopal C4
Bhubaneswar E4
Bhuj A4
Bihar E3
Bijapur B5
Bikaner B3
Bilaspur D4
Bishnupur ....Inset II
Borivli ....Inset I
Buj-Buj ....Inset II
Burdwan E4
Burhanpur C4
Chandannagar ....Inset II
Chandigarh C2
Chandrapur C5

Chembur ....Inset II
Chene ....Inset II
Chennai (Madras) D6
Cherrapunji F3
Chirner ....Inset I
Cochin (Kochi) C7
Coimbatore C6
Cuddalore C6
Cuttack E4
Daman B4
Darbhanga E3
Darjiling E3
Dehra Dun C3
Delhi C3
Dhulagarh ....Inset II
Dibrugarh F3
Dispur F3
Diu B4
Dum-Dum ....Inset II
Dumjor ....Inset II
Faizabad D3

Gandhinagar B4
Ganganagar B3
Gangtok E3
Garden Reach ....Inset II
Garulia ....Inset II
Gauhati F3
Gaya D3
Ghatkopar ....Inset I
Gorakhpur D3
Gulbarga C5
Guntur C5
Gwalior C3
Halisahar ....Inset II
Haora ....E4, Inset II
Hisabpur ....Inset II
Hubli-Dharwar C5
Hugli-Chunchura ....Inset II
Hyderabad C5
Imphal F4
Indore C4
Itanagar F3
Jabalpur D4
Jadabpur ....Inset II
Jagdalpur D5
Jaipur C3
Jammu B2
Jamnagar A4
Jampur ....Inset II
Jamshedpur E4
Janai ....Inset II
Jejur ....Inset I
Jhansi C3
Jodhpur B3
Joka ....Inset II
Jullundur B2
Junagadh B4
Kakinada D5
Kalwa ....Inset I
Kaman ....Inset I
Kamarhati ....Inset II
Kanchipuram C6
Kanchrapara ....Inset II
Kanpur D3
Kansaripara ....Inset II
Kasinathpur ....Inset II
Kathgodam C3
Kharagpur E4
Kohima F3
Kolhapur B5
Kolkata (Calcutta) ....E4, Inset II
Kolshet ....Inset I
Konnagar ....Inset II
Kota C3
Kozhikode C6
Kurla ....Inset I
Kurnool C5
Lakhpat A4
Lucknow D3
Ludhiana C2
Madurai C7
Malad ....Inset I
Malegaon B4
Mangalore B6
Mathura C3
Meerut C3
Moradabad C3
Mulund ....Inset I
Mumbai (Bombay) ....B5, Inset I
Mumbra ....Inset I
Mysore C6
Nagpur C4
Naihati ....Inset II
Nalikul ....Inset II
Nanded C5
Nangi ....Inset I
Nanole ....Inset I
Nasik B4
Nellore C6
New Delhi, capital C3
Nizamabad C5
Ongole C5
Panaji B5
Panihati ....Inset II
Patiala C2
Patna D3
Paye ....Inset I
Polba ....Inset II
Pondicherry C6
Port Blair F6
Pune B5
Raipur D4
Rajkot B4
Rajpur D4
Rambanti ....Inset II
Ranchi E4
Raurkela E4
Rishra ....Inset II
Saharanpur Panipat C3
Salem C6
Sambalpur D4
Sankrail ....Inset II
Sasaram D4
Sheva ....Inset I
Shillong F3
Sholapur C5
Shrirampur ....Inset II
Silvassi B4
Simla C2
Singur ....Inset II
Sonarpur ....Inset II
South Dum-Dum ....Inset II
Srinagar B2
Sugandha ....Inset II
Surat B4
Thane ....Inset I
Thanjavur C6
Tiruchchirappalli C6
Titagarh ....Inset II
Trivandrum
  (Thiruvananthapuram) C7

India map with National Capital and Other City legend. Scale 1:20,000,000. Lambert Conformal Conic Projection.

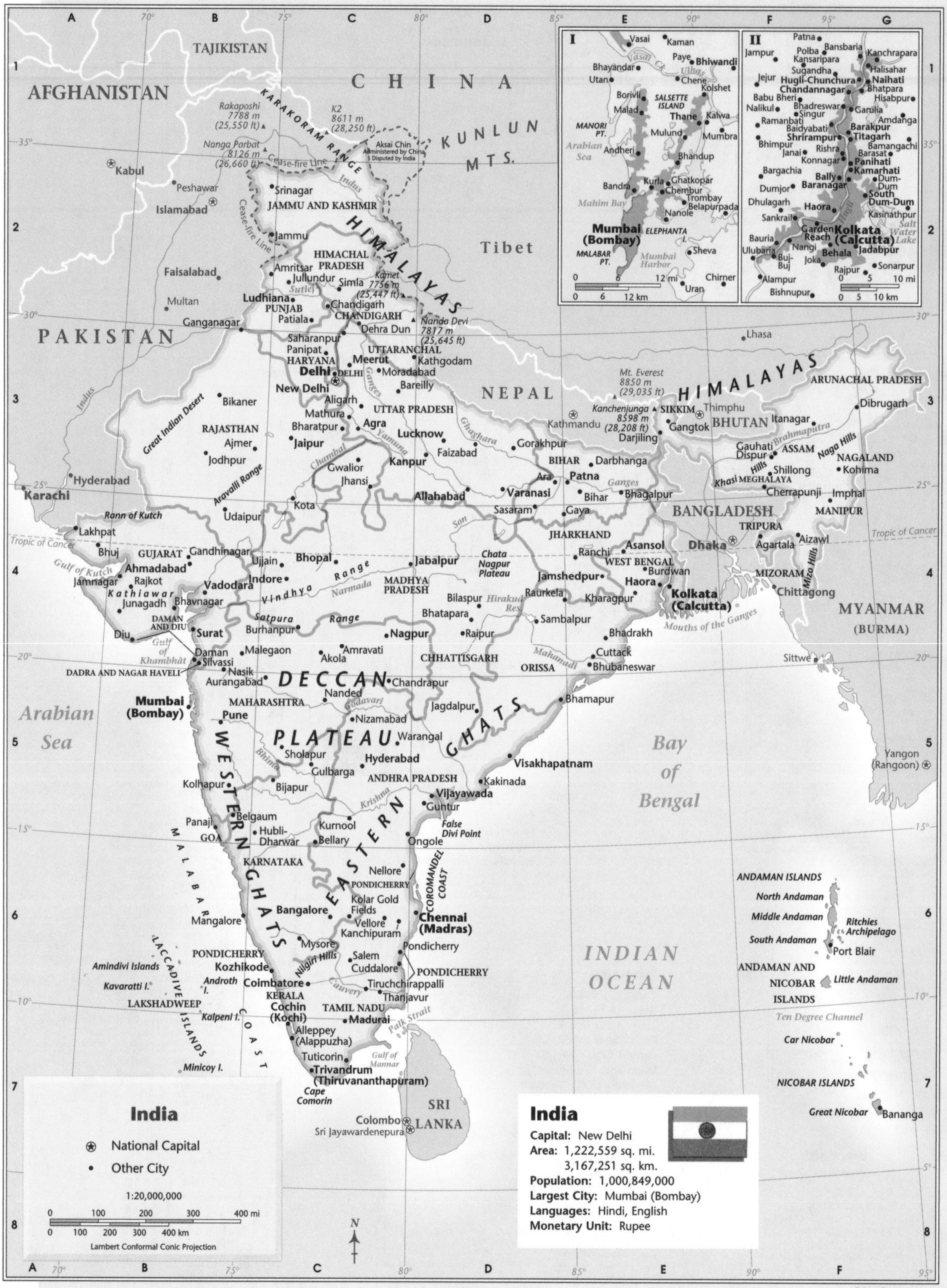

India
Capital: New Delhi
Area: 1,222,559 sq. mi.
  3,167,251 sq. km.
Population: 1,000,849,000
Largest City: Mumbai (Bombay)
Languages: Hindi, English
Monetary Unit: Rupee

© MapQuest.com, Inc.

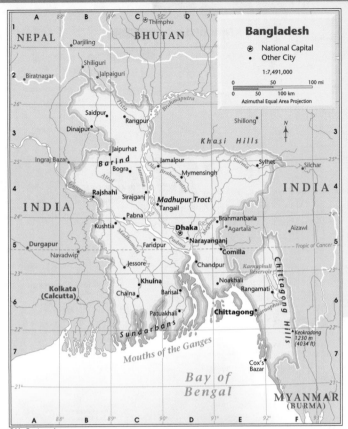

India: Map Index

Trombay ....Inset I
Tuticorin C7
Udaipur B4
Ujjain C4
Ulubaria ....Inset II
Uran ....Inset I
Utan ....Inset I
Vadodara B4
Varanasi D3
Vasai ....Inset I
Vellore C6
Vijayawada D5
Visakhapatnam D5
Warangal C5

Other Features

Amindivi, islands B6
Andaman, islands F6
Androth, island B6
Arabian, sea ....A5, Inset I
Aravalli, range B3
Bengal, bay E5
Bhima, river C5
Brahmaputra, river F3
Car Nicobar, island F7
Cauvery, river C6
Chambal, river C3
Chata Nagpur, plateau D4
Comorin, cape C7
Coromandel, coast D6
Deccan, plateau C5
Eastern Ghats, mts. D5
Elephanta, island ....Inset I
False Divi, point D5
Ganges, river E3
Ghaghara, river D3
Godavari, river C5
Great Indian, desert B3
Great Nicobar, island F7
Himalayas, mts. C2, E3
Hirakud, reservoir D4
Hugli, river ....Inset II
Indus, river C2
Kalpeni, island B7
Kamet, mt. C2
Kanchenjunga, mt. E3
Karakoram, range C1
Kathiawar, peninsula B4
Kavaratti, island B6
Khambhat, gulf B4
Khasi, hills F3
Kolar, gold fields C6
Krishna, river C5
Kutch, gulf A4
Laccadive, islands B6
Little Andaman, island F6
Mahanadi, river D4
Mahim, bay ....Inset I
Malabar, coast B6
Malabar, point ....Inset I
Mannar, gulf C7
Manori, point ....Inset I
Middle Andaman, island F6
Minicoy, island B7
Mizo, hills F4
Mouths of the Ganges, delta E4
Mumbai, harbor ....Inset I
Naga, hills F3
Nanda Devi, mt. C2
Narmada, river C4
Nicobar, islands F7
Nilgiri, hills C6
North Andaman, island F6
Palk, strait C7
Rann of Kutch, mud flat B4
Ritchies, archipelago F6
Salsette, island ....Inset I
Salt Water, lake ....Inset II
Satpura, range C4
Son, river D4
South Andaman, island F6
Sutlej, river C2
Ten Degree, channel F7
Ulhas, river ....Inset I
Vasai, creek ....Inset I
Vindhya, range C4
Western Ghats, mts. B5
Yamuna, river C3

Bangladesh

Capital: Dhaka
Area: 57,295 sq. mi.
148,433 sq. km.
Population: 127,118,000
Largest City: Dhaka
Language: Bengali
Monetary Unit: Taka

Bangladesh: Map Index

Cities and Towns

Barisal D6
Bogra C4
Brahmanbaria E5
Chalna C6
Chandpur D5
Chittagong E6
Comilla E5
Cox's Bazar E7
Dhaka, capital D5
Dinajpur B3
Faridpur C5
Jaipurhat B3
Jamalpur C4
Jessore C5
Khulna C6
Kushtia C5
Mymensingh D4
Narayanganj D5
Noakhali E6
Pabna C4
Patuakhali D6
Rajshahi B4
Rangamati F6
Rangpur C3
Saidpur B3
Sirajganj C4
Sylhet E4
Tangail C4

Other Features

Atrai, river B4
Barind, region B4
Bengal, bay D7
Brahmaputra, river D3
Chittagong Hills, region F5
Ganges, river B4
Jamuna, river C4
Karnaphuli, reservoir F6
Karnaphuli, river E6
Keokradong, mt. F7
Madhumati, river C5
Madhupur Tract, region D4
Meghna, river D5
Mouths of the Ganges, delta C7
Old Brahmaputra, river C4
Padma, river D5
Sundarbans, region C7
Surma, river E3
Tista, river C2

Pakistan

Capital: Islamabad
Area: 339,697 sq. mi.
880,044 sq. km.
Population: 138,123,000
Largest City: Karachi
Languages: Urdu, English
Monetary Unit: Pakistani rupee

Pakistan: Map Index

Internal Divisions

Azad Kashmir Province D2
Baluchistan Province B4
Federally Administrated
    Tribal Areas C3
Islamabad Capital Territory D3
Northern Areas D2
North-West Frontier Province D2
Punjab Province D3
Sind Province C5

Cities and Towns

Bahawalpur D4
Bela C4
Chiniot D3
Chitral D2
Dadu C4
Dera Ghazi Khan D3
Dera Ismail Khan D3
Faisalabad D3
Gilgit E2
Gujranwala E3
Gujrat E3
Gwadar B5
Hyderabad C5
Islamabad, capital D3
Jhang Sadar D3
Jhelum D3
Karachi C5
Kasur E3
Khuzdar C4
Lahore E3
Larkana C4
Mardan D2
Mianwali D3
Mirpur Khas C5
Multan D3
Muzaffarabad D2
Nawabshah C4
Nok Kundi B4
Okara D3
Panjgur B4
Peshawar D3
Quetta C3
Rahimyar Khan D4
Rawalpindi D3
Sahiwal D3
Sargodha D3
Shikarpur C4
Sialkot E3
Sukkur C4
Surab C4

Other Features

Arabian, sea B6
Central Makran, range B4
Chagai, hills B4
Chenab, river D3
Hindu Kush, mts. D2
Indus, river C4, E2
Jhelum, river D3
Karakoram, range E2
Khojak, pass C3
Khyber, pass D2
Kirthar, range C4
Konar, river D2
K2 (Godwin Austen), mt. E2
Makran Coast, range B5
Mouths of the Indus, delta B4
Nal, river B4
Nanga Parbat, mt. E2
Nara, canal C4
Nowshak, mt. D2
Rakaposhi, mt. E2
Ravi, river D3
Safed Koh, range C3
Siahan, range B4
Sulaiman, range C4
Sutlej, river D3
Thar, desert C4
Tirich Mir, mt. D2
Toba Kakar, range C3
Zhob, river C3

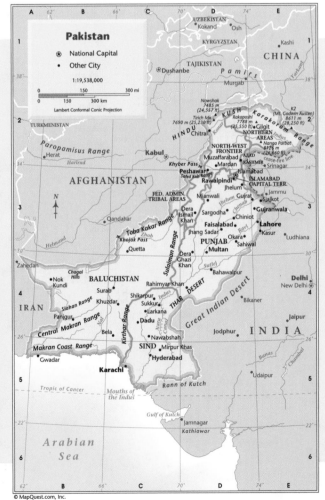

© MapQuest.com, Inc.

Afghanistan: Map Index

Cities and Towns

Asadabad	C2
Baghlan	B1
Balkh	B1
Bamian	B2
Baraki Barak	B2
Chaghcharan	B2
Charikar	B1
Farah	A2
Feyzabad	C1
Gardez	B2
Ghazni	B2
Herat	A2
Jalalabad	C2
Kabul, *capital*	B2
Khowst	B2
Konduz	B1

Kowt-e Ashrow	B2
Lashkar Gah	A2
Mazar-e Sharif	B1
Meymaneh	A1
Qalat	B2
Qaleh-ye Now	A2
Qaleh-ye Panjeh	C1
Qandahar	B2
Samangan	B2
Sar-e Pol	B1
Sheberghan	B1
Shindand	A2
Taloqan	B1
Tarin Kowt	B2
Zaranj	A2
Zareh Sharan	B2

Farah, *river*	A2
Fuladi, *mt.*	B2
Gowd-e Zereh, *lake*	A3
Hamun-e Saberi, *lake*	A2
Harirud, *river*	A2
Helmand, *river*	A2
Hindu Kush, *range*	B1
Kabul, *river*	B2
Khojak, *pass*	B2
Khyber, *pass*	C2
Konar, *river*	C1
Konduz, *river*	B1
Morghab, *river*	A1
Nowshak, *mt.*	C1
Panj, *river*	C1
Paropamisus, *range*	A2
Registan, *region*	A2
Shibar, *pass*	B2
Vakhan, *region*	C1

Other Features

Amu Darya, *river*	B1
Arghandab, *river*	B2

Afghanistan

Capital: Kabul
Area: 251,825 sq. mi.
　　　652,396 sq. km.
Population: 25,825,000
Largest City: Kabul
Languages: Pashto, Dari Persian
Monetary Unit: Afghani

Iran

Capital: Tehran
Area: 632,457 sq. mi.
　　　1,638,490 sq. km.
Population: 65,180,000
Largest City: Tehran
Languages: Persian, Turkic, Luri, Kurdish
Monetary Unit: Rial

Iran: Map Index

Cities and Towns

Abadan	B3
Ahvaz	B3
Arak	B3
Ardabil	B2
Bakhtaran	B3
Bam	D4
Bandar Beheshti	E4
Bandar-e Abbas	D4
Bandar-e Anzali	B2
Bandar-e Bushehr	C4
Bandar-e Khomeyni	B3
Bandar-e Torkeman	D3
Birjand	D3
Dezful	B3

Esfahan	C3
Hamadan	B3
Ilam	B3
Iranshahr	E4
Jask	D4
Karaj	C2
Kashan	C3
Kerman	D3
Khorramabad	B3
Khorramshahr	B3
Khvoy	B2
Mashhad	D2
Neyshabur	D2
Orumiyeh (Urmia)	A2
Qazvin	B2
Qom	C3
Rasht	B2
Sabzevar	D2
Sari	C2
Shahr-e Kord	C3
Shiraz	C4
Sirjan	C4
Tabriz	B2
Tehran, *capital*	C2
Yasuj	C3
Yazd	C3
Zabol	E3
Zahedan	E4
Zanjan	B2

Other Features

Aras, *river*	B2
Atrak, *river*	D2
Azerbaijan, *region*	B2
Bakhtiari, *region*	B3
Baluchistan, *region*	E4
Caspian, *sea*	C2
Damavand, *mt.*	C2
Dasht-e Kavir, *desert*	D3
Dasht-e Lut, *desert*	D3
Elburz, *mts.*	C2
Halil, *river*	D4
Hamun-e Jaz Murian, *lake*	D4
Hashtadan, *region*	E3
Hormuz, *strait*	D4
Karun, *river*	B3
Kavir-e Namak, *desert*	D3
Kerman, *region*	D4
Kharg, *island*	C4
Khorasan, *region*	D2
Khuzestan, *region*	B3
Kopet, *mts.*	D2
Kul, *river*	D4
Larestan, *region*	C4
Mand, *river*	C4
Mazandaran, *region*	C2
Oman, *gulf*	D5
Persian, *gulf*	C4
Qareh, *river*	B3
Qeshm, *island*	D4
Shatt al-Arab, *river*	B3
Urmia, *lake*	B2
Yazd, *region*	C3
Zagros, *mts.*	B3

Turkmenistan: Map Index

Cities and Towns

Ashgabat, *capital*	C3
Bakhardok	C2
Bayramaly	D3
Büzmeyin	C2
Chardzhou	D2
Cheleken	A2
Dashhowuz	C2
Ensenguly	A3
Gazanjyk	B2
Gumdag	B2
Gushgy	D3
Gyzylarbat	B2
Kerki	D3
Mary	C3
Nebitdag	B2

Tedzhen	C3
Turkmenbashi	A2

Other Features

Amu Darya, *river*	D2
Caspian, *sea*	A2
Etrek, *river*	B3
Garabil, *plateau*	D3
Garabogazköl, *lake*	A2
Gushgy, *river*	D3
Kara-Kum, *canal*	D3
Kara-Kum, *desert*	C2
Kopet, *mts.*	B2
Murgab, *river*	D3
Sarygamysh Koli, *lake*	B2
Sumbar, *river*	B2
Tedzhen, *river*	C3
Turan, *lowland*	C2

Turkmenistan

Capital: Ashgabat
Area: 188,417 sq. mi.
　　　488,127 sq. km.
Population: 4,366,000
Largest City: Ashgabat
Languages: Turkmen, Russian, Uzbek
Monetary Unit: Manat

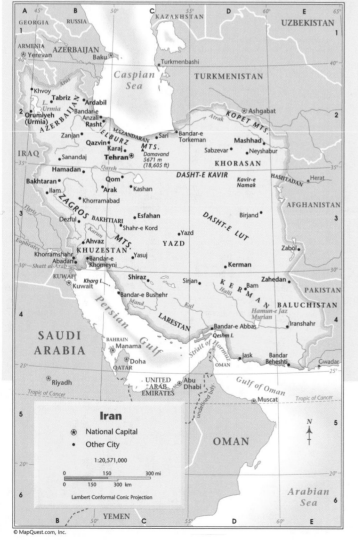

© MapQuest.com, Inc.

Beyneu B2
Ekibastuz D1
Embi B2
Esil C1
Kokshetau C1
Leneinsk C2
Lepsi D2
Oral B1
Öskemen
(Ust-Kamenogorsk) E1
Pavlodar D1
Petropavl C1
Qaraghandy (Karaganda) ..D2
Qostanay C1
Qyzylorda C2
Rudnyy C1
Saryshaghan D2
Semey (Semipalatinsk) ...E1
Shalqar B2
Shymkent (Chimkent) C2
Taldyqorghan D2
Temirtau D1
Zaysan E2
Zhambyl (Dzhambul) ...D2
Zhezqazgham C2

Other Features
Alakol, *lake* E2
Aral, *sea* B2
Balkhash, *lake* D2
Betpak Dala, *plain* ...C2
Caspian, *depression* ...B2
Caspian, *sea* A2
Ili, *river* D2
Irtysh, *river* D1
Ishim, *river* C1
Kazakh Upland *region* ...C2
Khan-Tengri, *mt.* E2
Muyun Kum, *desert* ...C2
Syrdarya, *river* C2
Tengiz, *lake* C1
Tobol, *river* C1
Torghay, *plateau* C1
Ural, *river* B2
Ustyurt, *plateau* B2
Zaysan, *lake* E2

Kazakhstan

Capital: Astana (Aqmola)
Area: 1,049,200 sq. mi.
2,718,135 sq. km.
Population: 16,825,000
Largest City: Almaty (Alma-Ata)
Language: Kazakh
Monetary Unit: Tenge

Kazakhstan: Map Index

Cities and Towns
Astana (Aqmola), *capital* D1
Almaty (Alma-Ata) B2
Aqtau B2
Aqtobe B1
Aral C2
Arqalyq C1
Atbasar C1
Atyrau B2
Ayagöz E2
Balkhash D2

Kazakhstan
⊛ National Capital
● Other City

1:26,667,000
0   125   250 mi
0   125   250 km
Lambert Conformal Conic Projection

© MapQuest.com, Inc.

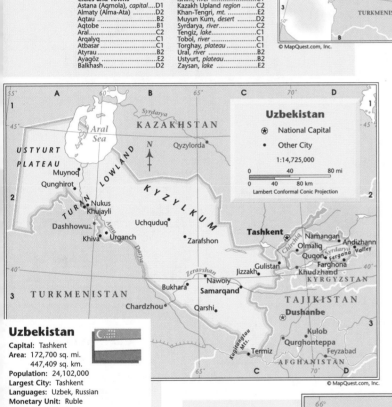

© MapQuest.com, Inc.

Uzbekistan
⊛ National Capital
● Other City

1:14,725,000
0   40   80 mi
0   40   80 km
Lambert Conformal Conic Projection

Uzbekistan

Capital: Tashkent
Area: 172,700 sq. mi.
447,409 sq. km.
Population: 24,102,000
Largest City: Tashkent
Languages: Uzbek, Russian
Monetary Unit: Ruble

Uzbekistan:
Map Index

Cities and Towns
Andizhan D2
Bukhara B3
Farghona C2
Gulistan C2
Jizzakh C2
Khujayli A2
Muynoq A2
Namangan D2
Nawoiy B2
Nukus A2
Olmaliq C2
Qarshi C3
Qunghirot A2
Quqon D2
Samarqand C3
Tashkent, *capital* C2
Termiz C3
Uchquduq B2
Urganch B2
Zarafshon B2

Other Features
Amu Darya, *river* B2
Aral, *sea* A2
Chirchiq, *river* C2
Fergana, *valley* D2
Kyzylkum, *desert* B2
Syrdarya, *river* C2
Turan, *lowland* A2
Ustyurt, *plateau* A2
Zeravshan, *river* B2

Kyrgyzstan:
Map Index

Cities and Towns
At-Bashy D2
Balykchy E1
Bishkek, *capital* D1
Cholpon-Ata E1
Jalal-Abad C2
Jangy-Bazar B2
Karakol F1
Kara-Say F2
Kyzyl-Kyya C2
Naryn E2
Osh C2
Özgön C2
Sary Tash C3
Songköl D2
Sülüktü A3
Talas B2
Tash Kömür C2
Tokmok D1
Toktogul C2

Other Features
Alay, *mts.* C3
Chatkal, *river* B2
Chu, *river* D1
Jengish Chokusu, *mt.* ...G1
Kyzyl-Suu, *river* C3
Naryn, *river* E2
Tien Shan, *mts.* E2
Toxkan, *river* E2
Ysyk-Köl, *lake* E1

Kyrgyzstan

Capital: Bishkek
Area: 76,642 sq. mi.
198,554 sq. km.
Population: 4,546,000
Largest City: Bishkek
Language: Kirghiz
Monetary Unit: Som

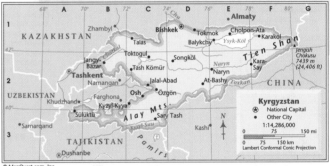

Kyrgyzstan
⊛ National Capital
● Other City
1:14,286,000
0   75   150 mi
0   75   150 km
Lambert Conformal Conic Projection

© MapQuest.com, Inc.

Tajikistan

Capital: Dushanbe
Area: 55,300 sq. mi.
143,264 sq. km.
Population: 6,103,000
Largest City: Dushanbe
Language: Tajik
Monetary Unit: Ruble

Tajikistan:
Map Index

Cities and Towns
Dangara A1
Dushanbe, *capital* A1
Jirgatol B1
Kalai Khum B1
Kansay A1
Khorugh B2
Khudzhand A1
Konibodom A1
Kulob A2
Morghob B1
Navabad A1
Norak A1
Panj A2
Panjakent A1
Qurghonteppa A2
Tursunzoda A1
Uroteppa A1
Zarafobod A1

Other Features
Alay, *mts.* B1
Bartang, *river* B1

Darya, *river* A2
Imeni Ismail Samani, *mt.* ...B1
Kofarnihon, *river* B1
Morghob, *river* B1
Oqsu, *river* C2

Pamirs, *mts.* B2
Panj, *river* B2
Pyandzh, *river* B1
Qarokul, *lake* B1
Surkhob, *river* B1

Syrdarya, *river* A1, B1
Turkeston, *mts.* A1
Vahsh, *river* A1
Zeravshan, *mts.* A1
Zeravshan, *river* A1

Tajikistan
⊛ National Capital
● Other City
1:7,622,000
0   40   80 mi
0   40   80 km
Lambert Conformal Conic Projection

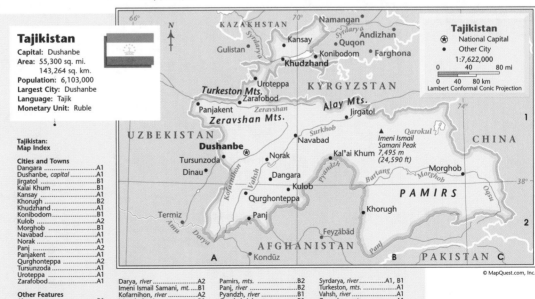

© MapQuest.com, Inc.

**Iraq:
Map Index**

Cities and Towns
Amarah, al- C2
Baghdad, *capital* B2
Baqubah B2
Basra C2
Dahuk B1
Diwaniyah, ad- C2
Fallujah, al- B2
Hadithah, al- B2
Hillah, al- B2
Irbil B1
Karbala B2
Khanaqin C1
Kirkuk C1
Kut, al- C2
Mosul B1
Najaf, an- C2
Nasiriyah, an- C2
Qayyarah, al- B1
Ramadi, ar- B2
Rutbah, ar- B2

Samarra B2
Samawah, as- C2
Sulaymaniyah, as- C1
Tall Afar B1
Tikrit B2
Umm Qasr C2

Other Features
Babylon, *ruins* B2
Diyala, *river* C2

Euphrates, *river* C2
Great Zab, *river* B1
Haji Ibrahim, *mt.* B1
Little Zab, *river* B1
Mesopotamia, *region*....B2
Milh, *lake* B2
Persian, *gulf* C3
Shatt al-Arab, *river*......C2
Syrian, *desert* B2
Tigris, *river* B1

Iraq
Capital: Baghdad
Area: 167,975 sq. mi.
435,169 sq. km.
Population: 22,427,000
Largest City: Baghdad
Language: Arabic
Monetary Unit: Dinar

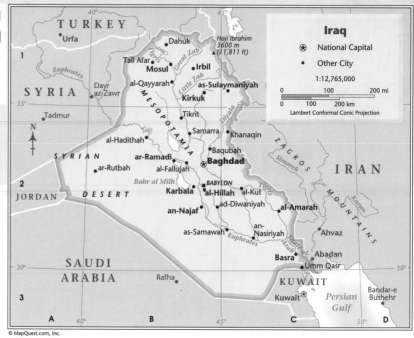

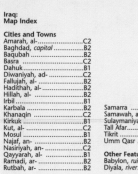

Kuwait
Capital: Kuwait
Area: 6,880 sq. mi.
17,924 sq. km.
Population: 1,991,000
Largest City: Kuwait
Language: Arabic
Monetary Unit: Dinar

**Kuwait:
Map Index**

Cities and Towns
Abdali B1
Ahmadi, al- C2
Fuhayhil, al- C2
Hawalli C2
Jahrah, al- B2
Khiran, al- C3
Kuwait, *capital* B2
Qasr as-Sabiyah C2
Rawdatayn, ar- B2
Sulaybikhat, as- B2
Wafrah, al- B3

Other Features
Bubiyan, *island* C2
Faylakah, *island* C2
Kuwait, *bay* B2
Persian, *gulf* C2
Wadi al-Batin, *river* A2
Warbah, *island* C1

Saudi Arabia
Capital: Riyadh
Area: 865,000 sq. mi.
2,240,933 sq. km.
Population: 21,505,000
Largest City: Riyadh
Language: Arabic
Monetary Unit: Riyal

**Saudi Arabia:
Map Index**

Cities and Towns
Abha B2
Badanah B1
Buqayq C1
Buraydah B1
Dammam, ad- C1
Dhahran C1
Hail B1
Harad C1
Hillah, al- B2
Hufuf, al- C1
Jawf, al- A1
Jeddah A2
Jizan B2
Jubayl, al- C1

Khamis Mushayt B2
Kharj, al- B1
Mecca A2
Medina A1
Najran B2
Qalat Bishah B2
Qunfudhah, al- B2
Rafha B1
Ras al-Khafji C1
Ras Tanura C1
Riyadh, *capital* B1
Sulayyil, as- B2
Tabuk A1
Taif, at- A2
Turayf A1
Unayzah B1
Wajh, al- A1
Yanbu al-Bahr A1

Other Features
Asir, *region* B2
Dahna, ad-, *desert* B2
Farasan, *islands* B2
Hasa, al-, *region* C1
Hijaz, al-, *region* A1
Jabal Tuwayq, *mts.* B1
Nafud, an-, *desert* B1
Najd, *region* B1
Persian, *gulf* C1
Red, *sea* A1
Rub al-Khali
(Empty Quarter), *desert* ..C2
Sabkhat Matti, *salt flat* ..C2
Sawda, *mt.* B2
Syrian, *desert* A1
Umm as-Samim, *salt flat* ..C2
Wadi al-Hamd, *river* A1

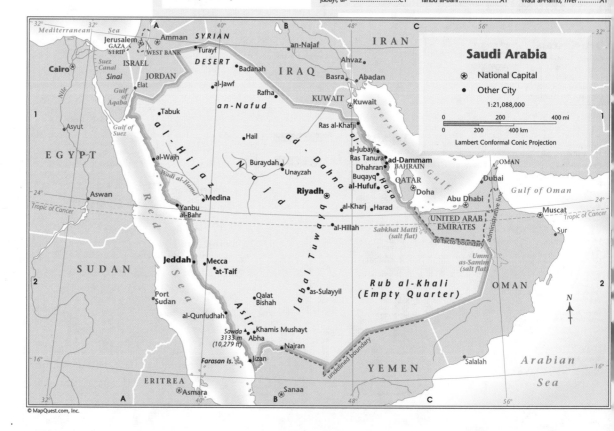

© MapQuest.com, Inc.

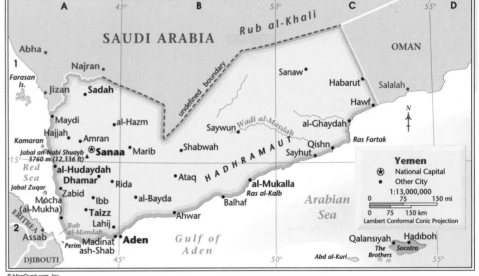

Bahrain and Qatar

Bahrain and Qatar:
Map Index

Bahrain
Cities and Towns
Askar.....................................B1
Mamtalah, al-.........................B2
Manama, *capital*....................B1
Mina Salman..........................B1

Other Features
Bahrain, *gulf*.........................A2
Hawar, *islands*......................B2
Jiddah, *island*.......................A1
Muharraq, al-, *island*.............B1
Ras al-Barr, *cape*..................B2
Sitrah, *island*.......................B1
Umm an-Nasan, *island*.........A1

Qatar
Cities and Towns
Doha, *capital*........................D3
Dukhan...................................B3
Jumayliyah, al-.......................C2
Khawr, al-...............................D2
Ruways, ar-............................C1
Umm Bab................................B3
Umm Said (Musayid)..............D4
Wakrah, al-............................D3

Other Features
Dawhat as-Salwa, *bay*..........B3
Ras Laffan, *cape*..................D2
Ras Rakan, *cape*..................C1
Tuwayyir al-Hamir, *hill*..........C4

Bahrain

Capital: Manama
Area: 268 sq. mi.
694 sq. km.
Population: 629,000
Largest City: Manama
Language: Arabic
Monetary Unit: Dinar

Qatar

Capital: Doha
Area: 4,412 sq. mi.
11,430 sq. km.
Population: 724,000
Largest City: Doha
Language: Arabic
Monetary Unit: Riyal

United Arab Emirates

United Arab Emirates (U.A.E.)

Capital: Abu Dhabi
Area: 30,000 sq. mi.
77,720 sq. km.
Population: 2,344,000
Largest City: Abu Dhabi
Language: Arabic
Monetary Unit: Dirham

United Arab Emirates:
Map Index

Cities and Towns
Abu Dhabi, *capital*............C2
Ajman...................................C2
Aradah.................................B3
Ayn, al-................................C2
Dubai...................................C2
Fujayrah, al-........................D2
Masfut..................................D2
Nashshash, an-....................C3
Ras al-Khaymah..................C2

Ruways, ar-..........................B2
Sham, ash-...........................D1
Sharjah.................................C2
Tarif......................................B2
Umm al-Qaywayn..................C2

Other Features
Hormuz, *strait*.....................D1
Matti, *salt flat*.....................B3
Oman, *gulf*.........................D2
Persian, *gulf*.......................B1
Salamiyah, *salt flat*.............C3

Yemen:
Map Index

Cities and Towns
Aden.....................................B2
Ahwar...................................B2
Amran...................................A1
Ataq.....................................B2
Balhaf...................................B2
Bayda, al-.............................A2
Dhamar.................................A2
Ghaydah, al-.........................C1
Habarut.................................C1
Hadiboh................................C1
Hajjah...................................A1
Hawf.....................................C1
Hazm, al-..............................A1
Hudaydah, al-........................A2
Ibb.......................................A2
Lahij.....................................A2
Madinat ash-Shab.................A2
Marib....................................B1
Maydi...................................A1

Mocha (Mukha, al-)..............A2
Mukalla, al-...........................B2
Qalansiyah............................C2
Qishn....................................C1
Rida......................................A2
Sadah...................................A1
Sanaa, *capital*....................A1
Sanaw..................................C1
Sayhut..................................C1
Saywun................................B1
Shabwah...............................B1
Taizz....................................A2
Zabid....................................A2

Other Features
Abd al-Kuri, *island*..............C2
Aden, *gulf*..........................B2
Arabian, *sea*.......................A2
Bab al-Mandab, *strait*.........A2
Hadhramaut, *district*...........B1
Jabal an-Nabi Shuayb, *mt.*...A1
Jabal Zuqar, *island*.............A2
Kamaran, *island*.................A1

Perim, *island*......................A2
Ras al-Kalb, *cape*...............B2
Ras Fartak, *cape*.................C1
Red, *sea*............................A2
Socotra, *island*...................C2
The Brothers, *islands*..........C2
Wadi al-Masilah, *river*.........B1

Yemen

Capital: Sanaa
Area: 205,356 sq. mi.
532,010 sq. km.
Population: 16,942,000
Largest City: Sanaa
Language: Arabic
Monetary Unit: Riyal

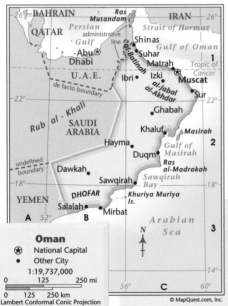

Oman

Oman

Oman:
Map Index

Cities and Towns
Dawkah..................................B2
Duqm....................................C2
Ghabah..................................C2
Hayma...................................C2
Ibri.......................................C1
Izki.......................................C1
Khaluf...................................C2
Matrah...................................C1

Mirbat....................................B3
Muscat, *capital*....................C1
Salalah..................................B3
Sawqirah...............................C2
Shinas...................................C1
Sur..C1

Other Features
Arabian, *sea*.......................C3
Batinah, al-, *region*.............C1
Dhofar, *region*....................B3

Hormuz, *strait*.....................C1
Jabal al-Akhdar, al-, *mts.*....C1
Khuriya Muriya, *islands*.......C3
Masirah, *gulf*......................C2
Masirah, *island*...................C2
Oman, *gulf*.........................C1
Persian, *gulf*.......................B1
Ras al-Madrakah, *cape*.......C2
Ras Musandam, *cape*..........C1
Sawqirah, *bay*....................C2

Oman

Capital: Muscat
Area: 118,150 sq. mi.
305,829 sq. km.
Population: 2,447,000
Largest City: Muscat
Language: Arabic
Monetary Unit: Rial Omani

Lebanon

Capital: Beirut
Area: 3,950 sq. mi.
10,233 sq. km.
Population: 3,563,000
Largest City: Beirut
Languages: Arabic, French
Monetary Unit: Pound

Lebanon: Map Index

Cities and Towns

Amyun	A1
Baalbek	B1
Babda	A2
Batrun, al-	A1
Beirut, *capital*	A2
Bint Jubayl	A2
Bsharri	B1
Damur, ad-	A2
Duma	A1
Halba	B1
Hirmil, al-	B1
Jazzin	A2
Jubayl	A1
Juniyah	A2
Marj Uyun	A2
Nabatiyah at-Tahta, an-	A2
Qubayyat, al-	B1
Rashayya	B2
Riyaq	B1
Sidon (Sayda)	A2
Sur (Tyre)	A2
Tripoli (Tarabulus)	A1
Zahlah	A2

Other Features

Anti-Lebanon, *mts.*	B1
Awwali, *river*	A2
Bekaa, *valley*	A2
Byblos, *ruins*	A2
Hermon, *mt.*	B2
Ibrahim, *river*	A1
Kebir, *river*	B1
Lebanon, *mts.*	B1
Litani, *river*	A2
Orontes, *river*	B1
Qurnat as-Sawda, *mt.*	B1

© MapQuest.com, Inc.

Israel

Capital: Jerusalem
Area: 7,992 sq. mi.
20,705 sq. km.
Population: 5,750,000
Largest City: Jerusalem
Languages: Hebrew, Arabic
Monetary Unit: New Shekel

Israel: Map Index

Districts

Central	B1
Haifa	B1
Jerusalem	B2
Northern	B1
Southern	B2
Tel Aviv	B1

Cities and Towns

Acre (Akko)	B1
Ashdod	B2
Ashqelon	B2
Beersheba	B2
Dimona	B2
Elat	B3
Hadera	B1
Haifa	B1
Herzliyya	B1
Holon	B1
Jerusalem, *capital*	B
Lod (Lydda)	B
Mizpe Ramon	B
Nahariyya	B
Nazareth	B
Netanya	B
Petah Tiqwa	B
Qiryat Gat	B
Qiryat Shemona	B
Ramat Gan	B
Ramla	B
Rehovot	B
Tel Aviv-Jaffa	B
Tiberias	B
Yotvata	B
Zefat	B

Other Features

Aqaba, *gulf*	B
Arabah, al-, *river*	B
Besor, *river*	B
Dead, *sea*	B
Galilee, *region*	B
Haifa, *bay*	B
Jezreel (Esdraelon), *plain*	B
Jordan, *river*	B
Judea, *plain*	B
Masada, *ruins*	B
Meron, *mt.*	B
Negev, *region*	B
Ramon, *mt.*	B
Samarian, *hills*	B
Sharon, *plain*	B
Tiberias (Galilee), *lake*	B
Zevulun, *plain*	B

© MapQuest.com, Inc.

Jordan

Capital: Amman
Area: 34,342 sq. mi.
88,969 sq. km.
Population: 4,561,000
Largest City: Amman
Language: Arabic
Monetary Unit: Dinar

Jordan: Map Index

Cities and Towns

Amman, *capital*	A2
Aqabah, al-	A3
Azraq ash-Shishan	B2
Bair	B2
Irbid	A1
Jafr, al-	B2
Jarash	A1
Karak, al-	A2
Maan	A2
Madaba	A2
Mafraq, al-	B1
Mudawwarah, al-	B3
Qatranah, al-	B2
Ramtha, ar-	B1
Ras an-Naqb	A2
Salt, as-	A1
Tafilah, at-	A2
Zarqa, az-	B1

Other Features

Aqaba, *gulf*	A3
Arabah, al-, *river*	A2
Dead Sea, *lake*	A2
Jabal Ramm, *mt.*	A3
Jordan, *river*	A2
Petra, *ruins*	A2
Syrian, *desert*	B1
Tiberias, *lake*	A1
Wadi as-Sirhan, *depression*	B2

© MapQuest.com, Inc.

Turkey

Capital: Ankara
Area: 300,948 sq. mi.
　　　779,658 sq. km.
Population: 65,599,000
Largest City: İstanbul
Language: Turkish
Monetary Unit: Lira

Turkey

⊛ National Capital
● Other City

1:11,125,000

0　　75　　150 mi
0　　75　　150 km
Lambert Conformal Conic Projection

© MapQuest.com, Inc.

Turkey: Map Index

Cities and Towns

Adana	C3
Adapazarı	B2
Afyon	B2
Ağrı	E2
Aksaray	C2
Alanya	C3
Amasya	C2
Ankara, *capital*	C2
Antalya	B3
Antioch (Antakya)	D3
Artvin	E2
Aydın	A3
Balıkesir	A2
Batman	E3
Bolu	B2
Bursa	B2
Çanakkale	A2
Çankırı	C2
Çorum	C2
Denizli	B3
Divriği	D2
Diyarbakır	E3
Edirne	A2
Elâzığ	D2
Erzincan	D2
Erzurum	E2
Eskişehir	B2
Eyüp	B2
Fethiye	B3
Gaziantep	D3
Gelibolu (Gallipoli)	A2
Giresun	D2
İskenderun	D3
Isparta	B3
İstanbul	B2
İzmir	A2
İzmit	B2
Kadıköy	A2
Karaman	C3
Kars	E2
Kastamonu	C2
Kayseri	C2
Kırıkkale	C2
Kırşehir	C2
Konya	C3
Kütahya	B2
Malatya	D2

Manisa	A2
Maraş	D3
Mardin	E3
Mersin	C3
Muğla	B3
Muş	E2
Niğde	C2
Ordu	D2
Samsun	D2
Siirt	E3

Silifke	C3
Sinope	C2
Sivas	D2
Tarsus	C3
Tekirdağ	A2
Thrace	A2
Tokat	D2
Trabzon	D2
Urfa	D3
Usak	B2

Üsküdar	B2
Van	E2
Zonguldak	C1

Other Features

Aegean, *sea*	A3
Anatolia, *region*	B2
Antalya, *gulf*	B3
Ararat (Ağrı Dağı), *mt.*	F2
Aras, *river*	E2

Atatürk, *reservoir*	D3
Beyşehir, *lake*	B3
Black, *sea*	C1
Bosporus, *strait*	B2
Burdur, *lake*	B3
Büyük Menderes, *rivers*	A3
Ceyhan, *river*	D3
Cilician Gates, *pass*	C3
Çoruh, *river*	E2
Çukorova, *region*	C3

Eğridir, *lake*	B2
Erciyas Dağı, *mt.*	C2
Euphrates, *river*	D3
Great Zab, *river*	E3
İskenderum, *gulf*	C3
Keban, *reservoir*	D2
Kızıl Irmak, *river*	C2
Kura, *river*	E2
Marmara, *sea*	A2
Mediterranean, *sea*	B4

Murat, *river*	E2
Pontic, *mts.*	C2
Sakarya, *river*	B2
Seyhan, *river*	C3
Taurus, *mts.*	B3
Tigris, *river*	E2
Tuz, *lake*	C2
Ulu Dağ (Mt. Olympus), *mt.*	B2
Van, *lake*	E2
Yeşilırmak, *river*	D2

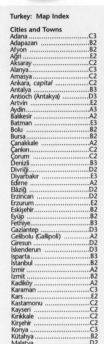

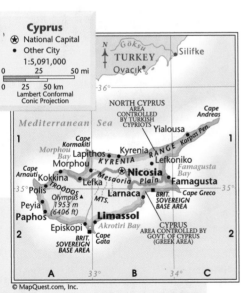

Cyprus

⊛ National Capital
● Other City

1:5,091,000

0　　25　　50 mi
0　　25　　50 km
Lambert Conformal Conic Projection

© MapQuest.com, Inc.

Cyprus

Capital: Nicosia
Area: 3,572 sq. mi.
　　　9,254 sq. km.
Population: 754,000
Largest City: Nicosia
Languages: Greek, Turkish
Monetary Unit: Pound

Cyprus: Map Index

Cities and Towns

Episkopi	A2
Famagusta	B1
Kokkina	A1
Kyrenia	B1
Lapithos	B1
Larnaca	B2
Lefka	A1
Lefkoniko	B1
Limassol	B2
Morphou	A1
Nicosia, *capital*	B1
Paphos	A2
Peyia	A2
Polis	A1

Yialousa	C1

Other Features

Akrotiri, *bay*	B2
Andreas, *cape*	C1
Arnauti, *cape*	A1
British Sovereign Base Area	A2, B2
Famagusta, *bay*	B2
Gata, *cape*	B2
Greco, *cape*	C2
Karpas, *peninsula*	C1
Kormakiti, *cape*	A1
Kyrenia, *range*	B1
Mesaoria, *plain*	B1
Morphou, *bay*	A1
Olympus, *mt.*	A2
Troódos, *mts.*	A2

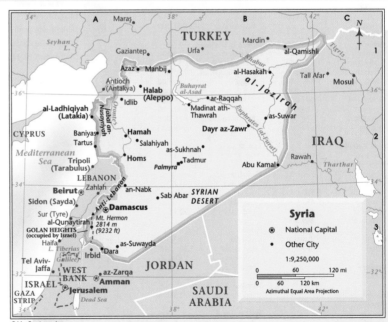

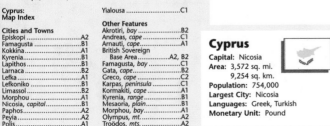

Syria: Map Index

Cities and Towns

Abu Kamal	B2
Azaz	A1
Baniyas	A2
Damascus, *capital*	A3
Dara	A3
Dayr az-Zawr	B2
Halab (Aleppo)	A1
Hamah	A2
Hasakah, al-	B1
Homs	A2
Idlib	A2
Ladhiqiyah, al- (Latakia)	A2
Madinat ath-Thawrah	A1
Manbij	A1
Nabk, an-	A2
Qamishli, al-	B1

Qunaytirah, al-	A3
Raqqah, ar-	B2
Sab Abar	A3
Salahiyah	A2
Sukhnah, as-	B2
Suwar, as-	B2
Suwayda, as-	A3
Tadmur	B2
Tartus	A2

Other Features

Anti-Lebanon, *mts.*	A3
Buhayrat al-Asad, *lake*	A2
Euphrates (al-Furat), *river*	B2
Golan Heights, occupied territory	A3
Hermon, *mt.*	A3
Jabal an-Nusayriyah, *mts.*	A2
Jazirah, al-, *region*	B1
Khabur, *river*	B1

Mediterranean, *sea*	A2
Orontes, *river*	A2
Palmyra, *ruins*	B2
Syrian, *desert*	B3
Tigris, *river*	C1

Syria

⊛ National Capital
● Other City

1:9,250,000

0　　60　　120 mi
0　　60　　120 km
Azimuthal Equal Area Projection

© MapQuest.com, Inc.

Syria

Capital: Damascus
Area: 71,498 sq. mi.
　　　185,228 sq. km.
Population: 17,214,000
Largest City: Damascus
Language: Arabic
Monetary Unit: Pound

MAJOR CITIES

Albania		Italy	
Tirana	244,000	Rome	2,645,000
		Milan	1,304,000
Andorra		Naples	1,046,000
Andorra la Vella	16,000	Turin	920,000
		Palermo	688,000
Armenia	(metro)	Genoa	654,000
Yerevan	1,278,000		
		Latvia	
Austria		Riga	821,000
Vienna	1,540,000		
		Liechtenstein	
Azerbaijan	(metro)	Vaduz	5,000
Baku	1,848,000		
		Lithuania	
Belarus	(metro)	Vilnius	580,000
Minsk	1,708,000		
		Luxembourg	
Belgium	(metro)	Luxembourg	77,000
Brussels	948,000		
Antwerp	456,000	**F.Y.R. Macedonia**	
		Skopje	430,000
Bosnia and Hercegovina			
Sarajevo	416,000	**Malta**	
		Valletta	7,000
Bulgaria			
Sofia	1,117,000	**Moldova**	
		Chişinău	656,000
Croatia	(metro)		
Zagreb	981,000	**Monaco**	
		Monaco	27,000
Czech Republic			
Prague	1,200,000	**Netherlands**	
		Amsterdam	717,000
Denmark		Rotterdam	591,000
Copenhagen	632,000		
		Norway	
Estonia		Oslo	492,000
Tallinn	424,000		
		Poland	
Finland		Warsaw	1,633,000
Helsinki	532,000	Łódź	820,000
		Kraków	745,000
France		Wrocław	642,000
Paris	2,152,000		
Lyon	1,260,000	**Portugal**	
Marseille	1,200,000	Lisbon	582,000
Georgia	(metro)	**Romania**	
Tbilisi	1,342,000	Bucharest	2,037,000
Germany		**Russia (European)**	
Berlin	3,458,000	Moscow	8,368,000
Hamburg	1,708,000	St. Petersburg	4,232,000
Munich	1,226,000	Nizh. Novgorod	1,376,000
Cologne	964,000	Samara	1,184,000
Frankfurt	647,000	Ufa	1,093,000
Essen	612,000	Kazan	1,076,000
Dortmund	597,000	Perm	1,031,000
Stuttgart	586,000	Rostov-na-Donu	1,014,000
Düsseldorf	571,000	Volgograd	999,000
Leipzig	549,000		
		San Marino	
Great Britain		San Marino	3,000
London	7,074,000		
Birmingham	1,021,000	**Slovakia**	
Leeds	727,000	Bratislava	452,000
Glasgow	616,000		
Sheffield	530,000	**Slovenia**	
Bradford	483,000	Ljubljana	273,000
Liverpool	468,000		
Edinburgh	449,000	**Spain**	
		Madrid	2,867,000
Greece	(metro)	Barcelona	1,509,000
Athens	3,073,000	Valencia	747,000
		Seville	697,000
Hungary			
Budapest	1,897,000	**Sweden**	
		Stockholm	718,000
Iceland			
Reykjavík	105,000	**Switzerland**	
		Zürich	342,000
Ireland		Bern	129,000
Dublin	482,000		
		Turkey (European)	
		İstanbul	6,620,000
		Ukraine	
		Kiev	2,630,000
		Kharkiv	1,555,000
		Dnipropetrovsk	1,147,000
		Donetsk	1,088,000
		Odesa	1,046,000
		Yugoslavia	(metro)
		Belgrade	1,204,000

International comparability of city population data is limited by various data inconsistencies.

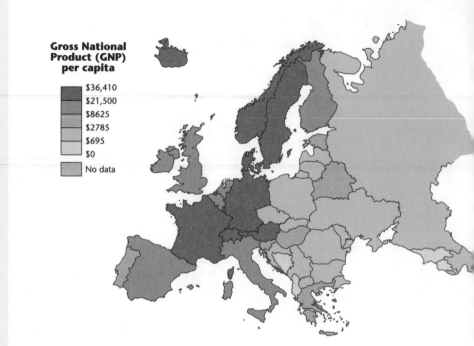

Gross National Product (GNP) per capita

- $36,410
- $21,500
- $8625
- $2785
- $695
- $0
- No data

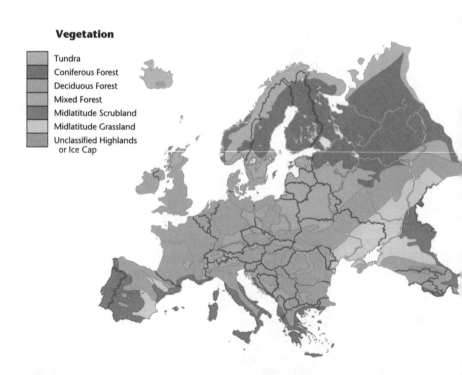

Vegetation

- Tundra
- Coniferous Forest
- Deciduous Forest
- Mixed Forest
- Midlatitude Scrubland
- Midlatitude Grassland
- Unclassified Highlands or Ice Cap

Europe: Population, by nation (in millions)*

| RUSSIA 146.4* | GER. 82.1 | GR. BRIT. 59.1 | FRANCE 59.0 | ITALY 56.7 | UKRAINE 49.8 | SPAIN 39.1 | POLAND 38.6 | ROM. 22.3 | NETH. 15.8 | All other European countries 158.3 |

*Including Asian Russia as well as the more populous European portion of the country.

© MapQuest.com, Inc.

CITIES
⊕ National Capital
★ Territorial Capital
• Other City

ELEVATIONS

Feet	Meters
13,120	4000
6560	2000
1640	500
656	200
0	0
Below sea level	

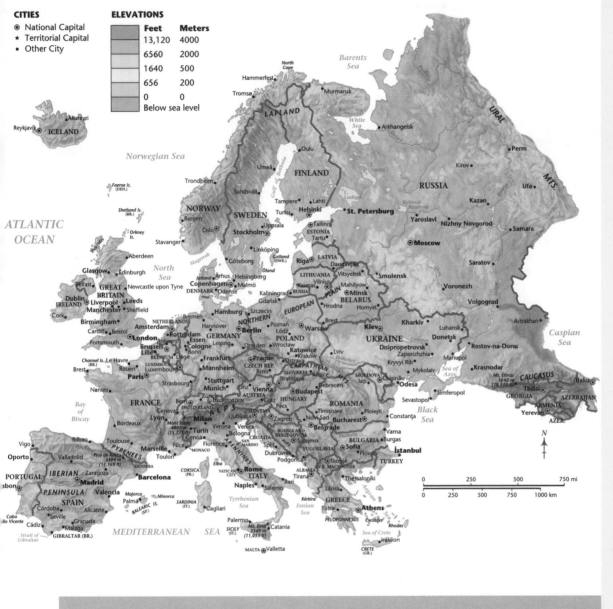

CLIMATE

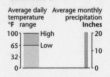

Average daily temperature °F range
Average monthly precipitation Inches
High
Low

ARKHANGELSK, Russia
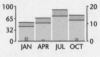

ATHENS, Greece
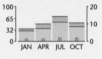

COPENHAGEN, Denmark

DUBLIN, Ireland
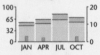

LISBON, Portugal

MOSCOW, Russia

NAPLES, Italy
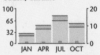

ODESA, Ukraine
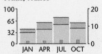

PARIS, France
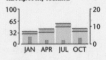

REYKJAVÍK, Iceland

TROMSØ, Norway

VIENNA, Austria
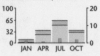

Population

Persons per sq mi	Persons per sq km
Over 520	Over 200
260–519	100–199
130–259	50–99
25–129	10–49
1–24	1–9
0	0

WORLD POPULATION

Asia 60.7%*
Oceania 0.5%
South America 5.7%
North America 7.9%
Africa 13.0%
Europe 2.1%**

*Excluding Russia   **Including Russia

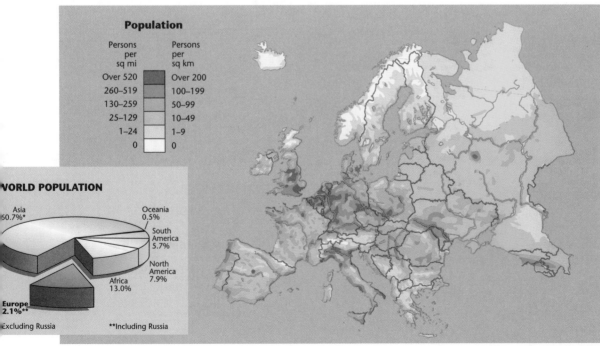

Great Britain:
Map Index

CHANNEL ISLANDS
Features
Alderney, island ....Inset
Guernsey, island ....Inset
Jersey, island ....Inset
St. Malo, gulf ....Inset
Sark, island ....Inset

ENGLAND
Cities and Towns
Aylesbury ....Inset
Banbury C
Barnsley C
Barnstaple ....B
Barrow-in-Furness C
Basildon ....Inset
Bath C
Bedford C
Berwick-upon-Tweed C
Birkenhead C
Birmingham C
Blackburn C
Blackpool C
Bolton C
Boston C
Bournemouth C
Bradford C
Braintree ....Inset
Brentwood ....Inset
Brighton C
Bristol C
Burnley C
Bury C
Bury St. Edmunds ....D
Buxton C
Camberley ....Inset
Cambridge ....D
Canterbury ....D
Carlisle C
Chatham ....Inset
Chelmsford ....D3, Inset
Cheltenham C
Chester C
Chesterfield C
Chichester C
Colchester ....D
Coventry C
Cowes C
Crawley ....Inset
Crewe C
Darlington C
Derby C
Doncaster C
Dorchester C
Dorking ....Inset
Dover ....D
Dudley C
Dunstable ....Inset
Durham C
Eastbourne C
Ely ....D
Epsom ....Inset
Ewell ....Inset
Exeter ....B
Farnham ....Inset
Felixstowe ....D
Fleetwood C
Folkestone ....D
Gateshead C
Gillingham ....D
Glastonbury C
Gloucester C
Gosport C
Grantham C
Gravesend ....Inset
Great Yarmouth ....D
Grimsby C
Guildford C
Halifax C
Harlow ....Inset
Harrogate C
Haslemere ....Inset
Hastings ....D
Hereford C
Hertford ....Inset
High Wycombe ....Inset
Hove C
Huddersfield C
Ipswich ....D
Kendal C
Kenilworth C
Kidderminster C
King's Lynn ....D
Kingston upon Hull..........C
Kingston upon Thames Inset
Lancaster C
Launceston ....B
Leeds C
Leicester C
Lewes ....D
Lichfield C
Lincoln C
Liverpool C
London, capital ....C3, Inset
Lowestoft ....D
Luton C
Maidstone ....D
Manchester C
Margate ....D
Matlock C
Middlesbrough C
Newcastle-under-Lyme C
Newcastle upon Tyne C
Newmarket ....D
Newquay ....B
Northallerton C
Northampton C
North Shields C
Norwich ....D
Nottingham C
Oldham C
Oxford C
Penrith C
Penzance ....B
Peterborough C
Plymouth ....B
Poole C
Portsmouth C
Preston C
Reading C
Reigate ....Inset
Rochdale C
Rotherham C
St. Albans ....C3, Inset

Great Britain

● National Capital
• Other City

1:4,375,000

Great Britain
Capital: London
Area: 94,251 sq. mi.
244,174 sq. km.
Population: 59,133,000
Largest City: London
Language: English
Monetary Unit: Pound

Republic of Ireland

Capital: Dublin
Area: 27,137 sq. mi.
70,303 sq. km.
Population: 3,632,000
Largest City: Dublin
Languages: English, Irish
Monetary Unit: Punt, Euro

Republic of Ireland:
Map Index

Counties
Carlow C2
Cavan C2
Clare B2
Cork B3
Donegal B1
Dún Laoghaire-Rathdown ..C2
Fingal C2
Galway B2
Kerry B2
Kildare C2
Kilkenny C2
Laois C2
Leitrim B1
Limerick B2
Longford C2
Louth C2
Mayo B2
Meath C2
Monaghan C1
Offaly C2
Roscommon B2
Sligo B1
South Dublin C2
Tipperary North Riding B2
Tipperary South Riding B2
Waterford C2
Westmeath C2
Wexford C2
Wicklow C2

County Boroughs
Cork B3
Dublin D2
Galway B2
Limerick B2
Waterford C2

Cities and Towns
Ardara B1
Arklow C2
Athlone C2
Ballina B1
Bantry B3
Blarney B3
Carlingford C1
Carlow C2
Carrick-on-Shannon B2
Cashel C2
Castlebar B2
Cavan C2
Clara C2
Clifden A2
Clonmel C2
Cóbh B3
Cork B3
Dingle A2
Donegal B1
Drogheda C2
Dublin, capital C2
Dundalk C2
Dungarvan C2
Dún Laoghaire C2
Ennis B2
Ennistymon B2
Galway B2
Kildare C2
Kilkee B2
Kilkenny C2
Killarney B2
Letterkenny C1
Lifford C1
Limerick B2
Longford C2
Mallow B2
Maynooth C2

Monaghan C1
Mullingar C2
Naas C2
Nenagh B2
Port Laoise C2
Roscommon B2
Roscrea C2
Rosslare C2
Shannon B2
Sligo B1
Swords C2
Tipperary B2
Tralee B2
Trim C2
Tuam B2
Tullamore C2
Waterford C2
Westport B2
Wexford C2
Wicklow C2
Youghal C3

Other Features
Achill, island A2
Allen, lake B1
Aran, islands B2
Bantry, bay B3
Barrow, river C2
Benwee Head, cape B1
Blackwater, river B2
Blackwater, river C1
Boggeragh, mts. B2
Boyne, river C2
Caha, mts. B3
Carlingford, lake C1
Carnsore, point C2
Carrantuohill, mt. B3
Celtic, sea B3
Clear, cape B3
Conn, lake B1
Connaught, province B2
Connemara, region B2
Corrib, lake B2
Derg, lake B2
Dingle, bay A2
Donegal, bay B1
Erne, river B1
Errigal, mt. B1
Finn, river C1
Foyle, inlet C1
Galway, bay B2
Grand, canal C2
Irish, sea D2
Killala, bay B1
Knockboy, mt. B3
Lee, river B3
Leinster, province C2
Loop Head, cape B2
Malin Head, cape C1
Mask, lake B2
Maumturk, mts. B2
Mizen Head, cape B3
Moher, cliffs B2
Munster, province B2
Ree, lake B2
Royal, canal B2
Saint George's, channel ...C3
Shannon, river C2
Suir, river C2
Twelve Pins, mt. B2
Ulster, province C1
Wicklow, mts. C2
Wicklow Head, cape D2

Great Britain: Map Index
St. Austell B4
St. Helens C3
Salford C3
Salisbury C3
Scarborough C2
Scunthorpe C3
Sheffield C3
Shrewsbury C3
Slough ....Inset III
Solihull C3
Southampton C4
Southend-on-Sea D3
Southport C3
South Shields C2
Stafford C3
Stevenage ....Inset III
Stoke-on-Trent C3
Stratford-upon-Avon C3
Sunderland C2
Swindon C3
Taunton C3
Telford C3
Tewkesbury C3
Thetford D3
Tiverton B4
Tonbridge ....Inset III
Torbay B4
Trowbridge C3
Truro B4
Tunbridge Wells D3
Wakefield C3
Walsall C3
Warrington C3
Warwick C3
Watford ....Inset III
Westminster ....Inset III
Whitehaven B2
Wigan C3
Winchester C3
Windsor ....Inset III
Wolverhampton C3
Worcester C3
Yeovil C4
York C3

Other Features
Avon, river C3
Black Country, region ...C3
Bristol, channel B3
Cheviot, hills C2
Cotswold, hills C3
Cumbrian, mts. B2
Dartmoor, plateau B4
Dee, river B3
Dover, strait D4
English, channel C4
Exmoor, plateau B3
Fens, region D3
Flodden Field, plain C2
Humber, river D3
Irish, sea B3
Lake, district B2
Land's End, promontory ...B4
Liverpool, bay B3
Lyme, bay C4
Mersey, river C3
Midlands, region C3
North, sea D2
North Downs, hills C3
North Foreland,
  promontory D3
Ouse, river C2, D3
Pennines, mts. C2
Scafell Pike, mt. B2
Scilly, islands A4
Severn, river C3
South Downs, hills C3
Spithead, channel C4
Start, point B4
Tees, river C2
Thames, river ......C3, Inset III
Trent, river C2
Tweed, river C2
Tyne, river C2
Wash, bay D3
Wight, island C4
Wye, river C3
Ware, river D3

ISLE OF MAN
City
Douglas B2

NORTHERN IRELAND
Cities and Towns
Armagh A2
Ballymena B2
Bangor B2
Belfast B2
Coleraine B2
Holywood B2
Larne B2
Londonderry A2
Newry B2
Omagh A2
Portadown B2
Strafford B2

Other Features
Antrim, mts. A2

Bann, river A2
Erne, river A2
Foyle, lake A2
Foyle, river A2
Giant's Causeway,
  headland A2
Irish, sea B3
Lough Erne, lake A2
Mourne, mts. A2
Neagh, lake A2
North, channel A2
Rathlin, island A2
Slieve Donard, mt. B2
Sperrin, mts. A2
Upper Lough Erne, lake ..A2

SCOTLAND
Cities and Towns
Aberdeen C1
Aviemore B1
Ayr B2
Campbeltown B2
Clydebank B2
Cupar B2
Dornoch B1
Dumfries B2
Dundee C2
Dunfermline B2
Edinburgh B2
Elgin B1
Fort William B1
Fraserburgh C1
Glasgow B2
Greenock B2
Hamilton B2
Hawick C2
Inverness B1
Kilmarnock B2
Kirkcaldy B2
Kirkwall ....Inset I
Kyle of Lochalsh B1
Lairg B1

Lerwick ....Inset I
Mallaig B1
Montrose C2
Motherwell B2
Newtown St. Boswells ..C2
Oban B2
Paisley B2
Perth B2
Peterhead C1
Pitlochry B2
Portree A1
St. Andrews C2
Scone B2
Sconser A1
Stirling B2
Stornoway A1
Stranraer B2
Thurso B1
Ullapool B1
Wick B1

Other Features
Arran, island B2
Barra, island A2
Bass Rock, islet C2
Bell Rock (Inchcape),
  reef C2
Ben Nevis, mt. B2
Bute, island B2
Cheviot, hills B2
Clyde, estuary B2
Clyde, river B2
Coll, island A2
Colonsay, island A2
Dee, river C1
Dornoch, estuary B1
Duncansby, cape B1
Dunsinane, mt. B2
Eigg, island B2
Fair, island ....Inset I
Forth, estuary C2
Forth, river B2

Grampian, mts. B2
Hebrides, sea A1
Hoy, island ....Inset I
Inner Hebrides, islands ..A2
Islay, island A2
Jura, island B2
Katrine, lake B2
Kinnairds, cape C1
Lammermuir, hills C2
Lewis, island A1
Linnhe, lake B2
Lomond, lake B2
Lorne, estuary B2
Mainland, island ....Inset I
Merrick, mt. B2
Minch, strait B1
Moray, estuary B1
Mull, island B2
Ness, lake B1
North Uist, island A1
Ochil, hills B2
Orkney, islands ....Inset I
Outer Hebrides, islands ..A1
Rhum, island A2
Sanday, island ....Inset I
Shetland, islands ....Inset I
Sidlaw, hills B2
Skye, island A1
Solway, estuary B2
Southern Uplands, mts. ..B2
South Ronaldsay,
  island ....Inset I
South Uist, island A1
Spey, river B1
Stronsay, island ....Inset I
Tay, estuary C2
Tay, lake B2
Tay, river B2
Tiree, island A2
Tweed, river C2
Unst, island ....Inset I
Westray, island ....Inset I

Wrath, cape B1
Yell, island ....Inset I

WALES
Cities and Towns
Aberystwyth B3
Bangor B3
Caerleon C3
Caernarfon B3
Cardiff B3
Carmarthen B3
Conwy B3
Fishguard B3
Holyhead B3
Lampeter B3
Llandrindod Wells B3
Merthyr Tydfil B3
Milford Haven B3
Mold B3
Newport C3
Pembroke B3
Port Talbot B3
Rhondda B3
St. David's B3
Swansea B3
Welshpool B3

Other Features
Anglesey, island B3
Bala, lake B3
Brecon Beacons, mts. ...B3
Bristol, channel B3
Cambrian, mts. B3
Cardigan, bay B3
Dee, river B3
Lleyn, peninsula B3
Menai, strait B3
Snowdon, mt. B3
Teifi, river B3
Tywi, river B3
Usk, river C3
Wye, river C3

Ireland

⊛ National Capital
• Other City

1:3,960,000

0   30   60 mi
0 30 60 km
Lambert Conformal Conic Projection

Denmark

Capital: Copenhagen
Area: 16,639 sq. mi.
43,080 sq. km.
Population: 5,357,000
Largest City: Copenhagen
Language: Danish
Monetary Unit: Krone

Denmark: Map Index

Counties

Århus C2
Bornholm E3
Frederiksborg D2
Fyn C3
København D3
Nordjylland B2
Ribe B2
Ringkøbing B2
Roskilde D3
Sønderjylland B3
Storstrøm C4
Vejle B3
Vestsjælland C3
Viborg B2

Cities and Towns

Åbenrå B3
Ålborg B1
Århus C2
Ballerup D3
Copenhagen, *capital* D3
Esbjerg B3
Fredericia B3
Frederiksberg D3
Frederikshavn C1
Gentofte D3
Grenå C2
Greve D3
Haderslev B3
Helsingør D2
Herning B2
Hillerød D3
Hirtshals B1
Hjørring B1
Holbæk C3
Holstebro B2
Horsens B3
Kalundborg C3
Kastrup D3
Køge D3
Kolding B3
Næstved C3
Nakskov C4
Nyborg C3
Nykøbing C3
Odense C2
Randers C2
Ribe B3
Ringkøbing B2
Rønne E3
Roskilde D3
Sandur .... Inset
Silkeborg B2
Skagen C1
Skive B2
Slagelse C3
Sønderborg B4
Sorø C3
Svendborg C3
Thisted B2
Tórshavn .... Inset
Trongisvágur .... Inset
Vejle B3
Vestmanna .... Inset
Viborg B2

Other Features

Ærø, *island* C4
Ålborg, *bay* C2
Anholt, *island* C2
Baltic, *sea* D3
Bordøy, *island* .... Inset
Bornholm, *island* E3
Eysturoy, *island* .... Inset
Faeroe, *islands* .... Inset
Falster, *island* D4
Fanø, *island* B3
Fehmarn, *strait* C4
Fyn, *island* C3
Gudenå, *river* B2
Jutland, *peninsula* B3
Kattegat, *strait* C2
Læsø, *island* C1
Langeland, *island* C4
Lille, *strait* B3
Limfjorden, *channel* ... B2
Lolland, *island* C4
Møn, *island* D4
Mors, *island* B2
North, *sea* A3
North Frisian, *islands* .. B4
Norwegian, *sea* .... Inset
Odense, *fjord* C3
Øresund, *sound* D3
Rømø, *island* B3
Samsø, *island* C3
Samsø, *strait* C3
Sandoy, *island* .... Inset
Sjælland, *island* C3
Skagerrak, *strait* B1
Skaw, *cape* C1
Skjern, *river* B3
Storå, *river* B2
Store, *strait* C3
Streymoy, *island* .... Inset
Suduroy, *island* .... Inset
Vágar, *island* .... Inset
Varde, *river* B3
Yding Skovhøj, *hill* B2

Netherlands: Map Index

Provinces

Drenthe D2
Flevoland C2
Friesland C1
Gelderland D2
Groningen D1
Limburg C3
North Brabant C3
North Holland B2
Overijssel D2
South Holland B2
Utrecht C2
Zeeland A3

Cities and Towns

Alkmaar B2
Almelo D2
Amersfoort C2
Amsterdam, *capital* B2
Apeldoorn C2
Arnhem C2
Assen D2
Bergen op Zoom B3
Breda B3
Delft B2
Delfzijl D1
Den Helder B2
Deventer D2
Doetinchem D2
Dordrecht B3
Edam C2
Ede C2
Eindhoven C3
Emmeloord C2
Emmen D2
Enschede D2
Gouda B2
Groningen D1
Haarlem B2
Heerenveen C1
Heerlen C4
Hengelo D2
Hilversum C2
Hoogeveen D2
Hoorn C2
Leeuwarden C1
Leiden B2
Lelystad C2
Maastricht C4
Meppel D2
Middelburg A3
Nijmegen C3
Oss C3
Otterlo C2
Roermond D3
Rotterdam B3
Scheveningen B2
Schiedam B3
's Hertogenbosch C3
Sittard C4
Sneek C1
The Hague B2
Tilburg C3
Utrecht C2
Venlo D3
Vlaardingen B3
Vlissingen A3
Weert C3
Zaanstad B2
Zwolle D2

Other Features

Ameland, *island* C1
Eems, *river* D1
Flevoland, *polder* C2
IJssel, *river* D2
IJsselmeer, *sea* C2
Maas, *river* C3, D3
Neder Rijn, *river* C2
New Waterway, *channel* .. B3
Northeast, *polder* C2
North Holland, *canal* ... B2
North Sea, *canal* B2
Oosterschelde, *channel* . A3
Overflakkee, *island* B3
Princess Margriet, *canal* .. C1
Schiermonnikoog, *island* .. D1
Schouwen, *island* A3
Terschelling, *island* C1
Texel, *island* B1
Tholen, *island* B3
Vaalserberg, *mt.* D4
Vlieland, *island* B1
Waal, *river* C3
Waddenzee, *sound* C1
Walcheren, *island* A3
Westerschelde, *channel* . A3
West Frisian, *islands* ... B1
Wilhelmina, *canal* C3
Zuid-Willemsvaart, *canal* .. C3

Netherlands

Capital: Amsterdam
Area: 16,033 sq. mi.
41,536 sq. km.
Population: 15,808,000
Largest City: Amsterdam
Language: Dutch
Monetary Unit: Guilder, Euro

© MapQuest.com, Inc.

Belgium

- ⊛ National Capital
- • Other City
- ⊥⊥⊥ Canal

1:2,381,000

0   20   40 mi
0 20 40 km
Lambert Conformal Conic Projection

Belgium:
Map Index

Internal Divisions

Antwerp (province)	C1
Brussels Cap. Region	C2
East Flanders (province)	B2
Flanders (region)	C1
Flemish Brabant (province)	C2
Hainaut (province)	B2
Liège (province)	D2
Limburg (province)	D1
Luxembourg (province)	D3
Namur (province)	C2
Walloon Brabant (province)	C2
Wallonia (region)	C2
West Flanders (province)	B1

Cities and Towns

Aalst	C2
Anderlecht	C2
Antwerp	C1
Arlon	D3
Ath	B2
Bastogne	D2
Binche	C2
Brugge	B1

Brussels, *capital*	C2
Charleroi	C2
Chimay	C2
Dinant	C2
Gembloux	C2
Genk	D2
Ghent	B1
Halle	C2
Hasselt	D2
Ixelles	C2
Knokke	B1
Kortrijk	B2
La Louvière	C2
Leuven	C2
Liège	D2
Limbourg	D2
Malmédy	D2
Mechelen	C1
Mons	B2
Mouscron	B2
Namur	C2
Neufchâteau	D3
Oostende	A1
Poperinge	A2
Roeselare	B2
Schaerbeek	C2
Sint-Niklaas	C1
Sint-Truiden	D2

Spa	D2
Tournai	B2
Turnhout	C1
Uccle	C2
Verviers	D2
Wavre	C2
Ypres	A2
Zeebrugge	B1

Other Features

Albert, *canal*	C1
Ardennes, *plateau*	D2
Botrange, *mt.*	E2
Brugge-Ghent, *canal*	B1
Dender, *river*	B2
Kempenland, *region*	D1
Leie, *river*	B2
Maas, *river*	D2
Meuse, *river*	D2
Oostende-Brugge, *canal*	B1
Ourthe, *river*	D2
Rupel, *river*	C1
Sambre, *river*	C2
Schelde, *river*	B2
Semois, *river*	D3
Senne, *river*	C2

Belgium

Capital: Brussels
Area: 11,787 sq. mi.
        30,536 sq. km.
Population: 10,182,000
Largest City: Brussels
Languages: Flemish, French, German
Monetary Unit: Belgian franc, Euro

© MapQuest.com, Inc.

Luxembourg

- ⊛ National Capital
- • Other City

1:1,700,000

0   10   20 mi
0 10 20 km
Azimuthal Equal Area Projection

Luxembourg:
Map Index

Cities and Towns

Clervaux	B1
Diekirch	B2
Differdange	A2
Dudelange	B2
Echternach	B2
Esch-sur-Alzette	A2
Ettelbruck	B2
Grevenmacher	B2
Larochette	B2
Luxembourg, *capital*	B2
Mersch	B2
Redange	A2
Remich	B2
Troisvierges	B1
Vianden	B2
Wiltz	A2

Other Features

Alzette, *river*	B2
Ardennes, *plateau*	A1
Bon Pays, *region*	B2
Buurgplaatz, *mt.*	B1
Clerve, *river*	B1
Mosel, *river*	B2
Our, *river*	B1
Sûre, *river*	A2, B2

Luxembourg

Capital: Luxembourg
Area: 999 sq. mi.
        2,588 sq. km.
Population: 429,000
Largest City: Luxembourg
Languages: French, German
Monetary Unit: Luxembourg franc, Euro

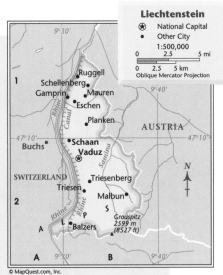

© MapQuest.com, Inc.

Liechtenstein

- ⊛ National Capital
- • Other City

1:500,000

0   2.5   5 mi
0 2.5 5 km
Oblique Mercator Projection

Liechtenstein

Capital: Vaduz
Area: 62 sq. mi.
        161 sq. km.
Population: 32,000
Largest City: Vaduz
Language: German
Monetary Unit: Swiss franc

Liechtenstein:
Map Index

Cities and Towns

Balzers	B2
Eschen	B1
Gamprin	B1
Malbun	B2
Mauren	B1
Planken	B1
Ruggell	B1
Schaan	B2
Schellenberg	B1
Triesen	B2
Triesenberg	B2
Vaduz, *capital*	B2

Other Features

Alps, *range*	A2
Grauspitz, *mt.*	B2
Rhine, *canal*	B1, B2
Rhine, *river*	A1, A2
Samina, *river*	B2

France

⊛ National Capital
• Other City

1:5,625,000

| 0 | 50 | 100 mi |
| 0 | 50 | 100 km |

Lambert Conformal Conic Projection

Same scale as main map

CORSE

II

Switzerland

Capital: Bern
Area: 15,943 sq. mi.
41,303 sq. km.
Population: 7,275,000
Largest City: Zürich
Languages: German, French, Italian
Monetary Unit: Swiss franc

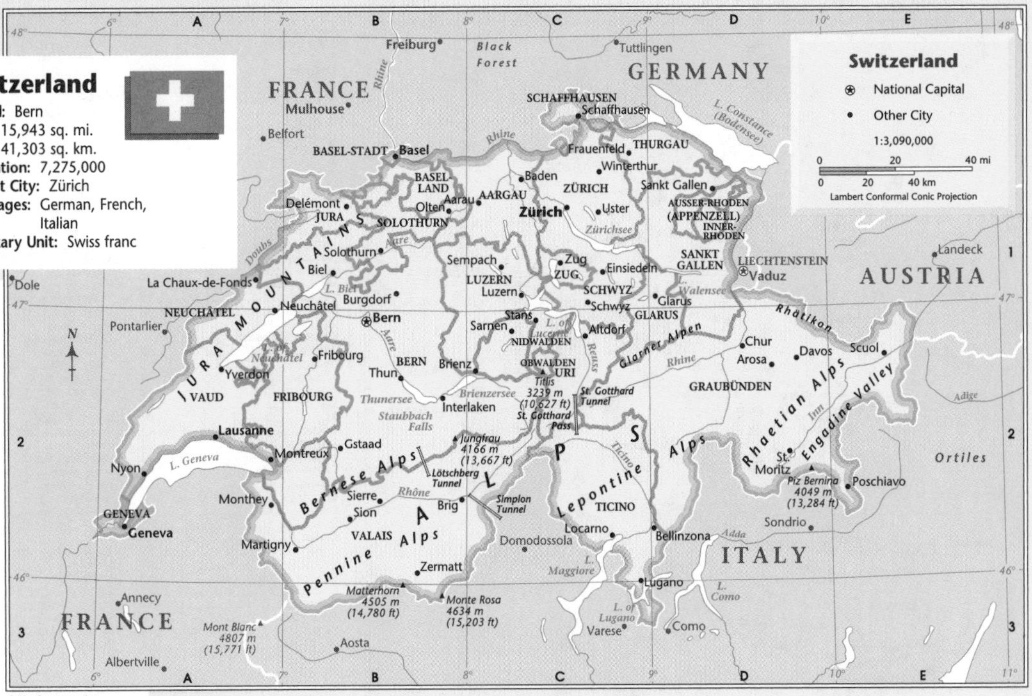
Switzerland
National Capital
Other City
1:3,090,000
0 20 40 mi
0 20 40 km
Lambert Conformal Conic Projection
FRANCE
GERMANY
AUSTRIA
ITALY
LIECHTENSTEIN
Black Forest
Freiburg
Tuttlingen
Mulhouse
Belfort
BASEL-STADT
Basel
SCHAFFHAUSEN
Schaffhausen
L. Constance (Bodensee)
THURGAU
Frauenfeld
Winterthur
Baden
AARGAU
Aarau
ZÜRICH
Zürich
Uster
Zürichsee
Sankt Gallen
AUSSER-RHODEN (APPENZELL) INNER-RHODEN
SANKT GALLEN
Vaduz
Landeck
Delémont
JURA
BASEL-LAND
Olten
SOLOTHURN
Solothurn
Biel
L. Biel
Burgdorf
La Chaux-de-Fonds
Dole
Pontarlier
NEUCHÂTEL
Neuchâtel
Bern
Sempach
LUZERN
Luzern
Zug
ZUG
Einsiedeln
SCHWYZ
Schwyz
Glarus
GLARUS
Walensee
Stans
Sarnen
NIDWALDEN
OBWALDEN
URI
Altdorf
Titlis 3239 m (10,627 ft)
St. Gotthard Pass
St. Gotthard Tunnel
JURA MOUNTAINS
Yverdon
VAUD
Fribourg
FRIBOURG
Thun
BERN
Brienz
Brienzersee
Thunersee
Staubbach Falls
Interlaken
Glarner Alpen
Rhätikon
Chur
Arosa
Davos
Scuol
GRAUBÜNDEN
Rhaetian Alps
Engadine Valley
Adige
Ortiles
Lausanne
L. Geneva
Nyon
Montreux
Gstaad
Jungfrau 4166 m (13,667 ft)
Lötschberg Tunnel
Bernese Alps
Sierre
Sion
Rhône
Brig
Simplon Tunnel
ALPS
Lepontine Alps
TICINO
St. Moritz
Piz Bernina 4049 m (13,284 ft)
Poschiavo
Sondrio
GENEVA
Geneva
Monthey
Martigny
VALAIS
Pennine Alps
Zermatt
Locarno
Bellinzona
Domodossola
L. Maggiore
Lugano
L. Lugano
L. Como
Como
Varese
Adda
Annecy
Mont Blanc 4807 m (15,771 ft)
Matterhorn 4505 m (14,780 ft)
Monte Rosa 4634 m (15,203 ft)
Aosta
Albertville
© MapQuest.com, Inc.

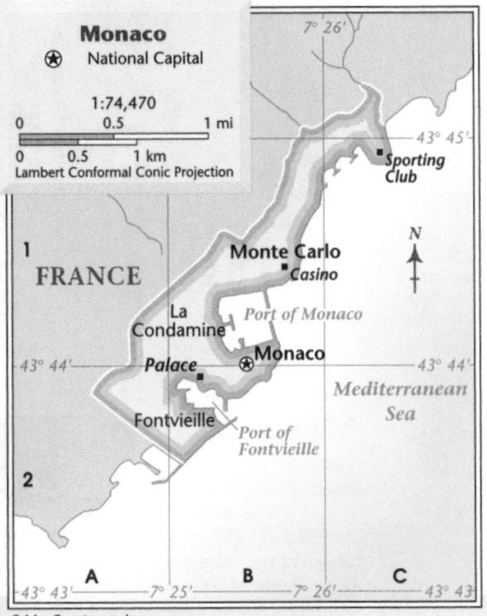
Monaco
National Capital
1:74,470
0 0.5 1 mi
0 0.5 1 km
Lambert Conformal Conic Projection
FRANCE
Sporting Club
Monte Carlo
Casino
Port of Monaco
La Condamine
Monaco
Palace
Mediterranean Sea
Fontvieille
Port of Fontvieille
© MapQuest.com, Inc.

Monaco: Map Index

Districts
Fontvieille A2
La Condamine B1
Monaco, *capital* B1
Monte Carlo B1

Other Features
Casino B1
Fontvieille, *port* B2
Monaco, *port* B1
Palace B2
Sporting Club C1

Monaco

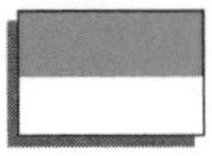

Capital: Monaco
Area: 0.75 sq. mi.
1.94 sq. km.
Population: 32,000
Language: French
Monetary Unit: French franc or Monégasque franc

Switzerland: Map Index

Cantons
Aargau C1
Appenzell Ausser-Rhoden D1
Appenzell Inner-Rhoden D1
Basel-Land B1
Basel-Stadt B1
Bern B2
Fribourg B2
Geneva A2
Glarus D2
Graubünden D2
Jura B1
Lucerne C1
Neuchâtel A2
Nidwalden C2
Obwalden C2
Sankt Gallen D1
Schaffhausen C1
Schwyz C1
Solothurn B1
Thurgau C1
Ticino C2
Uri C2
Valais B2
Vaud A2
Zug C1
Zürich C1

Cities and Towns
Aarau C1
Altdorf C2
Baden C1
Basel B1
Bellinzona D2
Bern, *capital* B2
Biel B1
Bolligen B2
Bulle B2
Chur D2
Davos D2
Einsiedeln C1
Fribourg B2
Frutigen B2
Geneva A2
Horgèn C1
Interlaken B2
La Chaux-de-Fonds A1
Lausanne A2
Locarno C2
Lucerne C1
Lugano C3
Montreux A2
Morges A2
Neuchâtel A2
St. Moritz D2
Sankt Gallen D1
Schaffhausen C1
Schwyz C1
Sempach C1
Sion B2
Thun B2
Uster C1
Winterthur C1
Yverdon A2
Zermatt B2
Zug C1
Zürich C1

Other Features
Aare, *river* B1, B2
Alps, *mts.* B2
Bernese Alps, *mts.* B2
Biel, *lake* B1
Brienzersee, *lake* B2
Constance (Bodensee), *lake* D1
Doubs, *river* A1
Dufourspitze, *mt.* B3
Engadine, *valley* D2
Geneva, *lake* A2
Inn, *river* D1
Jungfrau, *mt.* B2
Jura, *mts.* A2
Lepontine Alps, *mts.* C2
Lucerne, *lake* C2
Lugano, *lake* C3
Maggiore, *lake* C2
Matterhorn, *mt.* B3
Neuchâtel, *lake* A2
Pennine Alps, *mts.* B2
Reuss, *river* C2
Rhaetian Alps, *mts.* D2
Rhine, *river* C1, D2
Rhône, *river* B2
St. Gotthard, *pass* C2
St. Gotthard, *tunnel* C2
Splügen, *pass* D2
Staubbach, *falls* B2
Thunersee, *lake* B2
Ticino, *river* C2
Walensee, *lake* D1
Zürichsee, *lake* C1

France

Capital: Paris
Area: 210,026 sq. mi.
544,109 sq. km.
Population: 58,978,000
Largest City: Paris
Language: French
Monetary Unit: Franc, Euro

France: Map Index

Regions
Alsace D2
Aquitaine B4
Auvergne C4
Basse-Normandie B2
Bourgogne C3
Bretagne B2
Centre C3
Champagne-Ardenne D2
Corse ....Inset I
Franche-Comté D3
Haute-Normandie C2
Île-de-France C2
Languedoc-Roussillon C5
Limousin C4
Lorraine D2
Midi-Pyrénées C5
Nord-Pas-de-Calais C1
Pays De La Loire B3
Picardie C2
Poitou-Charentes C3
Provence-Alpes-Côte-d'Azur D4
Rhône-Alpes D4

Cities and Towns
Abbeville C1
Agen C4
Aix-en-Provence D5
Aix-les-Bains D4
Ajaccio ....Inset I
Albi C5
Alençon C2
Alès D4
Amiens C2
Angers B3
Angoulême C4
Annecy D4
Arachon B4
Argenteuil ....Inset II
Arles D5
Arpajon ....Inset II
Arras C1
Auch C5
Aurillac C4
Auxerre C3
Avignon D5
Ballancourt-sur-Essonne ....Inset II
Bar-le-Duc D2
Bastia ....Inset I
Bayeux B2
Bayonne B5
Beauvais C2
Belfort D3
Bergerac C4
Besançon D3
Béziers C5
Biarritz B5
Blois C3
Bondy ....Inset II
Bordeaux B4
Boulogne-Billancourt ....Inset II
Boulogne-sur-Mer C1
Bourg-en-Bresse D3
Bourges C3
Brest A2
Briançon D4
Brive-la-Gallarde C4
Caen B2
Cahors C4
Calais C1
Calvi ....Inset I
Cambrai C1
Cannes D5
Carcassonne C5
Carnac B3
Châlons-sur-Marne D2
Chambéry D4
Chamonix-Mont-Blanc D4
Chantilly C2
Charleville Mézières D2
Chartres C2
Châteauroux C3
Châtellerault C3
Chaumont D2
Chelles ....Inset II
Cherbourg B2
Chevreuse ....Inset II
Choisy-le Roi ....Inset II
Cholet B3
Clermont-Ferrand C4
Clichy ....Inset II
Cluny D3
Cognac B4
Colmar D2
Compiègne C2
Conflans-Sainte-Honorine ....Inset II
Corbeil-Essonnes ....Inset II
Coubert ....Inset II
Créteil ....Inset II
Dammartin-en-Goële ....Inset II
Deauville C2
Dieppe C2
Digne D4
Dijon D3
Dôle D3
Domont ....Inset II
Douai C1
Draguignan D5
Dreux C2
Dunkirk (Dunkerque) C1
Épinal D2
Étrechy ....Inset II
Évreux C2
Évry ....Inset II
Foix C5
Fontainebleau C2
Fréjus D5
Gap D4
Gentilly ....Inset II
Grenoble D4
Guéret C3
Laon C2
La Rochelle B3
La-Roche-sur-Yon B3
Laval B2
Le Creusot D3
Le Havre C2
Le Mans C2
Lens C1
Le Puy C4
Les Ulis ....Inset II
Levallois-Perret ....Inset II
Lille C1
Limoges C4
Limours ....Inset II
L'Isle-Adam ....Inset II
Lorient B3
Lourdes B5
Louvres ....Inset II
Luzarches ....Inset II
Lyon D4
Mâcon D3
Maisons-Laffitte ....Inset II
Marseille D5
Massy ....Inset II
Maurepas ....Inset II
Melun ....Inset II
Mende C4
Mennecy ....Inset II
Metz D2
Meulan ....Inset II
Montargis C2
Montauban C4
Montélimar D4
Montluçon C3
Montpellier C5
Montreuil ....Inset II
Mont-Saint-Michel B2
Morlaix B2
Mulhouse D3
Nancy D2
Nanterre ....Inset II
Nantes B3
Narbonne C5
Nevers C3
Nice D5
Nîmes D5
Niort B3
Orléans C3
Ozoir-la-Ferrière ....Inset II
Palaiseau ....Inset II
Paris, *capital* ....C2, Inset II
Pau B5
Périgueux C4
Perpignan C5
Poissy ....Inset II
Poitiers C3
Pontchartrain ....Inset II
Pontoise ....Inset II
Porto-Vecchio ....Inset I
Privas D4
Quimper A2
Reims D2
Rennes B2
Roanne D3
Rochefort B4
Rodez C4
Roubaix C1
Rouen C2
Saint-Brieuc B2
Saint-Cloud ....Inset II
Saint-Denis ....Inset II
Saint-Dizier D2
Saintes B4
Saint-Étienne D4
Saint-Germain-en-Laye ....Inset II
Saint-Lô B2
Saint-Malo B2
Saint-Nazaire B3
Saint-Tropez D5
Sarcelles ....Inset II
Saumur B3
Savigny-sur-Orge ....Inset II
Sedan D2
Sevran ....Inset II
Sèvres ....Inset II
Soissons C2
Strasbourg D2
Tarbes C5
Taverny ....Inset II
Toulon D5
Toulouse C5
Tourcoing C1
Tours C3
Trouville C2
Troyes D2
Valence D4
Valenciennes C1
Vannes B3
Verdun D2
Versailles ....C2, Inset II
Vesoul D3
Vichy C3
Vierzon C3
Villeneuve-Saint-Georges ....Inset II
Vincennes ....Inset II

Other Features
Adour, *river* B5
Aisne, *river* D2
Allier, *river* C3
Alps, *range* D4
Ardennes, *region* D1
Argonne, *forest* D2
Aube, *river* D3
Belfort, *gap* D3
Belle, *island* B3
Biscay, *bay* B4
Blanc, *mt.* D4
Cévennes, *mts.* C4
Charente, *river* B4
Corsica, *island* ....Inset I
Cotentin, *peninsula* B2
Dordogne, *river* C4
Dover, *strait* C1
Durance, *river* D5
English, *channel* B2
Garonne, *river* C4
Geneva, *lake* D3
Gironde, *river* B4
Hague, *cape* B2
Isère, *river* D4
Jura, *mts.* D3
Landes, *region* B5
Lion, *gulf* D5
Little St. Bernard, *pass* D4
Loire, *river* C3
Lot, *river* C4
Maritime Alps, *range* D4
Marne, *river* ....C2, Inset II
Massif Central, *plateau* C4
Meuse, *river* D2
Moselle, *river* D2
Oise, *river* ....C2, Inset II
Oléron, *island* B4
Omaha, *beach* B2
Orne, *river* B2
Pyrenees, *range* C5
Rance, *river* B2
Raz, *point* A3
Ré, *island* B3
Rhine, *river* D2
Rhône, *river* D4
Saint-Malo, *gulf* B2
Sambre, *river* C1
Saône, *river* D3
Seine, *river* ....C2, Inset II
Somme, *river* C2
Utah, *beach* B2
Vienne, *river* C3
Vignemale, *mt.* B5
Vilaine, *river* B3
Vosges, *mts.* D2
Yeu, *island* B3
Yonne, *river* C2

Portugal: Map Index

Districts
Aveiro A2
Beja A4
Braga A2
Bragança B2
Castelo Branco B3
Coimbra A2
Évora B3
Faro A4
Guarda B2
Leiria A3
Lisbon A3
Oporto (Porto) A2
Portalegre B3
Santarém A3
Setúbal A3
Viana do Castelo A2
Vila Real B2
Viseu B2

Cities and Towns
Abrantes A3
Almada A3
Amadora A3
Aveiro A2
Barreiro A3
Beja A4
Braga A2
Bragança B2
Caldasm da Rainha A3
Castelo Branco B3
Chaves B2
Coimbra B2
Covilhã B2
Elvas B3
Estoril A3
Évora B3
Faro B4
Figueira da Foz A3
Grândola A3
Guarda B2
Guimarães A2
Lagos A4
Leiria A3

Leixões A2
Lisbon, capital A3
Mafra A3
Moura B3
Odemira A4
Oeiras A3
Oporto (Porto) A2
Peniche A3
Portalegre B3
Portimão A4
Queluz A3
Santarém A3
Setúbal A3
Sines A4
Valença A1
Viana do Castelo A2
Vila do Conde A2
Vila Nova de Gaia A2
Vila Real B2
Vila Real
    de Santo Antonio B4
Viseu B2

Other Features
Algarve, region A4
Cádiz, gulf B4
Carvoeiro, cape A3
Chança, river B4
Douro, river B2
Espichel, cape A3
Estrela, mt. B2
Guadiana, river B3
Lima, river A2
Minho, river A1
Mondego, cape A2
Mondego, river B2
Roca, cape A3
Sado, river A3
São Vicente, cape A4
Seda, river B3
Setúbal, bay A3
Sor, river B3
Sorraia, river A3
Tagus, river B2
Tâmega, river B2
Zêzere, river A3

Portugal
Capital: Lisbon
Area: 35,672 sq. mi.
    92,415 sq. km.
Population: 9,918,000
Largest City: Lisbon
Language: Portuguese
Monetary Unit: Escudo, Euro

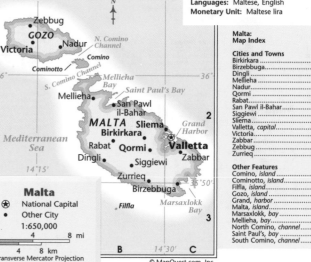

Malta
Capital: Valletta
Area: 122 sq. mi.
    316 sq. km.
Population: 382,000
Largest City: Valletta
Languages: Maltese, English
Monetary Unit: Maltese lira

Malta: Map Index

Cities and Towns
Birkirkara C2
Birzebbuga C2
Dingli B2
Mellieha B2
Nadur B1
Qormi B2
Rabat B2
San Pawl il-Bahar B2
Siggiewi B2
Sliema C2
Valletta, capital C2
Victoria A1
Zabbar C2
Zebbug A1
Zurrieq B2

Other Features
Comino, island B1
Cominotto, island B1
Filfla, island B3
Gozo, island A1
Grand, harbor C2
Malta, island B2
Marsaxlokk, bay C2
Mellieha, bay B2
North Comino, channel B1
Saint Paul's, bay B2
South Comino, channel B2

Gibraltar
Area: 2.25 sq. mi.
    5.83 sq. km.
Population: 29,000
Language: English
Monetary Unit: British Pound

Gibraltar: Map Index

Features
Catalan, bay A2
Detached, mole A2
Eastern, beach A2
Fortress Headquarters A3
Gibraltar, bay A2
Gibraltar, harbor A2
Gibraltar, strait A4
Governor's Residence A2
Great Europa, point A4
Highest point A3
Little, bay A4
Mediterranean, sea A3
North, mole A2
North Front, airfield A1
Rosia, bay A3
Saint Michael's, cave A3
Sandy, bay A3
Signal, hill A2
South, mole A3
The Rock, prom. A2

Gibraltar
1:82,200

0   0.5   1 mi
0   0.5   1 km
Miller Cylindrical Projection

© MapQuest.com, Inc.

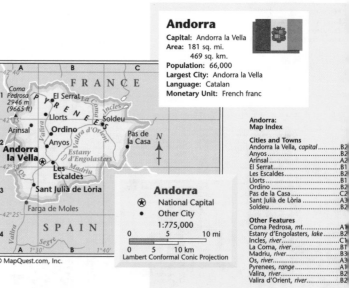

Andorra
Capital: Andorra la Vella
Area: 181 sq. mi.
    469 sq. km.
Population: 66,000
Largest City: Andorra la Vella
Language: Catalan
Monetary Unit: French franc

Andorra: Map Index

Cities and Towns
Andorra la Vella, capital B2
Anyos B2
Arinsal A2
El Serrat B1
Les Escaldes B2
Llorts B1
Ordino B2
Pas de la Casa C2
Sant Julià de Lòria A3
Soldeu B2

Other Features
Coma Pedrosa, mt. A1
Estany d'Engolasters, lake ...B2
Incles, river C1
La Coma, river B1
Madriu, river B3
Os, river A3
Pyrenees, range A1
Valira, river A3
Valira d'Orient, river B2

Spain:
Map Index

Regions

Andalusia	D4
Aragón	F2
Asturias	C1
Balearic Islands	G3
Basque Country	E1
Canary Islands	Inset I
Cantabria	D1
Castile-La Mancha	E3
Castile-León	D1, E1
Catalonia	G2
Estremadura	C3
Galicia	B1
La Rioja	E1
Madrid	E2
Murcia	F4
Navarra	F1
Valencia	F2, F3

Cities and Towns

Águilas	F4
Albacete	F3
Alcalá de Henares	Inset II
Alcañiz	F2
Alcázar de San Juan	E3
Alcira	F3
Alcobendas	Inset II
Alcorcón	E2, Inset II
Alcoy	F3
Algeciras	D4
Alicante	F3
Almadén	D3
Almansa	F3
Almendralejo	C3
Almería	E4
Antequera	D4
Aranda de Duero	E2
Aranjuez	E2
Astorga	C1
Ávila	D2
Avilés	D1
Badajoz	C3
Badalona	H2
Baracaldo	E1
Barcelona	H2

Baza	E4
Béjar	D2
Benavente	D1
Benidorm	F3
Bilbao	E1
Burgos	E1
Cáceres	C3
Cádiz	C4
Calatayud	F2
Cartagena	F4
Castellón de la Plana	F3
Ceuta	D5
Cieza	F4
Ciudadela	H2
Ciudad Real	D3
Ciudad Rodrigo	C2
Córdoba	D4
Cornellá de Llogregat	Inset II
Coslada	Inset II
Cuenca	E2
Don Benito	D3
Dos Hermanas	D4
Écija	D4
Elche	F3
Figueras	H1
Fuenlabrada	Inset II
Gerona	H2
Getafe	E2, Inset II
Gijón	D1
Granada	E4
Guadalajara	E2
Guecho	E1
Guernica y Luno	E1
Hellín	F3
Hospitalet	H2
Huelva	C4
Huesca	F1
Ibiza	G3
Jaén	E4
Jerez de la Frontera	C4
La Coruña	B1
La Laguna	Inset I
La Roda	E3
Las Palmas	Inset I
Leganés	Inset II
León	D1
Lérida	G2

Linares	E3
Logroño	E1
Loja	D4
Lorca	F4
Lucena	D4
Lugo	C1
Madrid, capital	E2, Inset II
Mahón	J3
Málaga	D4
Marbella	D4
Mataró	H2
Medina del Campo	D2
Mérida	C3
Mieres	D1
Miranda de Ebro	E1
Monforte	C1
Morón de la Frontera	D4
Móstoles	Inset II
Murcia	F4
Orense	C1
Oviedo	D1
Palencia	D1
Palma	H3
Pamplona	F1
Plasencia	C2
Ponferrada	C1
Pontevedra	B1
Puertollano	D3
Reinosa	D1
Reus	G2
Sabadell	H2
Sagunto	F3
Salamanca	D2
San Baudilio de Llobregat	G2
San Fernando	C4
San Sebastián	F1
Santa Coloma de Gramanet	H2
Santa Cruz de Tenerife	Inset I
Santander	E1
Santiago de Compostela	B1
Segovia	D2
Seville	D4
Soria	E2
Talavera de la Reina	D3
Tarragona	G2
Tarrasa	H2
Telde	Inset I

Teruel	F2
Toledo	D3
Tomelloso	E3
Torrejón de Ardoz	Inset II
Torrelavega	D1
Torrente	F3
Tortosa	G2
Úbeda	E3
Valdepeñas	E3
Valencia	F3
Valladolid	D2
Vich	H2
Vigo	B1
Villarreal de los Infantes	F3
Vitoria	E1
Yecla	F3
Zafra	C3
Zamora	D2
Zaragoza	F2

Other Features

Alarcón, reservoir	E3
Alboran, sea	E4
Alcántara, reservoir	C3
Almendra, reservoir	C2
Aneto, mt.	G1
Balearic, islands	G3
Balearic, sea	G2
Béticos, mts.	D4
Biscay, bay	D1
Brava, coast	H2
Buendía, reservoir	E2
Cabrera, island	H3
Cádiz, gulf	C4
Canaray, islands	Inset I
Cíjara, reservoir	D3
Cantábrica, mts.	C1
Cíjara, reservoir	D3
Duero, river	D2
Ebro, river	F1
Esla, river	D2
Finisterre, cape	B1
Formentera, island	G3
Fuerteventura, island	Inset I
Gata, cape	E4
Gibraltar, strait	D5
Gomera, island	Inset I
Gran Canaria, island	Inset I
Gredos, mts.	D2

Guadalquivir, river	D4
Guadarrama, mts.	D2
Guadiana, river	C3
Hierro, island	Inset I
Ibérico, mts.	E1
Ibiza, island	G3
Jarama, river	Inset II
Júcar, river	F3
Lanzarote, island	Inset I
La Palma, island	Inset I
Majorca, island	H3
Mediterranean, sea	E4
Mequinenza, reservoir	F2
Meseta, plateau	D3
Miño, river	B1
Minorca, island	H2
Morena, mts.	D4
Mulhacén, mt.	E4
Nao, cape	F3
Nevada, mts.	E4
Orellana, reservoir	D3
Ortegal, cape	C1
Palos, cape	F4
Pyrenees, mts.	F1
Ricobayo, reservoir	D2
Segura, river	E3
Sol, coast	D4
Tagus, river	D3
Tenerife, island	Inset I
Toledo, mts.	D3
Tormes, river	D2
Tortosa, cape	G2
Valdecañas, reservoir	D3
Valencia, gulf	G3
Zújar, reservoir	D3

Spain

Capital: Madrid
Area: 194,898 sq. mi.
504,917 sq. km.
Population: 39,168,000
Largest City: Madrid
Language: Spanish
Monetary Unit: Peseta, Euro

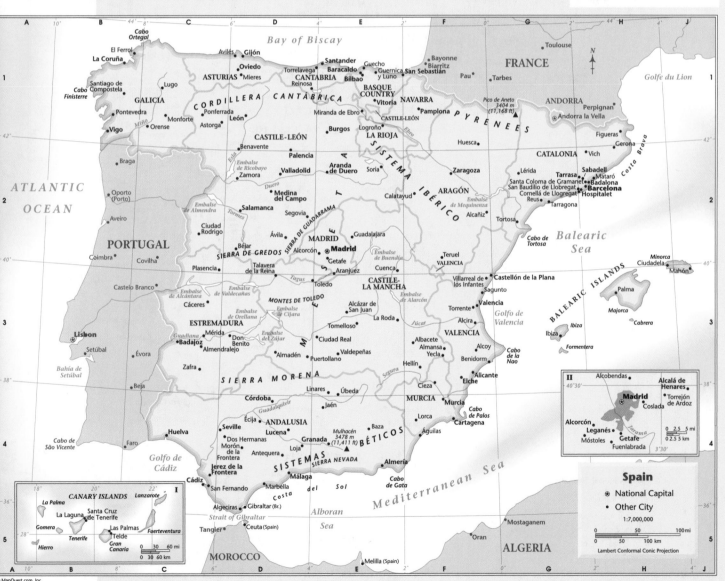

Austria:
Map Index

Provinces
Burgenland......................E3
Carinthia.........................C4
Lower Austria..................D2
Salzburg..........................C3
Styria..............................D3
Tirol............................B3, C4
Upper Austria.................C2
Vienna.............................E2
Vorarlberg.......................A3

Cities and Towns
Amstetten.......................D2
Baden..............................E2
Bad Ischl........................C3
Braunau...........................C2
Feldkirch.........................A3
Fürstenfeld......................E3
Gmünd.............................D3
Graz.................................D3
Hieflau............................D3
Innsbruck........................B3
Kapfenberg.....................D3
Klagenfurt.......................D4
Köflach.............................D3
Kufstein..........................C3
Lech.................................B3
Leoben.............................D3
Lienz...............................C3
Mistelbach.......................E2
Salzburg..........................C3

Sankt Pölten...................D2
Steyr................................D2
Stockerau.........................E2
Vienna, capital................E2
Villach.............................C4
Vöcklabruck.....................C2
Wels.................................C2
Wiener Neustadt..............E3
Wolfsberg.........................D4

Other Features
Alps, range......................B3
Bavarian Alps, range.......B3
Brenner, pass...................B3
Carnic Alps, range...........C4
Constance, lake...............A3
Danube, river...................D2
Drava, river......................C4
Enns, river.......................D3
Grossglockner, mt............C3
Hohe Tauern, mts............C3
Inn, river......................B3, C2
Karawanken, range..........D4
Mur, river........................D3
Mürz, river.......................D3
Neusiedler, lake...............E3
Niedere Tauern, range.....D3
Ötztal Alps, range............B4
Salzach, river...................C3
Salzburg Alps, range........C3
Semmering, pass..............D3
Traun, river......................D2
Ybbs, river.......................D2
Zillertal Alps, range..........B3

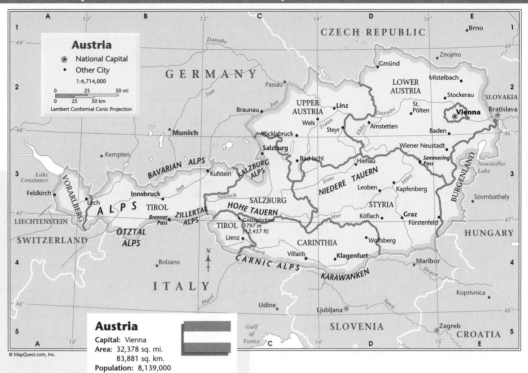

© MapQuest.com, Inc.

Austria
Capital: Vienna
Area: 32,378 sq. mi.
83,881 sq. km.
Population: 8,139,000
Largest City: Vienna
Language: German
Monetary Unit: Schilling, Euro

Vatican City
Area: 108.7 acres
Population: 811
Languages: Italian,
Latin
Monetary Unit: Lira

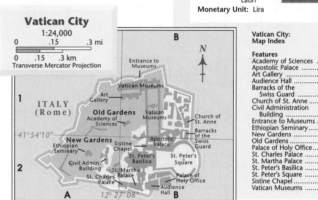

© MapQuest.com, Inc.

Vatican City:
Map Index

Features
Academy of Sciences B1
Apostolic Palace B2
Art Gallery B1
Audience Hall B2
Barracks of the
Swiss Guard B1
Church of St. Anne B1
Civil Administration
Building A2
Entrance to Museums B1
Ethiopian Seminary...........A2
New Gardens A2
Old Gardens A1
Palace of Holy Office........B2
St. Charles Palace B2
St. Martha Palace B2
St. Peter's Basilica B2
St. Peter's Square B2
Sistine Chapel B2
Vatican Museums B1

Italy:
Map Index

Regions
Abruzzi.............................C2
Apulia..............................C2
Basilicata.........................C2
Calabria...........................D3
Campania.........................C2
Emilia-Romagna...............B1
Friuli-Venezia Giulia........C1
Latium.............................C2
Liguria.............................B1
Lombardy.........................B1
Marche............................C2
Molise..............................C2
Piedmont.........................A1
Puglia..............................C2
Sardinia...........................B3
Sicily...............................C3
Trentino-Alto Adige..........B1
Tuscany...........................B2
Umbria.............................C2
Valle d'Aosta...................A1
Veneto.............................C2

Cities and Towns
Agrigento.........................C3
Alessandria......................B1
Alghero............................B2
Ancona.............................C2
Aosta...............................A1
Aquileia...........................C1
Arezzo.............................B2
Ascoli Piceno...................C2
Asti..................................B1
Avellino............................C2
Bari.................................D2
Barletta............................D2
Belluno............................C1
Benevento........................C2
Bergamo..........................B1
Bologna...........................B1
Bolzano............................B1
Brescia.............................B1
Brindisi............................D2
Cagliari............................B3
Caltanissetta....................C3
Campobasso.....................C2
Canossa...........................B1
Capua..............................C2
Carbonia..........................B3
Caserta............................C2
Castel Gandolfo...............C2
Catania............................C3
Catanzaro........................D3
Cefalù..............................C3
Chieti..............................C2
Chioggia...........................C1
Civitavecchia....................B2
Como...............................B1
Cortina d'Ampezzo...........C1
Cortona............................B2
Cosenza...........................D3
Cremona...........................B1
Crotone............................D3
Cuneo..............................A2
Enna................................C3
Faenza.............................B1
Ferrara.............................B1
Florence...........................B2
Foggia..............................C2
Forlì.................................C1
Frosinone.........................C2
Gaeta...............................C2
Gela.................................C3

Genoa..............................B1
Gorizia.............................C1
Grosseto...........................B2
Isernia..............................C2
L'Aquila............................C2
La Spezia.........................B1
Latina..............................C2
Lecce...............................D2
Livorno.............................B2
Lucca...............................B2
Macerata..........................C2
Manfredonia.....................C2
Mantova...........................B1
Mantua (Mantova)............B1
Marsala............................C3
Matera.............................D2
Merano............................B1
Messina............................C3
Milan...............................B1
Modena............................B1
Monopoli..........................D2
Montepulciano..................B2
Monza..............................B1
Naples..............................C2
Novara.............................B1
Nuoro...............................B2
Olbia................................B2
Oristano...........................B3
Otranto.............................D2
Padova.............................B1
Padua (Padova)................B1
Palermo............................C3
Parma..............................B1
Pavia................................B1
Perugia.............................C2
Pesaro..............................C2
Pescara............................C2
Pisa..................................B2
Pistoia..............................B2
Placenza...........................B1
Potenza............................C2
Prato................................B2
Ragusa.............................C3
Ravenna...........................C1
Reggio di Calabria...........C3
Reggio nell'Emilia............B1
Rieti.................................C2
Rimini..............................C1
Rome, capital...................C2
Rovigo..............................B1
Salerno............................C2
San Gimignano................B2
San Remo.........................A2
San Severo.......................C2
Sassari.............................B2
Savona.............................B1
Siena................................B2
Siracusa...........................C3
Sondrio.............................B1
Sorrento...........................C2
Spoleto.............................C2
Syracuse (Siracusa)..........C3
Taranto............................D2
Teramo............................C2
Termoli.............................C2
Terni.................................C2
Torre del Greco................C2
Trapani............................C3
Trento..............................B1
Treviso.............................C1
Trieste..............................C1
Turin................................A1
Udine...............................C1
Venice..............................C1
Ventimiglia.......................A2
Vercelli.............................B1

Verona.............................B1
Vicenza............................B1
Viterbo.............................C2

Other Features
Adige, river......................B1
Adriatic, sea.....................C2
Alps, mts....................A1, B1
Apennines, range..............B1
Arno, river........................B2
Asinara, island.................B2
Blanc, mt..........................A1
Bolsena, lake....................B2
Botte Donato, mt..............D3
Bracciano, lake.................C2
Brenner, pass....................B1
Cagliari, gulf.....................B3
Campagna di Roma, region.C2
Caprara, point...................C2
Capri, island.....................C2
Carbonara, cape................B3
Cervati, mt........................C2
Cimone, mt.......................B1
Como, lake........................B1
Corno, mt..........................C2
Dolomites, range...............B1
Egadi, islands...................C3
Elba, island.......................B2
Etna, mt............................C3
Garda, lake.......................B1
Gennargentu, mts..............B3
Genoa, gulf.......................B1
Giglio, island.....................B2
Ionian, sea........................D3
Ischia, island....................C2
Ligurian, sea.....................B2
Lipari, island.....................C3
Lombardy, plain................B1
Lugano, lake......................B1
Maggiore, lake...................B1
Maremma, region..............B2
Mediterranean, sea...........C3
Messina, strait..................C3
Montalto, mt.....................C3
Montecristo, island...........B2
Naples, bay.......................C2
Oglio, river........................B1
Pantelleria, island............C3
Passero, cape....................C3
Pianosa, island.................B2
Piave, river.......................C1
Po, river.......................A1, B1
Pontine, islands................C2
Pontine, marshes..............C2
Rosa, mt...........................A1
Salerno, gulf......................C2
Sangro, river.....................C2
San Pietro, island.............B3
Santa Maria di Leuca, cape.D3
Sant'Antioco, island..........B3
San Vito, cape...................C2
Sardinia, island.................B3
Sicily, island.....................C3
Sicily, strait......................B3
Spartivento, cape..............D3
Stromboli, island...............C3
Taranto, gulf.....................D2
Testa del Gargano, point...D2
Teulada, cape....................B3
Tiber, river........................C1
Tirso, river........................B2
Trasimeno, lake.................C2
Tyrrhenian, sea.................B2
Ustica, island...................C3
Venice, gulf.......................C1
Vesuvius, volcano.............C2

San Marino
Capital: San Marino
Area: 24 sq. mi.
62 sq. km.
Population: 25,000
Largest City: San Marino
Language: Italian
Monetary Unit: Italian lira

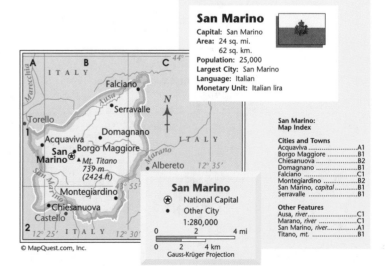

© MapQuest.com, Inc.

San Marino:
Map Index

Cities and Towns
Acquaviva.........................A1
Borgo Maggiore B1
Chiesanuova.....................B2
Domagnano.......................B1
Falciano...........................C1
Montegiardino..................B2
San Marino, capital..........B1
Serravalle.........................B1

Other Features
Ausa, river........................C1
Marano, river....................C1
San Marino, river..............A1
Titano, mt.........................B1

Germany
Capital: Berlin
Area: 137,735 sq. mi.
356,826 sq. km.
Population: 82,087,000
Largest City: Berlin
Language: German
Monetary Unit: Mark, Euro

Germany
⊛ National Capital
● Other City

1:4,066,000

0   25   50   75 mi
0   25 50 75 km
Lambert Conformal Conic Projection

© MapQuest.com, Inc.

Poland

Capital: Warsaw
Area: 120,727 sq. mi.
       312,764 sq. km.
Population: 38,609,000
Largest City: Warsaw
Language: Polish
Monetary Unit: Zloty

Poland:
Map Index

Cities and Towns
Biała Podlaska..................F2
Białystok.........................F2
Bielsko-Biała....................D4
Bydgoszcz.......................C2
Bytom..............................D3
Chełm..............................F3
Chojnice...........................C2
Chorzów...........................D3
Ciechanów.......................E2
Częstochowa....................D3
Darłowo............................C1
Elbląg..............................D1
Ełk...................................F2
Gdańsk............................D1
Gdynia.............................D1
Gliwice.............................D3
Głogów.............................C3
Gorzów Wielkopolski.........B2
Grudziądz.........................D2
Hel...................................D1
Jelenia Góra.....................B3
Katowice..........................D3
Kielce...............................E3
Kołobrzeg.........................B1
Konin...............................C1
Koszalin............................C1
Kraków.............................D3
Krosno.............................E4
Kutno...............................D2
Legnica............................C3
Leszno.............................C3
Łódź.................................D3
Łomża..............................F2
Lublin...............................F3
Nowy Sącz.......................E4
Nysa................................C3
Olsztyn.............................E2
Opole...............................C3
Ostrołęka.........................E2
Piła..................................C2
Piotrków Trybunalski.........D3
Płock...............................D2
Poznań.............................C2
Przemyśl..........................F4
Puck.................................D1
Puławy.............................E3
Radom..............................E3
Ruda Śląska......................D3
Rybnik..............................D3
Rzeszów...........................F3
Szczecinek.......................C2
Siedlce.............................F2
Sieradz.............................D3
Skierniewice.....................E3
Słupsk..............................C1
Sosnowiec........................D3
Suwałki............................F1
Świnoujście......................B2
Szczecin...........................B2
Tarnobrzeg.......................E3
Tarnów.............................E3
Toruń...............................D2
Tychy...............................D3
Ustka...............................C1
Wałbrzych........................C3
Warsaw, capital.................E2
Władysławowo...................D1
Włocławek........................D2
Wodzisław Śląski..............D3
Wrocław...........................C3
Zabrze..............................D3
Zakopane..........................D4
Zamość............................F3
Zielona Góra.....................B3

Other Features
Baltic, sea........................B1
Beskid, mts.......................D4
Bug, river..........................E2, F3
Carpathian, mts.................E4
Frisches Haff, bay..............D1
Gdańsk, gulf......................D1
High Tatra, mts..................D4
Mamry, lake......................E1
Narew, river......................E2
Neisse, river......................B3
Noteć, river.......................C2, D2
Oder, river.........................B2, D2
Pilica, river........................D3
Pomeranian, bay................B1
Rysy, mt............................E4
San, river..........................E3
Silesia, region....................C3
Śniardwy, lake...................E2
Sudeten, mts.....................B3
Vistula, river.....................D2, E3
Warta, river.......................B2, C2
Wieprz, river......................F3

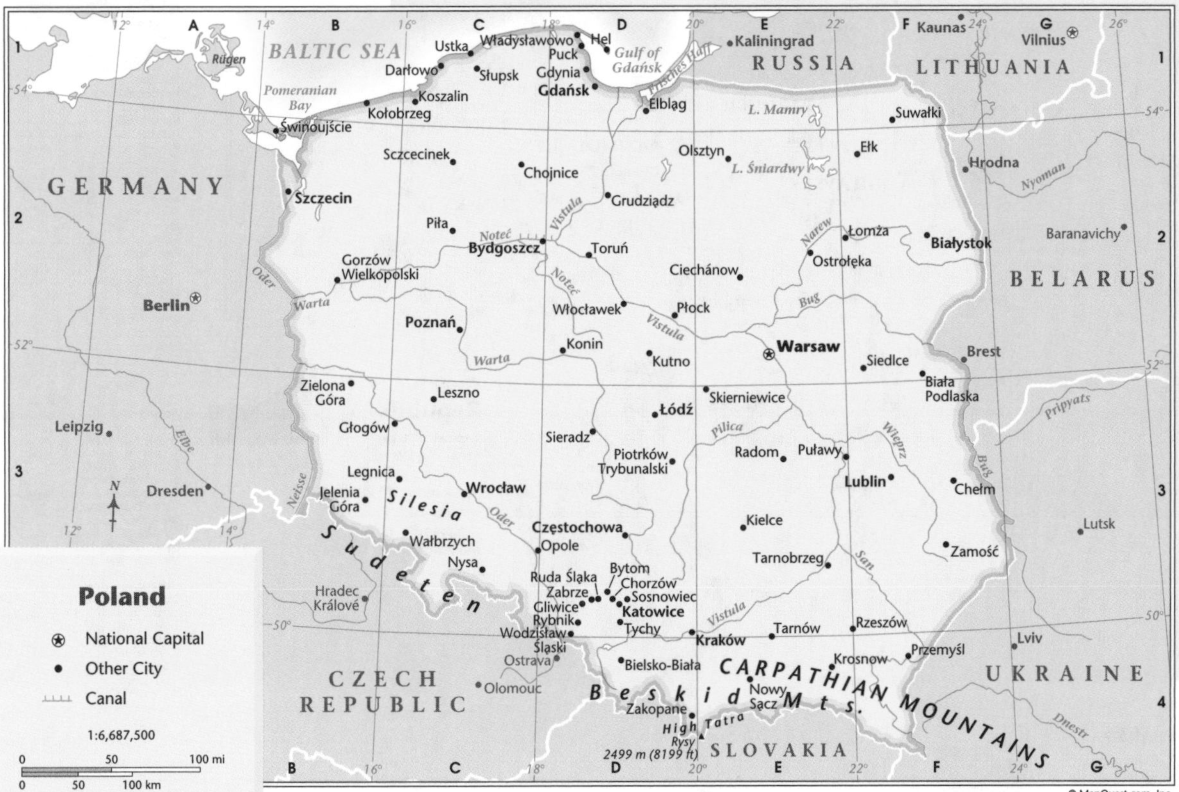

Poland

⊛ National Capital
• Other City
⊥⊥⊥ Canal

1:6,687,500

| 0 | 50 | 100 mi |
| 0 | 50 | 100 km |

Lambert Conformal Conic Projection

© MapQuest.com, Inc.

Germany:
Map Index

States
Baden-Württemberg............B4
Bavaria.............................B4
Berlin................................C2
Brandenburg......................C2
Bremen.............................B2
Hamburg...........................B2
Hesse...............................B3
Lower Saxony....................B2
Mecklenburg-Western
  Pomerania.......................C2
North Rhine-Westphalia.......A3
Rhineland-Palatinate...........A4
Saarland...........................A4
Saxony..............................C3
Saxony-Anhalt...................B3
Schleswig-Holstein.............B2
Thuringia...........................B3

Cities and Towns
Aachen.............................A3
Amberg.............................B4
Ansbach............................B4
Arnsberg...........................B3
Augsburg..........................B4
Bad Ems...........................A3
Baden-Baden.....................B4
Bad Kreuznach...................A4
Bad Reichenhall.................C5
Bamberg...........................B4
Bautzen............................C3
Bayreuth...........................B4
Bergisch Gladbach..............A3
Berlin, capital....................C2
Bernburg...........................B3
Bielefeld...........................B2
Bingen..............................A4
Bocholt..............................A3
Bochum.............................A3
Bonn.................................A3
Bottrop..............................A3
Brandenburg......................C2
Bremen.............................B2
Bremerhaven.....................B2
Brunswick.........................B2
Büren...............................B3
Chemnitz..........................C3
Coburg..............................B3
Cologne............................A3
Constance.........................B5
Cottbus.............................C3
Cuxhaven.........................B2
Dachau.............................B4
Darmstadt.........................B4
Dessau.............................C3
Detmold............................B3
Dortmund..........................A3
Dresden............................C3
Duisburg...........................A3
Düsseldorf.........................A3
Eberswalde.......................C2
Eisenach...........................B3
Eisenhüttenstadt................C2
Eisleben............................B3
Emden..............................A2
Erfurt................................B3
Erlangen...........................B4
Essen...............................A3
Esslingen..........................B4
Flensburg..........................B1
Frankfurt am Main..............B3
Frankfurt an der Oder.........C2
Freiberg............................C3
Freiburg............................A5
Friedrichshafen..................B5
Fulda................................B3
Fürth................................B4
Garmisch-Partenkirchen......B5
Gelsenkirchen....................A3
Gera.................................B3
Giessen.............................B3
Göppingen.........................B4
Görlitz...............................C3
Goslar...............................B3
Gotha...............................B3
Göttingen..........................B3
Greifswald.........................C1
Guben..............................C2
Güstrow............................C2
Hagen...............................A3
Halberstadt.......................B3
Halle.................................B3
Hamburg...........................B2
Hameln.............................B2
Hamm...............................A3
Hanau..............................B3
Hannover..........................B2
Heidelberg........................B4
Heidenheim.......................B4
Heilbronn..........................B4
Herne...............................A3
Hildesheim........................B2
Hindelang..........................B5
Hof...................................B3
Ingolstadt..........................B4
Jena.................................B3
Kaiserslautern....................A4
Karlsruhe...........................B4
Kassel...............................B3
Kaufbeuren.......................B5
Kempten............................B5
Kiel...................................B1
Kleve................................A3
Koblenz.............................A3
Krefeld..............................A3
Kulmbach..........................B3
Landshut...........................B4
Leipzig..............................C3
Leverkusen........................A3
Lindau..............................B5
Lippstadt...........................B3
Lübeck..............................B2
Luckenwalde......................C2
Ludwigsburg......................B4
Ludwigshafen am Rhein......B4
Lüneburg...........................B2
Lünen...............................A3
Magdeburg........................B2
Mainz...............................B4
Mannheim.........................B4
Marburg............................B3
Marl.................................A3
Meissen............................C3
Memmingen......................B5
Moers...............................A3
Mönchengladbach..............A3
Mühlhausen.......................B3
Mülheim an der Ruhr..........A3
Munich.............................B4
Münster............................A3
Naumburg.........................B3
Neubrandenburg................C2
Neumünster......................B1
Neunkirchen......................A4
Neuss...............................A3
Neustrelitz........................C2
Nienburg..........................B2
Nordenham.......................B2
Nordhausen......................B3
Nordhorn..........................A2
Northeim..........................B3
Nuremberg........................B4
Oberammergau.................B5
Oberhausen......................A3
Offenbach.........................B3
Oldenburg.........................B2
Osnabrück........................B2
Paderborn.........................B3
Passau.............................C4
Pforzheim.........................B4
Pirmasens.........................A4
Plauen..............................C3
Potsdam...........................C2
Puttgarden........................B1
Ratingen...........................A3
Ravensburg.......................B5
Recklinghausen.................A3
Regensburg.......................B4
Remagen..........................A3
Remscheid........................A3
Reutlingen.........................B4
Riesa...............................C3
Rosenheim........................C5
Rostock............................C1
Saarbrücken......................A4
Salzgitter...........................B2
Sassnitz............................C1
Schleswig..........................B1
Schwäbisch Gmünd............B4
Schwedt............................C2
Schweinfurt.......................B3
Schwerin...........................B2
Siegen..............................B3
Singen..............................B5
Solingen............................A3
Spandau............................C2
Speyer..............................B4
Stendal.............................B2
Stralsund...........................C1
Straubing...........................C4
Stuttgart............................B4
Suhl.................................B3
Trier.................................A4
Tübingen...........................B4
Uelzen..............................B2
Ulm..................................B4
Weiden.............................C4
Weimar.............................B3
Wetzlar.............................B3
Wiesbaden........................B3
Wilhelmshaven..................B2
Wismar.............................B2
Witten..............................A3
Wittenberg........................C3
Wittenberge......................B2
Wolfsburg..........................B2
Worms..............................B4
Wuppertal.........................A3
Würzburg..........................B4
Zittau...............................C3
Zwickau............................C3

Other Features
Ammersee, lake..................B4
Baltic, sea.........................C1
Bavarian Alps, mts.............B5
Bayerischer Wald, mts........C4
Black, forest......................A4
Bohemian, forest...............C4
Chiem, lake.......................C5
Constance, lake.................B5
Danube, river....................B4
East Frisian, islands...........A2
Eifel, plateau.....................A3
Elbe, river..........................B2, C3
Erzgebirge, mts..................C3
Fehmarn, island.................B1
Fichtelberg, mts.................B4
Fichtelgebirge, mts.............B4
Franconian Jura, mts..........B4
Frankenwald, mts...............B3
Fulda, river........................B3
Harz, mts..........................B3
Havel, river........................C2
Helgoland, island...............A1
Hünsruck, mts....................A4
Inn, river............................C4
Isar, river...........................C4
Kiel, bay............................B1
Lahn, river.........................B3
Lech, river.........................B4
Lüneburger Heide, region....B2
Main, river.........................B4
Main-Danube, canal...........B4
Mecklenburg, bay..............B1
Mittelland, canal................B2
Mosel, river.......................A4
Mulde, river.......................C3
Müritz, lake.......................C2
Neckar, river.....................B4
Neisse, river......................C3
Nord-Ostsee, canal............B1
North, sea.........................A1
Northern European, plain....B2
North Frisian, islands..........B1
Oberpfälzer Wald, mts........C4
Odenwald, forest...............B4
Oder, river.........................C2
Oderhaff, lake....................C2
Pomeranian, bay................C1
Rhine, river........................A3, A4
Rügen, island....................C1
Ruhr, river.........................B3
Saale, river........................B3
Saar, river..........................A4
Salzach, river.....................C4
Schwerin, lake...................B2
Spessart, mts.....................B4
Spree, river........................C3
Starnberg, lake...................B5
Swabian Jura, mts..............B5
Taunus, mts.......................B3
Thuringian, forest...............B3
Werra, river........................B3
Weser, river.......................B2
Zugspitze, mt.....................B5

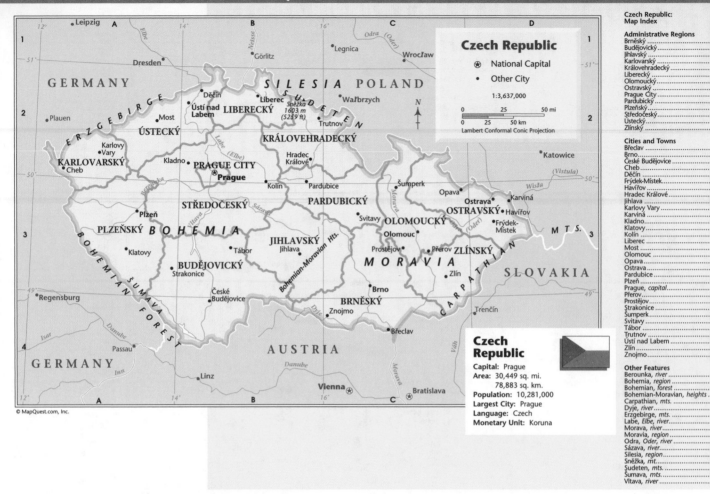

Czech Republic:
Map Index

Administrative Regions
Brněský C4
Budějovický B3
Jihlavský B3
Karlovarský A2
Královéhradecký B2
Liberecký B2
Olomoucký C3
Ostravský D3
Prague City B2
Pardubický C3
Plzeňský A3
Středočeský B3
Ústecký A2
Zlínský D3

Cities and Towns
Břeclav C4
Brno C3
České Budějovice B4
Cheb A2
Děčín B2
Frýdek-Místek D3
Havířov D3
Hradec Králové B2
Jihlava B3
Karlovy Vary A2
Karviná D3
Kladno B2
Klatovy A3
Kolín B2
Liberec B2
Most A2
Olomouc C3
Opava C3
Ostrava D3
Pardubice B2
Plzeň A3
Prague, capital B2
Přerov C3
Prostějov C3
Štrakonice A3
Šumperk C3
Svitavy C3
Tábor B3
Trutnov B2
Ústí nad Labem B2
Zlín C3
Znojmo C4

Other Features
Berounka, river A3
Bohemia, region A3
Bohemian, forest A3
Bohemian-Moravian, heights ..B3
Carpathian, mts. B4
Dyje, river B4
Erzgebirge, mts. A2
Labe, Elbe, river B2
Morava, river C3
Moravia, region C3
Odra, Oder, river C3
Sázava, river B3
Silesia, region B2
Sněžka, mt. B2
Sudeten, mts. B2
Šumava, mts. A3
Vltava, river B3

Czech Republic

Capital: Prague
Area: 30,449 sq. mi.
78,883 sq. km.
Population: 10,281,000
Largest City: Prague
Language: Czech
Monetary Unit: Koruna

Slovakia

Capital: Bratislava
Area: 18,933 sq. mi.
49,049 sq. km.
Population: 5,396,000
Largest City: Bratislava
Language: Slovak
Monetary Unit: New Koruna

Slovakia:
Map Index

Regions
Banskobystrický C2
Bratislavský A2
Košický C2
Nitriansky B2
Prešovský C2
Trenčiansky B2
Trnavský A2
Žilinský B2

Cities and Towns
Banská Bystrica B2
Bardejov C2
Bratislava, capital A2
Humenné C2
Komárno B3
Košice C2
Levice B2
Liptovský Mikuláš B2
Lučenec B2
Martin B2
Michalovce C2
Nitra B2
Nové Zamky B3
Piešťany A2
Poprad C2
Považská Bystrica B2
Prešov C2
Prievidza B2
Ružomberok B2
Spišská Nová Ves C2
Trenčín B2
Trnava A2
Žilina B2
Zvolen B2

Other Features
Biele Karpaty, mts. A2
Carpathian, mts. A2
Danube, river A3
Gerlachovka, mt. C2
Hornád, river C2
Hron, river B2
Ipeľ, river B2
Laborec, river C2
Male Karpaty, mts. A2
Morava, river A2
Ondava, river C2
Slaná, river B2
Slovenskérudohorie, mts. ..B2
Tatra, range A2
Váh, river A2

Romania:
Map Index

Cities and Towns
Alba Iulia ....B.
Alexandria ....C.
Arad ....A.
Bacău ....D.
Baia Mare ....B.
Bîrlad ....D.
Bistriţa ....C.
Botoşani ....D.
Brăila ....D.
Braşov ....C.
Bucharest, capital ....D
Buzău ....D.
Călăraşi ....D.
Cernavodă ....E.
Cluj-Napoca ....C.
Constanţa ....E.
Craiova ....B.
Dej ....C.
Deva ....B.
Dorohoi ....D.
Drobeta-Turnu Severin ......B.
Făgăraş ....C.
Feteşti ....D.
Focşani ....D.
Galaţi ....E.
Giurgiu ....C.
Hunedoara ....B.
Iaşi ....D.
Lugoj ....A.
Lupeni ....B.
Medgidia ....E.
Mediaş ....C.
Miercurea Ciuc ....C.
Olteniţa ....D.
Oneşti ....D.
Oradea ....A.
Petrila ....B.
Petroşani ....B.
Piatra Neamţ ....D.
Piteşti ....D
Ploieşti ....D
Rădăuţi ....C.
Reghin ....C.
Reşiţa ....A.
Rîmnicu Vîlcea ....C.
Roman ....D
Salonta ....A.
Satu Mare ....B.
Sfîntu Gheorghe ....C.
Sibiu ....B.
Sighetul Marmaţiei ....B.

© MapQuest.com, Inc.

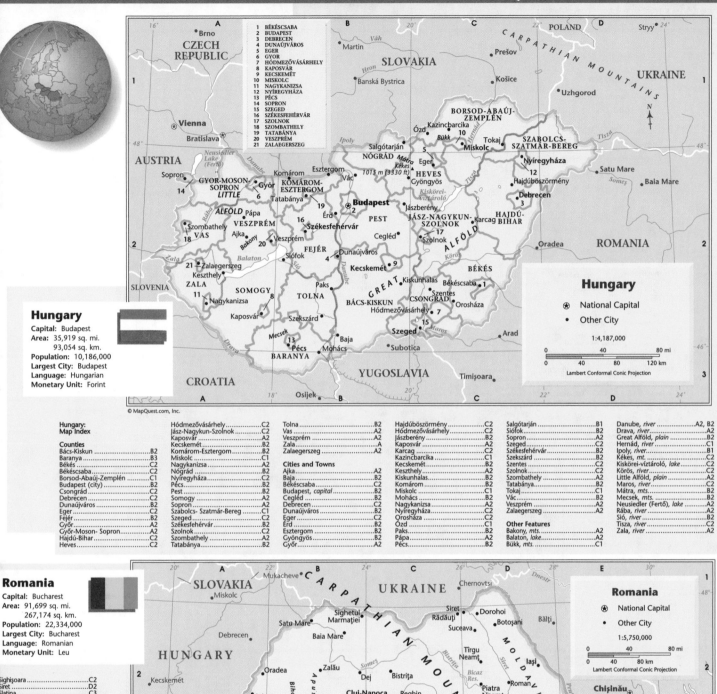

Map legend (numbered locator list):

1 BÉKÉSCSABA
2 BUDAPEST
3 DEBRECEN
4 DUNAÚJVÁROS
5 EGER
6 GYŐR
7 HÓDMEZŐVÁSÁRHELY
8 KAPOSVÁR
9 KECSKEMÉT
10 MISKOLC
11 NAGYKANIZSA
12 NYÍREGYHÁZA
13 PÉCS
14 SOPRON
15 SZEGED
16 SZÉKESFEHÉRVÁR
17 SZOLNOK
18 SZOMBATHELY
19 TATABÁNYA
20 VESZPRÉM
21 ZALAEGERSZEG

Hungary

Capital: Budapest
Area: 35,919 sq. mi.
 93,054 sq. km.
Population: 10,186,000
Largest City: Budapest
Language: Hungarian
Monetary Unit: Forint

Hungary
⊛ National Capital
• Other City
1:4,187,000
0   40   80 mi
0   40   80   120 km
Lambert Conformal Conic Projection

© MapQuest.com, Inc.

Hungary: Map Index

Counties

Bács-Kiskun	B2	
Baranya	B3	
Békés	C2	
Békéscsaba	C2	
Borsod-Abaúj-Zemplén	C1	
Budapest (city)	B2	
Csongrád	C2	
Debrecen	C2	
Dunaújváros	B2	
Eger	C2	
Fejér	B2	
Győr	A2	
Győr-Moson- Sopron	A2	
Hajdú-Bihar	C2	
Heves	C2	
Hódmezővásárhely	C2	
Jász-Nagykun-Szolnok	C2	
Kaposvár	A2	
Kecskemét	B2	
Komárom-Esztergom	B2	
Miskolc	C1	
Nagykanizsa	A2	
Nógrád	B2	
Nyíregyháza	C1	
Pécs	B2	
Pest	B2	
Somogy	A2	
Sopron	A2	
Szabolcs- Szatmár-Bereg	C1	
Szeged	C2	
Székesfehérvár	B2	
Szolnok	C2	
Szombathely	A2	
Tatabánya	B2	
Tolna	B2	
Vas	A2	
Veszprém	A2	
Zala	A	
Zalaegerszeg	A2	

Cities and Towns

Ajka	A2
Baja	B2
Békéscsaba	C2
Budapest, capital	B2
Cegléd	B2
Debrecen	C2
Dunaújváros	B2
Eger	C2
Érd	B2
Esztergom	B2
Gyöngyös	B2
Győr	A2
Hajdúböszörmény	C2
Hódmezővásárhely	C2
Jászberény	B2
Kaposvár	A2
Karcag	C2
Kazincbarcika	C1
Kecskemét	B2
Keszthely	A2
Kiskunhalas	B2
Komárom	B2
Miskolc	C1
Mohács	B2
Nagykanizsa	A2
Nyíregyháza	C1
Oroszháza	C2
Ózd	C1
Paks	B2
Pápa	A2
Pécs	B2
Salgótarján	B1
Siófok	B2
Sopron	A2
Szeged	C2
Székesfehérvár	B2
Szekszárd	B2
Szentes	C2
Szolnok	C2
Szombathely	A2
Tatabánya	B2
Tokaj	C1
Vác	B2
Veszprém	A2
Zalaegerszeg	A2

Other Features

Bakony, mts.	A2
Balaton, lake	A2
Bükk, mts.	C1
Danube, river	A2, B2
Drava, river	A2
Great Alföld, plain	B2
Hernád, river	C1
Ipoly, river	B1
Kékes, mt.	B2
Kiskörei-víztároló, lake	C2
Körös, river	C2
Little Alföld, plain	A2
Maros, river	C2
Mátra, mts.	B2
Mecsek, mts.	A2
Neusiedler (Fertő), lake	A2
Rába, river	A2
Sió, river	B2
Tisza, river	B2
Zala, river	A2

Romania

Capital: Bucharest
Area: 91,699 sq. mi.
 267,174 sq. km.
Population: 22,334,000
Largest City: Bucharest
Language: Romanian
Monetary Unit: Leu

Sighișoara	C2
Siret	D2
Slatina	C3
Slobozia	D3
Suceava	D2
Tecuci	D3
Timișoara	A3
Tîrgoviște	C3
Tîrgu Jiu	B3
Tîrgu-Mureș	C2
Tîrgu Neamț	D2
Tîrgu Ocna	D2
Tulcea	E3
Turda	B2
Turnu Măgurele	C4
Vaslui	D2
Zalău	B2

Other Features

Apuseni, mts.	B2
Argeș, river	C3
Banat, region	A3
Bicaz, reservoir	D2
Bihor, mts.	B2
Bistrița, river	D2
Carpathian, mts.	B1
Danube, river	B3, D3, E3
Dobruja, region	E4
Ialomița, river	D3
Iron Gate, reservoir	B3
Jiu, river	B3
Moldavia, region	D2
Moldoveanu, mt.	C3
Mouths of the Danube, delta	E3
Mureș, river	B2
Olt, river	C3
Prut, river	E2
Razelm, lake	E3
Siret, river	D2
Someș, river	B2
Transylvanian Alps, mts.	B3
Walachia, region	B3

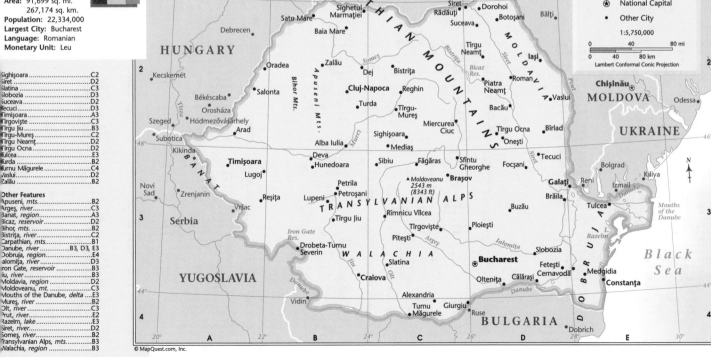

Romania
⊛ National Capital
• Other City
1:5,750,000
0   40   80 mi
0   40   80 km
Lambert Conformal Conic Projection

© MapQuest.com, Inc.

Part of Russia extends onto the continent of Asia.

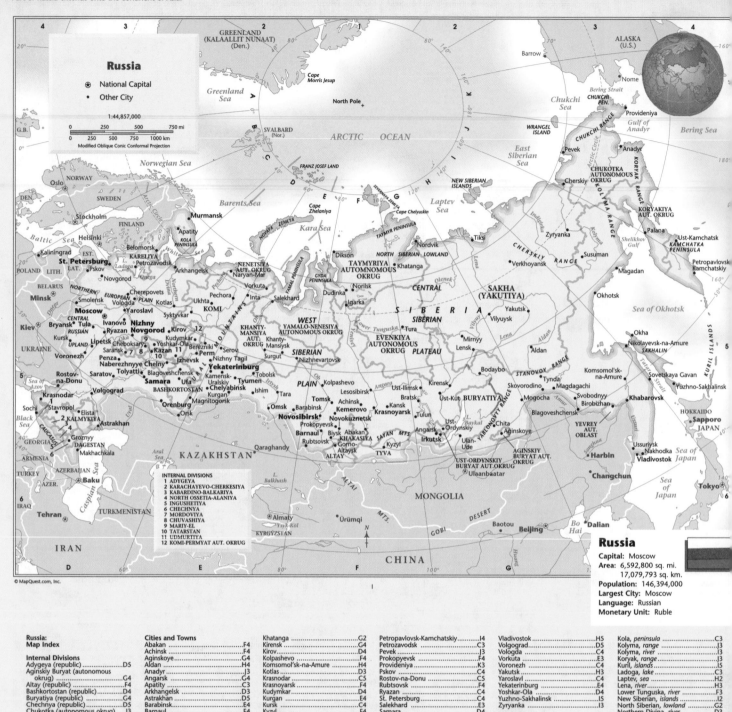

Russia

Capital: Moscow
Area: 6,592,800 sq. mi.
17,079,793 sq. km.
Population: 146,394,000
Largest City: Moscow
Language: Russian
Monetary Unit: Ruble

© MapQuest.com, Inc.

Russia:
Map Index

Internal Divisions
Adygeya (republic) D5
Aginskiy Buryat (autonomous
 okrug) G4
Altay (republic) F4
Bashkortostan (republic) D4
Buryatiya (republic) G4
Chechnya (republic) D5
Chuvashiya (republic) D4
Dagestan (republic) D5
Evenkiya (autonomous okrug) ...F3
Ingushetiya (republic) D5
Kabardino-Balkariya (republic) ...D5
Kalmykiya (republic) D5
Karachayevo-Cherkesiya
 (republic) D5
Kareliya (republic) C3
Khakasiya (republic) F4
Khanty-Mansiya
 (autonomous okrug) E3
Komi (republic) D3
Komi-Permyat
 (autonomous okrug) D4
Koryakiya (autonomous okrug) ...J3
Mariy-El (republic) D4
Mordoviya (republic) D4
Nenetsiya (autonomous okrug) ...D3
North Ossetia Alaniya (republic) ...D4
Tatarstan (republic) D4
Taymyriya (autonomous okrug) ...F2
Tyva (republic) F4
Udmurtiya (republic) D4
Ust-Ordynskiy Buryat (autonomous
 okrug) G5
Sakha (Yakutiya) (republic) H3
Yamalo-Nenesiya
 (autonomous okrug) E3
Yevrey (autonomous oblast) H5

Cities and Towns
Abakan F4
Achinsk F4
Aginskoye G4
Aldan H4
Anadyr J3
Angarsk G4
Apatity C3
Arkhangelsk D3
Barabinsk E4
Barnaul F4
Belomorsk C3
Berezniki D4
Birobizhan H5
Biysk F4
Blagoveshchensk G4
Blagoveshchensk H4
Bodaybo G4
Bratsk G4
Bryansk C4
Cheboksary D4
Chelyabinsk E4
Cherepovets C4
Cherskiy J3
Chita G4
Dikson F2
Dudinka F3
Elista D5
Gorno-Altaysk F4
Groznyy D5
Igarka F3
Inta E3
Irkutsk G4
Ishim E4
Ivanovo D4
Izhevsk D4
Kaliningrad A4
Kamensk-Uralskiy E4
Kansk F4
Kazan D4
Kemerovo F4
Khabarovsk H5
Khanty-Mansiysk E3

Khatanga G2
Kirensk G4
Kirov D4
Kolpashevo F4
Komsomol'sk-na-Amure H4
Kotlas D3
Krasnodar C5
Krasnoyarsk F4
Kudymkar D4
Kurgan E4
Kursk C4
Lensk G3
Lesosibirsk F4
Lipetsk C4
Magadan I4
Magdagachi H4
Magnitogorsk D4
Makhachkala D5
Mirnyy G3
Mogocha G4
Moscow, capital C4
Murmansk C3
Naberezhnyye Chelny D4
Nakhodka H5
Naryan-Mar D3
Nikolayevsk-na-Amure H4
Nizhnevartovsk E3
Nizhny Novgorod D4
Nizhny Tagil D4
Nordvik G2
Norilsk F3
Novgorod C4
Novokuznetsk F4
Novosibirsk F4
Okha I4
Okhotsk I4
Omsk E4
Orenburg D4
Orsk D4
Palana J4
Pechora D3
Penza D4
Perm D4

Petropavlovsk-Kamchatskiy I4
Petrozavodsk C3
Pevek J3
Prokopyevsk F4
Providenlya K3
Pskov C4
Rostov-na-Donu C5
Rubtsovsk F4
Ryazan C4
St. Petersburg C4
Salekhard E3
Samara D4
Saransk D4
Saratov D4
Serov E4
Skovorodino H4
Smolensk C4
Sochi C5
Sovetskaya Gavan I5
Stavropol D5
Surgut E3
Susuman I3
Svobodnyy H4
Syktyvkar D3
Tara E4
Tiksi H2
Tobolsk E4
Tolyatti D4
Tomsk F4
Tula C4
Tulun G4
Tura G3
Tynda H4
Tyumen D4
Ufa D4
Ukhta D3
Ulan-Ude G4
Ussuriysk H5
Ust-Ilimsk G4
Ust-Kamchatsk J4
Ust-Kut G4
Ust-Ordynskiy G4
Verkhoyansk H3
Vilyuysk H3

Vladivostok H5
Volgograd D5
Vologda C4
Vorkuta E3
Voronezh C4
Yakutsk H3
Yaroslavl C4
Yekaterinburg D4
Yoshkar-Ola D4
Yuzhno-Sakhalinsk I5
Zyryanka I3

Other Features
Aldan, river H4
Amur, river H4
Anadyr, gulf J3
Angara, river F4
Azov, sea C5
Baltic, sea B4
Barents, sea D2
Baykal, lake G4
Bering, sea K3
Bering, strait K3
Black, sea C5
Caspian, sea D6
Caucasus, mts. D5
Central Russian, upland C4
Central Siberian, plateau G3
Central, range I4
Chelyuskin, cape G2
Cherskiy, range H3
Chukchi, peninsula J3
Chukchi, range J3
Chukchi, sea K2
Dnepr, river C4
Dzhugdzhur, range H4
East Siberian, sea I2
Franz Josef Land, islands D1
Gyda, peninsula E2
Indigirka, river I3
Irtysh, river D4
Kamchatka, peninsula J4
Kara, sea E2

Kola, peninsula C3
Kolyma, range I3
Kolyma, river I3
Koryak, range J3
Kuril, islands I5
Ladoga, lake C3
Laptev, sea H2
Lena, river H3
Lower Tunguska, river F3
New Siberian, islands I2
North Siberian, lowland G2
Northern Divina, river D3
Northern European, plain C4
Novaya Zemlya, islands E3
Ob, river D4
Oka, river D4
Okhotsk, sea I4
Olenek, river G3
Onega, lake C3
Pechora, river D3
Sakhalin, island I4
Sayan, mts. F4
Severnaya Zemlya, islands F1
Shelikhov, gulf I3
Siberia, region F3
Sikhote Alin, range H5
Stanovoy, range H4
Tatar, strait H5
Taymyr, peninsula G2
Ural, mts. D5
Ural, river D4
Ussuri, river H5
Verkhoyansk, range H3
Vilyuy, river G3
Volga, river D5
West Siberian, plain E3
White, sea C3
Wrangel, island K2
Yablonovyy, range G4
Yamal, peninsula E3
Yenisey, river F3
Zhelaniya, cape E2

Armenia

Capital: Yerevan
Area: 11,500 sq. mi.
29,793 sq. km.
Population: 3,409,000
Largest City: Yerevan
Language: Armenian
Monetary Unit: Dram

Armenia:
Map Index

Cities and Towns
Alaverdi B1
Ararat B3
Artashat B3
Artik A2
Artsvashen C2
Dilijan B2
Ejmiatsin B2
Gavarr C2
Goris D3

Gyumri A2
Hoktemberyan B2
Hrazdan B2
Ijevan C2
Kafan D3
Kirovakan B2
Martuni C2
Meghri D4
Sisian D3
Sotk C2
Stepanavan B2
Tashir B1
Vardenis C2

Vayk C3
Yerevan, *capital* B2

Other Features
Akhuryan, *river* A2
Aragats, *mt.* B2
Aras, *river* C3
Arpa, *river* C3
Debed, *river* B2
Hrazdan, *river* B2
Lesser Caucasus, *mts.* B1
Sevan, *lake* C2
Vorotan, *river* C3

Georgia:
Map Index

Cities and Towns
Akhalkalaki B4
Akhaltsikhe B4
Akhmeta C4
Batumi A4
Bolnisi C4
Borjomi B4
Chiatura B3
Gagra A2
Gori C4
Gudauta A2
Jvari B3
Khashuri C4
Kobuleti A4
Kutaisi B3
Lagodekhi D4
Marneuli C4
Mtskheta C4
Ochamchire A3
Ozurgeti A3
Poti A3
Rustavi C4
Samtredia B3
Senaki B3
Sukhumi A3
Tbilisi, *capital* C4
Telavi C4
Tqvarcheli A3
Tsiteli-Tsqaro D4
Tskhinvali B3

Tsnori C4
Zestaponi B3
Zugdidi A3

Other Features
Abkhazia, *autonomous*
republic A3
Ajaria, *autonomous republic* A4
Alazani, *river* C4
Caucasus, *mts.* A2
Enguri, *river* A3
Iori, *river* C4
Lesser Caucasus, *mts.* ...B4
Mqinvartsveri, *mt.* ...C3
Mtkvari, *river* C4
Rioni, *river* B3
Shkhara, *mt.* B3
South Ossetia, *region* ...B4

Georgia

Capital: Tbilisi
Area: 26,900 sq. mi.
69,689 sq. km.
Population: 5,067,000
Largest City: Tbilisi
Language: Georgian
Monetary Unit: Lari

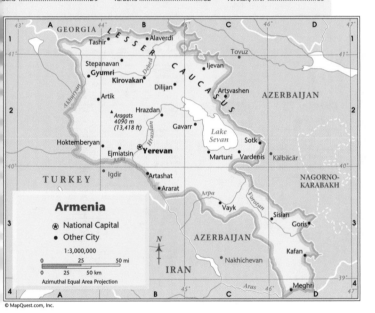

Azerbaijan

Capital: Baku
Area: 33,400 sq. mi.
86,528 sq. km.
Population: 7,908,000
Largest City: Baku
Language: Azerbaijani
Monetary Unit: Manat

Azerbaijan:
Map Index

Cities and Towns
Ağcabädi B2
Ağdam B3
Ağstafa A2
Älät C3
Äli Bayramli C3
Astara C3
Baku, *capital* C2
Balakän B2
Bärdä B2
Biläsuvar C3
Gäncä B2
Göyçay B2
Kälbäcär B2
Länkäran C3
Mingäçevir B2
Nakhichevan A3
Quba B2
Şahbuz A3
Şaki B2

Salyan C3
Sumqayit C2
Tovuz A2
Xaçmaz C2
Xankändi B3
Yevlax B2
Zaqatala B2

Other Features
Abşeron, *peninsula* C2
Aras, *river* B3
Bazardüzü Daği, *mt.* ..B2
Caucasus, *range* A1
Karabakh, *canal* B2
Kür, *river* A2, C2
Kür-Aras, *lowland* B2
Lesser Caucasus, *range* ...A2
Mingäçevir, *reservoir* ...B2
Nagorno-Karabakh,
autonomous region ...B3
Samur, *river* B2
Talish, *mts.* C3

Estonia:
Map Index

Cities and Towns
Haapsalu B2
Kärdla...................................B1
Keila......................................C1
Kohtla-Järve D1
Kunda D1
Kuressaare B2
Mustvee D2
Narva....................................E1
Paldiski.................................C2
Pärnu....................................C2
Rapla....................................C1
Tallinn, *capital* C1
Tapa.....................................C1
Tartu D2
Tõrva C2
Türi C2

Valga D3
Viljandi.................................C2
Virtsu B2
Võru D3

Other Features
Baltic, *sea* A1
Finland, *gulf* C1
Hiiumaa, *island*.................B2
Irbe, *strait*..........................A3
Munamägi, *mt.* D3
Narva, *river*........................D1
Pärnu, *river*........................C2
Pedja, *river*........................D2
Peipus, *lake* D2
Pskov, *lake* D3
Riga, *gulf*............................B3
Saaremaa, *island* B2
Vörts Järv, *lake*..................D2

Estonia
Capital: Tallinn
Area: 17,413 sq. mi.
45,111 sq. km.
Population: 1,409,000
Largest City: Tallinn
Language: Estonian
Monetary Unit: Kroon

Estonia
⍟ National Capital
● Other City
1:7,000,000

0   50   100 mi
0   50   100 km
Lambert Conformal Conic Projection

© MapQuest.com, Inc.

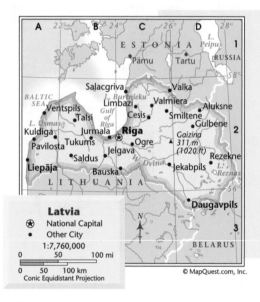

Latvia
Capital: Riga
Area: 24,900 sq. mi.
64,508 sq. km.
Population: 2,354,000
Largest City: Riga
Language: Latvian
Monetary Unit: Lat

Latvia
⍟ National Capital
● Other City
1:7,760,000

0   50   100 mi
0   50   100 km
Conic Equidistant Projection

© MapQuest.com, Inc.

Latvia:
Map Index

Cities and Towns
Aluksne D2
Bauska..................................C2
Cesis.....................................C2
Daugavpils...........................D3
Gulbene................................D2
Jekabpils...............................C2
Jelgava B2
Jurmala.................................B2
Kuldiga A2
Liepāja..................................A2
Limbazi.................................C2
Ogre C2
Pavilosta...............................A2
Rezekne................................D2
Riga, *capital* C2
Salacgriva.............................C2
Saldus B2
Smiltene...............................C2
Talsi......................................B2
Tukums.................................B2
Valka.....................................C2
Valmiera...............................C2
Ventspils...............................A2

Other Features
Baltic, *sea* A2
Burtnieku, *lake*...................C2
Gaizina, *mt.*........................C2
Reznas, *lake*.......................D2
Riga, *gulf*............................B2
Usmas, *lake*........................B2
Western Dvina, *river* C2

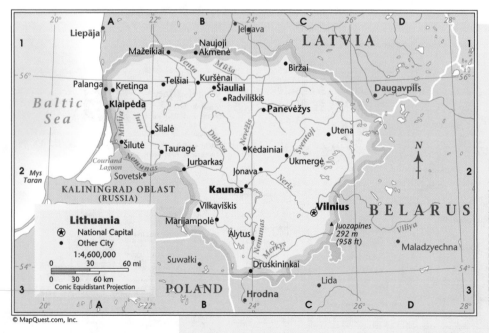

Lithuania
Capital: Vilnius
Area: 25,213 sq. mi.
65,319 sq. km.
Population: 3,585,000
Largest City: Vilnius
Language: Lithuanian
Monetary Unit: Litas

Lithuania
⍟ National Capital
● Other City
1:4,600,000

0   30   60 mi
0   30   60 km
Conic Equidistant Projection

© MapQuest.com, Inc.

Lithuania:
Map Index

Cities and Towns
Alytus....................................C2
Biržai.....................................C1
Druskininkai.........................B2
Jonava..................................C2
Jurbarkas.............................B2
Kaunas.................................B2
Kėdainiai..............................B2
Klaipėda...............................A2
Kretinga...............................A2
Kuršenai...............................B1
Marijampolė.........................B2
Mažeikiai..............................B1
Naujoji Akmenė....................B1
Palanga................................A2
Panevėžys............................B2
Radviliškis............................B2
Šiauliai..................................B2
Šilalė.....................................B2

Šilutė A2
Tauragé B2
Telšiai B2
Ukmergé...............................C2
Utena....................................C2
Vilkaviškis.............................B2
Vilnius, *capital*....................C2

Other Features
Baltic, *sea* A2
Courland, *lagoon* A2
Dubysa, *river* B2
Juozapines, *mt.* C2
Jura, *river*............................A2
Merkys, *river* C2
Minija, *river*.........................A2
Mūša, *river* B1
Nemunas, *river* A2, B2
Neris, *river* C2
Nevėžis, *river*......................B2
Šventoji, *river*......................B2
Venta, *river*.........................A2

© MapQuest.com, Inc.

Belarus

Capital: Minsk
Area: 80,134 sq. mi.
207,601 sq. km.
Population: 10,402,000
Largest City: Minsk
Languages: Belarussian, Russian
Monetary Unit: Belarus ruble

Belarus

⊛ National Capital
• Other City

1:8,000,000

0   75   150 mi
0   75   150 km

Lambert Conformal Conic Projection

Belarus:
Map Index

Cities and Towns

Asipovichy	D3
Babruysk	D3
Baranavichy	C3
Brest	A3
Homyel	E3
Hrodna	A3
Krychaw	E3
Lida	B3
Mahilyow	E3
Maladzyechna	C2
Mazyr	D3
Minsk, capital	C3
Orsha	E2
Pastavy	C2
Pinsk	C3
Polotsk	D2
Rechytsa	E3

Salihorsk	C3
Smilovichi	D3
Smolevichi	D2
Vawkavysk	B3
Vitsyebsk	E2
Zhlobin	D3

Other Features

Bug, river	A3
Byarezina, river	D3
Byelaruskaya Hrada, range	C3
Dnepr, river	E3
Dnepr-Bug, canal	B3
Dzyarzhynskaya Hara, mt.	C3
Nyoman, river	B3
Pripyats, marshes	C4
Pripyats, river	C3
Ptsich, river	D3
Sozh, river	E3
Western Dvina, river	D2

Ukraine:
Map Index

Cities and Towns

Balaklava	C4
Belaya Tserkov	C2
Berdyansk	D3
Cherkassy	C2
Chernigov	C1
Chernivtsi	B2
Chornobyl'	C1
Dneprodzerzhinsk	C2
Dnipropetrovsk	D2
Donetsk	D2
Feodosiya	D3

Gorlovka	D2
Ivano-Frankovsk	A2
Izmail	B3
Kachovka	C3
Kerch	D3
Kharkiv	C1
Kherson	C3
Khmelnytskyy	B2
Khust	A2
Kiev, capital	C1
Kirovograd	C2
Konotop	C1
Korosten	B1
Kotovsk	B2
Kovel	A1

Kramatorsk	D2
Kremenchug	C2
Kryvyi Rih	C2
Lisichansk	D2
Luhansk	D2
Lutsk	B1
Lviv	A2
Makeyevka	D2
Mariupol	D3
Melitopol	D3
Mogilev Podolskiy	B2
Mykolaiv	C3
Nikopol	C2
Odesa	C2
Pervomaysk	C2

Poltava	C2
Priluki	C1
Rovno	B1
Sevastopol	C4
Shostka	C1
Simferopol	C4
Sumy	C1
Ternopol	B2
Uman	C2
Uzhgorod	A2
Vinnitsa	B2
Yalta	C4
Yevpatoriya	C3
Zaporizhzhia	D2
Zhitomir	B1

Other Features

Azov, sea	D3
Black, sea	C3
Bug, river	A1
Carpathian, mts.	A2
Crimean, mts.	C4
Crimean, peninsula	C3
Desna, river	C1
Dneprodzerzhinsk, reservoir	C2
Dnieper, river	C1,C3
Dniester, river	B2
Donets, basin	D2
Donets, river	D2
Hoverla, mt.	A2
Kakhovka, reservoir	C3

Karkinit, bay	C3
Kerch, strait	D3
Kiev, reservoir	C1
Kremenchug, reservoir	C2
Pripyat, river	A1
Prut, river	B2
Psel, river	C1
Sluch, river	B1
Southern Bug, river	B2
Tisza, river	A2
Volyno-Podol'skaya Vozvyshennost, uplands	B2
Vorskla, river	C1

Ukraine

Capital: Kiev
Area: 233,100 sq. mi.
603,886 sq. km.
Population: 49,811,000
Largest City: Kiev
Languages: Ukrainian, Russian
Monetary Unit: Hryvnya

Ukraine

⊛ National Capital
• Other City

1:9,625,000

0   75   150 mi
0   75   150 km

Lambert Conformal Conic Projection

Slovenia

Capital: Ljubljana
Area: 7,821 sq. mi.
20,262 sq. km.
Population: 1,971,000
Largest City: Ljubljana
Languages: Slovenian, Serbo-Croatian
Monetary Unit: Tolar

Slovenia:
Map Index

Cities and Towns
Celje C2
Idrija B2
Jesenice B2
Kočevje B3
Koper A3
Kranj B2
Krško C3
Ljubljana, capital B2
Maribor C2
Murska Sobota D2
Nova Gorica A3
Novo Mesto C3
Postojna B3
Ptuj C2

Other Features
Adriatic, sea A3
Drava, river C2
Julian Alps, mts. A2
Krka, river B3
Kupa, river B3
Mura, river C2
Sava, river B2
Savinja, river B2
Trieste, gulf A3
Triglav, mt. A2

Slovenia
⊛ National Capital
● Other City
1:5,100,000
0   25   50 mi
0   25   50 km
Lambert Conformal Conic Projection

© MapQuest.com, Inc.

Croatia
⊛ National Capital
● Other City
1:9,700,000
0   50   100 mi
0   50   100 km
Lambert Conformal Conic Projection

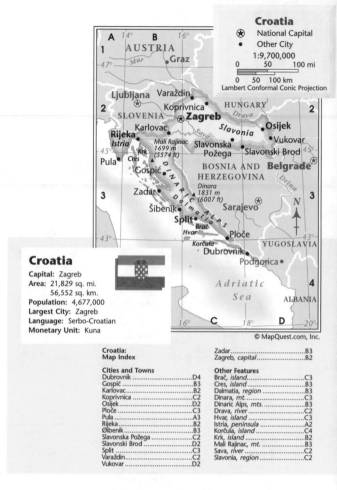

© MapQuest.com, Inc.

Croatia

Capital: Zagreb
Area: 21,829 sq. mi.
56,552 sq. km.
Population: 4,677,000
Largest City: Zagreb
Language: Serbo-Croatian
Monetary Unit: Kuna

Croatia:
Map Index

Cities and Towns
Dubrovnik D4
Gospić B3
Karlovac B2
Koprivnica C2
Osijek D2
Ploče C3
Pula A3
Rijeka B2
Øibenik B3
Slavonska Požega D2
Slavonski Brod D2
Split C3
Varaždin C2
Vukovar D2
Zadar B3
Zagreb, capital B2

Other Features
Brač, island C3
Cres, island B3
Dalmatia, region B3
Dinara, mt. C3
Dinaric Alps, mts. B3
Drava, river C2
Hvar, island C3
Istria, peninsula A2
Korčula, island C4
Krk, island B2
Mali Rajinac, mt. B3
Sava, river C2
Slavonia, region C2

Bosnia and Hercegovina:
Map Index

Cities and Towns
Banja Luka B1
Bihać A1
Bijeljina C1
Bosanska Gradiška B1
Bosanska Krupa A1
Brčko B1
Bugojno B1
Derventa B1
Doboj B1
Foča B2
Gacko B2
Goražde B2
Gračanica B1
Jajce B1
Livno B2
Mostar B2
Pale B2
Prijedor A1
Sanski Most A1
Sarajevo, capital B2
Srebrenica C1
Teslić B1
Trebinje B2
Tuzla B1
Zavidovići B1
Zenica B1
Zvornik C1

Other Features
Bosna, river B1
Dinara, mt. A2
Dinaric Alps, mts. A1
Drina, river C1
Neretva, river B2
Sava, river B1
Una, river A1
Vrbas, river B1

Bosnia and Herzegovina
⊛ National Capital
● Other City
1:5,500,000
0   40   80 mi
0   40   80 km
Lambert Conformal Conic Projection

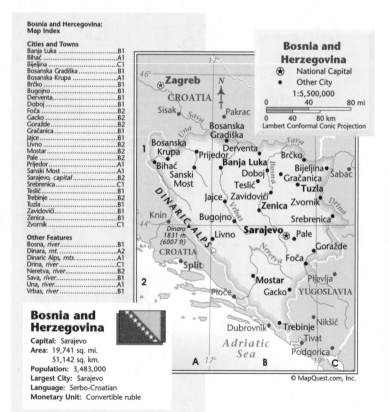

© MapQuest.com, Inc.

Bosnia and Herzegovina

Capital: Sarajevo
Area: 19,741 sq. mi.
51,142 sq. km.
Population: 3,483,000
Largest City: Sarajevo
Language: Serbo-Croatian
Monetary Unit: Convertible ruble

F.Y.R. Macedonia

Capital: Skopje
Area: 9,928 sq. mi.
25,720 sq. km.
Population: 2,023,000
Largest City: Skopje
Languages: Macedonian, Albanian, Serbo-Croatian, Turkish
Monetary Unit: Denar

F.Y.R. Macedonia:
Map Index

Cities and Towns
Bitola B2
Blatec C2
Debar A2
Gevgelija C2
Kavadarci C2
Kičevo A2
Kočani C2
Kruševo B2
Kumanovo B1
Ohrid A2
Prilep B2
Skopje, capital B2
Øtip C2
Struga A2
Strumica C2
Tetovo A1
Titov Veles B2

Other Features
Belasica, mts. C2
Bregalnica, river C2
Crna, river B2
Crna Gora, mts. B1
Doiran, lake C2
Jakupica, mts. B2
Korab, mt. A2
Kožuf, mts. B3
Nidže, mts. B3
Ograzden, mts. C2
Ohrid, lake A2
Prespa, lake B3
Treska, river B2
Vardar, river C2

F.Y.R. Macedonia
⊛ National Capital
● Other City
1:4,000,000
0   25   50 mi
0   25   50 km
Lambert Conformal Conic Projection

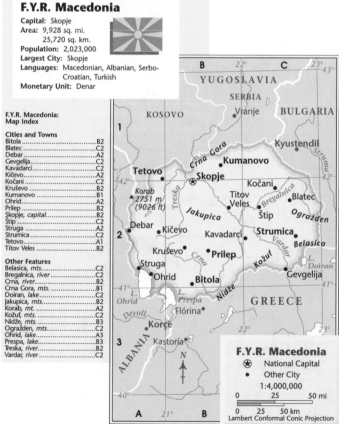

© MapQuest.com, Inc.

Albania

⊛ National Capital
• Other City

1:3,750,000

0   15   30 mi
0   15   30 km

Lambert Conformal
Conic Projection

Federal Republic of Yugoslavia

⊛ National Capital
• Other City

1:3,682,000

0   30   60 mi
0   30   60 km

Lambert Conformal Conic Projection

© MapQuest.com, Inc.

Albania:
Map Index

Cities and Towns
Berat....................................A3
Durrës..................................A2
Elbasan................................B2
Ersekë.................................B3
Fier......................................A3
Gjirokastër...........................B3
Kavajë.................................A2
Korçë...................................B3
Krujë...................................A2
Kukës..................................B1
Laç.....................................A2
Lushnjë................................A3
Peshkopi..............................B2
Pogradec..............................B3
Pukë...................................A1
Sarandë...............................A4
Shëngjin..............................A2
Shkodër...............................A1
Tirana, *capital*.....................A2
Vlorë..................................A3

Other Features
Adriatic, *sea*........................A2
Buene, *river*.........................A2
Devoll, *river*........................B3

Drin, *river*............................A1
Erzen, *river*..........................A2
Ionian, *sea*...........................A4
Korab, *mt.*............................B2
Mat, *river*.............................B2
North Albanian Alps, *range*.....A1
Ohrid, *lake*...........................B2
Osum, *river*..........................B3
Otranto, *strait*.......................A3
Prespa, *lake*..........................C3
Scutari, *lake*.........................A1
Seman, *river*.........................A3
Shkumbin, *river*.....................A2
Vijosë, *river*..........................A3

Albania

Capital: Tirana
Area: 11,100 sq. mi.
          28,756 sq. km.
Population: 3,365,000
Largest City: Tirana
Languages: Albanian, Greek
Monetary Unit: Lek

Yugoslavia:
Map Index

Internal Divisions
Kosovo (province)................B3
Montenegro (republic)...........A3
Serbia (republic)..................B2
Vojvodina (province)..............A2

Cities and Towns
Bačka Palanka.....................A2
Bar.....................................A3
Bečej..................................B2
Belgrade, *capital*.................B2
Bor.....................................C2
Čačak.................................A3
Cetinje................................A3
Đakovica.............................B3
Kikinda...............................B2
Kosovska Mitrovica...............B3
Kragujevac..........................B3
Kraljevo..............................B3
Kruševac............................B3
Leskovac.............................B3
Nikšić.................................A3
Niš.....................................B3
Novi Pazar..........................B3
Novi Sad.............................A2
Pančevo..............................B2
Peć....................................B3
Pirot...................................C3
Pljevlja...............................A3
Podgorica............................A3

Požarevac............................B2
Priboj..................................A3
Priština...............................B3
Prizren................................B3
Prokuplje.............................B3
Šabac.................................A2
Senta..................................B2
Smederevo...........................B2
Sombor...............................A2
Sremska Mitrovica.................A2
Subotica..............................A1
Svetozarevo.........................B3
Uroševac.............................B3
Užice..................................A3
Valjevo...............................A2
Vranje.................................B3
Vrbas.................................A2
Vršac.................................B2
Zaječar...............................C3
Zrenjanin.............................B2

Other Features
Adriatic, *sea*........................A4
Balkan, *mts.*........................C3
Beli Drim, *river*....................B3
Crna Gora, *mts.*....................B3
Danube, *river*...................A2, B2
Đaravica, *mt.*.......................B3
Dinaric Alps, *mts.*.................A3
Drina, *river*.........................A2
Durmitor, *mt.*.......................A3
Fruška Gora, *mts.*..................A2
Ibar, *river*...........................B3

Jastrebac, *mts.*.....................B3
Južna, *river*.........................B3
Kopaonik, *mts.*.....................B3
Kotor, *gulf*...........................A3
Morava, *river*........................B3
Nišava, *river*.........................C3
North Albanian Alps, *mts.*.......B3
Šar Planina, *mts.*...................B3
Sava, *river*...........................A2
Scutari, *lake*.........................A3
Tara, *river*............................A3
Tisa, *river*............................B2
Velika Morava, *river*................B2
Veliki, *canal*.........................A2
Zapandna Morava, *river*...........B3
Zeta, *river*............................A3
Zlatibor, *mts.*........................A3

Yugoslavia

Capital: Belgrade
Area: 39,449 sq. mi.
          102,199 sq. km.
Population: 11,207,000
Largest City: Belgrade
Language: Serbo-Croatian
Monetary Unit: New Yugoslav dinar

© MapQuest.com, Inc.

Moldova

National Capital (⊛)
Other City (•)

0   35   70 mi
0   35   70 km

1:4,800,000
Lambert Conformal Conic Projection

Moldova

Capital: Chişinău
Area: 13,012 sq. mi.
33,710 sq. km.
Population: 4,461,000
Largest City: Chişinău
Languages: Moldovan, Russian
Monetary Unit: Moldovan leu

Moldova:
Map Index

Cities and Towns
Bălţi	A2
Basarabeasca	B2
Bender (Tighina)	B2
Briceni	A1
Cahul	B3
Căuşeni	B2
Chişinău, *capital*	B2
Comrat	B2
Dubăsari	B2
Fălești	A2
Floreşti	B2
Leova	B2
Orhei	B2
Rîbniţa	B2
Rîşcani	A2
Soroca	B1
Tiraspol	B2
Ungheni	A2

Other Features
Botna, *river*	B2
Bugeac, *region*	B3
Codri, *region*	A3
Cogalnic, *river*	B2
Dnestr, *river*	B2
Ialpug, *river*	B2
Prut, *river*	A1, B3
Raut, *river*	B2

Bulgaria:
Map Index

Administrative Regions
Blagoevgrad	B4
Burgas	F3
Dobrich	F2
Gabrovo	D3
Haskovo	D4
Jambol	E3
Kardzhali	D4
Kjustendil	A3
Lovech	C3
Montana	B2
Pazardzhik	C3
Pernik	A3
Pleven	C2
Plovdiv	C3
Razgrad	E2
Ruse	D2
Shumen	F2
Silistra	E1
Sliven	E3
Smoljan	C4
Sofia, *capital*	B3
Sofia City	B3
Stara Zagora	D3
Targovishte	E2
Varna	F2
Veliko Tarnovo	D2
Vidin	A2
Vraca	B2

Pleven	C2
Plovdiv	C3
Primorsko	F3
Razgrad	E2
Ruse	D2
Samokov	B3
Shumen	E2
Silistra	F1
Sliven	E3
Smoljan	C4
Sofia, *capital*	B3
Stara Zagora	D3
Svilengrad	E4
Svishtov	D2
Targovishte	E2
Varna	F2
Veliko Tarnovo	D2
Vidin	A2
Vratsa	B2

Other Features
Arda, *river*	C4
Balkan, *mts.*	B2
Danube, *river*	B2
Golyama Kamchiya, *river*	E2
Iskŭr, *river*	C3
Kamchiya, *river*	F2
Luda Kamchiya, *river*	E3
Ludogorie, *region*	E2
Maritsa, *river*	D3
Mesta, *river*	B4
Musala, *mt.*	B3
Ogosta, *river*	B2
Osŭm, *river*	C3
Rhodope, *mts.*	C4
Rila, *mts.*	B3
Sredna Gora, *mts.*	C3
Struma, *river*	A3
Stryama, *river*	C3
Thrace, *region*	D4
Thracian, *plain*	C3
Tundzha, *river*	E3
Yantra, *river*	D2

Cities and Towns
Asenovgrad	C3
Aytos	F3
Blagoevgrad	B4
Burgas	F3
Dimitrovgrad	D3
Dobrich	F2
Elkhovo	E3
Gabrovo	D3
Haskovo	D4
Jambol	E3
Kardzhali	D4
Kazanlŭk	D3
Kjustendil	A3
Kozloduy	B2
Lom	B2
Lovech	C2
Madan	C4
Montana	B2
Oryakhovo	B2
Panagyurishte	C3
Pazardzhik	C3
Pernik	B3
Petrich	B4

Bulgaria

Capital: Sofia
Area: 42,855 sq. mi.
111,023 sq. km.
Population: 8,195,000
Largest City: Sofia
Language: Bulgarian
Monetary Unit: Lev

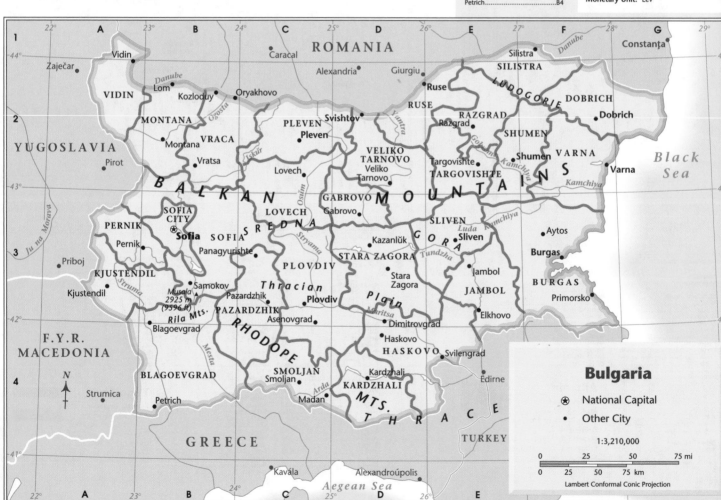

Bulgaria

National Capital (⊛)
Other City (•)

1:3,210,000

0   25   50   75 mi
0   25   50   75 km

Lambert Conformal Conic Projection

Greece

(*) National Capital

• Other City

1:6,500,000

| 0 | 75 | 150 mi |
| 0 | 75 | 150 km |

Lambert Conformal Conic Projection

© MapQuest.com, Inc.

Greece:
Map Index

Regions

Attica	B2
Central Greece	B2
Central Macedonia	B1
Crete	C4
Eastern Macedonia and Thrace	C1
Epirus	B2
Ionian Islands	B2
Northern Aegean	C2
Peloponnesus	B3
Southern Aegean	B2
Thessaly	B2
Western Greece	B2
Western Macedonia	B1

Cities and Towns

Agrínion	B2
Akharnaí	Inset
Alexandroúpolis	C1
Árgos	B3
Asprópirgos	Inset
Athens, *capital*	B3, Inset
Áyios Dhimítrios	Inset
Corinth	B3
Dháfni	Inset
Elevsís	Inset
Ellinikón	Inset
Glifádha	Inset
Ioánnina	B2
Iráklion	C4
Kalámai	B3
Kalamáki	Inset
Kallithéa	Inset
Kastoría	B1
Kateríni	B1
Kavála	C1
Keratsínion	Inset
Kérkira	A2
Khalándrion	Inset
Khalkís	B2
Khaniá	B4
Kifisiá	Inset
Komotiní	C1
Kozáni	B1
Lamía	B2
Lárisa	B2
Mándra	Inset
Mesolóngion	B2
Mitilíni	C2
Néa Liósia	Inset
Neápolis	B3
Níkaia	Inset
Paianía	Inset
Pátrai	B2
Peristéri	Inset
Pílos	B3
Piraiévs	B3, Inset
Préveza	B2
Rhodes	D3
Selínia	Inset
Sérrai	B1
Sparta	B3
Thásos	C1
Thessaloníki	B1
Tríkala	B2
Véroia	B1
Vólos	B2
Xánthi	C1

Other Features

Aegean, *sea*	C2
Aigáleo, *mts.*	Inset
Aíyina, *island*	B3
Akhelóös, *river*	B2
Alfíos, *river*	B3
Aliákmon, *river*	B1
Ándros, *island*	C3
Astipálaia, *island*	C3
Áthos, *mt.*	C1
Corinth, *gulf*	B2
Corinth, *isthmus*	B3
Crete, *island*	C4
Crete, *sea*	C4
Cyclades, *islands*	C3
Delos, *island*	C3
Dodecanese, *islands*	C3
Elevsís, *bay*	Inset
Euboea, *island*	B2
Ikaría, *island*	C3
Ionian, *sea*	A2
Ionian, *islands*	B2
Itháki, *island*	B2
Kárpathos, *island*	C4
Kefallínía, *island*	B2
Kérkira, *island*	A2
Khalkidhikí, *peninsula*	B1
Khíos, *island*	C2
Kifissós, *river*	B2
Kíthira, *island*	B3
Kos, *island*	C3
Lésvos, *island*	C2
Límnos, *island*	C2
Míkonos, *island*	C3
Milos, *island*	C3
Náxos, *island*	C3
Northern Sporades, *islands*	B2
Olympus, *mt.*	B1
Páros, *island*	C3
Pindus, *mts.*	B2
Piniós, *river*	B2
Prespa, *lake*	B1
Rhodes, *island*	D3
Salamís, *island*	Inset
Sámos, *island*	C3
Samothráki, *island*	C1
Saronic, *gulf*	Inset
Skíros, *island*	C2
Struma, *river*	B1
Thásos, *island*	C1
Thíra, *island*	C3
Zákinthos, *island*	B3

Greece

Capital: Athens
Area: 50,949 sq. mi.
 131,992 sq. km.
Population: 10,707,000
Largest City: Athens
Language: Greek
Monetary Unit: Drachma

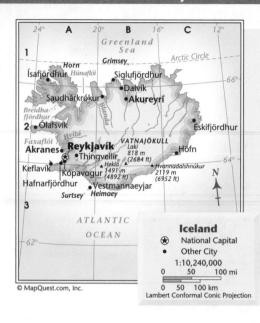

Iceland

Capital: Reykjavík
Area: 36,699 sq. mi.
95,075 sq. km.
Population: 273,000
Largest City: Reykjavík
Language: Icelandic
Monetary Unit: New Icelandic króna

Iceland
⊛ National Capital
• Other City

1:10,240,000

0   50   100 mi

0   50   100 km

Lambert Conformal Conic Projection

Iceland:
Map Index

Cities and Towns

Akranes	A2	**Other Features**	
Akureyri	B2	Blanda, *river*	B2
Dalvík	B2	Breidhafjördhur, *fjord*	A2
Eskifjördhur	C2	Faxaflói, *bay*	A2
Hafnarfjördhur	A3	Greenland, *sea*	B1
Höfn	C2	Grímsey, *island*	B1
Ísafjördhur	A1	Heimaey, *island*	A3
Keflavík	A3	Hekla, *volcano*	B3
Kópavogur	A2	Horn, *cape*	A1
Ólafsvík	A2	Húnaflói, *bay*	A2
Reykjavík, *capital*	A2	Hvannadalshnúkur, *mt.*	B3
Saudhárkrókur	B2	Hvítá, *river*	A2
Siglufjördhur	B1	Laki, *volcano*	B2
Thingvellir	A2	Surtsey, *island*	A3
Vestmannaeyjar	A3	Vatnajökull, *ice cap*	B2

Norway

Capital: Oslo
Area: 125,050 sq. mi.
323,964 sq. km.
Population: 4,439,000
Largest City: Oslo
Language: Norwegian
Monetary Unit: Norwegian krone

Norway:
Map Index

Cities and Towns

Ålesund	B3
Alta	E1
Arendal	B4
Bergen	B3
Bodø	C2
Drammen	C4
Dumbås	B3
Egersund	B4
Florø	A3
Fredrikstad	C4
Gjøvik	C3
Hamar	C3
Hammerfest	E1
Harstad	D2
Haugesund	B4
Kinsarvik	B3
Kirkenes	F2
Kristiansand	B4
Kristiansund	B3
Lakselv	F1
Leikanger	B3
Lillehammer	C3
Mo	C2
Molde	B3
Mosjøen	C2
Moss	C4
Namsos	C3
Narvik	D2
Oslo, *capital*	C3
Skien	B4
Stavanger	B4
Steinkjer	C3
Tromsø	D2
Trondheim	C3
Vadsø	F1

Other Features

Barents, *sea*	E1
Boknafjord, *fjord*	B4
Dovrefjell, *mts.*	B3
Finnmark, *plateau*	E2
Glåma, *river*	B3
Glittertinden, *mt.*	B3
Hallingdal, *valley*	B3
Hardangerfjord, *fjord*	B4
Hardangervidda, *plateau*	B3
Jotunheimen, *mts.*	B3
Lofoten, *islands*	C2
Mjøsa, *lake*	C3
North, *cape*	F1
North, *sea*	A3
Norwegian, *sea*	A2
Oslofjord, *fjord*	C4
Skagerrak, *strait*	B4
Sognefjord, *fjord*	B3
Tana, *river*	F1
Trondheimsfjord, *fjord*	B3
Vesterålen, *islands*	C2

Norway
⊛ National Capital
• Other City

1:12,075,000

0   50   100   150   200 mi

0   100   200   300 km

Lambert Conformal Conic Projection

Finland: Map Index

Internal Divisions

Eastern Finland (province)	C2
Lapland (province)	C1
Oulu (province)	C1
Southern Finland (province)	C2
Western Finland (province)	B2
Central Finland (region)	C2
Central Ostrobothnia (region)	B2
Etelä-Savo (region)	C2
Häme (region)	B2
Itä-Uusimaa (region)	C2
Kainuu (region)	C2
Kymenlaakso (region)	C2
North Karelia (region)	C2
Northern Ostrobothnia (region)	B2
Ostrobothnia (region)	B2
Päijät Häme (region)	B2
Pirkanmaa (region)	B2
Satakunta (region)	B2
Savo (region)	C2
South Karelia (region)	C2
South Ostrobothnia (region)	B2
South-West Finland (region)	B2
Uusimaa (region)	B2

Cities and Towns

Espoo	B2
Hämeenlinna	B2
Hangö	B3
Helsinki, capital	B2
Hyvinkää	B2
Iisalmi	C2
Imatra	C2
Ivalo	C1
Jakobstad	B2
Järnsä	C2
Joensuu	C2
Jyväskylä	B2
Kajaani	C2
Kemi	B1
Kemijärvi	C1
Kokkola	B2
Kolari	B1
Kotka	C2
Kouvola	C2
Kuopio	C2
Lahti	B2
Lappeenranta	C2
Lieksa	D2
Mariehamn (Maarianhamina)	A2
Mikkeli	C2
Muonio	B1
Oulu	C1
Pori	B2
Raahe	B2
Rauma	B2
Rovaniemi	C1
Salo	B2
Savonlinna	C2
Seinäjoki	B2
Tampere	B2
Tornio	B1
Turku	B2
Vaasa	B2
Vantaa	B2
Varkaus	C2
Ylivieska	B2

Other Features

Åland, islands	B2
Baltic, sea	B3
Bothnia, gulf	B2
Finland, gulf	C3
Haltiatunturi, mt.	B1
Iijoki, river	C1
Inari, lake	C1
Kemijoki, river	C1
Kivi, lake	C2
Lapland, region	B1
Lokka, reservoir	C1
Muoniojoki, river	B1
Näsi, lake	B2
Oulu, lake	C1
Oulujoki, river	C2
Ounasjoki, river	B1
Päijänne, lake	C2
Pielinen, lake	C2
Saimaa, lake	C2
Tenojoki, river	C1
Torniojoki, river	B1
Ylikitka, lake	C1

Finland

Capital: Helsinki
Area: 130,559 sq. mi.
338,236 sq. km.
Population: 5,158,000
Largest City: Helsinki
Languages: Finnish, Swedish
Monetary Unit: Markka, Euro

Finland
- National Capital
- Other City
1:10,000,000

Sweden

- National Capital
- Other City
1:11,333,000
Lambert Conformal Conic Projection

Sweden

Capital: Stockholm
Area: 173,732 sq. mi.
450,083 sq. km.
Population: 8,911,000
Largest City: Stockholm
Language: Swedish
Monetary Unit: Krona

Sweden: Map Index

Counties

Blekinge	C3
Dalarna	B2
Gävleborg	C2
Gotland	C3
Halland	B3
Jämtland	B2
Jönköping	B3
Kalmar	C3
Kronoberg	B3
Malmöhus	B3
Norrbotten	C1
Örebro	B3
Östergötland	C3
Skåne	B3
Södermanland	C3
Stockholm	C3
Uppsala	C3
Värmland	B3
Västerbotten	C2
Västernorrland	C2
Västmanland	C3
Västra Götaland	B3

Cities and Towns

Borås	B3
Eskilstuna	C3
Falun	C2
Gällivare	D1
Gävle	C2
Göteborg	B3
Halmstad	B3
Haparanda	D1
Härnösand	C2
Helsingborg	B3
Hudiksvall	C2
Jönköping	B3
Kalmar	C3
Karlskrona	C3
Karlstad	B3
Kiruna	D1
Kristianstad	B3
Kristinehamn	B3
Linköping	C3
Luleå	D1
Lund	B3
Malmberget	D1
Malmö	B3
Norrköping	C3
Örebro	C3
Örnsköldsvik	C2
Orrefors	C3
Östersund	C2
Sarjektjakko	C1
Skellefteå	C2
Söderhamn	C2
Stockholm, capital	C3
Sundsvall	C2
Trollhättan	B3
Uddevalla	B3
Umeå	C2
Uppsala	C3
Västerås	C3
Växjö	B3
Visby	C3

Other Features

Ångermanälven, river	C2
Baltic, sea	C3
Bothnia, gulf	D2
Dalälven, river	C2
Faxälven, river	C2
Göta, canal	B3
Gotland, island	C3
Hornavan, lake	C1
Indalsälven, river	B2
Kalixälven, river	D1
Kattegat, strait	B3
Kebnekaise, mt.	C1
Kjølen, mts.	C1
Klarälven, river	B2
Ljusnanälven, river	B2
Luleälven, river	D1
Mälaren, lake	C3
Muonioälven, river	C1
Norra Storfjället, mt.	C1
Öland, island	C3
Öresund, sound	B3
Österdalälven, river	B2
Skagerrak, strait	A3
Skellefteälven, river	C1
Småland, region	B3
Storavan, lake	C1
Storsjön, lake	B2
Torneälven, river	D1
Uddjaur, lake	C1
Umeälven, river	C2
Vänern, lake	B3
Vättern, lake	B3
Vindelälven, river	C2

© MapQuest.com, Inc.

MAJOR CITIES

Algeria
Algiers 1,483,000
Oran 590,000
Constantine 483,000

Angola (metro)
Luanda 2,081,000

Benin
Cotonou 402,000
Porto-Novo 144,000

Botswana
Gaborone 183,000

Burkina Faso
Ouagadougou 824,000

Burundi
Bujumbura 235,440

Cameroon (metro)
Douala 1,320,000
Yaoundé 1,119,000

Cape Verde
Praia 61,000

Central African Republic
Bangui 474,000

Chad (metro)
N'Djamena 826,000

Comoros (metro)
Moroni 30,000

Congo, Democratic Republic of the
Kinshasa 3,800,000
Lubumbashi 739,000

Congo, Republic of the
Brazzaville (metro) 1,004,000

Côte d'Ivoire
Abidjan 2,793,000
Yamoussoukro 107,000

Djibouti (metro)
Djibouti 450,000

Egypt
Cairo 6,789,000
Alexandria 3,328,000
Port Said 470,000
Suez 418,000

Equatorial Guinea
Malabo 38,000

Eritrea
Asmara 358,000

Ethiopia
Addis Ababa 2,085,000

Gabon
Libreville 275,000

The Gambia
Banjul 40,000

Ghana (metro)
Accra 1,673,000

Guinea (metro)
Conakry 1,558,000

Guinea-Bissau
Bissau 138,000

Kenya
Nairobi 959,000
Mombasa 401,000

Lesotho
Maseru 109,000

Liberia (metro)
Monrovia 962,000

Libya (metro)
Tripoli 1,682,000

Madagascar (metro)
Antananarivo 876,000

Malawi
Blantyre 332,000
Lilongwe 234,000

Mali
Bamako 810,000

Mauritania
Nouakchott 550,000

Mauritius
Port Louis 146,000

Morocco
Casablanca 2,943,000
Fez 564,000
Rabat 1,220,000

Mozambique (metro)
Maputo 2,212,000

Namibia
Windhoek 114,000

Niger
Niamey 392,000

Nigeria
Lagos 1,300,000
Ibadan 1,300,000
Abuja 250,000

Rwanda
Kigali 237,000

São Tomé & Príncipe
São Tomé 43,000

Senegal
Dakar 1,641,000

Seychelles (metro)
Victoria 24,000

Sierra Leone
Freetown 470,000

Somalia
Mogadishu 997,000

South Africa
Cape Town 2,350,000
Johannesburg 1,916,000
Durban 1,137,000
Pretoria 1,080,000
Port Elizabeth 853,000
Bloemfontein 300,000

Sudan
Omdurman 1,271,000
Khartoum 947,000

Swaziland
Mbabane 38,000

Tanzania (metro)
Dar es-Salaam 1,747,000

Togo
Lomé 600,000

Tunisia
Tunis 674,000

Uganda (metro)
Kampala 954,000

Western Sahara
el-Aaiún 90,000

Zambia (metro)
Lusaka 1,317,000

Zimbabwe (metro)
Harare 1,410,000

International comparability of city population data is limited by various data inconsistencies.

© MapQuest.com, Inc.

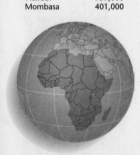

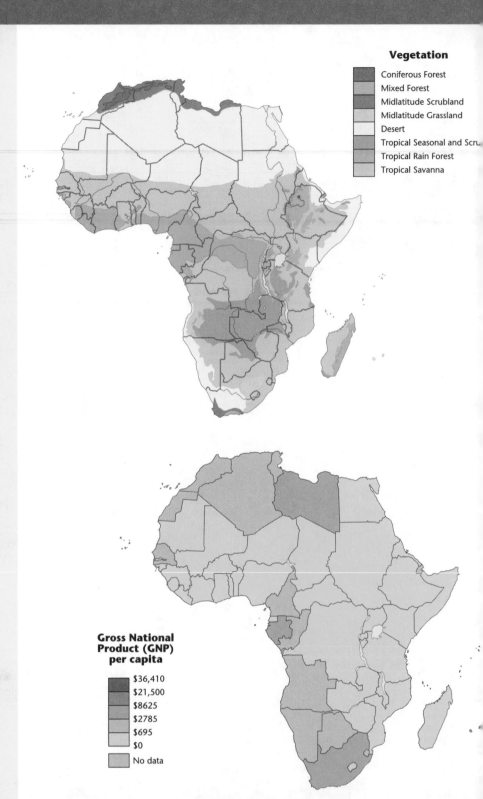

Vegetation

- Coniferous Forest
- Mixed Forest
- Midlatitude Scrubland
- Midlatitude Grassland
- Desert
- Tropical Seasonal and Scru...
- Tropical Rain Forest
- Tropical Savanna

Gross National Product (GNP) per capita

- $36,410
- $21,500
- $8625
- $2785
- $695
- $0
- No data

Africa: Population, by nation (in millions)

| NIGERIA 113.8 | EGYPT 67.3 | ETHIOPIA 59.7 | CONGO, DEM.REP. 50.5 | S. AFR. 43.4 | SUDAN 34.5 | TANZ. 31.3 | ALGERIA 31.1 | MOROC. 29.7 | KENYA 28.8 | All other African countries 288.3 |

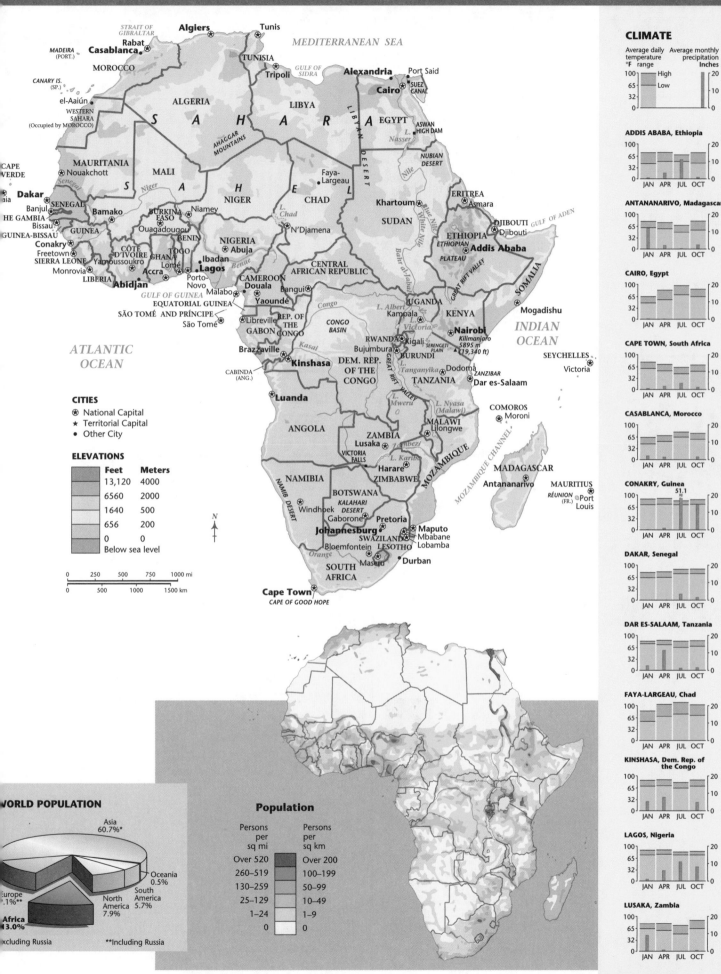

CLIMATE

Average daily temperature °F range — Average monthly precipitation Inches

High / Low

ADDIS ABABA, Ethiopia
ANTANANARIVO, Madagascar
CAIRO, Egypt
CAPE TOWN, South Africa
CASABLANCA, Morocco
CONAKRY, Guinea 51.1
DAKAR, Senegal
DAR ES-SALAAM, Tanzania
FAYA-LARGEAU, Chad
KINSHASA, Dem. Rep. of the Congo
LAGOS, Nigeria
LUSAKA, Zambia

CITIES
⊛ National Capital
★ Territorial Capital
• Other City

ELEVATIONS

Feet	Meters
13,120	4000
6560	2000
1640	500
656	200
0	0
Below sea level	

Scale: 0 250 500 750 1000 mi
0 500 1000 1500 km

N

WORLD POPULATION

Asia 60.7%*
Oceania 0.5%
Europe .1%**
North America 7.9%
South America 5.7%
Africa 13.0%

*Excluding Russia
**Including Russia

Population

Persons per sq mi	Persons per sq km
Over 520	Over 200
260–519	100–199
130–259	50–99
25–129	10–49
1–24	1–9
0	0

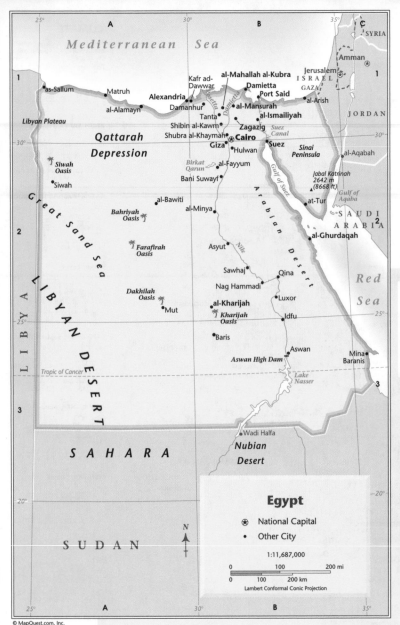

Mediterranean Sea

as-Sallum
Matruh
al-Alamayn
Alexandria
Kafr ad-Dawwar
Damanhur
Tanta
Shibin al-Kawm
Shubra al-Khaymah
al-Mahallah al-Kubra
Damietta
Port Said
al-Mansurah
al-Ismailiyah
Zagazig
Cairo
Giza
Suez
Hulwan
al-Arish
JORDAN
Jerusalem
ISRAEL
GAZA
Amman
SYRIA

Libyan Plateau
Qattarah Depression
Siwah Oasis
Siwah
al-Bawiti
Bahriyah Oasis
Farafirah Oasis
al-Minya
Dakhilah Oasis
Mut
al-Kharijah
Kharijah Oasis
Baris

Birkat Qarun
al-Fayyum
Bani Suwayf
Asyut
Sawhaj
Nag Hammadi
Qina
Luxor
Idfu
Aswan

Sinai Peninsula
al-Aqabah
Gulf of Aqaba
Jabal Katrinah 2642 m (8668 ft)
at-Tur
SAUDI ARABIA
al-Ghurdaqah
Red Sea

Suez Canal
Gulf of Suez
Arabian Desert
Nile

Great Sand Sea
LIBYA
LIBYAN DESERT
Tropic of Cancer
SAHARA
SUDAN

Aswan High Dam
Lake Nasser
Wadi Halfa
Nubian Desert
Mina Baranis

Egypt
Capital: Cairo
Area: 385,229 sq. mi.
998,003 sq. km.
Population: 67,273,906
Largest City: Cairo
Language: Arabic
Monetary Unit: Pound

Egypt
⊛ National Capital
● Other City
1:11,687,000
0   100   200 mi
0 100 200 km
Lambert Conformal Conic Projection

Egypt:
Map Index

Cities and Towns
Alamayn, al- A1
Alexandria A1
Arish, al- B1
Aswan B3
Asyut B2
Bani Suwayf B2
Baris B3
Bawiti, al- A2
Cairo, capital B1
Damanhur B1
Damietta B1
Fayyum, al- B2
Ghurdaqah, al- B2
Giza B1
Hulwan B2
Idfu B3
Ismailiyah, al- B1
Kafr ad-Dawwar B1
Kharijah, al- B2
Luxor B2
Mahallah al-Kubra, al- B1
Mansurah, al- B1
Matruh A1
Mina Baranis C3
Minya, al- B2
Mut A2
Nag Hammadi B2
Port Said B1
Qina B2
Sallum, as- A1

Sawhaj B2
Shibin al-Kawm B1
Shubra al-Khaymah B1
Siwah A2
Suez B1
Tanta B1
Tur, at- B2
Zagazig B1

Other Features
Aqaba, gulf B2
Arabian, desert B2
Aswan High, dam B3
Bahriyah, oasis A2
Birkat Qarun, lake B2
Dakhilah, oasis A2
Damietta, river B1
Farafirah, oasis A2
Great Sand Sea, desert A2
Jabal Katrinah, mt. B2
Kharijah, oasis B2
Libyan, desert A2
Libyan, plateau A1
Nasser, lake B3
Nile, river B2
Qattarah, depression A2
Red, sea C2
Rosetta, river B1
Sahara, desert A3
Sinai, peninsula B2
Siwah, oasis A2
Suez, canal B1
Suez, gulf B2

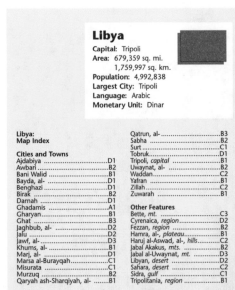

Libya
Capital: Tripoli
Area: 679,359 sq. mi.
1,759,997 sq. km.
Population: 4,992,838
Largest City: Tripoli
Language: Arabic
Monetary Unit: Dinar

Libya:
Map Index

Cities and Towns
Ajdabiya D1
Awbari B2
Bani Walid B1
Bayda, al- D1
Benghazi D1
Birak B2
Darnah D1
Ghadamis A1
Gharyan B1
Ghat B3
Jaghbub, al- D2
Jalu D2
Jawf, al- D3
Khums, al- B1
Marj, al- D1
Marsa al-Burayqah C1
Misurata C1
Murzuq B2
Qaryah ash-Sharqiyah, al- B1

Qatrun, al- B3
Sabha B2
Surt C1
Tobruk D1
Tripoli, capital B1
Uwaynat, al- B2
Waddan C2
Yafran B1
Zillah C2
Zuwarah B1

Other Features
Bette, mt. C3
Cyrenaica, region D2
Fezzan, region B2
Hamra, al-, plateau B1
Haruj al-Aswad, al-, hills C2
Jabal Akakus, mts. B2
Jabal al-Uwaynat, mt. D3
Libyan, desert D2
Sahara, desert C2
Sidra, gulf C1
Tripolitania, region B1

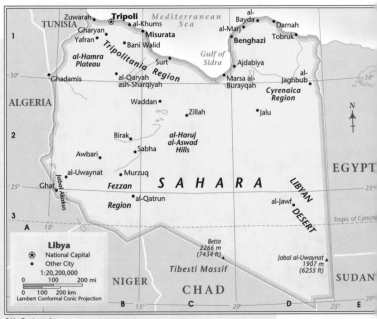

TUNISIA
Zuwarah
Gharyan
Yafran
al-Hamra Plateau
Ghadamis
ALGERIA
Tripoli
al-Khums
Misurata
Bani Walid
Surt
al-Qaryah ash-Sharqiyah
Waddan
Tripolitania Region
Mediterranean Sea
Gulf of Sidra
Ajdabiya
Marsa al-Burayqah
al-Bayda
al-Marj
Benghazi
Darnah
Tobruk
Cyrenaica Region
Jaghbub
al-

Birak
Awbari
al-Uwaynat
Ghat
Jabal Akakus
Fezzan Region
Sabha
Murzuq
al-Qatrun
al-Haruj al-Aswad Hills
Zillah
Jalu
SAHARA
LIBYAN DESERT
al-Jawf
Tropic of Cancer
EGYPT

Bette 2266 m (7434 ft)
Jabal al-Uwaynat 1907 m (6255 ft)
Tibesti Massif
NIGER
CHAD
SUDAN

Libya
⊛ National Capital
● Other City
1:20,200,000
0   100   200 mi
0 100 200 km
Lambert Conformal Conic Projection

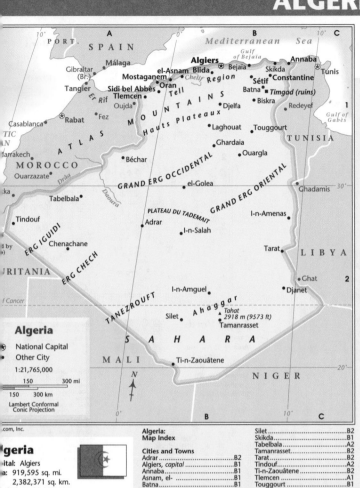

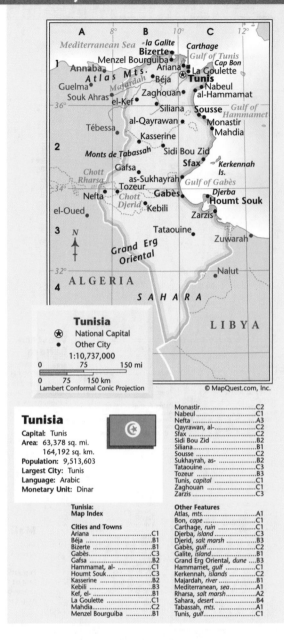

Algeria

- ⊛ National Capital
- • Other City

1:21,765,000

150 ... 300 mi

150 ... 300 km

Lambert Conformal Conic Projection

Algeria

Capital: Algiers
Area: 919,595 sq. mi.
2,382,371 sq. km.
Population: 31,133,486
Largest City: Algiers
Language: Arabic
Monetary Unit: Dinar

Algeria:
Map Index

Cities and Towns
Adrar	B2
Algiers, *capital*	B1
Annaba	B1
Asnam, el-	B1
Batna	B1
Béchar	A1
Bejaïa	B1
Biskra	B1
Blida	B1
Chenachane	A2
Constantine	B1
Djanet	B2
Djelfa	B1
Ghardaia	B1
Golea, el-	B2
I-n-Amenas	B2
I-n-Amguel	B2
I-n-Salah	B2
Laghouat	B1
Mostaganem	B1
Oran	A1
Ouargla	B1
Sétif	B1
Sidi bel Abbès	A1
Silet	B2
Skikda	B1
Tabelbala	A2
Tamanrasset	B2
Tarat	B2
Tindouf	A2
Ti-n-Zaouâtene	B2
Tlemcen	A1
Touggourt	B1

Other Features
Ahaggar, *mts.*	B2
Atlas, *mts.*	A1
Bejaïa, *gulf*	B1
Chelif, *river*	B1
Daoura, *river*	A2
Drâa, *river*	A1
Erg Chech, *desert*	A2
Erg Iguidi, *desert*	A2
Grand Erg Occidental, *desert*	B1
Grand Erg Oriental, *desert*	B2
Hauts Plateaux, *plateau*	B1
Sahara, *desert*	B2
Tademait, *plateau*	B2
Tahat, *mt.*	B2
Tanezrouft, *mts.*	A2
Tell Region	B1
Timgad, *ruins*	B1

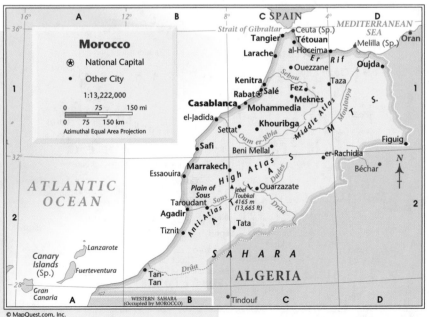

Tunisia

- ⊛ National Capital
- • Other City

1:10,737,000

0 ... 75 ... 150 mi

0 ... 75 ... 150 km

Lambert Conformal Conic Projection

© MapQuest.com, Inc.

Tunisia

Capital: Tunis
Area: 63,378 sq. mi.
164,192 sq. km.
Population: 9,513,603
Largest City: Tunis
Language: Arabic
Monetary Unit: Dinar

Tunisia:
Map Index

Cities and Towns
Ariana	C1
Béja	B1
Bizerte	B1
Gabès	C3
Gafsa	B2
Hammamet, al-	C1
Houmt Souk	C3
Kasserine	B2
Kebili	B3
Kef, el-	B1
La Goulette	C1
Mahdia	C2
Menzel Bourguiba	B1

Monastir	C2
Nabeul	C1
Nefta	A3
Qayrawan, al-	C2
Sfax	C2
Sidi Bou Zid	B2
Siliana	B1
Sousse	C2
Sukhayrah, as-	B2
Tataouine	C3
Tozeur	B3
Tunis, *capital*	C1
Zaghouan	C1
Zarzis	C3

Other Features
Atlas, *mts.*	A1
Bon, *cape*	C1
Carthage, *ruin*	C1
Djerba, *island*	C3
Djerid, *salt marsh*	B3
Gabès, *gulf*	C2
Galite, *island*	B1
Grand Erg Oriental, *dune*	B3
Hammamet, *gulf*	C1
Kerkennah, *islands*	C2
Majardah, *river*	B1
Mediterranean, *sea*	A1
Rharsa, *salt marsh*	A2
Sahara, *desert*	B4
Tabassah, *mts.*	A1
Tunis, *gulf*	C1

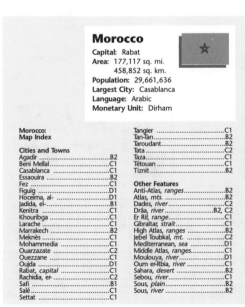

Morocco

Capital: Rabat
Area: 177,117 sq. mi.
458,852 sq. km.
Population: 29,661,636
Largest City: Casablanca
Language: Arabic
Monetary Unit: Dirham

Morocco

- ⊛ National Capital
- • Other City

1:13,222,000

0 ... 75 ... 150 mi

0 ... 75 ... 150 km

Azimuthal Equal Area Projection

Morocco:
Map Index

Cities and Towns
Agadir	B2
Beni Mellal	C1
Casablanca	C1
Essaouira	B2
Fez	C1
Figuig	D1
Hoceima, al-	D1
Jadida, el-	B1
Kenitra	C1
Khouribga	C1
Larache	C1
Marrakech	B2
Meknès	C1
Mohammedia	C1
Ouarzazate	C2
Ouezzane	C1
Oujda	D1
Rabat, *capital*	C1
Rachidia, er-	C2
Safi	B1
Salé	C1
Settat	C1

Tangier	C1
Tan-Tan	B2
Taroudant	B2
Tata	C2
Taza	C1
Tétouan	C1
Tiznit	B2

Other Features
Anti-Atlas, *ranges*	B2
Atlas, *mts.*	C1
Dades, *river*	C2
Drâa, *river*	B2, C2
Er Rif, *range*	C1
Gibraltar, *strait*	C1
High Atlas, *ranges*	B2
Jebel Toubkal, *mt.*	B2
Mediterranean, *sea*	D1
Middle Atlas, *ranges*	C1
Moulouya, *river*	D1
Oum er-Rbia, *river*	C1
Sahara, *desert*	C2
Sebou, *river*	C1
Sous, *plain*	B2
Sous, *river*	B2

© MapQuest.com, Inc.

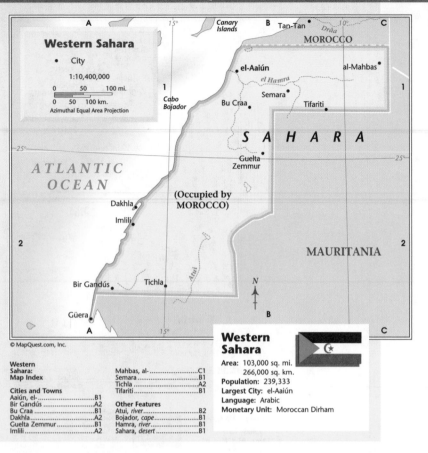

Western Sahara

- • City

1:10,400,000

0 50 100 mi.

0 50 100 km.

Azimuthal Equal Area Projection

© MapQuest.com, Inc.

Western Sahara:
Map Index

Cities and Towns
Aaiún, el-	B1
Bir Gandús	A2
Bu Craa	B1
Dakhla	A2
Guelta Zemmur	B1
Imlili	A2

Mahbas, al-	C1
Semara	B1
Tichla	A2
Tifariti	B1

Other Features
Atui, river	B2
Bojador, cape	B1
Hamra, river	B1
Sahara, desert	B1

Western Sahara

Area: 103,000 sq. mi.
266,000 sq. km.
Population: 239,333
Largest City: el-Aaiún
Language: Arabic
Monetary Unit: Moroccan Dirham

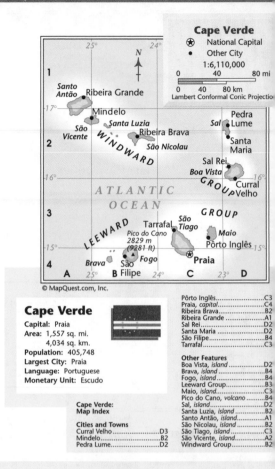

Cape Verde

- ⊛ National Capital
- • Other City

1:6,110,000

0 40 80 mi.

0 40 80 km.

Lambert Conformal Conic Projection

© MapQuest.com, Inc.

Cape Verde

Capital: Praia
Area: 1,557 sq. mi.
4,034 sq. km.
Population: 405,748
Largest City: Praia
Language: Portuguese
Monetary Unit: Escudo

Cape Verde:
Map Index

Cities and Towns
Curral Velho	D3
Mindelo	B2
Pedra Lume	D2

Pôrto Inglês	C3
Praia, capital	C4
Ribeira Brava	B2
Ribeira Grande	A1
Sal Rei	D2
Santa Maria	D2
São Filipe	B4
Tarrafal	C3

Other Features
Boa Vista, island	D2
Brava, island	B4
Fogo, island	B4
Leeward Group	B3
Maio, island	C3
Pico do Cano, volcano	B4
Sal, island	D2
Santa Luzia, island	B2
Santo Antão, island	A1
São Nicolau, island	B2
São Tiago, island	C3
São Vicente, island	A2
Windward Group	B2

Mali:
Map Index

Cities and Towns
Ansongo	D2
Bafoulabé	A3
Bamako, capital	B3
Bougouni	B3
Bourem	C2
Djenné	C3
Gao	D2
Goundam	C2
Kayes	A3
Kidal	D2
Kita	B3
Koulikoro	B3
Koutiala	B3
Ménaka	D2
Mopti	C3
Niono	B3
Nioro du Sahel	B2

San	C3
Ségou	B3
Sikasso	B3
Taoudenni	C1
Tessalit	D1
Timbuktu	C2

Other Features
Adrar des Iforas, massif	D2
Azaouâd, region	C2
Bani, river	B3
Baoulé, river	B3
Djouf, el-, desert	B1
Erg Chech, desert	C1
Hombori, mts.	C2
Hombori Tondo, mt.	C2
Niger, river	B3
Sahara, desert	C1
Sahel, region	C2
Senegal, river	A3

Mali

Capital: Bamako
Area: 482,077 sq. mi.
1,248,904 sq. km.
Population: 10,429,124
Largest City: Bamako
Language: French
Monetary Unit: Franc

Mauritania

Capital: Nouakchott
Area: 398,000 sq. mi.
1,031,088 sq. km.
Population: 2,581,738
Largest City: Nouakchott
Languages: Arabic, Wolof
Monetary Unit: Ouguiya

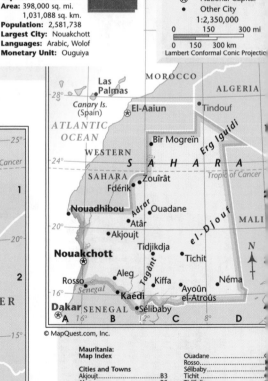

Mauritania

- ⊛ National Capital
- • Other City

1:2,350,000

0 150 300 mi.

0 150 300 km.

Lambert Conformal Conic Projection

© MapQuest.com, Inc.

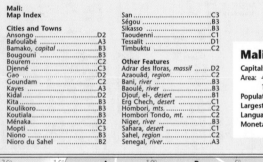
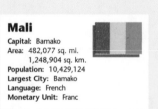

Mali

- ⊛ National Capital
- • Other City

1:21,265,000

0 200 400 mi.

0 200 400 km.

Lambert Conformal Conic Projection

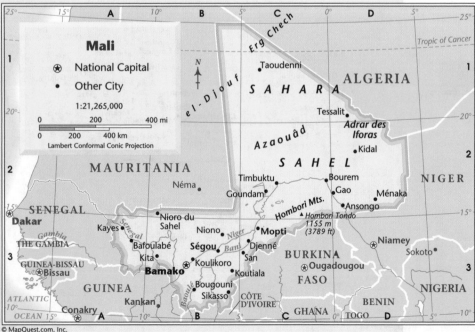

© MapQuest.com, Inc.

Mauritania:
Map Index

Cities and Towns
Akjoujt	B3
Aleg	B3
Atâr	B2
Ayoûn el-Atroûs	C3
Bîr Mogreïn	C1
Fdérik	B2
Kaédi	B3
Kiffa	B3
Néma	D3
Nouadhibou	A2
Nouakchott, capital	A3

Ouadane	B2
Rosso	A3
Sélibaby	B3
Tichit	C2
Tidjikdja	B2
Zouîrât	B2

Other Features
Adrar, region	B2
Djouf, el-, desert	C2
Erg Iguidi, desert	C1
Sahara, desert	B2
Senegal, river	A3
Tagânt, region	B2

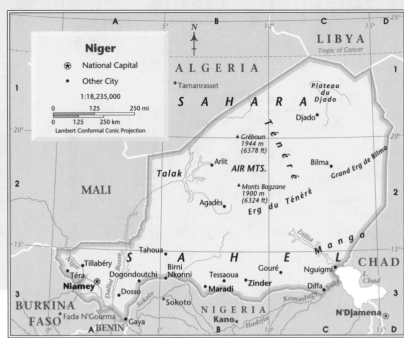

Niger:
Map Index

Cities and Towns
Agadès B2
Arlit B2
Bilma C2
Birni Nkonni B3
Diffa C3
Djado C1
Dogondoutchi A3
Dosso A3
Gaya A3
Gouré C3
Maradi B3
Nguigmi C3
Niamey, capital A3
Tahoua A3
Téra A3
Tessaoua B3
Tillabéry A3
Zinder B3

Other Features
Air, mts. B2
Bagzane, mt. B2
Chad, lake C3
Dallol Bosso, river ...A3
Dillia, river C2
Djado, plateau C1
Erg du Ténéré, desert ..B2
Grand Erg de Bilma,
  desert C2
Gréboun, mt. B1
Komadugu Yobe, river ..C3
Manga, region C2
Niger, river A3
Sahara, desert A1
Sahel, region A3
Talak, region B2
Ténéré, desert C1

Niger

Capital: Niamey
Area: 497,000 sq. mi.
 1,287,565 sq. km.
Population: 9,962,242
Largest City: Niamey
Language: French
Monetary Unit: CFA franc

Chad

Capital: N'Djamena
Area: 495,755 sq. mi.
 1,248,339 sq. km.
Population: 7,557,436
Largest City: N'Djamena
Languages: French, Arabic
Monetary Unit: CFA franc

Chad:
Map Index

Cities and Towns
Abéché C4
Abou Deïa B5
Am Timan C5
Aozou B2
Ati B4
Bardaï B2
Berdoba C4
Biltine C4
Bol A4
Bongor A5
Bousso B5
Doba B5
Fada C3
Faya-Largeau B3
Koro Toro B3
Laï B5
Mao A4
Massenya B5
Melfi B5
Mongo B4
Moundou B5
N'Djamena, capital ..A4
Pala A5
Sarh B5
Zouar B2

Other Features
Bahr Salamat, river ...B5
Batha, river C4
Bodélé, depression ..B3
Chad, lake A4
Chari, river A5
Emi Koussi, mt. B3
Ennedi, plateau C3
Enneri Ke, river B3
Ghazal, river B4
Grand Erg de Bilma,
  desert A3
Logone, river A5
Ouadi Maba, river ...C3
Sahara, desert A2
Tibesti, massif B2

Sudan:
Map Index

Cities and Towns
Atbarah C2
Babanusah B3
Damazin, ad- C3
Dunqulah C1
Fashir, al- B2
Halaib D1
Juba C4
Junaynah, al- A2
Kaduqli B3
Kassala D2
Khartoum, capital C2
Khartoum North C2
Khashm al-Qirbah C2
Kuraymah C1
Kusti C2
Malakal C3
Nuhud, an- B2
Nyala B2
Omdurman C2
Pibor Post C3
Port Sudan D1
Qadarif, al- C2
Rumbek B3
Sannar C2
Ubayyid, al- B3
Wadi Halfa C1
Wad Madani C2
Waw B3
Yambio B4

Other Features
Akobo, river C3
Atbarah, river C2
Bahr al-Arab, river B3
Bahr al-Ghazal, river ..C3
Bahr al-Jabal, river C3
Blue Nile, river C2
Kangen, river C3
Kinyeti, mt. C4
Libyan, desert B1
Lol, river B3
Nasser, lake C1
Nile, river C1, C2
Nuba, mts. B3
Nubian, desert C1
Red, sea D1
Red Sea, hills D1
Sobat, river C3
Sudd, region B3
Sue, river B3
Wadi al-Malik, river ...B2
Wadi Howar, river B2
White Nile, river C3

Sudan

Capital: Khartoum
Area: 966,757 sq. mi.
 2,530,459 sq. km.
Population: 34,475,690
Largest City: Khartoum
Language: Arabic
Monetary Unit: Pound

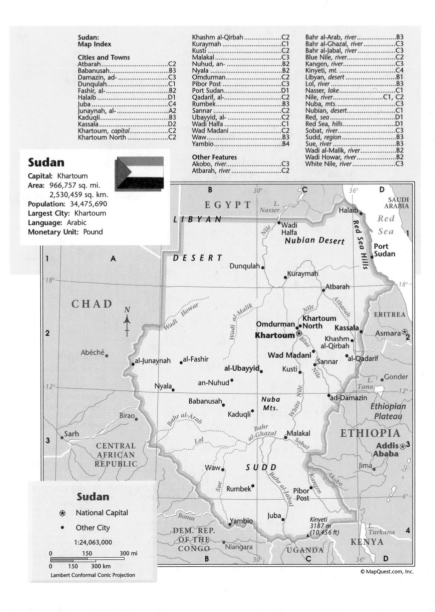

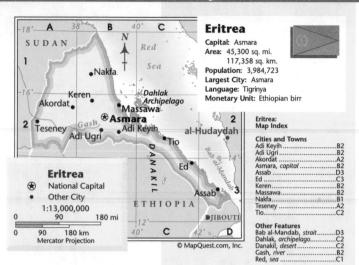

Eritrea

Capital: Asmara
Area: 45,300 sq. mi.
117,358 sq. km.
Population: 3,984,723
Largest City: Asmara
Language: Tigrinya
Monetary Unit: Ethiopian birr

Eritrea

⊛ National Capital
• Other City

1:13,000,000

0   90   180 mi
0   90   180 km
Mercator Projection

Eritrea:
Map Index

Cities and Towns
Adi Keyih B2
Adi Ugri B2
Akordat A2
Asmara, *capital* B2
Assab D3
Ed C3
Keren B2
Massawa B2
Nakfa B1
Teseney A2
Tio C2

Other Features
Bab al-Mandab, *strait* D3
Dahlak, *archipelago* C2
Danakil, *desert* C2
Gash, *river* B2
Red, *sea* C1

© MapQuest.com, Inc.

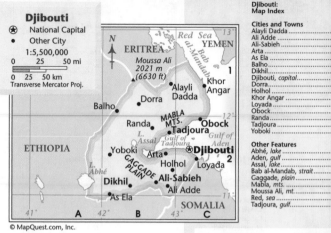

Djibouti

⊛ National Capital
• Other City

1:5,500,000

0   25   50 mi
0   25   50 km
Transverse Mercator Proj.

© MapQuest.com, Inc.

Djibouti:
Map Index

Cities and Towns
Alayli Dadda ....B
Ali Adde ....B
Ali-Sabieh ....B
Arta ....B
As Ela ....B
Balho ....A
Dikhil ....B
Djibouti, *capital* C
Dorra ....B
Holhol C
Khor Angar C
Loyada C
Obock C
Randa ....B
Tadjoura ....B
Yoboki ....B

Other Features
Abhé, *lake* ....A
Aden, *gulf* C
Assal, *lake* ....A
Bab al-Mandab, *strait* ...C
Gaggade, *plain* ....B
Mabla, *mts.* C
Moussa Ali, *mt.* C
Red, *sea* C
Tadjoura, *gulf* ....B

Djibouti

Capital: Djibouti
Area: 8,950 sq. mi.
23,187 sq. km.
Population: 447,439
Largest City: Djibouti
Languages: Cushitic languages
Monetary Unit: Franc

Ethiopia

⊛ National Capital
• Other City

1:15,053,000

0   100   200 mi
0   100   200 km
Mercator Projection

© MapQuest.com, Inc.

Ethiopia

Capital: Addis Ababa
Area: 437,794 sq. mi.
1,134,181 sq. km.
Population: 59,680,383
Largest City: Addis Ababa
Language: Amharic
Monetary Unit: Birr

Somalia:
Map Index

Cities and Towns
Baraawe A3
Baydhabo A3
Beledweyne B3
Benderbeyla C2
Berbera B1
Boosaaso B1
Burco ....B
Ceerigaabo ....B
Dhuusamareeb ....B
Eyl ....B
Gaalkacyo ....B
Garoowe ....B
Hargeysa ....A
Hobyo ....A
Jamaame ....A
Jawhar ....A
Jilib ....A
Kismayu ....A
Luuq ....A
Marka ....A
Mogadishu, *capital* ...B
Qardho ....B
Xuddur ....A

Other Features
Aden, *gulf* ....B
Gees Gwardafuy, *cape* ...C
Juba, *river* ....A
Nugaal, *valley* ....B
Raas Xaafun, *cape* ....B
Surud Ad, *mt.* ....B
Webi Shabeelle, *river* ...B

Somalia

Capital: Mogadishu
Area: 246,300 sq. mi.
638,083 sq. km.
Population: 7,140,643
Largest City: Mogadishu
Language: Somali, Arabic
Monetary Unit: Shilling

Somalia

⊛ National Capital
• Other City

1:22,100,000

0   150   300 mi
0   150   300 km
Miller Cylindrical Projection

© MapQuest.com, Inc.

Ethiopia:
Map Index

Cities and Towns
Addis Ababa, *capital* ...C2
Adwa C1
Arba Minch B3
Asela C3
Asosa B2
Awasa C3
Bahir Dar B2
Debre Birhan C2
Debre Markos B2
Degeh Bur D2
Dese C2
Dire Dawa D2
Goba C3
Gonder B1
Gore B2

Harer D2
Imi D3
Jima B3
Mekele C2
Nazret C2
Negele C3
Nekemte B2
Shewa Gimira B3
Weldiya C2
Werder D3

Other Features
Abaya, *lake* B3
Abhe, *lake* C2
Akobo, *river* A3
Atbara, *river* B1
Awash, *river* C2
Baro, *river* B2
Blue Nile, *river* B2

Choke, *mts.* B2
Dawa, *river* C3
Denakil, *desert* C1
Dinder, *river* B1
Ethiopian, *plateau* C2
Genale, *river* C3
Great Rift, *valley* C3
Ogaden, *region* D3
Omo, *river* B3
Provisional
Administrative Line D3
Ras Dashen, *mt.* C1
Tana, *lake* B1
Tekeze, *river* B1
Turkana, *lake* B3
Wabe Gestro, *river* D3
Wabe Shebele, *river* D3
Ziway, *lake* C3

© MapQuest.com, Inc.

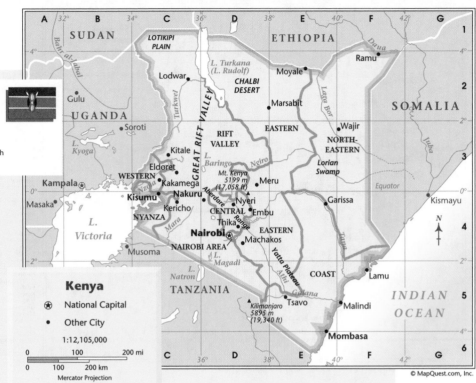

Kenya

Capital: Nairobi
Area: 224,961 sq. mi.
582,801 sq. km.
Population: 28,808,658
Largest City: Nairobi
Language: Swahili, English
Monetary Unit: Shilling

Kenya:
Map Index

Provinces
Central D4
Coast E5
Eastern E3
Nairobi Area D4
North-Eastern F3
Nyanza C4
Rift Valley D3
Western C3

Cities and Towns
Eldoret C3
Embu D4
Garissa E4
Kakamega C3
Kericho C4
Kisumu C4
Kitale C3
Lamu F5
Lodwar C2
Machakos D4
Malindi F5
Marsabit E2
Meru D3
Mombasa E5
Moyale E2

Nairobi, *capital* D4
Nakuru D4
Nyeri D4
Ramu F2
Thika D4
Tsavo E5
Wajir F3

Other Features
Aberdare, *range* D4
Athi, *river* E5
Baringo, *lake* D2
Chalbi, *desert* D1
Daua, *river* F1
Galana, *river* E5
Great Rift, *valley* C3
Kenya, *mt.* D4
Laga Bor, *river* E3
Lorian, *swamp* E3
Lotikipi, *plain* C1
Magadi, *lake* D4
Mara, *river* C4
Ngiro, *river* D3
Nzoia, *river* C3
Tana, *river* F4
Turkana (Rudolf), *lake* D2
Turkwel, *river* C2
Victoria, *lake* B4
Yatta, *plateau* E5

Kenya

⊛ National Capital
• Other City

1:12,105,000

0   100   200 mi
0   100   200 km
Mercator Projection

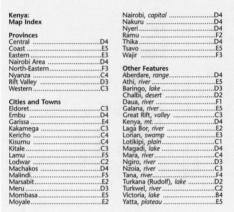

Uganda

Capital: Kampala
Area: 93,070 sq. mi.
241,114 sq. km.
Population: 22,804,973
Largest City: Kampala
Language: English
Monetary Unit: Shilling

Uganda:
Map Index

Cities and Towns
Arua B2
Atiak C2
Entebbe C3
Fort Portal B3
Gulu C2
Jinja C3
Kabale A4
Kampala, *capital* C3
Kitgum C2
Lira C2
Loyoro D2
Masaka B4
Masindi B3
Mbale D3
Mbarara B4
Moroto D2

Mubende B3
Soroti C3
Tororo D3

Other Features
Achwa, *river* C2
Albert, *lake* B3
Albert Nile, *river* B2
Bahr al-Jabal, *river* B2
Edward, *lake* A4
Elgon, *mt.* D3
George, *lake* B4
Kafu, *river* B3
Kagera, *river* B4
Kyoga, *lake* C3
Margherita, *peak* A3
Ruwenzori, *range* B3
Sese, *islands* C4
Victoria, *lake* C4
Victoria Nile, *river* B2,C3

Uganda

⊛ National Capital
• Other City

1:11,600,000

0   75   150 mi
0   75   150 km
Mercator Projection

© MapQuest.com, Inc.

Burundi

Capital: Bujumbura
Area: 10,740 sq. mi.
27,824 sq. km.
Population: 5,735,937
Largest City: Bujumbura
Languages: French, Kirundi
Monetary Unit: Franc

Burundi:
Map Index

Cities and Towns
Bubanza B2
Bujumbura, *capital* B2
Bururi B2
Cankuzo C2
Gitega C2
Karuzi C2
Makamba B3
Muramvya B2
Muyinga C1
Ngozi B1

Rutana B2
Ruyigi C2

Other Features
Heha, *mt.* B2
Kagera, *river* C1
Malagarasi, *river* C2
Ruvubu, *river* C2
Ruzizi, *river* A1
Tanganyika, *lake* B2

Burundi

⊛ National Capital
• Other City

1:6,548,000

0   50   100 mi
0   50   100 km
Conic Equidistant Projection

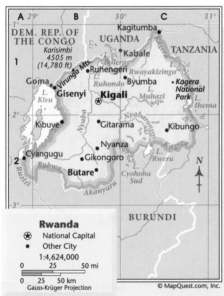

Rwanda

⊛ National Capital
• Other City

1:4,624,000

0   25   50 mi
0   25   50 km
Gauss-Krüger Projection

© MapQuest.com, Inc.

Rwanda

Capital: Kigali
Area: 10,169 sq. mi.
26,345 sq. km.
Population: 8,154,933
Largest City: Kigali
Languages: French, Kinyarwanda
Monetary Unit: Franc

Rwanda:
Map Index

Cities and Towns
Butare B2
Byumba C1
Cyangugu A2
Gikongoro B2
Gisenyi B1
Gitarama B2
Kagitumba C1
Kibungo C2
Kibuye B2
Kigali, *capital* B1
Nyanza B2
Ruhengeri B1

Other Features
Akanyaru, *river* B2

Bulera, *lake* B1
Cyohoha Sud, *lake* C2
Ihema, *lake* C1
Kagera National Park C1
Kagera, *river* C1, C2
Karisimbi, *mt.* B1
Kivu, *lake* A1
Muhazi, *lake* C1
Nyaba, *river* B2
Nyabarongo, *river* B2
Ruhondo, *lake* B1
Ruhwa, *river* B2
Ruzizi, *river* A2
Rwayakizinga, *lake* C1
Rweru, *lake* C2
Virunga, *mts.* B1

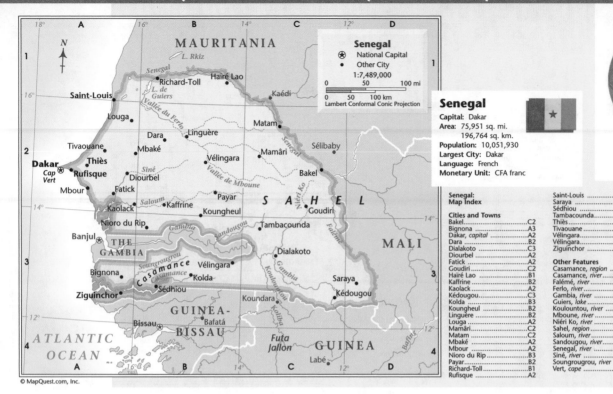

Senegal

- **National Capital**
- **Other City**

1:7,489,000

0   50   100 mi
0   50   100 km

Lambert Conformal Conic Projection

© MapQuest.com, Inc.

Senegal

Capital: Dakar
Area: 75,951 sq. mi.
    196,764 sq. km.
Population: 10,051,930
Largest City: Dakar
Language: French
Monetary Unit: CFA franc

Senegal:
Map Index

Cities and Towns
Bakel	C2
Bignona	A3
Dakar, *capital*	A2
Dara	B2
Dialakoto	C3
Diourbel	A2
Fatick	A2
Goudiri	C2
Hairé Lao	B1
Kaffrine	B2
Kaolack	A2
Kédougou	C3
Kolda	B3
Koungheul	B2
Linguère	B2
Louga	A2
Mamâri	C2
Matam	C2
Mbaké	A2
Mbour	A2
Nioro du Rip	B3
Payar	B2
Richard-Toll	B1
Rufisque	A2

Saint-Louis	A1
Saraya	D3
Sédhiou	B3
Tambacounda	C3
Thiès	A2
Tivaouane	A2
Vélingara	B2
Vélingara	B3
Ziguinchor	A3

Other Features
Casamance, *region*	B3
Casamance, *river*	B3
Falémé, *river*	C3
Ferlo, *river*	B2
Gambia, *river*	C3
Guiers, *lake*	B1
Koulountou, *river*	C3
Mboune, *river*	B2
Niéri Ko, *river*	C2
Sahel, *region*	C2
Saloum, *river*	B2
Sandougou, *river*	B3
Senegal, *river*	B1, C2
Siné, *river*	B2
Soungrougrou, *river*	B3
Vert, *cape*	A2

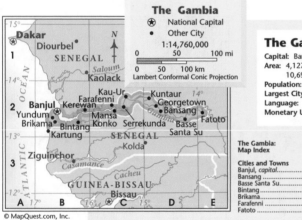

The Gambia

- **National Capital**
- **Other City**

1:14,760,000

0   50   100 mi
0   50   100 km

Lambert Conformal Conic Projection

© MapQuest.com, Inc.

The Gambia

Capital: Banjul
Area: 4,127 sq. mi.
    10,692 sq. km.
Population: 1,336,320
Largest City: Banjul
Language: English
Monetary Unit: Dalasi

The Gambia:
Map Index

Cities and Towns
Banjul, *capital*	B2
Bansang	D2
Basse Santa Su	D2
Bintang	B2
Brikama	B2
Farafenni	C2
Fatoto	E2

Georgetown	D2
Kartung	B2
Kau-Ur	C2
Kerewan	B2
Kuntaur	D2
Mansa Konko	C2
Serrekunda	C2
Yundum	B2

Other Feature
Gambia, *river*	D2

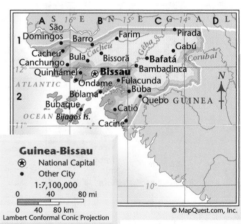

Guinea-Bissau

- **National Capital**
- **Other City**

1:7,100,000

0   40   80 mi
0   40   80 km

Lambert Conformal Conic Projection

© MapQuest.com, Inc.

Guinea-Bissau

Capital: Bissau
Area: 13,948 sq. mi.
    36,135 sq. km.
Population: 1,234,555
Largest City: Bissau
Language: Portuguese
Monetary Unit: CFA franc

Guinea-Bissau:
Map Index

Cities and Towns
Bafatá	C1
Bambadinca	C1
Barro	B1
Bissau, *capital*	B2
Bissorã	B1
Bolama	B2
Buba	C2
Bubaque	B2
Bula	B1
Cacheu	A1
Cacine	C2
Canchungo	A1
Catió	B2
Farim	B1
Fulacunda	B2
Gabú	C1
Ondame	B2
Pirada	C1
Quebo	C2
Quinhámel	B2
São Domingos	A1

Other Features
Bijagós, *islands*	A2
Cacheu, *river*	B1
Corubal, *river*	D1
Gêba, *river*	C1

Guinea:
Map Index

Cities and Towns
Beyla	D3
Conakry, *capital*	B3
Coyah	B3
Dabola	C2
Fria	B2
Guéckédou	C3
Kailahun	C3
Kali	A2
Kamsar	A2
Kankan	D2
Kérouané	D3
Kindia	B3
Kissidougou	C3
Kouroussa	D2
Labé	B2
Lélouma	B2
Macenta	D3
Mamou	B2
Niagassola	D1
Nzérékoré	D4
Siguiri	D2
Tougué	C2
Yomou	D4

Other Features
Bafing, *river*	C2
Futa Jallon, *plateau*	B1
Gambia, *river*	B2
Los, *islands*	A3
Milo, *river*	D3
Niger, *river*	D2
Nimba, *mts.*	D4
Tinkissa, *river*	C2

Guinea

Capital: Conakry
Area: 94,926 sq. mi.
    245,922 sq. km.
Population: 7,538,953
Largest City: Conakry
Language: French
Monetary Unit: Guinea franc

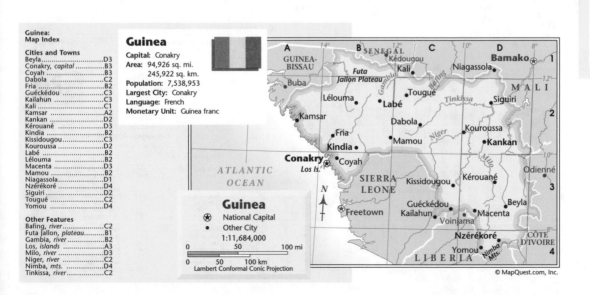

Guinea

- **National Capital**
- **Other City**

1:11,684,000

0   50   100 mi
0   50   100 km

Lambert Conformal Conic Projection

© MapQuest.com, Inc.

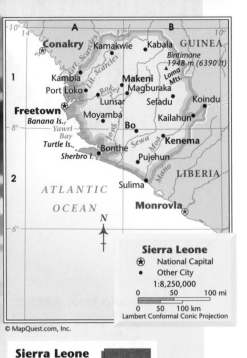

© MapQuest.com, Inc.

Sierra Leone

- National Capital
- Other City

1:8,250,000

0   50   100 mi

0   50   100 km

Lambert Conformal Conic Projection

Sierra Leone

Capital: Freetown
Area: 27,699 sq. mi.
71,759 sq. km.
Population: 5,296,651
Largest City: Freetown
Language: English
Monetary Unit: Leone

Sierra Leone:
Map Index

Cities and Towns
Bo B2
Bonthe A2
Freetown, capital A1
Kabala B1
Kailahun B1
Kamakwie A1
Kambia A1
Kenema B2
Koindu B1
Lunsar A1
Magburaka B1
Makeni B1
Moyamba A1
Port Loko A1

Pujehun B2
Sefadu B1
Sulima B2

Other Features
Banana, islands A1
Bintimane, mt. B1
Great Scarcies, river A1
Jong, river A2
Little Scarcies, river A1
Loma, mts. B1
Mano, river B2
Moa, river B2
Rokel, river A1
Sewa, river B2
Sherbro, island A2
Turtle, islands A2
Yawri, bay A2

Côte d'Ivoire (Ivory Coast)

- National Capital
- Other City

1:9,789,000

0   75   150 mi

0   75   150 km

Lambert Conformal Conic Projection

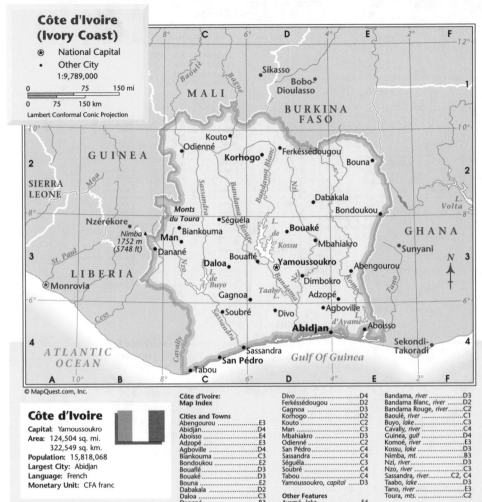

© MapQuest.com, Inc.

Côte d'Ivoire

Capital: Yamoussoukro
Area: 124,504 sq. mi.
322,549 sq. km.
Population: 15,818,068
Largest City: Abidjan
Language: French
Monetary Unit: CFA franc

Côte d'Ivoire:
Map Index

Cities and Towns
Abengourou E3
Abidjan D4
Aboisso E4
Adzopé E3
Agboville D4
Biankouma C3
Bondoukou E2
Bouaflé D3
Bouaké D3
Bouna E2
Dabakala D2
Daloa C3
Danané B3
Dimbokro D3

Divo D4
Ferkéssédougou D2
Gagnoa D3
Korhogo D2
Kouto D2
Man C3
Mbahiakro D3
Odienné C2
San Pédro C4
Sassandra C4
Séguéla C3
Soubré C4
Tabou C4
Yamoussoukro, capital D3

Other Features
Ayamé, lake E4
Bagoé, river.....................C1

Bandama, river D3
Bandama Blanc, river D2
Bandama Rouge, river C2
Baoulé, river C2
Buyo, lake C3
Cavally, river C4
Guinea, gulf D4
Komoé, river E3
Kossu, lake D3
Nimba, mt. B3
Nzi, river D3
Nzo, river C3
Sassandra, river C2, C4
Taabo, lake D3
Tano, river E3
Toura, mts. C2

Liberia

Capital: Monrovia
Area: 38,250 sq. mi.
99,093 sq. km.
Population: 2,923,725
Largest City: Monrovia
Language: English
Monetary Unit: Dollar

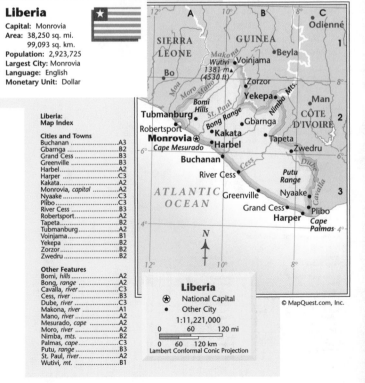

© MapQuest.com, Inc.

Liberia:
Map Index

Cities and Towns
Buchanan A3
Gbarnga B2
Grand Cess B3
Greenville B3
Harbel A2
Harper C3
Kakata A2
Monrovia, capital A2
Nyaake C3
Plibo C3
River Cess B3
Robertsport A2
Tapeta B2
Tubmanburg A2
Voinjama B1
Yekepa B2
Zorzor B2
Zwedru B2

Other Features
Bomi, hills A2
Bong, range A2
Cavalla, river C3
Cess, river B3
Dube, river A2
Makona, river A1
Mano, river A2
Mesurado, cape A2
Moro, river A2
Nimba, mts. B2
Palmas, cape B3
Putu, range B3
St. Paul, river A2
Wutivi, mt. B1

Liberia

- National Capital
- Other City

1:11,221,000

0   60   120 mi

0   60   120 km

Lambert Conformal Conic Projection

São Tomé & Príncipe

Capital: São Tomé
Area: 386 sq. mi.
1,000 sq. km.
Population: 154,878
Largest City: São Tomé
Language: Portuguese
Monetary Unit: Dobra

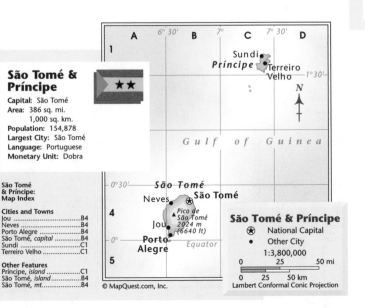

© MapQuest.com, Inc.

São Tomé & Príncipe:
Map Index

Cities and Towns
Jou B4
Neves B4
Porto Alegre B4
São Tomé, capital B4
Sundi C1
Terreiro Velho C1

Other Features
Príncipe, island C1
São Tomé, island B4
São Tomé, mt. B4

São Tomé & Príncipe

- National Capital
- Other City

1:3,800,000

0   25   50 mi

0   25   50 km

Lambert Conformal Conic Projection

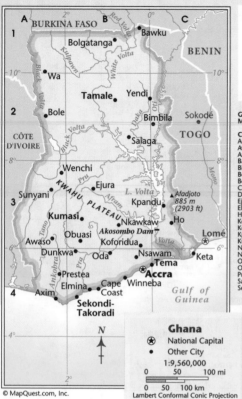

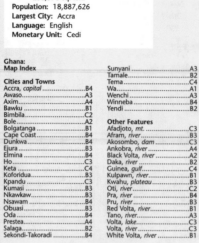

Ghana

Capital: Accra
Area: 92,098 sq. mi.
238,596 sq. km.
Population: 18,887,626
Largest City: Accra
Language: English
Monetary Unit: Cedi

Ghana:
Map Index

Cities and Towns

Accra, *capital*	B4
Awaso	A3
Axim	A4
Bawku	B1
Bimbila	C2
Bole	A2
Bolgatanga	B1
Cape Coast	B4
Dunkwa	B4
Ejura	B3
Elmina	B4
Ho	C3
Keta	C4
Koforidua	B4
Kpandu	C3
Kumasi	B3
Nkawkaw	B3
Nsawam	B4
Obuasi	B3
Oda	B4
Prestea	A4
Salaga	B2
Sekondi-Takoradi	B4

Sunyani	A3
Tamale	B2
Tema	C4
Wa	A1
Wenchi	A3
Winneba	B4
Yendi	B2

Other Features

Afadjoto, *mt.*	C3
Afram, *river*	B3
Akosombo, *dam*	C3
Ankobra, *river*	A4
Black Volta, *river*	A2
Daka, *river*	B2
Guinea, *gulf*	C4
Kulpawn, *river*	B1
Kwahu, *plateau*	B3
Oti, *river*	C2
Pra, *river*	B3
Pru, *river*	B3
Red Volta, *river*	B1
Tano, *river*	A3
Volta, *lake*	C3
Volta, *river*	C3
White Volta, *river*	B1

Ghana
⊛ National Capital
● Other City
1:9,560,000
0   50   100 mi
0   50   100 km
Lambert Conformal Conic Projection

© MapQuest.com, Inc.

Burkina Faso

Capital: Ouagadougou
Area: 105,946 sq. mi.
274,472 sq. km.
Population: 11,575,898
Largest City: Ouagadougou
Language: French
Monetary Unit: CFA franc

Burkina Faso
⊛ National Capital
● Other City
1:14,785,000
0   100   200 mi
0   100   200 km
Lambert Conformal Conic Projection

© MapQuest.com, Inc.

Burkina Faso:
Map Index

Cities and Towns

Bobo-Dioulasso	B3
Dédougou	C2
Dori	D1
Gaoua	C3
Koudougou	C2
Léo	C3
Ouagadougou, *capital*	D2
Ouahigouya	C2
Tenkodogo	D3

Other Features

Black Volta, *river*	B3
Red Volta, *river*	D3
Sirba, *river*	D2
Téna Kourou, *mt.*	B3
White Volta, *river*	D2

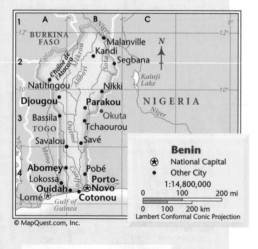

Benin
⊛ National Capital
● Other City
1:14,800,000
0   100   200 mi
0   100   200 km
Lambert Conformal Conic Projection

© MapQuest.com, Inc.

Benin

Capital: Porto-Novo
Area: 43,500 sq. mi.
112,694 sq. km.
Population: 6,305,567
Largest City: Cotonou
Language: French
Monetary Unit: CFA franc

Benin:
Map Index

Cities and Towns

Abomey	A4
Bassila	A3
Cotonou	B4
Djougou	A3
Kandi	B2
Lokossa	A4
Malanville	B2
Natitingou	A2
Nikki	B3
Ouidah	B4
Parakou	B3
Pobé	B4

Porto-Novo, *capital*	B4
Savalou	A3
Savé	B3
Segbana	B2
Tchaourou	B3

Other Features

Alibori, *river*	B2
Chaîne de l'Atacora, *mts.*	A2
Couffo, *river*	B4
Guinea, *gulf*	A4
Mékrou, *river*	A2
Mono, *river*	A4
Niger, *river*	B1
Ouémé, *river*	B3
Sota, *river*	B2

Togo

Capital: Lomé
Area: 21,925 sq. mi.
56,801 sq. km.
Population: 5,081,413
Largest City: Lomé
Language: French
Monetary Unit: CFA franc

Togo:
Map Index

Cities and Towns

Amlamé	B3
Aného	B3
Anié	B3
Atakpamé	B3
Badou	B3
Bafilo	B2
Bassar	B2
Blitta	B2
Dapaong	B1
Kanté	B2
Kara	B2
Kpalimé	B3
Kpémé	B3
Lomé, *capital*	B3
Mango	B1
Niamtougou	B2
Sokodé	B2
Sotouboua	B3
Tabligbo	B3
Tchamba	B3
Tsévié	B3

Other Features

Agou, *mt.*	B3
Benin, *bight*	B4
Mono, *river*	B2
Oti, *river*	B1

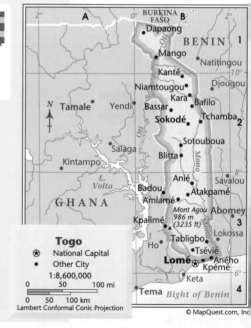

Togo
⊛ National Capital
● Other City
1:8,600,000
0   50   100 mi
0   50   100 km
Lambert Conformal Conic Projection

© MapQuest.com, Inc.

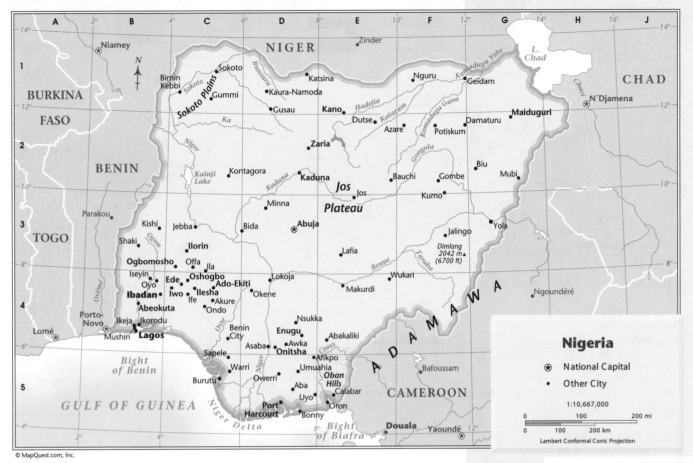

© MapQuest.com, Inc.

Nigeria

⊛ National Capital
• Other City

1:10,667,000

| 0 | 100 | 200 mi |

| 0 | 100 | 200 km |

Lambert Conformal Conic Projection

Nigeria

Capital: Abuja
Area: 356,669 sq. mi.
924,013 sq. km.
Population: 113,828,587
Largest City: Lagos
Language: English
Monetary Unit: Naira

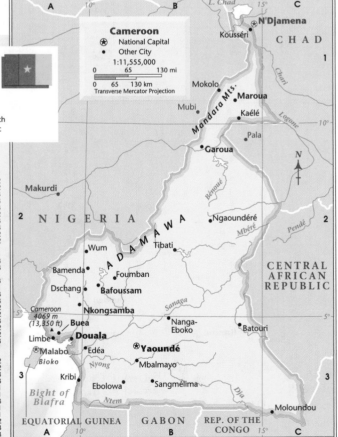

© MapQuest.com, Inc.

Cameroon

⊛ National Capital
• Other City

1:11,555,000

| 0 | 65 | 130 mi |

| 0 | 65 | 130 km |

Transverse Mercator Projection

Cameroon

Capital: Yaoundé
Area: 183,569 sq. mi.
475,567 sq. km.
Population: 15,456,092
Largest City: Douala
Languages: English, French
Monetary Unit: CFA franc

Cameroon:
Map Index

Cities and Towns
Bafoussam	B2
Bamenda	B2
Batouri	B3
Buea	A3
Douala	A3
Dschang	B2
Ebolowa	B3
Edéa	B3
Foumban	B2
Garoua	B2
Kaélé	B1
Kousséri	B1
Kribi	A3
Limbe	A3
Maroua	B1
Mbalmayo	B3
Mokolo	B1
Moloundou	C3
Nanga-Eboko	B3
Ngaoundéré	B2
Nkongsamba	A2
Sangmélima	B3
Tibati	B2
Wum	B2
Yaoundé, capital	B3

Other Features
Adamawa, massif	B2
Bénoué, river	B2
Biafra, bight	A3
Cameroon, mt.	A3
Chad, lake	B1
Chari, river	C1
Dja, river	B3
Logone, river	C1
Mandara, mts.	B1
Mbéré, river	B2
Ntem, river	B3
Nyong, river	B3
Sanaga, river	B2

Nigeria:
Map Index

Cities and Towns
Aba	D5
Abakaliki	E4
Abeokuta	B4
Abuja, capital	D3
Ado-Ekiti	C4
Akure	C4
Asaba	D4
Awka	D4
Azare	F2
Bauchi	E2
Benin City	C4
Bida	D3
Birnin Kebbi	C1
Biu	G2
Bonny	D5
Burutu	C5
Calabar	E5
Damaturu	F2
Dutse	E2
Ede	C4
Enugu	D4
Geidam	F1
Gombe	F2
Gummi	C1
Gusau	D1
Ibadan	B4
Ife	C4
Ikeja	B4
Ikorodu	B4
Ila	C3
Ilesha	C4
Ilorin	C3
Iseyin	B4
Iwo	C4
Jalingo	F3
Jebba	C3
Jos	E3
Kaduna	D2
Kano	E1
Katsina	D1
Kaura-Namoda	D1
Kishi	B3
Kontagora	C2
Kumo	F2
Lafia	E3
Lagos	B4
Lokoja	D4
Maiduguri	G2

Makurdi	E4
Minna	D3
Mubi	G2
Mushin	B4
Nguru	F1
Nsukka	D4
Offa	C3
Ogbomosho	C4
Okene	D4
Ondo	C4
Onitsha	D4
Oron	E5
Oshogbo	C4
Owerri	D5
Oyo	B4
Port Harcourt	D5
Potiskum	F2
Sapele	C5
Shaki	B3
Sokoto	C1
Umuahia	D5
Uyo	D5
Warri	C5
Wukari	E4
Yola	G3
Zaria	D2

Other Features
Adamawa, massif	E5
Benin, bight	B5
Benue, river	E3
Bunsuru, river	D1
Chad, lake	G1
Cross, river	E4
Dimlang, mt.	F3
Gongola, river	F2
Guinea, gulf	B5
Hadejia, river	E1
Jos, plateau	E2
Ka, river	C2
Kaduna, river	D2
Kainji, lake	C2
Katagum, river	E2
Komadugu Gana, river	F2
Komadugu Yobe, river	F1
Niger, delta	C5
Niger, river	C2, D5
Oban, hills	E5
Ogun, river	B3
Osse, river	C4
Sokoto, plains	C1
Sokoto, river	C1
Taraba, river	F3

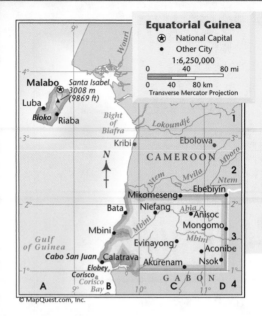

Equatorial Guinea

⊛ National Capital
• Other City

1:6,250,000

0   40   80 mi
0   40   80 km
Transverse Mercator Projection

© MapQuest.com, Inc.

Equatorial Guinea

Capital: Malabo
Area: 10,831 sq. mi.
        28,060 sq. km.
Population: 465,746
Largest City: Malabo
Language: Spanish
Monetary Unit: CFA franc

Equatorial Guinea: Map Index

Cities and Towns
Aconibe C3
Akurenam C3
Añisoc C3
Bata B3
Calatrava B3
Ebebiyín D2
Evinayong C3
Luba A1
Malabo, *capital* A1
Mbini B3
Mikomeseng C2
Mongomo D3

Niefang C3
Nsok D3
Riaba A1

Other Features
Abia, *river* C3
Biafra, *bight* B1
Bioko, *island* A1
Corisco, *bay* B4
Corisco, *island* B4
Elobey, *islands* B3
Guinea, *gulf* A3
Mbini, *river* C3
Mboro, *river* D4
San Juan, *cape* B3
Santa Isabel, *peak* A1

Gabon

Capital: Libreville
Area: 103,347 sq. mi.
        267,738 sq. km.
Population: 1,225,853
Largest City: Libreville
Language: French
Monetary Unit: CFA franc

Gabon

⊛ National Capital
• Other City

1:11,850,000

0   75   150 mi
0   75   150 km
Azimuthal Equal Area Projection

© MapQuest.com, Inc.

Gabon: Map Index

Cities and Towns
Bélinga B1
Bitam A1
Booué A2
Franceville B2
Koula-Moutou B2
Lambaréné A2
Libreville, *capital* A1
Makokou B1
Mayumba A2
Mékambo B1
Mitzic A1
Moanda B2
Mouila A2
Ndendé A2
Ndjolé A2

Okondja B2
Omboué A2
Owendo A1
Oyem A1
Port-Gentil A2
Tchibanga A2

Other Features
Chaillu, *mts.* B2
Cristal, *mts.* A1
Djouah, *river* B1
Iboundji, *mt.* A2
Ivindo, *river* B1
Lopez, *cape* A2
Ndogo, *lagoon* A2
Ngounié, *river* A2
Nyanga, *river* A2
Ogooué, *river* A2

Republic of the Congo

⊛ National Capital
• Other City

1:18,000,000

0   100   200 mi
0   100   200 km
Azimuthal Equal Area Projection

© MapQuest.com, Inc.

Republic of the Congo

Capital: Brazzaville
Area: 132,047 sq. mi.
        342,091 sq. km.
Population: 2,716,814
Largest City: Brazzaville
Language: French
Monetary Unit: CFA franc

Republic of the Congo: Map Index

Cities and Towns
Bétou E2
Brazzaville, *capital* C6
Djambala C5
Ewo C4
Impfondo D3
Kinkala C6
Loubomo B6
Makoua C4
Mossendjo B5
Ouesso D3
Owando C4
Pointe-Noire A6

Sembé C3
Sibiti B5

Other Features
Alima, *river* D4
Batéké, *plateau* C5
Congo, *basin* D3
Congo, *river* D4
Ivindo, *river* B3
Lékéti, *mts.* C5
Lengoué, *river* C4
Mayombé, *massif* B6
Niari, *river* B5
Nyanga, *river* A5
Sangha, *river* D2
Ubangi, *river* E2

Central African Republic (C.A.R.)

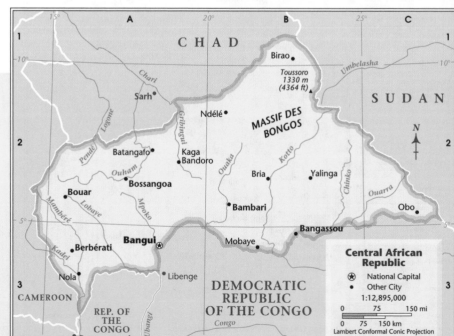

Capital: Bangui
Area: 240,324 sq. mi.
        622,601 sq. km.
Population: 3,444,951
Largest City: Bangui
Language: French
Monetary Unit: CFA franc

Central African Republic: Map Index

Cities and Towns
Bambari B2
Bangassou B3
Bangui, *capital* A3
Batangafo A2
Berbérati A3
Birao B1
Bossangoa A2
Bouar A2
Bria B2
Kaga Bandoro A2
Mobaye B3
Ndélé B2
Nola A3
Obo C2
Yalinga B2

Other Features
Chari, *river* A2
Chinko, *river* B2
Gribingui, *river* A2
Kadéi, *river* A3
Kotto, *river* B2
Lobaye, *river* A2
Mambéré, *river* A2
Massif des Bongos, *range* ..B2
Mpoko, *river* A2
Ouaka, *river* B2
Ouarra, *river* C2
Ouham, *river* A2
Pendé, *river* A2
Toussoro, *mt.* B2
Ubangi, *river* A3

Central African Republic

⊛ National Capital
• Other City

1:12,895,000

0   75   150 mi
0   75   150 km
Lambert Conformal Conic Projection

© MapQuest.com, Inc.

Democratic Republic of the Congo

Capital: Kinshasa
Area: 905,446 sq. mi.
2,345,715 sq. km.
Population: 50,481,305
Largest City: Kinshasa
Language: French
Monetary Unit: Congolese franc

Democratic Republic of the Congo:
Map Index

Regions
Bandundu B2
Bas-Congo A2
Équateur B1
Kasai-Occidental B2
Kasai-Oriental B2
Katanga C3
Kinshasa B2
Maniema C2
Nord-Kivu C2
Orientale C1
Sud-Kivu C2

Cities and Towns
Banana A2
Bandundu B2
Boende B2
Bolobo B2
Boma A2
Bondo B1
Bukavu C2
Bumba B1
Bunia C1
Buta C1
Dilolo B3
Gemena B1
Goma C2
Ikela B2
Ilebo B2
Inga A2
Isiro C1
Kabalo C2
Kahemba B2
Kalemie C2
Kamina C3
Kananga B2
Kikwit B2
Kindu C2
Kinshasa, *capital* A2
Kisangani C1
Kolwezi C3

Likasi C3
Lisala B1
Lodja B2
Lubumbashi C3
Lusambo B2
Manono C2
Matadi A2
Mbandaka B2
Mbanza-Ngungu A2
Mbuji-Mayi B2
Moba C2
Mwene-Ditu B2
Tshikapa B2
Uvira C2
Watsa C1
Yangambi C1

Other Features
Albert, *lake* C1
Aruwimi, *river* C1
Bomu, *river* C1
Congo, *river* B1
Congo Basin, *region* B1
Edward, *lake* C2
Kasai, *river* B2
Katanga, *plateau* B3
Kivu, *lake* C2
Kwa, *river* B2
Kwango, *river* B2
Lomami, *river* C2
Lualaba, *river* C2
Luapula, *river* C3
Lukuga, *river* C2
Luvua, *river* C2
Mai-Ndombe, *lake* B2
Margherita, *peak* C1
Mitumba, *mts.* C2
Mweru, *lake* C3
Sankuru, *river* B2
Tanganyika, *lake* C2
Tshuapa, *river* B2
Tumba, *lake* B2
Ubangi, *river* B1
Uele, *river* C1
Upemba, *lake* C3

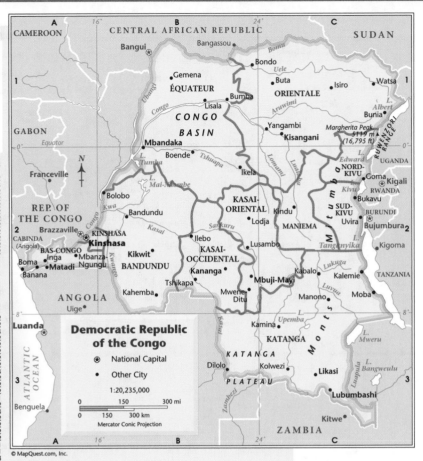

Democratic Republic of the Congo

⊛ National Capital
• Other City

1:20,235,000

0   150   300 mi
0   150   300 km
Mercator Conic Projection

© MapQuest.com, Inc.

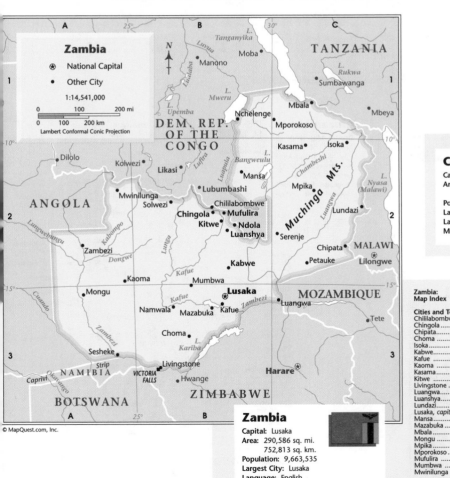

Zambia

⊛ National Capital
• Other City

1:14,541,000

0   100   200 mi
0   100   200 km
Lambert Conformal Conic Projection

© MapQuest.com, Inc.

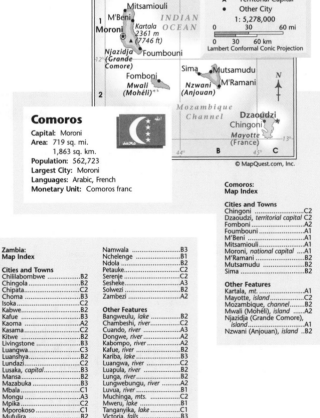

Comoros

⊛ National Capital
★ Territorial Capital
• Other City

1: 5,278,000

0   30   60 mi
0   30   60 km
Lambert Conformal Conic Projection

© MapQuest.com, Inc.

Comoros

Capital: Moroni
Area: 719 sq. mi.
1,863 sq. km.
Population: 562,723
Largest City: Moroni
Languages: Arabic, French
Monetary Unit: Comoros franc

Comoros:
Map Index

Cities and Towns
Chingoni C2
Dzaoudzi, *territorial capital* C2
Fomboni A2
Foumbouni A1
M'Beni A1
Mitsamiouli A1
Moroni, *national capital* A1
M'Ramani B2
Mutsamudu B2
Sima B2

Other Features
Kartala, *mt.* A1
Mayotte, *island* C2
Mozambique, *channel* B2
Mwali (Mohéli), *island* A2
Njazidja (Grande Comore),
island A1
Nzwani (Anjouan), *island* B2

Zambia:
Map Index

Cities and Towns
Chililabombwe B2
Chingola B2
Chipata C2
Choma B3
Isoka C2
Kabwe B2
Kafue B3
Kaoma A2
Kasama C2
Kitwe B2
Livingstone B3
Luangwa C3
Luanshya B2
Lundazi C2
Lusaka, *capital* B3
Mansa B2
Mazabuka B3
Mbala C1
Mongu A3
Mpika C2
Mporokoso C1
Mufulira B2
Mumbwa B3
Mwinilunga A2

Namwala B3
Nchelenge B1
Ndola B2
Petauke C2
Serenje C2
Sesheke A3
Solwezi B2
Zambezi A2

Other Features
Bangweulu, *lake* B2
Chambeshi, *river* C2
Cuando, *river* A3
Dongwe, *river* B2
Kabompo, *river* A2
Kafue, *river* B2
Kariba, *lake* B3
Luangwa, *river* B2
Luapula, *river* B2
Lunga, *river* B2
Lungwebungu, *river* A2
Luvua, *river* B1
Muchinga, *mts.* C2
Mweru, *lake* B1
Tanganyika, *lake* C1
Victoria, *falls* B3
Zambezi, *river* A3, B3

Zambia

Capital: Lusaka
Area: 290,586 sq. mi.
752,813 sq. km.
Population: 9,663,535
Largest City: Lusaka
Language: English
Monetary Unit: Kwacha

© MapQuest.com, Inc.

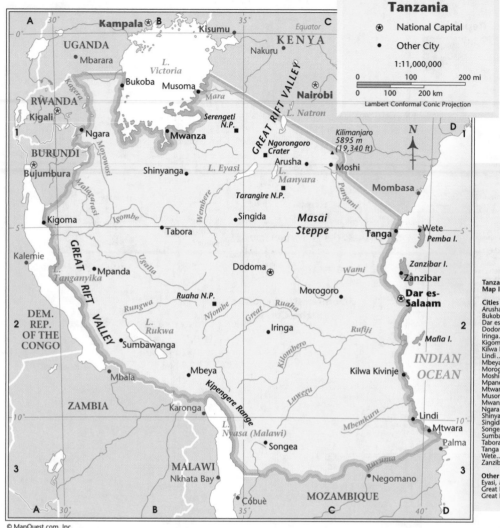

Tanzania

⊛ National Capital

• Other City

1:11,000,000

0   100   200 mi

0   100   200 km

Lambert Conformal Conic Projection

Tanzania
Capital: Dar es-Salaam, Dodoma
Area: 364,017 sq. mi.
943,049 sq. km.
Population: 31,270,820
Largest City: Dar es-Salaam
Languages: Swahili, English
Monetary Unit: Shilling

Tanzania: Map Index

Cities and Towns

Arusha	C1
Bukoba	B1
Dar es-Salaam, capital	C2
Dodoma, capital	C2
Iringa	C2
Kigoma	A1
Kilwa Kivinje	C2
Lindi	C2
Mbeya	B2
Morogoro	C2
Moshi	C1
Mpanda	B2
Mtwara	D3
Musoma	B1
Mwanza	B1
Ngara	B1
Shinyanga	B1
Singida	B1
Songea	C3
Sumbawanga	B2
Tabora	B2
Tanga	C2
Wete	C1
Zanzibar	C2

Other Features

Eyasi, lake	B1
Great Rift, valley	B2, C1
Great Ruaha, river	C2
Igombe, river	B1
Kagera, river	B1
Kilimanjaro, mt.	C1
Kilombero, river	C2
Kipengere, range	B2
Luwegu, river	C2
Mafia, island	C2
Malagarasi, river	B1
Manyara, lake	C1
Mara, river	B1
Masai, steppe	C1
Mbemkuru, river	C3
Moyowosi, river	B1
Natron, lake	C1
Ngorongoro, crater	C1
Njombe, river	B2
Nyasa (Malawi), lake	B3
Pangani, river	C1
Pemba, island	C2
Ruaha Natl. Park	B2
Rufiji, river	C2
Rukwa, lake	B2
Rungwa, river	B2
Ruvuma, river	C3
Serengeti Natl. Park	B1
Tanganyika, lake	A2
Tarangire Natl. Park	C1
Ugalla, river	B2
Victoria, lake	B1
Wami, river	C2
Wembere, river	B1
Zanzibar, island	C2

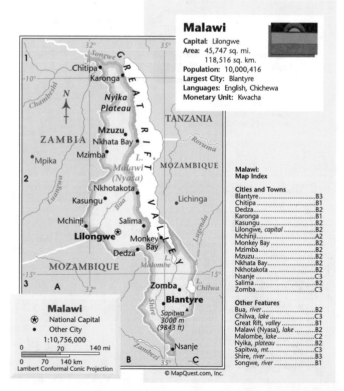

Malawi
Capital: Lilongwe
Area: 45,747 sq. mi.
118,516 sq. km.
Population: 10,000,416
Largest City: Blantyre
Languages: English, Chichewa
Monetary Unit: Kwacha

Malawi: Map Index

Cities and Towns

Blantyre	B3
Chitipa	B1
Dedza	B2
Karonga	B1
Kasungu	B2
Lilongwe, capital	B2
Mchinji	A2
Monkey Bay	B2
Mzimba	B2
Mzuzu	B2
Nkhata Bay	B2
Nkhotakota	B2
Nsanje	C3
Salima	B2
Zomba	B3

Other Features

Bua, river	B2
Chilwa, lake	C3
Great Rift, valley	B1
Malawi (Nyasa), lake	B1
Malombe, lake	C2
Nyika, plateau	B1
Sapitwa, mt.	B3
Shire, river	B3
Songwe, river	B1

Malawi
⊛ National Capital
• Other City
1:10,756,000

0   70   140 mi

0   70   140 km

Lambert Conformal Conic Projection

© MapQuest.com, Inc.

Mozambique
Capital: Maputo
Area: 313,661 sq. mi.
812,593 sq. km.
Population: 19,124,335.
Largest City: Maputo
Language: Portuguese
Monetary Unit: Metical

Mozambique: Map Index

Cities and Towns

Angoche	C3
Beira	B3
Chimoio	B3
Chinde	C3
Cuamba	C2
Inhambane	B5
Lichinga	B2
Maputo, capital	B5
Moçambique	D2
Moçimboa da Praia	D1
Nacala	D2
Nampula	C2
Pebane	C3
Pemba	D2
Quelimane	C3
Tete	B3
Vilanculos	B4
Xai-Xai	B5

Other Features

Binga, mt.	B3
Búzi, river	B4
Cabora Bassa, dam	B2
Cabora Bassa, lake	A2
Changane, river	B4
Chilwa, lake	B2
Chire, river	B3
Lebombo, mts.	A4
Limpopo, river	B4
Lugenda, river	C2
Lúrio, river	C2
Mozambique, channel	C3
Namuli, highlands	C2
Nyasa (Malawi), lake	B2
Rovuma, river	C1
Save, river	B4
Zambezi, river	B3

Mozambique
⊛ National Capital
• Other City
1:25,181,000

0   150   300 mi

0   150   300 km

Modified Lambert Conformal Conic Projection

© MapQuest.com, Inc.

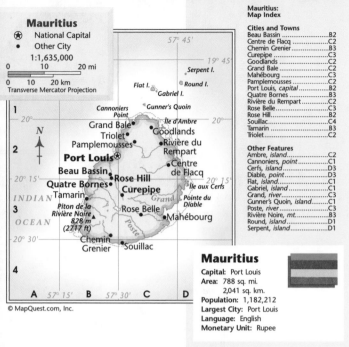

Mauritius
⊛ National Capital
• Other City
1:1,635,000
0   10   20 mi
0   10   20 km
Transverse Mercator Projection

© MapQuest.com, Inc.

Mauritius: Map Index

Cities and Towns
Beau Bassin	B2
Centre de Flacq	C2
Chemin Grenier	B3
Curepipe	C3
Goodlands	C2
Grand Bale	C2
Mahébourg	C3
Pamplemousses	C2
Port Louis, capital	B2
Quatre Bornes	B3
Rivière du Rempart	C2
Rose Belle	C3
Rose Hill	B2
Souillac	C4
Tamarin	B3
Triolet	C2

Other Features
Ambre, island	C2
Cannoniers, point	C1
Cerfs, island	D3
Diable, point	D3
Flat, island	C1
Gabriel, island	C1
Grand, river	C3
Gunner's Quoin, island	C1
Poste, river	C3
Rivière Noire, mt.	B3
Round, island	D1
Serpent, island	D1

Mauritius
Capital: Port Louis
Area: 788 sq. mi.
2,041 sq. km.
Population: 1,182,212
Largest City: Port Louis
Language: English
Monetary Unit: Rupee

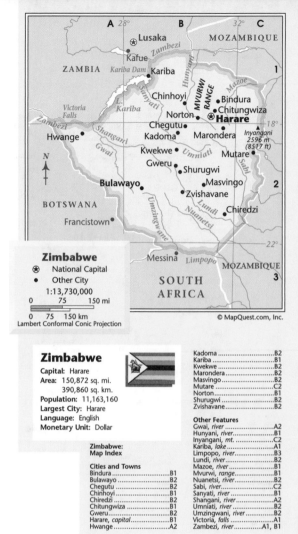

Zimbabwe
⊛ National Capital
• Other City
1:13,730,000
0   75   150 mi
0   75   150 km
Lambert Conformal Conic Projection

© MapQuest.com, Inc.

Zimbabwe
Capital: Harare
Area: 150,872 sq. mi.
390,860 sq. km.
Population: 11,163,160
Largest City: Harare
Language: English
Monetary Unit: Dollar

Zimbabwe: Map Index

Cities and Towns
Bindura	B1
Bulawayo	B2
Chegutu	B2
Chinhoyi	B1
Chiredzi	B2
Chitungwiza	B1
Gweru	B2
Harare, capital	B1
Hwange	A2
Kadoma	B2
Kariba	B1
Kwekwe	B2
Marondera	B2
Masvingo	B2
Mutare	C2
Norton	B1
Shurugwi	B2
Zvishavane	B2

Other Features
Gwai, river	A2
Hunyani, river	B1
Inyangani, mt.	C2
Kariba, lake	A1
Limpopo, river	B3
Lundi, river	B2
Mazoe, river	B1
Mvurwi, range	B1
Nuanetsi, river	B2
Sabi, river	C2
Sanyati, river	A2
Shangani, river	A2
Umniati, river	B2
Umzingwani, river	B2
Victoria, falls	A1
Zambezi, river	A1, B1

© MapQuest.com, Inc.

Botswana
⊛ National Capital
• Other City
1:16,700,000
0   75   150 mi
0   75   150 km
Lambert Conformal Conic Proj.

Botswana
Capital: Gaborone
Area: 224,607 sq. mi.
581,883 sq. km.
Population: 1,464,167
Largest City: Gaborone
Language: English
Monetary Unit: Pula

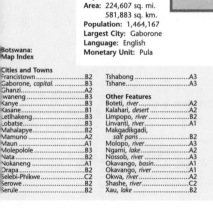

Botswana: Map Index

Cities and Towns
Francistown	B2	Tshabong	A3
Gaborone, capital	B3	Tshane	A3
Ghanzi	A2		
Jwaneng	B3	**Other Features**	
Kanye	B3	Boteti, river	A2
Kasane	B1	Kalahari, desert	A2
Letlhakeng	B3	Limpopo, river	B2
Lobatse	B3	Linvanti, river	A1
Mahalapye	B2	Makgadikgadi,	
Mamuno	A2	salt pans	B2
Maun	A1	Molopo, river	A3
Molepolole	B3	Ngami, lake	A2
Nata	B2	Nossob, river	A3
Nokaneng	A1	Okavango, basin	A1
Orapa	B2	Okavango, river	A1
Selebi-Phikwe	C2	Okwa, river	A2
Serowe	B2	Shashe, river	C2
Serule	B2	Xau, lake	B2

Madagascar
⊛ National Capital
• Other City
1:17,474,000
0   100   200 mi
0   100   200 km
Lambert Conformal Conic Projection

© MapQuest.com, Inc.

Madagascar
Capital: Antananarivo
Area: 226,658 sq. mi.
587,197 sq. km.
Population: 14,873,387
Largest City: Antananarivo
Languages: Malagasy, French
Monetary Unit: Malagasy franc

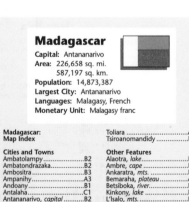

Madagascar: Map Index

Cities and Towns
Ambatolampy	B2
Ambatondrazaka	B2
Ambositra	B3
Ampanihy	A3
Andoany	B1
Antalaha	C1
Antananarivo, capital	B2
Antsirabe	B2
Antsiranana	B1
Antsohihy	B1
Farafangana	B3
Fianarantsoa	B3
Ihosy	B3
Mahajanga	B2
Maintirano	A2
Manakara	B3
Marovoay	B2
Morombe	A3
Morondava	A3
Toamasina	B2
Tôlanaro	B3

Toliara	A3
Tsiroanomandidy	B2

Other Features
Alaotra, lake	B2
Ambre, cape	B1
Ankaratra, mts.	B2
Bemaraha, plateau	A2
Betsiboka, river	B2
Kinkony, lake	B2
L'Isalo, mts.	B3
Mahajamba, river	B2
Mangoky, river	A3
Maromokotro, mt.	B1
Menarandra, river	A3
Mozambique, channel	A2
Nosy Be, island	B1
Nosy Sainte Marie, island	B2
Onilahy, river	A3
Saint-André, cape	A2
Sainte-Marie, cape	B4
Sofia, river	B2
Tsaratanana, mts.	B1
Tsiribihina, river	B2

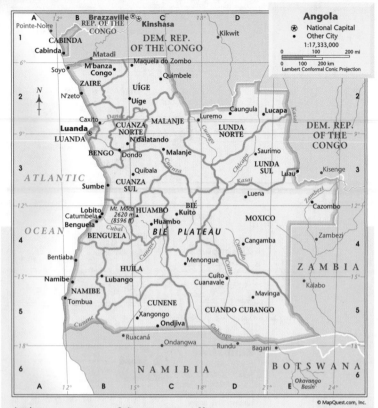

Angola

Capital: Luanda
Area: 481,354 sq. mi.
1,247,031 sq. km.
Population: 11,177,537
Largest City: Luanda
Language: Portuguese
Monetary Unit: Kwanza

Angola: Map Index

Provinces

Bengo	B3
Benguela	B4
Bié	C4
Cabinda	B1
Cuando Cubango	D5
Cuanza Norte	B2
Cuanza Sul	B3
Cunene	C5
Huambo	C4
Huila	B4
Luanda	B3
Lunda Norte	D2
Lunda Sul	D3
Malanje	C2
Moxico	D4
Namibe	B5
Uíge	C2
Zaire	B2

Cities and Towns

Benguela	B4
Bentiaba	B4
Cabinda	B1
Cangamba	D4
Catumbela	B4
Caungula	D2
Caxito	B2
Cazombo	E3
Cuíto Cuanavale	D5
Dondo	B3
Huambo	C4
Kuito	C4
Lobito	B4
Luanda, capital	B2
Luau	E3
Lubango	B5
Lucapa	D2
Luena	D3
Luremo	C2
Malanje	C2
Maquela do Zombo	C2
Mavinga	D5
Menongue	C4
Namibe	B5
N'dalatando	B3
N'zeto	B2
Ondjiva	C5
Quibala	C3
Quimbele	C2
Saurimo	D3
Soyo	B2
Sumbe	B3
Tombua	B5
Uíge	C2
Xangongo	C5

Other Features

Bié, plateau	C4
Chicapa, river	D3
Cuando, river	D4
Cuango, river	D2
Cuanza, river	C3
Cubal, river	B4
Cubango, river	D5
Cuito, river	D4
Cunene, river	B5, C4
Dande, river	B2
Kasai, river	D3
Môco, mt.	C4
Zambezi, river	E3

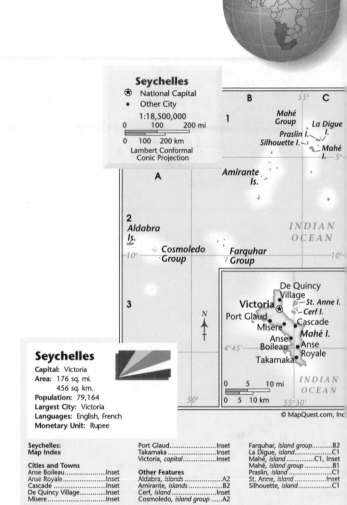

Seychelles

Capital: Victoria
Area: 176 sq. mi.
456 sq. km.
Population: 79,164
Largest City: Victoria
Languages: English, French
Monetary Unit: Rupee

Seychelles: Map Index

Cities and Towns

Anse Boileau	Inset
Anse Royale	Inset
Cascade	Inset
De Quincy Village	Inset
Misere	Inset
Port Glaud	Inset
Takamaka	Inset
Victoria, capital	Inset

Other Features

Aldabra, islands	A2
Amirante, islands	B2
Cerf, island	Inset
Cosmoledo, island group	A2
Farquhar, island group	B2
La Digue, island	C1
Mahé, island	C1, Inset
Mahé, island group	B1
Praslin, island	C1
St. Anne, island	Inset
Silhouette, island	C1

Namibia

Capital: Windhoek
Area: 318,146 sq. mi.
824,212 sq. km.
Population: 1,648,270
Largest City: Windhoek
Language: English, Afrikaans
Monetary Unit: Rand

Namibia: Map Index

Cities and Towns

Bethanien	C4
Gobabis	C2
Grootfontein	C1
Karasburg	C4
Karibib	B2
Katima Mulilo	E1
Keetmanshoop	C4
Khorixas	B2
Lüderitz	B4
Maltahöhe	B3
Mariental	C3
Okahandja	B2
Okakarara	C2
Omaruru	B2
Ondangwa	A1
Opuwo	A1
Oranjemund	B4
Oshakati	B1
Otavi	C1
Otjiwarongo	B2
Outjo	B2
Rehoboth	C3
Rundu	C1
Swakopmund	B2
Tsumeb	C1
Tsumkwe	D1
Walvis Bay	B2
Windhoek, capital	C2

Other Features

Auob, river	C3
Brandberg, mt.	B2
Caprivi, strip	D1
Eiseb, river	D2
Etosha, pan	B1
Fish, river	C4
Kalahari, desert	C3
Kaoko Veld, mts.	A1
Kaukau Veld, region	C2
Kunene, river	A1
Linyanti, river	E1
Namib, desert	A1, B3
Nossob, river	C3
Okavango, river	C1
Omatako, river	C1
Orange, river	C4
Ruacana, falls	B1
Skeleton, coast	A1
Ugab, river	B2
Zambezi, river	E1

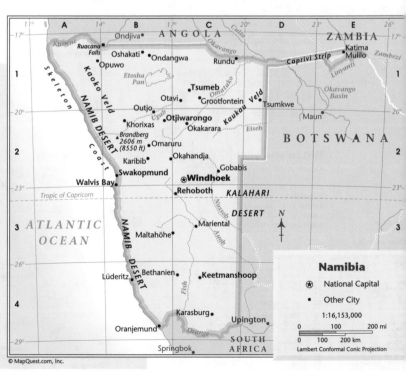

© MapQuest.com, Inc.

South Africa

* National Capital
* Other City

1:12,778,000

0   100   200 mi
0   100   200 km

Lambert Conformal Conic Projection

© MapQuest.com, Inc.

South Africa

Capital: Cape Town, Pretoria, Bloemfontein
Area: 473,290 sq. mi.
1,226,140 sq. km.
Population: 43,426,386
Largest City: Johannesburg
Languages: Afrikaans, English
Monetary Unit: Rand

South Africa: Map Index

Provinces

Eastern Cape	C3
Free State	C2
Gauteng	C2
Kwazulu Natal	C2
Northern Province	C1
North-West	B2
Mpumalanga	C2
Northern Cape	B3
Western Cape	A3

Cities and Towns

Alice	C3
Aliwal North	C3
Beaufort West	B3
Bellville	A3
Benoni	C2
Bethlehem	C2
Bloemfontein, *judicial apital*	C2
Boksburg	C2
Brakpan	C2
Calvinia	A3
Cape Town, *legislative capital*	A3
Carnarvon	B3
Cradock	C3
De Aar	B3
Durban	D2
East London	C3
Ellisras	C1
Ermelo	C2

George	B3
Germiston	C2
Graaf-Reinet	B3
Grahamstown	C3
Griquatown	B2
Johannesburg	C2
Kimberley	B2
Kroonstad	C2
Krugersdorp	C2
Kuruman	B2
Ladysmith	C2
Mafeking	C2
Messina	D1
Middelburg	C3
Mmabatho	C2
Mossel Bay	B3
Nelspruit	D2
Newcastle	C2
Oudtshoorn	B3

Pietermaritzburg	D2
Pietersburg	C1
Port Edward	D3
Port Elizabeth	C3
Port Nolloth	A2
Pretoria, *administrative capital*	C2
Queenstown	C3
Richards Bay	D2
Roodepoort	C2
Saldanha	A3
Soweto	C2
Springbok	A2
Springs	C2
Stellenbosch	A3
Sun City	C2
Uitenhage	C3
Umtata	C3
Upington	B2
Vanrhynsdorp	A3

Vereeniging	C2
Vryburg	B2
Welkom	C2
Worcester	A3

Other Features

Agulhas, *cape*	B3
Auob, *river*	A2
Bloemhof, *reservoir*	C2
Bushmanland, *plain*	A2
Caledon, *river*	C2
Drakensberg, *mts.*	C3
Good Hope, *cape*	A3
Great Fish, *river*	C3
Great Karroo, *plateau*	B3
Griqualand East, *region*	C3
Griqualand West, *region*	B2
Grootvloer, *pan*	B2
Hendrik Verwoerd, *reservoir*	C3

Kalahari, *desert*	B2
Kruger Natl. Park	D1
Langeberg, *mts.*	B3
Lebombo, *mts.*	D1
Limpopo, *river*	C1
Molopo, *river*	B2
Namib, *desert*	A2
Nossob, *river*	B2
Olifants, *river*	A3
Olifants, *river*	C1
Orange, *river*	B2
Sak, *river*	B3
St. Lucia, *lake*	D2
Swartberg, *mts.*	B3
Tugela, *river*	D2
Vaal, *reservoir*	C2
Vaal, *river*	C2
Wilge, *river*	C2
Zululand, *region*	D2

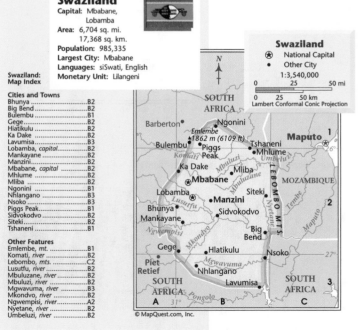

Swaziland

Capital: Mbabane, Lobamba
Area: 6,704 sq. mi.
17,368 sq. km.
Population: 985,335
Largest City: Mbabane
Languages: siSwati, English
Monetary Unit: Lilangeni

Swaziland: Map Index

Cities and Towns

Bhunya	B2
Big Bend	B2
Bulembu	B1
Gege	B2
Hiatikulu	B2
Ka Dake	B2
Lavumisa	B3
Lobamba, *capital*	B2
Mankayane	B2
Manzini	B2
Mbabane, *capital*	B2
Mhlume	B2
Mliba	B2
Ngonini	B1
Nhlangano	B3
Nsoko	B3
Piggs Peak	B1
Sidvokodvo	B2
Siteki	B2
Tshaneni	B1

Other Features

Emlembe, *mt.*	B1
Komati, *river*	B2
Lebombo, *mts.*	B2
Lusutfu, *river*	B2
Mbuluzane, *river*	B2
Mbuluzi, *river*	B2
Mgwavuma, *river*	B3
Mkondvo, *river*	B2
Ngwempisi, *river*	A2
Nyetane, *river*	B2
Umbeluzi, *river*	B2

Swaziland

* National Capital
* Other City

1:3,540,000

0   25   50 mi
0   25   50 km

Lambert Conformal Conic Projection

© MapQuest.com, Inc.

Lesotho

Capital: Maseru
Area: 11,716 sq. mi.
30,352 sq. km.
Population: 2,128,950
Largest City: Maseru
Language: English
Monetary Unit: Loti

Lesotho: Map Index

Cities and Towns

Butha-Buthe	B1
Leribe	B1
Libono	B1
Mafeteng	A2
Maseru, *capital*	A2
Mohales Hoek	A3
Mokhotlong	C2
Morija	A2
Pitseng	B2
Qachas Nek	A3
Quthing	A3
Roma	A2
Sekake	B2
Teyateyaneng	A2
Thaba-Tseka	B2

Other Features

Caledon, *river*	A1
Central, *range*	B2
Drakensberg, *mts.*	B3
Makhaleng, *river*	A2
Maloti, *mts.*	B2
Matsoku, *river*	B2
Orange, *river*	A3, B2
Sources, *river*	B1
Thabana Ntlenyana, *mt.*	C2
Tsedike, *river*	B3

Lesotho

* National Capital
* Other City

1:5,811,000

0   30   60 mi
0   30   60 km

Lambert Conformal Conic Projection

© MapQuest.com, Inc.

MAJOR CITIES

Argentina
Buenos Aires	2,961,000
Córdoba	1,148,000
Rosario	895,000

Bolivia
La Paz	739,000
Santa Cruz	833,000
El Alto	527,000

Brazil
São Paulo	10,018,000
Rio de Janeiro	5,606,000
Salvador	2,263,000
Belo Horizonte	2,097,000
Fortaleza	1,917,000
Brasília	1,738,000
Curitiba	1,409,000
Recife	1,330,000
Pôrto Alegre	1,296,000
Belém	1,168,000
Manaus	1,138,000

Chile
Santiago	4,641,000
Puente Alto	363,000

Colombia
Bogotá	4,945,000
Cali	1,666,000
Medellín	1,630,000
Barranquilla	994,000

Ecuador
Guayaquil	1,974,000
Quito	1,444,000

Falkland Islands
Stanley	1,200

French Guiana
Cayenne	41,000

Guyana
Georgetown	195,000

Paraguay
Asunción	547,000

Peru
Lima	5,682,000
Arequipa	619,000
Trujillo	509,000

Suriname
Paramaribo	216,000

Uruguay
Montevideo	1,303,000

Venezuela
Caracas	3,673,000
Maracaibo	1,221,000
Barquisimeto	954,000
Valencia	911,000

International comparability of city population
data is limited by various data inconsistencies.

CITIES
⊗ National Capital
★ Territorial Capital
● Other City

ELEVATIONS
	Feet	Meters
	13,120	4000
	6560	2000
	1640	500
	656	200
	0	0
	Below sea level	

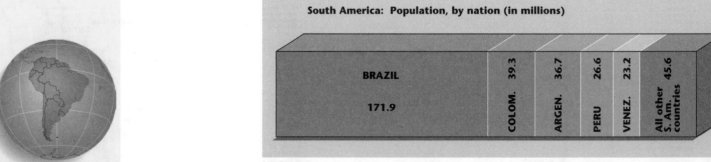

South America: Population, by nation (in millions)

BRAZIL 171.9	COLOM. 39.3	ARGEN. 36.7	PERU 26.6	VENEZ. 23.2	All other S. Am. countries 45.6

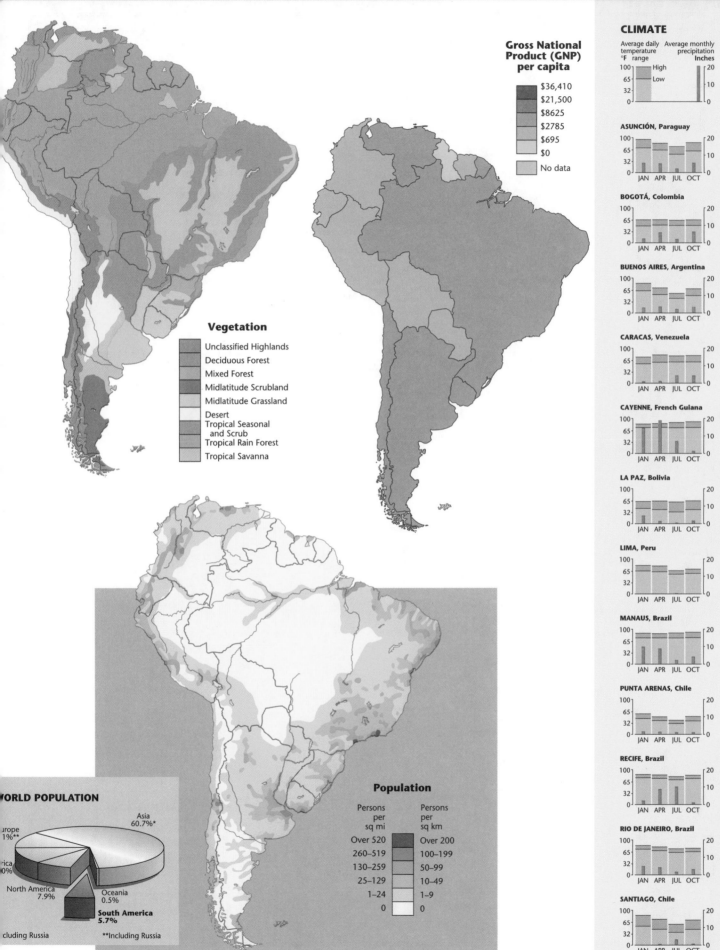

Gross National Product (GNP) per capita

- $36,410
- $21,500
- $8625
- $2785
- $695
- $0
- No data

Vegetation

- Unclassified Highlands
- Deciduous Forest
- Mixed Forest
- Midlatitude Scrubland
- Midlatitude Grassland
- Desert
- Tropical Seasonal and Scrub
- Tropical Rain Forest
- Tropical Savanna

CLIMATE

Average daily temperature °F range Average monthly precipitation Inches

ASUNCIÓN, Paraguay

BOGOTÁ, Colombia

BUENOS AIRES, Argentina

CARACAS, Venezuela

CAYENNE, French Guiana

LA PAZ, Bolivia

LIMA, Peru

MANAUS, Brazil

PUNTA ARENAS, Chile

RECIFE, Brazil

RIO DE JANEIRO, Brazil

SANTIAGO, Chile

Population

Persons per sq mi	Persons per sq km
Over 520	Over 200
260–519	100–199
130–259	50–99
25–129	10–49
1–24	1–9
0	0

WORLD POPULATION

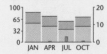

- Asia 60.7%*
- Europe 11%**
- ...rica 0%
- North America 7.9%
- Oceania 0.5%
- South America 5.7%

*...cluding Russia **Including Russia

A   **B**   **C**   **D**   **E**

BOLIVIA

Chuquicamata

PARAGUAY

Antofagasta

Tropic of Capricorn

JUJUY

Embarcación

Concepción

BRAZIL

Llullaillaco
6723 m
(22,057 ft)

San Salvador
de Jujuy

Asunción

Salta

FORMOSA

Foz do Iguaçu

Curitiba

SALTA

Formosa

Iguaçu
Falls

PACIFIC
OCEAN

San Miguel
de Tucumán

CHACO

Presidencia Roque Sáenz Peña

MISIONES

Posadas

Ojos del Salado
6880 m
(22,572 ft)

TUCUMÁN

SANTIAGO
DEL
ESTERO

Resistencia

Corrientes

CATAMARCA

Catamarca

Santiago
del Estero

CORRIENTES

Curuzú Cuatiá

Santa Maria

La Rioja

Reconquista

La Serena

LA RIOJA

SANTA FE

Pôrto Alegre

L.
dos
Patos

SAN JUAN

CÓRDOBA

San
Francisco

ENTRE
RÍOS

Mercedario
6770 m
(22,211 ft)

San Juan

Córdoba

Champaquí
2850 m
(9350 ft)

Santa Fe

Paraná

Concordia

Pelotas

Aconcagua
6960 m
(22,834 ft)

Mendoza

Villa
María

Rosario

Godoy Cruz

San Luis

Río
Cuarto

San Nicolás

URUGUAY

Santiago

Tupungato
6800 m
(22,310 ft)

SAN
LUIS

DISTRITO FEDERAL

San
Rafael

Buenos Aires

Avellaneda

Montevideo

MENDOZA

Lanús

CHILE

Lomas de
Zamora

La
Plata

Concepción

Domuyo
4709 m
(15,450 ft)

LA PAMPA

Santa Rosa

BUENOS AIRES

Cabo
San Antonio

Olavarría

Tandil

NEUQUÉN

Mar del Plata

Neuquén

Bahía Blanca

Necochea

Lanín
3776 m
(12,389 ft)

San Antonio
Oeste

ATLANTIC
OCEAN

San Carlos
de Bariloche

RÍO NEGRO

Viedma

Punta Rasa

Puerto Montt

Golfo
San Matías

Chiloé

Península Valdés

Esquel

CHUBUT

Rawson

Comodoro Rivadavia

Golfo San Jorge

Coihaique

Cabo Tres Puntas

Península
Taitao

L.
Buenos
Aires

Puerto Deseado

SANTA CRUZ

Fitzroy
3375 m
(11,073 ft)

L. San
Martín

L. Cardiel

L.
Viedma

Santa Cruz

Puerto Santa Cruz

Calafate

L.
Argentino

Bahía
Grande

West
Falkland I.

East
Falkland I.

Río Gallegos

Punta Dungeness

Stanley

Gallegos

Strait of Magellan

Falkland Islands
(Islas Malvinas)
(Br.)
(claimed by Argentina)

Punta Arenas

TIERRA
DEL
FUEGO

Ushuaia

Isla de
los Estados

Beagle
Channel

Cape Horn

A   **B**   **C**   **D**   **E**   **F**

Argentina

⊛ National Capital

★ Territorial Capital

● Other City

1:17,760,000

0   200   400 mi

0   200   400 km

Modified Chamberlain Trimetric Projection

ANDES

ATACAMA DESERT

GRAN CHACO

PAMPAS

PATAGONIA

Sierras de Córdoba

© MapQuest.com, Inc.

Argentina

Capital: Buenos Aires
Area: 1,073,518 sq. mi.
2,781,134 sq. km.
Population: 36,737,664
Largest City: Buenos Aires
Language: Spanish
Monetary Unit: Peso

Argentina:
Map Index

Provinces
Buenos Aires C4
Catamarca B2
Chaco C2
Chubut B5
Córdoba C3
Corrientes D2
Distrito Federal D3
Entre Ríos D3
Formosa D1
Jujuy B1
La Pampa B4
La Rioja B2
Mendoza B3
Misiones E2
Neuquén B5
Río Negro B5
Salta B1
San Juan B3
San Luis B3
Santa Cruz A6
Santa Fe C2
Santiago del Estero C2
Tierra del Fuego B7
Tucumán B2

Cities and Towns
Avellaneda D3
Bahía Blanca C4
Buenos Aires, *capital* D3
Calafate A7
Catamarca B2
Comodoro Rivadavia B6
Concordia D3
Córdoba C3
Corrientes D2
Curuzú Cuatiá D2
Embarcación C1
Esquel A5
Formosa D2
Godoy Cruz B3
Lanús D3

La Plata D4
La Rioja B2
Lomas de Zamora D4
Mar del Plata D4
Mendoza B3
Necochea D4
Neuquén B4
Olavarría C4
Paraná C3
Posadas D2
Presidencia Roque
Sáenz Peña C2
Puerto Deseado B6
Puerto Santa Cruz B5
Rawson B5
Reconquista D2
Resistencia D2
Río Cuarto C3
Río Gallegos B7
Rosario C3
Salta B1
San Antonio Oeste B5
San Carlos de Bariloche ...A5
San Francisco C3
San Juan B3
San Luis B3
San Miguel de Tucumán ...B2
San Nicolás C3
San Rafael B3
San Salvador de Jujuy B1
Santa Fe C3
Santa Rosa C4
Santiago del Estero C2
Tandil D4
Ushuaia B7
Viedma C5
Villa María C3

Other Features
Aconcagua, *mt.* A3
Andes, *mts.* A6–B1
Argentino, *lake* A7
Atuel, *river* B4
Beagle, *channel* B7
Bermejo, *river* C2

Blanca, *bay* C4
Buenos Aires, *lake* A6
Cardiel, *lake* A6
Champaquí, *mt.* C3
Chico, *river* B6
Chubut, *river* A5
Colorado, *river* B4
Córdoba, *range* B3
Desaguadero, *river* B2
Deseado, *river* B6
Domuyo, *volcano* A4
Dungeness, *point* B7
Estados, *island* B7
Fitzroy, *mt.* A6
Gallegos, *river* A7
Gran Chaco, *region* C1
Grande, *bay* B7
Iguaçu, *falls* E2
Iguaçu, *river* E2
Lanín, *volcano* A4
Llullaillaco, *volcano* B1
Magellan, *strait* B7
Mar Chiquita, *lake* C3
Mercedario, *mt* B3
Negro, *river* B4
Ojos del Salado, *mt.* B2
Pampas, *plain* C4
Paraguay, *river* D2
Paraná, *river* D2
Patagonia, *region* A6
Pilcomayo, *river* C1
Plata, Río de la, *estuary* ..D3
Rasa, *point* C5
Salado, *river* B4
Salado, *river* C2
San Antonio, *cape* D4
San Jorge, *gulf* B6
San Martín, *lake* A6
San Matías, *gulf* C5
Santa Cruz, *river* A7
Tres Puntas, *cape* B6
Tupungato, *mt.* B3
Uruguay, *river* D3
Valdés, *peninsula* C5
Viedma, *lake* A6

Paraguay

 National Capital
• Other City

1:10,375,000

0   50   100 mi
0   50   100 km
Conic Equidistant Projection

© MapQuest.com, Inc.

Paraguay

Capital: Asunción
Area: 157,048 sq. mi.
406,752 sq. km.
Population: 5,434,095
Largest City: Asunción
Language: Spanish
Monetary Unit: Guaraní

Paraguay:
Map Index

Departments
Alto Paraguay C2
Alto Paraná E4
Amambay E3
Asunción D4
Boquerón B3
Caaguazú D4
Caazapá D5
Canendiyú E4
Central D4
Concepción D3
Cordillera D4
Guairá D4
Itapúa E5
Misiones D5
Neembucú C5
Paraguarí D5
Presidente Hayes C4
San Pedro D4

Cities and Towns
Abaí...............................E4
Asunción, *capital* D4
Caacupé D4
Caaguazú E4
Caazapá D5
Capitán Pablo Lagerenza ..B1
Ciudad del Este E4
Concepción D3
Coronel Oviedo D4
Doctor Pedro P. Peña A3
Encarnación E5

Filadelfia........................B3
Fuerte Olimpo D2
General
Eugenio A. Garay A2
Mariscal Estigarribia B3
Paraguarí D4
Pedro Juan Caballero E3
Pilar C5
Pozo Colorado C3
Puerto Bahía C2
Puerto Pinasco D3
Salto del Guairá E4
San Juan Bautista D5
San Lorenzo D4
San Pedro D4
Villa Hayes D4
Villarrica D4

Other Features
Acaray, *river* E4
Amambay, *mts.* E3
Apa, *river* D3
Chaco Boreal, *region* B2
Gran Chaco, *region* B3
Iguazú, *falls* E4
Itaipú, *reservoir* E4
Jejuí-Guazú, *river* D4
Montelindo, *river* C3
Paraguay, *river* C2, C5
Paraná, *river* C5, E5
Pilcomayo, *river* B3, C4
Tebicuary, *river* D5
Verde, *river* C3
Ypané, *river* D3
Ypoá, *lake* D4

Uruguay

 National Capital
• Other City

1:6,625,000

0   40   80 mi
0   40   80 km
Lambert Conformal Conic Projection

© MapQuest.com, Inc.

Uruguay

Capital: Montevideo
Area: 68,037 sq. mi.
176,215 sq. km.
Population: 3,308,523
Largest City: Montevideo
Language: Spanish
Monetary Unit: New peso

Uruguay:
Map Index

Cities and Towns
Artigas B1
Bella Unión B1
Canelones B3
Carmelo A2
Colonia B3
Durazno B2
Florida B3
Fray Bentos A2
Las Piedras B3
Melo C2
Mercedes A2
Minas C3
Montevideo, *capital* B3
Nueva Palmira A2
Pando C3
Paso de los Toros B2
Paysandú A2
Piedra Sola B2
Punta del Este C3
Rivera C1
Rocha C3
Salto B1
San Carlos C3
San José B3
Tacuarembó C1
Treinta y Tres C2
Trinidad B2

Other Features
Arapey Grande, *river* B1
Baygorria, *lake* B2
Cebollatí, *river* C2
Cuareim, *river* B1
Daymán, *river* B1
Grande, *range* C2
Haedo, *range* B2
Merín, *lagoon* D2
Mirador Nacional, *mt.* C3
Negra, *lagoon* D2
Negro, *river* B2
Paso de Palmar, *lake* B2
Plata, *river* B3
Queguay Grande, *river* B2
Rincón del Bonete, *lake* ...B2
Salto Grande, *reservoir* ...B1
San José, *river* B2
San Salvador, *river* A2
Santa Ana, *range* C1
Santa Lucía, *river* B3
Tacuarembó, *river* C1
Tacuarí, *river* C2
Uruguay, *river* A1
Yaguarí, *river* C1
Yaguarón, *river* D2
Yi, *river* C2

Chile

Capital: Santiago
Area: 292,135 sq. mi.
756,826 sq. km.
Population: 14,973,843
Largest City: Santiago
Language: Spanish
Monetary Unit: Peso

Chile:
Map Index

Regions
Aisén del General Carlos
  Ibáñez del Campo B8
Antofagasta C2
Atacama B3
Bío-Bío B6
Coquimbo B4
El Libertador General
  Bernardo O'Higgins B4
La Araucanía B6
Los Lagos B7
Magallanes y Antártica
  Chilena B9
Maule B5, B6
Región Metropolitana B4,
  Inset
Tarapacá C1
Valparaíso ....B4, Inset

Cities and Towns
Aguada de Cachinal C2
Aguas Blancas C2
Algarrobo ....Inset
Altamira C3
Ancud B7
Angol B6
Antofagasta B2
Arica B1
Balmaceda B8
Calama C2
Casablanca ....Inset
Cerro Castillo B9
Castro B7
Chaitén B7
Chañaral B3
Chiapa C1
Chile Chico B8
Chillán B6
Chuquicamata C2
Cochrane B8
Coihaique B8
Colina ....Inset
Collaguasi C2
Concepción B6
Conchalí ....Inset
Constitución B5
Copiapó B3
Coquimbo B3
Curicó B4
El Tabo ....Ins
El Trebolar ....Ins
Freirina ....B
Gatico C
Illapel ....B
Iquique C
Lampa ....Ins
La Serena ....B
Lebu ....B
Linares ....B
Los Andes ....B
Los Ángeles ....B
Maipú ....Ins
Mamiña ....Ins
Melipilla ....Ins
Ñuñoa ....Ins
Osorno ....B
Ovalle ....B
Parral ....B
Pisagua ....B
Porvenir ....B
Potrerillos C
Puente Alto ....Ins
Puerto Aisén ....Ins
Puerto Cisnes ....B
Puerto Montt ....B
Puerto Natales ....B
Puerto Varas C
Puerto Williams C
Punta Arenas C
Punta Delgada C
Putre C
Quellón ....B
Quillota ....B
Quilpué ....Ins
Rancagua ....B
Rungue ....Ins
San Antonio ....B4, Ins
San Bernardo ....Ins
San Félix ....B
San Fernando ....B
San Pedro de Atacama C
Santa Inés ....Inse
Santiago, capital .....B4, Ins
Socompa C
Talagante ....Ins
Talca ....B
Talcahuano ....B
Taltal ....B
Temuco ....B
Tilomonte C
Tocopilla ....B
Tomé ....B
Unión ....B
Valdivia ....B
Vallenar ....B
Valparaíso ....B4, Ins
Victoria ....B
Viña del Mar ....B4, Inse

Other Features
Aconcagua, river ....B
Ancud, gulf ....B
Andes, mts. ....B8, C
Atacama, desert C
Bascuñán, cape C
Bío-Bío, river ....B
Brunswick, peninsula ......B
Buenos Aires, lake C
Campana, island ....A
Chiloé, island ....B
Chonos, archipelago ....B
Cochrane, lake ....B
Concepción, bay ....B
Copiapó, river ....B
Corcovado, gulf ....B
Desolación, island ....B
Domeyko, mts. C
Dungeness, point C
Duque de York, island .....A
Elqui, river ....B
Fitzroy, mt. ....B
Galera, point ....B
Horn, cape C
Hoste, island C
Imperial, river ....B
Lanín, volcano ....B
Lengua de Vaca, point .....B
Llanquihue, lake ....B
Llullaillaco, volcano ....B
Loa, river ....B
Madre de Dios, island .....A
Magdalena, island ....B
Magellan, strait ....B
Maipo, river ....B4, Inse
Maule, river ....B
Navarino, island C
Occidental, mts. C
Ojos del Salado, mt. C
Ollagüe, volcano C
Penas, gulf ....B
Rapel, river ....B
Reina Adelaida, archipelago B
San Martín, lake ....B
San Valentín, mt. ....B
Santa Inés, island ....B
Taitao, peninsula ....A
Tierra del Fuego, island ...C
Toltén, river ....A
Wellington, island ....A

Chile
⊛ National Capital
• Other City

1:22,062,000
0   100   200 mi
0   100   200 km
Modified Chamberlain Trimetric Projection

REGIÓN METROPOLITANA
0   10   20 mi
0   10   20 km

Peru

Capital: Lima
Area: 496,225 sq. mi.
1,285,216 sq. km.
Population: 26,624,582
Largest City: Lima
Languages: Spanish, Quechua
Monetary Unit: Nuevo Sol

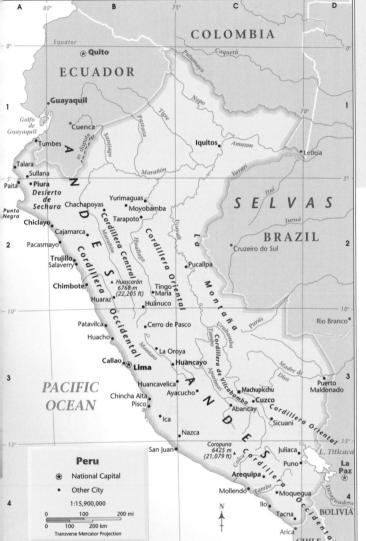

Peru
⊛ National Capital
• Other City
1:15,900,000
0 100 200 mi
0 100 200 km
Transverse Mercator Projection

Peru: Map Index

Cities and Towns
Abancay	C3
Arequipa	C4
Ayacucho	C3
Cajamarca	B2
Callao	B3
Cerro de Pasco	B3
Chachapoyas	B2
Chiclayo	B2
Chimbote	B2
Chincha Alta	B3
Cuzco	C3
Huacho	B3
Huancavelica	B3
Huancayo	B3
Huánuco	B2
Huaraz	B2
Ica	B3
Ilo	C4
Iquitos	C1
Juliaca	C4
La Oroya	B3
Lima, capital	B3
Mollendo	C4
Moquegua	C4

Moyobamba	B2
Nazca	C3
Pacasmayo	B2
Paita	A2
Patavilca	B3
Pisco	B3
Piura	A2
Pucallpa	C2
Puerto Maldonado	D3
Puno	C4
Salaverry	B2
San Juan	B4
Sicuani	C3
Sullana	A1
Tacna	C4
Talara	A1
Tarapoto	B2
Tingo María	B2
Trujillo	B2
Tumbes	A1
Yurimaguas	B2

Other Features
Amazon, river	C1
Andes, mts.	B1, C3
Apurímac, river	C3
Central, mts.	B2
Colca, river	C4

Coropuna, mt.	C4
Guayaquil, gulf	A1
Huallaga, river	B2
Huascarán, mt.	B2
La Montaña, region	C2
Machupicchu, ruins	C3
Madre de Dios, river	C3
Mantaro, river	B3
Marañón, river	B1, B2
Napo, river	C1
Negra, point	A2
Occidental, mts.	B2, C4
Oriental, mts.	B2, C3
Pastaza, river	B1
Purús, river	C1
Putumayo, river	C1
Santiago, river	B1
Sechura, desert	A2
Tambo, river	C3
Tambo, river	C4
Tigre, river	B1
Titicaca, lake	D4
Ucayali, river	C2
Urubamba, river	C3
Vilcabamba, mts.	C3
Yavarí, river	C1

© MapQuest.com, Inc.

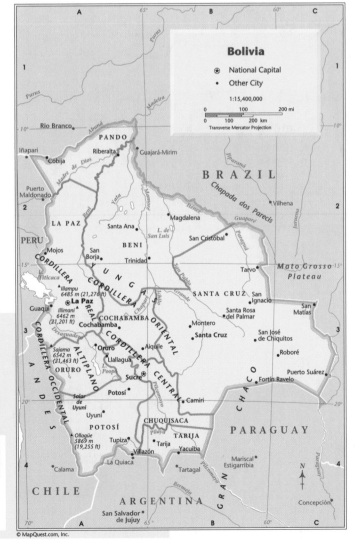

Bolivia
⊛ National Capital
• Other City
1:15,400,000
0 100 200 mi
0 100 200 km
Transverse Mercator Projection

Bolivia: Map Index

Departments
Beni	A2
Chuquisaca	B4
Cochabamba	A3
La Paz	A2
Oruro	A3
Pando	A2
Potosí	A4
Santa Cruz	B3
Tarija	B4

Cities and Towns
Aiquile	A3
Camiri	B4
Cobija	A2
Cochabamba	A3
Fortín Ravelo	B3
Guaqui	A3
La Paz, capital	A3
Llallagua	A3
Magdalena	A2
Mojos	A2
Montero	B3
Oruro	A3
Potosí	A4
Puerto Suárez	C3
Riberalta	A2
Roboré	C3
San Borja	A2

San Cristóbal	B2
San Ignacio	B3
San José de Chiquitos	B3
San Matías	C3
Santa Ana	A2
Santa Cruz	B3
Santa Rosa del Palmar	B3
Sucre, capital	A3
Tarija	B4
Tarvo	B3
Trinidad	B2
Tupiza	A4
Uyuni	A4
Villazón	A4
Yacuiba	B4

Other Features
Abuná, river	A2
Altiplano, plateau	A3
Beni, river	A2
Chaparé, river	A3
Cordillera Central, mts.	A3
Cordillera Occidental, mts.	A3
Cordillera Oriental, mts.	A3
Cordillera Real, mts.	A3
Desaguadero, river	A3
Gran Chaco, region	B4
Grande, river	B3
Guaporé, river	B2
Ichilo, river	B3
Illampu, mt.	A3
Illimani, mt.	A3

Iténez, river	B2
Madre de Dios, river	A2
Mamoré, river	A2
Ollagüe, volcano	A4
Paraguá, river	B2
Paraguay, river	C4
Pilaya, river	B4
Pilcomayo, river	B3
Poopó, lake	A3
Sajama, mt.	A3
Salar de Uyuni, salt flat	A4
San Luis, lake	B2
San Pablo, river	B3
Titicaca, lake	A3
Yata, river	A2
Yungas, region	A3

Bolivia

Capital: La Paz, Sucre
Area: 424,164 sq. mi.
1,098,871 sq. km.
Population: 7,982,850
Largest City: La Paz
Languages: Spanish, Quechua, Aymara
Monetary Unit: Boliviano

© MapQuest.com, Inc.

Caribbean Sea

PANAMA

PACIFIC OCEAN

VENEZUELA

ECUADOR

PERU

BRAZIL

Colombia

⊛ National Capital
● Other City

1:13,825,000

0   100   200 mi
0 100 200 km
Transverse Mercator Projection

© MapQuest.com, Inc.

Colombia

Capital: Bogotá
Area: 440,831 sq. mi.
   1,142,049 sq. km.
Population: 39,309,422
Largest City: Bogotá
Language: Spanish
Monetary Unit: Peso

Colombia:
Map Index

Internal Divisions

Amazonas (commissary)	B5
Antioquia (dept.)	B3
Arauca (intendency)	C3
Atlántico (dept.)	B2
Bolívar (dept.)	B2
Boyacá (dept.)	B3
Caldas (dept.)	B3
Capital District	B4
Caquetá (dept.)	B4
Casanare (intendency)	C3
Cauca (dept.)	A4
César (dept.)	B2
Chocó (dept.)	A3
Córdoba (dept.)	B2
Cundinamarca (dept.)	B3
Guainía (commissary)	C4
Guaviare (commissary)	B4
Huila (dept.)	A4
La Guajira (dept.)	B2
Magdalena (dept.)	B2
Meta (dept.)	B4
Nariño (dept.)	A4
Norte de Santander (dept.)	B2
Putumayo (intendency)	A4
Quindío (dept.)	B3
Risaralda (dept.)	B3
San Andrés y Providencia (intendency)	Inset
Santander (dept.)	B2
Sucre (dept.)	B2
Tolima (dept.)	B4
Valle del Cauca (dept.)	A4
Vaupés (commissary)	C4
Vichada (commissary)	C3

Cities and Towns

Arauca	C3
Armenia	B3
Barrancabermeja	B3
Barranquilla	B2
Bogotá, *capital*	B3
Bucaramanga	B3
Buenaventura	A4
Cali	A4
Cartagena	B2
Cravo Norte	C3
Cúcuta	B3
El Encanto	B5
Florencia	B4
Ibagué	B3
Leticia	C6
Manizales	B3
Medellín	B3
Miraflores	B4
Mitú	C4

Mocoa	A4
Montería	B2
Neiva	B4
Orocué	C3
Palmira	A4
Pasto	A4
Pereira	B3
Popayán	A4
Puerto Carreño	D3
Puerto Inírida	D4
Puerto Leguízamo	B5
Quibdó	A3
Riohacha	B2
San Felipe	D4
San José del Guaviare	B4
Santa Marta	B2
Sincelejo	B2
Tumaco	A4
Tunja	B3
Turbo	A2
Valledupar	B2
Villavicencio	B3
Vista Hermosa	B4
Yopal	B3

Other Features

Albuquerque, *cays*	Inset
Amazon, *river*	C5
Andes, *range*	A4
Apaporis, *river*	C4
Atrato, *river*	A3
Caquetá, *river*	B5
Cauca, *river*	B3
Cordillera Central, *range*	A4
Cordillera Occidental, *range*	A4
Cordillera Oriental, *range*	B4
Cristóbal Colón, *peak*	B2
Gallinas, *point*	C1
Guainía, *river*	C4
Guajira, *peninsula*	C1
Guaviare, *river*	C4
Huila, *mt.*	A4
Llanos, *prairie*	C3
Magdalena, *river*	B3
Meta, *river*	C3
Orinoco, *river*	D3
Patía, *river*	A4
Providencia, *island*	Inset
Putumayo, *river*	B5
Roncador, *cay*	Inset
San Andrés, *island*	Inset
San Juan, *river*	A3
Serranilla, *bank*	Inset
Sierra Nevada de Santa Marta, *mts.*	B2
Tolima, *mt.*	B3
Vaupés, *river*	B4
Vichada, *river*	C3

Venezuela:
Map Index

Internal Divisions

Amazonas (territory)	C3
Anzoátegui (state)	D2
Apure (state)	C2
Aragua (state)	C2
Barinas (state)	C2
Bolívar (state)	D2
Carabobo (state)	C2
Cojedes (state)	C2
Delta Amacuro (territory)	D2
Dependencias Federales	C1
Distrito Federal	C1
Falcón (state)	B1
Guárico (state)	C2
Lara (state)	B1
Mérida (state)	B2
Miranda (state)	C1
Monagas (state)	D2
Nueva Esparta (state)	D1
Portuguesa (state)	C2
Sucre (state)	D1
Táchira (state)	B2
Trujillo (state)	B2
Yaracuy (state)	C1
Zulia (state)	B2

Cities and Towns

Acarigua	C2
Anaco	D2
Barcelona	D1
Barinas	B2
Barquisimeto	C1
Baruta	C1
Cabimas	B1
Calabozo	C2
Canaima	D2
Caracas, *capital*	C1
Carora	C1
Carúpano	D1
Ciudad Bolívar	D2
Ciudad Guayana	D2
Coro	C1
Cumaná	D1
El Tigre	D2
Guanare	C2
Güiria	D1
La Asunción	D1
La Guaira Maiquetía	C1
Los Teques	C1
Maiquetía	C1
Maracaibo	B1
Maracay	C1
Maturín	D2
Mérida	B2

Petare	C1
Puerto Ayacucho	C2
Puerto Cabello	C1
Puerto La Cruz	D1
Punto Fijo	B1
San Cristóbal	B2
San Felipe	C1
San Fernando de Apure	C2
San Juan de Los Morros	C2
Santa Elena de Uairén	D3
Trujillo	B2
Tucupita	D2
Valencia	C1
Valera	B2

Other Features

Angel, *falls*	D2
Apure, *river*	C2
Arauca, *river*	C2
Bolívar, *mt.*	B2
Caroní, *river*	D2
Casiquiare, *river*	C3
Caura, *river*	D2
Cojedes, *river*	C2
Guri, *reservoir*	D2
Guiana, *highlands*	D2
La Tortuga, *island*	C1
Llanos, *plain*	B2

Maracaibo, *lake*	B2
Margarita, *island*	D1
Mérida, *mts.*	B2
Meta, *river*	C2
Neblina, *mt.*	C3
Negro, *river*	B3
Orinoco, *river*	C3, D2
Pacaraima, *mts.*	D3
Paria, *gulf*	D1
Parima, *mts.*	D3
Roraima, *mt.*	D2
Venezuela, *gulf*	B1

Venezuela

Capital: Caracas
Area: 352,144 sq. mi.
   912,050 sq. km.
Population: 23,203,466
Largest City: Caracas
Language: Spanish
Monetary Unit: Bolívar

COLOMBIA

Tumaco
San Lorenzo
Pasto
Punta Galera
Esmeraldas
ESMERALDAS
Tulcán
CARCHI
IMBABURA
Ibarra
Puerto Asís
PICHINCHA
Otavalo
Cayambe
5790 m
(18,996 ft)
Nueva Loja
SUCUMBÍOS
Quito
Cotopaxi
5897 m
(19,347 ft)
Santo Domingo
de los Colorados
NAPO
Nuevo
Rocafuerte
PACIFIC
OCEAN
Equator
Bahía de Manta
Manta
MANABÍ
Quevedo
Chone
Chimborazo
6267 m
(20,561 ft)
Latacunga
Tena
Ambato
TUNGURAHUA
Puyo
Cabo San Lorenzo
Portoviejo
Isla de la Plata
Jipijapa
LOS
RÍOS
Guaranda
BOLÍVAR
Riobamba
PASTAZA
Babahoyo
CHIMBORAZO
Punta Santa Elena
Milagro
GUAYAS
Macas
La Libertad
Guayaquil
Isla
Puná
CAÑAR
Azogues
MORONA-
SANTIAGO
Golfo de
Guayaquil
Cuenca
AZUAY
Puerto Bolívar
Machala
Santa Rosa
Tumbes
EL ORO
Loja
Zamora
ZAMORA-
CHINCHIPE
Sullana
LOJA
Borja

PERU

CORDILLERA OCCIDENTAL
CORDILLERA ORIENTAL
ANDES

GALÁPAGOS (inset)

Isla Pinta
Isla Marchena
Wolf
1707 m
(5602 ft)
Isla
San Salvador
Isla
Fernandina
GALÁPAGOS
Isla
Santa Cruz
Isla
Isabela
Baquerizo
Moreno
Isla San
Cristóbal
Isla
Santa María
Isla
Española
PACIFIC
OCEAN
0 20 40 mi
0 20 40 km

Ecuador

Capital: Quito
Area: 105,037 sq. mi.
272,117 sq. km.
Population: 12,562,496
Largest City: Guayaquil
Language: Spanish
Monetary Unit: Sucre

**Ecuador:
Map Index**

Provinces

Azuay B4
Bolívar B3
Cañar B4
Carchi C2
Chimborazo B3
Cotopaxi B3
El Oro B4
Esmeraldas B2
Galápagos .... Inset
Guayas A4
Imbabura B2
Loja B5
Los Ríos B3
Manabí A3
Morona-Santiago C4
Napo C3
Pastaza C3
Pichincha B2
Sucumbíos C2
Tungurahua B3
Zamora-Chinchipe B5

Cities and Towns

Ambato B3
Azogues B4
Babahoyo B3
Baquerizo Moreno .... Inset
Chone A3
Cuenca B4

Esmeraldas B2
Guaranda B3
Guayaquil B4
Ibarra B2
Jipijapa A3
La Libertad A4
Latacunga B3
Loja B4
Macas B4
Machala B4
Manta A3
Milagro B4
Nueva Loja C2
Nuevo Rocafuerte D3
Otavalo B2
Portoviejo A3
Puerto Bolívar B4
Puyo B3
Quevedo B3
Quito, capital B3
Riobamba B3
San Lorenzo B2
Santa Rosa B4
Santo Domingo
  de los Colorados ... B3
Tena C3
Tulcán C2
Zamora B5

Other Features

Aguarico, river C3
Andes, mts. B4
Cayambe, mt. C3

Chimborazo, mt. B3
Chira, river A5
Cordillera Occidental, mts. .. B4
Cordillera Oriental, mts. .. C4
Cotopaxi, mt. B3
Curaray, river C3
Daule, river B3
Española, island ...... Inset
Fernandina, island ... Inset
Galera, point A2
Guaillabamba, river .. B2
Guayaquil, gulf A4
Guayas, river B4
Isabela, island .... Inset
Manta, bay A3
Marchena, island .... Inset
Napo, river C3
Pastaza, river C3
Pinta, island .... Inset
Plata, island A3
Puná, island A4
Putumayo, river D2
San Cristóbal, island . Inset
San Lorenzo, cape ... A3
San Salvador, island . Inset
Santa Cruz, island ... Inset
Santa Elena, point ... A4
Santa María, island .. Inset
Santiago, river B4
Tigre, river C3
Vinces, river B3
Wolf, mt. .... Inset
Zamora, river B4

Ecuador
⊛ National Capital
• Other City
1:8,250,000
0 40 80 mi
0 40 80 km
Transverse Mercator Projection

Venezuela map

Caribbean Sea
NETHERLANDS ANTILLES
(Neth.)
Willemstad
DEPENDENCIAS
FEDERALES
GRENADA
St. George's
Ríohacha
Punto Fijo
Coro
Golfo de
Venezuela
FALCÓN
La Guaira
Maiquetía
NUEVA
ESPARTA
Isla de
Margarita
La Asunción
TRINIDAD
AND TOBAGO
Barranquilla
Maracaibo
Puerto Cabello
Maracay
Caracas
Isla
La Tortuga
Carúpano
Güiria
Port of
Spain
Cartagena
Valledupar
Cabimas
LARA
San Felipe
YARACUY
DISTRITO FEDERAL
Petare
Baruta
SUCRE
Cumaná
Gulf of
Paria
Carora
Barquisimeto
Valencia
Los Teques
Barcelona
Puerto
La Cruz
Maturín
ATLANTIC
OCEAN
L.
Maracaibo
Trujillo
Acarigua
COJEDES
CARABOBO
San Juan
de los Morros
ARAGUA
MIRANDA
Anaco
MONAGAS
Tucupita
DELTA
ZULIA
Valera
PORTUGUESA
Guanare
Calabozo
GUÁRICO
El Tigre
ANZOÁTEGUI
AMACURO
Mabaruma
MÉRIDA
Mérida
Cordillera de Mérida
Barinas
Pico Bolívar
5007 m
(16,427 ft)
BARINAS
Ciudad
Guayana
TÁCHIRA
Cúcuta
San Cristóbal
San Fernando
de Apure
Ciudad
Bolívar
Georgetown
Bucaramanga
Guri
Res.
Arauca
APURE
BOLÍVAR
Cuyuni
Nieuw Nickerie
Medellín
LLANOS
Meta
Puerto
Carreño
Orinoco
Canaima
Angel
Falls
Mt. Roraima
2772 m
(9094 ft)
GUYANA
COLOMBIA
Puerto Ayacucho
GUIANA HIGHLANDS
Bogotá
Caura
Caroní
Santa Elena
de Uairén
Lethem
SURINAME
Guaviare
Puerto
Inírida
AMAZONAS
Sierra Pacaraima
Uraricoera
Essequibo
Courantyne
Guainía
Orinoco
Sierra
Parima
Boa Vista
Branco
Acarai Mts.
Pico da Neblina
3014 m
(9889 ft)
BRAZIL
Uaupés
Casiquiare
Negro
Cafuini
ANDES
Magdalena
Cauca
Arauca
Apure

Venezuela
⊛ National Capital
• Other City
1:11,110,000
0 100 200 mi
0 100 200 km
Transverse Mercator Projection

Guyana

Capital: Georgetown
Area: 83,000 sq. mi.
  214,969 sq. km.
Population: 705,156
Largest City: Georgetown
Language: English
Monetary Unit: Guyana dollar

Guyana
★ National Capital
• Other City
1:10,660,000

0   75   150 mi
0   75   150 km
Transverse Mercator Projection

© MapQuest.com, Inc.

Guyana:
Map Index

Cities and Towns
Anna Regina....................B2
Apoteri...........................B4
Bartica..........................B2
Biloku............................B5
Charity...........................B2
Georgetown, capital.........B2
Isherton.........................B4
Lethem...........................B4
Linden............................B3
Mabaruma.......................B1
Mahdia...........................B3
Matthews Ridge...............A2
New Amsterdam...............C2
Suddie...........................B2

Other Features
Acarai, mts. B5
Barama, river...................B2
Berbice, river..................B3
Courantyne, river.............B3
Cuyuni, river...................A2
Demerara, river...............B3
Essequibo, river..........B3, B5
Kaieteur, falls.................B3
Kanuku, mts. B4
Mazaruni, river................A2
Merume, mts. A2
New, river.......................C4
Pakaraima, mts. A3
Potaro, river...................B3
Rawa, river......................B4
Roraima, mt. A3
Takutu, river...................B4

Suriname

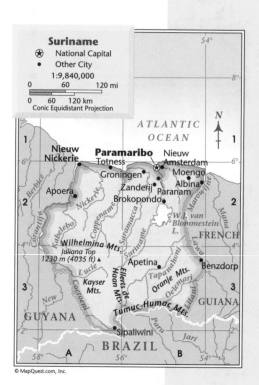

© MapQuest.com, Inc.

Suriname
★ National Capital
• Other City
1:9,840,000

0   60   120 mi
0   60   120 km
Conic Equidistant Projection

Suriname

Capital: Paramaribo
Area: 63,037 sq. mi.
  163,265 sq. km.
Population: 431,156
Largest City: Paramaribo
Language: Dutch
Monetary Unit: Suriname guilder

Suriname:
Map Index

Cities and Towns
Albina...........................B2
Apetina.........................B3
Apoera..........................A2
Benzdorp.......................B3
Brokopondo B2
Groningen......................B2
Moengo.........................B2
Nieuw Amsterdam B2
Nieuw Nickerie................A2
Paramaribo, capital..........B2
Paranam.........................B2
Sipaliwini......................A3
Totness.........................A2
Zanderij.........................B2

Other Features
Coeroeni, river................A3
Coppename, river.............A2
Corantijn, river...............A2
Ellerts de Haan, mts. A3
Juliana Top, mt. A3
Kabelebo, river................A2
Kayser, mts. A3
Lawa, river......................B2
Litani, river....................B3
Lucie, river.....................A3
Marowijne, river B2
Nickerie, river.................A2
Oelemari, river................B3
Oranje, mts. B3
Saramacca, river..............B3
Suriname, river...............B3
Tapanahoni, river............B3
Tumuc-Humac, mts. B3
Wilhelmina, mts. A2
W.J. van Blommestein, lake.......B2

French Guiana

French Guiana:
Map Index

Cities and Towns
Apatou...........................A1
Cacao............................B1
Camopi..........................B2
Cayenne, capital..............B1
Grand Santi....................A1
Iracoubo........................B1
Kaw...............................B1
Kourou...........................B1
Mana.............................B1
Maripasoula....................A2
Ouanary.........................C1
Régina...........................B1
Rémire...........................B1
Saint-Élie.......................B1
Saint-Georges C2
Saint-Laurent du Maroni....A1
Saül..............................B2

Other Features
Camopi, river..................B2
Devil's, island.................B1
Lawa, river......................A2
Litani, river....................A2
Mana, river.....................B1
Maroni, river...................A1
Oyapock, river.................B2
Salut, islands..................B1
Tampok, river..................B2
Tumuc-Humac, mts. A2

French Guiana

Capital: Cayenne
Area: 35,135 sq. mi.
  91,000 sq. km.
Population: 167,982
Largest City: Cayenne
Language: French
Monetary Unit: French franc

© MapQuest.com, Inc.

French Guiana
★ Territorial Capital
• Other City
1:8,410,000

0   50   100 mi
0   50   100 km
Conic Equidistant Projection

Brazil

Capital: Brasília
Area: 3,286,470 sq. mi.
8,514,171 sq. km.
Population: 171,853,126
Largest City: São Paulo
Language: Portuguese
Monetary Unit: Real

Brazil: Map Index

States and Federal District

Acre	A2
Alagoas	E2
Amapá	C1
Amazonas	B2
Bahia	D3
Ceará	E2
Espírito Santo	D3
Federal District	D3
Goiás	D3
Maranhão	D2
Mato Grosso	C3
Mato Grosso do Sul	C4
Minas Gerais	D3
Pará	C2
Paraíba	E2
Paraná	C4
Pernambuco	E2
Piauí	D2
Rio de Janeiro	D4, Inset I
Rio Grande do Norte	E2
Rio Grande do Sul	C4
Rondônia	B3
Roraima	B1
Santa Catarina	C4
São Paulo	C4, Inset II
Sergipe	E3
Tocantins	D3

Cities and Towns

Alagoinhas	E3
Altamira	C2
Anápolis	D3
Aracaju	E3
Bacabal	D2
Bauru	D4
Belém	D2
Belford Roxo	Inset I
Belo Horizonte	D3
Boa Vista	B1
Bom Jesus da Lapa	D3
Brasília, *capital*	D3
Cáceres	C3
Cachimbo	C2
Campina Grande	E2
Campinas	D4
Campo Grande	C4
Campos	D4
Campos Elísios	Inset I
Carapicuíba	Inset II
Corumbá	C3
Cotia	Inset II
Cruzeiro do Sul	A2
Cubatão	Inset II
Cuiabá	C3
Curitiba	D4
Diadema	Inset II
Dourados	C4
Duque de Caxias	Inset I
Feira de Santana	E3
Floriano	D2
Florianópolis	D4
Fortaleza	E2
Foz do Iguaçu	C4
Goiânia	D3
Governador Valadares	D3
Guajara Mirim	B3
Guarujá	Inset II
Guarulhos	Inset II
Ilhéus	E3
Imbariê	Inset I
Imperatriz	D2
Inhomirim	Inset I
Ipiiba	Inset I
Itabira	D3
Itabuna	E3
Itaipu	Inset I
Itajaí	D4
Itapecerica da Serra	Inset II
Itapeva	Inset II
Itaquaquecetuba	Inset II
Jaboatão	E2
Jacare-Acanga	C2
Japeri	Inset I
Jir Paraná	B3
João Pessoa	E2
Joinville	D4
Juàzeiro	D2
Juàzeiro do Norte	E2
Juiz de Fora	D4
Jundiaí	C4
Lajes	C4
Londrina	C4
Macapá	C1
Maceió	E2
Majé	Inset I
Manaus	B2
Maraba	D2
Mariana	D3
Mauá	Inset II
Mogi das Cruzes	Inset II
Monjolo	Inset I
Montes Claros	D3
Mozzoro	E2
Natal	E2
Neves	Inset I
Nilópolis	Inset I
Niterói	D4, Inset I
Nova Iguaçu	Inset I
Olinda	E2
Osasco	Inset II
Palmas	D3
Paranaguá	D4
Parnaiba	D2
Passo Fundo	C4
Paulo Afonso	E2
Pelotas	C5
Petrólina	D2
Petrópolis	D4, Inset I
Piracicaba	D4
Poá	Inset II
Pôrto Alegre	C5
Pôrto Velho	B2
Queimados	Inset I
Randonopolis	C3
Recife	E2
Ribeirão Pires	Inset II
Ribeirão Prêto	D4
Rio Branco	B2
Rio de Janeiro	D4, Inset I
Rio Grande	C5
Rio Verde	C3
Salvador	E3
Santa Maria	C4
Santana do Livramento	C5
Santarém	C2
Santo André	D4
Santos	D4, Inset II
São Bernardo do Campo	Inset II
São Caetano do Sul	Inset II
São Gonçalo	Inset I
São João de Meriti	Inset I
São José do Rio Prêto	D4
São Luís	D2
São Paulo	D4, Inset II
São Vincente	Inset II
Sobral	D2
Sorocaba	D4
Suzano	Inset II
Taboão da Serra	Inset II
Tefé	B2
Teresina	D2
Tubarão	D4
Uberaba	D3
Uberlândia	D3
Vincente de Carvalho	Inset II
Vitória	D4
Vitória da Conquista	D4
Volta Redonda	D4

Other Features

Acaraí, *range*	C1
Açúcar, *mt.*	Inset I
Amazon, *basin*	B2
Amazon, *river*	B2
Araguaia, *river*	C3
Aripuanã, *river*	B2
Baleia, *point*	E3
Bandeira, *mt.*	E3
Billings, *reservoir*	Inset II
Branco, *river*	B1
Brazilian, *highlands*	D3
Caviana, *island*	D1
Chapada dos Parecis, *range*	C3
Corcovado, *mt.*	Inset I
Corumbau, *point*	E3
Furnas, *reservoir*	D4
Geral, *range*	C4
Grande, *river*	D3
Guandu, *river*	Inset I
Guaporé, *river*	B3
Guiana, *highlands*	B1
Içá, *river*	B2
Iguaçu, *falls*	C4
Itaipu, *reservoir*	C4
Japurá, *river*	B2
Jari, *river*	C1
Javari, *river*	A2
Juruá, *river*	B2
Juruena, *river*	C3
Madeira, *river*	B2
Mantiqueira, *range*	D4
Mar, *range*	D4
Marajó, *island*	D2
Mato Grosso, *plateau*	C3
Mexiana, *island*	D1
Neblina, *mt.*	B1
Negro, *river*	B2
Órgãos, *range*	Inset I
Pantanal, *lowland*	C3
Pará, *river*	C2
Paraguai, *river*	C3
Paraná, *river*	C4
Parima, *range*	B1
Parnaíba, *river*	D2
Patos, *lagoon*	C5
Paulo Afonso, *falls*	E2
Pedra Açú, *mt.*	Inset I
Purus, *river*	B2
Roncador, *range*	C3
São Francisco, *river*	D3
Selvas, *region*	B2
Sobradinho, *reservoir*	D3
Tapajós, *river*	C3
Taquari, *river*	C3
Teles Pires, *river*	C3
Tietê, *river*	Inset II
Tocantins, *river*	D2
Tucuruí, *reservoir*	D2
Tumucumaque, *range*	C1
Uruguai, *river*	C4
Xingu, *river*	C3

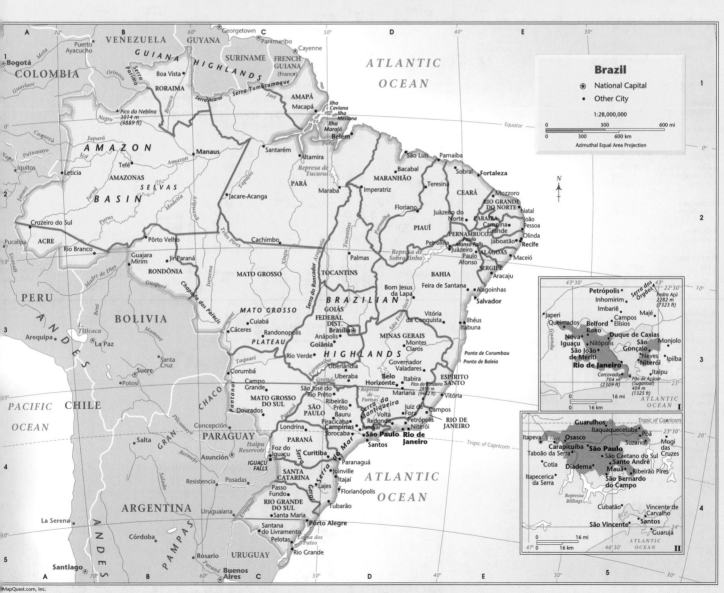

MAJOR CITIES

Antigua & Barbuda
St. Johns 27,000

Bahamas
Nassau 172,000

Barbados
Bridgetown 6,000

Belize
Belize City 45,000
Belmopan 4,000

Canada (metro)
Toronto 4,264,000
Montréal 3,327,000
Vancouver 1,832,000
Ottawa 1,010,000

Costa Rica
San José 324,000

Cuba
Havana 2,185,000

Dominica
Roseau 16,000

Dominican Republic
Santo Domingo 2,135,000

El Salvador (metro)
San Salvador 1,214,000

Grenada
St. George's 30,000

Guatemala (metro)
Guatemala 2,205,000

Haiti
Port-au-Prince 884,000

Honduras (metro)
Tegucigalpa 995,000

Jamaica (metro)
Kingston 587,000

Mexico
Mexico City 8,489,000
Guadalajara 1,633,000
Puebla 1,223,000

Nicaragua (metro)
Managua 1,124,000

Panama
Panamá 465,000

Puerto Rico
San Juan 428,000

St. Kitts & Nevis
Basseterre 15,000

St. Lucia
Castries 45,000

St. Vincent & Grenadines
Kingstown 15,000

Trinidad & Tobago
Port of Spain 43,000

United States (Census 2000)
New York 8,008,000
Los Angeles 3,695,000
Chicago 2,896,000
Houston 1,954,000
Philadelphia 1,518,000
Phoenix 1,321,000
San Diego 1,223,000
Washington, D.C. 572,000

International comparability of city population data is limited by various data inconsistencies.

CITIES
⊗ National Capital
★ Territorial Capital
• Other City

ELEVATIONS

Feet	Meters
13,120	4000
6560	2000
1640	500
656	200
0	0
Below sea level	

N

0 250 500 750 1000 mi
0 500 1000 1500 km

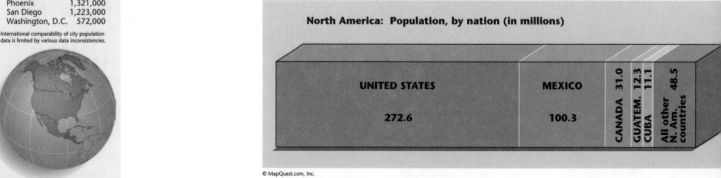

North America: Population, by nation (in millions)

UNITED STATES	MEXICO	CANADA	GUATEM.	CUBA	All other N. Am. countries
272.6	100.3	31.0	12.3	11.1	48.5

© MapQuest.com, Inc.

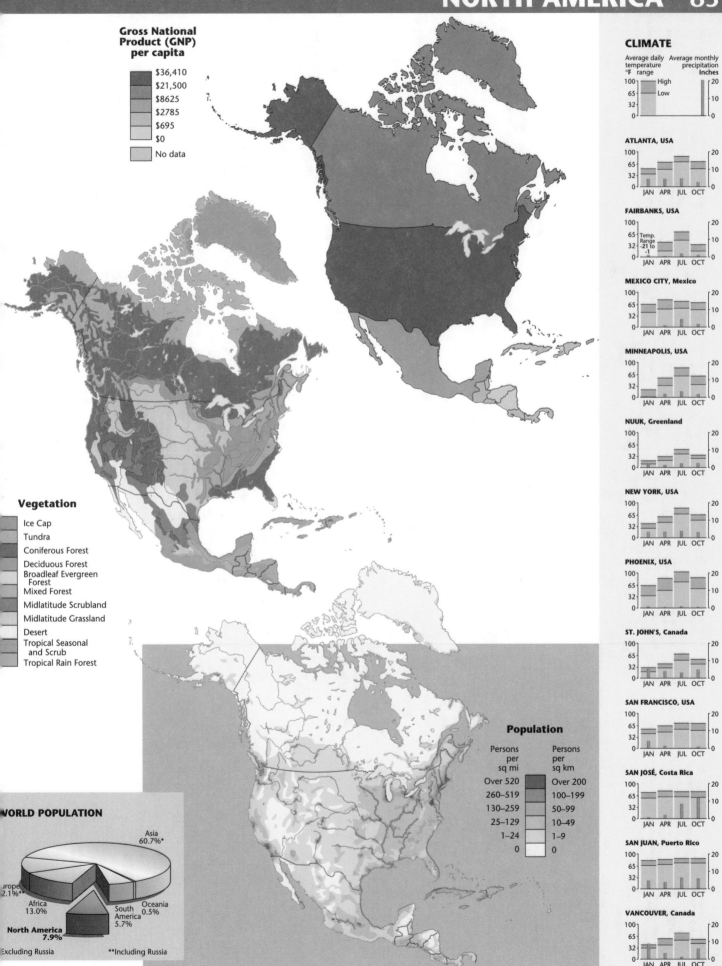

Gross National Product (GNP) per capita

- $36,410
- $21,500
- $8625
- $2785
- $695
- $0
- No data

Vegetation

- Ice Cap
- Tundra
- Coniferous Forest
- Deciduous Forest
- Broadleaf Evergreen Forest
- Mixed Forest
- Midlatitude Scrubland
- Midlatitude Grassland
- Desert
- Tropical Seasonal and Scrub
- Tropical Rain Forest

CLIMATE

Average daily temperature °F range   Average monthly precipitation Inches

- 100 — High
- 65 — Low
- 32
- 0

- 20
- 10
- 0

ATLANTA, USA

JAN APR JUL OCT

FAIRBANKS, USA

Temp. Range -21 to -1

JAN APR JUL OCT

MEXICO CITY, Mexico

JAN APR JUL OCT

MINNEAPOLIS, USA

JAN APR JUL OCT

NUUK, Greenland

JAN APR JUL OCT

NEW YORK, USA

JAN APR JUL OCT

PHOENIX, USA

JAN APR JUL OCT

ST. JOHN'S, Canada

JAN APR JUL OCT

SAN FRANCISCO, USA

JAN APR JUL OCT

SAN JOSÉ, Costa Rica

JAN APR JUL OCT

SAN JUAN, Puerto Rico

JAN APR JUL OCT

VANCOUVER, Canada

JAN APR JUL OCT

Population

Persons per sq mi	Persons per sq km
Over 520	Over 200
260–519	100–199
130–259	50–99
25–129	10–49
1–24	1–9
0	0

WORLD POPULATION

- Asia 60.7%*
- Europe 12.1%**
- Africa 13.0%
- South America 5.7%
- Oceania 0.5%
- North America 7.9%

*Excluding Russia   **Including Russia

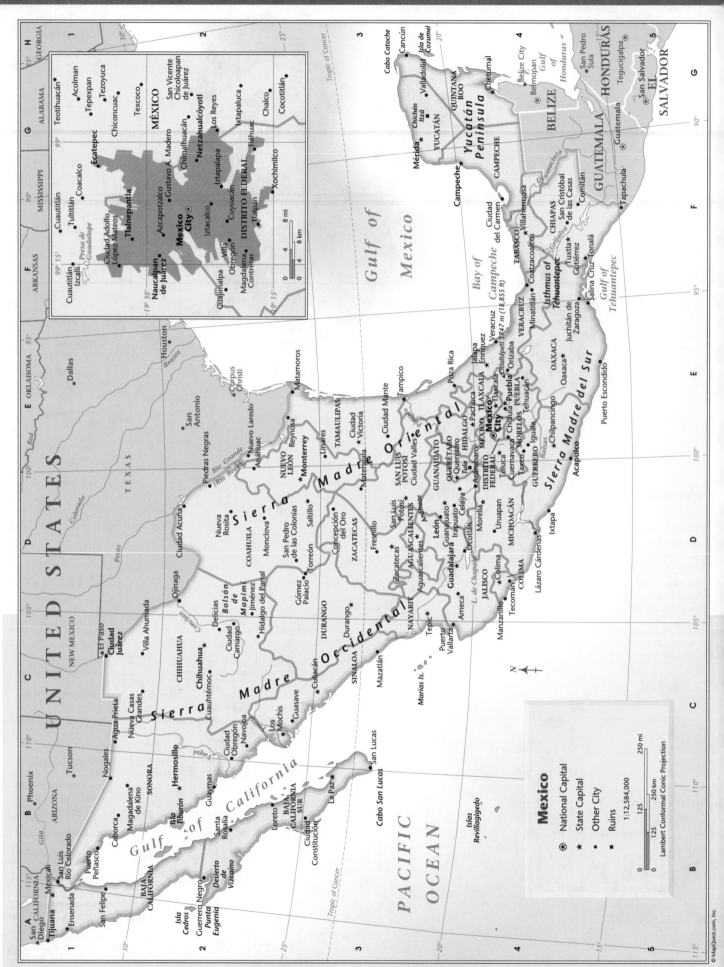

Mexico
⊛ National Capital
★ State Capital
• Other City
■ Ruins

1:12,584,000
Lambert Conformal Conic Projection

MapQuest.com, Inc.

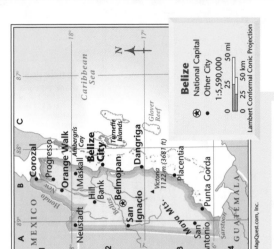

Belize

National Capital
Other City
1:5,590,000
0 25 50 km
0 25 50 mi
Lambert Conformal Conic Projection

Belize

Capital: Belmopan
Area: 8,867 sq. mi.
22,972 sq. km.
Population: 235,789
Largest City: Belize City
Language: English
Monetary Unit: Belize dollar

Belize:
Map Index

Cities and Towns
Belize City B2
Belmopan, capital B2
Corozal B1
Dangriga B2
Hill Bank B2
Maskall B2
Neustadt A2
Orange Walk B1
Placentia B3
Progresso B1
Punta Gorda B3
San Antonio A3
San Ignacio A2

Other Features
Ambergris Cay, *island* B2
Belize, *river* B2
Glover, *reef* C3
Hondo, *river* B1
Maya, *mts.* A3
New, *river* B1
Sarstoon, *river* A4
Turneffe, *islands* C2
Victoria, *peak* B3

Guatemala

National Capital
Other City
1:8,150,000
0 50 100 km
0 50 100 mi
Lambert Conformal Conic Projection

Guatemala

Capital: Guatemala City
Area: 42,042 sq. mi.
108,917 sq. km.
Population: 12,335,580
Largest City: Guatemala City
Language: Spanish
Monetary Unit: Quetzal

Guatemala:
Map Index

Cities and Towns
Antigua C5
Champerico B5
Chinajá C4
Cobán C4
Escuintla C5
Flores D3
Guatemala City, *capital* ..B4
Huehuetenango B4
Jutiapa D5
La Libertad D3
Mazatenango B5
Paxbán C2
Puerto Barrios E4
Quetzaltenango B5
Salamá C4
San José C6
San Luis D3
Santo Tomás de Castilla ..E4
Tikal D2
Zacapa D5

Other Features
Atitlán, *lake* B5
Chixoy, *river* C4
Honduras, *gulf* E4
Izabal, *lake* D4
Motagua, *river* C4
Pasión, *river* C3
Paz, *river* C6
Petén-Itzá, *lake* D3
San Pedro, *river* C2
Sarstún, *river* D4
Sierra Madre, *mts.* A5
Suchiate, *river* A4
Tacaná, *volcano* A4
Tajumulco, *volcano* B4
Usumacinta, *river* C3

Mexico

Capital: Mexico City
Area: 756,066 sq. mi.
1958,720 sq. km.
Population: 100,294,036
Largest City: Mexico City
Language: Spanish
Monetary Unit: New peso

Mexico:
Map Index

States
Aguascalientes D3
Baja California A1
Baja California Sur B2
Campeche F4
Chiapas E5
Chihuahua C2
Coahuila D2
Colima D4
Distrito Federal ...E4, Inset
Durango C3
Guanajuato D3
Guerrero E4
Hidalgo E3
Jalisco D3
México ....E4, Inset
Michoacán D4
Morelos E4
Nayarit C3
Nuevo León D2
Oaxaca E4
Puebla E4
Querétaro D3
Quintana Roo G3
San Luis Potosí D3
Sinaloa C3
Sonora B1
Tabasco F4
Tamaulipas E3
Tlaxcala E4
Veracruz E4
Yucatán F3
Zacatecas D3

Cities and Towns
Acámbaro D4
Acapulco E4
Acolman ....Inset
Agua Prieta C1
Aguascalientes, *state capital* ..D3
Ameca D3
Anáhuac D2
Azcapotzalco ....Inset
Caborca B1
Campeche, *state capital* F4
Cancún G3
Celaya D3
Chalco ....Inset
Chetumal, *state capital* G4
Chiconcuac ....Inset
Chihuahua, *state capital* C2
Chilpancingo, *state capital* ..E4
Chimalhuacán ....Inset
Cholula E4
Ciudad Acuña D2
Ciudad Adolfo López Mateos ..Inset
Ciudad Camargo C2
Ciudad Constitución B3
Ciudad del Carmen F4
Ciudad Juárez C1
Ciudad Mante E3
Ciudad Obregón C2
Ciudad Valles E3
Ciudad Victoria, *state capital* ..E3
Coacalco ....Inset
Coatzacoalcos F4
Cocotitlán ....Inset
Colima, *state capital* D4
Comitán F4
Concepción del Oro D3

Coyoacán ....Inset
Cuajimalpa ....Inset
Cuauhtémoc C2
Cuautitlán ....Inset
Cuautitlán Izcalli ....Inset
Cuernavaca, *state capital* ...E4
Culiacán, *state capital* C3
Delicias C2
Durango, *state capital* D3
Ecatepec ....Inset
Ensenada A1
Fresnillo D3
Gómez Palacio D2
Guadalajara, *state capital* ..D3
Guanajuato, *state capital* ...D3
Guasave C2
Guaymas B2
Guerrero Negro B2
Gustavo A. Madero ..Inset
Hermosillo, *state capital* ...B2
Hidalgo del Parral C2
Iguala E4
Irapuato D3
Ixtapa D4
Ixtapaluca ....Inset
Iztacalco ....Inset
Iztapalapa ....Inset
Jalapa Enríquez, *state capital* ..E4
Jiménez D2
Juchitán de Zaragoza ...F4
La Paz, *state capital* B3
Lázaro Cárdenas D4
León D3
Linares E3
Loreto B2
Los Mochis C2
Los Reyes ....Inset
Magdalena de Kino B1
Magdalena Contreras ...Inset
Manzanillo D4
Matamoros E2
Matehuala D3
Mazatlán C3
Mérida, *state capital* G3
Mexicali, *state capital* A1
Mexico City, *national capital* ....E4, Inset
Minatitlán F4
Monclova D2
Monterrey, *state capital* D2
Morelia, *state capital* D4
Naucalpan de Juárez ...Inset
Navojoa B2
Nogales B1
Nueva Casas Grandes C1
Nueva Rosita D2
Nuevo Laredo E2
Oaxaca, *state capital* E4
Ocotlán D3
Ojinaga D2
Orizaba E4
Pachuca, *state capital* E3
Piedras Negras D2
Poza Rica E3
Puebla, *state capital* E4
Puerto Escondido E4
Puerto Peñasco B1
Puerto Vallarta D3
Querétaro, *state capital* D3
Reynosa E2
Salina Cruz F4
Saltillo, *state capital* D3

San Cristóbal de las Casas F4
San Felipe B1
San Lucas C3
San Luis Potosí, *state capital* ..D3
San Pedro de las Colonias ..D2
Santa Rosalía B2
San Vicente Chicoloapan ..Inset
Tampico E3
Tapachula F5
Taxco E4
Tehuacán E4
Tehuantepec F4
Teotihuacán ....Inset
Tepexpan ....Inset
Tepic, *state capital* D3
Texcoco ....Inset
Tezoyuca ....Inset
Tijuana A1
Tlalnepantla ....Inset
Tlaxcala, *state capital* E4
Toluca, *state capital* E4
Tonalá F4
Torreón D2
Tultitlán ....Inset
Tuxtla Gutiérrez, *state capital* ..F4
Uruapan D4
Valladolid G3
Veracruz E4
Villa Ahumada C1
Villahermosa, *state capital* ..F4
Villa Obregón ....Inset
Xochimilco ....Inset
Zacatecas, *state capital* D3

Other Features
Anáhuac, *depression* D3
Balsas, *river* E4
Bolsón de Mapimí, *depression* ..D2
California, *gulf* B1
Campeche, *bay* F4
Catoche, *cape* G3
Cedros, *island* A2
Chapala, *lake* D3
Chichén Itzá, *ruins* G3
Citaltépetl, *mt.* E4
Conchos, *river* C2
Cozumel, *island* G3
Eugenia, *point* A2
Fuerte, *river* C2
Grijalva, *river* F4
Guadalupe, *reservoir* ....Inset
Marías, *islands* C3
Pánuco, *river* E3
Revillagigedo, *islands* B4
Río Grande (Río Bravo), *river* ..D2
San Lucas, *cape* B3
Sierra Madre del Sur, *mts.* ..D4
Sierra Madre Occidental, *mts.* ..C2
Sierra Madre Oriental, *mts.* ..D2
Tehuantepec, *gulf* F4
Tehuantepec, *isthmus* F4
Tiburón, *island* B2
Tula, *ruins* E3
Usumacinta, *river* F4
Vizcaíno, *desert* B2
Yaqui, *river* C2
Yucatán, *peninsula* G4

© MapQuest.com, Inc.

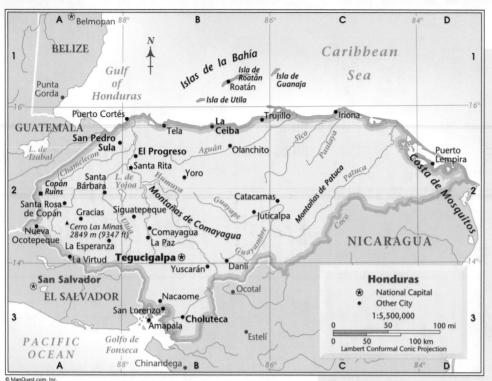

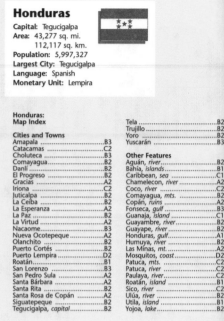

Honduras

Capital: Tegucigalpa
Area: 43,277 sq. mi.
112,117 sq. km.
Population: 5,997,327
Largest City: Tegucigalpa
Language: Spanish
Monetary Unit: Lempira

Honduras:
Map Index

Cities and Towns
Amapala B3
Catacamas C2
Choluteca B3
Comayagua B2
Danlí B2
El Progreso B2
Gracias A2
Iriona C2
Juticalpa B2
La Ceiba B2
La Esperanza A2
La Paz B2
La Virtud A2
Nacaome B3
Nueva Ocotepeque A2
Olanchito B2
Puerto Cortés B2
Puerto Lempira D2
Roatán B1
San Lorenzo B3
San Pedro Sula A2
Santa Bárbara A2
Santa Rita B2
Santa Rosa de Copán A2
Siguatepeque B2
Tegucigalpa, capital B2

Tela B2
Trujillo B2
Yoro B2
Yuscarán B3

Other Features
Aguán, river B2
Bahía, islands B1
Caribbean, sea C1
Chamelecon, river A2
Coco, river C2
Comayagua, mts. B2
Copán, ruins A2
Fonseca, gulf B3
Guanaja, island C1
Guayambre, river B2
Guayape, river B2
Honduras, gulf A1
Humuya, river B2
Las Minas, mt. A2
Mosquitos, coast D2
Patuca, mts. C2
Patuca, river C2
Paulaya, river C2
Roatán, island B1
Sico, river C2
Ulúa, river B2
Utila, island B1
Yojoa, lake B2

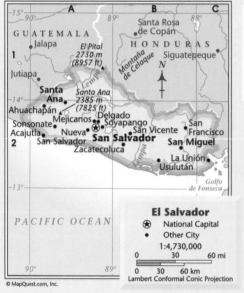

El Salvador

Capital: San Salvador
Area: 8,124 sq. mi.
21,047 sq. km.
Population: 5,839,079
Largest City: San Salvador
Language: Spanish
Monetary Unit: Colón

El Salvador:
Map Index

Cities and Towns
Acajutla A2
Ahuachapán A2
Delgado A2
La Unión C2
Mejicanos A2
Nueva San Salvador A2
San Francisco B2
San Miguel B2
San Salvador, capital A2
Santa Ana A2
San Vicente B2
Sonsonate A2
Soyapango A2
Usulután B2
Zacatecoluca B2

Other Features
El Pital, mt. A1
Fonseca, gulf C2
Lempa, river A1, B2
Santa Ana, volcano A2

Costa Rica:
Map Index

Cities and Towns
Alajuela B2
Cartago C3
Colorado C2
Golfito C4
Heredia B2
La Cruz A1
Liberia A2
Limón C3
Los Chiles B1
Puerto Jiménez C4
Puerto Quepos B3
Puntarenas B3
San José, capital B3
Santa Cruz A2

Other Features
Arenal, lake B2
Central, range B2
Chirripó, mt. C3
Chirripó, river C2
Coronado, bay B3
Dulce, gulf C4
Frío, river B2
General, river C3

Grande, river B3
Guanacaste, range A2
Irazú, volcano C3
Nicoya, gulf B3
Papagayo, gulf A2
Pirris, river B3
Reventazón, river C3
San Carlos, river B2
San Juan, river B2
Sarapiquí river B2
Sixaola, river C3
Talamanca, range C3
Tempisque, river A2

Costa Rica

Capital: San José
Area: 19,730 sq. mi.
51,114 sq. km.
Population: 3,674,490
Largest City: San José
Language: Spanish
Monetary Unit: Colón

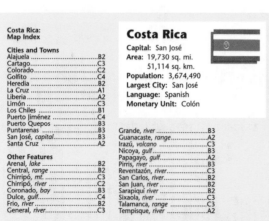

© MapQuest.com, Inc.

Nicaragua
Capital: Managua
Area: 50,880 sq. mi.
131,813 sq. km.
Population: 4,717,132
Largest City: Managua
Language: Spanish
Monetary Unit: Córdoba

**Nicaragua:
Map Index**

Cities and Towns

Bluefields	C3
Boaco	B2
Bocay	B1
Chinandega	A2
Colonia Nueva Guinea	B3
Corinto	A2
Diriamba	A3
Estelí	A2
Granada	B3
Jinotega	B2
Jinotepe	A3
Juigalpa	B2
La Rosita	B2
León	A2
Managua, capital	A2
Masaya	A3
Matagalpa	B2
Nagarote	A2
Ocotal	A2
Prinzapolka	C2
Puerto Cabezas	C1
Puerto Sandino	A2
Rama	B2
Río Blanco	B2
Río Grande	A2
Rivas	B3
San Carlos	B3
San Juan del Norte	C3
San Juan del Sur	B3
Siuna	B2
Somoto	A2
Waspam	C1
Wiwili	B2

Other Features

Bambana, river	B2
Bismuna, lagoon	C1
Bluefields, bay	C3
Bocay, river	B2
Chontaleña, mts.	B2
Coco, river	A2, C1
Cosigüina, mt.	A2
Cosigüina, point	A2
Dariense, mts.	B2
Escondido, river	B2
Fonseca, gulf	A2
Gracias a Dios, cape	C1
Grande de Matagalpa, river	B2
Huapí, mts.	B2
Isabelia, mts.	B2
Kurinwás, river	B2
Maíz, islands	C2
Managua, lake	A2
Mico, river	B2
Miskitos, cays	C1
Mogotón, mt.	A2
Mosquitos, coast	C3
Nicaragua, lake	B3
Ometepe, island	B3
Perlas, lagoon	C2
Perlas, point	C2
Prinzapolka, river	B2
San Juan, river	B3
San Juan del Norte, bay	C3
Siquia, river	B2
Solentiname, island	B3
Tipitapa, river	A2
Tuma, river	B2
Wawa, river	B1
Zapatera, island	B3

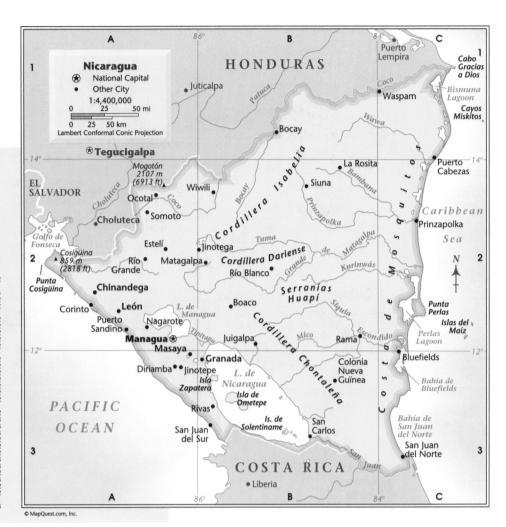

© MapQuest.com, Inc.

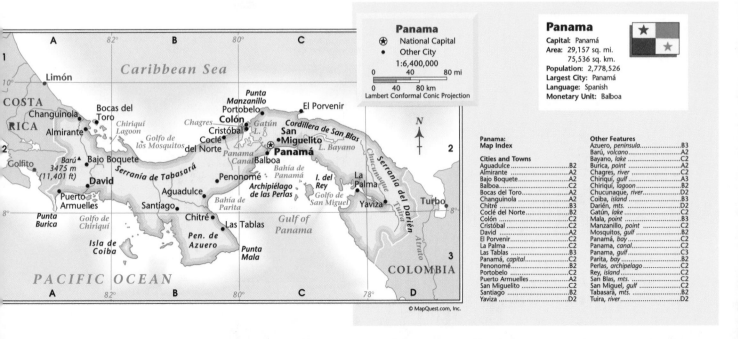

Panama
Capital: Panamá
Area: 29,157 sq. mi.
75,536 sq. km.
Population: 2,778,526
Largest City: Panamá
Language: Spanish
Monetary Unit: Balboa

**Panama:
Map Index**

Cities and Towns

Aguadulce	B2
Almirante	A2
Bajo Boquete	A2
Balboa	C2
Bocas del Toro	A2
Changuinola	A2
Chitré	B2
Coclé del Norte	B2
Colón	C2
Cristóbal	C2
David	A2
El Porvenir	C2
La Palma	C2
Las Tablas	B3
Panamá, capital	C2
Penonomé	B2
Portobelo	C2
Puerto Armuelles	A2
San Miguelito	C2
Santiago	B2
Yaviza	D2

Other Features

Azuero, peninsula	B3
Barú, volcano	A2
Bayano, lake	C2
Burica, point	A2
Chagres, river	C2
Chiriquí, gulf	A3
Chiriquí, lagoon	B2
Chucunaque, river	D2
Coiba, island	B3
Darién, mts.	D2
Gatún, lake	C2
Mala, point	B3
Manzanillo, point	C2
Mosquitos, gulf	B2
Panamá, bay	C2
Panama, canal	C2
Parita, bay	B2
Perlas, archipelago	C2
Rey, island	C2
San Blas, mts.	C2
San Miguel, gulf	C2
Tabasará, mts.	B2
Tuira, river	D2

© MapQuest.com, Inc.

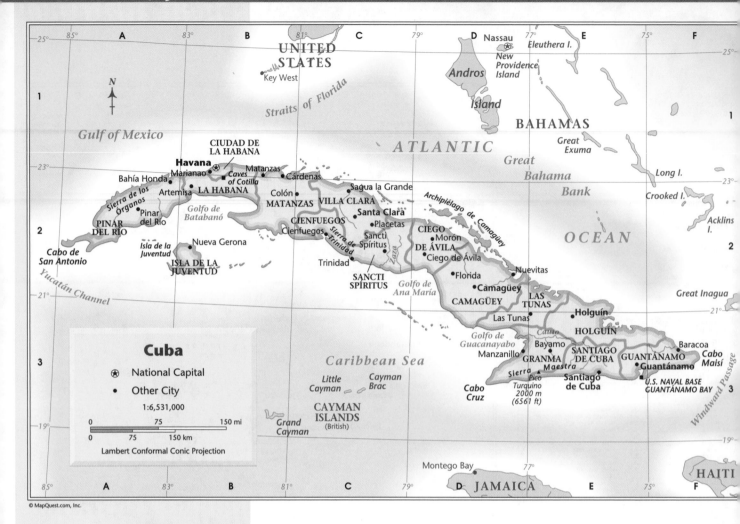

Cuba

Capital: Havana
Area: 42,804 sq. mi.
110,890 sq. km.
Population: 11,096,395
Largest City: Havana
Language: Spanish
Monetary Unit: Peso

Cuba:
Map Index

Provinces
Camagüey.........................D2
Ciego de Ávila.................D2
Cienfuegos......................C2
Ciudad de La Habana......B1
Granma............................E3
Guantánamo....................E3
Holguín.............................E3
Isla de la Juventud
(special municipality)......B2
La Habana........................B2
Las Tunas........................E2
Matanzas..........................B2
Pinar del Río....................A2
Sancti Spíritus.................C2
Santiago de Cuba.............E3
Villa Clara........................C2

Cities and Towns
Artemisa...........................B2
Bahía Honda....................A2
Baracoa............................F3
Bayamo............................E3
Camagüey........................D2
Cárdenas..........................B1
Ciego de Ávila.................D2
Cienfuegos......................C2
Colón................................C2
Florida..............................D2
Guantánamo....................E3
Havana, capital................B1
Holguín.............................E3
Las Tunas........................E3

Manzanillo........................D3
Marianao..........................B1
Matanzas..........................B1
Morón...............................D2
Nueva Gerona..................B2
Nuevitas...........................D2
Pinar del Río....................A2
Placetas...........................C2
Sagua la Grande..............C2
Sancti Spíritus.................C2
Santa Clara......................C2
Santiago de Cuba.............E3
Trinidad............................C2

Other Features
Ana María, gulf................D2
Batabanó, gulf.................B2
Camagüey, archipelago....D2
Cauto, river......................E3
Cotilla, caves...................B2
Cruz, cape........................D3
Florida, straits..................B1
Guacanayabo, gulf...........D3
Juventud, island...............B2
Maestra, mts....................D3
Maisí, cape.......................F3
Mexico, gulf......................A1
Órganos, mts....................A2
San Antonio, cape............A2
Trinidad, mts.....................C2
Turquino, mt.....................E3
U.S. Naval Base
Guantánamo Bay..............E3
Windward, passage..........F3
Yucatán, channel.............A2
Zaza, river........................C2

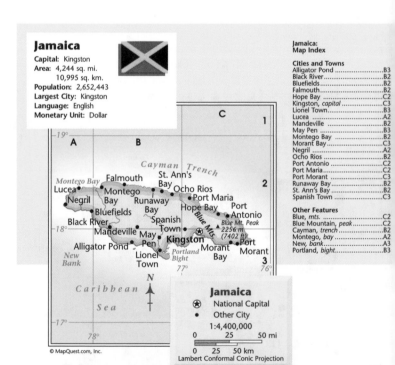

Jamaica

Capital: Kingston
Area: 4,244 sq. mi.
10,995 sq. km.
Population: 2,652,443
Largest City: Kingston
Language: English
Monetary Unit: Dollar

Jamaica:
Map Index

Cities and Towns
Alligator Pond..................B3
Black River......................B2
Bluefields........................B2
Falmouth..........................B2
Hope Bay.........................C2
Kingston, capital..............C3
Lionel Town.....................B3
Lucea...............................A2
Mandeville.......................B2
May Pen...........................B3
Montego Bay....................B2
Morant Bay......................C3
Negril...............................A2
Ocho Rios........................B2
Port Antonio....................C2
Port Maria........................C2
Port Morant.....................C3
Runaway Bay...................B2
St. Ann's Bay..................B2
Spanish Town..................C3

Other Features
Blue, mts.........................C2
Blue Mountain, peak........C2
Cayman, trench...............B2
Montego, bay...................A2
New, bank........................A3
Portland, bight.................B3

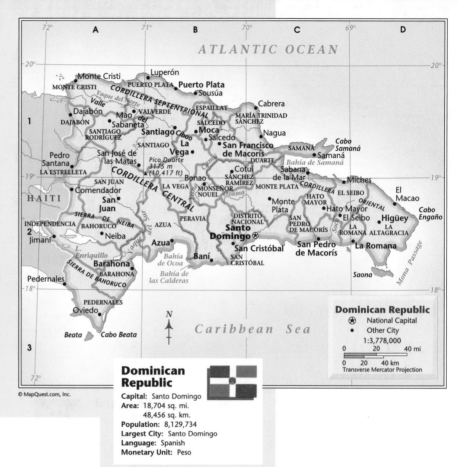

Bonao B2
Cabrera C1
Comendador A2
Cotuí B1
Dajabón A1
El Macao D2
El Seibo C2
Hato Mayor C2
Higüey D2
Jimaní A2
La Romana D2
La Vega B1
Luperón B1
Mao A1
Miches C2
Moca B1
Monte Cristi A1
Monte Plata C2
Nagua C1
Neiba A2
Oviedo A3
Pedernales A3
Pedro Santana A1
Puerto Plata B1
Sabana de la Mar C1
Sabaneta B1
Salcedo B1
Samaná C1
San Cristóbal B2
San Francisco de Macorís B1
San José de las Matas A1
San Juan A2
San Pedro de Macorís C2
Santiago B1
Santo Domingo, capital C2
Sousúa B1

**Dominican Republic:
Map Index**

Provinces
Azua B2
Bahoruco A2
Barahona A2
Dajabón A1
Distrito Nacional B2
Duarte C1
El Seibo C2
Espaillat B1
Hato Mayor C2
Independencia A2
La Altagracia D2
La Estrelleta A1
La Romana D2
La Vega B2
María Trinidad Sánchez B1
Monseñor Nouel B2
Monte Cristi A1
Monte Plata C2
Pedernales A3
Peravia B2
Puerto Plata B1
Salcedo B1
Samaná C1
Sánchez Ramírez B1
San Cristóbal B2
San Juan A2
San Pedro de Macorís C2
Santiago B1
Santiago Rodríguez A1
Valverde B1

Cities and Towns
Azua B2
Baní B2
Barahona A2

Other Features
Bahoruco, mts. A2
Beata, cape A3
Beata, island A3
Calderas, bay B2
Camú, river B1
Central, range B2
Cibao, valley A1
Duarte, mt. B1
Engaño, cape D2
Enriquillo, lake A2
Mona, passage D2
Neiba, mts. A2
Ocoa, bay B2
Oriental, range C2
Ozama, river B2
Samaná, bay C1
Samaná, cape C1
Saona, island D2
Septentrional, range A1
Soco, river C2
Yaque del Norte, river A1
Yaque del Sur, river A2
Yuna, river B2

Dominican Republic

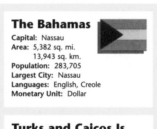

Capital: Santo Domingo
Area: 18,704 sq. mi.
    48,456 sq. km.
Population: 8,129,734
Largest City: Santo Domingo
Language: Spanish
Monetary Unit: Peso

Haiti

Capital: Port-au-Prince
Area: 10,695 sq. mi.
    27,614 sq. km.
Population: 6,884,264
Largest City: Port-au-Prince
Languages: French, Creole
Monetary Unit: Gourde

Haiti

⊛ National Capital
• Other City

1:5,593,000

0   30   60 mi
0 30 60 km
Lambert Conformal Conic Projection

apQuest.com, Inc.

i
Index

artments
onite C1
re D1
nd Ande B2
....C1
-Est D1
-Ouest B1
st C2
....B2
....C2

s and Towns
-à-Galets C2
-Anse C2
-Haïtien C1
ne-Marie A2
ives C1
el C2
nie A2
gâne C2
Cayes B2
goâne C2
alais C2
au-Prince, capital C2
de-Paix C1
Salut B2
Marc C1

Other Features
Artibonite, river C1
Gonâve, gulf B1
Gonâve, island B2
Gravois, point B3
Pic de la Selle, mt. D2
Port-au-Prince, bay C2
Tortuga, island C1
Vache, island B2
Windward, passage B1

The Bahamas

Capital: Nassau
Area: 5,382 sq. mi.
    13,943 sq. km.
Population: 283,705
Largest City: Nassau
Languages: English, Creole
Monetary Unit: Dollar

Turks and Caicos Is.

Capital: Grand Turk
Area: 193 sq. mi.
    500 sq. km.
Population: 16,863
Largest City: Grand Turk
Language: English
Monetary Unit: U.S. Dollar

**Bahamas and
Turks & Caicos Islands:
Map Index**

Bahamas

Cities and Towns
Alice Town B2
Arthur's Town B3
Freeport A2
Kemps Bay B3
Marsh Harbour B2
Matthew Town C4
Nassau, capital B2
Nicholls' Town A2
Sandy Point B2

Other Features
Acklins, island C4
Andros, island A3
Cat, island B3
Crooked, island C4
Crooked Island, passage C4
Eleuthera, island B2
Exuma, sound B3
Grand Bahama, island A2
Great Abaco, island B2
Great Bahama, bank A3

Great Exuma, island B3
Great Inagua, island C4
Harbour, island B2
Little Inagua, island C4
Long, island C3
Mayaguana, island C4
Mayaguana, passage C4
New Providence, island B3
Northeast Providence,
    channel B2
Rum, cay C3
Samana, cay C3
San Salvador, island C3
Water, cays A3

Turks & Caicos Islands

Cities and Towns
Cockburn Harbour D4
Grand Turk, capital D4

Other Features
Ambergris, cay. D4
Caicos, islands D4
Grand Turk, island D4
Providenciales, island C4
Salt, cay D4
Turks, islands D4

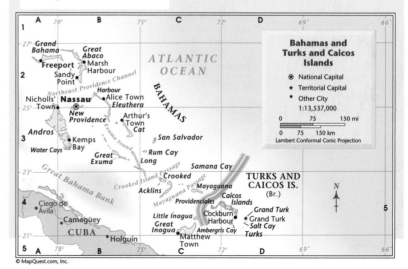

Bahamas and Turks and Caicos Islands

⊛ National Capital
★ Territorial Capital
• Other City

1:13,537,000

0   75   150 mi
0 75 150 km
Lambert Conformal Conic Projection

© MapQuest.com, Inc.

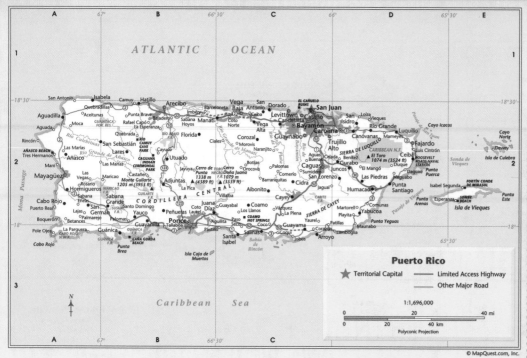

Puerto Rico

Capital: San Juan
Area: 3,492 sq. mi.
9,047 sq. km.
Population: 3,887,652
Largest City: San Juan
Languages: Spanish, English
Monetary Unit: U.S. dollar

Puerto Rico: Map Index

Cities and Towns

Adjuntas	B2
Aguada	A2
Aguadilla	A2
Aguas Buenas	C2
Aguilita	B2
Aibonito	C2
Añasco	B2
Arecibo	B2
Arroyo	C2
Bajadero	B2
Barceloneta	B2
Barranquitas	C2
Bayamón	C2
Cabo Rojo	A2
Caguas	C2
Camuy	B2
Candelaria	C2
Canóvanas	D2
Carolina	D2
Cataño	C2
Cayey	C2
Ceiba	C2
Ceiba	D2
Celada	C2
Ciales	C2
Cidra	C2
Coamo	C2
Coco	C2
Comerío	C2
Coquí	C3
Corazón	C2
Corozal	C2
Coto Laurel	B2
Dorado	C2
Fajardo	D2
Florida	B2
Guánica	B3
Guayama	C2
Guayanilla	B2
Guaynabo	C2
Gurabo	D2
Hatillo	B2
Hormigueros	A2
Humacao	D2
Imbéry	B2
Isabela	A1
Jayuya	B2
Jobos	C3
Juana Díaz	C2
Juncos	D2
Lajas	A2
Lares	B2
Las Piedras	D2
Levittown	C2
Loíza	D2
Luquillo	D2
Manatí	B2
Martorell	D2
Maunabo	D2
Mayagüez	A2
Moca	A2
Naguabo	D2
Pastillo	C3
Patillas	D2
Peñuelas	B2
Ponce	B2
Puerto Real	A2
Punta Santiago	D2

Quebradillas	B2
Río Grande	D2
Sabana Grande	A2
Salinas	C2
San Antonio	A2
San Germán	A2
San Isidro	D2
San Juan, *capital*	C2
San Lorenzo	C2
San Sebastián	A2
Santa Isabel	C2
Santo Domingo	A2
Trujillo Alto	C2
Utuado	B2
Vega Alta	C2
Vega Baja	C2
Villalba	C2
Yabucoa	D2
Yauco	B2

Other Features

Añasco, *beach*	A2
Arenas, *point*	D2
Bayamón, *river*	C2
Brea, *point*	B3
Cabo Rojo Natl. Wildlife Refuge	A3
Caguana Indian Ceremonial Park	B2
Caja de Muertos, *island*	C3
Caña Gorda, *beach*	B3
Caribbean, *sea*	C3
Caribbean Natl. Forest	D2
Carite Forest Reserve	C2
Coamo Hot Springs	C2
Cordillera Central, *mts.*	B2
Culebra, *island*	E2
Culebrinas, *river*	A2
Doña Juana, *mt.*	B2
El Cañuelo, *ruins*	C2
El Toro, *mt.*	D2
Este, *point*	E2
Fortín Conde de Mirasol, *fort*	E2
Grande de Añasco, *river*	A2
Grande de Manatí, *river*	B2
Guajataca Forest Reserve	A2
Guánica Forest Reserve	B3
Guilarte, *mt.*	B2
Guilarte Forest Reserve	B2
Icacos, *key*	E2
La Plata, *river*	C2
Maricao Forest Reserve	A2
Mona, *passage*	A2
Norte, *key*	E2
Puerca, *point*	D2
Punta, *mt.*	B2
Rincón, *bay*	A2
Río Abajo Forest Reserve	B2
Río Camuy Cave Park	B2
Rojo, *cape*	A3
Roosevelt Roads Naval Station	D2
San Juan, *bay*	C2
Sierra de Cayey, *mts.*	C2
Sierra de Luquillo, *mts.*	D2
Sombe, *beach*	E2
Susua Forest Reserve	B2
Toro Negro Forest Reserve	B2
Vieques, *island*	E2
Vieques, *passage*	D2
Vieques, *passage*	E2
Vieques, *sound*	D2
Yeguas, *point*	D2

Antigua & Barbuda

⊛ National Capital
• Other City

1:1,480,000

0   10   20 mi
0   10   20 km
Transverse Mercator Projection

Antigua and Barbuda

Capital: St. John's
Area: 171 sq. mi.
443 sq. km.
Population: 64,246
Largest City: St. John's
Language: English
Monetary Unit: East Caribbean dollar

Antigua and Barbuda: Map Index

Cities and Towns

Bolands	D5
Cedar Grove	E5
Codrington	E2
Falmouth	E5
Freetown	E5
Old Road	D5
St. John's, *capital*	D5

Other Features

Antigua, *island*	D4
Barbuda, *island*	E3
Boggy, *peak*	D5
Cobb, *cove*	E1
Codrington, *lagoon*	D1
Goat, *point*	D1
Gravenor, *bay*	E2
Palmetto, *point*	D2
Redonda, *island*	A6
Shirley, *cape*	E6
Spanish, *point*	E2
Willoughby, *bay*	E5

Dominica: Map Index

Cities and Towns

Berekua	B4
Castle Bruce	B2
Colihaut	A2
Glanvillia	A2
La Plaine	B3
Laudat	B3
Marigot	B2
Massacre	B3
Pointe Michel	B3
Pont Cassé	B3
Portsmouth	A2
Rosalie	B3
Roseau, *capital*	B3
Saint Joseph	B2
Salibia	B2
Salisbury	B3
Soufrière	B4
Vieille Case	B1
Wesley	B2

Other Features

Boiling, *lake*	B3
Dominica, *passage*	A1
Grand, *bay*	B4
Layou, *river*	B3
Morne Diablotin, *mt.*	B2
Roseau, *river*	B3
Toulaman, *river*	B2

Dominica

Capital: Roseau
Area: 290 sq. mi.
751 sq. km.
Population: 64,881
Largest City: Roseau
Language: English
Monetary Unit: East Caribbean dollar

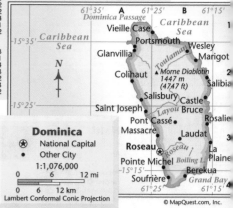

Dominica

⊛ National Capital
• Other City

1:1,076,000

0   6   12 mi
0   6   12 km
Lambert Conformal Conic Projection

© MapQuest.com, Inc.

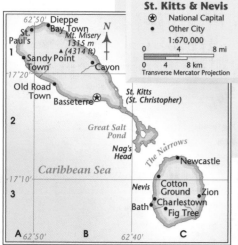

St. Kitts & Nevis

⊛ National Capital
• Other City

1:670,000

0   4   8 mi
0   4   8 km
Transverse Mercator Projection

St. Kitts & Nevis: Map Index

Cities and Towns

Basseterre, *capital*	B2
Bath	C3
Cayon	B1
Charlestown	C3
Cotton Ground	C2
Dieppe Bay Town	B1
Fig Tree	C3
Newcastle	C2
Old Road Town	B2
St. Paul's	A1
Sandy Point Town	A1
Zion	C3

Other Features

Great Salt, *pond*	C2
Nag's Head, *cape*	C2
Narrows, *strait*	C2
Nevis, *island*	C3
St. Kitts (St. Christopher), *island*	B2

St. Kitts & Nevis

Capital: Basseterre
Area: 104 sq. mi.
269 sq. km.
Population: 42,838
Largest City: Basseterre
Language: English
Monetary Unit: East Caribbean dollar

© MapQuest.com, Inc.

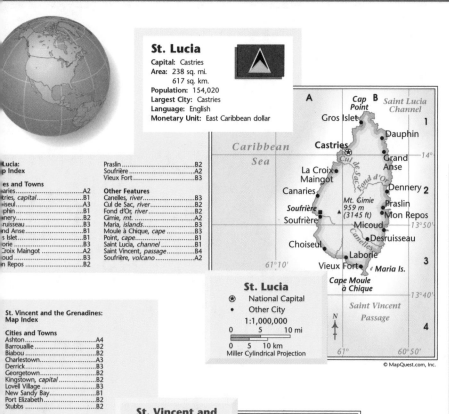

St. Lucia

Capital: Castries
Area: 238 sq. mi.
617 sq. km.
Population: 154,020
Largest City: Castries
Language: English
Monetary Unit: East Caribbean dollar

...Lucia:
...p Index

...es and Towns
...naries.....................................A2
...tries, *capital*........................B1
...iseul....................................A3
...phin......................................B1
...anery.....................................B2
...ruisseau.................................B3
...nd Anse..................................B1
...s Islet...................................B1
...orie.......................................B3
...Croix Maingot............................A2
...oud.......................................B3
...n Repos..................................B3

Other Features
Canelles, *river*...........................B3
Cul de Sac, *river*........................B2
Fond d'Or, *river*.........................B2
Gimie, *mt.*................................A2
Maria, *islands*...........................B3
Moule à Chique, *cape*....................B3
Point, *cape*..............................B1
Saint Lucia, *channel*.....................B1
Saint Vincent, *passage*...................B4
Soufrière, *volcano*.......................A2

St. Lucia

- ⊛ National Capital
- • Other City

1:1,000,000

0   5   10 mi
0 5 10 km
Miller Cylindrical Projection

© MapQuest.com, Inc.

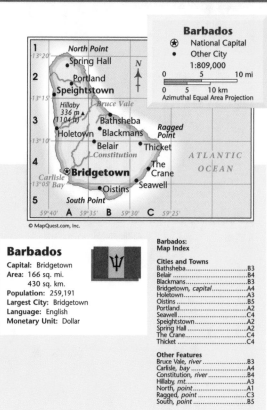

Barbados

Capital: Bridgetown
Area: 166 sq. mi.
430 sq. km.
Population: 259,191
Largest City: Bridgetown
Language: English
Monetary Unit: Dollar

Barbados

- ⊛ National Capital
- • Other City

1:809,000

0   5   10 mi
0   5   10 km
Azimuthal Equal Area Projection

© MapQuest.com, Inc.

Barbados:
Map Index

Cities and Towns
Bathsheba...................................B3
Belair.......................................B4
Blackmans...................................B3
Bridgetown, *capital*......................A4
Holetown....................................A3
Oistins......................................B5
Portland....................................A2
Seawell.....................................C4
Speightstown...............................A2
Spring Hall.................................A2
The Crane...................................C4
Thicket.....................................C4

Other Features
Bruce Vale, *river*........................B3
Carlisle, *bay*............................A4
Constitution, *river*......................B4
Hillaby, *mt.*.............................A3
North, *point*.............................A1
Ragged, *point*............................C3
South, *point*.............................B5

St. Vincent and the Grenadines:
Map Index

Cities and Towns
Ashton......................................A4
Barrouallie................................B2
Biabou......................................B2
Charlestown................................A3
Derrick.....................................B3
Georgetown.................................B2
Kingstown, *capital*.......................B2
Lovell Village.............................B3
New Sandy Bay..............................B1
Port Elizabeth.............................B2
Stubbs......................................B2

Other Features
Baleine, *bay*.............................B1
Baliceaux, *island*........................B3
Bequia, *island*...........................B2
Canouan, *island*..........................B3
Grenadines, *islands*......................A3
Mayreau, *island*..........................A4
Mt. Wynn, *bay*............................B2
Mustique, *island*.........................B3
North Mayreau, *channel*...................A3
Palm, *island*.............................A4
Petit Canouan, *island*....................B3
Petit Mustique, *island*...................B3
Petit St. Vincent, *island*................A4
St. Vincent, *island*......................B2
Savan, *island*............................B3
Soufrière, *mt.*...........................B1
Tobago, *cays*.............................A4
Union, *island*............................A4
Windward, *islands*........................B4

St. Vincent and the Grenadines

- ⊛ National Capital
- • Other City

1:1,900,000

0   10   20 mi
0   10   20 km
Miller Cylindrical Projection

St. Vincent and The Grenadines

Capital: Kingstown
Area: 150 sq. mi.
389 sq. km.
Population: 120,519
Largest City: Kingstown
Languages: English, French patois
Monetary Unit: East Caribbean dollar

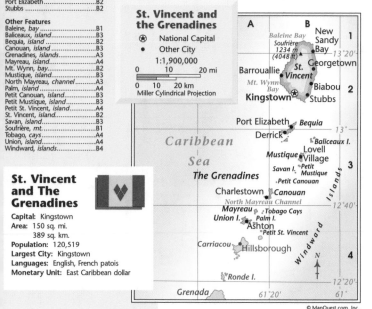

© MapQuest.com, Inc.

Trinidad & Tobago

Capital: Port of Spain
Area: 1,980 sq. mi.
5,130 sq. km.
Population: 1,102,096
Largest City: Port of Spain
Language: English
Monetary Unit: Dollar

Trinidad & Tobago:
Map Index

Cities and Towns
Arima.......................................A2
Canaan......................................B1
Chaguanas...................................A2
Charlotteville.............................B1
Couva.......................................A2
Fullarton...................................A2
Guayaguayare...............................A2
Matelot.....................................A2
Moruga......................................A2
Pierreville.................................A2
Plymouth....................................B1
Point Fortin...............................A2
Port of Spain, *capital*...................A2
Princes Town...............................A2
Rio Claro...................................A2
St. Augustine..............................A2
San Fernando...............................A2
San Francique..............................A2
Sangre Grande..............................A2
Scarborough................................B1
Siparia.....................................A2
Toco..B2

Other Features
El Cerro del Aripo, *mt.*..................A2
Paria, *gulf*..............................A2
Pitch, *lake*..............................A2
Tobago, *island*...........................B1
Trinidad, *island*.........................A2

Trinidad & Tobago

- ⊛ National Capital
- • Other City

1:2,700,000

0   15   30 mi
0   15   30 km
Azimuthal Equal Area Projection

© MapQuest.com, Inc.

Grenada:
Map Index

Cities and Towns
Grand Bay...................................C1
Grand Roy...................................B2
Hillsborough...............................C1
Marquis.....................................B2
St. David's................................B2
St. George's, *capital*....................B2
Sauteurs....................................B2
Tivoli......................................B2

Other Features
Bird, *island*.............................B2

Caille, *island*...........................B1
Carriacou, *island*........................C1
Diamond, *island*..........................B1
Frigate, *island*..........................B1
Grenada, *island*..........................B2
Grenadines, *island group*................B1, C1
Large, *island*............................C1
Les Tantes, *island*.......................B1
Petit Martinique, *island*.................C1
Ronde, *island*............................B1
St. Catherine, *mt.*.......................B2
Salines, *point*...........................A2
Sandy, *island*............................B2

Grenada

- ⊛ National Capital
- • Other City

1:1,260,000

0   8   16 mi
0   8   16 km
Transverse Mercator Projection

© MapQuest.com, Inc.

Grenada

Capital: St. George's
Area: 133 sq. mi.
345 sq. km.
Population: 97,008
Largest City: St. George's
Language: English
Monetary Unit: East Caribbean dollar

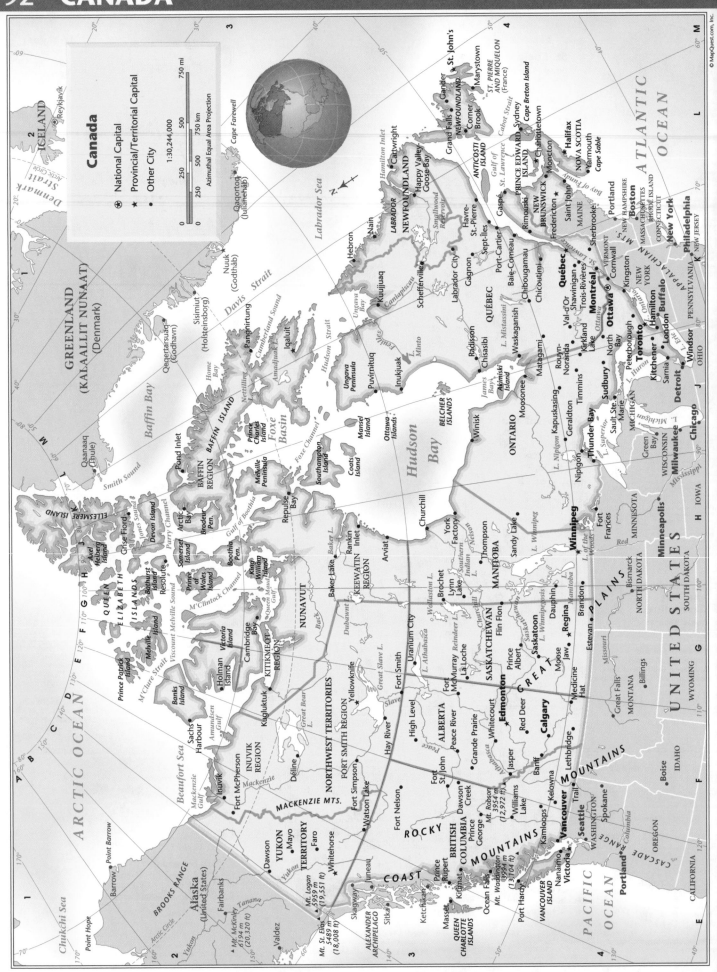

Canada

⊛ National Capital
★ Provincial/Territorial Capital
• Other City

1:30,244,000
Azimuthal Equal Area Projection

Map Index

Canada:
Map Index

ALBERTA
Cities and Towns
Banff ...F3
Calgary ...F3
Edmonton, capital ...F3
Fort McMurray ...G3
Grande Prairie ...F3
High Level ...F2
Jasper ...F3
Lethbridge ...F3
Medicine Hat ...F3
Peace River ...F2
Red Deer ...F3
Whitecourt ...F3

Other Features
Athabasca, river ...G3
Peace, river ...F3

BRITISH COLUMBIA
Cities and Towns
Dawson Creek ...E3
Fort Nelson ...E2
Fort St. John ...E3
Kamloops ...E3
Kelowna ...E4
Kitimat ...D3
Masset ...D3
Nanaimo ...E4
Ocean Falls ...D3
Port Hardy ...D3
Prince George ...E3
Prince Rupert ...D3
Trail ...E4
Vancouver, capital ...E4
Victoria, capital ...E3
Williams Lake ...E3

Other Features
Coast, mts. ...D3
Fraser, river ...E3
Queen Charlotte, islands ...C3
Robson, mt. ...E3
Rocky, mts. ...E3
Vancouver, island ...E4
Waddington, mt. ...E3

MANITOBA
Cities and Towns
Brandon ...H4
Brochet ...G3
Churchill ...H3
Dauphin ...G3
Flin Flon ...G3
Lynn Lake ...G3
Thompson ...H3
Winnipeg, capital ...H4
York Factory ...H3

Other Features
Churchill, river ...G3
Hudson, bay ...H3
Manitoba, lake ...H3
Nelson, river ...H3
Saskatchewan, river ...H3
Southern Indian, lake ...G3
Winnipeg, lake ...H3
Winnipegosis, lake ...G3

NEW BRUNSWICK
Cities and Towns
Fredericton, capital ...L4
Moncton ...L4
Saint John ...L4

Other Feature
Fundy, bay ...L4

NEWFOUNDLAND
Cities and Towns
Cartwright ...K3
Corner Brook ...L4
Gander ...L4
Grand Falls ...L4
Happy Valley-Goose Bay ...K3
Hebron ...K3
Labrador City ...K3
Marystown ...L4
Nain ...E3
St. John's, capital ...E4

Other Features
Cabot, strait ...M4
Hamilton, inlet ...M3
Labrador, region ...L3
St. Lawrence, gulf ...L4
Smallwood, reservoir ...L3

NORTHWEST TERRITORIES
Cities and Towns
Arviat ...H2
Déline ...E2
Fort McPherson ...E2
Fort Simpson ...F2
Fort Smith ...F2
Hay River ...D2
Holman Island ...E1
Inuvik ...E1
Sachs Harbour ...E1
Yellowknife, capital ...F2

Other Features
Amundsen, gulf ...E1
Banks, island ...D1
Beaufort, sea ...D1
Fort Smith, region ...F2
Great Bear, lake ...E2
Great Slave, lake ...D2
Home, bay ...D2
Mackenzie, river ...D2
Mackenzie, mts. ...D2
M'Clure, strait ...E1
Melville, island ...E1
Prince Patrick, island ...D1
Slave, river ...F2
Victoria, island ...F1
Viscount Melville, sound ...F1

NUNAVUT
Cities and Towns
Arctic Bay ...H1
Baker Lake ...H2
Cambridge Bay ...G2
Gjoa Haven ...J1
Iqaluit, capital ...L2
Kugluktuk ...F2
Pangnirtung ...K1
Pond Inlet ...K1
Rankin Inlet ...H2
Repulse Bay ...J2
Resolute ...H1

Other Features
Amadjuak, lake ...K2
Axel Heiberg, island ...H1
Back, river ...L1
Baffin, bay ...J1
Baffin, island ...K1
Baffin, region ...H2
Bathurst, island ...H1
Belcher, islands ...K3
Boothia, gulf ...D2
Boothia, peninsula ...E1
Brodeur, peninsula ...J2
Coats, island ...J2
Cumberland, sound ...M2
Davis, strait ...J1
Devon, island ...D1
Dubawnt, lake ...F2
Ellesmere, island ...K2
Foxe, basin ...L2
Foxe, channel ...D2
Home, bay ...D2
Hudson, bay ...D2
Hudson, strait ...J3
James, bay ...J3
Jones, sound ...H1
Keewatin, region ...H2
King William, island ...F2
Kitikmeot, region ...G1
M'Clintock, channel ...J2
Melville, peninsula ...J3
Nettilling, lake ...K2
Ottawa, islands ...K3
Parry, channel ...J1
Prince Charles, island ...K2
Prince of Wales, island ...H1
Queen Elizabeth, islands ...G2
Smith, sound ...K1
Somerset, island ...H1
Southampton, island ...J2
Victoria, island ...G1

NOVA SCOTIA
Cities and Towns
Halifax, capital ...H1
Sydney ...L1
Yarmouth ...L1

Other Features
Cabot, strait ...M4
Cape Breton, island ...M4
Fundy, bay ...L4
Sable, cape ...L4

ONTARIO
Cities and Towns
Cornwall ...K4
Fort Frances ...H4
Geraldton ...J4
Hamilton ...J4
Kapuskasing ...J4
Kingston ...K4
Kirkland Lake ...J4
Kitchener ...J4
London ...J4
Moosonee ...J3
Nipigon ...J4
North Bay ...K4
Ottawa, national capital ...K4
Peterborough ...K4
Sarnia ...J4
Sault Ste. Marie ...J4
Sudbury ...J4
Thunder Bay ...J4
Timmins ...J4
Toronto, capital ...J4
Windsor ...J4
Winisk ...J3

Other Features
Akimiski, island ...J3
Albany, river ...H4
Erie, lake ...J4
Hudson, bay ...J3
Huron, lake ...J4
James, bay ...J3
Nipigon, lake ...J4
Ontario, lake ...J4
Ottawa, river ...K4
Superior, lake ...J4
Woods, lake ...H4

PRINCE EDWARD ISLAND
Cities and Towns
Charlottetown, capital ...L4

QUÉBEC
Cities and Towns
Baie-Comeau ...L4
Chibougamau ...K4
Chicoutimi ...K4
Chisasibi ...K3
Gagnon ...L4
Gaspé ...L4
Havre-St-Pierre ...L4
Inukjuak ...K3
Kuujjuaq ...L3
Matagami ...K4
Montréal ...K4
Port-Cartier ...L4
Povungnituk ...K3
Québec, national capital ...K4
Rimouski ...L4
Rouyn-Noranda ...K4
Radisson ...K3
Schefferville ...L3
Sept-Îles ...L4
Shawinigan ...K4
Sherbrooke ...K4
Trois-Rivières ...K4
Val-d'Or ...K4
Waskaganish ...K3

Other Features
Anticosti, island ...L3
Caniapiscau, river ...L3
Feuilles, river ...J3
Hudson, bay ...J3
Hudson, strait ...K2
James, bay ...J3
Minto, lake ...K3
Mistassini, lake ...K4
Ontario, lake ...J4
St. Lawrence, gulf ...L4
St. Lawrence, river ...K4
Ungava, bay ...L3
Ungava, peninsula ...K2

SASKATCHEWAN
Cities and Towns
Estevan ...G4
La Loche ...G3
Moose Jaw ...G3
Prince Albert ...G3
Regina, capital ...G3
Saskatoon ...G3
Uranium City ...G3

Other Features
Athabasca, lake ...G3
Churchill, river ...G3
Great Plains, plain ...G3
Reindeer, lake ...G3
Saskatchewan, river ...G3
Wollaston, lake ...G3

YUKON TERRITORY
Cities and Towns
Dawson ...D2
Faro ...D2
Mayo ...D2
Watson Lake ...E2
Whitehorse, capital ...D2

Other Features
Beaufort, sea ...D1
Logan, mt. ...C2
St. Elias, mt. ...C2
Yukon, river ...D2

Manitoba
Capital: Winnipeg
Area: 250,947 sq. mi.
650,122 sq. km.
Population: 1,113,898
Largest City: Winnipeg

Nunavut
Capital: Iqaluit
Area: 800,775 sq. mi.
2,074,000 sq. km.
Population: 24,730
Largest City: Iqaluit

Yukon Territory
Capital: Whitehorse
Area: 186,661 sq. mi.
483,578 sq. km.
Population: 30,766
Largest City: Whitehorse

British Columbia
Capital: Victoria
Area: 365,947 sq. mi.
948,049 sq. km.
Population: 3,724,500
Largest City: Vancouver

Nova Scotia
Capital: Halifax
Area: 21,425 sq. mi.
55,505 sq. km.
Population: 909,282
Largest City: Halifax

Saskatchewan
Capital: Regina
Area: 251,866 sq. mi.
652,503 sq. km.
Population: 990,237
Largest City: Saskatoon

Alberta
Capital: Edmonton
Area: 255,287 sq. mi.
661,265 sq. km.
Population: 2,696,826
Largest City: Edmonton

Northwest Territories
Capital: Yellowknife
Area: 520,850 sq. mi.
1,349,000 sq. km.
Population: 39,672
Largest City: Yellowknife

Québec
Capital: Québec
Area: 594,860 sq. mi.
1,541,088 sq. km.
Population: 7,138,795
Largest City: Montréal

Canada
Capital: Ottawa
Area: 3,849,674 sq. mi.
9,973,249 sq. km.
Population: 31,006,347
Largest City: Toronto
Languages: English, French
Monetary Unit: Canadian dollar

Newfoundland
Capital: St. John's
Area: 156,949 sq. mi.
406,604 sq. km.
Population: 551,792
Largest City: St. John's

Prince Edward Island
Capital: Charlottetown
Area: 2,185 sq. mi.
5,661 sq. km.
Population: 134,557
Largest City: Charlottetown

New Brunswick
Capital: Fredericton
Area: 28,355 sq. mi.
73,459 sq. km.
Population: 738,133
Largest City: Saint John

Ontario
Capital: Toronto
Area: 412,581 sq. mi.
1,068,863 sq. km.
Population: 10,753,573
Largest City: Toronto

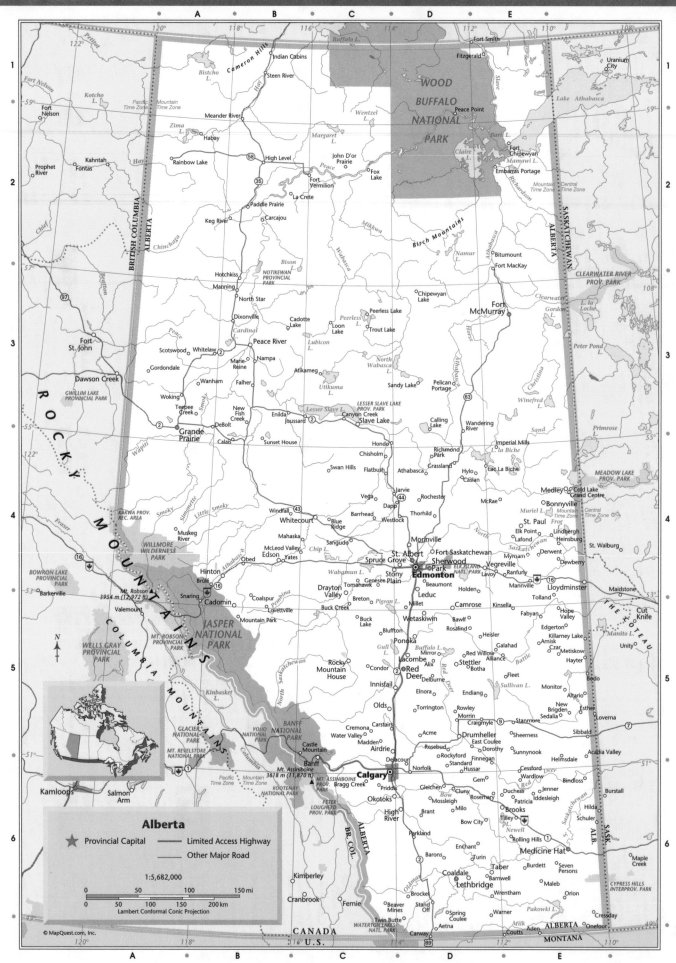

Alberta

★ Provincial Capital — Limited Access Highway
 — Other Major Road

1:5,682,000

0   50   100   150 mi
0 50 100 150 200 km
Lambert Conformal Conic Projection

© MapQuest.com, Inc.

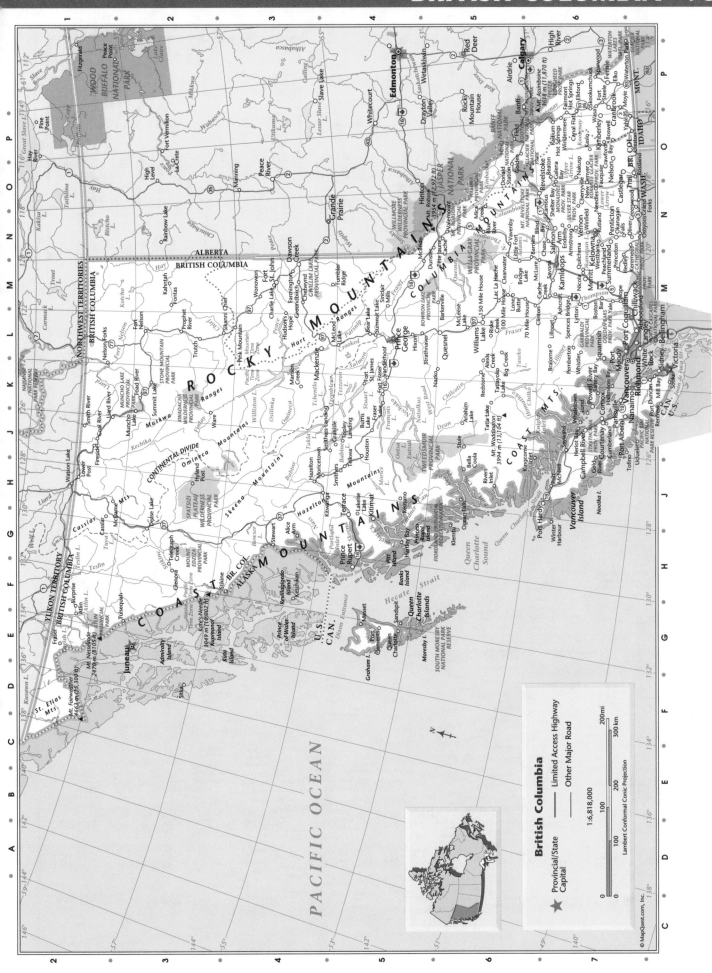

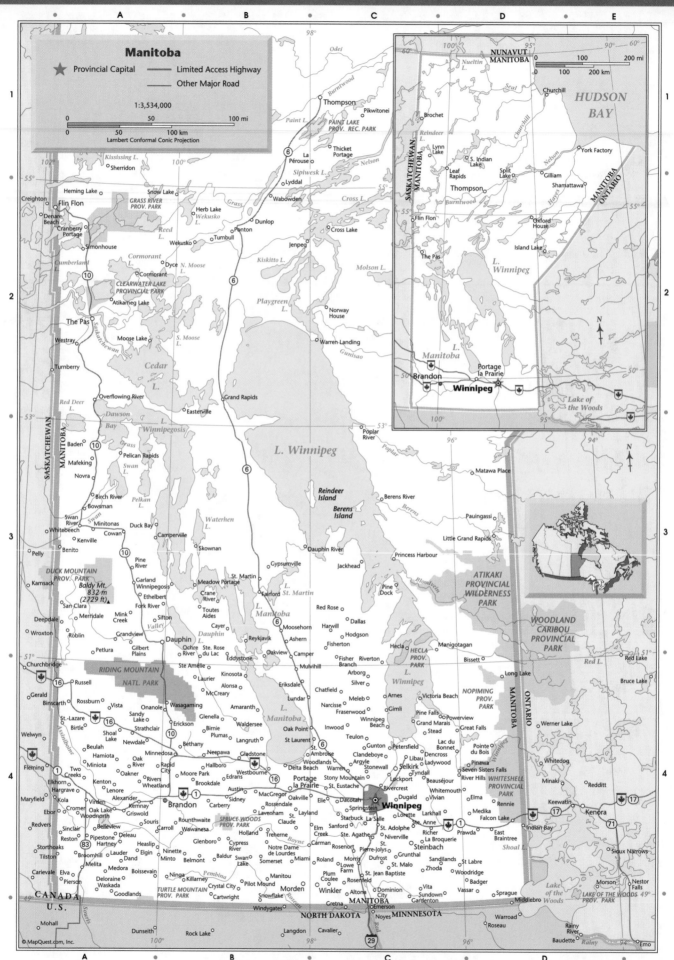

Manitoba

★ Provincial Capital ── Limited Access Highway
── Other Major Road

1:3,534,000

0   50   100 mi
0   50   100 km
Lambert Conformal Conic Projection

HUDSON BAY

NUNAVUT MANITOBA

SASKATCHEWAN | MANITOBA

MANITOBA | ONTARIO

Churchill
York Factory
Brochet
Lynn Lake
S. Indian Lake
Leaf Rapids
Split Lake
Gilliam
Shamattawa
Thompson
Flin Flon
Oxford House
The Pas
Island Lake
L. Winnipeg
L. Manitoba
Brandon
Portage la Prairie
Winnipeg
Lake of the Woods

Thompson
Pikwitonei
PAINT LAKE PROV. REC. PARK
La Pérouse
Thicket Portage
Nelson
Lyddal
Wabowden
Cross L.
Snow Lake
Herb Lake
Wekusko
Dunlop
Ponton
Cross Lake
Jenpeg
Norway House
Warren Landing

Creighton
Flin Flon
Denare Beach
Cranberry Portage
Simonhouse
Heming Lake
Sherridon
Kissising L.
Sipiwesk L.
GRASS RIVER PROV. PARK
Grass

Cumberland L.
Reed L.
Wekusko
Dyce
N. Moose L.
Cormorant
Atikameg Lake
CLEARWATER LAKE PROVINCIAL PARK
Kiskitto L.
Playgreen L.
Molson L.

The Pas
Westray
Turnberry
Moose Lake
S. Moose L.
Cedar L.
Saskatchewan
Red Deer L.
Overflowing River
Dawson Bay
Easterville
Grand Rapids
L. Winnipeg
Poplar River
Matawa Place

Baden
Mafeking
Novra
Pelican Rapids
Swan L.
Birch River
Bowsman
Pelkan L.
Winnipegosis
Grass
Reindeer Island
Berens Island
Berens River
Pauingassi

Swan River
Whitebeech
Minitonas
Cowan
Duck Bay
Waterhen L.
Camperville
Skownan
Dauphin River
Little Grand Rapids
ATIKAKI PROVINCIAL WILDERNESS PARK

Pelly
Benito
Kenville
Pine River
Garland
Winnipegosis
Ethelbert
Fork River
Sifton
DUCK MOUNTAIN PROV. PARK
Baldy Mt. 832 m (2729 ft)▲
Meadow Portage
Crane River
Toutes Aides
Cayer
Gypsumville
L. St. Martin
St. Martin
Fairford
Jackhead
Red Rose
Princess Harbour
Pine Dock
WOODLAND CARIBOU PROVINCIAL PARK

Kamsack
San Clara
Merridale
Mink Creek
Grandview
Dauphin
Ste. Rose du Lac
Ochre River
Reykjavik
Oakview
Camper
Moosehorn
Harwill
Dallas
Hodgson
Fisherton
Manigotagan
Bloodvein

Deepdale
Wroxton
Roblin
Petlura
Gilbert Plains
Eddystone
Mulvihill
Fisher Branch
Riverton
Hecla
Bissett
Red L.
Red Lake

Churchbridge
Gerald
Russell
Vista
Onanole
Wasagaming
RIDING MOUNTAIN NATL. PARK
Laurier
McCreary
Kinosota
Eriksdale
Arborg
Silver
HECLA PROV. PARK
Long Lake
Bruce Lake

Binscarth
Rossburn
Sandy Lake
Glenella
Amaranth
Alonsa
Chatfield
Meleb
Narcisse
Victoria Beach
Pine Falls
NOPIMING PROV. PARK
Werner Lake

St.-Lazare
Birtle
Shoal Lake
Strathclair
Erickson
Birnie Plumas
Waldersee
Langruth
Lundar
Fraserwood
Gimli
Grand Marais
Powerview
Great Falls
Whitedog

Welwyn
Beulah
Hamiota
Minnedosa
Neepawa
Gladstone
Oak Point
St Laurent
Inwood
Teulon
Winnipeg Beach
Stead
Lac du Bonnet
Pointe du Bois
Minaki
Redditt

Fleming
Elkhorn
Two Creeks
Miniota
Oak River
Rapid City
Hallboro
Westbourne
Delta Beach
Gunton
Petersfield
Dencross
Pinawa
Seven Sisters Falls
River Hills
WHITESHELL PROVINCIAL PARK

Maryfield
Hargrave
Kola
Kenton
Lenore
Rivers
Wheatland
Brookdale
Austin
MacGregor
Portage la Prairie
St. Eustache
Clandeboye
Argyle
Stonewall
Selkirk
Ladywood
Beauséjour
Keewatin
Kenora

Pierson
Cromer
Oak Lake
Woodnorth
Kemnay
Brandon
Carberry
Sidney
Rossendale
Oakville
Elie
Dacotah
Springstein
Winnipeg
Lorette
Ste. Anne
Medika
Falcon Lake
Indian Bay
71

Redvers
Ebor
Sinclair
Belleview
Griswold
Souris
Rounthwaite
Wawanesa
Holland
Treherne
Elm Creek
Starbuck
La Salle
Larkhall
Prawda
Rennie
17

Storthoaks
Tilston
Reston
Pipestone
Hartney
Deleau
Carroll
Glenboro
SPRUCE WOODS PROV. PARK
Cypress River
Lavenham
Claude
Sanford
Ste. Agathe
Niverville
Richer
East Braintree
Shoal L.

Carievale
Elva
Medora
Boissevain
Ninette
Baldur
Swan Lake
Notre Dame de Lourdes
Somerset
Miami
Roland
Lowe Farm
Pierre-Jolys
Dufrost
Steinbach
Sandilands
St Labre
Woodridge

Mohall
Deloraine
Waskada
Goodlands
TURTLE MOUNTAIN PROV. PARK
Killarney
Crystal City
Pilot Mound
Snowflake
Manitou
Morden
Winkler
Altona
St. Jean Baptiste
St. Malo
Zhoda
Vita
Sundown
Vassar
Sprague
Badger
LAKE OF THE WOODS PROV. PARK

Dunseith
Rock Lake
Langdon
Cavalier
Windygates
Gretna
MANITOBA
Emerson
Noyes
Dominion City
Gardenton
Middlebro
Warroad
Roseau
Rainy River
Baudette
Emo
CANADA U.S.
NORTH DAKOTA
MINNNESOTA
Rainy

29

© MapQuest.com, Inc.

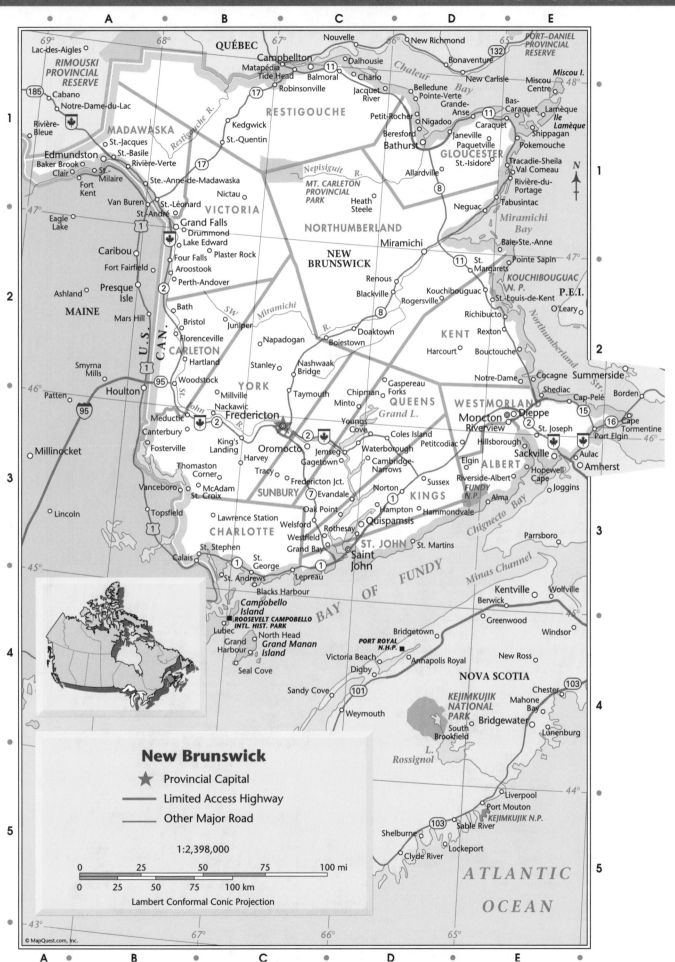

69°

Lac-des-Aigles

RIMOUSKI
PROVINCIAL
RESERVE

185 Cabano
Notre-Dame-du-Lac

Rivière-
Bleue

Edmundston
Baker Brook
Clair
Fort
Kent

St.-Jacques
St.-Basile
Rivière-Verte
Ste.-Anne-de-Madawaska

MADAWASKA

Van Buren
St.-André
St.-Léonard

Eagle
Lake

Caribou

Fort Fairfield

Ashland

Presque
Isle

MAINE

Mars Hill

St.-
Milaire

Grand Falls
Drummond
Lake Edward
Four Falls Plaster Rock
Aroostook
Perth-Andover

VICTORIA

Nictau

Kedgwick

St.-Quentin

QUÉBEC

Matapédia
Tide Head

Robinsonville

RESTIGOUCHE

Nouvelle
Campbellton
Dalhousie

Balmoral Charlo

Jacquet
River

Petit-Rocher

New Richmond

Bonaventure

132

New Carlisle

Miscou I.

Belledune
Pointe-Verte
Grande-
Anse
Nigadoo
Bathurst

Beresford

Janeville
Caraquet

GLOUCESTER
St.-Isidore

Allardville

Miscou
Centre

Lamèque
Ile
Lamèque
Shippagan

Pokemouche

Tracadie-Sheila
Val Comeau

Rivière-du-
Portage

PORT-DANIEL
PROVINCIAL
RESERVE

Chaleur Bay

Nepisiguit R.

MT. CARLETON
PROVINCIAL
PARK

Heath
Steele

NORTHUMBERLAND

NEW
BRUNSWICK

Bath
Bristol
Florenceville
Hartland

CARLETON

Smyrna
Mills

Patten

Houlton

Millinocket

Woodstock

Napadogan

Stanley

YORK

Nashwaak
Bridge

Taymouth

Bristol

Juniper

Meductic
Canterbury
Fosterville

Thomaston
Corner

Vanceboro

Lincoln

Topsfield

Millville
Nackawic
Fredericton

King's
Landing

Harvey

McAdam
St. Croix

Lawrence Station

Renous

Blackville

Doaktown
Boiestown

Miramichi R.

St.

Margarets

Pointe Sapin

St.-Louis-de-Kent

KOUCHIBOUGUAC
W. P.

P.E.I.

O'Leary

Kouchibouguac
Rogersville

Harcourt

KENT
Richibucto

Rexton
Bouctouche

Notre-Dame

Cocagne
Shediac

Summerside
Borden

Cap-Pelé

15

Cape
Tormentine

Port Elgin

Amherst

Aulac

Sackville

ALBERT

Hillsborough

Hopewell
Cape

Joggins

Parrsboro

Chignecto Bay

Minas Channel

Kentville
Wolfville
Berwick

Greenwood

Windsor

New Ross

Chester
103

Mahone
Bay

Bridgewater

Lunenburg

Campobello
Island
ROOSEVELT CAMPOBELLO
INTL. HIST. PARK

Lubec

Grand
Harbour

North Head

Seal Cove

Grand Manan
Island

PORT ROYAL
N.H.P.

Victoria Beach

Digby

Sandy Cove

Weymouth

Bridgetown

Annapolis Royal

NOVA SCOTIA

KEJIMKUJIK
NATIONAL
PARK

South
Brookfield

L.
Rossignol

Liverpool

Port Mouton

KEJIMKUJIK N.P.

Shelburne

Sable River

Lockeport

Clyde River

ATLANTIC

OCEAN

New Brunswick

★ Provincial Capital
— Limited Access Highway
⋯ Other Major Road

1:2,398,000

| 0 | 25 | 50 | 75 | 100 mi |

| 0 | 25 | 50 | 75 | 100 km |

Lambert Conformal Conic Projection

© MapQuest.com, Inc.

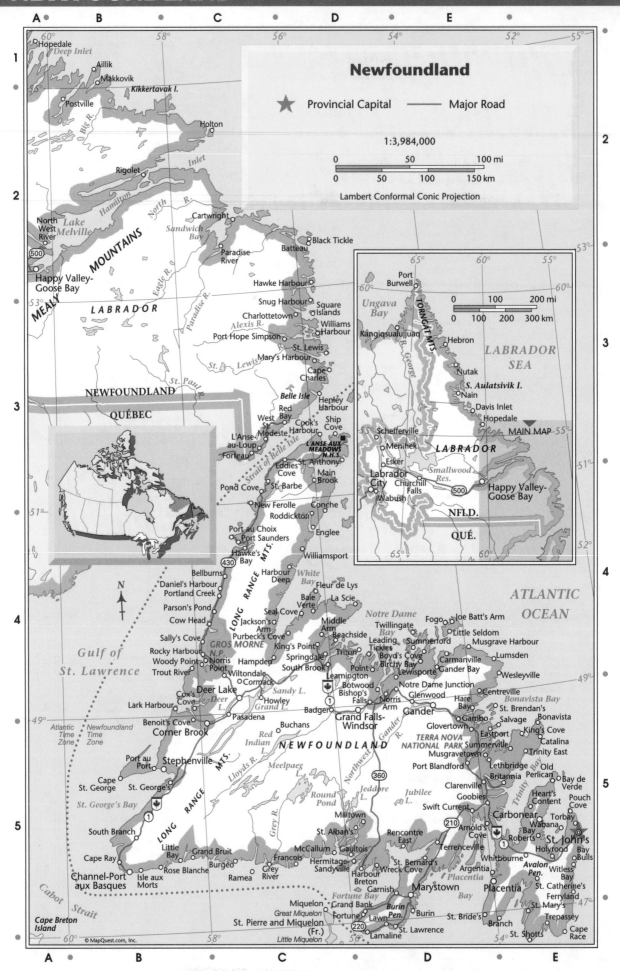

Newfoundland

★ Provincial Capital   ———— Major Road

1:3,984,000

0   50   100 mi

0   50   100   150 km

Lambert Conformal Conic Projection

Hopedale
Deep Inlet
Aillik
Makkovik
Kikkertavak I.
Postville
Holton
Rigolet
Hamilton Inlet
North West River
Lake Melville
Cartwright
Sandwich Bay
MEALY MOUNTAINS
Happy Valley-Goose Bay
LABRADOR
Black Tickle
Batteau
Paradise River
Hawke Harbour
Snug Harbour
Square Islands
Charlottetown
Williams Harbour
Port Hope Simpson
St. Lewis
Alexis R.
Mary's Harbour
Cape Charles
Belle Isle
Henley Harbour
West St. Modeste
Red Bay
Cook's Harbour
Ship Cove
L'Anse-au-Loup
Forteau
L'ANSE AUX MEADOWS N.H.S.
Eddies Cove
St. Anthony
Main Brook
Pond Cove
St. Barbe
New Ferolle
Conche
Roddickton
Port au Choix
Port Saunders
Englee
Hawke's Bay
Williamsport

NEWFOUNDLAND
QUÉBEC

Bellburns
Harbour Deep
White Bay
Fleur de Lys
Daniel's Harbour
La Scie
Portland Creek
Baie Verte
Parson's Pond
Seal Cove
Cow Head
Notre Dame Bay
Fogo
Joe Batt's Arm
Jackson's Arm
Middle Arm
Twillingate
Little Seldom
Purbeck's Cove
Beachside
Leading Tickles
Musgrave Harbour
Sally's Cove
King's Point
Summerford
Lumsden
Rocky Harbour
Springdale
Triton
Boyd's Cove
Carmanville
Woody Point
Hampden
South Brook
Birchy Bay
Gander Bay
Wesleyville
Norris Point
Point Leamington
Lewisporte
Trout River
Wiltondale
Botwood
Notre Dame Junction
Centreville
Cormack
Bishop's Falls
Glenwood
Bonavista Bay
Deer Lake
Howley
Badger
Norris Arm
Hare Bay
St. Brendan's
Cox's Cove
Grand L.
Gander
Gambo
Salvage
Bonavista
Lark Harbour
Pasadena
Grand Falls-Windsor
Glovertown
King's Cove
Catalina
Benoit's Cove
Buchans
Eastport
Corner Brook
Red Indian L.
TERRA NOVA NATIONAL PARK
Summerville
Trinity East
Port au Port
Meelpaeg L.
Lloyds R.
NEWFOUNDLAND
Musgravetown
Lethbridge
Old Perlican
Stephenville
Port Blandford
Britannia
Bay de Verde
Cape St. George
Jeddore L.
Clarenville
Heart's Content
St. George's
St. George's Bay
Round Pond
Jubilee L.
Goobies
Pouch Cove
South Branch
Milltown
Swift Current
Carbonear
Torbay
St. Alban's
Rencontre East
Arnold's Cove
Wabana
Little Bay
Grand Bruit
McCallum
Gaultois
Terrenceville
Roberts
Holyrood
St. John's
Cape Ray
Rose Blanche
Burgeo
Francois
Hermitage
Sandyville
St. Bernard's
Whitbourne
Bay Bulls
Channel-Port aux Basques
Isle aux Morts
Ramea
Grey River
Wreck Cove
Harbour Breton
Argentia
Avalon Pen.
Witless Bay
Garnish
Marystown
Placentia
St. Catherine's
Miquelon
Grand Bank
Burin Pen.
Placentia Bay
Ferryland
Great Miquelon
Fortune
Burin
St. Bride's
St. Mary's
St. Pierre and Miquelon (Fr.)
Lawn
St. Lawrence
Branch
St. Shotts
Little Miquelon
Lamaline
Trepassey
Cape Race

GROS MORNE N.P.
LONG RANGE MTS.
Gulf of St. Lawrence
Cabot Strait
Cape Breton Island
Atlantic Time Zone
Newfoundland Time Zone

ATLANTIC OCEAN

500
430
1
360
210
1
220

Strait of Belle Isle
St. Paul R.
St. Lewis R.
Eagle R.
Paradise R.
North R.
Big R.
Sandy L.
Northwest Gander R.
Grey R.
Trinity Bay
Fortune Bay

Inset map (top right)
Port Burwell
Ungava Bay
TORNGAT MTS.
Kangiqsualujjuaq
Hebron
LABRADOR SEA
Nutak
S. Aulatsivik I.
Nain
Davis Inlet
Hopedale
Schefferville
MAIN MAP
Menihek
LABRADOR
Esker
Smallwood Res.
Labrador City
Churchill Falls
Happy Valley-Goose Bay
Wabush
NFLD.
QUÉ.
George R.
500

© MapQuest.com, Inc.

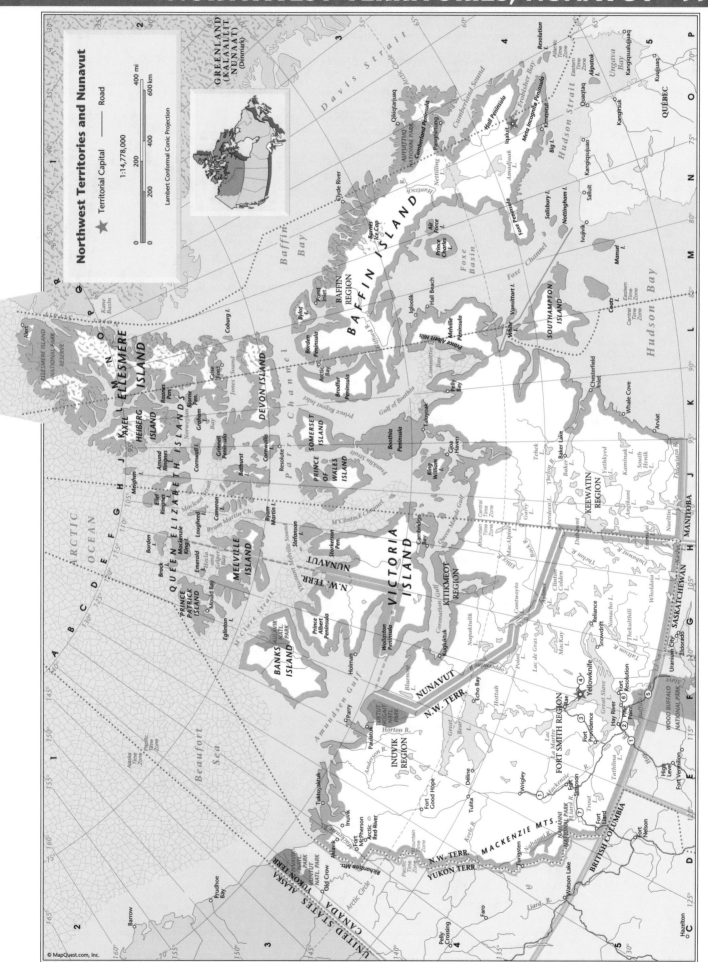

Northwest Territories and Nunavut

★ Territorial Capital
— Road

1:14,778,000

400 mi
600 km
200
400
200
0
0

Lambert Conformal Conic Projection

© MapQuest.com, Inc.

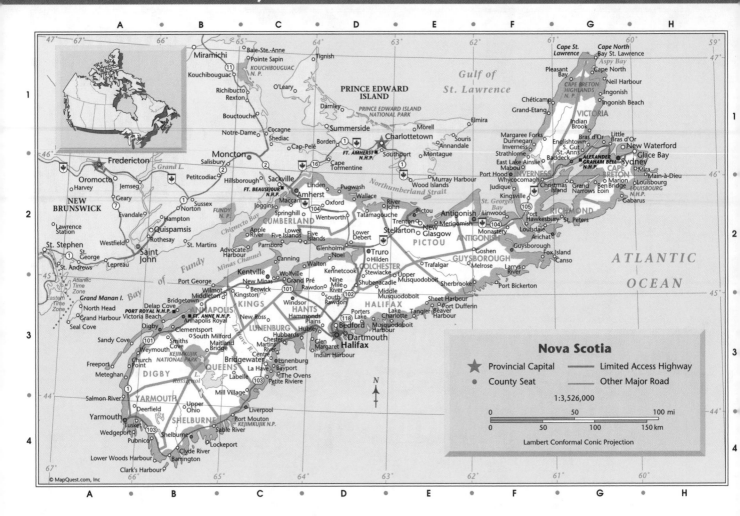

Nova Scotia

★ Provincial Capital
● County Seat
— Limited Access Highway
— Other Major Road

1:3,526,000

0   50   100 mi
0   50   100   150 km

Lambert Conformal Conic Projection

© MapQuest.com, Inc

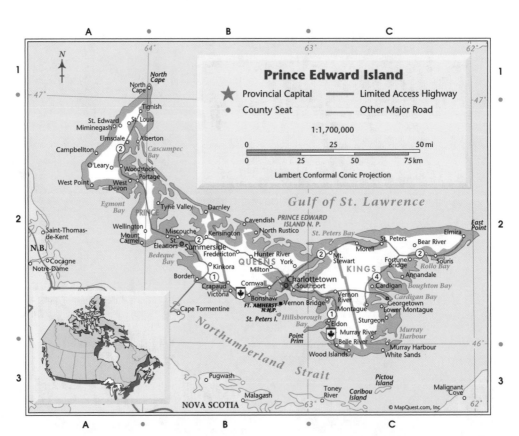

Prince Edward Island

★ Provincial Capital
● County Seat
— Limited Access Highway
— Other Major Road

1:1,700,000

0   25   50 mi
0   25   50   75 km

Lambert Conformal Conic Projection

© MapQuest.com, Inc

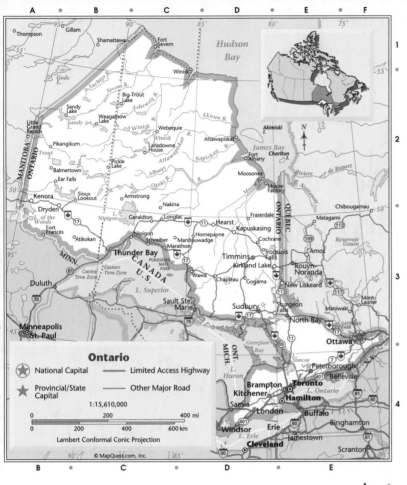

Ontario

⬢ National Capital — Limited Access Highway

★ Provincial/State Capital — Other Major Road

1:15,610,000

0   200   400 mi
0   200   400   600 km

Lambert Conformal Conic Projection

© MapQuest.com, Inc.

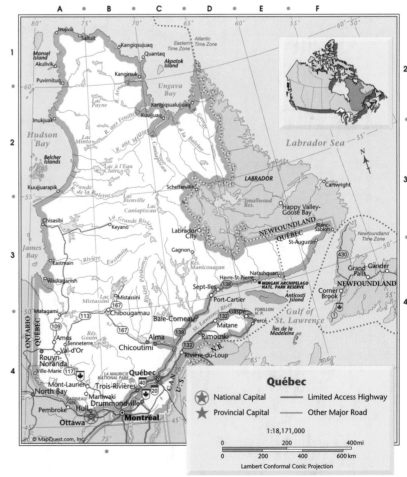

Québec

⬢ National Capital — Limited Access Highway

★ Provincial Capital — Other Major Road

1:18,171,000

0   200   400mi
0   200   400   600 km

Lambert Conformal Conic Projection

© MapQuest.com, Inc.

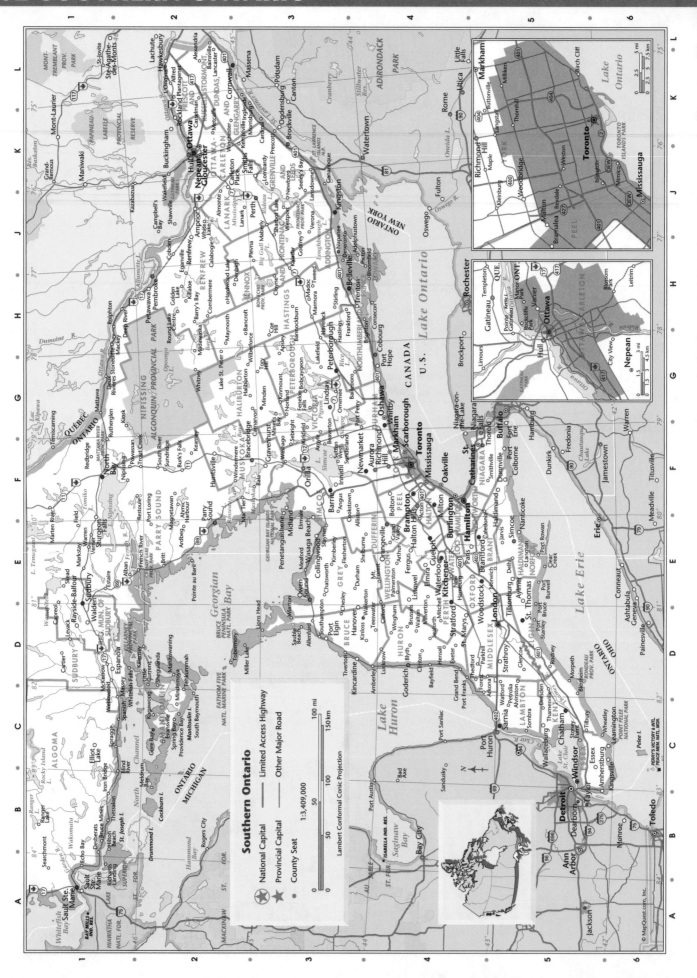

Southern Ontario

★ National Capital
★ Provincial Capital
● County Seat

— Limited Access Highway
— Other Major Road

1:3,409,000

Lambert Conformal Conic Projection

0   50   100 mi
0   50   100   150 km

© MapQuest.com, Inc.

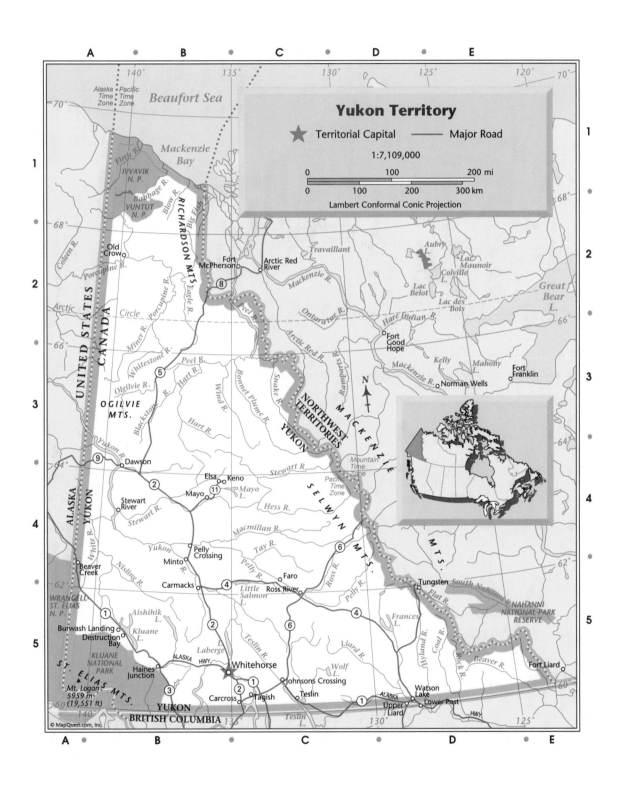

Yukon Territory

★ Territorial Capital ——— Major Road

1:7,109,000

0	100	200 mi
0	100	200	300 km

Lambert Conformal Conic Projection

Beaufort Sea

Mackenzie Bay

Alaska Time Zone · Pacific Time Zone

IVVAVIK N. P.

Babbage R.
Blow R.
Firth R.
Big Fish R.

VUNTUT N. P.

RICHARDSON MTS

Coleen R.
Porcupine R.
Old Crow
Porcupine R.
Eagle R.

UNITED STATES
CANADA

Arctic
Circle

Miner R.
Whitestone R.
Olgilvie R.
Blackstone R.
Peel R.
Hart R.

OGILVIE MTS.

Fort McPherson
Arctic Red River
Peel R.
Travaillant
Mackenzie R.
Ontaratue R.
Arctic Red R.

Aubry L.
Lac Maunoir
Lac Colville L.
Lac Belot
Lac des Bois

Great Bear L.

Hare Indian R.
Fort Good Hope

Kelly L.
Mahony L.
Fort Franklin

Mackenzie R.
Norman Wells

Wind R.
Bonnet Plume R.
Snake R.
Hart R.

NORTHWEST TERRITORIES

YUKON

M A C K E N Z I E   M T S.

N

Mountain Time Zone
Pacific Time Zone

Yukon R.
Dawson

Elsa Keno
Mayo
Stewart R.
Mayo L.
Stewart River
Stewart R.
Hess R.

S E L W Y N   M T S.

Macmillan R.
Tay R.
Yukon R.
Pelly Crossing
Minto
Pelly R.
Ross R.

Faro
Ross River
Little Salmon
Carmacks
Pelly R.

Tungsten
South Nahanni R.
Flat R.
Hyland R.
Coal R.
Rock R.
Beaver R.

NAHANNI NATIONAL PARK RESERVE

Beaver Creek
Nisling R.
White R.

WRANGELL ST. ELIAS N. P.

ALASKA
YUKON

Aishihik L.
Kluane L.
Burwash Landing
Destruction Bay

KLUANE NATIONAL PARK

Teslin R.
Teslin L.
Frances L.

Fort Liard

Mt. Logan 5959 m (19,551 ft)

ST. ELIAS MTS.

Haines Junction
ALASKA HWY

Laberge L.
Whitehorse
Johnsons Crossing
Teslin
Wolf R.
Liard R.

Watson Lake
ALASKA HWY
Upper Liard
Lower Post

Carcross
Tagish

YUKON
BRITISH COLUMBIA
Teslin L.

© MapQuest.com, Inc.

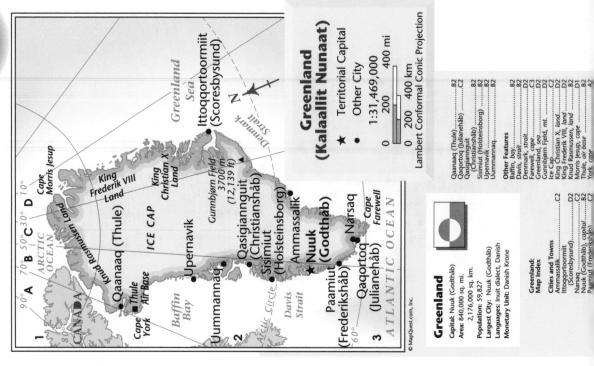

King Frederik VIII Land

Cape Morris Jesup

King Christian X Land

Gunnbjørn Field 3700 m (12,139 ft)

Ittoqqortoormiit (Scoresbysund)

Greenland Sea

Denmark Strait

N

ICE CAP

Qaanaaq (Thule)

Thule Air Base

Upernavik

Qasigiannguit (Christianshåb)

Sisimiut (Holsteinsborg)

Ammassalik

Nuuk (Godthåb)

Narsaq

Cape Farewell

Paamiut (Frederikshåb)

Qaqortoq (Julianehåb)

Knud Rasmussen Land

Uummannaq

Cape York

Baffin Bay

Davis Strait

Arctic Circle

CANADA

ARCTIC OCEAN

ATLANTIC OCEAN

90° A 70° B 50° C 30° D 10°

1 2 3

80° 60°

Greenland (Kalaallit Nunaat)

★ Territorial Capital
● Other City

1:31,469,000

Lambert Conformal Conic Projection

0   200   400 km
0   200   400 mi

Greenland

Capital: Nuuk (Godthåb)
Area: 840,000 sq. mi.
2,176,000 sq. km.
Population: 59,827
Largest City: Nuuk (Godthåb)
Languages: Inuit dialect, Danish
Monetary Unit: Danish Krone

Greenland: Map Index

Cities and Towns

Qaanaaq (Thule)	B2
Qaqortoq (Julianehåb)	C2
Qasigiannguit (Christianshåb)	B2
Sisimiut (Holsteinsborg)	B2
Upernavik	B2
Uummannaq	B2

Other Features

Baffin, bay	B2
Davis, strait	B2
Farewell, cape	C3
Greenland, sea	D2
Gunnbjørn Field, mt.	D2
Ice Cap	C2
King Christian X, land	D2
King Frederik VIII, land	D1
Knud Rasmussen, land	B2
Morris Jesup, cape	B2
York, cape	A2

Ammassalik	C2
Ittoqqortoormiit (Scoresbysund)	D2
Narsaq	C2
Nuuk (Godthåb), capital	B2
Paamiut (Frederikshåb)	C2

© MapQuest.com, Inc.

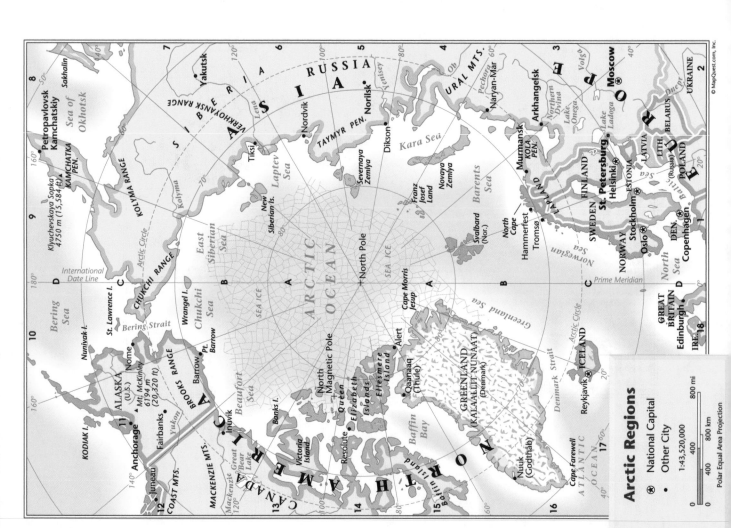

Arctic Regions

⊛ National Capital
● Other City

1:43,520,000

Polar Equal Area Projection

0   400   800 km
0   400   800 mi

Petropavlovsk Kamchatskiy

Klyuchevskaya Sopka 4750 m (15,584 ft)

KAMCHATKA PEN.

Sea of Okhotsk

Sakhalin

Yakutsk

RUSSIA

Nordvik

Norilsk

Dikson

Kara Sea

Novaya Zemlya

Barents Sea

URAL MTS.

Naryan-Mar

Arkhangelsk

Moscow

UKRAINE

BELARUS

POLAND

LATVIA

LITH.

ESTONIA

FINLAND

St. Petersburg

Helsinki

SWEDEN

NORWAY

Stockholm

Oslo

DEN.

Copenhagen

GREAT BRITAIN

Edinburgh

IRE.

ICELAND

Reykjavik

GREENLAND (KALAALLIT NUNAAT) (Denmark)

Cape Farewell

Nuuk (Godthåb)

Qaanaaq (Thule)

Baffin Bay

Baffin Island

Resolute

Victoria Island

Banks I.

Queen Elizabeth Islands

Ellesmere Island

Alert

North Magnetic Pole

North Pole

ARCTIC OCEAN

SEA ICE

Cape Morris Jesup

Greenland Sea

Denmark Strait

Svalbard (Nor.)

North Cape

Hammerfest

Tromsø

Franz Josef Land

Severnaya Zemlya

TAYMYR PEN.

Laptev Sea

New Siberian Is.

Tiksi

East Siberian Sea

KOLYMA RANGE

VERKHOYANSK RANGE

International Date Line

CHUKCHI RANGE

Wrangel I.

Chukchi Sea

St. Lawrence I.

Bering Strait

Nunivak I.

Nome

KODIAK I.

Anchorage

Juneau

Fairbanks

ALASKA (U.S.)

Mt. McKinley 6194 m (20,320 ft)

BROOKS RANGE

Barrow

Pt. Barrow

Beaufort Sea

MACKENZIE MTS.

COAST MTS.

Great Bear Lake

CANADA

NORTH AMERICA

ATLANTIC OCEAN

Bering Sea

© MapQuest.com, Inc.

N
8 7 6 5 4 3 2
D C B A B C D
9 1
10
11 A
12 17 18
13 14 15 16

© MapQuest.com, Inc.

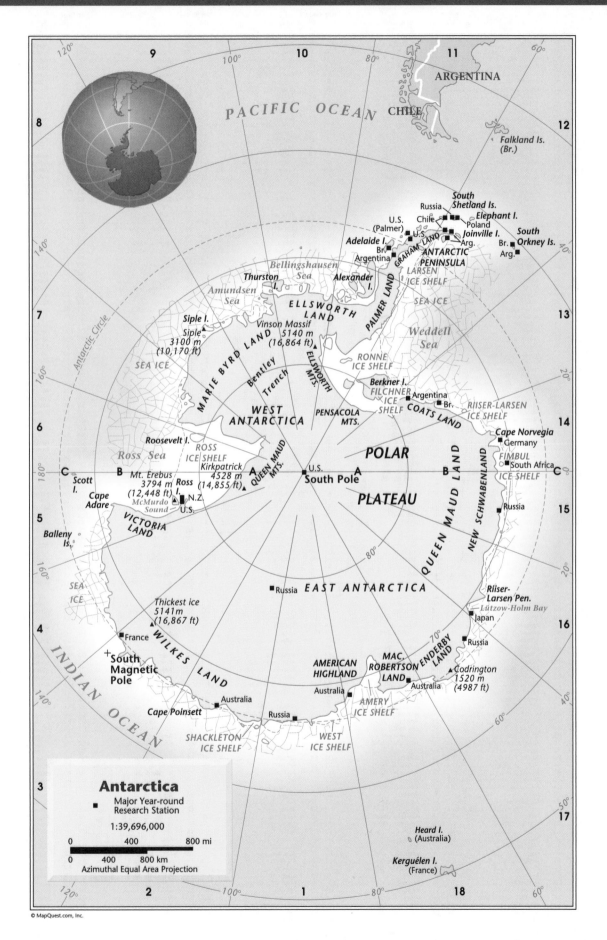

PACIFIC OCEAN

CHILE

ARGENTINA

Falkland Is.
(Br.)

South
Shetland Is.
Russia
U.S.
(Palmer)
Chile
Elephant I.
Poland
Joinville I.
Adelaide I.
Br.
Argentina
U.S.
Arg.
South
Orkney Is.
Br.
Arg.

GRAHAM LAND
ANTARCTIC
PENINSULA
LARSEN
ICE SHELF

Bellingshausen
Sea
Thurston
I.
Alexander
I.

PALMER LAND

SEA ICE

Weddell
Sea

Amundsen
Sea

ELLSWORTH
LAND

Siple I.
Siple
3100 m
(10,170 ft)

Vinson Massif
5140 m
(16,864 ft)

RONNE
ICE SHELF

Berkner I.
FILCHNER
ICE
SHELF
Argentina
Br.

RIISER-LARSEN
ICE SHELF

SEA ICE

MARIE BYRD LAND

Bentley
Trench

ELLSWORTH
MTS.

WEST
ANTARCTICA

PENSACOLA
MTS.

COATS LAND

Cape Norvegia
Germany

Roosevelt I.

ROSS
ICE SHELF

QUEEN MAUD
MTS.

POLAR

FIMBUL
South Africa
ICE SHELF

Ross Sea

Kirkpatrick

Scott
I.

Mt. Erebus
3794 m
(12,448 ft)
Ross
I.
N.Z.
U.S.
McMurdo
Sound

4528 m
(14,855 ft)

U.S.
South Pole

A

B

PLATEAU

QUEEN MAUD LAND
NEW SCHWABENLAND

Russia

Cape
Adare

VICTORIA
LAND

EAST ANTARCTICA

Russia

Riiser-
Larsen Pen.
Lützow-Holm Bay
Japan

Balleny
Is.

SEA
ICE

Thickest ice
5141m
(16,867 ft)

Russia

France

WILKES LAND

South
Magnetic
Pole

AMERICAN
HIGHLAND

MAC.
ROBERTSON
LAND

ENDERBY
LAND

Australia

Codrington
1520 m
(4987 ft)

INDIAN OCEAN

Cape Poinsett

Australia

Australia

Russia

AMERY
ICE SHELF

SHACKLETON
ICE SHELF

WEST
ICE SHELF

Heard I.
(Australia)

Kerguélen I.
(France)

Antarctica

■ Major Year-round
Research Station

1:39,696,000

0   400   800 mi

0   400   800 km

Azimuthal Equal Area Projection

A

	Key	Page
Aachen	A3	40
Aaiún, el-	B1	58
Aalst	C2	33
Aarau	C1	35
Aare, river	B1, B2	35
Aba	D5	65
Abadan	B3	22
Abaí	E4	75
Abakaliki	E4	65
Abakan	D6	44
Abancay	C3	77
Abaya, lake	B3	60
Abbeville	C1	34
Abbey	B10	104
Abbotsford	L6	95
Abdali	B1	24
Abéché	C4	59
Abemama, island	A1	17
Abengourou	E3	63
Abenrå	B3	32
Abeokuta	B4	65
Aberdeen	Inset	10
Aberdeen	C1	30
Aberdeen	H4	99
Aberdeen, S. Dak.	D1	126
Aberystwyth	B3	30
Abha	B2	24
Abhe, lake	C2	60
Abia, river	C3	66
Abidjan	D4	63
Abilene, Tex.	D2	126
Abkhazia, autonomous republic	A3	45
Aboisso	E4	63
Abomey	A4	64
Abou Deïa	B5	59
Abrantes	A3	36
Abruzzi	C2	38
Abşeron, peninsula	C2	45
Abu Dhabi, capital	C2	25
Abu Kamal	B2	27
Abuja, capital	D3	65
Abuná, river	A2	77
Acadia Valley	E5	94
Acajutla	A2	86
Acámbaro	D4	84
Acapulco	E4	84
Acarai, mts.	B5	80
Acaray, river	E4	75
Acarigua	C2	79
Accra, capital	B4	64
Achill, island	A2	31
Achinsk	D6	44
Achwa, river	C2	61
Acklins, island	C4	89
Acme	D5	94
Acolman	Inset	84
Aconcagua, mt.	A3	74
Aconcagua, river	B4	76
Aconibe	C3	66
Acquaviva	A1	39
Acre	A2	81
Acre (Akko)	B1	26
Acton	E4	102
Acton Vale	D6	103
Açúcar, mt.	Inset	81
Adamawa, massif	B2, E5	65
Adams, lake	N5	95
Adana	C3	27
Adapazarı	B2	27
Adare, cape	B5	107
Addis Ababa, capital	C2	60
Addu, atoll	A5	19
Adelaide, island	C11	107
Adelaide, S.A., capital	C3, Inset II	14
Aden	B2	25
Aden	E6	94
Aden, gulf	B1, C2	60
Adi Keyih	B2	60
Adi Ugri	B2	60
Adige, river	B1	38
Adirondack, mts., N.Y.	F1	126
Adjuntus	B2	90
Admiralty, islands	A2	15
Ado-Ekiti	C4	65
Adolphustown	H3	102
Adour, river	B5	34
Adra	B2	57
Adrar des Iforas, massif	D2	58
Adriatic, sea	C2	38
Advocate Harbour	C2	100
Adwa	C1	60
Adygeya, republic	E4	44
Adzopé	E3	63
Aegean, sea	C2	51
Ærø, island	C4	32
Aetna	D6	94
Afadjoto, mt.	C3	64
Afghanistan		22
Afikpo	D5	65
Afram, river	B3	64
Afyon	B2	27
Agadès	B2	59
Agadir	B2	57
Agartala	F4	20
Agboville	D4	63
Ağcabädi	B2	45
Ağdam	B3	45
Agen	C4	34
Aginskiy Buryat, autonomous okrug	D7	44
Aginskoye	D7	44
Agou, mt.	B3	64
Agra	C3	20
Ağrı	E2	27
Agrigento	B2	51
Agrínion	B2	51
Ağstafa	A2	45
Agua Prieta	C1	84
Aguada	A2	90
Aguadilla	A2	90
Aguadulce	B2	87
Aguán, river	B2	86
Aguarico, river	C3	79
Aguas Blancas	C2	76

	Key	Page
Aguas Buenas	C2	90
Aguascalientes, state capital	D3	84
Águilas	F4	37
Aguililla	B2	90
Agung, mt.	C2	13
Agusan, river	C4	12
Ahmadabad	B4	20
Ahmadi, al-	C2	24
Ahmic Harbour	F2	102
Ahuachapán	A2	86
Ahvaz	B3	22
Ahwar	B2	25
Aibonito	C2	90
Aigáleo, mts.	Inset	51
Aiguile	A3	77
Aïr Ronge	E5	104
Air, mts.	B2	59
Airdrie	C5	94
Aishihik, lake	B5	105
Aisne, river	D2	34
Aiwo	A2	16
Aix-en-Provence	D5	34
Aix-les-Bains	D4	34
Aíyina, island	B3	51
Aizawl	F4	20
Aizuwakamatsu	C2	8
Ajaccio	Inset I	34
Ajaria, autonomous republic	A4	45
Ajdabiya	D1	56
Ajka	A2	43
Ajman	C2	25
Ajmer	B3	20
Akanyaru, river	B2	61
Akashi	B3	8
Akhalkalaki	B4	45
Akhaltsikhe	B4	45
Akharnaí	Inset	51
Akhelóös, river	B2	51
Akhmeta	C3	45
Akhuryan, river	A2	45
Akita	D2	8
Akjoujt	B3	58
Aklavik	A3	99
Akobo, river	B3	60
Akola	C4	20
Akordat	A2	60
Akosombo, dam	C3	64
Akpatok, island	P4	99
Akranes	A2	52
Akron, Ohio	E1	126
Aksaray	C2	27
Aksu	B1	10
Akulivik	A1	101
Akure	C4	65
Akurenam	C3	66
Akureyri	B2	52
Akuseki, island	A4	8
Alabama	E2	126
Alagoas	E3	81
Alagoinhas	E3	81
Alajuela	B2	86
Alakol, lake	E1	23
Alamayn, al-	A1	56
Alameda	H11	104
Alampur	Inset II	20
Åland, islands	B2	53
Alanya	C3	27
Alarcón, reservoir	E3	37
Alaska	Inset I	126
Alaska, gulf, Alaska	Inset I	126
Alaska, range, Alaska	Inset I	126
Älät	C3	45
Alaverdi	B1	45
Alay, mts.	B1, C3	23
Alayli Dadda	B1	60
Alazani, river	C4	45
Alba Iulia	B2	43
Albacete	F3	37
Alban	E1	102
Albania		49
Albany, capital, N.Y.	F1	126
Albany, Ga.	E2	126
Albany, Oreg.	A2	101
Albany, W.A.	A3	14
Albert Nile, river	B2	61
Albert, canal	C1	33
Albert, lake	B3	61
Alberton	A2	100
Albi	C5	34
Albina	B2	80
Ålborg	B1	32
Ålborg, bay	C2	32
Albuquerque, cays	Inset	78
Albuquerque, N. Mex.	C2	126
Albury, N.S.W.	D3	14
Alcalá de Henares	Inset II	37
Alcañiz	F2	37
Alcántara, reservoir	C3	37
Alcázar de San Juan	E3	37
Alcira	F3	37
Alcobendas	Inset II	37
Alcorcón	E2, Inset II	37
Alcoy	F3	37
Aldabra, islands	A2	70
Aldan	D8	44
Aldan, river	D8	44
Alderney, island	Inset II	30
Aleg	B3	58
Alençon	C2	34
Alert	Q1	99
Alès	D4	34
Alessandria	B1	38
Ålesund	B3	52
Aleutian islands, Alaska	Inset I	126
Alexander	A4	96
Alexander, island	B11	107
Alexandra	A4	15
Alexandria	A4	43
Alexandria	A1	56
Alexandria, La.	D2	126
Alexandroúpolis	C1	51
Alexis Creek	L5	95

	Key	Page
Alexis, river	C3	98
Alfios, river	B3	51
Alfred	L2	102
Algarve, region	A4	36
Algeciras	D4	37
Algeria		57
Alghero	B2	38
Algiers, capital	B1	57
Ali Adde	B2	60
Áli Bayramli	C3	45
Ali-Sabieh	B2	60
Aliákmon, river	B1	51
Alibori, river	B2	64
Alicante	F3	37
Alice	C3	71
Alice Arm	H3	95
Alice Springs, N.T.	C2	14
Alice Town	B2	89
Aligarh	C3	20
Alima, river	D4	66
Aliwal North	C3	71
Alix	D5	94
Alkmaar	B2	32
Allahabad	D3	20
Allardville	D1	97
Allen, lake	B1	31
Allenford	D3	102
Allentown, Pa.	F1	126
Alleppey (Alappuzah)	C7	20
Alliance	E5	94
Alliston	F3	102
Alligator Pond	B3	88
Alma	E3	103
Almada	A3	36
Almadén	D3	37
Almansa	F3	37
Almelo	D2	32
Almendra, reservoir	C2	37
Almería	E4	37
Almirante	A2	87
Almonte	J2	102
Alonsa	B4	96
Alor Setar	A1	13
Alor, island	D2	13
Alotau	B3	15
Alpena, Mich.	E1	126
Alps, mts.		
Alsace	D2	34
Alsask	A9	104
Alta	E1	52
Altai, mts.	B1	10
Altamira	C2	81
Altamira	C3	76
Altario	E5	94
Altay	B1	10
Altay	B2	11
Altay, republic	F4	44
Altdorf	C2	35
Altiplano, plateau	A3	77
Altona	C4	96
Altun, range	A2	10
Aluksne	D2	46
Alvinston	D5	102
Alytus	C2	46
Alzette, river	B2	33
Amadjuak, lake	O4	99
Amadora	A3	36
Amagasaki	B3	8
Amahai	D2	13
Amakusa, islands	A3	8
Amami, island	Inset II	8
Amapá	C1	81
Amapala	B3	86
Amarah, al-	C2	24
Amaranth	B4	96
Amarillo, Tex.	C2	126
Amasya	C2	27
Amazon, basin	B2	81
Amazon, river	B2	81
Amazonas	B2	81
Ambato	B3	79
Ambatolampy	B2	69
Ambatondrazaka	B2	69
Amberg	B4	40
Ambergris Cay, island	C2	85
Ambergris, cay	D4	89
Amberley	D3	102
Ambon	D2	13
Ambositra	B3	69
Ambre, cape	B1	69
Ambrym, island	C2	18
Amdanga	Inset II	20
Ameca	D3	84
Ameland, island	C1	32
American Samoa		18
Amersfoort	C2	32
Amherst	C2	100
Amherstburg	B5	102
Amiens	C2	34
Amindivi, islands	B6	20
Amirante, islands	B2	70
Amisk	E5	94
Amistad, lake	H6	104
Amlamé	B3	64
Amman, capital	A2	26
Ammassalik	C2	106
Ammersee, lake	B4	40
Amos	A4	101
Amparai	C4	19
Amqui	J3	103
Amran	A1	25
Amravati	B4	20
Amritsar	B2	20
Amsterdam, capital	C2	32
Amstetten	D2	39
Amu Darya, river	B1, D2	23
Amund Ringnes, island	J1	99
Amundsen, gulf	C2	99
Amundsen, sea	B9	107

	Key	Page
Amur, river	D8	44
Amyun	A1	26
Ana María, gulf	D2	88
Anabar	C1	16
Anaco	D2	79
Anadyr	C10	44
Anadyr, gulf	C11	44
Anaheim Lake	K5	95
Anáhuac	D2	84
Anápolis	D3	81
Añasco	A2	90
Añasco, beach	A2	90
Anatolia, region	B2	27
Anatom, island	C5	18
Anchorage, Alaska	Inset I	126
Ancona	C2	38
Ancud	B7	76
Ancud, gulf	B7	76
Andalusia	D4	37
Andaman, islands	F6	20
Andaman, sea	B3	12
Anderlecht	C2	33
Anderson, river	C1	99
Andes, mts.		73
Andheri	Inset I	
Andizhan	D2	23
Andoany	B1	69
Andong	C4	9
Andorra		36
Andorra la Vella, capital	B2	36
Andreas, cape	C1	27
Andros	A3	89
Ándros, island	C3	51
Androth, island	B6	20
Aného	B3	64
Anelghowhat	C5	18
Anetan	B1	16
Aneto, mt.	G1	37
Angara, river	D6	44
Angarsk	D7	44
Angaur	B4	17
Angel, falls	D2	79
Angeles	B3	12
Ångermanälven, river	C2	53
Angers	B3	34
Angikuni, lake	H4	99
Angkor Thom, ruins	B2	11
Angkor Wat, ruins	B2	11
Anglesey, island	B3	30
Angoche	C3	68
Angol	B6	76
Angola		70
Angoulême	C4	34
Angus	F3	102
Anholt, island	C2	32
Anhui	E2	10
Anibare	B2	16
Anié	B3	64
Añisoc	C3	66
Anjou	J5	103
Anju	A3	9
Ankang	D2	10
Ankara, capital	C2	27
Ankaratra, mts.	B2	69
Ankobra, river	A4	64
Ann Arbor, Mich.	E1	126
Anna Regina	B2	80
Annaba	B1	57
Annam, mts.	A2	11
Annandale	C2	100
Annapolis Royal	B3	100
Annapolis, capital, Md.	F2	126
Annapurna, mt.	B2	19
Annecy	D4	34
Anqing	E2	10
Ansbach	B4	40
Anse Boileau	Inset	70
Anse Royale	Inset	70
Anse-à-Galets	C2	89
Anshan	F1	10
Ansongo	D2	58
Antalaha	C1	69
Antalya	B3	27
Antalya, gulf	B3	27
Antananarivo, capital	B2	69
Antarctic, peninsula	C12	107
Antarctica		107
Antequera	D4	37
Anti-Atlas, ranges	B2	57
Anti-Lebanon, mts.	B1	26
Anticosti, island	D4	101
Antigonish	F2	100
Antigua	C5	85
Antigua, island	D4	90
Antigua and Barbuda		90
Antioch (Antakya)	D3	27
Antofagasta	B2	76
Antrim, mts.	A2	30
Antsirabe	B2	69
Antsiranana	B1	69
Antsohihy	B1	69
Antwerp	C1	33
Anuradhapura	B3	19
Anyang	E2	10
Anyang	B4	9
Anyos	B2	36
Aoa	C1	18
Aoba, island	B2	18
Aomori	D1	8
Aoral, mt.	C3	11
Aosta	A1	38
Aozou	B2	59
Apa, river	D3	75
Apaporis, river	C4	78
Apatity	C3	44
Apatou	A1	80
Apeldoorn	C2	32
Apennines, range	B1	38
Apetina	B3	80
Api, mt.	C2	19
Apia, capital	C2	18
Apo, volcano	C4	12
Apolima, island	A2	18
Apolima, strait	B2	18
Apoteri	B4	80
Appalachian, mts.	E2	126
Apple River	C2	100
Apsley	G3	102

	Key	Page
Apulia	C2	38
Apure, river	C2	79
Apurímac, river	C3	77
Apuseni, mts.	B2	43
Aqaba, gulf	A3, B3	26
Aqaba, al-	A3	26
Aqtau	B2	23
Aqtobe	B1	23
Aquila	C1	38
Aquitaine	B4	34
Ara	D3	20
Arabah, al-, river	A2, B2	26
Arabian, desert	B2	56
Arabian, sea	A5, Inset I	20
Aracaju	E3	81
Arachon	B4	34
Arad	A2	43
Aradah	B3	25
Arafura, sea	E2	13
Aragats, mt.	B2	45
Aragón	F2	37
Araguaia, river	C3	81
Arak	B2	22
Arakabesan, island	B3	17
Arakan Yoma, mts.	B2	12
Aral	C2	23
Aral, sea	A2, B2	23
Aran, islands	B2	31
Aranda de Duero	E2	37
Aranjuez	E2	37
Aranyaprathet	C3	12
Arapey Grande, river	B1	75
Ararat	B3	45
Ararat (Ağri Daği), mt.	F2	27
Aras, river	E2	27
Arauca	C3	78
Arauca, river	C2	79
Aravalli, range	B3	20
Arawa	B2	15
Arba Minch	B3	60
Arborfield	G7	104
Arborg	C4	96
Archerwill	G8	104
Arcola	H11	104
Arctic Bay	L2	99
Arctic Red River	B3	99
Arda, river	C4	50
Ardabil	B2	22
Ardara	B1	31
Ardbeg	B2	102
Ardennes, plateau	D1	33
Ardennes, region	D1	34
Arecibo	B2	90
Arekalong, peninsula	C2	17
Arenal, lake	B2	86
Arenas, point	D2	90
Arendal	B4	52
Arequipa	C4	77
Arezzo	B2	38
Argenteuil	Inset II	34
Argentina		74
Argentino, lake	A7	74
Argeş, river	C3	43
Arghandab, river	B2	22
Argonne, forest	D2	34
Árgos	B3	51
Argyle	C4	96
Argyle	F3	102
Århus	C2	32
Ari, atoll	A3	19
Ariana	C1	57
Arica	B1	76
Arichat	F2	100
Arima	A2	91
Arinsal	A2	36
Aripuanã, river	C2	81
Arish, al-	B1	56
Arizona	B2	126
Arkansas	D2	126
Arkansas, river	D2	126
Arkhangelsk	C4	44
Arklow	D4	102
Arkona	D4	102
Arles	D5	34
Arlit	D3	33
Arlon	D3	33
Armenia		45
Armenia	B3	78
Armidale, N.S.W.	E3	14
Armstrong	N6	95
Armstrong	C2	101
Arnaud, river	B2	101
Arnes	C4	96
Arnhem	C3	32
Arnhem Land, region	C1	14
Arnhem, cape	C1	14
Arno, island	C1	16
Arno, river	B2	38
Arnold's Cove	D5	98
Arnprior	J2	102
Arnsberg	B3	40
Aroostook	B2	97
Arorae, island	A2	17
Arpa, river	C3	45
Arpajon	Inset II	34
Arqalyq	C1	23
Arran, island	B2	30
Arras	C1	34
Arroyo	C3	90
Arta	B2	51
Artashat	B3	45
Artemisa	B2	88
Arthur	E4	102
Arthur's Town	B3	89
Artibonite, river	C1	89
Artigas	B1	75
Artik	A2	45
Artsvashen	B2	45
Artvin	E2	27
Aru, islands	E2	13
Arua	B2	61
Aruba, island	A2	90
Arun, river	D2	19
Arusha	C1	68
Aruvi, river	B3	19
Aruwimi, river	C1	67
Arvayheer	C2	11

	Key
As Ela	B2
Asaba	D4
Asadabad	C2
Asahi Dake, mt.	Inset I
Asahikawa	Inset I
Asama, mt.	C2
Asansol	E4
Asau	A2
Asbestos	E6
Ascoli Piceno	C2
Asela	C3
Asenovgrad	C3
Ashburton	B3
Ashburton, river	A2
Ashcroft	M6
Ashdod	A2
Ashern	B3
Asheville, N.C.	E2
Asheweig, river	C2
Ashgabat, capital	B2
Ashikaga	C2
Ashizuri, cape	B3
Ashmore and Cartier, islands	B1
Ashqelon	A2
Ashton	A4
Ashuapmushuan, river	C3
Asinara, island	D3
Asipovichy	B2
Asir, region	B2
Askar	B2
Asmara, capital	B2
Asnam, el-	B1
Aso, mt.	B3
Asosa	B2
Aspiring, mt.	A3
Asprópirgos	Inset
Asquith	C8
Assab	D3
Assal, lake	C2
Assen	D1
Assiniboia	D11
Assiniboine, mt.	P6
Assiniboine, river	D1
Astana (Akmola), capital	D1
Astara	B1
Asti	B1
Astipálaia, island	C3
Astorga	C1
Astrakhan	E2
Astrolabe, reefs	C2
Asturias	C1
Asunción, capital	D4
Aswan	B3
Aswan High, dam	B2
Asyut	B2
At-Bashy	D2
Atacama, desert	B2
Atakpamé	B2
Ataq	B2
Atâr	B2
Atatürk, reservoir	D3
Atbara, river	C2
Atbarah	C2
Atbarah, river	C1
Atbasar	C1
Ath	B2
Athabasca	D4
Athabasca, lake	A1
Athabasca, river	B4, D3, Inset
Athens, capital	B3, Inset
Athens, Ga.	E2
Athi, river	C2
Athlone	C2
Áthos, mt.	C1
Ati	C3
Atiak	B2
Atikameg	C3
Atikameg Lake	A2
Atikokan	B3
Atitlán, lake	B5
Atlanta, capital, Ga.	E2
Atlantic City, N.J.	F1
Atlas, mts.	A1, B2
Atlin	F1
Atlin, lake	F1
Atrai, river	B4
Atrak, river	A3
Atrato, river	A3
Attapu	D2
Attawapiskat	C2
Attawapiskat, river	B4
Atuel, river	B4
Atyrau	C1
Aua	C1
Aube, river	D3
Auch	B5
Auckland	B2
Augsburg	B4
Augusta, capital, Maine	G1
Augusta, Ga.	E2
Auki	B1
Aulac	C1
Aunuu, island	C1
Auob, river	C5
Aur, island	C2
Aurangabad	C5
Aurillac	C4
Aurora	C3
Ausa, river	C1
Austin, capital, Tex.	D2
Australia	
Australian Alps, mts.	D3
Australian Capital Territory	D3
Austria	
Auvergne	C4
Auxerre	C3
Avalon, peninsula	E5
Aveiro	A2
Avellaneda	D3
Avellino	C2
Aviemore	C2
Avignon	D5
Ávila	D2
Avilés	D1
Avon, islands	A2
Avon, river	E10
Avonlea	E10
Awaji	B3

Key Page
ji, *island* B3 8
sa C3 60
sh, *river* C2 60
so A3 64
ari B2 56
a D4 65
vali, *river* A2 26
Heiberg, *island* K1 99
n A4 64
cucho C3 77
göz E2 23
n A3 27
Chawan, *island* A1 13
's Cliff D6 103
s Dhimítrios Inset 51
sbury Inset III 30
ner E5 102
ner A6 103
ner, *lake* G4 99
ner, *lake* E6 103
al- C2 25
in el-Atroûs C3 58
B2 30
s F3 50
ouâd, *region* C2 58
re F2 65
z A1 27
apotzalco Inset 84
baijan 45
baijan, *region* B2 22
gues B4 79
res, *islands* 5
v, *sea* D3 47
aq ash-Shishan B2 26
a B2 89
ero, *peninsula* B3 87
river B3 11
bek B1 26
al-Mandab, *strait* C1 60
ahoyo B3 79
anusah B3 59
ar, *island* D2 13
bage, *river* B1 105
da A2 26
elthuap, *island* C3 17
ine, *lake* J4 95
ine, *river* J3 95
ruysk D3 47
u Bheri Inset II 20
uyan, *channel* B2 12
uyan, *islands* B2 12
ylon, *ruins* B2 24
Lieu A5 11
abal D2 81
äu D2 43
k, *river* H3 99
ka Palanka A2 49
olod B4 12
Ems A3 40
Ischl C3 39
Kreuznach A4 40
Reichenhall C5 40
ajoz C3 37
alona H2 37
anah B1 24
as A2 13
deck G1 100
len C1 35
len E2 39
len A3 96
len-Baden B4 40
len-Württemberg B4 40
ger D4 96
ger C5 98
ou B3 64
atá C1 62
in, *bay* L1 92
in, *island* M2 99
in, *region* N2 99
lo B2 64
ng, *river* C2 62
oulabé A3 58
oussam B2 65
hdad, *capital* B2 24
hlan B1 22
lung B2 19
mati, *river* C2 19
oé, *river* C1 63
uio B2 12
zane, *mt.* B2 59
amas 89
awalpur D4 21
ia D3 81
ía Blanca C4 74
ía Honda A2 88
ía, *islands* B1 86
ir Dar B2 60
oruco, *mts.* A2 89
r al-Arab, *river* B3 59
r al-Ghazal, *river* C3 59
r al-Jabal, *river* C3 59
r Salamat, *river* B5 59
rain 25
rain, *gulf* A2 25
Mare B2 43
cheng F1 10
dyabati Inset II 20
e Verte C4 98
e-Comeau H2 103
e-des-Sables J3 103
e-St-Paul F4 103
e-Ste.-Anne E1 97
e-Ste-Catherine G3 103
lieboro G3 102
nsville L2 102
B2 26
ti B1 16
a B2 43
a California A1 84
a California Sur B2 84
adero B2 90
o Boquete A2 87
kel C2 62
ker Brook A1 97
ker Lake J4 99
kersfield, Calif. B2 126

Key Page
Bakhardok C2 22
Bakhtaran B3 22
Bakhtiari, *region* B3 22
Bakony, *mts.* A2 43
Baku, *capital* C2 45
Bala F2 102
Bala, *lake* B3 30
Balabac, *island* A5 12
Balabac, *strait* A5 12
Balakän B2 45
Balaklava C4 47
Balaton, *lake* A2 43
Balboa C2 87
Balcarres G10 104
Baldur B4 96
Baldy, *mt.* A3 96
Balearic, *islands* G3 37
Balearic, *sea* G2 37
Baleia, *point* E3 81
Baleine, *river* C2 101
Balgonie F10 104
Balhaf B2 25
Balho B1 60
Bali, *island* C2 13
Baliceaux, *island* B3 91
Balıkesir A2 27
Balikpapan C2 13
Balkan, *mts.* B2 50
Balkh B1 22
Balkhash D2 23
Balkhash, *lake* D2 23
Ballancourt-sur-Essonne Inset II 34
Ballarat, Vic. D3 14
Balleny, *islands* C5 107
Ballerup D3 32
Ballina B1 31
Bally Inset II 20
Ballymena A2 30
Balmaceda B8 76
Balmertown B2 101
Balmoral C1 97
Balsas, *river* E4 84
Bălţi A2 50
Baltic, *sea* 29
Baltimore, Md. F2 126
Baluchistan, *region* E4 22
Balykchy E1 23
Balzers B2 33
Bam D4 22
Bamako, *capital* B3 58
Bamangachi Inset II 20
Bambadinca C1 62
Bambana, *river* B2 87
Bambari B2 66
Bamberg B4 40
Bamenda B2 65
Bamian B2 22
Ban Houayxay A1 11
Ban Phai C2 12
Banaba, *island* A2 17
Banana A2 67
Banana, *islands* A1 63
Bananga F7 20
Banat, *region* A3 43
Banbury C3 30
Bancroft H2 102
Banda Aceh A1 13
Banda, *sea* D2 13
Bandama Blanc, *river* D2 63
Bandama Rouge, *river* C2 63
Bandama, *river* D3 63
Bandar Beheshti E4 22
Bandar Lampung B2 13
Bandar Seri Begawan, *capital* B2 13
Bandar-e Abbas D4 22
Bandar-e Anzali B2 22
Bandar-e Bushehr C4 22
Bandar-e Khomeyni B3 22
Bandar-e Torkeman C2 22
Bandeira, *mt.* D4 81
Bandra Inset I 20
Bandundu B2 67
Bandung B2 13
Banff C5 94
Bangalore C6 20
Bangar C2 13
Bangassou B3 66
Banggi, *island* D1 13
Banghiang, *river* C3 11
Bangka, *island* B2 13
Bangkok, *capital* B3 12
Bangladesh 21
Bangor B2 30
Bangor B3 30
Bangor, Maine G1 126
Bangui, *capital* A3 66
Bangweulu, *lake* B2 67
Baní B2 89
Bani Suwayf B2 56
Bani Walid B1 56
Bani, *river* B3 58
Baniyas A2 27
Banja Luka B1 48
Banjarmasin C2 13
Banjul, *capital* B2 62
Banks, *island* G4 95
Banks, *island* D2 99
Banks, *islands* B1 18
Banks, *peninsula* B3 15
Bann, *river* A2 30
Bannockburn H3 102
Bansang D2 62
Bansbaria Inset II 20
Banská Bystrica B2 42
Bantry B3 31
Bantry, *bay* B3 31
Baoding E2 10
Baoshan C3 10
Baotou E1 10
Baoulé, *river* B3 58
Baqubah B2 24
Baquerizo Moreno Inset 79
Bar A3 49
Bar-le-Duc D2 34
Baraawe A3 60
Barabinsk D5 44
Baracaldo E1 37
Barachois M3 103

Key Page
Baracoa F3 88
Barahona A2 89
Baraki Barak B2 22
Barakpur Inset II 20
Baram, *river* D2 13
Barama, *river* B2 80
Baranagar Inset II 20
Baranavichy C3 47
Barasat Inset II 20
Barbados 91
Barbuda, *island* E3 90
Barcelona D1 79
Barcelona H2 37
Barceloneta B2 90
Bärdä B2 45
Bardaï B2 59
Bardejov C2 42
Bareilly C3 20
Barents, *sea* B3 44
Bargachia Inset II 20
Bari D2 38
Baril, *lake* E2 94
Barinas B2 79
Barind, *region* B4 21
Baris B3 56
Barisal D6 21
Bark, *lake* H2 102
Barkerville M4 95
Barkly, *tableland* C1 14
Barletta D2 38
Barnaul D6 44
Barnes, *ice cap* O3 99
Barnsley C3 30
Barnstaple B3 30
Barnwell D6 94
Baro, *river* B2 60
Barons D6 94
Barquisimeto C1 79
Barra, *island* A2 30
Barrancabermeja B3 78
Barranquilla B2 78
Barranquitas C2 90
Barreiro A3 36
Barrhead C4 94
Barrie F3 102
Barrière M5 95
Barrington B4 100
Barro B1 62
Barrouallie B2 91
Barrow, Alaska Inset I 126
Barrow, *river* C2 31
Barrow-in-Furness B2 30
Barry's Bay H2 102
Bartang, *river* B1 23
Bartica B2 80
Barú, *volcano* A2 87
Baruta C1 79
Baruun-Urt D2 11
Bas-Caraquet E1 97
Basarabeasca B2 50
Basel B1 35
Bashi, *channel* B1 12
Basilan B5 12
Basilan, *island* B5 12
Basildon Inset III 30
Basilicata C2 38
Baskatong, *reservoir* A5 103
Basque Country E1 37
Basra C2 24
Bass Rock, *islet* C2 30
Bass, *strait* D3 14
Bassar B2 64
Basse Santa Su D2 62
Basse-Normandie B2 34
Bassein B3 12
Basseterre, *capital* B2 90
Bassila A3 64
Bastia Inset I 34
Bastogne D2 33
Bata B3 66
Bataan, *peninsula* B3 12
Batabanó, *gulf* B2 88
Batan, *islands* B1 12
Batang C3 10
Batang Duri C2 13
Batangafo A2 66
Batangas B3 12
Batdambang B2 11
Bate, *bay* Inset IV 14
Batéké, *plateau* C5 66
Bath C3 90
Bath C3 30
Bath B2 97
Batha, *river* C4 59
Bathsheba B3 91
Bathurst D1 97
Bathurst, *island* J1 99
Batin, Wadi al-, *river* A2 24
Batinah, al-, *region* C1 25
Batman E3 27
Batna B1 57
Baton Rouge, *capital*, La. D2 126
Batouri B3 65
Batrun, al- A1 26
Batteau D2 98
Batticaloa C4 19
Battle, *river* A7 104
Battleford B8 104
Batu Pahat B2 13
Batumi A4 45
Baubau D2 13
Bauchi E2 65
Bauria Inset II 20
Bauru D4 81
Bauska C2 46
Bautzen C3 40
Bavaria B4 40
Bavarian Alps, *mts.* B5 40
Bawiti, al- A2 56
Bawku B1 64
Bawlf D5 94
Bay Bulls E5 98
Bay de Verde E5 98
Bay Roberts E5 98
Bay St. Lawrence G1 100
Bayamo E3 88
Bayamón C2 90
Bayamón, *river* C2 90
Bayan Har, *range* C2 10

Key Page
Bayanhongor C2 11
Bayda, al- B2 25
Bayda, al- D1 56
Baydhabo A3 60
Bayerischer Wald, *mts.* C4 40
Bayeux B2 34
Bayfield D4 102
Baygorria, *lake* B2 75
Baykal, *lake* D7 44
Bayonne B5 34
Bayport C3 100
Bayramaly D3 22
Bayreuth B4 40
Bays, *lake* F2 102
Baza E4 37
Bazardüzü Daği, *mt.* B2 45
Bazin, *river* A4 103
Beachside D4 98
Beagle, *channel* B7 74
Bear Lake L4 95
Bear River C2 100
Beata, *cape* A3 89
Beata, *island* A3 89
Beaton O6 95
Beau Bassin B2 69
Beauceville F5 103
Beaufort West B3 71
Beaufort, *sea* B1 105
Beaulac E6 103
Beaumont D4 94
Beaumont, Tex. D2 126
Beauport L5 103
Beaupré F4 103
Beauséjour C4 96
Beauvais C2 34
Beauval C5 104
Beaver Creek A4 105
Beaver Harbour E3 100
Beaver Hill, *lake* D2 96
Beaver Mines C6 94
Beaver, *river* A6 104
Beaver, *river* D5 105
Beaverton F3 102
Bécancour D5 103
Bečej B2 49
Béchar A1 57
Bedeque, *bay* B2 100
Bedford C3 30
Bedford D3 100
Bedford D6 103
Bedok B1 13
Beechy C10 104
Beersheba B2 26
Behala Inset II 20
Bei'an F1 10
Beihai D3 10
Beijing, *capital* E2 10
Beira B3 68
Beirut, *capital* A2 26
Beja B3 36
Béja B1 57
Bejaïa B1 57
Bejaïa, *gulf* B1 57
Béjar D2 37
Bekaa, *valley* A2 26
Békéscsaba C2 43
Bela C4 21
Belair B2 91
Belapurpada Inset I 20
Belarus 47
Belasica, *mts.* C2 48
Belaya Tserkov C2 47
Beledweyne B3 60
Belém D2 81
Bélep, *islands* C2 18
Belfast B2 30
Belford Roxo Inset I 81
Belfort D3 34
Belfort, *gap* D3 34
Belgaum B5 20
Belgium 33
Belgrade, *capital* B2 49
Beli Drim, *river* B3 49
Bélinga B1 66
Belitung, *island* B2 13
Belize 85
Belize City B2 85
Belize, *river* B2 85
Bella Coola J5 95
Bella Unión B1 75
Bellary C5 20
Bellburns C4 98
Belle Isle, *strait* C3 98
Belle River C3 100
Belle, *island* B3 34
Belle, *island* C3 98
Belle-Anse C2 89
Belledune D1 97
Belleview A4 96
Belleville H3 102
Bellingham L7 95
Bellingham, Wash. A1 126
Bellingshausen, *sea* B10 107
Bellinzona D2 35
Bellona, *island* A2 16
Belluno C1 38
Bellville A3 71
Belmont B4 96
Belmopan, *capital* B2 85
Belo Horizonte D3 81
Beloeil C6 103
Belomorsk C3 44
Bemaraha, *plateau* A2 69
Bemidji, Minn. D1 126
Ben Eoin G2 100
Ben Nevis, *mt.* B2 30
Benavente D1 37
Bend, Oreg. A1 126
Bender (Tighina) B2 50
Benderbeyla C2 60
Bendigo, Vic. D3 14
Benevento C2 38
Bengal, *bay* E5 20
Bengbu E2 10
Benghazi D1 56
Bengkulu B2 13
Bengough E11 104
Benguela B4 70
Beni Mellal C1 57

Key Page
Beni, *river* A2 77
Benidorm F3 37
Benin 64
Benin City C4 65
Benin, *bight* B5 65
Benito A3 96
Benoit's Cove B5 98
Benoni C2 71
Bénoué, *river* B2 65
Benson G11 104
Bentiaba B4 70
Benue, *river* E3 65
Benxi F1 10
Benzdorp B3 80
Beqa, *island* B3 17
Bequia, *island* B2 91
Berat A3 49
Berbera B1 60
Berbérati A3 66
Berbice, *river* B3 80
Berdoba C4 59
Berdyansk D3 47
Berekua B4 90
Berens River C3 96
Berens, *island* C3 96
Berens, *river* C3 96
Beresford D1 97
Berezniki D4 44
Bergamo B1 38
Bergen B3 52
Bergen op Zoom B3 32
Bergerac C4 34
Bergisch Gladbach A3 40
Bering, *sea* Inset I 126
Bering, *strait* C11 44
Berkner, *island* B12 107
Berlin, *capital* C2 40
Bermejo, *river* C2 74
Bermuda, *island* 82
Bern, *capital* B2 35
Bernburg B3 40
Bernese Alps, *mts.* B2 35
Bernières K6 103
Berounka, *river* A3 42
Bertwell H8 104
Berwick C2 100
Berwick-upon-Tweed C2 30
Besançon D3 34
Beskid, *mts.* D4 41
Besnard, *lake* D5 104
Besor, *river* B2 26
Bethanien C4 70
Bethany B4 96
Bethel, Alaska Inset I 126
Bethierville C5 103
Bethlehem C2 71
Béticos, *mts.* E4 37
Bétou E2 66
Betsiamites H3 103
Betsiamites, *river* G2 103
Betsiboka, *river* B2 69
Bette, *mt.* C3 56
Beulah A4 96
Beyla D3 62
Beyneu B2 23
Beyşehir, *lake* B3 27
Béziers C5 34
Bhadrakh D4 20
Bhadreswar Inset II 20
Bhagalpur E3 20
Bhairahawa B2 19
Bhaktapur C2 19
Bhamapur D5 20
Bhamo C1 12
Bhandup Inset I 20
Bharatpur C3 20
Bhatapara D4 20
Bhatpara Inset II 20
Bhavnagar B4 20
Bhayandar Inset I 20
Bheri, *river* B2 19
Bhima, *river* C5 20
Bhimpur Inset II 20
Bhiwandi Inset I 20
Bhopal C4 20
Bhubaneswar E4 20
Bhuj A4 20
Bhunya B2 71
Bhutan 19
Biabou B2 91
Biafra, *bight* A3 65
Biak, *island* E2 13
Biała Podlaska F2 41
Białystok F2 41
Biankouma C3 63
Biarritz B5 34
Bicaz, *reservoir* D2 43
Biche, *lake* E4 94
Bida D3 65
Bié, *plateau* C4 70
Biel B1 35
Biel, *lake* B1 35
Biele Karpaty, *mts.* A2 42
Bielefeld B2 40
Bielsko-Biała D4 41
Bien Hoa B4 11
Bienville, *lake* B2 101
Big Beaver E11 104
Big Bend B2 71
Big Creek L5 95
Big Fish, *river* B1 105
Big Gull, *lake* J3 102
Big Muddy, *lake* F11 104
Big River C7 104
Big Trout Lake C2 101
Big, *island* O4 99
Big, *river* B2 98
Biggar C8 104
Bignona A3 62
Bigstone, *river* D1 96
Bihać A1 48
Bihar E3 20
Bihor, *mts.* B2 43
Bijagós, *islands* A2 62
Bijapur C5 20
Bijeljina C1 48
Bikaner B3 20
Bikar, *island* C1 16
Bikini, *island* B1 16

Key Page
Bilaspur D4 20
Biläsuvar C3 45
Bilauktaung, *range* B3, C3 12
Bilbao E1 37
Billings, Mont. C1 126
Billings, *reservoir* Inset II 81
Bilma C2 59
Biloku B5 80
Biloxi, Miss. E2 126
Biltine C4 59
Bimbila C2 64
Binche C2 33
Bindloss E6 94
Bindura B1 69
Binga, *mt.* B3 68
Bingen A4 40
Binscarth A4 96
Bint Jubayl A2 26
Bintang B2 62
Bintimane, *mt.* B1 63
Bío-Bío, *river* B6 76
Bioko, *island* A1 66
Bir Gandús A2 58
Bîr Mogreïn C1 58
Birak B2 56
Birao B1 66
Biratnagar D3 19
Birch Cliff K5 102
Birch Hills E7 104
Birch River A3 96
Birch, *mts.* D2 94
Birchy Bay D4 98
Bird, *island* B2 91
Birendranagar B2 19
Birganj C2 19
Birjand D3 22
Birkat Qarun, *lake* B2 56
Birkenhead B3 30
Birkirkara B2 36
Bîrlad D2 43
Birmingham C3 30
Birmingham, Ala. E2 126
Birni Nkonni B3 59
Birnie B4 96
Birnin Kebbi C1 65
Birobizhan E8 44
Birtle A4 96
Biržai C1 46
Birzebbuga C3 36
Biscay, *bay* B4 34
Bishkek, *capital* D1 23
Bishnupur Inset II 20
Bishop's Falls D4 98
Biskra B1 57
Bislig C4 12
Bismarck, *archipelago* A2 15
Bismarck, *capital*, N. Dak. C1 126
Bismarck, *range* A2 15
Bismarck, *sea* A2 15
Bismuna, *lagoon* C1 87
Bison, *lake* B2 94
Bissau, *capital* B2 62
Bissett D3 96
Bissorã B1 62
Bistcho, *lake* A1 94
Bistrița C2 43
Bistrița, *river* C2 43
Bitam A1 66
Bitola B2 48
Bitumount E2 94
Biu G2 65
Biwa, *lake* B3 8
Biysk D6 44
Bizard, *island* H5 103
Bizerte B1 57
Bjorne, *peninsula* L1 99
Black (Da), *river* A2 11
Black Country, *region* C3 30
Black Lake E1 104
Black River B2 88
Black Tickle D2 98
Black Volta, *river* A2, B3 64
Black, *forest* A4 40
Black, *hills*, S. Dak. C1 126
Black, *lake* E1 104
Black, *sea* 29
Blackburn C3 30
Blackmans B3 91
Blackpool C3 30
Blacks Harbour C3 97
Blackstone, *river* B3 105
Blackville D2 97
Blackwater, *river* B2, C1 31
Blagoevgrad B4 50
Blagoveshchensk D4 44
Blagoveshchensk D8 44
Blaine Lake D8 104
Blainville H5 103
Blanc, *mt.* D4 34
Blanc, *reservoir* C4 103
Blanc-Sablon E3 101
Blanca, *bay* C4 74
Blanda, *river* B2 52
Blantyre B3 68
Blarney B3 31
Blatec C2 48
Blenheim B3 15
Blenheim D5 102
Blida B1 57
Bligh Water, *sound* B2 17
Blind Bay N6 95
Blind River C1 102
Blitta B2 64
Bloemfontein, *judicial capital* C2 71
Blois C3 34
Bloodvein, *river* C3 96
Bloomfield H4 102
Bloomington, Ind. E2 126
Blossom Park H6 102
Blow, *river* B1 105
Blue Mountain, *peak* C2 88
Blue Nile, *river* C2 59
Blue Ridge C4 94
Blue River N5 95
Blue, *mts.* E3 14
Blue, *mts.* C2 88
Bluefields B2 88
Bluefields C3 87

Key Page
Bluenose, *lake* E3 99
Bluffton C5 94
Blyth D4 102
Bo B2 63
Bo Hai, *gulf* E2 10
Boa Vista B1 81
Boa Vista, *island* D2 58
Boaco B2 87
Bobcaygeon G3 102
Bobo-Dioulasso B3 64
Bocas del Toro A2 87
Bocay B1 87
Bocay, *river* B2 87
Bocholt A3 40
Bochum A3 40
Bodaybo D7 44
Bodo E5 94
Bodø C2 52
Boende B2 67
Boggeragh, *mts.* B2 31
Boggy, *peak* D5 90
Bogor B2 13
Bogotá, *capital* B3 78
Bogra C4 21
Bohemia, *region* A3 42
Bohemian, *forest* A3 42
Bohemian-Moravian, *heights* B3 42
Bohol, *island* C4 12
Bohol, *sea* C4 12
Boiestown C2 97
Boilleau F3 103
Bois-des-Filion H5 103
Boise, *capital*, Idaho B1 126
Boissevain A4 96
Boknafjord, *fjord* B4 52
Boksburg C2 71
Bol A4 59
Bolama B2 62
Bolands D5 90
Bole A2 64
Bolgatanga B1 64
Bolívar, *mt.* B2 79
Bolivia **77**
Bolligen B2 35
Bolnisi C4 45
Bolobo B2 67
Bologna B1 38
Bolovens, *plateau* D4 11
Bolsena, *lake* B2 38
Bolsón de Mapimí, *depression* D2 84
Bolton C3 30
Bolton F4 102
Bolu B2 27
Bolzano B1 38
Bom Jesus da Lapa D3 81
Boma A2 67
Bombay B5, Inset I 20
Bomu, *river* C1 67
Bon Pays, *region* B2 33
Bon, *cape* C1 57
Bonaire, *island* 82
Bonao B2 89
Bonaventure L3 103
Bonaventure, *river* L3 103
Bonavista E5 98
Bonavista, *bay* E5 98
Bondo B1 67
Bondoukou E2 63
Bondy Inset II 34
Bongor A5 59
Bonin, *islands* Inset III 8
Bonn A3 40
Bonnet Plume, *river* C3 105
Bonny D5 65
Bonnyville E4 94
Bonshaw B2 100
Bonthe A2 63
Bööntsagaan, *lake* B2 11
Boosaaso B1 60
Boothia, *gulf* K2 99
Boothia, *peninsula* K2 99
Booué A2 66
Bor C2 49
Borås B3 53
Bordeaux B4 34
Borden B2 100
Borden C8 104
Borden, *island* F1 99
Borden, *peninsula* M2 99
Borđoy, *island* Inset 32
Borgo Maggiore B1 39
Borivli Inset I 20
Borjomi B4 45
Borneo, *island* C1 13
Bornholm, *island* E3 32
Bosanska Gradiška B1 48
Bosanska Krupa A1 48
Bosna, *river* B1 48
Bosnia & Hercegovina **48**
Boso, *peninsula* D3 8
Bosporus, *strait* B2 27
Bossangoa A2 66
Bosten, *lake* B1 10
Boston C3 30
Boston Bar M6 95
Boston, *capital*, Mass. F1 126
Boswell O6 95
Botany, *bay* Inset IV 14
Boteti, *river* A2 69
Botha D5 94
Bothnia, *gulf* B2, D2 53
Botna, *river* B2 50
Botoşani D2 43
Botrange, *mt.* E2 33
Botswana **69**
Botte Donato, *mt.* D3 38
Bottrop A3 40
Botwood D4 98
Bouaflé D3 63
Bouaké D3 63
Bouar A2 66
Boucherville J5 103
Bouctouche E2 97
Bougainville, *island* B2 15
Boughton, *bay* C2 100
Bougouni B3 58
Boulder, Colo. C2 126
Key Page
Boulogne-Billancourt Inset II 34
Boulogne-sur-Mer C1 34
Bouna E2 63
Bourail C2 18
Bourem C2 58
Bourg-en-Bresse D3 34
Bourges C3 34
Bourgogne C3 34
Bourke, N.S.W. D3 14
Bournemouth C4 30
Bousso B5 59
Bow City D6 94
Bow, *river* D6 94
Bow, *river* E6 104
Bowen, Qld. D2 14
Bowling Green, Ky. E2 126
Bowser, *lake* H3 95
Bowsman A3 96
Boyd's Cove D4 98
Boyne, *river* C2 31
Boyne, *river* B4 96
Bozeman, Mont. B1 126
Brabant Lake G4 104
Brač, *island* C3 48
Bracciano, *lake* C2 38
Bracebridge F2 102
Bradford C3 30
Braga A2 36
Bragança B2 36
Bragg Creek C6 94
Brahmanbaria E5 21
Brahmaputra, *river* F3 20
Brăila D3 43
Braintree Inset III 30
Brakpan C2 71
Bralorne L6 95
Bramalea H5 102
Brampton F4 102
Branch E5 98
Branco, *river* B1 81
Brandberg, *mt.* B2 70
Brandenburg C2 40
Brandon B4, C2 96
Brant D6 94
Brantford E4 102
Bras d'Or G1 100
Brasília, *capital* D3 81
Braşov C3 43
Bratislava, *capital* A2 42
Bratsk D7 44
Braunau C2 39
Brava, *coast* H2 37
Brava, *island* B4 58
Brazil **81**
Brazilian, *highlands* D3 81
Brazzaville, *capital* C6 66
Brčko B1 48
Brea, *point* B2 90
Břeclav C4 42
Brecon Beacons, *mts.* B3 30
Breda B3 32
Bredenbury H10 104
Bregalnica, *river* C2 48
Breidhafjördhur, *fjord* A2 52
Bremen B2 40
Bremerhaven B2 40
Brenner, *pass* B3 39
Brentwood Inset III 30
Brescia B1 38
Brest A3 47
Brest A2 34
Bretagne B2 34
Breton C5 94
Bria B2 66
Briançon D4 34
Briceni A1 50
Bridge Lake M5 95
Bridgeport, Conn. F1 126
Bridgetown B3 100
Bridgetown, *capital* A4 91
Bridgewater C3 100
Brienzersee, *lake* B2 35
Brighton C4 30
Brighton H3 102
Brikama B2 62
Brindisi D2 38
Brisbane, Qld., *capital* E2, Inset III 14
Brisbane, *river* Inset III 14
Bristol C3 30
Bristol B2 97
Bristol, *channel* B3 30
Britannia E5 98
Britt E2 102
Brive-la-Gallarde C4 34
Brno C3 42
Broadview H10 104
Brochet C1 96
Brock, *island* F1 99
Brocket D6 94
Brockville K3 102
Brodfur, *peninsula* L2 99
Broken Hill, N.S.W. D3 14
Brokopondo B2 80
Brolin C3 30
Bromptonville E6 103
Brookdale B4 96
Brooks E6 94
Brooks *range*, Alaska Inset I 126
Broome, W.A. B1 14
Broomhill A4 96
Brossard J6 103
Brownsville, Tex. D3 126
Bruce Mines B1 102
Bruce Peninsula N.P. D2 102
Brugge B1 33
Brugge-Ghent, *canal* B1 33
Brûlé B4 94
Brunei **13**
Brunei, *bay* C1 13
Brunei, *river* B2 13
Brunswick D3 40
Brunswick, Ga. E2 126
Brunswick, *peninsula* B9 76
Brussels D4 102
Brussels, *capital* C2 33
Bryan, Tex. D2 126
Bryansk D3 44
Bsharri B1 26
Key Page
Bu Craa B1 58
Bua, *river* B2 68
Buada B2 16
Buala A1 16
Buba C2 62
Bubanza B2 61
Bubaque B2 62
Bubiyan, *island* C2 24
Bucaramanga B3 78
Buchanan A3 63
Buchanan H9 104
Buchans C5 98
Bucharest, *capital* D3 43
Buck Creek C4 94
Buck Lake C5 94
Buckingham A6 103
Budapest, *capital* B2 43
Buea A3 65
Buenaventura A4 78
Buendía, *reservoir* E2 37
Buene, *river* A2 49
Buenos Aires, *capital* D3 74
Buenos Aires, *lake* A6 74
Buffalo Narrows B5 104
Buffalo, *lake* D5 94
Buffalo, *lake* E4 99
Buffalo, N.Y. F1 126
Bug, *river* E2, F3 41
Bugeac, *region* B3 50
Bugojno B1 48
Buhayrat al-Asad, *lake* B1 27
Buj-Buj Inset II 20
Bujumbura, *capital* B2 61
Buka, *island* B2 15
Bukavu C2 67
Bukhara B3 23
Bukit Pagon, *mt.* C3 13
Bukit Panjang B1 13
Bukit Timah B1 13
Bükk, *mts.* C1 43
Bukoba B1 68
Bula B1 62
Bulawayo B2 69
Bulembu B1 71
Bulgan C2 11
Bulgaria **50**
Bulle B2 35
Bulyea F10 104
Bumba B1 67
Bunbury, W.A. A3 14
Bundaberg, Qld. E2 14
Bungo, *channel* B3 8
Bunia C1 67
Bunsuru, *river* D1 65
Buon Me Thuot B4 11
Buqayq C1 24
Buraydah B1 24
Burco B2 60
Burdekin, *river* D1 14
Burdett E6 94
Burdur, *lake* B3 27
Burdwan E4 20
Büren B3 40
Burgas F3 50
Burgeo C5 98
Burgos E1 37
Burhanpur C4 20
Burica, *point* A2 87
Burin D5 98
Burin, *peninsula* D5 98
Buriram C3 12
Burk's Falls F2 102
Burke, *channel* J5 95
Burkina Faso **64**
Burlington F4 102
Burlington, Vt. F1 126
Burma (Myanmar) **12**
Burnley C3 30
Burns Lake K4 95
Burntwood, *lake* A2 96
Burntwood, *river* B1, C1, D2 96
Bursa B2 27
Burtnieku, *lake* C2 46
Buru, *island* D2 13
Burundi **61**
Bururi B2 61
Burutu C5 65
Burwash Landing B5 105
Bury C3 30
Bury St. Edmunds D3 30
Buryatiya, *republic* D7 44
Bushmanland, *plain* A2 71
Buta C1 67
Butare B2 61
Bute, *island* B2 30
Butha-Buthe B1 71
Butte, Mont. B1 126
Buttonville K5 102
Butuan C4 12
Butwal B2 19
Buurgplaatz, *mt.* B1 33
Buxton C3 30
Buyant-Uhaa D3 11
Buyo, *lake* C3 63
Büyük Menderes, *lake* A3 27
Buzău D3 43
Búzi, *river* B4 68
Büzmeyin C2 22
Byam Martin, *channel* G1 99
Byam Martin, *island* H1 99
Byarezina, *river* D3 47
Byblos, *ruins* A1 26
Bydgoszcz C2 41
Byelaruskaya Hrada, *range* C3 47
Bylot, *island* N2 99
Bytom D3 41
Byumba C1 61

C

Ca Mau A5 11
Ca, *river* A2 11
Caacupé D4 75
Caaguazú E4 75
Caazapá D5 75
Cabanatuan B3 12
Cabano H4 103
Cabimas B1 79
Cabinda B1 70
Key Page
Cabo Rojo A2 90
Cabora Bassa, *dam* B2 68
Cabora Bassa, *lake* A2 68
Caborca B1 84
Cabrera C1 89
Cabrera, *island* H3 37
Cabri B10 104
Čačak B3 49
Cacao B1 80
Cáceres C3 81
Cáceres C3 37
Cache Creek M6 95
Cacheu A1 62
Cacheu, *river* B1 62
Cachimbo C2 81
Cacine B2 62
Cacouna G4 103
Cadiz B4 12
Cádiz C4 37
Cádiz, *gulf* C4 37
Cadomin B4 94
Cadotte Lake B3 94
Caen B2 34
Caerleon C3 30
Caernarfon B3 30
Cagayan de Oro C4 12
Cagayan Sulu, *island* A5 12
Cagayan, *islands* B4 12
Cagayan, *river* B2 12
Cagliari B3 38
Cagliari, *gulf* B3 38
Caguas C2 90
Caha, *mts.* B3 31
Cahors C4 34
Cahul B3 50
Caicos, *islands* D4 89
Caidasm da Rainha A3 36
Caille, *island* B1 91
Cairns, Qld. D1 14
Cairo, *capital* B1 56
Cairo, Ill. E2 126
Caja de Muertos, *island* B3 90
Cajamarca B2 77
Calabar E5 65
Calabogie J2 102
Calabozo C2 79
Calabria D3 38
Calafate A7 74
Calais C1 34
Calais B3 94
Calais B3 97
Calama C2 76
Calamian, *islands* A3 12
Calapan B3 12
Călăraşi D3 43
Calatayud F2 37
Calatrava B3 66
Calbayog C3 12
Calcutta E4, Inset II 20
Caledon, *river* A1, C2 71
Caledonia F4 102
Calgary C5 94
Cali A4 78
California B2 126
California, *gulf* B1 84
Callao B3 77
Calling Lake D3 94
Caltanissetta C3 38
Calvi Inset I 34
Calvinia A3 71
Cam Ranh B4 11
Camagüey D2 88
Camagüey, *archipelago* D2 88
Camberley Inset III 30
Cambodia **11**
Cambrai C1 34
Cambrian, *mts.* B3 30
Cambridge D3 30
Cambridge Bay G3 99
Cambridge-Narrows D3 97
Cameron, *hills* B1 94
Cameron, *island* H1 99
Cameroon **65**
Cameroon, *mt.* A3 65
Camiri B4 77
Camopi B2 80
Camopi, *river* B2 80
Campana, *island* A8 76
Campania C2 38
Campbell River K6 95
Campbellton C1 97
Campbellton A2 100
Campbellton K4 103
Campbelltown, N.S.W. Inset IV 14
Campbelltown, S.A. Inset II 14
Campbeltown B2 30
Campeche, *bay* F4 84
Campeche, *state capital* F4 84
Camper B3 96
Camperville A3 96
Campina Grande E2 81
Campinas D4 81
Campo Grande C4 81
Campobasso C2 38
Campobello, *island* C4 97
Campos D4 81
Campos Elísios Inset I 81
Camrose D4 94
Camsell Portage A1 104
Camú, *river* B1 89
Camuy B2 90
Can Tho A4 11
Caña Gorda, *beach* B3 90
Canaan B1 91
Canada **92**
Canaima D2 79
Çanakkale A2 27
Canal Flats P6 95
Canaray, *islands* Inset I 37
Canaries A2 91
Canary, *islands* 55
Canaveral, *cape*, Fla. E3 126
Canberra, A.C.T., *natl. capital* D3 14
Canchungo A1 62
Cancún G3 84
Candelaria C2 90
Candiac J6 103
Candle Lake E7 104
Key Page
Cando B8 104
Canelles, *river* B3 91
Canelones B3 75
Cangamba D4 70
Cangzhou E2 10
Caniapiscau, *lake* C3 101
Caniapiscau, *river* C2 101
Çankırı C2 27
Cankuzo C2 61
Cannes D5 34
Canning C2 100
Canning, *river* Inset I 14
Canoe Narrows B5 104
Canoe, *lake* B5 104
Canora H9 104
Canossa B1 38
Canouan, *island* B3 91
Canóvanas D2 90
Canso G2 100
Cantabria D1 37
Cantábrica, *mts.* C1 37
Canterbury D3 30
Canterbury B3 97
Canterbury, *bight* B3 15
Canterbury, *plains* B3 15
Canton, *island* B2 17
Canwood D7 104
Canyon Creek C3 94
Cao Bang B1 11
Cap-aux-Os M3 103
Cap-Chat K2 103
Cap-de-la-Madeleine D5 103
Cap-Haïtien C1 89
Cap-Pelé E2 97
Cap-Rouge K6 103
Cap-St-Ignace F4 103
Cape Charles D3 98
Cape Coast B4 64
Cape Girardeau, Mo. E2 126
Cape North G1 100
Cape Race E5 98
Cape Ray B5 98
Cape St. George B5 98
Cape Tormentine E2 97
Cape Town, *legislative capital* A3 71
Cape Verde **58**
Cape York, *peninsula* D1 14
Capitán Pablo Lagerenza B1 75
Caplan L3 103
Caprara, *point* B2 38
Capreol D1 102
Capri, *island* C2 38
Capua C2 38
Caquetá, *river* B5 78
Car Nicobar, *island* F7 20
Caracas, *capital* C1 79
Caramoan, *peninsula* B3 12
Carapicuíba Inset II 81
Caraquet E1 97
Carberry B4 96
Carbonara, *cape* B3 38
Carbonear E5 98
Carbonia B3 38
Carcajou B2 94
Carcassonne C5 34
Carcross C5 105
Cardamom, *mts.* A3 11
Cárdenas B1 88
Cardiel, *lake* A6 74
Cardiff B3 30
Cardigan C2 100
Cardigan, *bay* B3 30
Cardigan, *bay* C2 100
Cardinal K3 102
Cardinal, *lake* B3 94
Caribbean, *sea* 82
Carievale A4 96
Carleton K3 103
Carleton Place J2 102
Carlingford C1 31
Carlingford, *lake* C1 31
Carlisle C2 30
Carlisle, *bay* A4 91
Carlow C2 31
Carlsbad, N. Mex. C2 126
Carlyle H11 104
Carmacks B4 105
Carman B4 96
Carmanville D4 98
Carmarthen B3 30
Carmelo A2 75
Carnac B3 34
Carnarvon B3 71
Carnarvon G2 102
Carnarvon, W.A. A2 14
Carnduff J11 104
Carnic Alps, *range* C4 39
Carnsore, *point* C2 31
Carolina D2 90
Caroline, *island* D2 17
Caroline, *islands* B2 15
Caron E10 104
Caroni, *river* D2 79
Carora C1 79
Carpathian, *mts.* 43
Carpentaria, *gulf* C1 14
Carrantuohill, *mt.* B3 31
Carriacou, *island* C1 91
Carrick-on-Shannon B2 31
Carroll A4 96
Carrot River G7 104
Carson City, *capital*, Nev. B2 126
Carstairs C5 94
Cartagena B2 78
Cartagena F4 37
Cartago C3 86
Carthage, *ruin* C1 57
Cartier D1 102
Cartwright B4 96
Cartwright C2 98
Carúpano D1 79
Carvoeiro, *cape* A3 36
Carway D6 94
Casa Grande, Ariz. B2 126
Casablanca Inset 76
Casablanca C1 57
Casamance, *region* B3 62
Casamance, *river* B3 62
Key P
Cascade Inset
Cascade, *range* A1
Cascapedia, *river* K3
Cascumpec, *bay* B2
Caserta C2
Cashel C2
Casiquiare, *river* C3
Caslan D4
Casper, Wyo. C1
Caspian, *depression* B2
Caspian, *sea*
Casselman K2
Cassiar H1
Cassiar, *mts.* G1
Castel Gandolfo C2
Castellón de la Plana F3
Castelo Branco B3
Castile and León D1, E1
Castile-la Mancha E3
Castle Bruce B2
Castle Mountain C5
Castlebar B2
Castlegar O6
Castries, *capital* B1
Castro B7
Cat, *island* B3
Catacamas C2
Catalina E5
Catalonia G2
Catamarca B2
Catanduanes, *island* C3
Catania C3
Cataño C2
Catanzaro D3
Catió B2
Catoche, *cape* G3
Catumbela B4
Cauca, *river* B3
Caucasus, *mts.* A1, A2
Caungula D2
Caura, *river* D2
Causapscal J3
Căuşeni B2
Cauto, *river* E3
Cauvery, *river* C6
Cavalla, *river* C3
Cavally, *river* C4
Cavan C2
Cavendish B2
Caviana, *island* D1
Caxito B2
Cayambe, *mt.* C3
Cayenne, *capital* B1
Cayer B3
Cayey C2
Cayman, *trench* B2
Cayman, *islands*
Cayon B1
Cazombo E3
Ceará E3
Cebollatí, *river* C2
Cebu B4
Cebu, *island* B4
Cedar City, Utah B2
Cedar Grove E5
Cedar Rapids, Iowa D1
Cedar, *lake* A2
Cedros, *island* A2
Ceduna, S.A. C3
Ceerigaabo B1
Cefalù C3
Cegléd B2
Ceiba C2
Ceiba C2
Celada D2
Celaya D3
Celebes (Sulawesi), *island* D2
Celebes, *sea* D1
Celje C2
Celtic, *sea* B3
Central African Republic
Central Butte D10 1
Central Makran, *range* B4
Central Siberian, *plateau* C7
Centre C3
Centre C3 1
Centre de Flacq C2
Centreville E4
Ceram, *island* D2
Ceram, *sea* D2
Cerf, *island* Inset
Cernavodă E3
Cerro Castillo B9
Cerro de Pasco B3
Cervati, *mt.* C2
Cesis C2
České Budějovice B4
Cess, *river* B2
Cessford E6
Cetinje A3
Ceuta D5
Cévennes, *mts.* C4
Ceyhan, *river* D3
Chachapoyas B2
Chaco Boreal, *region* B2
Chad
Chad, *lake* A4, C3
Chaeryŏng, *river* A3
Chagai, *hills* B4
Chaghcharan B2
Chagres, *river* C2
Chaguanas A2
Chaitén B7
Chaiyaphum C3
Chalco Inset
Chaleur, *bay* D1
Chalna C6
Châlons-sur-Marne D2
Chambal, *river* C3
Chambéry D4
Chambeshi, *river* C2
Chambord D3 1
Chamelecon, *river* A2
Chamonix-Mont-Blanc D4
Champagne Castle, *mt.* C2
Champagne-Ardenne D2
Champaquí, *mt.* C3
Champasak C4
Champerico B5

	Key	Page
amplain	D5	103
añaral	B3	76
ança	B4	36
andannagar	Inset II	20
andigarh	C2	20
andler	M3	103
andpur	D5	21
andrapur	C5	20
ang (Yangtze), river	D2, E2	10
angane, river	B4	68
angchun	F1	10
angde	E3	10
anghua	B1	9
angi	B1	13
angjin	B2	9
angjin, river	B2	9
angsha	E3	10
anguinola	A2	87
angyŏn	A3	9
angzhou	C2	10
anghzou	F2	10
annel islands, Calif.	A2	126
annel-Port aux Basques	B5	98
antilly	C2	34
ao Phraya, river	B3	12
apada dos Parecis, range	C3	81
apala, lake	D3	84
aparé, river	A3	77
apleau	D3	101
aplin	D10	104
ardzhou	D2	22
arente, river	B4	34
ari, river	A5	59
arikar	B1	22
arity	B2	80
arleroi	C2	33
arles	A1	96
arlesbourg	E5, Inset	103
arleston, capital, W. Va.	E2	126
arleston, S.C.	F2	126
arlestown	C3	90
arlestown	A3	91
arleville Mézières	D2	34
arleville, Qld.	D2	14
arlie Lake	M3	95
arlie	C1	97
arlotte, N.C.	E2	126
arlottetown	C3	98
arlottetown	B2	100
arlotteville	B1	91
arters Towers, Qld.	D2	14
artres	C2	34
ase	N6	95
ateauguay	C6, H6	103
ateauroux	C3	34
atellerault	C3	34
atfield	C4	96
atham	Inset III	30
atham	C5	102
atham, sound	G4	95
atkal, river	B2	23
atsworth	E3	102
attanooga, Tenn.	E2	126
au Doc	A4	11
aumont	D2	34
aves	B2	36
eb	A2	42
eboksary	D4	44
ech'ŏn	C4	9
echnya, republic	E4	44
eduba, island	B2	12
egutu	B2	69
eju	Inset	9
eju, island	Inset	9
eju, strait	Inset	9
ek Keng	Inset	10
ekiang	G8	104
eleken	A2	22
elif, river	B1	57
elles	Inset II	34
elm	F3	41
elmsford	D3, Inset III	30
eltenham	C3	30
eltenham	D5	44
elyabinsk	D5	44
elyuskin, cape	B7	44
embur	Inset I	20
eméville	A6	103
engde	E1	10
engdu	D2	10
ennai (Madras)	D6	20
eporah	B2	34
erapovets	D3	44
erkassy	C2	47
ernigov	C1	47
ernivtsi	B2	47
errapunji	F3	20
erryville	N6	95
erskiy, range	C8	44
esapeake, bay	F2	126
ester	C3	30
ester	C3	100
esterfield	C3	30
esterfield Inlet	K4	99
esterfield, islands	A2	18
eticamp	G1	100
etumal, state capital	G4	84
etwynd	M3	95
eviot, hills	C2	30
evreuse	Inset II	34
eyenne, capital, Wyo.	C1	126
ezhukha	A2	19
i, river	C2	12
iang Mai	B2	12
iang Rai	B2	12
iapa	C1	76
iatura	B3	45
iba	D3	8
ibougamau	B2	103
ibougamau, lake	B2	103

	Key	Page
Chicago, Ill.	E1	126
Chicapa, river	D3	70
Chichén Itzá, ruins	G3	84
Chichester	C4	30
Chichi, island	Inset III	8
Chiclayo	B2	77
Chico, river	B6	74
Chiconcuac	Inset	84
Chicoutimi	E3	103
Chief, river	L2	95
Chiem, lake	C5	40
Chiesanuova	B2	39
Chieti	C2	38
Chifeng	E1	10
Chignecto, bay	C2	100
Chihuahua, state capital	C2	84
Chilcotin, river	K5	95
Chile		76
Chile Chico	B8	76
Chililabombwe	B2	67
Chilko, lake	K5	95
Chillán	B6	76
Chilliwack	M6	95
Chiloé, island	B7	76
Chilung	B1	9
Chilwa, lake	B2, C3	68
Chimalhuacán	Inset	84
Chimay	C2	33
Chimborazo, mt.	B3	79
Chimbote	B2	77
Chimoio	B3	68
Chin, hills	B2	12
China		10
Chinajá	C4	85
Chinandega	A2	87
Chincha Alta	B3	77
Chinchaga, river	A2	94
Chinde	C3	68
Chindwin, river	B1	12
Chingola	B2	67
Chingoni	C2	67
Chinhae	C5	9
Chinhoyi	B1	69
Chiniot	D3	21
Chinju	C5	9
Chinko, river	B2	66
Chioggia	C1	38
Chip, lake	C4	94
Chipata	C2	67
Chipewyan Lake	D3	94
Chipman	D2	97
Chira, river	A5	79
Chirchiq, river	C2	23
Chire, river	B3	68
Chiredzi	B2	69
Chiriquí, gulf	A3	87
Chiriquí, lagoon	B2	87
Chirner	Inset I	20
Chirripó, mt.	C3	86
Chirripó, river	C2	86
Chisasibi	A3	101
Chisholm	C4	94
Chişinău, capital	B2	50
Chita	D7	44
Chitipa	B1	68
Chitose	Inset I	8
Chitral	D2	21
Chitré	B3	87
Chittagong	E6	21
Chitungwiza	B1	69
Chixoy, river	C4	85
Choa Chu Kang	A1	13
Choiceland	F7	104
Choiseul	A3	91
Choiseul, island	A1	16
Choisy-le Roi	Inset II	34
Chojnice	C2	41
Choke, mts.	B2	60
Cholet	B3	34
Cholpon-Ata	E1	23
Cholula	E4	84
Choluteca	B3	86
Choma	B3	67
Chomo Lhari, mt.	A1	19
Chon Buri	B3	12
Chŏngch'ŏn, river	A3	9
Ch'ŏngjin	C2	9
Ch'ŏngju	B4	9
Chŏngju	A3	9
Chongqing	D3	10
Chonju	B5	9
Chonos, archipelago	B7	76
Chontaleña, mts.	B2	87
Chornobyl'	C1	47
Chorzów	D3	41
Choshui, river	B2	9
Choybalsan	D2	11
Christchurch	B3	15
Christina, river	E3	94
Christmas Island	G2	100
Chu, river	D1	23
Chubut, river	A5	74
Chucunaque, river	D2	87
Chugoku, mts.	B3	8
Chukchi, peninsula	C11	44
Chukchi, range	C10	44
Chukchi, sea	B11	44
Chukotka, autonomous okrug	C10	44
Chumphon	B4	12
Chunan	B1	9
Ch'unch'ŏn	B4	9
Chung Hau	Inset	10
Chungho	B2	9
Ch'ungju	B4	9
Chungli	B1	9
Chungqing, Ind. Mun.	D3	10
Chungyang, range	C2	9
Chur	D2	35
Church Point	A3	100
Churchbridge	A4	96
Churchbridge	J10	104
Churchill	D1	96
Churchill Falls	D3	98
Churchill, lake	B4	104
Churchill, river	D1	96

	Key	Page
Churia, mts.	B2	19
Chute-aux-Outardes	H2	103
Chuuk, islands	C2	15
Chuvashiya, republic	D4	44
Ciales	C2	90
Cibao, valley	A1	89
Cicia, island	C2	17
Cidra	C2	90
Ciechánow	E2	41
Ciego de Ávila	D2	88
Cienfuegos	C2	88
Cieza	F3	37
Cijara, reservoir	D3	37
Cikobia, island	C1	17
Cilacap	B2	13
Cilician Gates, pass	C3	27
Cimone, mt.	B1	38
Cincinnati, Ohio	E2	126
Cirebon	B2	13
Citlaltépetl, mt.	E4	84
City View	G6	102
Ciudad Acuña	D2	84
Ciudad Bolívar	D2	79
Ciudad Camargo	C2	84
Ciudad Constitución	B3	84
Ciudad del Carmen	F4	84
Ciudad del Este	E4	75
Ciudad Guayana	D2	79
Ciudad Juárez	C1	84
Ciudad Mante	E3	84
Ciudad Obregón	C2	84
Ciudad Real	E3	37
Ciudad Rodrigo	C2	37
Ciudad Valles	E3	84
Ciudad Victoria, state capital	E3	84
Ciudadela	H2	37
Civitavecchia	B2	38
Clair	A1	97
Claire, lake	D2	94
Clandeboye	C4	96
Clara	C2	31
Clarenville	D5	98
Clark's Harbour	B4	100
Clarksville, Tenn.	E2	126
Clear Creek	E5	102
Clear, cape	B3	31
Clearwater	M5	95
Clearwater, river	E3	94
Clementsport	B3	100
Clermont	F4	103
Clermont-Ferrand	C4	34
Clervaux	B1	33
Clerve, river	B1	33
Cleveland, Ohio	E1	126
Clichy	Inset II	34
Cliffden	A2	31
Clifford	E4	102
Climax	B11	104
Clinton	M5	95
Clinton	D4	102
Clinton Colden, lake	G4	99
Cloncurry, Qld.	D2	14
Cloridorme	M2	103
Clonmel	C2	31
Clovis, N. Mex.	C2	126
Cloyne	H3	102
Cluff Lake Mine	A2	104
Cluj-Napoca	B2	43
Cluny	D3	34
Cluny	D6	94
Clutha, river	A4	15
Clyde River	P2	99
Clyde, estuary	B2	30
Clyde, river	B2	30
Clydebank	B2	30
Coacalco	Inset	84
Coahuila	D2	84
Coal River	J1	95
Coal, river	D5	105
Coaldale	D6	94
Coalspur	B4	94
Coamo	C2	90
Coast, mts.	F2, J5	95
Coast, ranges	A1, A2	126
Coaticook	E6	103
Coats Land, region	B13	107
Coats, island	M4	99
Coatzacoalcos	F4	84
Cobán	C4	85
Cobden	J2	102
Cobh	B3	31
Cobham, river	D2	96
Cobija	A2	77
Cobourg	G4	102
Coburg	B3	40
Coburg, island	N1	99
Cocagne	E2	97
Cochabamba	A3	77
Cochin (Kochi)	C7	20
Cochrane	B8	76
Cochrane	D3	101
Cochrane, lake	B8	76
Cochrane, river	H2	104
Cockburn Harbour	D4	89
Cockburn, island	B2	102
Coclé del Norte	B2	87
Coco	C2	90
Coco, islands	B3	12
Coco, river	A2, C1	87
Cocos, islands		5
Cocotitlán	Inset	84
Cod, cape, Mass.	G1	126
Codri, region	A3	50
Codrington	A2	90
Codrington, mt.	C17	107
Cody, Wyo.	C1	126
Coe Hill	H3	102
Coeroeni, river	A3	80
Coeur d'Alene, Idaho	B1	126
Cogalnic, river	B2	50
Cognac	B4	34
Coiba, island	B3	87
Coihaique	B8	76
Coimbatore	C6	20
Coimbra	B2	36
Cojedes, river	C2	79
Colca, river	C4	77

	Key	Page
Colchester	D3	30
Cold Lake	E4	94
Coleraine	A2	30
Coles Island	D3	97
Coleville	A9	104
Colihaut	A2	90
Colima, state capital	A5	19
Colina	Inset	76
Coll, island	A2	30
Collaguasi	C2	76
Collingwood	B3	15
Collingwood	E3	102
Colmar	D2	34
Cologne	A3	40
Colombia		78
Colombier	H3	103
Colombo, capital	A5	20
Colón	C2	87
Colón	C2	88
Colonia	A2	15
Colonia	B3	75
Colonia Nueva Guinea	B3	87
Colonsay	E9	104
Colonsay, island	A2	30
Colorado	C2	86
Colorado	C2	126
Colorado, plateau	B2	126
Colorado, river	B4	74
Colorado, river	B2	126
Colorado Springs, Colo.	C2	126
Columbia, capital, S.C.	E2	126
Columbia, mts.	M4	95
Columbia, plateau	B1	126
Columbia, river	B1	126
Columbus, capital, Ohio	E2	126
Columbus, Ga.	E2	126
Coma Pedrosa, mt.	A1	36
Comayagua	B2	86
Comayagua, mts.	B2	86
Combermere	H2	102
Comendador	A2	89
Comerío	C2	90
Comilla	E5	21
Comino, island	B1	36
Cominotto, island	B1	36
Comitán	F4	84
Committee, bay	L3	99
Como	B1	38
Como, lake	B1	38
Comodoro Rivadavia	B6	74
Comorin, cape	C7	20
Comoros		67
Comox	K6	95
Compiègne	C2	34
Compton	E6	103
Comrat	B2	50
Con Son, islands	B5	11
Conakry, capital	A3	62
Concepción	B6	76
Concepción	D3	75
Concepción del Oro	D3	84
Conchalí	Inset	76
Conche	D4	98
Conchos, river	C2	84
Concord, capital, N.H.	F1	126
Concordia	D3	74
Condor	C5	94
Conche	D4	98
Congo, Dem Rep of		67
Congo, Rep of		66
Congo, basin	D3	66
Congo, river	D4	66
Conn, lake	B1	31
Connecticut	F1	126
Connemara, region	B2	31
Consecon	H4	102
Constance	B5	40
Constance (Bodensee), lake	D1	35
Constanţa	E3	43
Constanza	B1	57
Constitución	B5	76
Consul	A11	104
Contrecoeur	C6	103
Contwoyto, lake	G3	99
Conwy	B3	30
Coober Pedy, S.A.	C2	14
Cook's Harbour	D3	98
Cook, mt.	B3	15
Cook, strait	B3	15
Cookshire	E6	103
Cookstown	F3	102
Coos Bay, Oreg.	A1	126
Copán, ruins	A2	86
Copenhagen, capital	D3	32
Copiapó	B3	76
Copiapó, river	B3	76
Coppename, river	A2	80
Coppermine, river	F3	99
Coquí	C3	90
Coquimbo	B3	76
Coral, sea	E1	14
Corantijn, river	A2	80
Corazón	C3	90
Corbeil-Essonnes	Inset II	34
Corcovado, gulf	B7	76
Corcovado, mt.	Inset I	81
Córdoba	C3	74
Córdoba	D4	37
Córdoba, range	B3	74
Cork	B3	31
Cormack	C4	98
Cormorant	A2	96
Cormorant, reef	A2	96
Cornélia de Llobregat	G2	37
Corner Brook	C5	98
Corno, mt.	C2	38
Cornwall	B2	100
Cornwall	L2	102
Cornwall, island	K1	99
Cornwallis, island	J1	99
Coro	C1	79
Coromandel, peninsula	C2	15

	Key	Page
Coronach	E11	104
Coronado, bay	B3	86
Coronation, gulf	F3	99
Coronel Oviedo	D4	75
Coropuna, mt.	C4	77
Corozal	B1	85
Corozal	C2	90
Corpus Christi, Tex.	D3	126
Corregidor, island	B3	12
Corrib, lake	B2	31
Corrientes	D2	74
Corse	Inset I	34
Corsica, island	Inset I	34
Cortina d'Ampezzo	C1	38
Cortona	B2	38
Çoruh, river	H3	103
Çorum	E2	27
Çorum	C2	27
Corumbá	C3	81
Corumbau, point	E3	81
Corvallis, Oreg.	A1	126
Cosenza	D3	38
Coslada	Inset II	37
Cosmoledo, island group	A2	70
Costa Rica		86
Cotabato	C5	12
Côte d'Ivoire		63
Cotentin, peninsula	B2	34
Cotia	Inset II	81
Cotonou	B4	64
Cotopaxi, mt.	B3	79
Cotswold, hills	C3	30
Cottbus	C3	40
Cotton Ground	C2	90
Cotuí	B1	89
Coubert	Inset II	34
Couffo, river	B4	64
Courantyne, river	B3	80
Courland, lagoon	A2	46
Courtenay	K6	95
Courval	D10	104
Coutts	E6	94
Couva	A2	91
Coventry	C3	30
Covilhã	B2	36
Cow Head	C4	98
Cowan	A3	96
Cowansville	D6	103
Cowes	C4	30
Cox's Bazar	E7	21
Cox's Cove	B4	98
Coyah	B3	62
Coyoacán	Inset	84
Cozumel, island	G3	84
Cradock	C3	71
Craigmyle	D5	94
Craik	E9	104
Craiova	B3	43
Cranberry Portage	A2	96
Cranbrook	P6	95
Crane River	B3	96
Crane Valley	E11	104
Crapaud	B2	100
Cravo Norte	C3	78
Crawford Bay	O6	95
Crawley	Inset III	30
Crean, lake	D6	104
Cree Lake	D3	104
Cree, river	E2	104
Cremona	B1	38
Cremona	C5	94
Cres, island	B3	48
Cressday	E6	94
Creston	O6	95
Crete, island	C4	51
Crete, sea	C4	51
Créteil	Inset II	34
Crewe	C3	30
Crimean, mts.	C4	47
Crimean, peninsula	C3	47
Cristal, mts.	A1	66
Cristóbal	C2	87
Cristóbal Colón, peak	B2	78
Crna Gora, mts.	B3	49
Crna, river	B2	48
Croatia		48
Crocker, range	D2	13
Cromer	A4	96
Crooked River	G8	104
Crooked, island	C4	89
Crooked, river	L4	95
Cross Lake	C2	96
Cross, lake	E4	65
Cross, cape	A2	70
Crotone	D3	38
Cruz, cape	D3	88
Cruzeiro do Sul	A2	81
Crystal City	B4	96
Cu Lao Thu, island	B4	11
Cuajimalpa	Inset	84
Cuamba	C2	68
Cuando, river	D2	70
Cuango, river	D2	70
Cuanza, river	C3	70
Cuareim, river	B1	75
Cuauhtémoc	C2	84
Cuautitlán	Inset	84
Cuautitlán Izcalli	Inset	84
Cuba		88
Cubal, river	B5	70
Cubango, river	D5	70
Cubatão	Inset II	81
Cúcuta	B3	78
Cuddalore	C6	20
Cudworth	E8	104
Cuenca	B4	79
Cuenca	E2	37
Cuernavaca, state capital	E4	84
Cuiabá	C3	81
Cuíto Cuanavale	D5	70
Cuito, river	D4	70
Cukorova, region	C2	90
Culebra, island	E2	90
Culebrinas, river	A2	90
Culiacán, state capital	C3	84
Cumaná	D1	79
Cumberland	K6	95
Cumberland		30
Cumberland House	H7	104
Cumberland, lake	H6	104

	Key	Page
Cumberland, peninsula	P3	99
Cumberland, sound	P3	99
Cumbrian, mts.	B2	30
Cunene, river	B5, C4	70
Cuneo	A1	38
Cupar	B2	30
Cupar	F10	104
Curaçao, island		82
Curaray, river	C3	79
Curepipe	C3	69
Curicó	B4	76
Curitiba	D4	81
Curral Velho	D3	58
Curuzú Cuatiá	D2	74
Cut Knife	A8	104
Cuttack	E4	20
Cuxhaven	B2	40
Cuyo, islands	B4	12
Cuyuni, river	A2	80
Cuzco	C3	77
Cyangugu	A2	61
Cyclades, islands	C3	51
Cypress River	B4	96
Cyprus		27
Czar	E5	94
Czech Republic		42
Częstochowa	D3	41

D

	Key	Page
Da Lat	B4	11
Da Nang	B3	11
Dabakala	D2	63
Dabola	C2	62
Dachang	D3	10
Dachau	B4	40
Dacotah	C4	96
Dades, river	C2	57
Dadu	C4	21
Dafoe	F9	104
Dagestan, republic	E4	44
Dagupan	B2	12
Dahlak, archipelago	C2	60
Dahna, ad-, desert	B1	24
Dahuk	B1	24
Dajabón	A1	89
Daka, river	B2	64
Dakar, capital	A2	62
Dakhla	A2	58
Đakovica	B3	49
Dalälven, river	C2	53
Dalandzadgad	C3	11
Dalhousie	K3	103
Dali	D2	10
Dalian	F2	10
Dallas	C3	96
Dallas, Tex.	D2	126
Dallol Bosso, river	A3	59
Dalmatia, region	B3	48
Daloa	C3	63
Dalvík	B2	52
Daly, river	C1	14
Daman	B4	20
Damanhur	B1	56
Damascus, capital	A3	27
Damaturu	F2	65
Damavand, mt.	C2	22
Damazin, ad-	C3	59
Dame-Marie	A2	89
Damietta	B1	56
Damietta, river	B1	56
Dammam, ad-	C1	24
Dammartin-en-Goële	Inset II	34
Dampier, W.A.	A2	14
Damur, al-	A2	26
Danakil, desert	C2	60
Danané	B3	63
Dand	A4	96
Dande, river	B2	70
Dandeldhura	A2	19
Dandong	F1	10
Dangara	A1	23
Dangme, river	C2	19
Dangrek, mts.	B2	12
Dangriga	B2	85
Daniel's Harbour	C4	98
Danjiangkou	E2	10
Danlí	B2	86
Danube, river		29
Danville	D6	103
Danville, Va.	F2	126
Dao Phu Quoc, island	A4	11
Dapaong	B1	64
Dapp	B4	94
Daqing	F1	10
Dar es-Salaam, capital	C2	68
Dara	A3	27
Đaravica, mt.	B3	49
Darbhanga	E3	20
Darhan	C2	11
Darién, mts.	D2	87
Dariense, mts.	B2	87
Darjiling	E3	20
Darling, range	A3	14
Darling, river	D3	14
Darlington	C2	30
Darłowo	C1	41
Darmstadt	B4	40
Darnah	D1	56
Darnley	B2	100
Dartmoor, plateau	B4	30
Dartmouth	D3	100
Daru	A2	15
Darwin, N.T., capital	C1	14
Dashhowuz	A2	22
Dasht-e Kavir, desert	D3	22
Dasht-e Lut, desert	D3	22
Datong	E1	10
Daua, river	F1	61
Daugavpils	D3	46
Daule, river	B1	91
Dauphin	A3	96
Dauphin River	B3	96
Dauphin, lake	B3	96
Davao	C5	12
Davao, gulf	C5	12

Name	Key	Page
Davenport, Iowa	D1	126
David	A2	87
Davidson	D9	104
Davis Inlet	E3	98
Davis, strait	M2	91
Davos	D2	35
Dawa, river	C3	60
Dawhat as-Salwa, bay	B3	25
Dawkah	B2	25
Dawna, range	B2	12
Dawson	B3	105
Dawson Creek	M3	95
Dawson, river	A2	96
Daymán, river	B1	75
Dayr az-Zawr	B2	27
Dayton, Ohio	E2	126
Daytona Beach, Fla.	E3	126
De Aar	B3	71
De Quincy Village	Inset	70
Dead Sea, lake	A2	26
Dead, sea	B2	26
Dean, channel	J5	95
Dean, river	K5	95
Dease Lake	G2	95
Death, valley, Calif.	B2	126
Deauville	C2	34
Debar	A2	48
Debden	D7	104
Debed, river	B2	45
DeBolt	A3	94
Debre Birhan	C2	60
Debre Markos	B2	60
Debrecen	C2	43
Decatur, Ill.	E2	126
Deccan, plateau	C5	20
Děčín	B2	42
Dédougou	C2	64
Dedza	B2	68
Dee, river	B3, C1	30
Deep River	H1	102
Deep, inlet	B1	98
Deepdale	A3	96
Deer Lake	C4	98
Deerfield	A4	100
Degeh Bur	D2	60
Dégelis	H4	103
Dehiwala-Mt. Lavinia	A5	19
Dehra Dun	C2	20
Dej	B2	43
Del Rio, Tex.	C3	126
Delacour	D5	94
Delap Cove	B3	100
Delaronde, lake	C6	104
Delaware	F2	126
Delburne	D5	94
Deleau	A4	96
Delft	B2	32
Delft, island	A2	19
Delfzijl	D1	32
Delgado	A2	86
Delhi	C3	20
Delhi	E5	102
Delicias	C2	84
Déline	D3	99
Delisle	C9	104
Deloraine	A4	96
Delos, island	C3	51
Delson	J6	103
Delta Beach	B4	96
Demerara, river	B3	80
Den Helder	B2	32
Denakil, desert	C1	60
Denare Beach	H6	104
Denbigh	H2	102
Dencross	C4	96
Dender, river	B2	33
Denigomodu	A2	16
Denmark		32
Denmark, strait	D2	106
Dennery	B2	91
Denpasar	C2	13
D'Entrecasteaux, islands	B2	15
D'Entrecasteaux, reefs	C1	18
Denver, capital, Colo.	C2	126
Denzil	A8	104
Dera Ghazi Khan	D3	21
Dera Ismail Khan	D3	21
Derby	C3	30
Derg, lake	B2	31
Derrick	B3	91
Derventa	B1	48
Derwent	E4	94
Des Moines, capital, Iowa	D1	126
Desaguadero, river	B2	74
Desaguadero, river	A3	77
Desberats	B1	102
Deschaillons	D5	103
Deschambault Lake	G6	104
Dese	C2	60
Deseado, river	B6	74
Deseronto	H3	102
Desna, river	C1	47
Desolación, island	B9	76
Desruisseau	B3	91
Dessau	C3	40
Destruction Bay	B5	105
Detmold	B3	40
Detroit, Mich.	E1	126
Deux Rivieres	G1	102
Deux-Montagnes	H5	103
Deva	B3	43
Deventer	D2	32
Devil's, island	B1	80
Devoll, river	B3	49
Devon, island	L1	99
Devonport, Tas.	D4	14
Dewberry	E4	94
Dezful	B3	22
Dháfni	Inset	51
Dhahran	C1	24
Dhaka, capital	D5	21
Dhamar	A2	25
Dhangarhi	C1	19
Dhankuta	D2	19
Dharan	D2	19
Dhaulagiri, mt.	B2	19
Dhofar, region	C3	25
Dhulagarh	Inset II	20
Dhuusamareeb	B2	60

Name	Key	Page
Diadema	Inset II	81
Dialakoto	C3	62
Diamond, island	B1	91
Dibrugarh	F3	20
Diefenbaker, lake	C10	104
Diekirch	B2	33
Dien Bien Phu	A2	11
Dieppe	C2	34
Dieppe	E2	97
Dieppe Bay Town	B1	90
Diffa	B3	59
Differdange	A2	33
Digby	B3	100
Digne	D4	34
Digul, river	E2	13
Dikhil	B2	60
Dikson	B6	44
Dili	D2	13
Dilijan	B2	45
Dillon	B5	104
Dilolo	B3	67
Dimbokro	D3	63
Dimitrovgrad	D3	50
Dimlang, mt.	F3	65
Dimona	B2	26
Dinagat, island	C4	12
Dinajpur	B3	21
Dinant	C2	33
Dinara, mt.	A2, C3	48
Dinaric Alps, mts.	A1, B3	48
Dinder, river	B1	60
Dingle	A2	31
Dingle, bay	A2	31
Dingli	B2	36
Dinsmore	C9	104
Diourbel	A2	62
Dipolog	B4	12
Diriamba	A3	87
Dispur	F3	20
Diu	B4	20
Diuata, mts.	C4	12
Divo	D4	63
Divriği	C2	27
Diwaniyah, ad-	C2	24
Dixon Entrance, channel	F4	95
Dixonville	B3	94
Diyala, river	C2	24
Diyarbakir	E3	27
Dja, river	B3	65
Djado	C1	59
Djambala	B2	57
Djanet	B2	57
Djelfa	B1	57
Djénné	C3	58
Djerba, island	C3	57
Djibouti		60
Djibouti, capital	C2	60
Djouah, river	B1, C3	58
Djouf, el-, desert	B1, C3	58
Djougou	A3	64
Dnepr-Bug, canal	B3	47
Dneprodzerzhinsk	C2	47
Dnieper, river	C1, E3	47
Dniester, river	B2	43
Dnipropetrovsk	D2	47
Doaktown	C2	97
Doba	B5	59
Doboj	B1	48
Dobrich	F2	50
Dobruja, region	E3	43
Doctor Pedro P Peña	A3	75
Dodecanese, islands	C3	51
Dodge City, Kans.	C2	126
Dodoma, capital	C2	68
Dodsland	B9	104
Doetinchem	D3	32
Dogo, island	B2	8
Dogondoutchi	A3	59
Doha, capital	D3	25
Doiran, lake	C2	48
Dolbeau	D3	103
Dôle	D3	34
Dolomites, range	B1	39
Domagnano	B1	39
Domeyko, mts.	C3	76
Dominica		90
Dominica, passage	A1	90
Dominican Republic		89
Dominion City	C4	96
Domont	Inset II	34
Domremy	E8	104
Domuyo, volcano	A4	74
Don Benito	D3	37
Doña Juana, mt.	C2	90
Donald Station	O5	95
Doncaster	C3	30
Dondo	B3	70
Donegal	B1	31
Donegal, bay	B1	31
Donets, basin	D2	47
Donetsk	D2	47
Dong Hoi	B3	11
Dong Nai, river	B4	11
Dongting, lake	E3	10
Dongwe, river	A2	67
Donnacona	E5	103
Dor, lake	C6	104
Dorado	C2	90
Dorchester	C4	30
Dordogne, river	C4	34
Dordrecht	B3	32
Dore Lake	C6	104
Dörgön, lake	B2	11
Dori	D1	64
Dorintosh	B6	104
Dorking	Inset III	30
Dornoch	B1	30
Dorohoi	D2	43
Dorothy	D5	94
Dorra	B1	60
Dortmund	A3	40
Dorval	H6	103
Dos Hermanas	D4	37
Dosquet	E5	103
Dosso	A3	59
Dothan, Ala.	E2	126
Douai	C1	34

Name	Key	Page
Douala	A3	65
Doubs, river	A1	35
Douglas	B2	30
Douglas, channel	H4	95
Douglastown	M3	103
Douro, river	B2	36
Dourados	C4	81
Dover	D3	30
Dover, capital, Del.	F2	126
Dover, strait	D4	30
Dovrefjell, mts.	B3	52
Dozen, island	B2	8
Drâa, river	A1, B2, C2	57
Draguignan	D5	34
Drake	E9	104
Drakensberg, mts.	B3, C3	71
Drammen	C4	52
Drava, river	A2	43
Drayton Valley	C4	94
Dresden	C3	40
Dresden	C5	102
Dreux	C2	34
Drin, river	A1	49
Drina, river	A2	49
Drobeta-Turnu Severin	B3	43
Drogheda	C2	31
Drumheller	D5	94
Drummond	B2	97
Drummondville	D6	103
Druskininkai	B2	46
Dryden	B3	101
Dschang	B2	65
Duars, plain	A3	19
Duarte, mt.	B1	89
Dubai	C2	25
Dubăsari	B2	50
Dubawnt, lake	H4	99
Dubawnt, river	H4	99
Dubbo, N.S.W.	D3	14
Dublin, capital	C2	31
Dubrovnik	D4	48
Dubuque, Iowa	D1	126
Dubysa, river	B2	46
Duchess	E6	94
Duck Bay	A3	96
Duck Lake	D8	104
Dudelange	B2	33
Dudinka	D1	44
Dudley	C3	30
Dufourspitze, mt.	B3	35
Dufrost	C4	96
Dugald	C4	96
Duisburg	A3	40
Dukhan	B3	25
Dulce, gulf	C4	86
Duluth, Minn.	D1	126
Dum-Dum	Inset II	20
Duma	A1	26
Dumaguete	B4	12
Dumbás	B3	52
Dumfries	B2	30
Dumjor	Inset II	20
Dún Laoghaire	C2	31
Dunaújváros	B2	43
Duncan	L7	95
Duncansby, cape	B1	30
Dund-Us	B2	11
Dundalk	C2	31
Dundee	C2	30
Dundurn	D9	104
Dunedin	B4	15
Dunfermline	B2	30
Dungarvan	C2	31
Dunkirk (Dunkerque)	C1	34
Dunkwa	B4	64
Dunlop	B2	96
Dunnegan	F1	100
Dunnville	F5	102
Dunqulah	C1	59
Dunsinane, mt.	B2	30
Dunstable	Inset III	30
Dunster	N4	95
Duque	C2	25
Duque de Caxias	Inset I	81
Duque de York, island	A9	76
Durance, river	D5	34
Durango, Colo.	C2	126
Durango, state capital	D3	84
Durazno	B2	75
Durban	D2	71
Durham	C2	30
Durham	E3	102
Durham, N.C.	F2	126
Durmitor, mts.	A3	49
Durrës	A2	49
Dyce	A2	96
Dyje, river	B4	42
Dzaoudzi, territorial capital	C2	67
Dzavhan, river	B2	11
Dzhugdzhur, range	D8	44
Dzungaria, desert basin	B1	10
Dzyarzhynskaya Hara, mt.	C3	47

E

Name	Key	Page
Eagle, river	B2	98
Eagle, river	B2	105
Ear Falls	B2	101
East Angus	E6	103
East Antarctica	B1	107
East Braintree	D4	96
East China, sea		7
East Coast Bays	B2	15
East Coulee	D5	94
East Frisian, islands	A2	40
East Lake Ainslie	F1	100
East London	C3	71
East Point	C2	100
East Siberian, sea	B10	44
East York	K5	102
East, cape	C2	15
Eastbourne	D4	30
Eastend	B11	104
Eastern Ghats, mts.	C6	20
Easterville	B2	96
Eastmain	A3	101
Eastmain, river	B3	101
Eastport	E5	98
Eatonia	A9	104
Eau Claire, Wis.	D1	126
Eauripik, atoll	B2	15
Ebebiyín	D2	66
Eberswalde	C2	40
Ebolowa	B3	65
Ebon, island	B3	16
Ebor	A4	96
Ebro, river	F1	37
Ecatepec	Inset	84
Echo Bay	E3	99
Echo Bay	A1	102
Echternach	B2	33
Écija	D4	37
Ecuador		79
Ed	C3	60
Edam	C2	32
Edam	B7	104
Eddies Cove	C3	98
Eddystone	B3	96
Ede	C4	65
Ede	C2	32
Edéa	B3	65
Edgerton	E5	94
Edinburgh	B2	30
Edirne	A2	27
Edmonton, capital	D4	94
Edmundson	A1	97
Edmundston	H4	103
Édouard, lake	D4	103
Edrans	B2	96
Edson	B4	94
Edward, lake	A4	61
Edwards plateau, Tex.	C2	126
Eems, river	D1	32
Effingham	C1	89
Éfaté, island	C3	18
Egadi, islands	C3	38
Eganville	H2	102
Eger	C2	43
Egersund	B4	52
Eglinton, island	E1	99
Egmont, bay	A2	100
Egmont, cape	B2	15
Egmont, mt.	B2	15
Eğridir, lake	B2	27
Egypt		56
Eifel, plateau	A3	40
Eigg, island	A2	30
Eindhoven	C3	32
Einsiedeln	C1	35
Eiseb, river	D2	70
Eisenach	B3	40
Eisenhüttenstadt	C2	40
Eisleben	B3	40
Ejmiatsin	B2	45
Ejura	B3	64
Ekibastuz	D1	23
Ekwan, river	D2	101
El Cañuelo, ruins	C2	90
El Cerro del Aripo, mt.	A2	91
El Encanto	B5	78
El Ferrol	B1	37
El Macao	D2	89
El Paso, Tex.	C2	126
El Pital, mt.	A1	86
El Porvenir	C2	87
El Progreso	B2	86
El Salvador		86
El Seibo	C2	89
El Serrat	B1	36
El Tabo	Inset	76
El Tigre	D2	79
El Toro, mt.	D2	90
El Trebolar	Inset	76
Elat	B3	26
Elâzığ	D2	27
Elba, island	B2	38
Elbasan	B2	49
Elbe, river	B2, C3	40
Elbląg	D1	41
Elbow	D9	104
Elburz, mts.	C2	22
Elche	F3	37
Eldon	C2	100
Eldoret	C3	61
Elephant, island	C12	107
Elephanta, island	Inset I	20
Eleuthera, island	B2	89
Elevsís	Inset	51
Elfros	G9	104
Elgin	B1	30
Elgin	A4	96
Elgin	D3	97
Elgon, mt.	D3	61
Eli Malk, island	B3	17
Elie	C4	96
Elista	E4	44
Elk	F2	41
Elk Point	E4	94
Elkford	P6	95
Elkhorn	A4	96
Elkhovo	E3	50
Elko	P6	95
Elko, Nev.	B1	126
Ellef Ringnes, island	H1	99
Ellerts de Haan, mts.	A3	80
Ellesmere, island	M1	99
Ellice, river	G3	99
Ellinikón	Inset	51
Elliot Lake	C1	102
Ellisras	C1	71
Ellsworth Land, region	B10	107
Ellsworth, mts.	B10	107
Elm Creek	C4	96
Elma	D4	96
Elmina	B4	64
Elmira	C2	100
Elmira	E4	102
Elmsdale	A2	100
Elmvale	F3	102
Elnora	D5	94
Elqui, river	B3	76
Elrose	B9	104
Elsa	B4	105

Name	Key	Page
Elva	A4	96
Elvas	B3	36
Ely	D3	30
Ely, Nev.	B2	126
Embarcación	C1	74
Embarras Portage	E2	94
Embi	B2	23
Embu	D4	61
Emden	A2	40
Emerald, island	F1	99
Emerald, Qld.	D2	14
Emerson	C4	96
Emi Koussi, mt.	B3	59
Emilia-Romagna	B1	38
Emlembe, mt.	B1	71
Emmeloord	C2	32
Emmen	D2	32
Emporia, Kans.	D2	126
Ems, river	A2	40
Encarnación	E5	75
Enchant	D6	94
Ende	D2	13
Enderbury, island	B2	17
Enderby	N6	95
Enderby Land, region	C17	107
Endiang	D5	94
Enewetak, island	A1	16
Engaño, cape	D2	89
Enggano, island	B2	13
Englee	C4	98
English, channel	C4	30
Englishtown	G1	100
Enguri, river	A3	45
Enid, Okla.	D2	126
Enilda	B3	94
Enna	C3	38
Ennadai, lake	H4	99
Ennery	C1	89
Ennis	B2	31
Ennistymon	B2	31
Enns, river	D3	39
Enriquillo, lake	A2	89
Enschede	D2	32
Ensenada	A1	84
Ensenguly	A3	22
Entebbe	C3	61
Enugu	D4	65
Épi, island	C3	18
Épinal	D2	34
Episkopi	A2	27
Epsom	Inset III	30
Equatorial, channel	A5	19
Equatorial Guinea		66
Er Rif, range	C1	57
Erciyes Daği, mt.	C2	27
Érd	B2	43
Erdenet	C2	11
Erebus, mt.	B5	107
Erenhot	E1	10
Erfurt	B3	40
Erg Chech, desert	C1	58
Erg Iguidi, desert	D1	58
Erickson	B4	96
Erie, lake	E5	102
Erie, Pa.	E1	126
Eriksdale	B4	96
Erimo, cape	Inset I	8
Eritrea		60
Erlangen	B4	40
Ermelo	C2	71
Erne, river	A2	30
Errigal, mt.	B1	31
Erromango, island	C4	18
Erskë	B3	49
Erzen, river	A2	49
Ergebirge, mts.	C3	40
Erzincan	D2	27
Erzurum	E2	27
Esbjerg	B3	32
Esch-sur-Alzette	A2	33
Eschen	B1	33
Escondido, river	B2	87
Escuintla	C5	85
Escuminac	K3	103
Esfahan	C3	22
Esil	C1	23
Esker	D3	98
Eskifjördhur	C2	52
Eskilstuna	C3	53
Eskimo Point	K4	99
Eskisehir	B2	27
Esla, river	D2	37
Esmeraldas	B2	79
Espanola	D1	102
Española, island	Inset	79
Esperance, W.A.	B3	14
Espichel, cape	A3	36
Espírito Santo	D3	81
Espíritu Santo, island	B2	18
Espoo	B2	53
Esquel	A5	74
Essaouira	B2	57
Essen	A3	40
Essequibo, river	B3, B5	80
Essex	C5	102
Esslingen	B4	40
Estados, island	C7	74
Estaire	E1	102
Estany d'Engolasters, lake	B2	36
Este, point	E2	90
Esteli	A2	87
Esterhazy	H10	104
Estevan	G11	104
Esther	E5	94
Eston	B9	104
Estonia		46
Estoril	A3	36
Estrela, mts.	B2	36
Esztergom	B2	43
Etchemin, river	L6	103
Ethelbert	A3	96
Ethiopia		60
Ethiopia, plateau	C2	60
Etna, mt.	C3	38
Etobicoke	J5	102
Etosha, pan	B1	70
Etrechy	Inset II	34
Etrek, river	B3	22

Name	Key	Page
Ettelbruck	B2	
'Eua, island	B4	
Euboea, island	C3	
Eugene, Oreg.	A1	
Eugenia, point	A3	
Euphrates, river	C3	
Eureka, Calif.	J4	
Eutsuk, lake	I3	
Evandale	C3	
Evansville	A2	
Evansville, Ind.	E2	
Evenkiya, autonomous okrug	C6	
Everest, mt.	D2	
Everett, Wash.	A1	
Evinayong	C3	
Évora	B3	
Évreux	C2	
Évry	Inset II	
Ewa	B1	
Ewell	Inset III	
Ewo	B4	
Exeter	C4	
Exeter	D4	
Exmoor, plateau	C4	
Extremadura	C3	
Exuma, sound	C2	
Eyasi, lake	C3	
Eyebrow	D10	
Eyl	B2	
Eyre, lake	C3	
Eyre, peninsula	C3	
Eysturoy, island	Inset	

F

Name	Key	Page
Fabyan	E5	
Fada	C3	
Fadiffolu, atoll	A2	
Faenza	B1	
Faeroe, islands	Inset	
Fagamalo	A1	
Făgăras	C3	
Fagasa	B1	
Fagatogo	B1	
Fair, island	Inset I	
Fairbanks, Alaska	Inset I	
Fairford	B3	
Fairmont Hot Springs	P6	
Fairweather, mt.	D3	
Faisalabad	D3	
Faizabad	D2	
Fajardo	D2	
Fakfak	C3	
Falciano	C1	
Falcon Lake	D4	
Falelatai	A2	
Falelima	A2	
Falémé, river	B3	
Faleniu	B1	
Fălesti	B2	
Falher	B3	
Falkland, islands	C7	
Fallujah, al-	B2	
Falmouth	B4	
Falmouth	E5	
False Divi, point	D5	
Falster, island	D4	
Falun	C2	
Famagusta	B1	
Fan Si Pan, mt.	A2	
Fangliao	B2	
Fanø, island	B3	
Farafangana	B3	
Farafenni	A2	
Farah	A2	
Faraulep, atoll	B2	
Farewell, cape	B3	
Farewell, cape		
Farghona	D2	
Fargo, N. Dak.	D1	
Faridpur	C5	
Farim	A1	
Farmington	C3	
Farmington, N. Mex.	C2	
Farnham	Inset III	
Faro	C5	
Faro	B4	
Farquhar, island group	B2	
Farrellton	A6	
Fashir, al-	A2	
Fatick	A2	
Fatoto	C2	
Fauquier	N6	
Faxaflói, bay	A2	
Faxälven, river	C2	
Faya-Largeau	B2	
Faylakah, island	C3	
Fayyum, al-	B2	
Fdérik	B2	
Fehmarn, island	B1	
Fehmarn, strait	B1	
Feira de Santana	E3	
Feldkirch	A3	
Felidu, atoll	A3	
Felixstowe	D3	
Fen, river	E2	
Fenelon Falls	G3	
Fengshan	B2	
Fengyüan	B2	
Feni, islands	B2	
Feni, region	D3	
Feodosiya	D3	
Fergana, valley	E4	
Fergus	E4	
Ferkéssédougou	C3	
Ferlo, river	B2	
Ferme-Neuve	A5	
Fernandina, island	Inset	
Fernie	P6	
Ferrara	B1	
Ferryland	E5	
Fethiye	B3	
Feuilles, river	C1	
Feyzabad	C1	
Fez	C1	
Fianarantsoa	B3	
Fichtelberg, mt.	C3	

Name	Key	Page
...htelgebirge, mts.	B4	40
...ld	O5	95
...ld	E1	102
...ld, lake	A3	49
...ld, lake	E11	104
...Tree	C3	90
...ueira da Foz	A2	36
...ueres	H1	37
...iguig	D1	57
...adelfia		17
...adelphia	B3	75
...glacier	B12	107
...fla, island	B3	36
...more	G11	104
...nbul Ice Shelf, glacier	B14	107
...isterre, cape	B1	37
...nland		53
...land, gulf	C3	53
...alay, river	J2	95
...an, river	C1	31
...negan	D5	94
...anmark, plateau	E2	52
...eside	J1	95
...th, river	A1	105
...ther Branch	C3	96
...sherton	C3	96
...shguard	B3	30
...tzgerald	E1	94
...tzroy, mt.	B8	76
...tzroy, river	B1	14
...ve Islands	C2	100
...rli	C1	38
...rmentera, island	G3	37
...rmosa	D2	74
...ort Albany	D2	101
...ort Chipewyan	E2	94
...ort Collins, Colo.	C1	126
...ort Erie	G5	102
...ort Frances	B3	101
...ort Fraser	K4	95
...ort Good Hope	C3	99
...ort Lauderdale, Fla.	E3	126
...ort Liard	D4	99
...ort MacKay	E2	94
...ort McMurray	E3	94
...ort McPherson	B3	99
...ort Myers, Fla.	E3	126
...ort Nelson	L2	95
...ort Nelson, river	L1	95
...ort Norman	C4	99
...ort Portal	B3	61
...ort Providence	E4	99
...ort Qu'Appelle	G10	104
...ort Resolution	F4	99
...ort Saskatchewan	D4	94
...ort Severn	C1	101
...ort Simpson	D4	99
...ort Smith, Ark.	D2	126
...ort Smith, region	E4	99
...ort St. James	K4	95
...ort St. John	M3	95
...ort Steele	P6	95
...ort Stockton, Tex.	C2	126
...ort Vermilion	B2	94
...ort Wayne, Ind.	E1	126
...ort William	B2	30
...ort Worth, Tex.	D2	126
...ortaleza	E2	81
...orteau	C3	98
...orth, estuary	C3	30
...orth, river	B2	30

Name	Key	Page
Fortín Conde de Mirasol, fort	E2	90
Fortín Ravelo	B3	77
Fortune	D5	98
Fortune Bridge	C2	100
Fortune, bay	D5	98
Foster, river	E4	104
Fosterville	B3	97
Fouman	B2	65
Foumbouni	A1	67
Four Falls	B2	97
Foveaux, strait	A4	15
Fox Island	F2	100
Fox Lake	C2	94
Fox Valley	A10	104
Foxe, basin	N3	99
Foxe, channel	M3	99
Foxe, peninsula	N4	99
Foyle, inlet	C1	31
Foyle, lake	A2	30
Foyle, river	A2	30
Foz do Iguaçu	C4	81
France		34
Frances, lake	D5	105
Franceville	B2	66
Franche-Comté	D3	34
Francis	G10	104
Francistown	B2	69
Francois	C5	98
François, lake	K4	95
Franconian Jura, mts.	B4	40
Frankenwald, mts.	B3	40
Frankford	H3	102
Frankfort, capital, Ky.	E2	126
Frankfurt am Main	B3	40
Frankfurt an der Oder	C2	40
Franklin, strait	J2	99
Franquelin	J2	103
Franz Josef Land, islands	A4	44
Fraser	B1	40
Fraser Lake	K4	95
Fraser, river	L5, M4	95
Fraserburgh	C1	30
Fraserdale	D2	101
Fraserwood	A4	96
Fray Bentos	A2	75
Fredericia	B3	32
Fredericton	C3	97
Fredericton	B2	100
Fredericton Jct.	C3	97
Frederiksberg	D3	32
Frederikshavn	C1	32
Fredrikstad	C4	52
Freeport	A2	89
Freeport	A3	100
Freetown	E5	90
Freetown, capital	A1	63
Freiberg	C3	40
Freiburg	A5	40
Freirina	B3	76
Fréjus	D5	34
Fremantle, W.A.	A3, Inset	14
French Guiana		80
French River	E1	102
Frenchman, river	B11	104
Fresnillo	D3	84
Fresno, Calif.	B2	126
Fria	B2	62
Fribourg	B2	35
Friedrichshafen	B5	40
Frigate, island	C1	91
Frisches Haff, bay	D1	41
Friuli-Venezia Giulia	C1	38
Frobisher, lake	C4	104
Frog, lake	E4	94
Frome, lake	D2	14
Frontier	B11	104
Frosinone	C2	38
Fruška Gora, mts.	A2	49
Frutigen	B2	35
Frýdek-Místek	D3	42
Fua'amotu	B4	17
Fuenlabrada	Inset II	37
Fuerte Olimpo	D2	75
Fuerte, river	C2	84
Fuerteventura, island	Inset I	37
Fuhayhil, al-	C2	24
Fujairah, al-	D2	25
Fuji, mt.	C3	8
Fujian	E3	10
Fujisawa	C3	8
Fukue	A3	8
Fukue, island	A3	8
Fukui	C2	8
Fukuoka	A3	8
Fukushima	D2	8
Fukuyama	B3	8
Fulacunda	B2	62
Fuladi, mt.	B2	22
Fulda	B3	40
Fulda, river	B3	40
Fullarton	A2	91
Funabashi	D3	8
Funafuti, capital	C3	16
Funafuti, island	C3	16
Fundy, bay	A3	100
Furnas, reservoir	C4	81
Fürstenfeld	E3	39
Fürth	B4	40
Fushun	F1	10
Futa Jallon, plateau	B1	62
Futuna, island	C4	18
Fuxin	F1	10
Fuzhou	E3	10
Fyn, island	C3	32

G

Name	Key	Page
Gaalkacyo	B2	60
Gabarus	G2	100
Gabès	C2	57
Gabès, gulf	C2	57
Gaborone, capital	B3	69
Gabon		66
Gabriel, island	C1	69
Gabrovo	D3	50
Gabú	C1	62
Gacko	B2	48

Name	Key	Page
Gaeta	C2	38
Gafsa	B2	57
Gagetown	C3	97
Gagnoa	D3	63
Gagnon	C3	101
Gagra	A2	45
Gainesville, Fla.	E3	126
Gainsborough	J11	104
Gairdner, lake	C3	14
Gaizina, mt.	C2	46
Galahad	E5	94
Galana, river	E5	61
Galápagos, islands	Inset	79
Galaţi	E3	43
Galdhøpiggen, mt.	B3	52
Galena Bay	O6	95
Galicia	C1	37
Galilee, region	B1	26
Galle	B5	19
Gallegos, river	A7	74
Gallinas, point	C1	78
Gällivare	D1	53
Galoa	B3	17
Galveston, Tex.	D3	126
Galway	B2	31
Galway, bay	B2	31
Gambia, The		62
Gambia, river	B2, C3, D2	62
Gambo	C5	98
Gamprin	B1	33
Gan, river	E3	10
Gananoque	J3	102
Gäncä	B2	45
Gander	D5	98
Gander Bay	B4	98
Gandhinagar	B4	20
Ganganagar	B2	20
Ganges, river	E3	20
Gangtok	D1	96
Gansu	C1, D2	10
Ganzhou	E3	10
Gao	D2	58
Gaoua	C3	64
Gap	D4	34
Garabil, plateau	D3	22
Garabogazköl, lake	A2	22
Garda, lake	B1	38
Garden Hill	D2	96
Garden Reach	Inset II	20
Garden, island	Inset I	14
Garden, river	A1	102
Gardenton	C4	96
Gardez	B2	22
Gardner, canal	H4	95
Gardner, island	B2	17
Garissa	E4	61
Garland	A3	96
Garmisch-Partenkirchen	B5	40
Garnish	D5	98
Garonne, river	C4	34
Garoowe	B2	60
Garrou	B2	65
Garry, lake	H3	99
Garson Lake	A4	104
Garulia	Inset II	20
Gary, Ind.	E1	126
Gascoyne, river	A2	14
Gash, river	B3	60
Gaspé	M3	103
Gaspé, peninsula	L3	103
Gaspereau Forks	D2	97
Gatal, river	C4	37
Gateshead	C2	30
Gatico	B2	76
Gatineau	A6	103
Gatineau Park	A6	103
Gatineau, river	A4, A5	103
Gatún, lake	C2	87
Gau, island	B3	17
Gauhati	F3	20
Gaultois	D5	98
Gavarr	C2	45
Gävle	C2	53
Gaya	E4	20
Gaya	A3	59
Gazanjyk	B2	22
Gazelle, peninsula	B2	15
Gaziantep	D3	27
Gbarnga	B2	63
Gdańsk	D1	41
Gdańsk, gulf	D1	41
Gdynia	D1	41
Gêba, river	C1	62
Geelong, Vic.	D3	14
Gege	B2	71
Geikie, river	F1	65
Gejiu	J6	95
Gela	C3	38
Gelibolu (Gallipoli)	A2	27
Gelsenkirchen	A3	40
Gem	D6	94
Gembloux	C2	33
Gemena	B1	67
General Eugenio A. Garay	A2	75
General Santos	C5	12
General, river	C3	86
Genesee	C4	94
Geneva	A2	35
Geneva, lake	A2	35
Genk	D2	33
Gennargentu, mts.	B2	38
Genoa	B1	38
Genoa, gulf	B2	69
Gentilly	Inset II	34
Gentofte	D3	32
George	B3	71
George Town	A2	13
George, river	C2	101
Georgetown	B2	91
Georgetown	C2	62
Georgetown	C2	100
Georgetown, capital	B2	80
Georgia		45
Georgia	A1	89
Georgian, bay	E2	102
Gera	C3	40
Geral, range	C4	81

Name	Key	Page
Gerald	A4	96
Geraldton	C3	101
Geraldton, W.A.	A2	14
Gerlachovka, mt.	C2	42
Germany		40
Germiston	C2	71
Gerona	C2	37
Getafe	E2, Inset I	37
Gevgelija	C2	48
Geylegphug	B3	19
Ghadamis	A1	56
Ghaghara, river	D3	20
Ghana		64
Ghanzi	A2	69
Ghardaïa	B1	57
Gharyan	B1	56
Ghatkopar	Inset I	20
Ghaydah, al-	C1	25
Ghazal, river	B4	59
Ghazni	B2	22
Ghent	B1	33
Ghardaqah, al-	B1	56
Giant's Causeway, headland	A2	30
Gibraltar		36
Gibraltar, strait	D5	37
Gibson, desert	B2	14
Giessen	B3	40
Gifford, river	M2	99
Gifu	C3	8
Giglio, island	B2	38
Gijón	D1	37
Gikongoro	B2	61
Gilbert Plains	A3	96
Gilbert, islands	A1	17
Gilbert, river	D1	14
Gilgit	E2	21
Gilman	D1	96
Gillingham	D3	30
Gimie, mt.	A2	91
Gimli	C4	96
Gironde, river	B4	34
Gisborne	C2	15
Gisenyi	B1	61
Gitarama	B2	61
Gitega	B2	61
Giurgiu	C4	43
Giza	B2	56
Gjirokastër	B3	49
Gjoa Haven	J3	99
Gjøvik	C3	52
Glace Bay	H1	100
Gladstone	B4	96
Gladstone, Qld.	E2	14
Glâma, river	C3	52
Glasgow	B1	30
Glasgow, Mont.	C1	126
Glaslyn	B7	104
Glastonbury	C3	30
Gleichen	D6	94
Glenboro	B4	96
Glencoe	D5	102
Glenholme	D2	100
Glenora	G5	95
Glenwood	D5	98
Glidden	A9	104
Glifádha	Inset	51
Glittertinden, mt.	B3	52
Gliwice	D3	41
Głogów	C3	41
Gloucester	K2	102
Gloucester	C3	30
Glover, reef	C3	85
Glovertown	D5	98
Gmünd	C3	60
Goba	C3	60
Gobabis	C2	70
Gobi, desert	D1	10
Godavari, river	C5	20
Godbout	J2	103
Goderich	D4	102
Godfrey	J3	102
Godoy Cruz	B3	74
Gods, lake	D2	96
Gogama	D3	101
Goiânia	D3	81
Golan Heights, occ. terr.	A3	26
Gold Coast, Qld.	E2	14
Gold River	J6	95
Golden	O5	95
Golden Lake	H2	102
Golea, el-	B2	57
Golfito	C4	86
Golmud	C2	10
Golyama Kamchiya, river	E2	50
Goma	C2	67
Gomera, island	Inset I	37
Gómez Palacio	D2	84
Gonaïves	C1	89
Gonâve, gulf	B1	89
Gonâve, island	B2	89
Gonder	B1	60
Gongola, river	F2	65
Goobies	C5	98
Good Hope, cape	A3	71
Goodlands	A4	96
Goodlands	A4	96
Goodsoil	A6	104
Göppingen	B4	40
Gorakhpur	D3	20
Gordon, lake	E3	94
Gordondale	A3	94
Gore	B2	60
Gore Bay	C2	102
Gori	C4	45
Goris	D3	45
Gorizia	C1	38
Görlitz	C3	40
Gorlovka	D2	47

Name	Key	Page
Gorno-Altay, republic	D6	44
Gorno-Altaysk	D6	44
Goroka	A2	15
Gorontalo	D1	13
Gorzów Wielkopolski	B2	41
Gosford, N.S.W.	E3	14
Goshen	F2	100
Goslar	B3	40
Gospić	B3	48
Gosport	C4	30
Göta, canal	B3	53
Göteborg och Bohus	B3	53
Gotha	B3	40
Gotland, island	C3	53
Gotsu	B3	8
Göttingen	B3	40
Gouda	B2	32
Goudiri	C2	62
Gouin, reservoir	B3	103
Goundam	C2	58
Gouré	C3	59
Govan	E9	104
Governador Valadares	D3	81
Gowd-e Zereh, lake	A3	22
Göyçay	B2	45
Gozo, island	A1	36
Graaf-Reinet	B3	71
Gračanica	B1	48
Gracias	A2	86
Grafton, N.S.W.	E2	14
Graham Land, region	C11	107
Graham, island	F4	95
Graham, island	K1	99
Grahamstown	C3	71
Grampian, mts.	B2	30
Gran Canaria, island	Inset I	37
Gran Chaco, region	B3	75
Granada	B3	87
Granada	E4	37
Granby	D6	103
Grand Anse	B1	91
Grand Bahama, island	A2	89
Grand Bale	C2	69
Grand Bank	D5	98
Grand Bay	C1	91
Grand Bay	C3	97
Grand Bend	D4	102
Grand Bruit	B5	98
Grand Canyon, Ariz.	B2	126
Grand Centre	E4	94
Grand Cess	B3	63
Grand Erg Occidental, desert	B1	57
Grand Erg Oriental, desert	B2	57
Grand Falls	B1	97
Grand Falls-Windsor	D5	98
Grand Forks	N6	95
Grand Forks, N. Dak.	D1	126
Grand Island, Nebr.	D1	126
Grand Junction, Colo.	C2	126
Grand Manan, island	C4	97
Grand Marais	C4	96
Grand Narrows	G2	100
Grand Pré	C2	100
Grand Rapids	B2	96
Grand Rapids, Mich.	E1	126
Grand Roy	B2	91
Grand Santi	A1	80
Grand Turk, capital	D4	89
Grand Turk, island	D4	89
Grand Valley	E4	102
Grand, canal	C2	31
Grand, harbor	C2	36
Grand, lake	D2	97
Grand, lake	C4	98
Grand, river	C3	69
Grand-Anse	D1	97
Grand-Étang	F1	100
Grand-Mère	D5	103
Grand-Remous	A5	103
Grande Baleine, river	A2	101
Grande de Añasco, river	A2	90
Grande de Manatí, river	C2	90
Grande de Matagalpa, river	B2	87
Grande Prairie	A3	94
Grande, bay	A7	74
Grande, range	C2	75
Grande, river	B3	77
Grande, river	D3	81
Grande, river	B3	86
Grande-Anse	D1	97
Grande-Rivière	M3	103
Grande-Vallée	M2	103
Grândola	A3	36
Grandview	A3	96
Granisle	J4	95
Granthel	C3	30
Granville Lake	A1	96
Gras, lake	F4	99
Grass, river	A3, B2	96
Grassland	D4	94
Grauspitz, mt.	B2	33
Gravelbourg	D11	104
Gravenhurst	F3	102
Gravesend	Inset III	30
Gravois, point	B3	89
Graz	D3	39
Great Abaco, island	B2	89
Great Alfold, plain	B2	43
Great Artesian, basin	D2	14
Great Australian, bight	B3	14
Great Bahama, bank	B4	89
Great Barrier, island	C1	15
Great Barrier, reef	D1	14
Great Basin, Nev.	B2	126
Great Bear, lake	D3	99
Great Britain		30
Great Dividing, range	D1, D3	14
Great Exuma, island	C3	89
Great Falls	C4	96
Great Falls, Mont.	B1	126
Great Fish, river	C3	71
Great Inagua, island	C4	89
Great Indian, desert	B3	20
Great Karroo, plateau	B3	71
Great Nicobar, island	F7	20
Great Rift, valley		55
Great Ruaha, river	C2	68
Great Salt, lake, Utah	B1	126

Name	Key	Page
Great Sand Sea, desert	A2	56
Great Sandy, desert	B2	14
Great Scarcies, river	A1	63
Great Sea, reef	B1	17
Great Slave, lake	F4	99
Great Victoria, desert	C2	14
Great Wall of China	D2	10
Great Yarmouth	D3	30
Great Zab, river	B1	24
Great, plains	C1	126
Greater Hinggan, range	F1	10
Greater Sunda, islands	B2	13
Gréboun, mt.	B1	59
Gredos, mts.	D2	37
Greece		51
Greeley, Colo.	C1	126
Greely, fjord	L1	99
Green Bay, Wis.	E1	126
Green Lake	C6	104
Green, islands	B2	15
Greenland		106
Greenland, sea	D2	106
Greenock	B2	30
Greensboro, N.C.	F2	126
Greenville	B3	63
Greenville, S.C.	E2	126
Greenwood	N6	95
Greifswald	C1	40
Grená	C2	32
Grenada		91
Grenada, island	B2	91
Grenadines, islands	A3, B1, C1	91
Grenfell	H10	104
Grenoble	D4	34
Gretna	C4	96
Greve	D3	32
Grevenmacher	B2	33
Grey River	C5	98
Grey, range	D2	14
Greymouth	B3	15
Gribingui, river	A2	66
Griffin	G11	104
Griffith, N.S.W.	D3	14
Grijalva, river	F4	84
Grimsby	C3	30
Grimsey, island	B1	52
Grinnell, peninsula	J1	99
Griqualand East, region	C3	71
Griqualand West, region	B2	71
Griquatown	B2	71
Grise Ford	M1	99
Griswold	A4	96
Groningen	B2	80
Groningen	C1	32
Gronlid	F7	104
Groote Eylandt, island	C1	14
Grootfontein	C1	70
Grootvloer, pan	B2	71
Gros Islet	B1	91
Gros Morne Natl. Park	C4	98
Gros-Morne	L2	103
Grosseto	B2	38
Grossglockner, mt.	C3	39
Groundbirch	M3	95
Groznyy	D2	41
Grudziądz	D2	41
Grunthal	C4	96
Guacanayabo, gulf	D3	88
Guadalajara	E2	37
Guadalajara, state capital	D3	84
Guadalcanal, island	A1	16
Guadalquivir, river	D4	37
Guadalupe, reservoir	Inset	84
Guadarrama, mts.	D2	37
Guadeloupe, island		82
Guadiana, river	C3	37
Guaillabamba, river	B2	79
Guainía, river	C4	78
Guajara Mirim	C1	81
Guajira, peninsula	C1	78
Guam, island		5
Guanacaste, range	A2	86
Guanaja, island	C1	86
Guanajuato, state capital	D3	84
Guanare	B2	79
Guandu, river	Inset I	81
Guangdong	E3	10
Guangxi Zhuang	D3	10
Guangzhou	E3	10
Guánica	B3	90
Guantánamo	E3	88
Guaporé, river	A3	77
Guaqui	A3	77
Guaranda	B3	79
Guarda	B2	36
Guarujá	Inset II	81
Guarulhos	Inset II	81
Guasave	C2	84
Guatemala		85
Guatemala City, capital	C5	85
Guaviare, river	C4	78
Guayaguayare	A2	91
Guayama	C2	90
Guayambre, river	B2	86
Guayanilla	B2	90
Guayape, river	B2	86
Guayaquil	A4	79
Guayaquil, gulf	A4	79
Guayas, river	B2	79
Guaymas	C2	84
Guaynabo	C2	90
Guben	C3	40
Gudauta	A2	45
Gudeña, river	C2	32
Guecho	E1	37
Guéckédou	C3	62
Guelph	E4	102
Guelta Zemmur	B1	58
Guéret	C3	34
Guernica Y Luno	E1	37
Guernsey, island	Inset II	30
Guerrero	D4	84
Guerrero Negro	A2	84
Guiana, highlands	D2	79
Guiers, lake	B1	62
Guilarte, mt.	B2	90
Guildford	C3	30
Guilin	E3	10

	Key	Page
Guimarães	A2	36
Guinea		62
Guinea, gulf		55
Guinea-Bissau		62
Güiria	D1	79
Guiyang	D3	10
Guizhou	D3	10
Gujranwala	E3	21
Gujrat	E3	21
Gulbarga	C5	20
Gulbene	D2	46
Gulf Coastal, plain	D3	126
Gulistan	C2	23
Gull Lake	B10	104
Gull, lake	C5	94
Gulu	C2	61
Gumdag	B2	22
Gunisao, river	C2	96
Gunnbjørn Fjeld, mt.	D2	106
Gunton	C4	96
Guntur	D5	20
Gurabo	D2	90
Guri, reservoir	D2	79
Gushgy	D3	22
Gushgy, river	D3	22
Gushikawa	Inset II	8
Gustavo A. Madero	Inset	84
Güstrow	C2	40
Guyana		80
Guysborough	F2	100
Gwadar	B5	21
Gwai, river	A2	69
Gwalior	C3	20
Gweru	B2	69
Gyda, peninsula	B5	44
Gympie, Qld.	E2	14
Gyöngyös	A2	43
Győr	A2	43
Gypsumville	B3	96
Gyumri	A2	45
Gyzylarbat	B2	22

H

	Key	Page
Ha Giang	A1	11
Ha'apai, island group	B3	17
Haapsalu	B2	46
Haarlem	B2	32
Habarut	C1	25
Habay	A2	94
Haboro	Inset I	8
Hachijo, island	Inset I	8
Hachinohe	D1	8
Hachioji	C3	8
Haddummati, atoll	A4	19
Hadejia, river	E1	65
Hadera	B1	26
Haderslev	B3	32
Hadhramaut, district	B1	25
Hadithah, al-	B2	24
Haedo, range	B2	75
Hafford	C8	104
Hafnarfjördhur	A3	52
Hagen	A3	40
Hague, cape	B2	34
Haha, island	Inset III	8
Haifa	B1	26
Haifa, bay	B1	26
Haikou	E4	10
Hail	B1	24
Hailar	E1	10
Hainan	D4	10
Haines Junction	B5	105
Haiphong	B2	11
Hairé Lao	B1	62
Haiti		89
Hajdúböszörmény	C2	43
Haji Ibrahim, mt.	B1	24
Hajjah	A1	25
Haka	B2	12
Hakodate	D1, Inset I	8
Halab (Aleppo)	A1	27
Halaib	D1	59
Halba	B1	26
Halberstadt	B3	40
Haldimand	F5	102
Halfmoon Bay	L6	95
Haliburton	G2	102
Halifax	C3	30
Halifax, capital	D3	100
Halil, river	D4	22
Halisahar	Inset II	20
Hall Beach	M3	99
Hall, peninsula	P4	99
Halla-san, mt.	Inset	9
Hallboro	B4	96
Halle	C2	33
Halle	B3	40
Hallingdal, valley	B3	52
Halmahera, island	D1	13
Halmstad	B3	53
Haltiatunturi, mt	B1	53
Halton Hills	F4	102
Hamadan	B3	22
Hamah	A2	27
Hamamatsu	C3	8
Hamar	B3	52
Hambantota	C5	19
Hamburg	B2	40
Hämeenlinna	B2	53
Hameln	B2	40
Hamersley, range	A2	14
Hamgyŏng, mts.	C2	9
Hamhŭng	B3	9
Hami	C1	10
Hamilton	C2	15
Hamilton	B2	30
Hamilton	F4	102
Hamilton, inlet	B2	98
Hamiota	A4	96
Hamm	A3	40
Hammamat, al-	C1	57
Hammamet, gulf	C1	57
Hammerfest	E1	52
Hammonds Plains	D3	100
Hammondvale	D3	97

	Key	Page
Hampden	C4	98
Hampstead	J5	103
Hampton	D3	97
Hamun-e Jaz Murian, lake	D4	22
Hamun-e Saberi, lake	A2	22
Han, river	E2	10
Han, river	B4	9
Hanau	B3	40
Handan	E2	10
Hangayn, mts.	B2	11
Hangö	B3	53
Hangzhou	F2	10
Hanley	D9	104
Hannibal, Mo.	D2	126
Hannover	B2	40
Hanoi, capital	A2	11
Hanover	D3	102
Hantzsch, river	O3	99
Hanzhong	D1	53
Haora	E4, Inset II	20
Haparanda	B4	52
Happy Valley-Goose Bay	A2, E4	98
Har Us, lake	B2	11
Harad	C1	24
Harare, capital	B1	69
Harbel	A2	63
Harbin	F1	10
Harbour Breton	D5	98
Harbour Deep	C4	98
Harbour, island	B2	89
Harcourt	D2	97
Hardangerfjord, fjord	B4	52
Hardangervidda, plateau	B3	52
Hardwood Lake	H2	102
Hare Bay	D5	98
Harer	D2	60
Hargeysa	A2	60
Hargrave	A4	96
Harirud, river	A2	22
Harlow	Inset III	30
Härnösand	C2	53
Harper	C3	63
Harris	C9	104
Harrisburg, capital, Pa.	F1	126
Harrogate	C2	30
Harstad	D2	52
Hart, ranges	L3	95
Hart, river	B3	105
Hartford, capital, Conn.	F1	126
Hartland	B2	97
Hartley Bay	H4	95
Hartney	A4	96
Harvey	C3	97
Harwill	C3	96
Harz, mts.	B3	40
Hasa, al-, region	C1	24
Hasakah, al-	B1	27
Hashtadan, region	E3	22
Haslemere	Inset III	30
Hasselt	D2	33
Hastings	C2	15
Hastings	D4	30
Hastings	H3	102
Hat Yai	B5	12
Hatillo	B2	90
Hato Mayor	C2	89
Hatteras cape, N.C.	F2	126
Hattiesburg, Miss.	E2	126
Haugesund	B4	52
Haultain, river	D4	104
Haute-Normandie	C2	34
Havana, capital	B1	88
Havel, river	C2	40
Havelock	H3	102
Havířov	D3	42
Havre, Mont.	C1	126
Havre-St-Pierre	D3	101
Hawaii	Inset II	126
Hawaii island, Hawaii	Inset II	126
Hawalli	C2	24
Hawar, islands	B2	25
Hawea, lake	A3	15
Hawf	C1	25
Hawick	C2	30
Hawke Harbour	D2	98
Hawke's Bay	C4	98
Hawke, bay	C2	15
Hawkesbury	L2	102
Hay River	F5	102
Hay, river	A2, B1	94
Hayes, river	D1, D2	96
Hayma	C2	25
Hayter	E5	94
Hazelton	J3	95
Hazelton, mts.	H3	95
Hazlet	B10	104
Hazm, al-	A1	25
Hearst	D3	101
Heart's Content	E5	98
Heaslip	A4	96
Heath Steele	C1	97
Hebei	E2	10
Hebrides, sea	A1	30
Hebron	E3	98
Hecate, strait	G4	95
Hecla	C3	96
Hecla and Griper, bay	F1	99
Hedley	M6	95
Heerenveen	C2	32
Heerlen	C4	32
Hefei	E2	10
Hegang	G1	10
Heha, mt.	B2	61
Heidelberg	B4	40
Heidenheim	B4	40
Heilbronn	B4	40
Heilong (Amur), river	F1	10
Heilongjiang	F1	10
Heimaey, island	A3	52
Heinsburg	E4	94
Heisler	D5	94
Hekla, volcano	B3	52
Hel	D1	41
Helen, reef	Inset	18
Helena, capital, Mont.	B1	126
Helgoland, island	A1	40
Hellín	F3	37
Helmand, river	A2	22
Helmsdale	E5	94

	Key	Page
Helsingborg	B3	53
Helsingør	D2	32
Helsinki, capital	B2	53
Heming Lake	A2	96
Henan	E2	10
Henashi, cape	C1	8
Hengch'un	B2	9
Hengelo	D2	32
Hengyang	E3	10
Henley Harbour	D3	98
Hensall	D4	102
Henzada	B3	12
Herat	A2	22
Herb Lake	B2	96
Herbert	C10	104
Heredia	B2	86
Hereford	C3	30
Heriot Bay	K6	95
Hermitage-Sandyville	D5	98
Hermon, mt.	A3	27
Hermosillo, state capital	B2	84
Hernád, river	C1	43
Herne	A3	40
Herning	B2	32
Hertford	Inset III	30
Herzliyya	B1	26
Hess, river	C4	105
Hesse	B3	40
Hetauda	C2	19
Hiatikulu	B2	71
Hibbing, Minn.	D1	126
Hicks Bay	C2	15
Hidaka, mts.	Inset I	8
Hidalgo	E3	84
Hidalgo del Parral	C2	84
Hieflau	D3	39
Hierro, island	Inset I	37
Higashiosaka	B3	8
High Atlas, ranges	B2	57
High Level	B2	94
High River	D6	94
High Tatra, mts.	D4	41
High Wycombe	Inset III	30
Highrock	A1	96
Highrock, lake	A1	96
Higüey	D2	89
Hiiumaa, island	B2	46
Hijaz, al-, region	A1	24
Hilda	E6	94
Hilden	D2	100
Hildesheim	B2	40
Hill Bank	B2	85
Hillaby, mt.	A3	91
Hillah, al-	B2	24
Hillerød	D3	32
Hillsborough	C1	91
Hillsborough	E3	97
Hillsborough, bay	B2	100
Hilo, Hawaii	Inset II	126
Hilton Beach	B1	102
Hilversum	C2	32
Himalayas, mts.		7
Himeji	B3	8
Hinche	C1	89
Hindelang	B5	40
Hindu Kush, range	B1	22
Hino, cape	B3	8
Hinton	B4	94
Hirakata	B3	8
Hirakud, reservoir	D4	20
Hirara	Inset II	8
Hirmil, al-	B1	26
Hirosake	D1	8
Hiroshima	B3	8
Hirtshals	B1	32
Hisapbur	Inset II	20
Hitachi	D2	8
Hixon	L4	95
Hjørring	B1	32
Hkakabo Razi, mt.	C1	12
Ho	C3	64
Ho Chi Minh City	B4	11
Hoa Binh	A1	11
Hobart, Tas., capital	D4	14
Hobsons, bay	Inset V	14
Hobyo	B2	60
Hoceima, al-	D1	57
Hodgeville	D10	104
Hodgson	C3	96
Hódmezővásárhely	C2	43
Hoeryŏng	C1	9
Hof	B3	40
Höfn	C2	52
Hohe Tauern, mts.	C3	39
Hohhot	E1	10
Hokkaido, island	D1, Inset I	8
Hoktemberyan	B2	45
Holbæk	C3	32
Holden	D4	94
Holdfast	E10	104
Holetown	A3	91
Holguín	E3	88
Holhol	B2	60
Holland	B4	96
Holman	E2	99
Holon	B1	26
Holstebro	B2	32
Holton	C2	98
Holyhead	B3	30
Holyrood	E5	98
Holywood	B2	30
Homathko, river	K5	95
Hombori Tondo, mt.	C2	58
Hombori, mts.	C2	58
Homer, Alaska	Inset I	126
Homo, bay	B2	18
Homs	A2	27
Homyel	E3	47
Hon Gai	B2	11
Hondo	C3	94
Hondo, river	B1	85
Honduras		86
Honduras, gulf	A1	86
Hong Kong, S.A.R.	E3	10
Hong Kong, island	Inset	10
Hongze, lake	E2	10
Honiara, capital	A1	16
Honolulu, capital, Hawaii	Inset II	126

	Key	Page
Honshu, island	C2	8
Hoogeveen	D2	32
Hoorn	B2	32
Hope	M6	95
Hope Bay	C2	88
Hope Valley	E5	94
Hopedale	A1	98
Hopedale	E3	98
Hopewell Cape	E3	97
Horgen	C1	35
Hormigueros	A2	90
Hormuz, strait	D4	22
Horn, cape	C9	76
Horn, cape	A1	52
Hornád, river	C2	42
Hornavan, lake	C1	53
Hornepayne	D3	101
Horsburgh, atoll	A2	19
Horse, river	D3	94
Horsens	B3	32
Horton, river	D3	99
Hospitalet	H2	37
Hoste, island	C9	76
Hot Springs, Ark.	D2	126
Hotan	A2	10
Hotchkiss	B2	94
Hottah, lake	E3	99
Houghton, Mich.	E1	126
Houmt Souk	C3	57
Houston	J4	95
Houston, Tex.	D3	126
Hovd, river	B2	11
Hove	C4	30
Hoverla, mt.	A2	47
Hövsgöl, lake	C1	11
Howley	C4	98
Hoy, island	Inset I	30
Hradec Králové	B2	42
Hrazdan	A2	45
Hrazdan, river	B2	45
Hrodna	A3	47
Hron, river	B2	42
Hsinchu	B1	9
Hsinchuang	B1	9
Hsintien	B1	9
Hsinying	B2	9
Hua Hin	B3	12
Huacho	B3	77
Huai, river	E2	10
Huainan	E2	10
Hualien	C2	9
Huallaga, river	B2	77
Huambo	C4	70
Huancavelica	B3	77
Huancayo	B3	77
Huang (Yellow), river	D2, E2	10
Huánuco	B2	77
Huapí, mts.	B2	87
Huaraz	B2	77
Huascarán, mt.	B2	77
Hubbards	C3	100
Hubei	E2	10
Hubli-Dharwar	C5	20
Hudaydah, al-	A2	25
Huddersfield	C3	30
Hudiksvall	C2	53
Hudson Bay	H8	104
Hudson's Hope	M3	95
Hudson, bay	J3	92
Hudson, strait	O4	99
Hue	B3	11
Huehuetenango	A4	85
Huelva	C4	37
Huesca	F1	37
Hufuf, al-	C1	24
Hugli, river	Inset II	20
Hugli-Chunchura	Inset II	20
Hüichŏn	B2	9
Huila, mt.	A4	78
Hüksan Chedo, islands	A5	9
Hull	A6	103
Hulun, lake	E1	10
Hulwan	B2	56
Humacao	D2	90
Humber, river	D3	30
Humboldt	E8	104
Humenné	C2	42
Humuya, river	B2	86
Húnaflói, bay	A2	52
Hunan	E3	10
Hunedoara	B3	43
Hungary		43
Hüngnam	B3	9
Hünsruck, mts.	A4	40
Hunter River	B2	100
Huntington, W. Va.	E2	126
Huntsville	F2	102
Huntsville, Ala.	E2	126
Hunyani, river	B1	69
Huon, islands	B1	18
Huon, peninsula	A2	15
Huron, lake	E1	126
Hussar	D5	94
Hutchinson, Kans.	D2	126
Hvannadalshnúkur, mt.	B3	52
Hvar, island	C3	48
Hvíta, river	A2	52
Hwange	A2	69
Hyargas, lake	B2	11
Hyderabad	C5	20
Hyderabad	C2	21
Hyesan	C2	9
Hyland Post	H2	95
Hyland, river	D5	105
Hylo	D4	94
Hyvinkää	B2	53

I

	Key	Page
Ialomița, river	D3	43
Ialpug, river	B2	50
Iași	D2	43
Ibadan	B4	65
Ibagué	B3	78
Ibar, river	B3	49
Ibaraki	B3	8
Ibarra	B2	79
Ibb	A2	25

	Key	Page
Ibérico, mts.	F2	37
Ibiza	G4	37
Ibiza, island	G3	37
Iboundji, mt.	A2	66
Ibrahim, river	A1	26
Ibri	C1	25
Ica	B3	77
Içá, river	B2	81
Icacos, key	D2	90
Ice Cap	C2	106
Iceland		52
Ich'ŏn	B3	9
Ichihara	D3	8
Ichikawa	D3	8
Ichilo, river	B3	77
Ichinomiya	C3	8
Idaho	B1	126
Idaho Falls, Idaho	B1	126
Idfu	B3	56
Idhra, island	B3	51
Idlib	A2	27
Idrija	B2	48
Ife	C4	65
Igarka	C6	44
Igloolik	M3	99
Igombe, river	B1	68
Iguaçu, falls	C4	81
Iguaçu, river	E2	74
Iguala	E4	84
Iguazú, falls	E4	75
Ihavandiffulu, atoll	A1	19
Ihosy	B3	69
Ilan	B1	9
Iijoki, river	C1	53
Iisalmi	C2	53
Ijevan	C2	45
IJssel, river	D2	32
IJsselmeer, sea	C2	32
Ijuw	C2	16
Ikaría, island	C3	51
Ikeja	B4	65
Ikela	B2	67
Iki, island	A3	8
Ikorodu	B4	65
Ila	D3	19
Ilam	D3	19
Île-à-la-Crosse	C5	104
Île-de-France	C2	34
Ilebo	B2	67
Ilesha	C4	65
Ilford	D1	96
Ilhéus	E3	81
Ili, river	D2	23
Iligan	C4	12
Illampu, mt.	A3	77
Illapel	B4	76
Illimani, mt.	A3	77
Illinois	E1	126
Iloilo	B4	12
Ilorin	C3	65
Imatra	C2	53
Imbariê	Inset I	81
Imbéry	B2	90
Imeni Ismail Samani, peak	B1	23
Imi	D3	60
Imjin, river	B3	9
Imlili	A2	58
Imperatriz	D2	81
Imperial	E9	104
Imperial Mills	E4	94
Imperial, river	B6	76
Impfondo	D3	66
Imphal	F4	20
Inari, lake	C1	53
Inch'ŏn	B3	9
Incles, river	C1	36
Indalsälven, river	B2	53
India		20
Indian Bay	D4	96
Indian Brook	G1	100
Indian Cabins	B1	94
Indian Harbour	D3	100
Indian Head	G10	104
Indiana	E1	126
Indianapolis, capital, Ind.	E2	126
Indigirka, river	C9	44
Indispensable, reefs	B2	16
Indonesia		13
Indore	C4	20
Indus, river	C4, E2	21
Ingleside	K3	102
Ingolstadt	B4	40
Ingonish	G1	100
Ingonish Beach	G1	100
Ingushetiya, republic	E4	44
Inhambane	B5	68
Inhomirim	Inset I	81
Inland, sea	B3	8
Inn, river	B3, C2	39
Inner Hebrides, islands	A2	30
Inner Mongolia	E1	10
Innisfail	D5	94
Innisfil	F3	102
Innsbruck	B3	39
Inta	C5	44
Interlaken	B2	35
International Falls, Minn.	D1	126
Inthanon, mt.	B2	12
Inukjuak	A2	101
Inuvik	C3	99
Inuvik, region	C3	99
Invercargill	A4	15
Invermay	G9	104
Inverness	F1	100
Inverness	B1	30
Inwood	C4	96

	Key	Page
Ipoly, river	B1	
Ipswich	D3	
Iqaluit, capital, Nunivut	P4	
Iquique	C1	
Iquitos	C1	
Iracoubo	C1	
Iráklion	C4	
Iran	E4	
Iranshahr	E4	
Irapuato	D3	
Iraq		24
Irazú, volcano	C3	
Irbe, strait	A1	
Irbid	A1	
Irbil	B1	
Ireland	B5	
Iri	B5	
Irian Jaya, region	C2	
Iringa	C2	
Iriomote, island	Inset II	
Iriona	C2	
Irish, sea	B3	
Irkutsk	D7	
Iron Bridge	B1	1
Iron Gate Reservoir	B3	
Iroquois Falls	D3	1
Irrawaddy, river	B2	
Irtysh, river	D1	
Irtysh, river	C2	
Isabela	A1	
Isabela, island	Inset	
Isabelia, mts.	A1	
Ísafjördhur	A1	
Isangel	C4	
Isar, river	C4	
Ischia, island	C3	
Ise	C3	
Ise, bay	C3	
Isère, river	D4	
Isernia	C2	
Iseyin	B4	
Isherton	B4	
Ishigaki, island	Inset II	
Ishikari, river	Inset I	
Ishim	D5	
Ishim, river	C1	
Ishinomaki	D2	
Ishinomaki, bay	D2	
Ishizuchi, mt.	B3	
Isiro	C1	
Iskenderun	C2	
Iskŭr, river	C2	
Islamabad, capital	D2	
Island Lake	D2	
Island, lake	D2	
Islay, island	B5	
Isle aux Morts	B5	
Islington	J6	1
Ismailiyah, al-	B1	
Isoka	C2	
Isparta	B3	
Israel	B2	
Istanbul	B2	
Istria, peninsula	B2	
Italy		
Izmir	B2	
Izmit	B2	
Itabira	D3	
Itabuna	E3	
Itaipu	Inset I	
Itaipú, reservoir	E4	
Itajaí	F3	
Itanagar	F3	
Itapecerica da Serra	Inset II	
Itapeva	Inset II	
Itaquaquecetuba	Inset II	
Iténez, river	B2	
Itháki, island	B2	
Ittoqqortoormiit (Scoresbysund)	D2	1
Ituna	G9	1
Ivalo	C1	
Ivano-Frankivsk	A2	
Ivanovo	D3	
Ivindo, river	B1	
Ivujivik	A1	1
Iwaki	D2	
Iwakuni	B3	
Iwo	C4	
Iwo Jima, island	Inset III	
Ixelles	Inset	
Ixtapa	D4	
Ixtapaluca	Inset	
Izabal, lake	B2	
Izhevsk	D4	
Izki	C1	
Izmail	B2	
Iztacalco	Inset	
Iztapalapa	Inset	
Izu, islands	C3	
Izu, peninsula	C3	
Izuhara	A3	

J

	Key	Page
Jabal al-Akhdar, al-, mts.	C1	
Jabal al-Uwaynat, mt.	D3	
Jabal an-Nabi Shuayb, mt.	A2	
Jabal an-Nusayriyah, mts.	A1	
Jabal Katrinah, mt.	B2	
Jabal Ramm, mt.	A3	
Jabal Tuwayq, mts.	B2	
Jabal Zuqar, island	A2	
Jabalpur	C4	
Jaboatão	E2	
Jacare-Acanga	C3	
Jackhead	B1	
Jackson's Arm	C4	
Jackson, capital, Miss.	D2	12
Jackson, port	Inset IV	1
Jackson, Wyo.	B1	12
Jacksonville, Fla.	E2	12
Jacmel	C2	
Jacques-Cartier, river	E4	10
Jacquet River	C1	
Jadabpur	Inset II	
Jadida, el-	B1	
Jaén	E4	
Jaffna	C6	1

Key Page

al- ...B2 26
dalpur ...D5 20
nbub, al- ...D2 56
rah, al- ...B2 24
naica ...88
...C3 20
urhat ...B3 21
...B1 48
rta, capital ...B2 13
obstad ...B3 53
upica, mts. ...B2 48
l-Abad ...C2 23
labad ...C2 22
pa Enríquez,
 tate capital ...E4 84
...F3 65
...D4 84
...D2 56
t, island ...B2 16
...A3 60
alpur ...C4 21
abi ...B2 13
nes, bay ...J3 92
amu ...B2 20
nagar ...B4 20
pur ...Inset II
...C2 53
nshedpur ...E4 20
una, river ...C4 21
Lake ...H6 104
Mayen, island ...5
ai ...Inset II 20
akpur ...C3 19
vis ...D1 97
eville ...C4 77
gy-Bazar ...B2 23
an ...8
, sea ...B2 8
anese Alps, mts. ...Inset I 81
eri ...B2 81
urá, river ...B2 81
ana, river ...Inset II 81
ash ...A1 26
vie ...C1 81
us ...D4 94
vis ...E5 102
rebac, mts. ...B3 49
berény ...B2 43
a, island ...C2 13
a, sea ...C2 13
ari, river ...A2 81
vt, al- ...A1 24
...D3 56
whar ...B3 60
apura ...E2 13
uya ...B2 90
irah, al-, region ...B1 27
zin ...A2 26
...C3 65
el Toubkal, mt. ...C2 57
...A2 24
dore, lake ...D5 98
rson City, capital, Mo. ...D2 126
í-Guazú, river ...D4 75
r ...Inset II 20
abbils ...C2 46
enia Góra ...B3 41
gava ...B2 46
nseg ...C3 97
...B3 40
gish Chokusu, mt. ...G1 10
...E6 94
peg ...B2 96
mie ...A2 89
ez de la Frontera ...C4 37
sey, island ...Inset II 30
udong ...B2 13
elum ...D3 21
elum, river ...D3 21
...E3 10
musi ...G1 10
ngsu ...E2 10
ngxi ...A3 10
dah, island ...A1 25
lava ...B3 42
...A3 60
...F1 10
...F1 10
...B3 60
naní ...A2 89
ménez ...D2 84
...E2 10
gdezhen ...E3 10
...E2 10
ja ...C3 61
otega ...B2 87
otepe ...A3 87
sha (Yangtze), river ...C2 10
zhou ...F1 10
iijaba ...A3 79
Paraná ...B3 81
gatol ...B1 23
, river ...B3 43
jiang ...E3 10
...G1 10
...A2 24
zakh ...C2 23
o Pessoa ...E2 81
os ...C3 90
dhpur ...C2 20
s Batt's Arm ...D4 98
ensu ...C2 53
etsu ...C2 8
ggins ...C2 100
an D'or Prairie ...C2 94
nsons Crossing ...C5 105
nor Baharu ...B2 13
, strait ...B1 13
nville ...D4 81
nville, island ...C12 107

Key Page

Joka ...Inset II 20
Joliet, Ill. ...E1 126
Joliette ...C5 103
Jolo ...B5 13
Jolo, island ...B5 12
Jonava ...C2 46
Jong, river ...A2 63
Jönköping ...B3 53
Jonquière ...E3 103
Jonesboro, Ark. ...D2 126
Joplin, Mo. ...D2 126
Jordan ...26
Jordan, river ...A2 26
Jos ...E3 65
Jos, plateau ...E2 65
Jotunheimen, mts. ...B3 52
Jou ...B4 63
Joussard ...C3 94
Juan de Fuca, strait ...L7 95
Juana Díaz ...B2 90
Juàzeiro ...D2 81
Juàzeiro do Norte ...E2 81
Juba ...C4 59
Juba, river ...A3 60
Jubayl ...A1 26
Jubayl, al- ...C1 24
Jubilee, lake ...D5 98
Júcar, river ...F3 37
Juchitán de Zaragoza ...F4 84
Judique ...F2 100
Juigalpa ...B2 87
Juiz de Fora ...D4 81
Juliaca ...C4 77
Julian Alps, mts. ...A2 48
Juliana Top, mt. ...A3 80
Jullundur ...C2 20
Jumayliyah, al- ...C2 25
Jumla ...B2 19
Junagadh ...B4 20
Junaynah, al- ...A2 59
Juncos ...D2 90
Jundiai ...D4 81
Juneau, capital, Alaska ...Inset I 126
Jungfrau, mt. ...B2 35
Juniper ...B2 97
Juniyah ...A2 26
Juozapines, mt. ...C2 46
Jura, island ...B2 30
Jura, mts. ...A2 35
Jura ...C2 46
Jurbarkas ...B2 46
Jurmala ...B2 46
Jurong ...A1 13
Juruá, river ...C3 81
Juruena, river ...C3 81
Jutiapa ...D5 85
Juticalpa ...B2 86
Jutland, peninsula ...B3 32
Juventud, island ...B2 88
Južna, river ...B3 49
Jvari ...B3 45
Jwaneng ...B3 69
Jyväskylä ...C2 53

K

K2 (Godwin Austen), mt. ...A2 10
Ka Dake ...B2 71
Ka, river ...C2 65
Kabala ...B1 63
Kabale ...A4 61
Kabalo ...C2 67
Kabardino-Balkariya,
 republic ...E4 44
Kabelebo, river ...A2 80
Kabompo, river ...A2 67
Kabul, capital ...B2 22
Kabul, river ...B2 22
Kabwe ...B2 67
Kachovka ...C3 47
Kadavu, island ...B3 17
Kadei, river ...A3 66
Kadoma ...B2 69
Kaduna ...D2 65
Kaduna, river ...D2 65
Kaduqli ...B3 59
Kaédi ...B3 58
Kaélé ...B1 65
Kaeo ...B2 15
Kaesŏng ...B4 9
Kafan ...D3 45
Kaffrine ...B2 62
Kafr ad-Dawwar ...B1 56
Kafu, river ...B3 61
Kafue ...B3 67
Kafue, river ...B3 67
Kaga Bandoro ...A2 66
Kagawong ...C2 102
Kagera, river ...B4, C1, C2 61
Kagitumba ...C1 61
Kagoshima ...A4 8
Kahayan, river ...C2 13
Kahemba ...B2 67
Kahnawake ...H6 103
Kahoolawe island,
 Hawaii ...Inset II 126
Kai, islands ...E2 13
Kaieteur, falls ...B3 80
Kaifeng ...E2 10
Kaikoura ...B3 15
Kailahun ...C3 62
Kailahun ...B1 63
Kainji, lake ...D2 65
Kaiserslautern ...A4 40
Kaitaia ...B2 15
Kajaani ...C2 53
Kakamega ...C3 61
Kakata ...A2 63
Kakeroma, island ...Inset II 8
Kakhovka, reservoir ...C3 47
Kakinada ...H3 102
Kaladar ...H3 102
Kalahari, desert ...B3 51
Kalámai ...B3 51
Kalámaki ...Inset 51
Kälbäcär ...B2 45
Kalemie ...C2 67

Key Page

Kalgoorlie-Boulder, W.A. ...B3 14
Kali ...C1 62
Kali, river ...B2 19
Kalimantan, region ...C2 13
Kaliningrad ...D3 44
Kalixälven, river ...D1 53
Kallithéa ...Inset 51
Kalmar ...C3 53
Kalmykiya, republic ...E4 44
Kalpeni, island ...B7 20
Kalu, river ...B5 19
Kalundborg ...C3 32
Kalutara ...A5 19
Kalwa ...Inset I 20
Kamakwie ...A1 63
Kaman, island ...A1 63
Kaman ...Inset I 20
Kamarhati ...Inset II 20
Kambia ...A1 63
Kamchatka, peninsula ...D10 44
Kamchiya, river ...F2 50
Kamenets-Uralsky ...D5 44
Kamet, mt. ...C2 20
Kamloops ...M6 95
Kampala, capital ...C3 61
Kampong Cham ...D4 11
Kampong Chhnang ...C3 11
Kampong Saom ...B5 11
Kampong Thum ...C3 11
Kampot ...C5 11
Kamsack ...J9 104
Kamsar ...B2 62
Kamui, cape ...Inset I 8
Kananga ...B2 67
Kanazawa ...C2 8
Kanchenjunga, mt. ...D2 19
Kanchipuram ...C6 20
Kanchrapara ...Inset II 20
Kandi ...B4 65
Kandy ...B4 19
Kangaroo, island ...C3 14
Kangean, river ...C3 59
Kanggye ...B2 9
Kanghwa, bay ...A4 9
Kangiqsualujjuaq ...C2 101
Kangiqsujuaq ...B1 101
Kangirsuk ...B1 101
Kangnŭng ...C4 9
Kangshan ...B2 9
Kankan ...D2 62
Kano ...E1 65
Kansaripara ...Inset II 20
Kansas ...D2 126
Kansas City, Kans. ...D2 126
Kansas City, Mo. ...D2 126
Kansay ...A1 23
Kansk ...D6 44
Kanté ...B4 64
Kanuku, mts. ...B4 80
Kanye ...B3 69
Kaohsiung ...B2 9
Kaoko Veld, mts. ...A1 70
Kaolack ...A2 62
Kaoma ...A2 67
Kaop'ing, river ...B2 9
Kapfenberg ...D3 39
Kapingamarangi, atoll ...C2 15
Kapiskau, river ...D2 101
Kaposvár ...A2 43
Kapuskasing ...D3 101
Kara ...B2 64
Kara, sea ...B5 44
Kara-Kum, canal ...D3 22
Kara-Kum, desert ...C2 22
Kara-Say ...F2 23
Karabakh, canal ...B2 45
Karachayevo-Cherkesiya,
 republic ...E4 44
Karachi ...C5 21
Karaj ...C2 22
Karak, al- ...A2 26
Karakol ...F1 23
Karakoram, range ...C1 20
Karaman ...C3 27
Karamea ...C4 70
Karasburg ...C4 70
Karawanken, range ...D4 39
Karbala ...B2 24
Karcag ...C2 43
Kardiva, channel ...A2 19
Kärdla ...B1 46
Kareliya, republic ...C3 44
Kariba ...B1 69
Kariba, lake ...A1 69
Karibib ...B2 70
Karisimbi, mt. ...B1 61
Karkar, island ...A2 15
Karkinit, bay ...C3 47
Karlovac ...B2 48
Karlovy Vary ...A2 42
Karlskrona ...C3 53
Karlsruhe ...B4 40
Karlstad ...B3 53
Karnali, river ...B2 19
Karnaphuli, reservoir ...F6 21
Karnaphuli, river ...E6 21
Karonga ...B1 68
Karpas, peninsula ...C1 27
Kárpathos, island ...C4 51
Kars ...E2 27
Karsava, mt. ...A1 67
Kartung ...A2 62
Karun, river ...C2 22
Karuzi ...B3 61
Karviná ...D3 42
Kasai, river ...B2 67
Kasama ...A2 67
Kasane ...B1 69
Kasba, lake ...H4 99
Kashan ...C3 22
Kashi ...A2 10
Kashinathpur ...Inset II 20
Kaslo ...O6 95
Kassala ...D2 59
Kassel ...B3 40

Key Page

Kasserine ...B2 57
Kastamonu ...C2 27
Kastoría ...B1 51
Kastrup ...D3 32
Kasugai ...C3 8
Kasungu ...B2 68
Kasur ...E3 21
Katagum, river ...E2 65
Katanga, plateau ...B3 67
Katerini ...B1 51
Kate's Needle, mt. ...F2 95
Katherine, N.T. ...C1 14
Kathgodam ...C3 20
Kathiawar, peninsula ...B4 20
Kathmandu, capital ...C2 19
Katowice ...D3 41
Katrine, lake ...B2 30
Katsina ...D1 65
Kattegat, strait ...C2 32
Kau-Ur ...C2 62
Kauai island, Hawaii ...Inset I 126
Kaufbeuren ...B5 40
Kaukau Veld, region ...C2 70
Kaunas ...B2 46
Kaura-Namoda ...D1 65
Kavadarci ...C2 48
Kavajë ...A2 49
Kavála ...C1 51
Kavaratti, island ...B6 20
Kavieng ...B2 15
Kavir-e Namak, desert ...D3 22
Kawagoe ...C3 8
Kawaguchi ...C3 8
Kawasaki ...C3 8
Kawhia ...B2 15
Kawthaung ...C4 12
Kayangel, islands ...C1 17
Kayes ...A3 58
Kayser, mts. ...A3 80
Kayseri ...C2 27
Kazakh Upland, region ...C2 23
Kazakhstan ...23
Kazan ...D4 44
Kazanlŭk ...D3 50
Kazincbarcika ...C1 43
Kearney ...F2 102
Kearney, Nebr. ...D1 126
Keban, reservoir ...D2 27
Kebili ...B3 57
Kebir, river ...B1 26
Kebnekaise, mt. ...C1 53
Kechika, river ...J2 95
Kecskemét ...B2 43
Kédainiai ...B2 46
Kedgwick ...B1 97
Kediri ...C2 13
Kédougou ...C3 62
Keele, river ...C4 99
Keeley, lake ...B6 104
Keetmanshoop ...C4 70
Keewatin, region ...J4 99
Kef, el- ...B1 57
Kefallinía, island ...A3 52
Keflavík ...A3 52
Keg River ...B2 94
Keila ...C1 46
Kékes, mt. ...C2 43
Kelang ...A2 13
Kelani, river ...B4 19
Kelliher ...G9 104
Kelowna ...N6 95
Kelsey ...C1 96
Keluang ...B2 13
Kelvington ...G8 104
Kemano ...J4 95
Kemerovo ...D6 44
Kemi ...B1 53
Kemijärvi ...C1 53
Kemijoki, river ...C1 53
Kemnay ...A4 96
Kempenland, region ...D1 33
Kemps Bay ...B3 89
Kempt, lake ...B4 103
Kempten ...B5 40
Kemptville ...K2 102
Kenaston ...D9 104
Kendal ...C2 30
Kendari ...D2 13
Kenema ...B2 63
Keng Tung ...C2 12
Kenilworth ...C3 30
Kenitra ...C1 57
Kennetcook ...D2 100
Kennedy ...C3 30
Kennewick ...B2 100
Kenogami ...A4 96
Kenora ...B3 101
Kensington ...B2 100
Kenton ...A4 96
Kentucky ...E2 126
Kentville ...C2 100
Kenya ...61
Kenya, mt. ...D4 61
Keokradong, mt. ...F7 21
Kerangan Nyatan ...B3 13
Keratsinion ...Inset 51
Kerch ...D3 47
Kerch, strait ...D3 47
Kerema ...A2 15
Keremeos ...N6 95
Keren ...B2 60
Kerewan ...A2 62
Kerguelen, islands ...5
Kericho ...C4 61
Kerinci, mt. ...B2 13
Kerki ...C2 22
Kerki ...D3 22
Kerkrade ...D3 33
Kérkira ...A2 51
Kérkira, island ...A2 51
Kerman ...D4 22
Kerman, region ...D4 22
Kermanshah ...B2 22
Kerrobert ...A9 104
Kerulen, river ...D2 11
Keszthely ...A2 43
Keta ...C4 64
Ketchikan, Alaska ...Inset I 126
Key Lake Mine ...E3 104
Key West, Fla. ...E3 126

Key Page

Keyano ...B3 101
Khabarovsk ...E8 44
Khabur, river ...B1 27
Khakasiya, republic ...D6 44
Khalándrion ...Inset 51
Khalkhidikí, peninsula ...B1 51
Khalkís ...B2 51
Khaluf ...C2 25
Khambhât, gulf ...B4 20
Khamis Mushayt ...B2 24
Khan-Tengri, mt. ...E2 23
Khanaqin ...C2 24
Khaniá ...B2 51
Khanka, lake ...G1 10
Khanty-Mansiya,
 autonomous okrug ...C5 44
Khanty-Mansiysk ...C5 44
Kharagpur ...E4 20
Kharg, island ...C4 22
Kharijah, al- ...B2 56
Kharijah, oasis ...B2 56
Kharj, al- ...B1 24
Kharkiv ...D1 47
Khartoum North ...C2 59
Khartoum, capital ...C2 59
Khashm al-Qirbah ...C2 59
Khashuri ...B4 45
Khasi, hills ...F3 20
Khaskovo ...D4 50
Khatanga ...B7 44
Khawr, al- ...D2 25
Kherson ...C3 47
Khíos, island ...C2 51
Khiran, al- ...C2 24
Khmelnytskyy ...B2 47
Khojak, pass ...C3 21
Khok Angar ...C1 60
Khon Kaen ...C2 12
Khor Angar ...C1 60
Khorasan, region ...D2 22
Khorat, plateau ...C3 12
Khorixas ...B2 70
Khorramabad ...B2 22
Khorramshahr ...B3 22
Khorugh ...B3 23
Khouribga ...C1 57
Khowst ...B2 22
Khudzhand ...A2 23
Khujayli ...A2 23
Khulna ...C6 21
Khums, al- ...B1 56
Khuriya Muriya, islands ...C3 25
Khust ...A2 47
Khuzdar ...C4 21
Khuzestan, region ...B3 22
Khvoy ...A2 22
Khyber, pass ...D2 21
Kibungo ...C2 61
Kibuye ...A2 61
Kičevo ...A2 48
Kidal ...D2 58
Kidderminster ...C3 30
Kiel ...B1 40
Kiel, bay ...B1 40
Kielce ...E3 41
Kiev, capital ...C1 47
Kiev, reservoir ...C1 47
Kiffa ...C3 58
Kifisiá ...Inset 51
Kifissós, river ...B2 51
Kigali, capital ...B1 61
Kigoma ...A1 68
Kii, channel ...B3 8
Kii, peninsula ...B3 8
Kikinda ...B2 49
Kikkertavak, island ...B2 98
Kikwit ...B2 67
Kilchu ...C2 9
Kildare ...C2 31
Kilimanjaro, mt. ...C1 68
Kilinochchi ...B2 19
Kilkee ...B2 31
Kilkenny ...C2 31
Killala, bay ...B1 31
Killaloe ...H2 102
Killarney ...B2 31
Killarney ...B4 96
Killarney ...D1 102
Killarney Lake ...E5 94
Killdeer ...D11 104
Killeen, Tex. ...D2 126
Kilmarnock ...B2 30
Kilombero, river ...C2 68
Kilwa Kivinje ...C2 68
Kimbe ...B2 15
Kimberley ...O6 95
Kimberley ...B2 71
Kimberley ...E3 102
Kimberley, plateau ...B1 14
Kimch'aek ...C2 9
Kimch'ŏn ...C4 9
Kinabalu, mt. ...D1 13
Kinabatangan, river ...D2 13
Kinbasket ...B5 94
Kinbasket, lake ...O5 95
Kincaid ...C11 104
Kincardine ...D3 102
Kindersley ...A9 104
Kindia ...B2 62
Kindu ...C2 67
King Leopold, range ...B1 14
King William, island ...J3 99
King's Cove ...E5 98
King's Landing ...B3 97
King's Lynn ...D3 30
King's Point ...C4 98
Kingcome Inlet ...J6 95
Kingman, Ariz. ...B2 126
Kingston ...C3 100
Kingston ...J3 102
Kingston upon Hull ...D3 30
Kingston upon Thames ...Inset III 30
Kingston, capital ...B2 88
Kingstown, capital ...B2 91
Kingsville ...C5 102
Kinistino ...E8 104
Kinkala ...C6 66
Kinkora ...B2 100
Kinloss ...D3 102

Key Page

Kinmount ...G3 102
Kinnairds, cape ...C1 30
Kinosota ...B4 96
Kinsarvik ...B3 52
Kinsella ...E5 94
Kinshasa, capital ...A2 67
Kinyeti, mt. ...C4 59
Kioa, island ...B2 16
Kiosk ...G1 102
Kipengere, range ...B2 68
Kipling ...H10 104
Kirakira ...B2 16
Kirensk ...D7 44
Kiribati ...17
Kirikkale ...C2 27
Kiritimati (Christmas),
 island ...D1 17
Kirkcaldy ...B2 30
Kirkenes ...F2 52
Kirkfield ...G3 102
Kirkland Lake ...D3 101
Kirkpatrick, mt. ...A5 107
Kirkuk ...C2 24
Kirkwall ...Inset I 30
Kirov ...D4 44
Kirovakan ...B2 45
Kirovograd ...C2 47
Kirşehir ...C2 27
Kirthar, range ...C4 21
Kiruna ...D1 53
Kisangani ...C1 67
Kishi ...B3 65
Kiskitto, lake ...B2 96
Kiskörei-víztároló, lake ...C2 43
Kiskunhalas ...B2 43
Kismayo ...A4 60
Kissidougou ...C3 62
Kississing, lake ...A1 96
Kisumu ...C4 61
Kita ...B3 58
Kita, island ...Inset III 8
Kitakami, river ...D2 8
Kitakyushu ...A3 8
Kitale ...C3 61
Kitami ...Inset I 8
Kitami, mts. ...Inset I 8
Kitchener ...E4 102
Kitgum ...C2 61
Kíthira, island ...B3 51
Kitikmeot, region ...G3 99
Kitimat ...H4 95
Kitwanga ...H3 95
Kitwe ...B2 67
Kivi, lake ...B2 53
Kivu, lake ...B1 61
Kızıl Irmak, river ...C1 53
Kjølen, mts. ...C1 53
Kladno ...B2 42
Klagenfurt ...D4 39
Klaipėda ...A2 46
Klamath Falls, Oreg. ...A1 126
Klarälven, river ...B2 53
Klatovy ...A3 42
Kleinburg ...J5 102
Klemtu ...H5 95
Kleve ...A3 40
Klouklubed ...B3 17
Kluane, lake ...B5 105
Knee, lake ...D1 96
Knight, inlet ...K6 95
Knockboy, mt. ...B3 31
Knokke ...B1 33
Knoxville, Tenn. ...E2 126
Ko Chang, island ...C3 12
Ko Kut, island ...C3 12
Ko Phangan, island ...B4 12
Ko Samui, island ...B4 12
Ko Tarutao, island ...B5 12
Kobe ...B3 8
Koblenz ...A3 40
Kobuleti ...A2 45
Kočani ...C2 48
Kočevje ...B3 48
Kochi ...B3 8
Kodiak, Alaska ...Inset I 126
Kofarnihon, river ...A2 23
Köflach ...D3 39
Koforidua ...B3 64
Kofu ...C3 8
Køge ...D3 32
Kohima ...F3 20
Kohtla-Järve ...D1 46
Koindu ...B1 63
Koje-do, island ...C5 9
Kokkina ...A1 27
Kokkola ...B2 53
Kokshetau ...C1 23
Kola ...A4 96
Kola, peninsula ...C3 44
Kolari ...B3 62
Kolda ...B3 62
Kolding ...B5 20
Kolhapur ...B5 20
Kolín ...B1 42
Kołobrzeg ...B1 41
Kolpashevo ...D6 44
Kolshet ...Inset I 20
Kolumadulu, atoll ...A3 19
Kolwezi ...B2 67
Kolyma, range ...C10 44
Kolyma, river ...C9 44
Komadugu Gana, river ...F2 65
Komadugu Yobe, river ...F1 65
Komárno ...B3 42
Komárom ...B2 43
Komati, river ...B2 71
Komatsu ...C2 8
Komi, republic ...C4 44
Komi-Permyat,
 autonomous okrug ...D4 44
Komoé, river ...E3 63
Komotiní ...C1 51
Komsomolsk-na-Amure ...D8 44
Konar, river ...D2 21
Konduz ...B1 22
Konduz, river ...B2 22
Koné ...C2 18
Kong, river ...D4 11

Name	Key	Page
Konibodom	B1	23
Konin	D2	41
Konnagar	Inset II	20
Konotop	C1	47
Kontagora	C2	65
Kontum	B3	11
Konya	C3	27
Kootenay, lake	O6	95
Kootenay, river	P6	95
Kopaonik, mts.	B3	49
Kópavogur	A2	52
Koper	A3	48
Kopet, mts.	B2, D2	22
Koprivnica	C2	48
Korab, mt.	B2	49
Korab, mt.	A2	48
Korçë	B3	49
Korčula, island	C4	48
Korea, bay	A3	9
Korea, strait	C5	9
Korhogo	D2	63
Koriyama	D2	8
Korla	B1	10
Koro Toro	B4	59
Koro, island	B2	17
Koro, sea	B2	17
Koror, capital	B3	17
Koror, island	C3	17
Körös, river	C2	43
Korosten	B1	47
Kortrijk	B2	33
Koryak, range	C10	44
Koryakiya, autonomous okrug	C10	44
Kosŏng	C3	9
Kos, island	C3	51
Kosciusko, mt.	D3	14
Koshigaya	C3	8
Koshiki, islands	A4	8
Košice	C2	42
Kosovo, province	B3	49
Kosrae	D2	15
Kosrae, island	D2	15
Kossol, passage	C2	17
Kossol, reef	C2	17
Kossu, lake	D3	63
Koszalin	C1	41
Kota	C3	20
Kota Baharu	B1	13
Kota Kinabalu	D2	13
Kotcho, lake	M1	95
Kotka	C2	53
Kotlas	C4	44
Kotor, gulf	A3	49
Kotto, river	B2	66
Kouchibouguac	D2	97
Koudougou	C2	64
Koula-Moutou	B2	66
Koulikoro	B3	58
Koumac	C2	18
Koungheul	B2	62
Kourou	B1	80
Kouroussa	D2	62
Kousséri	B3	58
Koutiala	C3	63
Kouto	C2	63
Kouvola	C2	53
Kovel	A1	47
Kowŏn	B3	9
Kowloon	Inset	10
Kowt-e Ashrow	B2	22
Kozáni	B1	51
Kozhikode	C6	20
Kozloduy	B2	50
Kozu, island	C3	8
Kožuf, mts.	C2	49
Kpalimé	B3	64
Kpandu	C3	64
Kpémé	B4	64
Kra, isthmus	B4	12
Kracheh	B3	11
Kragujevac	B2	49
Krakatau, island	B2	13
Kraków	D3	41
Kraljevo	B3	49
Kramatorsk	D2	47
Kranj	B2	48
Kranji	B1	13
Krasnodar	B3	44
Krasnoyarsk	D6	44
Krefeld	A3	40
Kremenchug	C2	47
Kretinga	A2	46
Kribi	A3	65
Krishna, river	C5	20
Kristiansand	B4	52
Kristianstad	B3	53
Kristiansund	B3	52
Kristinehamn	B3	53
Krk, island	B3	48
Krka, river	B3	48
Krong Kaoh Kong	A4	11
Kroonstad	C2	71
Krosnow	E4	41
Krško	C3	48
Krugersdorp	C2	71
Krujë	A2	49
Kruševac	B3	49
Kruševo	B2	49
Krychaw	E3	47
Kryvyi Rih	C2	47
Kuala Abang	B3	13
Kuala Belait	A2	13
Kuala Lumpur, capital	A2	13
Kuala Terengganu	B2	13
Kuantan	B2	13
Kuching	C3	13
Kuchino, island	A4	8
Kudymkar	D4	22
Kufstein	E3	99
Kugluktuk	E3	39
Kuito	C4	70
Kukës	B1	49
Kul, river	D4	22
Kul Kangri, mt.	B1	19
Kuldiga	A2	46
Kulmbach	B3	40

Name	Key	Page
Kulob	A2	23
Kulpawn, river	B1	64
Kum, river	B4	9
Kumamoto	A3	8
Kumanovo	B1	48
Kumasi	B3	64
Kume, island	Inset II	8
Kumo	F2	65
Kunda	D1	46
Kunene, river	A1	70
Kunlun, mts.	B2	10
Kunming	D3	10
Kunsan	B5	9
Kuntaur	D2	62
Kuopio	C2	53
Kupa, river	B3	48
Kupang	D3	13
Kür, river	A2, C2	45
Kür-Aras, lowland	B2	45
Kura, river	E2	27
Kurashiki	B3	8
Kuraymah	C1	59
Kürdzhali	D4	50
Kure	B3	8
Kuressaare	B2	46
Kurgan	D5	44
Kuril, islands	E9	44
Kurinwás, river	B2	87
Kurla	Inset I	20
Kurnool	C5	20
Kuršėnai	B1	46
Kursk	D3	44
Kuruman	B2	71
Kurume	A3	8
Kurunegala	B4	19
Kushiro	Inset I	8
Kushtia	C5	21
Kusti	C2	59
Kut, al-	C2	24
Kütahya	B2	27
Kutaisi	B3	45
Kutch, gulf	A4	20
Kutno	D2	41
Kuujjuaq	C2	101
Kuujjuarapik	A2	101
Kuwait		**24**
Kuwait, bay	B2	24
Kuwait, capital	B2	24
Kwa, river	B2	67
Kwahu, plateau	B3	64
Kwajalein, island	B2	16
Kwangju	B5	9
Kwango, river	B2	67
Kwanza, river	B2	67
Kwekwe	B2	69
Kyaukpyu	B2	12
Kyle	B10	104
Kyle of Lochalsh	B1	30
Kyoga, lake	C3	61
Kyŏngju	C5	9
Kyoto	B3	8
Kyrenia	B1	27
Kyrgyzstan		**23**
Kyrenia, range	B1	27
Kyushu, island	A3	8
Kyustendil	A3	50
Kyzyl	D6	44
Kyzyl-Kyya	C2	23
Kyzyl-Suu, river	C3	23
Kyzylkum, desert	B2	23

L

Name	Key	Page
La Asunción	D1	79
La Baie	F3	103
La Broquerie	C4	96
La Ceiba	B2	86
La Chaux-de-Fonds	A1	35
La Coma, river	B1	36
La Conception	B5	103
La Condamine	B1	35
La Coruña	B1	37
La Crete	B2	94
La Croix Maingot	A2	91
La Crosse, Wis.	D1	126
La Cruz	A1	86
La Digue, island	C1	70
La Doré	D3	103
La Esperanza	A2	86
La Goulette	C1	57
La Grande, river	B3	101
La Guadeloupe	F6	103
La Guaira Maiquetía	C1	79
La Have	C3	100
La Laguna	Inset I	37
La Libertad	A4	79
La Libertad	C3	85
La Loche	A4	104
La Louvière	C2	33
La Malbaie	F4	103
La Martre	K2	103
La Martre, lake	E4	99
La Montaña, region	C2	77
La Oroya	B3	77
La Palma	B2	86
La Palma, island	Inset I	37
La Paz	B2	86
La Paz, capital	A3	77
La Paz, state capital	B3	84
La Pérouse	B1	96
La Pérouse, strait	Inset I	8
La Plaine	B3	90
La Plata	D4	74
La Plata, river	D4	74
La Plonge, lake	C5	104
La Pocatière	F4	103
La Prairie	J6	103
La Rioja	B2	74
La Rioja	E1	37
La Rochelle	B3	34
La Roda	E3	37
La Romana	D2	89
La Ronge	E5	104
La Ronge, lake	E6	104
La Rosita	B2	87
La Salle	C4	96
La Salle	J6	103
La Scie	D4	98

Name	Key	Page
La Serena	B3	76
La Spezia	B1	38
La Tortuga, island	C1	79
La Tuque	D4	103
La Unión	B7	76
La Unión	C2	86
La Vega	B1	89
La Virtud	A2	86
La-Roche-sur-Yon	B3	34
Labasa	B2	17
Labé	B2	62
Labe (Elbe), river	B2	42
Labelle	C3	100
Laberge, lake	B5	105
Labi	A3	13
Laborec, river	C2	42
Laborie	B3	91
Labrador City	D3	98
Labrieville	G2	103
Labu	C2	13
Labuan, island	D2	13
Laç	A2	49
Lac du Bonnet	C4	96
Lac La Biche	E4	94
Lac La Hache	M5	95
Lac Mégantic	F6	103
Lac-aux-Sables	D5	103
Lac-Bouchette	D3	103
Lac-des-Aigles	H4	103
Lac-des-Îles	A5	103
Lac-Édouard	D4	103
Lac-Etchemin	F5	103
Lac-Nominingue	A5	103
Lac-Saguay	A5	103
Laccadive, islands	B6	20
Lachenaie	J5	103
Lachine	H6	103
Lachute	B6	103
Lacombe	D5	94
Ladhiqiyah, al- (Latakia)	A2	27
Ladoga, lake	C3	44
Ladysmith	C2	71
Ladywood	C4	96
Lae	A2	15
Lae, island	B2	16
Laem, mt.	B3	12
Læsø, island	C1	32
Lafayette, La.	D2	126
Lafia	E3	65
Lafleche	D11	104
Lafond	E4	94
Laghouat	B1	57
Lagodekhi	D4	45
Lagos	B2	37
Lagos	A4	36
Laguna de Bay, lake	B3	12
Lahave, river	C3	100
Lahij	A2	25
Lahn, river	B3	40
Lahore	E3	21
Lahti	C2	53
Laï	B5	59
Lairg	B1	30
Lajas	A2	90
Lajes	C4	81
Lakatoro	B3	18
Lake Alma	F11	104
Lake Charlotte	E3	100
Lake Edward	B2	67
Lake Harbour	O4	99
Lake Lenore	F8	104
Lake St. Peter	G2	102
Lake, district	B2	30
Lakeba, island	C3	17
Lakeba, passage	C3	17
Lakefield	G3	102
Lakelse Lake	H4	95
Lakhpat	A4	20
Laki, volcano	B2	52
Lakselv	F1	52
Lalitpur	C2	19
Lamaline	D5	98
Lamap	B3	18
Lambaréné	A2	66
Lambton	E6	103
Lamèque	E1	97
Lamèque, island	E1	97
Lami	B3	17
Lamía	B2	51
Lammermuir, hills	C2	30
Lamon, bay	C2	12
Lampa	Inset	76
Lampang	B2	12
Lampeter	B3	30
Lampman	H11	104
Lamu	F5	61
Lan, island	B2	9
Lanai island, Hawaii	Inset II	126
Lanark	J2	102
Lancaster	C2	30
Lancaster	L2	102
L'Ancienne-Lorette	K5	103
Land's End, promontory	B4	30
Lander, Wyo.	C1	126
Landes, region	B5	34
Landis	B8	104
Landshut	C4	40
Lang Son	B2	11
Langeburg, mts.	B3	71
Langeland, island	C3	32
Langenburg	J10	104
Langham	D8	104
Langkawi, island	A1	13
Langley	L6	95
Langruth	B4	96
Langstaff	K5	102
Langton	E5	102
Languedoc-Roussillon	C5	34
Lanigan	E9	104
Lanín, volcano	A4	74
Länkäran	B4	45
L'Annonciation	B5	103
Lansdowne House	C2	101
Lansing, capital, Mich.	E1	126
L'Anse-à-Valleau	M2	103
L'Anse-au-Loup	C3	98
L'Anse-aux-Gascons	M3	103
L'Anse-St-Jean	F3	103

Name	Key	Page
Lantau, island	Inset	10
Lanús	D3	74
Lanzarote, island	Inset I	37
Lanzhou	D2	10
Lao Cai	A1	11
Laoag	B2	12
Laoang	C2	12
Laon	C2	34
Laos		**11**
Lapithos	B1	27
Lapland, region	B1	53
Lappeenranta	C2	53
Laptev, sea	B8	44
L'Aquila	C2	38
Larache	C1	57
Laramie, Wyo.	C1	126
Lares	B2	90
Larestan, region	C4	22
Large, island	C1	91
Lárisa	B2	51
Lark Harbour	B4	98
Larkana	C4	21
Larkhall	C4	96
Larnaca	B2	27
Larne	B2	30
Larochette	B2	33
Larrys River	F2	100
Larsen Ice Shelf, glacier	C12	107
Las Cruces, N. Mex.	C2	126
Las Minas, mt.	A2	86
Las Palmas	Inset I	37
Las Piedras	D2	90
Las Piedras	B3	75
Las Tablas	B3	87
Las Tunas	E3	88
Las Vegas, N. Mex.	C2	126
Las Vegas, Nev.	B2	126
L'Ascension	B5	103
Lashburn	A7	104
Lashio	C2	12
Lashkar Gah	A2	22
Last Mountain, lake	E9	104
Latacunga	B3	79
Late, island	C2	17
Latina	C2	38
Latvia		**46**
Lau, island group	C2	17
Laucala, island	C1	17
Laudat	B3	90
Lauder	A4	96
Launceston	B4	30
Launceston, Tas.	D4	14
Laurie River	A1	96
Laurier	B4	96
Lausanne	A2	35
Lautoka	A2	17
Laval	C2	34
Laval	C6, J5	103
Lavenham	B4	96
Lavoy	E4	94
Lavumisa	B3	71
Lawa, river	A2, B2	80
Lawn	D5	98
Lawrence Station	B3	97
Lawton, Okla.	D2	126
Layland	B4	96
Layou, river	B3	90
Lázaro Cárdenas	D4	84
Le Bic	H3	103
Le Creusot	D3	34
Le Havre	C2	34
Le Mans	C2	34
Le Puy	C4	34
Leader	A10	104
Leading Tickles	D4	98
Leaf Rapids	D1	96
Leamington	C5	102
l'Eau Claire, lake	B2	101
Lebanon		**26**
Lebanon, mts.	B1	26
Lebombo, mts.	C2, D1	71
Lebu	B6	76
Lecce	D2	38
Lech	B3	39
Lech, river	B4	40
Leduc	D4	94
Lee, river	B3	31
Leeds	C3	30
Leeuwarden	C1	32
Leeuwin, cape	A3	14
Leeward Group	B3	58
Lefka	A1	27
Lefkoniko	B1	27
Leganés	Inset II	37
Legazpi	B3	12
Legnica	C3	41
Leicester	C3	30
Leichhardt, river	D1	14
Leiden	B2	33
Leie, river	B2	33
Leikanger	B3	52
Leipzig	C3	40
Leiria	A3	36
Leitrim	H6	102
Leixões	A2	36
Lékéti, mts.	C5	66
Lékoumou	C2	66
Lékoua	B2	66
Lelystad	C2	33
Lempa, river	A1, B2	86
Lena, river	C8	44
Leneinsk	C2	23
Lenghu	C2	10
Lengoué, river	C2	66
Lenore	A4	96
Lens	C1	34
Lensk	C7	44
Léo	C3	64
Leoben	D3	39
Léogâne	C2	89
León	B3	84
León	C2	86
León	D1	37
Leone	B2	18
Leova	B2	50
Leoville	C7	104
Lepontine Alps, mts.	C2	35
Lepreau	C3	97

Name	Key	Page
Lepsi	D2	23
Leribe	B1	71
Lérida	G2	37
Lerwick	Inset I	30
Les Cayes	B2	89
Les Éboulements	F4	103
Les Escaldes	B2	36
Les Escoumins	G3	103
Les Islets-Caribou	J2	103
Les Méchins	K3	103
Les Tantes, island	B1	91
Les Ulis	Inset II	34
Leskovac	B3	49
Lesosibirsk	D6	44
Lesotho		**71**
Lesser Caucasus, mts.	A2, B4	45
Lesser Hinggan, range	F1	10
Lesser Slave, lake	C3	94
Lesser Sunda, islands	C2	13
Lestrock	G9	104
Lésvos, island	C2	51
Leszno	C3	41
Lethbridge	D6	94
Lethbridge	E5	98
Lethem	B4	80
Leticia	C6	78
Letlhakeng	B3	69
Letterkenny	C1	31
Leuven	C2	33
Levack	D1	102
Levallois-Perret	Inset II	34
Leveque, cape	B1	14
Leverkusen	A3	40
Levice	B2	42
Lévis	E5, L6	103
Levittown	C2	90
Lewes	D4	30
Lewis, island	A1	30
Lewisporte	D4	98
Lewiston, Idaho	B1	126
Lewiston, Maine	F1	126
Lexington, Ky.	E2	126
Leyte, island	C4	12
Lhasa	C3	10
Lhobrak, river	C2	19
Lhuntshi	C2	19
Lianyungang	E2	10
Liao, river	F1	10
Liaoning	F1	10
Liaoyang	F1	10
Liaoyuan	F1	10
Liard River	J1	95
Liard, river	K1	95
Liberec	B2	42
Liberia		**63**
Liberia	A2	86
Libreville, capital	A1	66
Libourne	C4	34
Libya		**56**
Libyan, desert	A2, D2	56
Lichfield	C3	30
Lichinga	B2	68
Lida	B3	47
Liechtenstein		**33**
Liège	D2	33
Lieksa	D2	53
Lienz	C4	39
Liepāja	A2	46
Lièvre, river	A5	103
Lifford	C1	31
Lifou, island	D2	18
Lifuka, island	C3	17
Liguria	B1	38
Ligurian, sea	B2	38
Lihir, group	B2	15
Likasi	C3	67
Likiep, island	B1	16
Lille	C1	34
Lille, strait	B3	32
Lillehammer	B3	52
Lillooet	M6	95
Lilongwe, capital	B2	68
Lima, capital	B3	77
Lima, river	A2	36
Limassol	B2	27
Limbazi	C2	46
Limbe	A3	65
Limbourg	D2	33
Limburg	C3	33
Limerick	B2	31
Limfjorden, channel	B2	32
Límnos, island	C2	51
Limoges	C4	34
Limón	C3	86
Limours	Inset II	34
Limousin	C4	34
Limpopo, river	C1	71
Linares	B5	76
Linares	E3	84
Linares	E3	37
Lincoln, capital, Nebr.	D1	126
Lindau	B5	40
Lindbergh	E4	94
Linden	B3	80
Linden	D2	100
Lindi	C2	68
Lindsay	G3	102
Line, islands	D1	17
Lingayen, gulf	B2	12
Lingga, island	B2	13
Lingshi	B2	19
Linguère	B2	62
Linköping	C3	53
Linnhe, lake	B2	30
Linwood	F2	100
Linz	D2	39
Lion, gulf	D5	34
Lions Head	D3	102
Lipa	B3	12
Lipari, islands	C3	38
Lipetsk	B3	44
Lippstadt	B3	40
Lira	C2	61

Name	Key	Page
Lisala	B1	
L'Isalo, mts.	B3	
Lisbon, capital	A3	
Lisichansk	D2	
Lismore, N.S.W.	E4	
Listowel	E4	
Litani, river	B1	
Litani, river	A2, B3	
Lithuania		
Little Alföld, plain	A2	
Little Andaman, island	F6	
Little Bay	B5	
Little Bras d'Or	G1	
Little Current	D2	
Little Fort	M5	
Little Grand Rapids	D3	
Little Inagua, island	C4	
Little Rock, capital, Ark.	D2	
Little Salmon, lake	C4	
Little Scarcies, river	A1	
Little Seldom	D4	
Little Smoky, river	A4	
Little St. Bernard, pass	B1	
Little Zab, river	B1	
Liuzhou	D3	
Liverpool	C3	
Liverpool	C3	
Liverpool, bay	B3	
Livingstone	B2	
Livno	B2	
Livorno	B2	
Ljubljana, capital	B2	
Ljusnanälven, river	A3	
Llallagua	A3	
Llandrindod Wells	B3	
Llanos, plain	C2	
Llanos, prairie	C2	
Llanquihue, lake	B7	
Lleyn, peninsula	B3	
Llorts	B1	
Lloyd, lake	E4	
Lloydminster	A7	
Lloyds, river	C5	
Llullaillaco, volcano	A3	
Lo Wu	Inset	
Loa, river	A1	
Loa, river	A3	
Lobamba, capital	B3	
Lobatse	B3	
Lobaye, river	A2	
Lobito	B4	
Locarno	C2	
Lockeport	B4	
Lockport	C4	
Lod (lydda)	B2	
Lodja	B2	
Łódź	D3	
Loei	B2	
Loess, plateau	D2	
Lofoten, islands	B2	
Logan, mt.	A5	
Logan, river	Inset III	
Logan, Utah	B1	
Logone, river	B2	
Logroño	E1	
Loi-kaw	C2	
Loire, river	C2	
Loíza	D2	
Loja	B4	
Loja	D4	
Lokka, reservoir	C1	
Lokoja	D4	
Lokossa	A4	
Lol, river	B3	
Lolland, island	C4	
Lom	B2	
Lomami, river	C2	
Lomawai	A3	
Lombardy	B1	
Lombok, island	J3	
Lombok, island	C2	
Lomé, capital	B3	
Lomond, lake	B2	
London	D5	
London, capital	C3, Inset III	
Londonderry	C2	
Londrina	C4	
Lone Butte	M5	
Long Beach, Calif.	B2	
Long Island, N.Y.	F1	
Long Lake	D4	
Long Range, mts.	B5, C4	
Long Xuyen	A4	
Long, island	C3	
Longford	C2	
Longlac	J5	
Longreach, Qld.	D2	
Longview, Tex.	D2	
Loon Lake	A6	
Loop Head, cape	A2	
Lop Buri	B3	
Lop, lake	C3	
Lorca	F4	
Loreburn	D9	
Lorengau	A2	
Loreto	B2	
Loretteville	K5	
L'Original	L2	
Lorne, estuary	D2	
Lorraine	H5	
Los Andes	B4	
Los Angeles	B6	
Los Angeles, Calif.	B2	
Los Chiles	B1	
Los Mochis	C2	
Los Reyes	Inset	
Los Teques	C1	
Lot, river	C4	

	Key	Page
uang Namtha	A1	11
ubomo	B6	66
uga	A2	62
ugh Erne, lake	A2	62
ughborough, lake	J3	102
ugheed, island	G1	99
uisburg	H2	100
uisdale	F2	100
uiseville	D5	103
uisiade, archipelago	B3	15
uisiana	D2	126
uisville, Ky.	E2	126
urdes	B5	34
uri	C2	19
uvres	Inset II	34
verall Village	B3	91
vettville	B4	94
ve Farm	C4	99
ver Arrow, lake	N6	95
ver Debert	D2	100
ver Five Islands	C2	100
ver Hutt	B3	15
ver Montague	C2	100
ver Post	H1	95
ver Saxony	B2	40
ver Tunguska, river	C6	44
ver Woods Harbour	B4	100
westoft	D3	30
vada	C2	60
valty, islands	C2	18
alaba, river	C2	67
anda, capital	B2	70
ang Prabang	B2	11
ang Prabang, range	A3	11
ang, mt.	B4	12
angwa	C3	67
angwa, river	C2	67
apula, river	B2, C3	67
au	E3	70
ba	A1	66
baba	B5	70
bbock, Tex.	C2	126
beck	B2	40
bicon, lake	C3	94
blin	F3	41
bumbashi	C3	67
capa	D2	70
cca	B2	38
cea	A2	88
cena	B3	12
cena	D4	37
cenec	B2	42
cern, lake	C2	35
cerne	C1	35
cie, river	A3	80
ckenwalde	C2	40
cknow	D3	20
cknow	D4	102
cky Lake	C9	104
da Kamchiya, river	E3	50
deritz	B4	70
dhiana	C2	20
dogorie, region	E2	50
dwigsburg	B4	40
dwigshafen am Rhein	B4	40
ena	D3	70
gano	C3	35
gano, lake	C3	35
ganville	B2	18
genda, river	C2	68
goj	C1	37
goj	A3	43
hansk	D2	47
kuga, river	C2	67
leá	D1	53
leälven, river	D1	53
mphat	F2	11
msden	E4	98
msden	F10	104
mut	A2	13
nd	B3	53
nd	K6	95
ndar	B4	96
ndazi	C2	67
ndi, river	B2	67
neburg	B2	40
nen	A3	40
nenburg	C3	100
nga, river	B2	67
ngwebungu, river	A2	67
nsar	A1	63
oyang	E2	10
peni	B3	43
perón	B1	89
quillo	D2	90
remo	C2	70
rio, river	C2	68
saka, capital	B3	67
sambo	B2	67
seland	A8	104
shnjë	A3	49
sutfu, river	B2	71
tsk	C3	30
utsk	D8	44
tzow-Holm, bay	C16	107
uq	A2	67
vua	B1, C2	67
wero, river	C2	68
xembourg		33
xembourg, capital	B2	33
xor	B2	56
zarches	Inset II	34
zhou	D3	10
zon, island	B3	12
zon, strait	B2	12
ddal	B1	96
bes, bay	C4	30
on Lake	C1	96
tton	M6	95

M

	Key	Page
a, river	A2	11
a	A2	26

	Key	Page
Maas, river	C3, D3	32
Maastricht	C4	32
Mabaruma	B1	80
Maberly	J3	102
Mabou	F1	100
Mac Tier	F2	102
MacAlpine, lake	H3	99
Macao, S.A.R.	E3	10
Macapá	C1	81
Macas	B4	79
Maccan	C2	100
Macdonnell, ranges	C2	14
Maceió	E2	81
Macenta	D3	62
Macerata	C2	38
Macfarlane, river	C2	104
Macgregor	B4	96
Machakos	D4	61
Machala	B4	79
Machida	C3	8
Machupicchu, ruins	C3	77
MacKay, lake	F4	99
Mackay, Qld.	D2	14
Mackenzie	L3	95
Mackenzie King, island	F1	99
Mackenzie, bay	B1	105
Mackenzie, mts.	C4	99
Mackenzie, river	B3, D4	99
Mackey	H1	102
Macklin	A8	104
Maclean, strait	G1	99
Macmillan, river	C4	105
Mâcon	D3	34
Macon, Ga.	E2	126
Madagascar		69
Madan	C4	50
Madang	A2	15
Madawaska	G2	102
Madden	C5	94
Madeira, island		55
Madeira, river	B2	81
Madhumati, river	C5	21
Madhupur Tract, region	D4	21
Madinat ath-Thawrah	B2	27
Madison, capital, Wis.	E1	126
Madiun	C2	13
Madoc	H3	102
Madre de Dios, island	A9	76
Madre de Dios, river	A2, C3	77
Madrid, capital	E2, Inset II	36
Madriu, river	B3	36
Madura, island	C2	13
Madurai	C7	20
Maebashi	C2	8
Maestra, mts.	D3	88
Maévo, island	C2	18
Mafeking	A3	96
Mafeteng	A2	71
Mafia, island	C2	68
Mafikeng	C2	71
Mafra	A3	36
Mafraq, al-	B1	26
Magadalena de Kino	B1	84
Magadan	D9	44
Magburaka	B1	63
Magdagachi	D8	44
Magdalena	B2	77
Magdalena Contreras	Inset	84
Magdalena, island	B7	76
Magdalena, river	B3	78
Magdeburg	B2	40
Magelang	C2	13
Magellan, strait	B9	76
Maggiore, lake	B1	38
Magnetawan	F2	102
Magnitogorsk	D4	44
Magog	D6	103
Mahabharat, range	B2	19
Mahajamba, river	B2	69
Mahajanga	B2	69
Mahalapye	B2	69
Mahallah al-Kubra, al-	B1	56
Mahanadi, river	D4	20
Mahaska	C2	67
Mahbas, al-	C1	58
Mahdia	B3	80
Mahdia	C2	57
Mahé, island	C1, Inset	70
Mahébourg	C3	69
Mahilyow	E3	47
Mahim, bay	Inset I	20
Mahón	J3	37
Mai-Ndombe, lake	B3	67
Maidstone	D3	30
Maidstone	A7	104
Maiduguri	G2	65
Main Brook	C4	98
Main, river	B4	40
Main-à-Dieu	H1	100
Main-Danube, canal	B4	40
Maine	G1	126
Mainland, island	Inset I	30
Maintirano	A2	69
Mainz	B4	40
Maio, island	B4	58
Maipo, river	B4, Inset	76
Maipú	Inset	76
Maisí, cape	F3	88
Maisons-Laffitte	Inset II	34
Maitland Bridge	B3	100
Maíz, islands	C2	87
Maizuru	B3	8
Majardah, river	B1	57
Majé	Inset I	87
Majorca, island	H3	37
Majuro	C2	16
Majuro, island	C2	16
Makamba	B3	61
Makassar, strait	C2	13
Makeni	B1	63
Makeyevka	D2	47
Makhachkala	E4	44
Makhaleng, river	A2	71
Makin, island	A1	17
Makkovik	B1	98
Makokou	B1	66
Makona, river	A1	63

	Key	Page
Makoua	C4	66
Makran Coast, range	B5	21
Makung	A2	9
Makurdi	E4	65
Malabar, coast	B6	20
Malabo, capital	A1	66
Malacca, strait	A1, A2	13
Malad	Inset I	20
Maladzyechna	C2	47
Malaga	D4	37
Malagarasi, river	B1	68
Malaita, island	B1	16
Malakal	C3	59
Malakula, island	B3	18
Malang	C2	13
Malanje	C3	70
Malanville	B2	64
Mälaren, lake	C3	53
Malatya	D2	27
Malawi		68
Malay, peninsula	A1	13
Malaysia		13
Malbaie, river	F4	103
Malbun	B2	33
Malcolm, atoll	A1	19
Malden, island	D2	17
Maldives		19
Male Karpaty, mts.	A2	42
Male, atoll	A2	19
Male, capital	A2	19
Maleb	E6	94
Malegaon	B4	20
Mali		58
Mali Rajinac, mt.	B3	48
Malindi	F5	61
Mallaig	B1	30
Mallow	B2	31
Malmberget	D1	53
Malmédy	E2	33
Malmö	B3	53
Maloelap, island	C2	16
Malombe, lake	C2	68
Maloti, mts.	B2	71
Malta		36
Maltahöhe	B3	70
Malton	J5	102
Mamâri	C2	62
Mamawi, lake	E2	94
Mambéré, river	A2	66
Mamburao	B3	12
Mamiña	C2	76
Mamoré, river	A2	77
Mamou	B2	62
Mamry, lake	E1	41
Mamtalah, al-	B2	25
Mamuno	A2	69
Man	C3	63
Mana	B1	80
Mana, river	B1	80
Manado	D1	13
Managua, capital	A2	87
Managua, lake	A2	87
Manakara	B3	69
Manama, capital	B1	25
Manatí	B2	90
Manaus	C2	81
Manawan, lake	G5	104
Manbij	A1	27
Manchester	C3	30
Manchester, N.H.	F1	126
Manchurian, plain	F1	10
Mand, river	C4	22
Mandalay	C2	12
Mandalgovĭ	C2	11
Mandara, mts.	B1	65
Mandaue	B4	12
Mandeville	B2	88
Mándra	Inset	51
Mandurah, W.A.	A3	14
Manfredonia	C2	38
Manga, region	C2	59
Mangalore	B6	20
Mango	B1	64
Mangoky, river	A3	69
Manicouagan, reservoir	C3	101
Manicouagan Deux, reservoir	H2	103
Manigotagan	C3	96
Manila, bay	B3	12
Manila, capital	B3	12
Manisa	A2	27
Manito, lake	B3	104
Manitoba, lake	B3, B4, D2	96
Manitou	B4	96
Manitoulin, island	C2	102
Manitouwadge	C3	101
Manitowaning	D2	102
Maniwaki	A5	103
Manizales	B3	78
Manja	A2	69
Mankato, Minn.	D1	126
Mankayane	B2	71
Mankota	C11	104
Mankulam	B2	19
Mannar	A3	19
Mannar, gulf	C7	20
Mannar, island	A2	19
Mannheim	B4	40
Manning	B3	94
Mannville	E4	94
Mano, river	A2, B2	63
Manokwari	E2	13
Manono	C2	67
Manono, river	B2	18
Manor Park	H5	102
Manori, point	Inset I	20
Manouane	A4	103
Manp'o	B2	9
Mansa	B2	67
Mansa Konko	C2	62
Mansel, island	M4	99
Manson Creek	K3	95
Mansurah, al-	B1	56
Manta	A3	79
Manta, bay	A3	79
Mantaro, river	B3	77
Mantiqueira, range	D4	81
Mantova	B1	38
Mantua (Mantova)	B1	38
Manukau	B2	15

	Key	Page
Manus, island	A2	15
Manyara, lake	C1	68
Manzanillo	D3	88
Manzanillo	D4	84
Manzini	B2	71
Mao	A1	89
Mao	A4	59
Maple Creek	A11	104
Maputo, capital	B5	68
Maquela do Zombo	C2	70
Mar Chiquita, lake	C3	74
Mar del Plata	D4	74
Mar, range	D4	81
Maraba	C4	81
Maracaibo	B1	79
Maracaibo, lake	B2	79
Maracay	C1	79
Maradi	B3	59
Marajó, island	D2	81
Marakei, island	A1	17
Maramasike, island	B1	16
Maranhão	D2	81
Marano	D3	27
Marañón, river	B1, B2	77
Marathon	C3	101
Marbella	D4	37
Marburg	B3	40
Marcelin	D8	104
Marche	C2	38
Marchena, island	Inset	79
Mardan	D2	21
Mardin	E3	27
Maré, island	D2	18
Maremma, region	B2	38
Margaree Forks	F1	100
Margaret, lake	C2	94
Margarita, island	D1	79
Margate	D3	30
Margherita, peak	A3	61
Maria	L3	103
Maria, islands	B3	91
Mariana	D3	81
Marianao	B1	88
Marías, islands	C3	84
Maribor	C2	48
Marie Byrd Land, region	B8	107
Marie-Reine	B3	94
Mariehamn (Maarianhamina)	A2	53
Mariental	C3	70
Marigot	B2	90
Marijampolė	B2	46
Marinduque, island	B3	12
Marino	C2	18
Marion Bridge	G2	100
Maripasoula	A2	80
Mariscal Estigarribia	B3	75
Maritime Alps, range	D4	34
Maritsa, river	D3	50
Mariupol	D3	47
Marj El, republic	A2	26
Marj Uyun	A2	26
Marj, al-	D1	56
Marka	A3	60
Markham	F4, K5	102
Markham, river	A2	15
Markstay	E1	102
Marl	A3	40
Marmara, sea	B2	27
Marmora	H3	102
Marne, river	C2, Inset II	34
Marneuli	C4	45
Maromokotro, mt.	B1	69
Marondera	B2	69
Maroni, river	A1	80
Maros, river	C2	43
Maroua	B1	65
Marovoay	B2	69
Marowijne, river	B2	80
Marquette, Mich.	E1	126
Marquis	B2	91
Marrakech	B2	71
Marsa al-Burayqah	C1	56
Marsabit	E2	61
Marsala	C3	38
Marsaxlokk, bay	C3	36
Marsden	A8	104
Marseille	D5	34
Marsh Harbour	B2	89
Marshall Is.		16
Marsoui	L2	103
Martaban, gulf	C3	12
Marten River	F1	102
Martensville	D8	104
Martigny	B2	42
Martinique, island		82
Martins River	C3	100
Martorell	D2	90
Martuni	C2	45
Mary	C3	22
Mary's Harbour	D3	98
Maryborough, Qld.	E2	14
Maryfield	A4	96
Maryfield	J11	104
Maryland	F2	126
Marystown	D5	98
Masada, ruins	B2	26
Masai, steppe	C1	68
Masaka	B4	61
Masan	C5	9
Masaya	A3	87
Masbate	B3	12
Masbate, island	B3	12
Mascouche	C6	103
Masfut	C2	25
Mashhad	D2	22
Masindi	B3	61
Masirah, gulf	C2	25
Masirah, island	C2	25
Mask, lake	B2	31
Maskall	B2	85
Massachusetts	F1	126
Massacre	B3	90
Massawa	B2	60

	Key	Page
Massenya	B5	59
Masset	F4	95
Massey	C1	102
Massif Central, plateau	C4	34
Massif des Bongos, range	B2	66
Massy	Inset II	34
Masuda	A3	8
Masvingo	B2	69
Mat, river	B2	49
Matadi	A2	67
Matagalpa	B2	87
Matagami	A4	101
Matale	B4	19
Matam	C2	62
Matamoros	E2	84
Matane	J3	103
Matanzas	B1	88
Matapédia	C1	97
Matapédia	K4	103
Matara	B6	19
Mataram	C2	13
Mataró	H2	37
Matautu	C2	18
Matawa Place	D3	96
Matehuala	D3	84
Matelot	A2	91
Matera	D2	38
Mathura	C3	20
Matlock	C3	30
Mato Grosso	C3	81
Mato Grosso do Sul	C4	81
Mato Grosso, plateau	C3	81
Mátra, mts.	B2	43
Matrah	C1	25
Matruh	A1	56
Matsoku, river	B2	71
Matsudo	C3	8
Matsue	B3	8
Matsumae	D1, Inset I	8
Matsumoto	C2	8
Matsuyama	B3	8
Mattawa	G1	102
Mattawin, river	C5	103
Matterhorn, mt.	B3	35
Matthew Town	C4	89
Matthews Ridge	A2	80
Mauá	Inset II	81
Maui, island, Hawaii	Inset II	126
Maule, river	B5	76
Maumturk, mts.	B2	31
Maun	A1	69
Mauna Loa, mt., Hawaii	Inset II	126
Maunabo	D2	90
Mauren	B2	33
Maurepas	Inset II	34
Mauritania		58
Mauritius		69
Mavinga	D5	70
May Pen	B3	88
Maya, mts.	A3	85
Mayaguana, island	C4	89
Mayaguana, passage	C4	89
Mayagüez	A2	90
Maydi	A1	25
Mayfair	C7	104
Maymont	C8	104
Maymyo	C2	12
Maynooth	C2	31
Maynooth	H2	102
Mayo	B4	105
Mayo, lake	C4	105
Mayo, volcano	A1	84
Mayon, volcano	B3	12
Mayotte, island	C2	67
Mayreau, island	A4	91
Mayumba	A2	66
Mayumbé, massif	B5	66
Mazabuka	B2	67
Mazandaran, region	C2	22
Mazar-e Sharif	B1	22
Mazaruni, river	A2	80
Mazatenango	B5	85
Mazatlán	C3	84
Mažeikiai	B1	46
Mazoe, river	B1	69
Mazyr	D3	47
Mbabane, capital	B2	71
Mbahiakro	D3	63
Mbaké	A2	62
Mbala	C1	67
Mbale	D3	61
Mbalmayo	B3	65
Mbandaka	B2	67
M'banza Congo	B2	70
Mbanza-Ngungu	A2	67
Mbarara	B4	61
Mbemkuru, river	C3	68
M'Beni	A1	67
Mbéré, river	B2	65
Mbeya	B2	68
Mbini	B3	66
Mbini, river	B3	66
Mboro, river	D4	66
Mbour	A2	62
Mbuji-Mayi	C2	67
Mbuluzane, river	B2	71
Mbuluzi, river	B2	71
McAdam	B3	97
McAllen, Tex.	D3	126
McBride	M4	95
McCallum	C5	98
McCreary	B4	96
McDame	H1	95
McGee	B9	104
Mchinji	A2	68
McKerrow	D1	102
McKinley mt., Alaska	Inset I	126
McLeese Lake	L5	95
McLeod Lake	L4	95
McLeod Valley	B2	94
M'Clintock, channel	H2	99
M'Clure, strait	D2	99
McLure	M5	95
McMurdo, sound	B5	107
McRae	E4	94
Meacham	E8	104
Meadow Lake	B6	104
Meadow Portage	B3	96
Meaford	E3	102

	Key	Page
Mealy, mts.	A3	98
Meander River	B1	94
Mecca	A2	24
Mechelen	C1	33
Mecklenburg, bay	B1	40
Mecklenburg- Western Pomerania	C2	40
Mecsek, mts.	B2	43
Medan	A1	13
Medellín	B3	78
Medford, Oreg.	A1	126
Medgidia	E3	43
Media,s	C2	43
Medicine Hat	D4	96
Medina	A1	24
Medina del Campo	D2	37
Medit	B2	13
Mediterranean, sea		29
Medley	E4	94
Medora	A4	96
Meductic	B3	97
Meelpaeg, lake	C5	98
Meerut	C2	20
Meghna, river	D5	21
Meghri	D4	45
Meighen, island	J1	99
Meiktila	B2	12
Meissen	C3	40
Mejicanos	A2	86
Mékambo	B1	66
Mekele	C1	60
Mékinac, lake	D4	103
Meknès	C1	57
Mekong, delta	D5	11
Mekong, river	A1, A4, C4, D3	11
Mékrou, river	B2	64
Melaka	B2	13
Melbourne, Fla.	E3	126
Melbourne, Vic., capital	D3	14
Meldrum Bay	B2	102
Meleb	C3	96
Melekeok	C3	17
Mélèzes, river	B2	101
Melfi	B5	59
Melfort	F8	104
Melipilla	Inset	76
Melita	A4	96
Melitopol	D3	47
Mellieha	B2	36
Mellieha, bay	B2	36
Melo	C2	75
Melrose	E2	100
Melun	Inset II	34
Melville	H10	104
Melville, island	C1	14
Melville, island	F1	99
Melville, lake	B2	98
Melville, peninsula	M3	99
Memmingen	B5	40
Memphis, Tenn.	D2	126
Memphrémagog, lake	D6	103
Menai, strait	B3	30
Ménaka	C4	34
Mende	C4	34
Mendoza	B3	16
Meneng	B3	16
Menihek	D3	98
Mennecy	Inset II	34
Menongue	C4	70
Mentawai, islands	A2	13
Menzel Bourguiba	B1	57
Meppel	D2	32
Mequinenza, lake	F2	37
Merano	B1	38
Merauke	F2	13
Mercedario, mt	B3	74
Mercedes	C2	75
Mergui	C3	12
Mergui, archipelago	C4	12
Mérida	B2	79
Mérida	D3	37
Mérida, mts.	B2	79
Mérida, state capital	G3	84
Meridian, Miss.	D2	126
Merigomish	E2	100
Merín, lagoon	C2	75
Merir, island	Inset	17
Merkys, river	C2	46
Meron, mt.	B1	26
Merredin, W.A.	A3	14
Merrick, mt.	B2	30
Merridale	A3	96
Merritt	M6	95
Mersch	B2	33
Mersey, river	C3	30
Mersin	B3	27
Merthyr Tydfil	B3	30
Meru	B3	61
Merume, mts.	A2	80
Mesaoria, plain	B1	27
Meseta, plateau	B2	37
Mesolóngion	B2	51
Mesopotamia, region	B2	24
Messina	D1	71
Messina	C3	38
Messina, strait	C3	38
Mesta, river	B4	50
Meta Incognita, peninsula	P4	99
Meta, river	C2	78
Métabetchouan	E3	103
Metcalfe	K2	102
Meteghan	A3	100
Métis-sur-Mer	J3	103
Metiskow	E5	94
Metz	B2	34
Meulan	Inset II	34
Meuse, river	D2	33
Mexiana, island	D1	81
Mexicali, state capital	A1	84
Mexico		84
Mexico City, national capital	E4, Inset	84
Mexico, gulf		82
Meymaneh	A1	22
Meyungs	B3	17
Mgwavuma, river	B3	71
Mhlume	B2	71
Miami	B4	96

	Key	Page
Miami, Fla.	E3	126
Mianwali	D3	21
Miaoli	B1	9
Mica Creek	N5	95
Michalovce	C2	42
Miches	C2	89
Michigan	E1	126
Michigan, lake	E1	126
Michoacán	D4	84
Mico, river	B2	87
Micoud	B3	91
Micronesia		15
Midale	G11	104
Middelburg	C3	71
Middelburg	A3	32
Middle Andaman, island	F6	20
Middle Arm	C4	98
Middle Atlas, ranges	C1	57
Middle Musquodoboit	D2	100
Middleboro	D4	96
Middlesbrough	C2	30
Middleton	B3	100
Midi-Pyrénées	C5	34
Midland	F3	102
Midland, Tex.	C2	126
Midlands, region	C3	30
Miercurea Ciuc	C2	43
Mieres	D1	37
Mikkeli	C2	53
Mikkwa, river	C2	94
Mikomeseng	C2	66
Mikura, island	C3	8
Miladummadulu, atoll	A1	19
Milagro	B4	79
Milan	B1	38
Milden	C9	104
Mildura, Vic.	D3	14
Miles City, Mont.	C1	126
Milestone	F10	104
Milford Haven	B3	30
Milford Sound	A3	15
Milh, lake	B2	24
Mili, island	C2	16
Milk, river	E6	94
Mill Bay	L7	95
Mill Village	C3	100
Miller Lake	D2	102
Millet	D4	94
Milliken	K5	102
Milltown	D5	98
Millville	B2	97
Milne, bay	B3	15
Milo	D6	94
Milo, river	D3	62
Mílos, island	C3	51
Milton	B2	100
Milton	F4	102
Milverton	E4	102
Milwaukee, Wis.	E1	126
Mimico	J6	102
Miminegash	A2	100
Mina Baranis	C3	56
Mina Salman	B1	25
Minami, island	Inset III	8
Minas	C3	75
Minas Gerais	D3	81
Minas, channel	C2	100
Minatitlán	F4	84
Minch, strait	B1	30
Mindanao, island	C5	12
Mindelo	B2	58
Mindemoya	C3	102
Minden	G3	102
Mindoro, island	B3	12
Mindoro, strait	B3	12
Miner's Bay	G3	102
Miner, river	B3	105
Mingãçevir	B2	45
Mingãçevir, reservoir	B2	45
Minho, river	A1	36
Minicoy, island	B7	20
Minija, river	A4	46
Miniota	A4	96
Minitonas	A3	96
Mink Creek	A3	96
Minna	D3	65
Minneapolis, Minn.	D1	126
Minnedosa	C1	96
Minnesota	D1	126
Minsk, capital	B4	47
Minto	B4	96
Minto	C2	97
Minto	B4	105
Minto, lake	B2	101
Minton	F11	104
Minya, al-	B2	56
Miquelon, island	M4	92
Mira	H1	100
Mirabel	B6	103
Mirador Nacional, mt.	C3	75
Miraflores	B4	78
Miragoâne	B2	89
Miramichi	D1	97
Miramichi, bay	E1	97
Miranda de Ebro	E1	37
Mirbat	B3	25
Mirebalais	C2	89
Miri	D2	13
Mirnyy	C7	44
Mirpur Khas	C5	21
Mirror	D5	94
Miscou, island	E1	97
Miscouche	B2	100
Misere	Inset	70
Misery, mt.	B3	90
Miskolc	C1	43
Misool, island	E2	13
Missinipe	F5	104
Mississauga	F4, J6	102
Mississippi	D2	126
Mississippi, lake	J2	102
Mississippi, river	D1	126
Missoula, Mont.	B1	126
Missouri	D2	126

	Key	Page
Missouri, river	D1	126
Mistassibi, river	D1	103
Mistassini	D3	103
Mistassini, lake	B3	101
Mistassini, river	D2	103
Mistatim	G8	104
Mistelbach	E2	39
Misurata	C1	56
Mitchell	D4	102
Mitchell, mt., N.C.	E2	126
Mitchell, river	D1	14
Mitilíni	C2	51
Mitla	D2	8
Mitsamiouli	A1	67
Mittelland, canal	B2	40
Mitú	C4	78
Mitumba, mts.	C2	67
Mitzic	A1	66
Miyake, island	C3	8
Miyako, island	Inset II	8
Miyakonojo	A4	8
Miyazaki	A4	8
Mizen Head, cape	B3	31
Mizo, hills	F4	20
Mjøsa, lake	C3	52
Mkondvo, river	B2	71
Mliba	B2	71
Mmabatho	C2	71
Mo	C2	52
Moa, island	D2	13
Moab, Utah	C2	126
Moala, island group	B3	17
Moanda	B2	66
Moba	C2	67
Mobaye	B3	66
Mobile, Ala.	E2	126
Moca	A2	90
Moçambique	D2	68
Moca, (Mukha, al-)	A2	25
Mocímboa da Praia	D1	68
Môco, mt.	C4	70
Mocoa	A4	78
Modena	B1	38
Moengo	B2	80
Moers	A3	40
Mogadishu, capital	B3	60
Mogami, river	D2	8
Mogi das Cruzes	Inset	81
Mogilev Podolskiy	B2	47
Mogocha	D7	44
Mogotón, mt.	A2	87
Moháks	B2	43
Mohales Hoek	A3	71
Mohammedia	C1	57
Moher, cliffs	B2	31
Mojave, desert, Calif.	B2	126
Mojos	A2	77
Mokhotlong	C2	71
Mokolo	B1	65
Mokpb	B5	9
Mold	B3	30
Moldavia, region	D2	43
Moldova		50
Moldoveanu, mt.	C3	43
Molepolole	B3	69
Molise	C2	38
Mollendo	C4	77
Molokai island, Hawaii	Inset II	126
Molopo, river	B2	71
Moloundou	C3	65
Molson, lake	C2	96
Molucca, sea	D2	13
Moluccas, islands	D2	13
Mombasa	Inset I	8
Mombetsu	Inset I	8
Mon Repos	B2	91
Møn, island	D4	32
Mona, passage	D2	89
Monaco		35
Monaco, capital	B1	35
Monaghan	C1	31
Monastery	F2	100
Monastir	C2	57
Mönchengladbach	A3	40
Monclova	D2	84
Moncton	E2	97
Mondego, cape	A2	36
Mondego, river	B2	36
Monforte	C1	37
Mongo	B4	59
Mongolia		11
Mongolian, plateau	C2	11
Mongomo	D3	66
Mongu	A3	67
Monitor	D6	94
Monjolo	Inset I	81
Monkey Bay	C2	67
Mono, river	A4, B2	64
Monopoli	D2	38
Monrovia, capital	A2	63
Mons	B2	33
Mont-Carmel	G4	103
Mont-Joli	H3	103
Mont-Laurier	A5	103
Mont-Royal	J5	103
Mont-Saint-Michel	B2	34
Mont-St-Pierre	L2	103
Mont-Tremblant-Village	B5	103
Montague	C2	100
Montalto, mt.	C3	38
Montana	B2	50
Montana	B2	126
Montargis	C2	34
Montauban	C4	34
Monte Carlo	B1	35
Monte Cristi	A1	89
Monte Plata	C2	89
Montebello	B6	103
Montecristo, island	B2	38
Montegiardino	B2	39
Montego Bay	B2	88
Montélimar	D4	34
Montelindo, river	C3	75

	Key	Page
Montenegro, republic	A3	49
Montepulciano	B2	38
Monterey, Calif.	A2	126
Montería	B2	78
Montero	B3	77
Monterrey, state capital	D2	84
Montes Claros	D3	81
Montevideo, capital	B3	75
Montgomery, capital, Ala.	E2	126
Montluçon	C3	34
Montmagny	F5	103
Montmartre	G10	104
Montpelier, capital, Vt.	F1	126
Montpellier	C5	34
Montréal	C6, J5	103
Montréal, island	J5	103
Montreal, lake	E6	104
Montreal, river	E6	104
Montreuil	Inset II	34
Montreux	A2	35
Montrose	C2	30
Monywa	B2	12
Monza	B1	38
Moore Park	B4	96
Moose Factory	D2	101
Moose Jaw	E10	104
Moose Lake	A2	96
Moose, river	D2	101
Moosehorn	B3	96
Moosomin	J10	104
Moosonee	D2	101
Mopti	C3	58
Moquegua	C4	77
Moradabad	C3	20
Morant Bay	C3	88
Moratuwa	A5	19
Morava, river	A2, C3	42
Morava, river	B3	49
Moravia, region	C3	42
Moray, estuary	B1	30
Morden	B4	96
Mordoviya, republic	E4	44
Moree, N.S.W.	D2	14
Morehead	A2	15
Morelia, state capital	D4	84
Morell	C2	100
Morelos	E4	84
Morena, mts.	D3	37
Moresby, island	F5	95
Moreton, bay	Inset III	14
Morgan City, La.	D3	126
Morges	A2	35
Morghab, river	A1	22
Morghob	B1	23
Morghob, river	B1	23
Morice, lake	J4	95
Moricetown	J3	95
Morija	A2	71
Morinville	D4	94
Morioka	D2	8
Morlaix	B2	34
Morne Diablotin, mt.	B2	90
Moro, gulf	B5	12
Moro, river	A2	63
Morocco		57
Morogoro	C2	68
Morombe	A3	69
Morón	D2	88
Morón	C2	11
Morón de la Frontera	D4	37
Morondava	A3	69
Moroni, national capital	A1	67
Morotai, island	D1	13
Moroto	D2	61
Morpeth	D5	102
Morphou	A1	27
Morrin	D5	94
Morris	C4	96
Morrisburg	K3	102
Mors, island	B2	32
Morse	C10	104
Mortlach	D10	104
Mortlock, islands	C2	15
Moruga	A2	91
Moscow, capital	D3	44
Mosel, river	A4	40
Moselle, river	D2	34
Moshi	C1	68
Mosjøen	C2	52
Mosquitos, coast	C3	87
Moss	C4	52
Mossbank	E11	104
Mossel Bay	B3	71
Mossendjo	B5	66
Mossleigh	D6	94
Mossy, river	F6	104
Most	A2	42
Mostaganem	B1	57
Mostar	B2	48
Móstoles	Inset II	37
Mosul	B1	24
Motagua, river	D4	85
Motherwell	B2	30
Mouila	A2	66
Mould Bay	E1	99
Moule à Chique, cape	B3	91
Moulmein	C3	12
Moulouya, river	D1	57
Moundou	B5	59
Mount Carmel	A2	100
Mt. Forest	E4	102
Mount Gambier, S.A.	D3	14
Mount Hagen	A2	15
Mount Isa, Qld.	C2	14
Mountain Park	B5	94
Moura	B3	36
Mourne, mts.	D2	30
Mouscron	A2	33
Moussa Ali, mt.	B1	60
Mouths of the Danube, delta	E3	43
Mouths of the Ganges, delta	C7	21
Mouths of the Indus, delta	C5	21
Moyale	E2	61
Moyamba	A1	63
Moyie	P6	95
Moyobamba	B2	77

	Key	Page
Moyowosi, river	B1	68
Mozambique		68
Mozambique, channel		55
Mozzoro	E2	81
Mpanda	B2	68
Mpika	C2	67
Mpoko, river	A2	66
Mporokoso	C1	67
M'Ramani	B2	67
Mtkvari, river	C4	45
Mtskheta	C4	45
Mtwara	D3	68
Muang Khammouan	C3	11
Muang Khôngxédôn	C4	11
Muang Paklay	A2	11
Muang Pakxan	B2	11
Muang Vangviang	B2	11
Muang Xaignabouri	A2	11
Muang Xay	A1	11
Muang Xépôn	D3	11
Muang Xon	B1	11
Muar	B2	13
Muara	C1	13
Mubende	B3	61
Mubi	G2	65
Muchinga, mts.	C2	67
Mudanjiang	F1	10
Mudawwarah, al-	B3	26
Mufulira	B2	67
Muğla	B3	27
Muharraq, al-, island	B1	25
Mühlhausen	B3	40
Mui Bai Bung, point	A5	11
Mukalla, al-	A5	19
Muko, island	Inset III	8
Mulaku, atoll	A3	19
Mulde, river	C3	40
Mulhacén, mt.	E4	37
Mülheim an der Ruhr	A3	40
Mulhouse	D3	34
Mull, island	A2	30
Mullaittivu	B2	19
Mullingar	C2	31
Multan	D3	21
Mulund	Inset I	20
Mulvihill	B4	96
Mumbai (Bombay)	B5, Inset I	20
Mumbai (Bombay), harbor	Inset I	20
Mumbra	Inset I	20
Mumbwa	B3	67
Mun, river	C3	12
Muna, island	D2	13
Munamägi, mt.	D3	46
Muncho Lake	K2	95
Munich	B4	40
Munsan	B4	9
Münster	A3	40
Munster, province	B2	31
Muonio	D1	53
Muonioälven, river	D1	53
Muoniojoki, river	B1	53
Mur, river	D3	39
Mura, river	C2	48
Muramvya	B2	61
Murat, river	E2	27
Murchison, river	A2	14
Murcia	F4	37
Murdochville	L3	103
Mureş, river	B2	43
Murgab, river	D3	22
Muriel	E4	94
Murilo, atoll	C2	15
Müritz, lake	C2	40
Murmansk	C3	44
Muroran	D1, Inset I	8
Muroto, cape	B3	8
Murray Harbour	C3	100
Murray River	C2	100
Murray, harbour	C2	100
Murray, lake	A2	15
Murray, river	D3	14
Murrumbidgee, river	D3	14
Murska Sobota	D2	48
Mürz, river	D3	39
Murzuq	B2	56
Muş	E2	27
Mûša, river	B1	46
Musala, mt.	B3	50
Musan	C1	9
Muscat, capital	C1	25
Musgrave Harbour	E4	98
Musgrave, ranges	C2	14
Musgravetown	E5	98
Mushin	B4	65
Muskeg River	A4	94
Muskegon, Mich.	E1	126
Muskogee, Okla.	D2	126
Muskoka, lake	F2	102
Muskwa, ranges	J2	95
Musoma	B1	68
Musquodoboit Harbour	D3	100
Mussau, island	A2	15
Mustang	B2	19
Mustique, island	B3	91
Mustvee	D2	46
Musu-dan, point	C2	9
Mut	A2	56
Mutare	C2	69
Mutsamudu	A2	67
Mutsu	D1	8
Muyinga	C1	61
Muyun Kum, desert	D2	23
Muzaffarabad	D2	21
Muynoq	A2	23
Mwali (Mohéli), island	A2	67
Mwanza	B1	68
Mwene-Ditu	C2	67
Mweru, lake	B1, C3	67
Mwinilunga	A2	67
My Tho	B4	11
Myanmar (Burma)		12
Myingyan	B2	12
Myitkyina	C1	12
Mykolaiv	C3	47
Mymensingh	D4	21
Myrnam	E4	94

	Key	Page
Mysore	C6	20
Mzimba	B2	68
Mzuzu	B2	68

N

	Key	Page
N'dalatando	B3	70
N'Djamena, capital	A4	59
N'zeto	B3	70
Naas	C2	31
Nabatiyah at-Tahta, an-	A2	26
Naberezhnyye Chelny	D4	44
Nabeul	C1	57
Nabk, an-	A2	27
Nabouwalu	B2	17
Nacala	D2	68
Nacaome	B3	86
Nackawic	B3	97
Nadi	A2	17
Nadi, bay	A2	17
Nadur	B1	36
Naduri	B2	17
Næstved	C3	32
Nafud, an-, desert	B1	24
Nag Hammadi	B2	56
Naga	B3	12
Naga, hills	F3	20
Nagano	C2	8
Nagaoka	C2	8
Nagarote	B2	87
Nagasaki	A3	8
Nagorno-Karabakh, autonomous region	B2	45
Nagoya	C3	8
Nagpur	C4	20
Nagua	C1	89
Naguabo	D2	90
Nagykanizsa	A2	43
Naha	Inset II	8
Nahanni, river	C4	99
Nahariyya	B1	26
Naicam	F8	104
Naihati	Inset II	20
Nain	E3	98
Nairobi, capital	C4	61
Najaf, an-	B2	24
Najd, region	B1	24
Najin	D1	9
Najran	B2	24
Nakadori, island	A3	8
Nakano, island	A4	8
Nakfa	B1	60
Nakhichevan	C2	45
Nakhodka	E8	44
Nakhon Phanom	C2	12
Nakhon Ratchasima	C3	12
Nakhon Sawan	B3	12
Nakhon Si Thammarat	B4	12
Nakina	C2	101
Nakodu	B2	17
Nakskov	C4	32
Naktong, river	C5	9
Nakuru	C4	61
Nakusp	O6	95
Nal, river	B4	21
Nalikul	Inset II	20
Nam Dinh	B2	11
Nam Ngum, reservoir	B2	11
Nam Tok	B3	12
Namangan	D2	23
Namew, lake	H6	104
Namib, desert	A1, B3	70
Namibe	B5	70
Namibia		70
Namoluk, atoll	C2	15
Namonuito, atoll	C2	15
Nampb	A3	9
Nampa	B3	94
Nampula	C2	68
Namsos	B2	52
Namu, island	B2	16
Namuli, highlands	C2	68
Namur	C2	33
Namur, lake	D2	94
Namwala	B3	67
Nan	B2	12
Nan Ling, mts.	E3	10
Nan, river	B2	12
Nanaimo	L6	95
Nanchang	E3	10
Nanchong	D2	10
Nancy	D2	34
Nanda Devi, mt.	C2	20
Nanded	C5	20
Nanga Parbat, mt.	E2	21
Nanga-Eboko	B2	65
Nangi	Inset II	20
Nangnim-sanmaek, mts.	B3	9
Nanjing	E2	10
Nanning	D3	10
Nanole	Inset I	20
Nantou	B2	9
Nanterre	Inset II	34
Nantes	B3	34
Nanticoke	E5	102
Nanumaga, island	B1	16
Nanumea, island	B1	16
Nanyang	E2	10
Nao, cape	G3	37
Napadogan	C2	97
Napaktulik, lake	F3	99
Napanee	J3	102
Napier	C2	15
Naples	C2	38
Naples, bay	C2	38
Napo, river	C1	77
Nara	B3	8
Nara, canal	C4	21
Narathiwat	B5	12
Narayanganj	C5	21
Narayani, river	B2	19
Narbonne	C5	34
Narcisse	C4	96
Nares, strait	O1	99
Narew, river	E2	41
Narmada, river	C4	20
Narrogin, W.A.	A3	14
Narrows, strait	C2	90
Narsaq	C2	106

	Key	Page
Narva	E1	
Narva, river	D1	
Narvik	C4	
Naryan-Mar	C4	
Naryn	E2	
Naryn, river	E2	
Nashshash, an-	C2	
Nashville, capital, Tenn.	E2	
Nashwaak Bridge	B2	
Näsi, lake	B4	
Nasiriyah, an-	C2	
Nassau, capital	B2	
Nasser, lake	B3	
Nata	C2	
Natal	B3	
Natalkuz, lake	K4	
Natashquan	D3	
Natitingou	A2	
Natron, lake	B2	
Natuna Besar, island	B1	
Naucalpan de Juárez	Inset	
Naujoji Akmenè	B3	
Naumburg	B3	
Nauru		
Navabad	A1	
Navarino, island	C9	
Navarra	F1	
Navojoa	C2	
Navua	B3	
Navua, river	A3	
Nawabshah	C4	
Náxos, island	C3	
Nayarit	C3	
Nazareth	B1	
Nazca	C3	
Naze	Inset II	
Nazko	L5	
Nazret	B1	
Nchelenge	B1	
Ndélé	A2	
Ndendé	A2	
Ndjolé	A2	
Ndola	B2	
Néa Liósia	Inset	
Neagh, lake	A2	
Neápolis	B3	
Nebitdag	B2	
Neblina, mt.	B1	
Nebraska	D1	
Nechako, river	K4	
Neckar, river	B4	
Necochea	D4	
Neder Rijn, river	C3	
Nee Soon	B1	
Needles	N6	
Neepawa	A3	
Nefta	A3	
Negele	B2	
Negev, region	B2	
Negombo	A4	
Negra, lagoon	A2	
Negra, point	A2	
Negril	A2	
Negro, river	B4	
Negro, river	C1	
Negro, river	C2	
Negros, island	B4	
Neguac	D1	
Neiafu	B4	
Neiba	A2	
Neiba, mts.	A2	
Neijiang	D3	
Neil Harbour	G1	
Neilburg	A8	
Neisse, river	C3	
Neiva	B3	
Nekemte	C6	
Nellore	C6	
Nelson	O6	
Nelson Forks	L1	
Nelson House	B2	
Nelson, river	C1, D1	
Nelspruit	D2	
Néma	D3	
Nemeiben, lake	E5	
Nemunas, river	A2, C2	
Nemuro	Inset I	
Nemuro, strait	Inset I	
Nenagh	C2	
Nendo, island	C2	
Nenetsiya, autonomous okrug	C4	
Nepal		
Nepalganj	B2	
Nepean	G6, K2	
Nepisiguit, river	C1	
Neretva, river	B2	
Neris, river	C2	
Neryungri	C4	
Nesselrode, mt.	E1	
Nestaocano, river	C2	
Netanya	B1	
Netherlands		
Nettilling, lake	O3	
Netzahualcóyotl	Inset	
Neubrandenburg	C2	
Neuchâtel	A2	
Neuchâtel, lake	A2	
Neudorf	G10	
Neufchâteau	D3	
Neumünster	B1	
Neunkirchen	A4	
Neuquén	B4	
Neusiedler, lake	A3	
Neuss	A3	
Neustadt	A2	
Neustrelitz	C2	
Nevada	B2	
Nevada, mts.	E4	
Neves	B4	
Neves	Inset I	
Nevėžis, river	C2	
Nevis, island	C3	
New Amsterdam	C2	106

Key Page
w Brigden E5 94
w Britain, *island* B2 15
w Caledonia, *island* C2 18
w Carlisle L4 103
w Delhi, *capital* C3 20
w Denver O6 95
w England, *range* E3 14
w Ferolle C4 98
w Fish Creek B3 94
w Georgia Group, *islands* A1 16
w Glasgow E2 100
w Guinea, *island* A2 15
w Hamburg E4 102
w Hampshire F1 126
w Hanover, *island* B2 15
w Haven, Conn. F1 126
w Ireland, *island* B2 15
w Jersey F1 126
w Kowloon Inset 10
w Liskeard E3 101
w Mexico C2 126
w Minas C2 100
w Orleans, La. D3 126
w Plymouth B2 15
w Providence, *island* B3 89
w Richmond L3 103
w Ross C3 100
w Sandy Bay B1 91
w Schwabenland,
egion B16 107
w Siberian, *islands* B9 44
w South Wales D3 14
w Territories, *island* Inset 10
w Waterford G1 100
w Waterway, *channel* B3 32
w York F1 126
w York, N.Y. F1 126
w Zealand 15
w, *river* C4 80
w, *river* B1 85
wark, N.J. F1 126
wboro J3 102
wcastle C2 90
wcastle C2 71
wcastle upon Tyne C2 30
wcastle, N.S.W. E3 14
wcastle-under-Lyme C3 30
wdale A4 96
well, *lake* E6 94
wman, W.A. A2 14
wmarket D3 30
wmarket F3 102
wport C3 30
wport News, Va. F2 126
wquay B4 30
wry A2 30
wtown St. Boswells C2 30
yagawa B3 8
yshabur D2 22
ami, *lake* A2 69
aoundéré B2 65
ara B1 68
aramasch B4 17
auruhoe, *mt.* C2 15
erkeel B3 17
emelis, *islands* B3 17
ermechau C2 17
etbong C2 17
ro, *river* D3 61
oc Linh, *mt.* B3 11
onini B1 71
orongoro, *crater* C1 68
ounié, *river* A2 66
ozi B1 61
igmi C3 59
lu, *atoll* A2 15
uru F1 65
wempisi, *river* A2 71
a Trang B4 11
angano B3 71
gara Falls F4 102
gara-on-the-Lake F4 102
gassola D1 62
mey, *capital* A3 59
mtougou B2 64
ri, *river* B5 66
s, *island* A1 13
ok B2 16
aragua 87
aragua, *lake* B3 87
e D5 34
holls' Town A2 89
kerie, *river* A2 80
obar, *islands* F7 20
ola M6 95
olet D5 103
osia, *capital* B1 27
oya, *gulf* B3 86
tau B1 97
že, *mts.* B3 48
dere Tauern, *range* D3 39
fang C3 66
nburg B2 40
i Ko, *river* C2 62
uw Amsterdam B2 80
uw Nickerie A2 80
adoo D1 97
de C3 27
er 59
er, *delta* C5 65
er, *river* B3 58
eria 65
island C3 8
gata C2 8
ama B3 8
hau, *island*, Hawaii Inset II 126
megen C3 32
aia Inset 51
ki B3 64
ko C2 8
olayevsk-na-Amure D9 44
opol C2 47
šić A3 49
unau, *island* A2 17
andu, *atoll* A3 19
, *river* B2 56
iri, *hills* C6 20
polis Inset I 81
ba, *mt.* B3 63

Key Page
Nimba, *mts.* B2 63
Nîmes D5 34
Nine Mile River D2 100
Ninette B4 96
Ninga B4 96
Ningbo F3 10
Ningxia Hui D2 10
Ninigo, *group* A2 15
Niono B3 58
Nioro du Rip B3 62
Nioro du Sahel B2 58
Niort B3 34
Nipawin F7 104
Nipigon C3 101
Nipigon, *lake* C3 101
Nipissing F1 102
Nipissing, *lake* F1 102
Niš B3 49
Nišava, *river* C3 49
Nishino, *island* Inset III 8
Nishinomiya B3 8
Nisling, *river* B4 105
Niterói D4, Inset I 81
Nitra B2 42
Niuafo'ou, *island* B1 17
Niuatoputapu, *island* C1 17
Niulakita, *island* C4 16
Niutao, *island* B2 16
Niverville C4 96
Nizamabad C5 20
Nizhnevartosk C5 44
Nizhny Novgorod D4 44
Nizhny Tagil D4 44
Njazidja
(Grande Comore), *island* A1 67
Njombe, *river* B2 68
Nkawkaw B3 64
Nkhata Bay B2 68
Nkhotakota B2 68
Nkongsamba A2 65
Noakhali E6 21
Nobeoka A3 8
Noel D2 100
Nogales B1 84
Nogales, Ariz. B2 126
Nojima, *cape* D3 8
Nok Kundi B4 21
Nokaneng A1 69
Nokomis E9 104
Nola A3 66
Nome, Alaska Inset I 126
Nonacho, *lake* G4 99
Nong Khai C2 12
Nonsan B4 9
Nonthaburi B3 12
Nootka, *island* J6 95
Norak A1 23
Nord-Ostsee, *canal* B1 40
Nord-Pas-de-Calais C1 34
Nordenham B2 40
Nordhausen B3 40
Nordhorn A2 40
Nordvik B7 44
Norfolk D5 94
Norfolk, Va. F2 126
Norilsk C6 44
Norland G3 102
Normandin D3 103
Norquay H9 104
Norra Storfjället, *mt.* C1 53
Norris Arm D4 98
Norris Point C4 98
Norrköping C3 53
Norte, *key* E2 90
N. Albanian Alps, *mts.* A1, B3 49
North Andaman, *island* F6 20
North Battleford B8 104
North Bay F1 102
North Cape B1 100
North Carolina F2 126
North China, *plain* E2 10
North Comino, *channel* B1 36
North Dakota C1 126
North Downs, *hills* C3 30
North Frisian, *islands* B4 32
North Holland, *canal* B2 32
North Korea 9
North Magnetic Pole B13 106
North Malosmadulu, *atoll* A2 19
N. Moose, *lake* B2 96
North Ossetiya, *republic* E4 44
North Platte, Nebr. C1 126
North Portal H11 104
North Rhine-Westphalia A3 40
North Rustico B2 100
North Saskatchewan, *river* D8 104
North Sea, *canal* B2 32
North Shields C2 30
North Siberian, *lowland* B6 44
North Star B3 94
North Taranaki, *bight* B2 15
N. Thompson, *river* N5 95
North Uist, *island* A1 30
North Wabasca, *lake* D3 94
North West River A2 98
North West, *cape* A2 14
North York K5 102
North, *cape* F1 52
North, *channel* A2 30
North, *channel* B1 102
North, *island* B2 15
North, *river* B2 98
North, *sea* 29
Northallerton C2 30
Northampton C3 30
Northeast, *polder* C2 32
Northeim B3 40
Northern Divina, *river* C4 44
Northern European, *plain* B2 40
Northern Sporades, *islands* B2 51
Northern Territory C2 14
Northgate H11 104
Northumberland, *strait* B3, D2 100
Northwest Gander, *river* D5 98
Norton D3 97
Norvegia, *cape* B14 107
Norway 52
Norway House C2 96
Norwegian, *bay* K1 99

Key Page
Norwegian, *sea* A2 52
Norwich D3 30
Norwich E4 102
Nossob, *river* C3 70
Nosy Be, *island* B1 69
Nosy Sainte Marie, *island* B2 69
Noteć, *river* C2, D2 41
Noto, *peninsula* C2 8
Notre Dame de Lourdes B4 96
Notre Dame Junction D4 98
Notre Dame, *bay* D4 98
Notre-Dame E2 97
Notre-Dame-de-la-Merci B5 103
Notre-Dame-de-la-Salette A6 103
Notre-Dame-de-Lorette D2 103
Notre-Dame-du-
Bon-Conseil D5 103
Notre-Dame-du-Lac H4 103
Notre-Dame-du-Laus A5 103
Nottingham C3 30
Nottingham, *island* N4 99
Nouadhibou A2 58
Nouakchott, *capital* A3 58
Nouméa, *capital* C2 18
Nouvelle K3 103
Nova Gorica A3 48
Nova Iguaçu Inset I 81
Novara B1 38
Novaya Zemlya, *islands* B4 44
Nové Zamky B3 42
Novgorod D3 44
Novi Pazar B3 49
Novi Sad A2 49
Novo Mesto C3 48
Novokuznetsk D6 44
Novosibirsk D6 44
Novra A3 96
Nowshak, *mt.* D2 21
Nowy Sącz E4 41
Nsanje C3 68
Nsawam B4 64
Nsok D3 66
Nsoko B3 71
Nsukka D4 65
Ntem, *river* B3 65
Nu'ulua, *island* D3 18
Nu'utele, *island* D3 18
Nuba, *mts.* C3 59
Nubian, *desert* C1 59
Nueltin, *lake* J4 99
Nueva Casas Grandes C1 84
Nueva Gerona B2 88
Nueva Loja C2 79
Nueva Ocotepeque A2 86
Nueva Palmira A2 75
Nueva Rosita D2 84
Nueva San Salvador A2 86
Nuevitas D2 88
Nuevo Laredo E2 84
Nuevo León D2 84
Nuevo Rocafuerte D3 79
Nuguria, *islands* B2 15
Nuhud, an- B2 59
Nui, *island* B2 16
Nuku'alofa, *capital* B4 17
Nukufetau, *island* C2 16
Nukulaelae, *island* C3 16
Nukuoro, *atoll* C2 15
Nukus A2 23
Nullarbor, *plain* B3 14
Numazu C3 8
Ñuñoa Inset 76
Nuoro B2 38
Nuremberg B4 40
Nutak E3 98
Nuuk (Godthåb), *capital* B2 106
Nuuuli B1 18
Nuwara Eliya B5 19
Nyaake C3 63
Nyaba, *river* B2 61
Nyala B2 59
Nyanga, *river* A2 66
Nyanza B2 61
Nyasa (Malawi), *lake* B2, B3 68
Nyborg C3 32
Nyeri D4 61
Nyetane, *river* B2 71
Nyika, *plateau* B2 68
Nyíregyháza C2 43
Nykøbing C4 32
Nyoman, *river* B3 47
Nyong, *river* B3 65
Nysa C3 41
Nzérékoré D4 62
Nzi, *river* D3 63
Nzo, *river* C3 63
Nzoia, *river* C3 61
Nzwani (Anjouan), *island* B2 67

O

O'Leary A2 100
Oahu, *island*, Hawaii Inset II 126
Oak Lake A4 96
Oak Point C4 96
Oak Point C3 97
Oak River A4 96
Oakland, Calif. A2 126
Oakner A4 96
Oakview B3 96
Oakville C4 96
Oakville F4 102
Oamaru B4 15
Oaxaca, *state capital* E4 84
Ob, *river* C5 44
Oban B2 30
Obed B4 94
Oberammergau B5 40
Oberhausen A3 40
Oberpfälzer Wald, *mts.* C4 40
Obi, *island* D2 13
Obihiro Inset I 8
Obo C2 66
Obock C2 60
Obuasi B3 64
Occidental, *mts.* B2, C4 77
Ocean Falls J5 95
Ochamchire A3 45
Ochil, *hills* B2 30

Key Page
Ocho Rios B2 88
Ochre River B3 96
Ocoa, *bay* B2 89
Ocotal A2 87
Ocotlán D3 84
Oda B4 64
Odei, *river* C1 96
Odemira A4 36
Odense C3 32
Odense, *fjord* C3 32
Odenwald, *forest* B4 40
Oder, *river* B2, C3 41
Oderhaff, *lake* C2 40
Odesa C3 47
Odessa, Tex. C2 126
Odienné C2 63
Oeiras A3 36
Oelemari, *river* B3 80
Offa C3 65
Offenbach B3 40
Ofu, *island* A1 18
Ogaden, *region* D3 60
Ogbomosho C3 65
Ogden, Utah B1 126
Ogema F11 104
Ogilvie, *mts.* B3 105
Oglio, *river* B1 38
Ogoki, *river* C2 101
Ogooué, *river* A2 66
Ogosta, *river* B2 50
Ogražden, *mts.* C2 48
Ogre C2 46
Ogun, *river* B3 65
Ohio E1 126
Ohio, *river* E2 126
Ohonua C4 17
Ohrid A2 48
Ohrid, *lake* B2 49
Øibenik B3 48
Oise, *river* C2, Inset II 34
Oistins B5 91
Oita A3 8
Ojinaga D2 84
Ojos del Salado, *mt.* B2 74
Oka, *river* D4 44
Okahandja B2 70
Okakarara C2 70
Okanagan Falls N6 95
Okanagan, *lake* N6 95
Okara D3 21
Okavango, *basin* A1 69
Okavango, *river* A1 69
Okayama B3 8
Okazaki C3 8
Okeechobee, *lake*, Fla. E3 126
Okene D4 65
Okha D9 44
Okhotsk D9 44
Okhotsk, *sea* D9 44
Oki, *islands* B2 8
Okinawa, *island* Inset II 8
Okino Erabu, *island* Inset II 8
Oklahoma D2 126
Oklahoma City, *capital*,
Okla. D2 126
Okondja B2 66
Okotoks C6 94
Okushiri, *island* C1, Inset I 8
Okwa, *river* A2 69
Ólafsvík A2 52
Olanchito B2 86
Öland, *island* C3 53
Olavarría C4 74
Olbia B2 38
Old Brahmaputra, *river* C4 21
Old Crow B2 105
Old Perlican E5 98
Old Road D5 90
Old Road Town B2 90
Old Wives, *lake* D10 104
Oldenburg B2 40
Oldham C3 30
Oldman, *river* D6 94
Olds C5 94
Olenek, *river* C7 44
Oléron, *island* B4 34
Olgilvie, *river* B3 105
Ölgiy A2 11
Olifants, *river* A3, C1 71
Olinda E2 81
Oliver N6 95
Ollagüe, *volcano* C2 76
Ollei C2 17
Olmaliq C2 23
Olomouc C3 42
Olongapo B3 12
Olosega, *island* A1 18
Olsztyn E2 41
Olt, *river* C3 43
Olteniţa D3 43
Olympia, *capital*, Wash. A1 126
Olympus *mt.*, Wash. A1 126
Olympus, *mt.* A2 27
Olympus, *mt.* B1 51
Omagh A2 30
Omaha, *beach* B2 34
Omaha, Nebr. D1 126
Oman 25
Oman, *gulf* C1, D2 25
Omaruru B2 70
Omatako, *river* C1 70
Omboué A2 66
Omdurman C2 59
Omemee G3 102
Ometepe, *island* B3 87
Omineca, *mts.* J2 95
Omineca, *river* K3 95
Omiya C3 8
Omo, *river* B3 60
Omsk D5 44
Omuta A3 8
Onanole B4 96
Ondame B2 62
Ondangwa B1 70
Ondava, *river* C2 42
Ondjiva C5 70
Ondo C4 65
Öndörhaan D2 11
Onefour E6 94

Key Page
Onega, *lake* C3 44
Oneşti D2 43
Ongjin A4 9
Ongole C5 20
Onilahy, *river* A3 69
Onion Lake A7 104
Onitsha D4 65
Ono, *island* B3 17
Onon, *river* D2 11
Onota, *island* A2 17
Onsŏng C1 9
Ontario, *lake* K4 92
Ontong Java, *island* A1 16
Oostende A1 33
Oostende-Brugge, *canal* B1 33
Oosterschelde, *channel* A3 32
Ootsa, *lake* J4 95
Opava C3 42
Opeongo, *lake* G2 102
Opole C3 41
Oporto (Porto) A2 36
Opuwo A1 70
Oqsu, *river* C2 23
Oradea A2 43
Oral B1 23
Oran A1 57
Orange Walk B1 85
Orange, N.S.W. D3 14
Orange, *river* A3, B2 71
Orangeville E4 102
Oranje, *mts.* B3 80
Oranjemund B4 70
Orapa B2 69
Ordino B2 36
Ordu D2 27
Örebro C3 53
Oregon A1 126
Orellana, *lake* D3 37
Orenburg D4 44
Orense C1 37
Øresund, *sound* D3 32
Órganos, *mts.* A2 88
Órgãos, *range* Inset I 81
Orhei B2 50
Orhon, *river* C2 11
Oriental, *mts.* B2, C3 77
Oriental, *range* C2 89
Orillia F3 102
Orinoco, *river* C3, D2 79
Orion E6 94
Oristano B3 38
Orizaba E4 84
Orkney, *islands* Inset I 30
Orlando, Fla. E3 126
Orléans C3 34
Orléans, *island* F5, L5 103
Ormoc C4 12
Orne, *river* B2 34
Örnsköldsvik C2 53
Orocué C3 78
Oroluk, *atoll* C2 15
Oromocto C3 97
Oron E5 65
Orontes, *river* A2 27
Orosháza C2 43
Orrefors C3 53
Orsha E2 47
Orsk D4 44
Ortegal, *cape* C1 37
Orumiyeh (Urmia) A2 22
Oruro A3 77
Oryakhovo B2 50
Os, *river* A3 36
Osaka B3 8
Osasco Inset II 81
Osh C2 23
Oshakati B1 70
Oshawa G4 102
Oshima, *peninsula* D1, Inset I 8
Oshogbo C4 65
Osijek D2 48
Osilinka, *river* K3 95
Öskemen
(Ust-Kamenogorsk) E1 23
Oslo, *capital* C3 52
Oslofjord, *fjord* C4 52
Osnabrück B2 40
Osorno B7 76
Osoyoos N6 95
Oss C3 32
Osse, *river* C4 65
Österdalälven, *river* B2 53
Östersund B2 53
Ostrava D3 42
Ostrołęka E2 41
Osum, *river* B3 49
Osumi, *islands* A4 8
Osumi, *peninsula* A4 8
Osumi, *strait* A4 8
Osŭm, *river* C3 50
Otaru Inset I 8
Otavalo B2 79
Otavi C1 70
Oti, *river* B1, C2 64
Otjiwarongo B2 70
Otranto D2 38
Otranto, *strait* A3 49
Otsu B3 8
Ottawa H5, K2 102
Ottawa, *river* G1, G5 H5, K2 102
Otterlo C2 32
Ötztal Alps, *range* B4 39
Ou, *mts.* D2 8
Ou, *river* B1 11
Ouadane C2 58
Ouagadougou, *capital* D2 64
Ouahigouya C2 64
Ouaka, river B2 66
Ouanary C1 80
Ouargla B1 57
Ouarra, river C2 66
Ouarzazate C2 57
Oudtshoorn B3 71
Ouémé, river B3 64
Ouesso D3 66
Ouezzane C1 57
Ouham, river A2 66
Ouidah B4 64
Oujda D1 57

Key Page
Oulu C1 53
Oulu, lake C2 53
Oulujoki, river C2 53
Oum er-Rbia, river C1 57
Ounasjoki, river B1 53
Oungre G11 104
Our, river B1 33
Ourthe, river D2 33
Ouse, river C2, D3 30
Outarde, river H2 103
Outer Hebrides, islands A1 30
Outjo B2 70
Outlook C9 104
Ouvéa, island C2 18
Ovalau, island B2 17
Ovalle B4 76
Overflakkee, island B3 32
Overflowing River A2 96
Oviedo A3 89
Oviedo D1 37
Owando C4 66
Owen Sound E3 102
Owen Stanley, range A2 15
Owendo A1 66
Owensboro, Ky. E2 126
Owerri D5 65
Oxbow H11 104
Oxford C3 30
Oxford D2 100
Oxford House D1, D2 96
Oxford, lake D2 96
Oyapock, river B2 80
Oyem A1 66
Oyo B4 65
Ozama, river B2 89
Ozark, plateau D2 126
Ózd C1 43
Özgön C2 23
Ozoir-la-Ferrière Inset II 34
Ozurgeti A4 45

P

Pa-an C3 12
Paamiut (Frederikshåb) C2 106
Pabna C4 21
Pacaraima, mts. D3 79
Pacasmayo B2 77
Pachuca, state capital E3 84
Padang B2 13
Paddle Prairie B2 94
Paderborn B3 40
Padma, river D5 21
Padua (Padova) B1 38
Paektu-san, mt. C2 9
Pagadian B5 12
Pago Pago, capital B1 18
Pahang, river B2 13
Paianía Inset 51
Päijänne, lake C2 53
Paint, lake B1 96
Paisley B2 30
Paita A2 77
Pakaraima, mts. A3 80
Pakistan 21
Pakowki, lake E6 94
Paks B2 43
Pakse C4 11
Pala A5 59
Palaiseau Inset II 34
Palana D10 44
Palanga A2 46
Palangkaraya C2 13
Palau 17
Palawan, island A4 12
Paldiski C1 46
Pale B2 48
Palembang B2 13
Palencia D1 37
Palermo C3 38
Palikir, capital C2 15
Palk, strait C7 20
Palliser, cape C3 15
Palm, island A4 91
Palma H3 37
Palmas D3 81
Palmer Land, region B11 107
Palmerston E4 102
Palmerston North C3 15
Palmira A4 78
Palmyra, ruins B2 27
Palos, cape F4 37
Palu C2 13
Pamirs, mts. B2 23
Pamirs, region A2 10
Pampas, plain C4 74
Pamplemousses C2 69
Pamplona F1 37
Panagyurishte C3 50
Panaji B5 20
Panama 87
Panama, canal C2 87
Panamá, capital C2 87
Panama, gulf C3 87
Panay, gulf B4 12
Panay, island B4 12
PanΔevo B2 49
Panch'iao B1 9
Pandan, strait A2 13
Pandaruan, river C2 13
Pando C3 75
Panev>«ys C2 46
Pangani, river C1 68
Pangkalpinang B2 13
Pangnirtung P3 99
Panihati Inset II 20
Panj A2 23
Panj, river B2 23
Panjakent A1 23
Panjgur B4 21
P'anmunj!m B4 9
Pantanal, lowland C4 81
Pantelleria, island C3 38
Pánuco, river E3 84
Panzhihua D3 10
Pápa A2 43
Papagayo, gulf A2 86
Paphos A2 27
Papua, gulf A2 15

	Key	Page
Papua New Guinea		15
Paquetville	D1	97
Pará	C2	81
Pará, river	C2	81
Paradise Hill	A7	104
Paradise River	C2	98
Paraguá, river	B2	77
Paraguai, river	C3	81
Paraguarí	D4	75
Paraguay		75
Paraguay, river	C2, C5	75
Paraíba	E2	81
Parakou	B3	64
Paramaribo, capital	C2	80
Paraná	C3	74
Paraná	C4	81
Paraná, river	D2	74
Paranaguá	D4	81
Paranam	B2	80
Pardubice	B2	42
Parent	B4	103
Parepare	C2	13
Paria, gulf	D1	79
Parima, range	B1	81
Paris, capital	C2, Inset II	34
Parkhill	D4	102
Parkland	D6	94
Parksville	K6	95
Parma	B1	38
Parnaíba	D2	81
Parnaíba, river	D2	81
Pärnu	C2	46
Pärnu, river	C2	46
Paro		19
Paropamisus, range	A2	22
Páros, island	C3	51
Parral	B6	76
Parrsboro	C2	100
Parry	D2	99
Parry Sound	E2	102
Parry, channel	J2	99
Parsnip, river	L4	95
Parson's Pond	C4	98
Pas de la Casa	C2	36
Pasadena	C5	98
Pasfield, lake	E2	104
Pasión, river	C3	85
Paso de los Toros	C2	75
Paso de Palmar, lake	B2	75
Passau	D4	40
Passero, cape	C3	38
Passo Fundo	C4	81
Pastavy	C2	47
Pastaza, river	B1	77
Pastillo	C3	90
Pasto	A4	78
Patagonia, region	A6	74
Patavilca	B3	77
Paterson, N.J.	F1	126
Patía, river	A4	78
Patiala	C2	20
Patillas	C2	90
Patna	E3	20
Patos, lagoon	C5	81
Pátrai	B2	51
Patricia	E6	94
Pattani	B5	12
Patuakhali	D6	21
Patuanak	C5	104
Patuca, mts.	C2	86
Patuca, river	C2	86
Pau	B5	34
Pauingassi	D3	96
Paulatuk	D3	99
Paulaya, river	C2	86
Paulo Afonso	E2	81
Pavaiai	B2	18
Pavia	B1	38
Pavilosta	A2	46
Pavlodar	D1	23
Paxbán	C2	85
Payar	B2	62
Paye	Inset I	20
Payne, lake	B2	101
Paynton	B7	104
Pays De La Loire	B3	34
Paysandú	A2	75
Paz, river	C6	85
Pazardzhik	C3	50
Peace Point	D1	94
Peace River	B3	94
Peace, river	A3, C2	94
Peachland	N6	95
Pebane	C3	68
Pe~	B3	49
Pechora	C4	44
Pechora, river	C4	44
Pécs	B2	43
Pedernales	A2	89
Pedja, river	D2	46
Pedra Açú, mt.	Inset I	81
Pedra Lume	D2	58
Pedro Juan Caballero	E3	75
Pedro Santana	A1	89
Peebles	H10	104
Peel, river	B3, C2	105
Peerless Lake	C3	94
Pegasus, bay	B3	15
Pegu	C3	12
Peipus, lake	D2	46
Pekalongan	B2	13
Pekanbaru	B1	13
Pelee, island	C6	102
Peleliu, island	A4	17
Peleng, island	D2	13
Pelican Narrows	H5	104
Pelican Portage	D3	94
Pelican Rapids	A3	96
Pelican, lake	A3	96
Pelkan, lake	A3	96
Pelly	J9	104
Pelly Bay	L3	99
Pelly Crossing	B4	105
Pelly, river	C4, C5	105
Pelotas	C5	81
Pematangsiantar	A1	13
Pemba	D2	68
Pemba, island	D2	68

	Key	Page
Pemberton	L6	95
Pembina, river	B4	94
Pembina, river	B4	96
Pembroke	B3	30
Pembroke	H2	102
Penas, gulf	B8	76
Pendé, river	A2	66
Pendleton, Oreg.	B1	126
Penetanguishene	F3	102
P'enghu (Pescadores),		
islands	A2	9
Peninsular Malaysia, region	B2	13
Pennant	B10	104
Pennine Alps, mts.	B2	35
Pennines, mts.	C2	30
Pennsylvania	F1	126
Penonomé	B2	87
Penrith	C2	30
Pensacola, Fla.	E2	126
Pensacola, mts.	A11	107
Penticton	N6	95
Peñuelas	B2	90
Penza	D4	44
Penzance	B4	30
Percé	M3	103
Perdue	C8	104
Pereira	B3	78
Péribonca, river	B3	101
Péribonka	D3	103
Périgueux	C4	34
Perim, island	A2	25
Peristéri	Inset	51
Perlas, archipelago	C2	87
Perlas, lagoon	C2	87
Perm	D4	44
Pernambuco	E2	81
Pernik	B3	50
Perpignan	C5	34
Perrot, island	G6	103
Persian, gulf	C1, C2, C3	24
Perth	B2	30
Perth, W.A., capital	A3, Inset I	14
Perth-Andover	B2	97
Peru		77
Perugia	C2	38
Pervomaysk	C2	47
Pescadores, channel	A2	9
Peshawar	D3	21
Peshkopi	B2	49
Petah Tiqwa	B1	26
Petare	C1	79
Petatauke	C2	67
Petawawa	H2	102
Petén-Itzá, lake	D3	85
Peterborough	C3	30
Peterborough	G3	102
Peterhead	C1	30
Petersfield	C4	96
Petit Canouan, island	B3	91
Petit Martinique, island	C1	91
Petit Mustique, island	B3	91
Petit St. Vincent, island	A4	91
Petit-Rocher	D1	97
Petitcodiac	D3	97
Petite Riviere	C3	100
Petlura	A3	96
Petra, ruins	A2	26
Petrich	B4	50
Petrolia	B3	43
Petrólia	C5	102
Petrolina	D2	81
Petropavl	C1	23
Petropavlovsk-Kamchatskiy	D9	44
Petrópolis	D4, Inset I	81
PetroΣani	B3	43
Petrozavodsk	C3	44
Pevek	C10	44
Peyia	A2	27
Pforzheim	B4	40
Phan Rang	B4	11
Phan Thiet	B4	11
Phatthalung	B5	12
Phayao	B2	12
Phetchabun	B2	12
Phetchabun, range	B2	12
Phetchaburi	B3	12
Phichit	B2	12
Philadelphia, Pa.	F2	126
Philippine, sea	C3	12
Philippine, sea	D2	17
Philippines		12
Phitsanulok	B2	12
Phnom Penh, capital	C4	11
Phnum Tbeng Meanchey	C2	11
Phoenix, capital, Ariz.	B2	126
Phoenix, island	B2	17
Phoenix, islands		17
Phôngsali	A1	11
Phou Bia, mt.	B2	11
Phra Nakhon Si Ayutthaya	B3	12
Phuket	B5	12
Phumi Samraong	B2	11
Phuntsholing	A3	19
Piapot	A10	104
Piauí	D2	81
Piave, river	C1	38
Pibor Post	C3	59
Pic de la Selle, mt.	D2	89
Pickle Lake	B2	101
Pico do Cano, volcano	H3	102
Picton	H3	102
Pidurutalagala, mt.	B4	19
Piedra Sola	B2	75
Piedras Negras	D2	84
Pielinen, lake	C2	53
Pierceland	A6	104
Pierre, capital, S. Dak.	C1	126

	Key	Page
Pierrefonds	G5	103
Pierreville	A2	91
Pierson	A4	96
Pie%t'any	A2	42
Pietermaritzburg	D2	71
Pietersburg	C1	71
Pigeon, lake	C4	94
Pigeon, lake	G3	102
Piggs Peak	B1	71
Pikangikum	B2	101
Pikes peak, Colo.	C2	126
Pikwitonei	C1	96
Pi¡a	C2	41
Pilar	C5	75
Pilaya, river	B4	77
Pilcomayo, river	B3, C4	75
Pilica, river	E3	41
Pilos	B3	51
Pilot Butte	F10	104
Pilot Mound	B4	96
Pinang, island	A2	13
Pinar del Río	A2	88
Pinawa	D4	96
Pindus, mts.	B2	51
Pine Bluff, Ark.	D2	126
Pine Dock	C3	96
Pine Falls	C4	96
Pine Point	F4	99
Pine River	A3	96
Pinehouse Lake	D5	104
Pines, island	D2	18
Ping, river	B2	12
Pingxiang	E3	10
Piniós, river	B2	51
Pink Mountain	L2	95
Pink, river	F4	104
Pinsk	B2	47
Pinta, island	Inset	79
Piotrków Trybunalski	D3	41
Pipestone	A4	96
Pipmuacan, reservoir	F2	103
Piracicaba	D4	81
Pirada	C1	62
Piraiévs	B3, Inset	51
Pirmasens	A4	40
Pirot	C3	49
Pirris, river	B3	86
Pisa	B2	38
Pisagua	B1	76
Pisco	B3	77
Pistoia	B2	38
Pite∑ti	C3	43
Pitlochry	B2	30
Pitseng	B2	71
Pitt, island	H4	95
Pittsburgh, Pa.	E1	126
Piura	A2	77
Placentia	B3	85
Placentia	D5	98
Placentia, bay	D5	98
Placenza	B1	38
Placetas	C2	88
Planken	B1	33
Plantagenet	K2	102
Plasencia	C2	37
Plaster Rock	B2	97
Plata, Río de la, estuary	D3	74
Plata, river	B3	75
Platte, river, Nebr.	C1	126
Plauen	C3	40
Playgreen, lake	B2	96
Pleasant Bay	G1	100
Pleiku	B4	11
Plenty, bay	C2	15
Plessisville	E5	103
Pleven	C2	50
Plevna	J3	102
Plibo	C3	63
Pljevlja	A3	49
Ploˆe	C3	48
P¡ock	D2	41
Ploie∑ti	D3	43
Plovdiv	C3	50
Plum Coulee	C4	96
Plumas	B4	96
Plymouth	B1	91
Plymouth	B4	30
Plze√	A3	42
Po, river	A1, B1	38
Poá	Inset II	81
Pobé	B4	64
Pocatello, Idaho	B1	126
Podgorica	A3	49
Pogradec	B3	49
P'ohang	C4	9
Pohnpei, island	D2	15
Poinsett, cape	C2	107
Point Fortin	A2	91
Point Leamington	D4	98
Point Pedro	B2	19
Point Prim	B2	100
Point, lake	F3	99
Pointe au Baril	E2	102
Pointe du Bois	D4	96
Pointe Michel	B3	90
Pointe Sapin	E2	97
Pointe-a-la-Croix	K3	103
Pointe-Claire	H6	103
Pointe-des-Monts	J2	103
Pointe-Lebel	H2	103
Pointe-Noire	A6	66
Pointe-Verte	D1	97
Poisson Blanc, reservoir	A6	103
Poissy	Inset II	34
Poitiers	C3	34
Poitou-Charentes	C3	34
Pokemouche	E1	97
Pokhara	B2	19
Poland		41
Polar, plateau	A14	107
Polba	D2	81
Polis	A1	27
Polonnaruwa	C4	19
Polotsk	D2	47
Poltava	D2	47
Poltimore	A6	103
Pomeranian, bay	C1	40
Ponce	B2	90

	Key	Page
Pond Cove	C3	98
Pond Inlet	N2	99
Pondicherry	C6	20
Ponferrada	C1	37
Ponoka	D5	94
Pont Cassé	B3	90
Pont-Rouge	E5	103
Pontchartrain	Inset II	34
Ponteix	C11	104
Pontevedra	B1	37
Pontianak	B2	13
Pontic, mts.	D2	27
Pontine, islands	C2	38
Pontine, marshes	C2	38
Pontoise	Inset II	34
Ponton	B2	96
Poole	C4	30
Poopó, lake	A3	77
Popayán	A4	78
Poperinge	A2	33
Poplar River	C3	96
Popomanaseu, mt.	B1	16
Popondetta	A2	15
Poprad	C2	42
Porcupine Plain	G8	104
Porcupine, river	B2	105
Pori	B2	53
Port Alberni	K6	95
Port Antonio	C2	88
Port au Choix	C4	98
Port au Port	B5	98
Port Augusta, S.A.	C3	14
Port Bickerton	F2	100
Port Blair	F6	20
Port Blandford	D5	98
Port Bruce	E5	102
Port Burwell	D3	98
Port Burwell	E5	102
Port Clements	F4	95
Port Colborne	F5	102
Port Coquitlam	L6	95
Port Dufferin	E3	100
Port Elgin	D3	97
Port Elgin	E3	102
Port Elizabeth	B2	91
Port Elizabeth	C3	71
Port Franks	D4	102
Port George	B2	100
Port Glaud	Inset	70
Port Harcourt	D5	65
Port Hardy	J6	95
Port Hawkesbury	F2	100
Port Hedland, W.A.	A2	14
Port Hood	F1	100
Port Hope	G4	102
Port Hope Simpson	C3	98
Port Laoise	C2	31
Port Lincoln, S.A.	C3	14
Port Loko	A1	63
Port Loring	E2	102
Port Louis, capital	B2	69
Port Macquarie, N.S.W.	E3	14
Port Maria	C2	88
Port McNeill	J6	95
Port Moody	L6	95
Port Morant	C3	88
Port Moresby, capital	A2	15
Port Mouton	C4	100
Port Nolloth	A2	71
Port of Spain, capital	A2	91
Port Perry	G3	102
Port Phillip, bay	Inset V	14
Port Pirie, S.A.	C3	14
Port Renfrew	K7	95
Port Rowan	E5	102
Port Said	B1	56
Port Saunders	C4	98
Port Stanley	D5	102
Port Sudan	D1	59
Port Talbot	B3	30
Port-au-Prince, bay	C2	89
Port-au-Prince, capital	C2	89
Port-Cartier	C3	101
Port-de-Paix	C1	89
Port-Gentil	A2	66
Port-Salut	B2	89
Portadown	A2	30
Portage	C2	48
Portage la Prairie	B4, D2	96
Portalegre	B3	36
Porter, lake	C4	104
Porters Lake	D3	100
Porth Edward	D3	71
Portimão	A4	36
Portland	A2	91
Portland Creek	C4	98
Portland, bight	B3	88
Portland, inlet	G4	95
Portland, Maine	F1	126
Portland, Oreg.	A1	126
Portneuf, river	G3	103
Porto Alegre	B4	63
Pôrto Alegre	C5	81
Pôrto Inglês	C3	58
Pôrto Velho	B2	81
Porto-Novo, capital	B4	64
Porto-Vecchio	Inset I	34
Portobelo	C2	87
Portoviejo	A3	79
Portree	A1	30
Portsmouth	C4	30
Portsmouth	A2	90
Portsmouth, Va.	F2	126
Portugal		36
Porvenir	B9	76
Posadas	D2	74
Poste, river	C3	69
Postojna	B3	48
Postville	B2	98
Potaro, river	B3	80
Potenza	C2	38
Poti	A3	45
Potiskum	F2	65
Potnarvin	C4	19
Potosí	A3	77
Potrerillos	C3	76
Potsdam	C2	40
Pottuvil	C5	19
Pouch Cove	E5	98

	Key	Page
Poutasi	C3	18
Pouthisat	B3	11
Pova«ská Bystrica	B2	42
Powassan	F1	102
Powell River	K6	95
Powerview	C4	96
Poyang, lake	E3	10
Poza Rica	E3	84
Po«arevac	B2	49
Pozna¡	C2	41
Pozo Colorado	C3	75
Pra, river	B4	64
Prachuap Khiri Khan	B4	12
Prague, capital	B2	42
Praia, capital	C4	58
Praslin	B2	91
Praslin, island	C1	70
Prato	B2	38
Prawda	D4	96
Preeceville	H9	104
Prelate	A10	104
Preparis, island	B3	12
Prescott	K3	102
Prescott, Ariz.	B2	126
Presidencia Roque		
Sáenz Peña	C2	74
Pre%ov	C2	42
Prespa, lake	A3	49
Presque Isle, Maine	G1	126
Prestea	A4	64
Preston	C3	30
Pretoria,		
administrative capital	C2	71
Préveza	B2	51
Prey Veng	D4	11
Priboj	A3	49
Priddis	C6	94
Prievidza	B2	42
Prijedor	A1	48
Prilep	B2	48
Priluki	C1	47
Primorsko	F3	50
Primrose, lake	A6	104
Prince Albert	E7	104
Prince Albert, hills	L3	99
Prince Albert, peninsula	D2	99
Prince Charles, island	N3	99
Prince George	L4	95
Prince of Wales, island	J2	99
Prince Patrick, island	E1	99
Prince Regent, inlet	K2	99
Prince Rupert	G4	95
Princes Town	A2	91
Princess Harbour	C3	96
Princess Margriet, canal	C1	32
Princess Royal, island	H4	95
Princeton	M6	95
Princeville	E5	103
Príncipe, island	C1	63
Prinzapolka	C2	87
Prinzapolka, river	B2	87
Pripyats, marshes	C4	47
Pripyats, river	C3	47
Pri%tina	B3	49
Privas	D4	34
Prizren	B3	49
Progresso	B1	85
Prokopyevsk	D6	44
Prokuplje	B3	49
Prome	B2	12
Prophet River	L2	95
Prost~jov	C2	42
Provence-Alpes-Côte-d'Azur	D4	34
Providence Bay	C2	102
Providence, capital, R.I.	F1	126
Providencia, island	Inset	78
Providenciales, island	C4	89
Provideniya	C11	44
Provo, Utah	B1	126
Pru, river	B3	64
Prut, river	B2	47
Przemyjl	F4	41
Pskov	D3	44
Pskov, lake	D3	46
Ptsich, river	D3	47
Pu'apu'a	B2	18
Pubnico	B4	100
Pucallpa	C2	77
Puck	D1	41
Puebla, state capital	E4	84
Pueblo, Colo.	C2	126
Puente Alto	Inset	76
Puerca, point	D2	90
Puerto Aisén	B8	76
Puerto Armuelles	A2	87
Puerto Ayacucho	C2	79
Puerto Bahía	C2	75
Puerto Barrios	E4	85
Puerto Bolívar	C1	79
Puerto Cabello	C1	79
Puerto Cabezas	C3	87
Puerto Carreño	D3	78
Puerto Cisnes	B7	76
Puerto Cortés	C2	86
Puerto Deseado	B6	74
Puerto Escondido	E4	84
Puerto Inírida	D3	78
Puerto Jiménez	C4	86
Puerto Leguízamo	B5	78
Puerto Lempira	D2	86
Puerto Maldonado	D3	77
Puerto Montt	B7	76
Puerto Natales	B9	76
Puerto Peñasco	B1	84
Puerto Pinasco	D3	75
Puerto Plata	B1	89
Puerto Princesa	A4	12
Puerto Real	A2	90
Puerto Rico		90
Puerto Quepos	B3	86
Puerto Sandino	A2	87
Puerto Santa Cruz	B7	74
Puerto Suárez	C3	77
Puerto Vallarta	C3	84
Puerto Varas	B7	76
Puerto Williams	C9	76

	Key	Page
Puertollano		D3
Puglia		C2
Pugwash	D2	1
Pukatawagan		A1
Pukch'lng		A1
Pukë		A3
Pula¡wy		A1
Pulangi, river		B4
Pulo Anna, island		Inset
Pulusuk, island		A4
Puná, island		A4
Punakha		A2
Pune		B5
Punggol		B1
P'ungsan		C4
Puno		C4
Punta, mt.		B1
Punta Arenas		B9
Punta del Este		C2
Punta Delgada		B9
Punta Gorda		D2
Punta Santiago		D2
Puntarenas		B3
Punto Fijo		B1
Purari, river		A1
Purbeck's Cove		C4
Purus, river		C5
Pusan		C5
Putao		C1
Putre		C1
Puttalam		B3
Puttgarden		B1
Putumayo, river		B5
Puvirnituq		A1
Puyo		C3
Puysegur, point		A4
Pyandzh, river		B1
P'yˆnggang		A3
P'yˆngsˆng		A3
P'yˆngsan		A3
P'yˆngyang, capital		A3
Pyrenees, range		C5

Q

	Key	Page
Qaanaaq (Thule)		B2
Qachas Nek		B3
Qadarif, al-		C2
Qaidam, basin		C2
Qalat		B2
Qalat Bishah		B2
Qaleh-ye Now		A1
Qaleh-ye Panjeh		C1
Qamea, island		C2
Qamishli, al-		B2
Qandahar		B2
Qaqortoq (Julianehåb)		D2
Qaraghandy (Karaganda)		D2
Qardho		B3
Qareh, river		B3
Qarokul, lake		B3
Qarshi		B3
Qaryah ash-Sharqiyah, al-		C1
Qasigiannguit		
(Christianshåb)		B2
Qasr as-Sabiyah		C2
Qatar		C2
Qatranah, al-		C2
Qatrun, al-		C2
Qattarah, depression		A2
Qayrawan, al-		B1
Qayyarah, al-		B1
Qazvin		C2
Qelelevu, island		D4
Qeshm, island		D4
Qilian, range		C2
Qin Ling, mts.		D2
Qina		B1
Qingdao		F2
Qinghai		C2
Qinghai, lake		C2
Qinhuangdao		E2
Qiqihar		F1
Qiryat Gat		B1
Qiryat Shemona		B1
Qishn		C3
Qom		C1
Qormi		B2
Qostanay		C1
Qu'Appelle		G10 1
Qu'Appelle, river		D10 1
Quang Ngai		C1 1
Quantaq		C1 1
Quanzhou		E3
Quatre Bornes		C2
Quba		C2
Qubayyat, al-		B1
Québec, capital		E5, L6 1
Quebo		B2
Quebradillas		A2
Queen Charlotte		F4
Queen Charlotte, islands		G4
Queen Charlotte, sound		H5
Queen Charlotte, strait		H5
Queen Elizabeth, islands		H1
Queen Maud Land, region		B16 1
Queen Maude, mts.		A5 1
Queen Maude, gulf		H3
Queensland		D2
Queenstown		A3
Queenstown		C3
Queenstown		A3
Queenstown, Tas.		D4
Queguay Grande, river		A2
Queimadas		Inset I
Quelimane		C2
Quellón		B7
Queluz		A3
Querétaro, state capital		D3
Quesnel		M5
Quesnel, lake		M5
Quetta		B2
Quetzaltenango		B5
Quezon City		B3
Qui Nhon		B4
Quibala		B4

	Key	Page
ló	A3	78
chena	M6	95
, lakes	F8	104
	F8	104
	B4	76
oué	Inset	76
mbele	C2	70
per	A2	34
hámel	B2	62
pamsis	D3	97
, capital	B3	79
aytirah, al-	A3	27
udhah, al-	B2	24
ghirot	A2	23
on	D2	23
honteppa	A2	23
at as-Sawda, mt.	A3	71
ing	A3	71
lorda	C2	23
	B2	53
es, peninsula	L1	99
	C2	13
, river	A2	43
	B2	36
t, capital	C1	57
ul	B2	15
it Lake	C7	104
it Lake Mine	G2	104
island	C2	17
Gia	A4	11
idia, er-	C2	57
	E1	126
Œuœi	C2	43
um Hot Springs	O6	95
	E3	41
ili%kis	B2	46
ille	F11	104
	E4	99
	B1	24
r	A1	96
ed, point	C3	91
eneau	H2	103
	C3	38
myar Khan	D4	21
oow Lake	A2	94
mar mt., Wash.	A1	126
	D4	20
ng, river	C2	13
raj	C3	19
et	B4	20
	Inset II	20
ahi	B4	21
oshi, mt.	A2	21
gh, capital, N.C.	F2	126
island chain	A1	16
	B2	87
adi, ar-	B2	24
anbati	Inset II	20
at Gan	B1	26
ea	C5	98
	B2	26
ree, island	B2	12
tha, ar-	B1	26
	F2	61
	A2	15
agua	B4	76
e, river	B2	20
hi	E4	20
	B2	60
ers	C2	32
onopolis	C3	81
urly	E4	94
gamati	F6	21
er Lake	B1	102
itikei, river	C2	15
pur	C3	21
ng	B4	76
d City	A4	96
d City, S. Dak.	C1	126
	C1	46
er	B2	19
gah, ar-	B2	27
al-Khalfi	C1	24
al-Khaymah	C2	25
an-Naqb	A2	26
Dashen, mt.	C1	60
Musandam, cape	C1	24
anura	C1	24
point	C5	74
ayya	A2	26
	B2	27
k, island chain	B1	16
haburi	B3	12
lin, island	A2	30
gen	A3	40
apura	B5	19
umara, range	C2	15
	B2	53
kela	D4	20
river	B2	50
nna	C1	38
nsburg	B5	40
river	D3	21
a, river	B4	80
alpindi	D3	21
atayn, ar-	B2	24
don	D2	100
son	B5	74
nore	F9	104
ng	B3	12
ide-Balfour	D1	102
point	A3	34
lm, lake	E3	43
	E2	50
island	B3	34
ing	C3	30
n, island	Inset I	8
ytsa	E3	47
	E2	81
inghausen	A3	40
nquista	D2	74
(Hong), river	A2	11
	C3	98

	Key	Page
Red Deer	D5	94
Red Deer, lake	A2	96
Red Deer, river	D5, E6	94
Red Indian, lake	C5	98
Red Rose	C3	96
Red Sucker, lake	E2	96
Red Volta, river	B1, D3	64
Red Willow	D5	94
Red, river	C4	96
Red, river	D2	126
Red, sea	A1	24
Redange	A2	33
Redbridge	F1	102
Redding, Calif.	A1	126
Redonda, island	A6	90
Redstone	L5	95
Redvers	A4	96
Redvers	J11	104
Ree, lake	B2	31
Reed, lake	A2	96
Regensburg	C4	40
Reggio di Calabria	C3	38
Reggio nell'Emilia	B1	38
Reghin	C2	43
Regina	F10	104
Régina	B1	80
Registan, region	A2	22
Rehoboth	C3	70
Rehovot	B2	26
Reigate	Inset III	30
Reims	D2	34
Reina Adelaida, archipelago	B9	76
Reindeer, island	C3	96
Reindeer, lake	H3	104
Reindeer, river	G4	104
Reinosa	D1	37
Reliance	G4	99
Remagen	A3	40
Remich	B2	33
Rémire	B1	80
Remscheid	A3	40
Rencontre East	D5	98
Renfrew	J2	102
Rennell, island	B2	16
Rennes	B2	34
Rennie	D4	96
Reno, Nev.	B2	126
Renous	D2	97
Repentigny	K5	103
Reserve	H8	104
Resistencia	D2	74
Re∑iœa	A3	43
Resolute	J2	99
Resolution, island	P4	99
Restigouche, river	B1	97
Reston	A4	96
Restoule	F1	102
Réunion, island		55
Reus	G2	37
Reuss, river	C2	35
Reutlingen	B4	40
Revelstoke	N6	95
Reventazón, river	C3	86
Revillagigedo, islands	B4	84
Rexdale	J5	102
Rexton	E2	97
Rey, island	C2	87
Reykjavik	B3	96
Reykjavík, capital	A2	52
Reynosa	E2	84
Reznas, lake	D2	46
Rhaetian Alps, mts.	D2	35
Rharsa, salt marsh	A2	57
Rhine, canal	B1, B2	33
Rhine, river	A3, A4	40
Rhineland-Palatinate	A4	40
Rhode Island	F1	126
Rhodes	D3	51
Rhodes, island	D3	51
Rhodope, mts.	C4	50
Rhondda	B3	30
Rhône, river	D4	34
Rhône-Alpes	D4	34
Rhum, island	A1	30
Riaba	A1	66
Ribe	B3	32
Ribeira Brava	B2	58
Ribeira Grande	A1	58
Ribeirão Pires	Inset II	81
Ribeirão Prêto	D4	81
Riberalta	A2	77
Ribnicœa	B2	50
Rice, lake	G3	102
Richard, lake	C1	104
Richard-Toll	B1	62
Richards Bay	D2	71
Richards Landing	A1	102
Richardson, mts.	B1	105
Richardson, river	E2	94
Richelieu, river	C6	103
Richer	C4	96
Richibucto	E2	97
Richmond	L6	95
Richmond	D6	103
Richmond Hill	F4, K5	102
Richmond Park	D4	94
Richmond, capital, Va.	F2	126
Ricobayo, reservoir	D2	37
Rida	A2	25
Rideau, lake	J3	102
Rideau, river	H6	102
Riesa	C3	40
Rieti	C2	38
Riga, capital	C2	46
Riga, gulf	B2, B3	46
Rigolet	B2	98
Riiser-Larsen Ice Shelf, glacier	B14	107
Riiser-Larsen, peninsula	C16	107
Rijeka	B2	48
Rila, mts.	B3	50
Rimini	C1	38
Rîmnicu Vîlcea	C3	43
Rimouski	H3	103
Rincón, bay	C3	90
Rincón del Bonete, lake	B2	75
Ringkøbing	B2	32
Río Blanco	B2	87

	Key	Page
Rio Branco	B2	81
Río Claro	A2	91
Río Cuarto	C3	74
Rio de Janeiro	D4, Inset I	81
Río Gallegos	B7	74
Río Grande	C5	81
Río Grande	D2	90
Río Grande	A2	87
Rio Grande (Río Bravo), river	D2	84
Rio Grande do Norte	E2	81
Rio Grande do Sul	C4	81
Rio Verde	C3	81
Riobamba	B3	79
Ríohacha	B2	78
Rioni, river	B3	45
Riou, lake	D1	104
Ri∑cani	A2	50
Rishiri, island	Inset I	8
Rishra	Inset II	20
Riske Creek	L5	95
Ritchies, archipelago	F6	20
Rivas	B3	87
River Cess	B3	63
River Hills	C4	96
River John	D2	100
Rivera	C1	75
Rivercrest	C4	96
Riverhurst	D10	104
Rivers	A4	96
Rivers Inlet	J5	95
Riverside, Calif.	B2	126
Riverside-Albert	E3	97
Riverton	C3	96
Riverview	E2	97
Rivière Bleue	G4	103
Rivière du Loup	C4	101
Rivière du Rempart	C2	69
Rivière Noire, mt.	B2	69
Rivière-à-Pierre	D4	103
Rivière-au-Renard	M3	103
Rivière-aux-Rats	B4	103
Rivière-du-Portage	G4	103
Rivière-du-Portage	E1	97
Rivière-Ste-Marguerite	G3	103
Rivière-Verte	A1	97
Riyadh, capital	B1	24
Riyaq	B2	26
Roanne	D3	34
Roanoke, Va.	F2	126
Roatán	B1	86
Roatán, island	B1	86
Robertsport	A2	63
Roberval	D3	103
Robinsonville	C1	97
Roblin	A3	96
Roboré	C3	77
Robson, mt.	N4	95
Roca, cape	A3	36
Rocanville	J10	104
Rocha	C3	75
Rochdale	C3	30
Rochefort	B4	34
Rochester	D4	94
Rochester, Minn.	D1	126
Rochester, N.Y.	F1	126
Rock Island	D6	103
Rock, river	D5	105
Rockcliffe Park	H5	102
Rockford, Ill.	E1	126
Rockglen	E11	104
Rockhampton, Qld.	E2	14
Rockland	K2	102
Rocky Harbour	C4	98
Rocky Island, lake	B1	102
Rocky Mountain House	C5	94
Rocky, mts.		82
Rockyford	D5	94
Roddickton	C4	98
Rodez	C4	34
Rodney	D5	102
Roermond	D3	32
Roeselare	B2	33
Rogersville	D2	97
Roi, island	B2	16
Roi Et	C2	12
Rojo, cape	A3	90
Rokel, river	A1	63
Roland	C4	96
Rolling Hills	E6	94
Rollo, bay	C2	100
Rolphton	H1	102
Roma	A2	71
Roma, Qld.	D2	14
Roman	D2	43
Romania		43
Rome, capital	C2	38
Rømø, island	B3	32
Roncador, cay	Inset	78
Roncador, range	C3	81
Ronde, island	B1	91
Rondônia	B3	81
Rongelap, island	B1	16
Rongerik, island	B1	16
Rønne	C3	32
Ronne Ice Shelf, glacier	B11	107
Roodeport	C2	71
Roosevelt, island	B6	107
Roosevelt Campobello Intl. Hist. Park	C4	97
Roper, river	C1	14
Roraima	B1	81
Roraima, mt.	A3	80
Rosa, mt.	A1	38
Rosalie	B3	90
Rosalind	D5	94
Rosario	C2	74
Roscommon	C2	31
Roscrea	C2	31
Rose Belle	C3	69
Rose Blanche	B5	98
Rose Hill	B2	69
Rose Valley	G8	104
Rose, island	B1	18
Roseau, capital	B3	90
Roseau, river	B4	96
Rosebud	D5	94
Rosemary	D6	94

	Key	Page
Rosenfeld	C4	96
Rosenheim	C5	40
Rosenort	C4	96
Rosetown	B9	104
Rosetta, river	B1	56
Roskilde	D3	32
Ross Ice Shelf, glacier	A6	107
Ross River	C4	105
Ross, island	B5	107
Ross, river	C4	105
Ross, sea	B6	107
Rossburn	A4	96
Rosseau, lake	F2	102
Rossel, island	B3	15
Rossendale	B4	96
Rossignol, lake	B3	100
Rossland	O6	95
Rosslare	C2	31
Rosso	B3	58
Rosthern	D8	104
Rostock	C1	40
Rostov-na-Donu	E3	44
Rotherham	C3	30
Rothesay	D3	97
Rotorua	C2	15
Rotterdam	B3	32
Roubaix	C1	34
Rouen	C2	34
Rouleau	F10	104
Round Lake Centre	H2	102
Round, island	D1	69
Round, pond	C5	98
Rounthwaite	A4	96
Rouyn-Noranda	A4	101
Rovaniemi	C1	53
Rovigo	B1	38
Rovno	B1	47
Rovuma, river	C1	68
Rowley	D5	94
Roxas	B4	12
Royal, canal	C2	31
Ruacana, falls	B1	70
Ruahine, range	C2	15
Ruapehu, mt.	C2	15
Rub al-Khali (Empty Quarter), desert	C2	24
Rubtsovsk	D6	44
Ruda ¿l]ka	D3	41
Rudnyy	C1	23
Rufiji, river	C2	68
Rufisque	A2	62
Rügen, island	C1	40
Ruggell	B1	33
Ruhengeri	B1	61
Ruhr, river	B3	40
Ruhwa, river	B2	61
Rukwa, lake	B2	68
Rum, cay	C3	89
Rumbek	B3	59
Runaway Bay	B2	88
Rundu	C1	70
Rungne	Inset	76
Rungwa, river	B2	68
Rupel, river	C1	33
Ruse	D2	50
Russell	A4	96
Russia		44
Rustavi	C4	45
Rutana	B2	61
Rutbah, ar-	B2	24
Rutherglen	F1	102
Rutland	N6	95
Ruvubu, river	C2	61
Ruvuma, river	C1	68
Ruways, ar-	B2, C1	25
Ruwenzori, range	B3	61
Ruyigi	C2	61
Ruzizi, river	A1, A2	61
Ru«omberok	B2	42
Rwanda		61
Rweru, lake	C2	61
Ryazan	D3	44
Rybinsk	D3	41
Ryotsu	E4	41
Rysy, mt.	B2	42
Ryukyu, islands	A4, Inset II	8
Rzeszów	F3	41

S

	Key	Page
's Hertogenbosch	C3	32
Saale, river	B3	40
Saar, river	A4	40
Saarbrücken	A4	40
Saaremaa, island	B2	46
Saarland	A4	40
Sab Abar	A3	27
sabac	A2	50
Sabadell	H2	37
Sabana de la Mar	C1	89
Sabana Grande	B2	90
Sabaneta	A1	89
Sabha	B2	56
Sable cape, Fla.	E3	126
Sable River	B4	100
Sabzevar	D2	22
Sachigo, river	B2	101
Sackville	E3	97
Sacramento, capital, Calif.	A2	126
Sadah	A1	25
Sado, island	C2	8
Sado, river	A3	36
Safata, bay	C3	18
Safed Koh, range	D3	21
Safi	B1	57
Safotu	B1	18
Saga	A3	8
Sagaing	B2	12
Sagami, bay	C3	8
Sagamihara	C3	8
Saginaw, Mich.	E1	126
Sagua la Grande	C2	88
Saguenay, river	F3	103
Sagunto	F3	37
Sahara, desert		55
Saharanpur Panipat	C3	20
≠ahbuz	A3	45

	Key	Page
Sahel, region		55
Sahiwal	D3	21
Sai Kung	Inset	10
Saidpur	B3	21
Saimaa, lake	C2	53
St. Adolphe	C4	96
St. Alban's	A1	98
St. Albans	C3, Inset III	30
St. Albert	D4	94
St.-Alexis-des-Monts	C5	103
St.-Ambroise	E3	103
St. Ambroise	B4	96
St.-André	C2	30
St. Andrews	C2	30
St. Andrews	B3	97
St.-Angèle-de-Mérici	J3	103
St. Ann's Bay	B2	88
St. Anne, island	Inset	70
St. Anthony	D3	98
St.-Antoine	C6	103
St.-Apollinaire	E5	103
St. Augustin	E3	101
St. Augustine	A2	91
St. Augustine, Fla.	E3	126
St. Austell	B4	30
St. Barbe	C3	98
St.-Basile	A1	97
St. Bernard's	D5	98
St. Brendan's	D5	98
St. Bride's	D5	98
Saint-Brieuc	B2	34
St. Brieux	F8	104
St.-Bruno	F8	104
St.-Camille-de-Lellis	F5	103
St. Catharines	E4	102
St. Catherine's	E5	98
St. Catherine, mt.	B2	91
St.-Charles, lake	K5	103
St. Clair, lake	C5	102
St. Clair, river	C5	102
St.-Claude	B4	96
Saint-Cloud	Inset II	34
St. Cloud, Minn.	D1	126
St.-Côme	C5	103
St. Croix	B3	97
St.-Cyprien	H4	103
St.-David-de-Falardeau	E3	103
St. David's	B2	91
St. David's	B2	30
Saint-Denis	Inset II	34
Saint-Dizier	D2	34
St.-Donat	B5	103
St. Edward	A2	100
St. Eleanors	B2	100
St. Elias, mts.	A5	105
Saint-Élie	B1	80
St.-Émile	K5	103
Saint-Étienne	D4	34
St. Eustache	C4	96
St.-Eustache	H5	103
St.-Fabien	H3	103
St.-Fabien-de-Panet	F5	103
St.-Félicien	D3	103
St.-Félix-d'Otis	F6	103
St.-François, lake	E6	103
St.-François, river	D5	103
St.-Gédéon	F6	103
St. George	C3	97
St. George's	B5	98
St. George's, bay	B5	98
St. George's, capital	A2	91
St. George's, channel	B2	15
St. George's, channel	C3	31
St. George, Utah	B2	126
St. Georges, bay	F2	100
St-Georges	F5	103
Saint-Georges	C2	80
St.-Germain	G4	103
Saint-Germain-en-Laye	Inset II	34
St. Gotthard, pass	C2	35
St. Gotthard, tunnel	C2	35
St. Helens	C3	30
St-Henri-de-Taillon	E3	103
St-Hubert	G4	103
St.-Hyacinthe	D6	103
St-Ignace-du-Lac	C5	103
St.-Isidore	D1	97
St.-Jacques	A1	97
St.-Jacques-de-Leeds	E5	103
St-Jean, lake	D3	103
St. Jean Baptiste	C4	96
St-Jean-Chrysostome	L6	103
St-Jean-de-Matha	C5	103
St-Jean-Port-Joli	F4	103
St-Jean-sur-Richelieu	C6	103
St-Jérôme	B6	103
Saint John	C3	97
St. John, river	C3	97
St. John's	E5	98
St. John's, capital	D5	90
Saint Joseph	A3	90
St. Joseph, island	B1	102
St. Joseph, Mo.	D2	126
St-Joseph-de-Beauce	F5	103
St. Kitts (St. Christopher), island	B2	90
St. Kitts and Nevis		90
St. Labre	C4	96
St-Lambert	J5	103
St. Laurent	B4	96
St-Laurent	J5	103
Saint-Laurent du Maroni	A1	80
St. Lawrence	D5	98
St. Lawrence, cape	G1	100
St. Lawrence, gulf	L4	92
St. Lawrence, river	K4	92
St. Lawrence Islands N.P.	J3	102
St.-Lazare	A4	96
St.-Léonard	J5	103
St.-Léonard	B1	97
St. Lewis	D3	98
St. Lewis, river	B2	98
Saint-Lô	B2	34
St. Louis	A2	100
St. Louis	E8	104

	Key	Page
St. Louis, Mo.	D2	126
St-Louis, lake	H6	103
St.-Louis-de-Kent	E2	97
St.-Louis-de-Kent	E2	97
St. Lucia	B1	91
Saint Lucia, channel	B1	91
St.-Ludger	F6	103
St. Ludger-de-Milot	E3	103
St. Malo	C4	96
St.-Malo	E6	103
Saint-Malo	B2	34
Saint-Malo, gulf	B2	34
St.-Marc	C1	89
St-Marc-du-Lac-Long	H4	103
St.-Marcel	F5	103
St.-Marcellin	H3	103
St. Margarets	D2	97
St. Martin	B3	96
St. Martin, lake	B3	96
St. Martins	E5	97
St. Mary's	E5	98
St. Marys	D4	102
St.-Maurice, river	C4	103
St.-Michel	F5	103
St.-Michel-des-Saints	C5	103
St.-Milaire	A1	97
St. Moritz	D2	35
Saint-Nazaire	B3	34
St.-Nicolas	E5	103
St.-Pacôme	F4	103
St.-Pamphile	G5	103
St.-Pascal	F4	103
St. Paul	E4	94
St. Paul, capital, Minn.	D1	126
St. Paul, river	A2	63
St. Paul, river	C3	98
St. Paul's	A1	90
Saint Paul's, bay	B2	36
St. Peters	F5	103
St. Peters	C2	100
St. Peters, bay	C2	100
St. Peters, island	B2	100
St. Petersburg	D3	44
St. Petersburg, Fla.	E3	126
St-Philémon	F5	103
St. Pierre, island	M4	92
St. Pierre-Jolys	C4	96
St.-Quentin	B1	97
St.-Raphaël	F5	103
St.-Rédempteur	K6	103
St-Rémi-d'Amherst	B5	103
St.-Romuald	L6	103
St. Shotts	E5	98
St.-Siméon	G4	103
St. Stephen	B3	97
St. Thomas	D5	102
St-Tite-des-Caps	F4	103
Saint-Tropez	D5	34
St-Vallier	F5	103
Saint Vincent, passage	B4	91
St. Vincent, gulf	Inset II	14
St. Vincent, island	B4	91
St. Vincent and the Grenadines		91
St. Walburg	A7	104
St-Zacharie	F5	103
Ste-Agathe-des-Monts	B5	103
Ste-Amélie	B4	96
Ste-Anne-des-Monts	K2	103
Ste-Anne-du-Lac	A5	103
Ste-Apolline	F5	103
Ste-Claire	F5	103
Ste-Croix	E5	103
Ste-Eulalie	D5	103
Ste-Foy	E5, K6	103
Ste-Luce	H3	103
Ste-Marie	E5	103
Ste-Monique	E3	103
Ste-Rose-du-Nord	F3	103
Ste-Thérèse	H5	103
Ste-Véronique	A5	103
Ste. Agathe	C4	96
Ste. Anne	C4	96
Ste. Rose du Lac	B3	96
Ste.-Anne-de-Madawaska	A1	97
Saintes	B4	34
Sajama, mt.	A3	77
Sak, river	B3	71
Sakai	B3	8
Sakarya, river	B2	45
Sakha (Yakutiya), republic	C8	44
Sakhalin, island	I4	44
≠aki	B2	45
Sakishima, islands	Inset II	8
Sakon Nakhon	C2	12
Sal Rei	D2	58
Sal, island	D2	58
Sala'ilua	A2	18
Salaberry-de-Valleyfield	B6	103
Salacgriva	C2	46
Salado, river	B3, C2	76
Salaga	B2	64
Salahiyah	A2	27
Salalah	B3	25
Salamá	C4	85
Salamanca	D2	37
Salamís, island	Inset	51
Salar de Uyuni, salt flat	A4	77
Salaverry	B2	77
Salcedo	B1	89
Saldanha	A3	71
Saldus	B2	46
Salé	C1	57
Salekhard	C5	44
Salelologa	B2	18
Salem	C6	20
Salem, capital, Oreg.	A1	126
Salerno	C2	38
Salerno, gulf	C2	38
Salford	C3	30
Salgótarján	B1	43
Salibia	C3	47
Salihorsk	C3	47
Salima	C3	68
Salina Cruz	E4	84
Salina, Kans.	D2	126
Salinas	C3	90
Salines, point	A2	91
Salisbury	A2	90
Salisbury	C3	30

Name	Key	Page
Salisbury, island	N4	99
Salluit	A1	101
Sallum, as-	A1	56
Sally's Cove	C4	98
Salmon Arm	N6	95
Salmon, Idaho	B1	126
Salmon River	A3	100
Salmon, river	L4	95
Salo	B2	53
Salonta	A2	43
Saloum, river	B2	62
Salsette, island	Inset I	20
Salt Lake City, capital, Utah	B1	126
Salt Water, lake	Inset II	20
Salt, as-	A1	26
Salt, cay	D4	89
Salta	B1	74
Saltcoats	H9	104
Saltery Bay	K6	95
Saltillo, state capital	D2	84
Salto	B1	75
Salto del Guairá	E4	75
Salut, islands	B1	80
Salvador	E3	81
Salvage	E5	98
Salween, river	C2	10
Salyan	C3	45
Salzach, river	C3	39
Salzburg	C3	39
Salzburg Alps, range	C3	39
Salzgitter	B2	40
Samaná	C1	89
Samaná, bay	C1	89
Samaná, cape	C1	89
Samana, cay	C1	89
Samangan	B1	22
Samar, island	C4	12
Samar, sea	C3	12
Samara	D4	44
Samarian, hills	B1	26
Samarinda	C2	13
Samarqand	C3	23
Samarra	B2	24
Samawah, as-	C2	24
Sambalpur	D4	20
Sambre, river	C2	33
Samch'ŏk	C4	9
Samina, river	B3	33
Samoa		18
Samokov	B3	50
Sámos, island	C3	51
Samothráki, island	C1	51
Samsø, island	C3	32
Samsø, strait	C3	32
Samsonvale, lake	Inset III	14
Samsun	D2	27
Samtredia	B3	45
Samur, river	B2	45
San	C3	58
San Andrés, island	Inset	78
San Angelo, Tex.	C2	126
San Antonio	B4, Inset	76
San Antonio	A3	85
San Antonio	C2	90
San Antonio Oeste	B5	74
San Antonio, cape	D4	74
San Antonio, cape	A2	88
San Antonio, Tex.	D3	126
San Baudilio de Llobregat	G2	37
San Bernardino, Calif.	B2	126
San Bernardo	Inset	76
San Blas, mts.	C2	87
San Borja	A2	77
San Carlos	B4	12
San Carlos	C3	75
San Carlos	B3	87
San Carlos de Bariloche	A5	74
San Carlos, river	B2	86
San Clara	A3	96
San Cristóbal	B2	77
San Cristóbal	B2	79
San Cristóbal	B2	89
San Cristóbal de las Casas	F4	84
San Cristóbal, island	B2	16
San Cristóbal, island	Inset	79
San Diego, Calif.	B2	126
San Felipe	D4	78
San Felipe	B1	84
San Félix	B3	76
San Fernando	B2	12
San Fernando	C4	37
San Fernando	B4	76
San Fernando	A2	91
San Fernando de Apure	C2	79
San Francique	A2	91
San Francisco	C3	74
San Francisco	B2	86
San Francisco de Macorís	B1	89
San Francisco, Calif.	A2	126
San Germán	A2	90
San Gimignano	B2	38
San Ignacio	B3	77
San Ignacio	A2	85
San Isidro	D2	90
San Jorge, gulf	B6	74
San José	B3	75
San José	C6	85
San José de Chiquitos	B3	77
San José de las Matas	A1	89
San José del Guaviare	B4	78
San Jose, Calif.	A2	126
San José, capital	B3	86
San José, river	B2	75
San Juan	B3	74
San Juan	B4	77
San Juan	A2	89
San Juan, capital	C2	90
San Juan, passage	D2	90
San Juan Bautista	D5	75
San Juan de Los Morros	C2	79
San Juan del Norte	C3	87
San Juan del Norte, bay	C3	87
San Juan del Sur	A3	87
San Juan, river	A3	78
San Lorenzo	D4	75
San Lorenzo	B2	79
San Lorenzo	B3	86
San Lorenzo	D2	90
San Lorenzo, cape	A3	79
San Lucas	C3	84
San Lucas, cape	B3	84
San Luis	B3	74
San Luis	D3	85
San Luis Potosí, state capital	D3	84
San Luis Río Colorado	B1	84
San Luis, lake	B2	77
San Marino		39
San Marino, capital	B1	39
San Marino, river	A1	39
San Martín, lake	A6	74
San Matías	A3	77
San Matías, gulf	C5	74
San Miguel	B2	86
San Miguel de Tucumán	B2	74
San Miguelito	C2	87
San Nicolás	C3	74
San Pablo	B3	12
San Pablo, river	B3	77
San Pawl il-Bahar	B2	36
San Pedro	D4	75
San Pédro	C4	63
San Pedro de Atacama	B2	76
San Pedro de las Colonias	D2	84
San Pedro de Macorís	C2	89
San Pedro Sula	A2	86
San Pedro, river	C2	85
San Pietro, island	B3	38
San Rafael	B2	74
San Remo	A2	38
San Salvador de Jujuy	B1	74
San Salvador, capital	A2	86
San Salvador, island	Inset	79
San Salvador, island	C3	89
San Salvador, river	A2	75
San Sebastián	F1	37
San Sebastián	B2	90
San Severo	C2	38
San Valentín, mt.	B8	76
San Vicente	B2	86
San Vito, cape	C3	38
San, river	E2	11
San, river	F3	41
Sanaa, capital	A1	25
Sanaga, river	B2	65
Sanandaj	B2	22
Sanaw	C1	25
Sancti Spíritus	C2	88
Sand, river	C3	94
Sandakan	D2	13
Sanday, island	Inset I	30
Sandilands	C4	96
Sandougou, river	B3	62
Sandoy, island	Inset	32
Sandspit	C4	95
Sandur	Inset	32
Sandwich, bay	C2	98
Sandy Bay	H5	104
Sandy Cove	A3	100
Sandy Lake	D3	94
Sandy Lake	A4	96
Sandy Lake	B2	101
Sandy Point	B2	89
Sandy Point Town	A1	90
Sandy Tash	D2	18
Sandy, island	A2	91
Sandy, lake	C4	98
Sanford	C4	96
Sangha, river	D2	66
Sangmélima	B3	65
Sangre Grande	A2	91
Sangro, river	C2	38
Sangudo	C4	94
Sankosh, river	C2	19
Sankrail	Inset II	20
Sankt Gallen	D1	35
Sankt Pölten	D2	39
Sankuru, river	B2	67
Sannar	B3	12
Sanski Most	A1	48
Sant Julià de Lòria	A3	36
Sant'Antioco, island	B3	38
Santa Ana	A2	86
Santa Ana, range	C1	75
Santa Ana, volcano	A2	86
Santa Bárbara	A2	86
Santa Barbara, Calif.	B2	126
Santa Catarina	C2	81
Santa Clara	C2	88
Santa Coloma de Gramanet	H2	37
Santa Cruz	B3	77
Santa Cruz	A2	91
Santa Cruz de Tenerife	Inset I	37
Santa Cruz, island	Inset	79
Santa Cruz, islands	C2	16
Santa Cruz, river	A7	74
Santa Elena de Uairen	D3	79
Santa Elena, point	A4	79
Santa Fe	C2	74
Santa Fe, N. Mex.	C2	126
Santa Inés	Inset	76
Santa Inés, island	B9	76
Santa Isabel	C3	90
Santa Isabel, island	A1	16
Santa Isabel, peak	A1	66
Santa Lucía, river	B3	75
Santa Luzia, island	B2	58
Santa Maria	D2	58
Santa Maria	C4	81
Santa Maria di Leuca, cape	D3	38
Santa María, island	B2	18
Santa María, island	Inset	79
Santa Marta	B2	78
Santa Rita	B2	86
Santa Rosa	C4	74
Santa Rosa	B4	79
Santa Rosa de Copán	A2	86
Santa Rosa del Palmar	B3	77
Santa Rosalía	B2	84
Santana do Livramento	B3	81
Santander	E1	37
Santarém	A3	36
Santarém	C2	81
Santiago	B2	87
Santiago	B1	89
Santiago de Compostela	B1	37
Santiago de Cuba	E3	88
Santiago del Estero	C2	74
Santiago, capital	B4, Inset	76
Santiago, river	B1	77
Santo André	Inset II	81
Santo Antão, island	A1	58
Santo Domingo	B2	90
Santo Domingo de los Colorados	B3	79
Santo Domingo, capital	C2	89
Santo Tomás de Castilla	E4	85
Santos	D4, Inset II	81
São Bernardo do Campo	Inset II	81
São Caetano do Sul	Inset II	81
São Domingos	A1	62
São Filipe	B4	58
São Francisco, river	D3	81
São Gonçalo	Inset I	81
São João de Meriti	Inset I	81
São José do Rio Prêto	D4	81
São Luís	D2	81
São Nicolau, island	B2	58
São Paulo	D4, Inset II	81
São Tiago, island	C3	58
São Tomé, capital	B4	63
São Tomé, island	B4	63
São Tomé and Príncipe		63
São Tomé, cape	A4	90
São Vicente, island	A2	58
São Vicente	Inset II	81
Saona, island	D2	89
Sapele	C5	65
Sapitwa, mt.	B2	68
Sapporo	Inset I	8
Sar, passage	B3	12
Sar-e Pol	B1	22
Sara Buri	B3	12
Sarajevo, capital	B2	48
Saramacca, river	B2	80
Sarandë	A4	49
Saransk	D4	44
Sarasota, Fla.	E3	126
Saratov	D4	44
Saravan	D4	11
Sarawak, state	C2	13
Saraya	D3	62
Sarbhang	B3	19
Sarcelles	Inset II	34
Sarda, river	A2	19
Sardinia, island	B2	38
Sargodha	D3	21
Sarh	B5	59
Sari	C2	22
Sariwŏn	A3	9
Sarjektjakko	C1	53
Sark, island	Inset II	30
Sarnia	C5	102
Saronic, gulf	Inset	51
Šar Planina, mts.	B3	49
Sarstoon, river	A4	85
Sarstún, river	D4	85
Sartène	C3	23
Sary Tash	C3	23
Sarygamysh Koli, lake	B2	22
Saryshaghan	D2	23
Sasamungga	A1	16
Sasaram	D4	20
Sasebo	A3	8
Saskatchewan, river	G3	92
Saskatoon	D8	104
Sassandra	A4	63
Sassandra, river	C2, C4	63
Sassari	B2	38
Sassnitz	C1	40
Sata, cape	A4	8
Satpura, range	C4	20
Satsuma, peninsula	A4	8
Sattahip	B3	12
Satu Mare	B2	43
Sauble Beach	D3	102
Saudhárkrókur	B2	52
Saudi Arabia		24
Saül	B2	80
Sault Ste. Marie	A1	102
Sault Ste. Marie, Mich.	E1	126
Sault-au-Mouton	G3	103
Saumur	B3	34
Saurimo	D3	70
Sauteurs	B2	91
Sava, river	B1, B2, C2	48
Savai'i, island	A2	18
Savalou	A3	64
Savan, island	B3	91
Savannah, Ga.	E2	126
Savannakhet	C3	11
Savé	B4	64
Savigny-sur-Orge	Inset II	34
Savinja, river	B2	48
Savona	B1	38
Savona	M6	95
Savonlinna	C2	53
Savu, sea	D2	13
Savu, mts.	B2	24
Sawhaj	B2	56
Sawqirah	C2	25
Sawqirah, bay	C2	25
Saxony	C3	40
Saxony-Anhalt	B3	40
Sayabec	J3	103
Sayan, mts.	D6	44
Sayhut	C1	25
Sayward	K6	95
Saywun	B1	25
Sázava, river	B3	42
Scafell Pike, mt.	B2	30
Scarborough	C2	30
Scarborough	B1	91
Scarborough	D4	102
Scarborough	F4, L5	102
Schaan	B2	33
Schaerbeek	Inset	33
Schaffhausen	C1	35
Schefferville	D3	98
Schefferville	C3	101
Schelde, river	B2	33
Schellenberg	B1	33
Scheveningen	B2	32
Schiedam	B3	32
Schiermonnikoog, island	D1	32
Schleswig	B1	40
Schleswig-Holstein	B2	40
Schouwen, island	A3	32
Schreiber	C3	101
Schuler	E6	94
Schwäbisch Gmünd	B4	40
Schwedt	C2	40
Schweinfurt	B3	40
Schwerin	B2	40
Schweriner, lake	B2	40
Schwyz	C1	35
Scilly, islands	A4	30
Scone	B2	30
Sconser	A1	30
Scotstown	E6	103
Scotswood	A3	94
Scott, island	C5	107
Scottsbluff, Nebr.	C1	126
Scugog, lake	G3	102
Scunthorpe	C3	30
Scutari, lake	A1, A3	49
Sczcecinek	C2	41
Seaforth	D4	102
Seal Cove	C4	98
Seal, river	D1	96
Searchmont	A1	102
Seattle, Wash.	A1	126
Seawell	C4	91
Sebright	F3	102
Sebou, river	C1	57
Sechura, desert	A2	77
Seda, river	B3	36
Sedalia	E5	94
Sédhiou	B3	62
Sedley	F10	104
Seeley's Bay	J3	102
Sefadu	B1	63
Segbana	B2	64
Ségou	B3	58
Segovia	D2	37
Séguéla	C3	63
Segura, river	E3	37
Seinäjoki	B2	53
Seine, river	C2, Inset II	34
Sekake	B2	71
Sekondi-Takoradi	B4	64
Selebi-Phikwe	C2	69
Selenge Mörön, river	C2	11
Sélibaby	B4	58
Sélinia	Inset	51
Selkirk	C4	96
Selvas, region	B2	81
Selwyn, mts.	C4	105
Seman, river	A3	49
Semara	B1	58
Semarang	C2	13
Sembawang	B1	13
Sembé	C3	66
Semeru, mt.	C2	13
Semey (Semipalatinsk)	E1	23
Semmering, pass	D3	39
Semois, river	D3	33
Sempach	C1	35
Sen, river	D2	11
Senaki	B3	45
Sendai	D2	8
Senegal		62
Senegal, river	B1, C2	62
Senkaku, islands	Inset II	8
Senmonorom	F3	11
Senne, river	C2	33
Senneterre	A4	101
Senta	B2	49
Seoul, capital	B4	9
Sepik, river	A2	15
Sept-Iles	C3	101
Septentrional, range	A1	89
Serangoon	B1	13
Serbia, republic	B2	49
Seremban	A2	13
Serenje	C2	67
Sergipe	E3	81
Seria	A2	13
Serov	D5	44
Serowe	B2	69
Serpent, island	D1	69
Sérrai	B1	51
Serranilla, bank	Inset	88
Serravalle	B1	39
Serrekunda	C2	62
Serule	B2	69
Sese, islands	C4	61
Seseke	A3	67
Seti, river	A2	19
Sétif	B1	57
Settat	C1	57
Setúbal	A3	36
Setúbal, bay	A3	36
Sevan, lake	C2	45
Sevastopol	C4	47
Seven Persons	E6	94
Seven Sisters Falls	C4	96
Severn, river	C3	30
Severn, river	B2	101
Severnaya Zemlya, islands	A6	49
Seville	D4	37
Sevran	Inset II	34
Sèvres	Inset II	34
Sewa, river	B2	63
Seward, Alaska	Inset I	126
Seychelles		70
Sfax	C2	57
Sfîntu Gheorghe	D3	43
Sha Tin	Inset	10
Shaanxi	D2	10
Shabwah	B1	25
Shache	A2	10
Shackleton Ice Shelf, glacier	C2	107
Shahr-e Kord	C3	22
Shaki	B3	65
Shalqar	B2	23
Sham, ash-	D1	25
Shamattawa	E2	96
Shamgong	B2	19
Shan, plateau	C2	12
Shanchung	B1	9
Shandong	E2	10
Shangani, river	A2	69
Shanghai	F2	10
Shannon	B2	31
Shannon, river	B2	31
Shantou	E3	10
Shanxi	E2	10
Shanxi	F3	10
Shaoguan	E3	10
Shaoxing	F3	10
Shaoyang	E3	10
Sharbot Lake	J3	102
Sharjah	C2	25
Shashe, river	C2	69
Shashi	E2	10
Shatt al-Arab, river	C2	24
Shaunavon	B11	104
Shawinigan	D5	103
Sheberghan	B1	22
Shediac	E2	97
Sheerness	E5	94
Sheet Harbour	E3	100
Sheffield	C3	30
Sheguianda	D2	102
Sheho	G9	104
Shek Pik	Inset	10
Shelburne	B4	100
Shelburne	E3	102
Shelikhov, gulf	C9	44
Shell Lake	C7	104
Shellbrook	D7	104
Shelter Bay	N6	95
Shëngjin	A2	49
Shenyang	F1	10
Sherbro, island	A2	63
Sherbrooke	E2	100
Sherbrooke	E6	103
Sheridan, Wyo.	C1	126
Sherridon	A1	96
Sherwood Park	D4	94
Shetland, islands	Inset I	30
Sheva	Inset I	20
Shewa Gimira	B3	60
Shibar, pass	B2	22
Shibin al-Kawm	B1	56
Shijiazhuang	E2	10
Shikarpur	C4	21
Shikoku, island	B3	8
Shillong	F3	20
Shimizu	C3	8
Shimonoseki	A3	8
Shimonoseki, strait	A3	8
Shinano, river	C2	8
Shinas	C1	25
Shindand	A2	22
Shinyanga	B1	68
Shiono, cape	B3	8
Ship Cove	D3	98
Shippagan	E1	97
Shirane, mt.	C3	8
Shiraz	C4	22
Shire, river	B3	68
Shiretoko, cape	Inset I	8
Shizuoka	C3	8
Shkhara, mt.	B3	45
Shkodër	A1	49
Shkumbin, river	A2	49
Shoal Lake	A4	96
Sholapur	C5	20
Shostka	C1	47
Shreveport, La.	D2	126
Shrewsbury	C3	30
Shrirampur	Inset II	20
Shubenacadie	D2	100
Shubra al-Khaymah	B1	56
Shumen	E2	50
Shurugwi	B2	69
Shwebo	B2	12
Shymkent (Chimkent)	C2	23
Siahan, range	B4	21
Sialkot	E3	21
Siargao, island	C4	12
şiauliai	B2	46
Sibbald	E5	94
Siberia, region	C7	44
Siberut, island	A2	13
Sibiti	B5	66
Sibiu	C3	43
Sibu	C2	13
Sibuyan, island	B3	12
Sibuyan, sea	B3	12
Sicamous	N6	95
Sichuan	D2	10
Sicily, island	C3	38
Sicily, strait	B3	38
Sico, river	C2	86
Sicuani	C3	77
Sidi bel Abbès	A1	57
Sidi Bou Zid	B2	57
Sidlaw, hills	C2	30
Sidney	L7	95
Sidney	B4	96
Sidon (Sayda)	A2	26
Sidra, gulf	C1	56
Sidvokodvo	B2	71
Siedlce	F2	41
Siegen	B3	40
Siempang	E1	11
Siemreab	B2	11
Siena	B2	38
Sieradz	D3	41
Sierra de Cayey, mts.	C2	90
Sierra de Loquillo, mts.	D2	90
Sierra Leone		63
Sierra Madre, mts.	B2	12
Sierra Madre, mts.	C5	85
Sierra Nevada de Santa Marta, mts.	B2	78
Sierra Nevada, mts., Calif.	A2	126
Sifton	A3	96
Siggiewi	B2	36
Sighetul Marmaœiei	B2	43
Sighişoara	C2	43
Siglufjördhur	B1	52
Siguatepeque	B2	86
Siguiri	D2	62
Siirt	E3	27
Sikanni Chief	L2	95
Sikasso	B3	58
Sikhote Alin, range	E8	
Sikkim (state)	B2	
ﬁlal>	B2	
Silay	C3	
Silesia, region	B2	
Silet	C3	
Silgarhi	B2	
Silhouette, island	C3	
Siliana	C1	
Silifke	B2	
Silisili, mt.	B1	
Silistra	F1	
Silkeborg	B2	
Sillery	K6	
ﬁlut>	A2	
Silvassa	B4	
Silver	C4	
Silver City, N. Mex.	C2	
Sima	B2	
Simcoe, lake	E4	
Simeulue, island	A2	
Simferopol	C4	
Simikot	A3	
Simla	C2	
Simon, lake	A6	
Simonette, river	A4	
Simonhouse	A3	
Simpson, desert	C2	
Sinai, peninsula	B2	
Sinaloa	C3	
Sincelejo	B2	
Sinclair	A4	
Sinclair Mills	M4	
Sindhuli Garhi	C2	
Siné, river	A3	
Sines	A4	
Singapore	B1	
Singapore, capital	B1	
Singapore, strait	B2	
Singen	B5	
Singida	B1	
Singur	Inset II	
Sinop	C2	
Sinp'o	C2	
Sint-Niklaas	C1	
Sint-Truiden	D2	
Sin»iju	B2	
Sió, river	B2	
Siófok	B2	
Sion	B2	
Sioux City, Iowa	D1	
Sioux Falls, S. Dak.	D1	
Sioux Lookout	C1	
Sipaliwini	B2	
Siparia	F1	
Siping	B2	
Sipiwesk, lake	C3	
Siple, island	B8	
Siple, mt.	B8	
Siquia, river	C4	
Sirajganj	C4	
Sirba, river	D2	
Siret	D2	
Siret, river	D4	
Sirjan	D4	
Sisaket	C3	
Sisian	D3	
Sisimiut (Holsteinsborg)	B2	
Sisophon	B2	
Siteki	B2	
Sitka, Alaska	Inset I	
Sittang, river	C4	
Sittard	C4	
Sittwe	B2	
Siuna	B2	
Sivas	A2	
Siwah	A2	
Sixaola, river	C3	
Sjælland, island	C3	
Skagen	C1	
Skagerrak, strait	A3	
Skaw, cape	C1	
Skead	E1	
Skeena, mts.	H3	
Skeena, river	H4	
Skeleton, coast	A1	
Skellefteå	C1	
Skelleftealven, river	C1	
Skien	B3	
Skierniewice	E3	
Skikda	B1	
Skíros, island	C2	
Skive	B2	
Skjern, river	B3	
Skookumchuck	B3	
Skopje, capital	B2	
Skovorodino	B3	
Skownan	B3	
Skye, island	A1	
Slagelse	C3	
Slaná, river	C3	
Slatina	C3	
Slave Lake	C3	
Slave, river	F2	
Slavonia, region	C2	
Slavonska Po≈ega	C2	
Slavonski Brod	D2	
Sliema	B2	
Slieve Donard, mt.	B2	
Sligo	B2	
Sliven	E3	
Slobozia	D3	
Slough	Inset III	
Slovakia		
Slovenia		
Slovenskérudohorie, mts.	B2	
Sluch', river	B2	
S{upsk	B1	
Småland, region	B3	
Smallwood, reservoir	D3	
Smeaton	D8	
Smederevo	B2	
Smilovichi	D3	
Smiltene	C2	
Smith River	J1	
Smithers	J4	
Smithers Landing	J4	
Smiths Cove	B3	

	Key Page
ths Falls	J3 102
thville	F4 102
oky, river	A3, A4 94
olensk	D3 44
olevichi	D2 47
olyan	C4 50
oothstone, lake	D6 104
oothstone, river	D6 104
ke, river	C3 105
ke, river	B1 126
ring	A4 94
ek	C1 32
ka, mt.	E2 41
ardwy, lake	A2 96
w Lake	A2 96
wdon, mt.	B3 30
wdrift	F4 99
wflake	B4 96
g Harbour	D3 98
ol	E3 11
n-kundo, islands	B5 9
ar, mts.	C3 59
at, river	C3 59
radinho, reservoir	D3 81
ral	D2 81
Trang	A5 11
hi	E3 44
orro, N. Mex.	C2 126
otra, island	C2 25
lerhamn	C2 53
a, capital	B3 50
a, river	B2 69
nafjord, fjord	B3 52
ssons	C2 34
sln, bay	A3 9
ch'o	C3 9
odé	B2 64
ol	C1 65
oto, plains	C1 65
oto, river	C1 65
coast	D4 37
	B1 18
deu	B2 36
ngen	A2 40
omon Is.	16
omon, sea	B2 15
osolo	C2 18
way, estuary	B2 30
wezi	B2 67
nalia	60
be, beach	E2 90
nbor	A2 49
nbra	C5 102
et, river	A4 96
nerset, island	K2 99
nΣ, me, river	C2 34
oto	A2 87
La	A2 11
, river	D4 20
arpur	Inset II 20
derborg	B4 32
drio	B1 38
ga	C3 68
ghua, river	F1 10
gkhla	B5 12
gkol	D2 23
gnam	B4 9
gnim	A3 9
gwe, river	B1 68
ora	B1 84
sonate	A2 86
soral, island	Inset 17
ke	L7 95
eron	A2 43
river	B3 36
el	C5 103
	E2 37
	C3 32
oca	B1 50
ocaba	D4 81
ong	E2 13
oti	C3 61
raia, river	A3 36
rento	C2 38
nowiec	D3 41
o, bay	B3 17
a, river	B2 64
	C2 45
ouboua	B2 64
	C4 63
frière	B4 90
frière	A2 91
frière	B1 91
frière, volcano	A2 91
llac	C2 69
ngrougrou, river	B3 62
rces, mt.	B1 71
ris	A4 96
ris	C2 100
ris, river	G11 104
s, plain	B2 57
s, river	B2 57
súa	B1 89
th Africa	71
th Andaman, island	F6 20
ulatsivik, island	E3 98
th Australia	C2 14
th Baymouth	C2 102
th Bend, Ind.	E1 126
th Branch	B5 98
th Brook	C4 98
th Carolina	E2 126
th China, sea	E4, Inset 10
th Comino, channel	B2 36
th Dakota	C3 126
th Downs, hills	C3 30
th Dum-Dum	Inset II 20
th Georgia, island	4
Gut St.-Anns	G1 100
th Henik, lake	J4 99
ndian Lake	D1 96
th Korea	9
th Magnetic Pole	C3 107
th Male, atoll	A3 19
th Malosmadulu, atoll	A2 19
th Milford	B3 100

	Key Page
S. Moose, lake	B2 96
South Orkney, islands	C12 107
South Ossetia, region	B3 45
South Pole	A17 107
South Rawdon	D3 100
South River	F2 102
South Ronaldsay, island	Inset I 30
South Saskatchewan, river	D8 104
South Shetland, islands	C12 107
South Shields	C2 30
South Taranaki, bight	B2 15
South Uist, island	A1 30
South West, cape	A4 15
South, island	A3 15
Southampton	C4 30
Southampton	D3 102
Southampton, island	L4 99
Southend	G4 104
Southend-on-Sea	D3 30
Southern Alps, mts.	A3 15
Southern Bug, river	B2 47
Southern Uplands, mts.	B2 30
Southport	C3 30
Southport	B2 100
Sovetskaya Gavan	E9 44
Soweto	C2 71
Soya, point	Inset I 8
Soyapango	A2 86
Soyo	B2 70
Sozh, river	E3 47
Spa	D2 33
Spain	37
Sousse	C2 40
Spandau	C1 102
Spanish	C1 102
Spanish Town	C3 88
Sparta	B3 51
Spartanburg, S.C.	E2 126
Spartivento, cape	D3 38
Sparwood	P6 95
Speightstown	A2 91
Spence Bay	K3 99
Spencer, gulf	C3 14
Spences Bridge	M6 95
Sperrin, mts.	A2 30
Spessart, mts.	B4 40
Spey, river	B1 30
Speyer	B4 40
Spiritwood	C7 104
Spi%ská Nová Ves	C2 42
Spithead, channel	C4 30
Split	C3 48
Split Lake	D1 96
Splügen, pass	D2 35
Spokane, Wash.	B1 126
Spoleto	C2 38
Spragge	C1 102
Sprague	D4 96
Spree, river	C3 40
Spring Bay	C2 102
Spring Coulee	D6 94
Spring Hall	A2 91
Springbok	A2 71
Springdale	C4 98
Springfield, capital, Ill.	E2 126
Springfield, Mass.	F1 126
Springfield, Mo.	D2 126
Springhill	C2 100
Springs	C2 71
Springside	H9 104
Springstein	C4 96
Springwater	B9 104
Spruce Grove	D4 94
Spy Hill	J10 104
Squamish	L6 95
Square Islands	D3 98
Sre Ambel	B4 11
Srebrenica	C1 48
Sredna Gora, mts.	C3 50
Sremska Mitrovica	A2 49
Sreng, river	B2 11
Sri Jayawardenepura, capital	A5 19
Sri Lanka	19
Srinagar	Inset I 20
Stafford	C3 30
Stand Off	D6 94
Standard	D5 94
Stanley	C2 97
Stanmore	E5 94
Stanovoy, range	D8 44
Star City	F8 104
Stara Zagora	D3 50
Starbuck	C4 96
Starbuck, island	D2 17
Starnberg, lake	B5 40
Start, point	B4 30
Staubbach, falls	C2 35
Stavanger	B4 52
Stavropol	E4 44
Stayner	E3 102
Stead	C4 96
Steen River	B1 94
Stefanson, island	G2 99
Steinbach	C4 96
Steinkjer	C3 52
Stellarton	E2 100
Stellenbosch	A3 71
Stendal	B2 40
Stepanavan	B2 45
Stephenville	B5 98
Stettler	D5 94
Stevenage	Inset III 30
Stevenson, lake	C2 96
Stewart	H3 95
Stewart River	B4 105
Stewart, island	A4 15
Stewart, river	B4, C3 105
Stewiacke	D2 100
Steyr	D2 39
Stikine	G3 95
Stikine, river	G2 95
Stirling	B2 30
Stirling	H3 102
Stockerau	E2 39
Stockholm, capital	C3 53
Stoeng Treng	D2 11
Stoke-on-Trent	C3 30

	Key Page
Stonecliffe	H1 102
Stoneham	E4 103
Stonewall	C4 96
Stoney Point	C5 102
Stony Mountain	C4 96
Stony Plain	D4 94
Stony Rapids	E1 104
Storå, river	B2 32
Storavan, lake	C1 53
Store, strait	C3 32
Storkerson, peninsula	G2 99
Stornoway	A1 30
Stornoway	E6 103
Storsjön, lake	B2 53
Storthoaks	A4 96
Stoughton	G11 104
Strakonice	A3 42
Stralsund	C1 40
Strangford	B2 30
Stranraer	B2 30
Strasbourg	D2 34
Strasbourg	F9 104
Stratford	D4 102
Stratford	E6 103
Stratford-upon-Avon	C3 30
Strathclair	A4 96
Strathlorne	F1 100
Strathnaver	L4 95
Strathroy	D5 102
Straubing	C4 40
Streymoy, island	Inset 32
Stromboli, island	C3 38
Stronsay, island	Inset I 30
Struga	A2 48
Struma, river	A3 50
Strumica	C2 48
Stryama, river	C3 50
Stuart, lake	K4 95
Stubbs	B2 91
Stuie	J5 95
Sturgeon	C2 100
Sturgeon Falls	D3 101
Sturgis	H9 104
Stuttgart	B4 40
Subotica	A1 49
Suceava	D2 43
Suchiate, river	A5 85
Sucre, capital	A3 77
Sudan	59
Sudbury	E1 102
Sudd, region	B3 59
Suddie	B2 80
Sudirman, range	E2 13
Su...uroy, island	Inset 32
Sue, river	B3 59
Suez	B2 56
Suez, canal	B1 56
Suez, gulf	B2 56
Sugandha	Inset II 20
Suhar	C1 25
Sühbaatar	C2 11
Suhl	B3 40
Suir, river	C2 31
Suita	B3 8
Sukabumi	B2 13
Sukang	B3 13
Sukhnah, as-	B2 27
Sukhothai	B2 12
Sukhumi	A3 45
Sukkur	C4 21
Sula, islands	D2 13
Sulaiman, range	C4 21
Sulaybikhat, as-	B2 24
Sulaymaniyah, as-	C1 24
Sulayyil, as-	B2 24
Sulima	B2 63
Sullana	A1 77
Sullivan, lake	E5 94
Sulu, archipelago	B5 12
Sulu, sea	A4 12
Sülüktü	A3 23
Sumatra, island	B2 13
umava, mts.	A3 42
Sumba, island	D2 13
Sumbar, river	B2 22
Sumbawa, island	C2 13
Sumbawanga	B2 68
Summerford	D4 98
Summerland	N6 95
Summerside	B2 100
Summerville	E5 98
Summit Lake	K2 95
Summit Lake	L4 95
umperk	C3 42
Sumqayit	C2 45
Sumy	C1 47
Sun City	C2 71
Sun Kosi, river	C2 19
Sunch'!n	B5 9
Sundarbans, region	C7 21
Sunderland	C2 30
Sunderland	F3 102
Sundi	C1 63
Sundown	C4 96
Sundridge	F2 102
Sundsvall	C2 53
Sunnynook	E5 94
Sunset House	B3 94
Sunyani	A3 64
Sup'ung, reservoir	A2 9
Superior, lake	J4 92
Superior, Wis.	D1 126
Sur	C1 25
Sur (Tyre)	A2 26
Surab	A3 21
Surabaya	C2 13
Surakarta	C2 13
Surat	B4 20
Surat Thani	B4 20
Süre, river	A2, B2 33
Surgut	C5 44
Surigao	C4 12
Surin	C3 12
Suriname	80
Surinam, river	B3 80
Surkhob, river	B1 23
Surma, river	E3 21

	Key Page
Surprise	F1 95
Surt	C1 56
Surtsey, island	A3 52
Surud Ad, mt.	B1 60
Sussex	D3 97
Susuman	C9 44
Sutlej, river	D4 21
Sutton West	F3 102
Suva, capital	B3 17
Suvadiva, atoll	A4 19
Suwa{ki	F1 41
Suwannee, river	B2 27
Suwanose, island	A4 8
Suwar, as-	B2 27
Suwayda, as-	A3 27
Suwln	9
Suzano	Inset II 81
Suzhou	F2 10
Svalbard, islands	C1 46
Svay Rieng	D4 11
Svendborg	C3 32
›ventoji, river	C2 46
Svetozarevo	B3 49
Svilengrad	E4 50
Svishtov	D2 50
Svitavy	C3 42
Svobodnyy	D8 44
Swabian Jura, mts.	B4 40
Swains, island	A1 18
Swakopmund	B2 70
Swan Hills	C4 94
Swan Lake	B4 96
Swan River	A3 96
Swan, lake	A3 96
Swan, river	A4 14
Swan, river	Inset I 14
Swansea	B3 30
Swaziland	71
Sweden	53
Swift Current	D5 98
Swift Current	C10 104
Swindon	C3 30
Świnoujście	B2 41
Switzerland	35
Swords	C2 31
Sydney	G1 100
Sydney, island	B2 17
Sydney, N.S.W., capital	E3, Inset IV 14
Syktyvkar	C4 44
Sylhet	E4 21
Syracuse (Siracusa)	C3 38
Syracuse, N.Y.	F1 126
Syrdarya, river	A1, C2 23
Syria	27
Syrian, desert	B1 26
Szczecin	B2 41
Szeged	C2 43
Székesfehérvár	B2 43
Szekszárd	B2 43
Szentes	C2 43
Szolnok	C2 43
Szombathely	A2 43

T

	Key Page
Taabo, lake	D3 63
Tabar, islands	B2 15
Tabasará, mts.	B2 87
Tabasco	F4 84
Tabelbala	A2 57
Taber	D6 94
Tablas, island	B3 12
Tabligbo	B3 64
Taboão da Serra	Inset II 81
Tábor	B3 42
Tabora	B2 68
Tabou	C4 63
Tabriz	B2 22
Tabuaeran, island	D1 17
Tabuk	A1 24
Tabusintac	D1 97
Tabwemasana, mt.	B2 18
Tacaná, volcano	A4 85
Tacloban	C4 12
Tacna	C4 77
Tacoma, Wash.	A1 126
Tacuarembó	C1 75
Tacuarembó, river	C1 75
Tacuarí, river	D2 75
Tadjoura	B2 60
Tadmur	B2 27
Tadoussac	G3 103
Taebaek-Sanmaek, mts.	C3 9
Taedong, river	B3 9
Taegu	C5 9
Taejn	B4 9
Tafahi, island	C1 17
Tafilah, at-	A2 26
Taga	A2 18
Taganrog, gulf	D3 47
Tagish	C5 105
Tagish, lake	E1 95
Tagula, island	B3 15
Tagus, river	D3 37
Tahan, mt.	B2 13
Tahat, mt.	B2 57
Tahoua	B3 59
Tai, lake	F2 10
Tai'an	E2 10
T'aichung	B1 9
Taif, at-	B2 24
T'ainan	B2 9
Taipei, capital	B1 9
Taitao, peninsula	A8 76
T'aitung	B2 9
Taiwan	9
Taiwan, strait	E3 10
Taiyuan	E2 10
Taizz	A2 25
Tajikistan	23
Tajumulco, volcano	B4 85
Tak	B2 12
Taka, island	B2 16
Takamaka	Inset 70
Takamatsu	B3 8
Takara, island	A4 8
Takatsuki	B3 8
Takev	C5 11
Takipy	A1 96

	Key Page
Takla Makan, desert	B2 10
Takla, lake	K3 95
Takua Pa	B4 12
Takutu, river	B4 80
Talagante	Inset 76
Talak, region	B2 59
Talamanca, range	C3 86
Talara	A1 77
Talas	D1 13
Talaud, islands	D1 13
Talavera de la Reina	D3 37
Talca	B5 76
Talcahuano	B6 76
Taldyqorghan	D2 23
Talish, mts.	C3 45
Tall Afar	B1 24
Tallahassee, capital, Fla.	E2 126
Tallinn, capital	C1 46
Taloqan	B1 22
Talsi	B2 46
Taltal	B3 76
Taltson, river	F4 99
Tamale	B2 64
Tamanrasset	B2 57
Tamarin	B3 69
Tamaulipas	E3 84
Tambacounda	C3 62
Tambo, river	C3, C4 77
Tâmega, river	B2 36
Tampa, Fla.	E2 126
Tampere	B2 53
Tampico	E3 84
Tampines	B1 13
Tampok, river	B2 80
Tamsagbulag	D2 11
Tamu	B1 12
Tamworth, N.S.W.	E3 14
Tan-Tan	B2 57
Tana, lake	B1 60
Tana, river	C4 61
Tana, river	F1 52
Tanabe	B3 8
Tanch'!n	C2 9
Tandil	D4 74
Tanega, island	A4 8
Tanen, range	B2 12
Tanezrouft, mts.	A2 57
Tanga	C2 68
Tanga, islands	B2 15
Tangail	C4 21
Tanganyika, lake	A2 68
Tanggula, range	C2 10
Tangier	C1 57
Tangier	E3 100
Tangshan	E2 10
Tanimbar, islands	E2 13
Tanjungpinang	B1 13
Tanna, island	C4 18
Tano, river	A3 64
Tanshui	B1 9
Tanta	B1 56
Tanzania	68
Taongi, island	B1 16
Taonudenni	C1 58
Taos	C1 126
Tapa	C1 46
Tapachula	F5 84
Tapajós, river	C2 81
Tapanahoni, river	B3 80
Tapeta	B2 63
Taquari, river	C3 81
Tara	D5 44
Tara, river	A3 49
Taraba, river	F3 65
Tarakan	C1 13
Taranto	D2 38
Taranto, gulf	D2 38
Tarapoto	B2 77
Tararua, range	C3 15
Tarat	B2 57
Tarawa, capital	A1 17
Tarbes	C5 34
Taree, N.S.W.	E3 14
Tarif	B2 25
Tarija	B4 77
Tarim, river	B1 10
Tarin Kowt	B2 22
Tarnobrzeg	E3 41
Tarnów	E3 41
Taroudant	B2 57
Tarrafal	C3 58
Tarragona	G2 37
Tarrasa	G2 37
Tarsus	C3 27
Tartu	D2 46
Tartus	A2 27
Tarvo	B3 77
Taseko, lake	L5 95
Tash Kömür	C2 23
Tashigang	C2 19
Tashir	B1 45
Tashkent, capital	C2 23
Tasikmalaya	B2 13
Tasman, bay	B3 15
Tasman, sea	14
Tasmania	D4 14
Tata	C2 57
Tatabánya	B2 43
Tatamagouche	D2 100
Tataouine	D2 57
Tatar, strait	D9 44
Tatarstan, republic	D4 44
Tathlina, lake	E4 99
Tatla Lake	K5 95
Tatlayoko Lake	K5 95
Tatra, range	B2 42
Tau, island	A1 18
Taumaruni	C2 15
Taung	C2 71
Taunggyi	B2 12
Taunton	C3 30
Taunus, mts.	A3 40
Taupo	C2 15
Taupo, lake	C2 15
Taurag>	B2 46
Tauranga	C2 15
Taureau, reservoir	C5 103
Taurus, mts.	B3 27
Tauu, islands	A1 18
Tavan Bogd Uul, mt.	A2 11

	Key Page
Taverny	Inset II 34
Taveuni, island	C2 17
Tavira	C3 12
Tavoy	C3 12
Tavoy, point	C3 12
Tawau	D2 13
Tawi Tawi, island	A5 12
Taxco	E4 84
Tay Ninh	B4 11
Tay, estuary	C2 30
Tay, lake	B2 30
Tay, river	C4 105
Taymouth	C2 97
Taymyr, peninsula	B6 44
Taymyriya, autonomous okrug	B6 44
Taza	C1 57
Tazin	A1 104
Tazin, river	B1 104
Tbilisi, capital	C4 45
Tchamba	B2 64
Tchaourou	B3 64
Tchentlo, lake	K3 95
Tchibanga	A2 66
Te Anau, lake	A4 15
Tebicuary, river	D5 75
Tecomán	D4 84
Tecuci	D3 43
Tedzhen	C3 22
Tedzhen, river	C3 22
Teepee Creek	A3 94
Tees, river	C2 30
Teeswater	D3 102
Tefé	B2 81
Tegal	B2 13
Tegucigalpa, capital	B2 86
Tehek, lake	J4 99
Tehkummah	D2 102
Tehran, capital	C2 22
Tehuacán	E4 84
Tehuantepec, gulf	E4 84
Tehuantepec, isthmus	F4 84
Teifi, river	B3 30
Tekapo, lake	B3 15
Tekeze, river	B1 60
TekirdaÆ	A2 27
Tekong, island	C1 13
Tel Aviv-Jaffa	B1 26
Tela	B2 86
Telavi	C4 45
Telegraph Creek	G2 95
Teles Pires, river	C2 81
Telford	C3 30
Telkwa	J4 95
Telok Anson	B2 46
Tel%iai	B2 46
Tema	C4 64
Temagami, lake	E1 102
Temburong, river	C2 13
Temirtau	D1 23
Tempisque, river	A2 86
Temuco	B6 76
Tena	C3 79
Téna Kourou, mt.	B3 64
Ténéré, desert	C1 59
Tenerife, island	Inset I 37
Tengiz, lake	C1 23
Tenkodogo	D3 64
Tennant Creek, N.T.	C1 14
Tennessee	E2 126
Tennessee, river	E2 126
Tenojoki, river	C1 53
Tenryu, river	C3 8
Teotihuacán	Inset 84
Tepexpan	Inset 84
Tepic, state capital	D3 84
Téra	A3 59
Terai, region	A2, C3 19
Teraina, island	D1 17
Teramo	C2 38
Teresina	D2 81
Tereul	F2 37
Termiz	C3 23
Termoli	C2 38
Ternate	D1 13
Terni	C2 38
Ternopil	B2 47
Terrace	H4 95
Terre Haute, Ind.	E2 126
Terrebonne	J5 103
Terreiro Velho	C1 63
Terrenceville	D5 98
Terschelling, island	C1 32
Teseney	A2 60
Teshio, river	Inset I 8
Tesiyn, river	B2 11
Tesli–	B1 48
Teslin	C5 105
Teslin, lake	C5 105
Teslin, river	C5 105
Tessalit	D1 58
Tessaoua	B3 59
Testa del Gargano, point	D2 38
Tete	B3 68
Tête Jaune Cache	N5 95
Tétouan	C1 57
Tetovo	A1 48
Teulada, cape	B3 38
Teulon	C4 96
Tewkesbury	C3 30
Texarkana, Tex.	D2 126
Texas	D2 126
Texcoco	Inset 84
Texel, island	B1 32
Teyateyaneng	A2 71
Tezoyuca	Inset 84
Tezzeron, lake	K4 95
Thaba-Tseka	B2 71
Thabana Ntlenyana, mt.	C2 71
Thai Nguyen	A2 11
Thailand	12
Thailand, gulf	B4, C4 12
Thames, river	C3, Inset III 30
Thamesville	D5 102
Thane	Inset II 20
Thanh Hoa	B2 11
Thanjavur	C6 20

	Key	Page
Thar, desert	C4	21
Thásos	C1	51
Thásos, island	C1	51
Thásos, island	C1	51
The Crane	C4	91
The Hague	B2	32
The Ovens	C3	100
The Pas	A2, C2	96
Thedford	D4	102
Thekulthili, lake		99
Thelon, river	H4, J4	99
Theodore	H9	104
Thessalon	B1	102
Thessaloníki	B1	51
Thetford	D3	30
Thetford Mines	E5	103
Thicket	C4	91
Thicket Portage	C1	96
Thiès	A2	62
Thika	D4	61
Thimphu, capital	A2	19
Thingvellir	A2	52
Thio	C2	18
Thíra, island	C3	51
Thisted	B2	32
Thlewiaza, river	J4	99
Tholen, island	B3	32
Thomaston Corner	B3	97
Thompson	C1, D2	96
Thompson, river	M6	95
Thong Hoe	A1	13
Thorhild	D4	94
Thornhill	K5	102
Thorold	F4	102
Thrace, region	D4	50
Thracian, plain	C3	50
Three Kings, islands	B1	15
Thule, air base	B2	106
Thun	B2	35
Thunder Bay	C3	101
Thunersee, lake	B2	35
Thuringia	B3	40
Thuringian, forest	B3	40
Thurso	B1	30
Thurston, island	B9	107
Ti'avea	D2	18
Ti-n-Zaouâtene	B2	57
Tiáhuac	Inset	84
Tianjin	E2	10
Tibati	B2	65
Tiber, river	C2	38
Tiberias	B1	26
Tiberias (Galilee), lake	A1, B1	26
Tibesti, massif	B2	59
Tibet (Xizang)	B2	10
Tibet, plateau	B2	10
Tiburón, island	B2	84
Tichit	B2	58
Tichla	A2	58
Ticino, river	C2	35
Tide Head	C1	97
Tidjikdja	C3	58
Tien Shan, range	A1	10
Tierra del Fuego, island	C9	76
Tietê, river	Inset II	81
Tignish	A2	100
Tigre, river	B1	77
Tigris, river	B1	24
Tijuana	A1	84
Tikal	D2	85
Tikrit	B2	24
Tiksi	B8	44
Tiladummati, atoll	A1	19
Tilburg	C3	32
Tilbury	C5	102
Tillabéry	A3	59
Tilley	E6	94
Tillsonburg	E5	102
Tilomonte	C2	76
Tilston	A4	96
Timaru	B3	15
Timbuktu	C2	58
Timgad, ruins	B1	57
TimiȘoara	A3	43
Timmins	D3	101
Timor, island	D2	13
Timor, sea	B1	14
Tindouf	A2	57
Tingo María	B2	77
Tinkissa, river	C2	60
Tio	C2	60
Tipitapa, river	B2	87
Tipperary	B2	31
Tirana, capital	A2	49
Tiraspol	B2	50
Tiree, island	A2	30
TirgoviȘte	C3	43
Tirgu Jiu	B3	43
Tirgu-MureȘ	D2	43
Tirgu Neamœ	D2	43
Tirgu Ocna	D2	43
Tirich Mir, mt.	D2	21
Tirso, river	B2	38
Tiruchchirappalli	C6	20
Tisa, river	A2	49
Tisdale	F8	104
Tista, river	C2	19
Tisza, river	C2	43
Titagarh	Inset II	20
Titano, mt.	B1	39
Titicaca, lake	A3, D4	77
Titov Veles	B2	48
Titova Mitrovica	B3	49
Tivaouane	A2	62
Tiverton	D4	30
Tiverton	D3	102
Tizi	B2	91
Tiznit	B2	57
Tlaipan	Inset	84
Tlalnepantla	Inset	84
Tlaxcala, state capital	E4	84
Tlemcen	A1	57
Toa Payoh	B2	13
Toad River	K2	95
Toamasina	B2	69
Toba Kakar, range	C3	21
Tobago, cays	A4	91
Tobago, island	B1	91
Tobermory	D2	102
Tobi, island	Inset	17

	Key	Page
Tobin, lake	G7	104
Tobol, river	C1	23
Tobolsk	D5	44
Tobruk	D1	56
Tocantins	D3	81
Tocantins, river	D2	81
Toco	B2	91
Tocopilla	B2	76
Tofino	K6	95
Tofua, island	B3	17
Togo		64
Tokachi, river	Inset I	8
Tokaj	C1	43
Tokara, islands	A4	8
Tokat	D2	27
Tokmok	C3	8
T!kch!k-kundo, islands	A4	9
Tokorozawa	C3	8
Toktogul	C2	23
Toku, island	C2	17
Tokuno, island	Inset II	8
Tokushima	B3	8
Tokuyama	A3	8
Tokyo, capital	C3	8
Tôlanaro	B3	69
Toledo	D3	37
Toledo, mts.	D3	37
Toledo, Ohio	E1	126
Toliara	A3	69
Tolima, mt.	B3	78
Tolland	E4	94
Toltén, river	B6	76
Toluca, state capital	E4	84
Tolyatti	D4	44
Tomakomai	Inset I	8
Tomanivi, mt.	B2	17
Tombua	B5	70
Tomé	B6	76
Tomelloso	E3	37
Tomiko, lake	F1	102
Tompkins	B10	104
Tomsk	D6	44
Tonalá	F4	84
Tonbridge	Inset III	30
Tone, river	C2	8
Tonga		17
Tongariro, mt.	C2	15
Tongatapu, island	B4	17
Tonghua	F1	10
Tongjos!n, bay	B3	9
Tongliao	F1	10
Tongsa	B2	19
Tongsa, river	B2	19
Tonkin, gulf	B2	11
Tonle Sap, lake	B2, C3	11
Tonle Sap, river	B2	11
Toowoomba, Qld.	E2	14
Topeka, Kans.	D2	126
Topley Landing	J4	95
Torbay	B4	30
Torbay	E5	98
Torghay, plateau	C1	23
Tormes, river	D2	37
Torneälven, river	D1	53
Torngat, mts.	D3	98
Tornio	B1	53
Torniojoki, river	B1	53
Toronto, capital	F4, K5	102
Tororo	D3	61
Torquay	G11	104
Torre del Greco	C2	38
Torrejón de Ardoz	Inset II	37
Torrelavega	D1	37
Torrens, lake	C3	14
Torrens, river	Inset II	14
Torrente	F3	37
Torreón	D2	84
Torres, islands	B1	18
Torres, strait	D1	14
Torrington	D5	94
Tórshavn	Inset	32
Tortosa	G2	37
Tortosa, cape	G2	37
Tortuga, island	C1	89
Toruł	D2	41
Tôrva	C2	46
Tory Hill	G3	102
Tosa, bay	B3	8
Totness	A2	80
Tottori	B3	8
Touggourt	B1	57
Tougué	C2	62
Toulaman, river	B2	90
Touliu	B2	9
Toulon	D5	34
Toulouse	C5	34
Toungoo	C2	12
Toura, mts.	C2	63
Tourcoing	C1	34
Tournai	B2	33
Tours	C3	34
Toussoro, mt.	B2	66
Toutes Aides	B3	96
Tovuz	A2	45
Towada, lake	D1	8
Townsville, Qld.	D1	14
Toxkan, river	E2	23
Toyama	C2	8
Toyama, bay	C2	8
Toyohashi	C3	8
Toyonaka	B3	8
Toyota	C3	8
Tozeur	B3	57
Tqvarcheli	A3	45
Trabzon	D2	27
Tracadie-Sheila	E1	97
Tracy	C3	97
Tracy	C5	103
Trafalgar	E2	100
Trail	O6	95
Tralee	B2	31
Trang	B5	12
Transantarctic, mts.		107
Transylvanian Alps, mts.	C3	43
Trapani	C3	38
Trasimeno, lake	C2	38
Trat	C3	12

	Key	Page
Traun, river	D2	39
Traverse City, Mich.	E1	126
Trebinje	B2	48
Treherne	B4	96
Treinta y Tres	C2	75
Trenche, river	C3	103
Trent, river	C3	30
TrenAín	B2	42
Trentino-Alto Adige	B1	38
Trento	B1	38
Trenton	E2	100
Trenton	H3	102
Trenton, capital, N.J.	F1	126
Trepassey	E5	98
Tres Puntas, cape	B6	74
Treska, river	B2	48
Treviso	C1	38
Trier	A4	40
Triesen	B2	33
Triesenberg	B2	33
Trieste	C1	38
Trieste, gulf	A3	48
Triglav, mt.	A2	48
Tríkala	B2	51
Trim	C2	31
Trincomalee	C3	19
Trinidad	B2	77
Trinidad	B2	75
Trinidad	C2	88
Trinidad, island	A2	91
Trinidad, mts.	C2	88
Trinidad and Tobago		91
Trinity East	E5	98
Trinity, bay	E5	98
Triolet	C2	69
Tripoli (Tarabulus)	A1	26
Tripoli, capital	B1	56
Tripolitania, region	B1	56
Triton	D4	98
Trivandrum (Thiruvananthapuram)	C7	20
Trnava	A2	42
Trois-Pistoles	G3	103
Trois-Rivières	D5	103
Troisvierges	B1	33
Trombay	Inset I	20
Trondheim	C3	52
Trondheimsfjord, fjord	B3	52
Trongisvágur	Inset	32
Troödos, mts.	A2	27
Trossachs	F11	104
Trout Creek	F1	102
Trout Lake	C3	94
Trout River	B4	98
Trout, lake	D4	99
Trout, lake	B2	101
Trouville	C2	34
Trowbridge	C3	30
Troyes	D2	34
Trujillo	B2	79
Trujillo	C2	37
Trujillo	B2	86
Trujillo Alto	C2	90
Truro	B4	30
Truro	D2	100
Trutch	L2	95
Trutnov	B2	42
Tsaratanana, mts.	B1	69
Tsavo	E5	61
Tsedike, river	B3	71
Tsengwen, river	B2	9
Tsetserleg	C2	11
Tsévié	B3	64
Tshabong	A3	69
Tshane	A3	69
Tshaneni	B1	71
Tshikapa	B2	67
Tshuapa, river	B2	67
Tsiribihina, river	A2	69
Tsiroanomandidy	B2	69
Tsiteli-Tsqaro	D4	45
Tskhinvali	B3	45
Tsnori	C4	45
Tsu, island	A3	8
Tsuen Wan	Inset	10
Tsugaru, strait	D1, Inset I	8
Tsumeb	C1	70
Tsumkwe	D1	70
Tsuruga	C3	8
Tsuruoka	C2	8
Tuam	B2	31
Tuas	A1	13
Tuasivi	B2	18
Tubarão	D4	81
Tübingen	B4	40
Tubmanburg	A2	63
Tucson, Ariz.	B2	126
Tucumán, N. Mex.	D2	126
Tucupita	D2	79
Tucurui, reservoir	D2	81
Tuela, river	D2	71
Tuguegarao	B2	12
Tuira, river	D2	87
Tuktoyaktuk	B3	99
Tuktut Nogait N.P.	D3	99
Tukums	B2	46
Tula	D3	44
Tula, ruins	D3	84
Tulcán	C2	79
Tulcea	E3	43
Tuléar	C2	31
Tulemalu, lake	F2	95
Tulsequah	F2	95
Tulsipur	B2	19
Tultitlán	Inset	84
Tulun	D7	44
Tuma, river	B2	87
Tumaco	A4	78
Tumba, lake	B2	67
Tumbes	A1	77
Tumbler Ridge	M3	95
Tumen, river	D1	9
Tumuc-Humac, mts.	A2, B3	80
Tumucumaque, range	C1	81

	Key	Page
Tunbridge Wells	D3	30
Tundzha, river	E3	50
Tungsten	C4	99
Tunis, capital	C1	57
Tunis, gulf	C1	57
Tunisia		57
Tunja	B3	78
Tupelo, Miss.	E2	126
Tupiza	A4	77
Tupungato, mt.	B3	74
Tur, at-	B2	56
Tura	C7	44
Turan, lowland	A2	23
Turayf	A1	24
Turbo	A2	78
Turda	B2	43
Turfan, depression	C1	10
T»rgovishte	E2	50
Türi	C2	46
Turin	A1	38
Turin	D6	94
Turkana (Rudolf), lake	D2	61
Turkestan, mts.	A1	23
Turkey		27
Turkmenbashi	A2	22
Turkmenistan		22
Turks and Caicos Islands		89
Turks, islands	D4	89
Turku	B2	53
Turkwel, river	C2	61
Turnberry	A2	96
Turnbull	B2	90
Turneffe, islands	C2	85
Turnhout	C1	33
Turnor Lake	B4	104
Turnu MŒEgurele	C4	43
Turquino, mt.	E3	88
Tursunzoda	A1	23
Turtle, lake	B7	104
Turtleford	B7	104
Turtleford	D4	98
Tuscaloosa, Ala.	E2	126
Tuscany	B2	38
Tusket	B4	100
Tuticorin	C7	20
Tutong	B2	13
Tutong, river	B2	13
Tutuila, island	AI, C2	11
Tuul, river	C2	11
Tuvalu		16
Tuxtla Gutiérrez, state capital	F4	84
Tuy Hoa	B4	11
Tuya, river	G1	95
Tuz, lake	C2	27
Tuzla	B1	48
Tweed	H3	102
Tweed, river	C2	30
Twillingate	D4	98
Twin Butte	D6	94
Twin Creeks	A4	96
Twin Falls, Idaho	B1	126
Two Creeks	A4	96
Tychy	D3	41
Tyndall	C4	96
Tyne Valley	B2	100
Tyne, river	C2	30
Tyrrhenian, sea	B2	38
Tyumen	D5	44
Tyva, republic	D6	44
Tywi, river	B3	30

U

	Key	Page
Uaboe	B1	16
Ubangi, river	B1	67
Ubayyid, al-	C2	59
Ube	A3	8
Úbeda	E3	37
Úbeda	E3	37
Uberaba	D3	81
Uberlândia	D3	81
Ubin, island	B1	13
Ubon Ratchathani	C3	12
Ucayali, river	C2	77
Uccle	C2	33
Uchiura, bay	Inset I	8
Uchquduq	B2	23
Ucluelet	K7	95
Udaipur	B4	20
Uddevalla	B3	53
Uddjaur, lake	C1	53
Udine	C1	38
Udmurtiya, republic	D4	44
Udon Thani	C2	12
Udu, point	C2	17
Uele, river	C1	67
Uelzen	B2	40
Ufa	D4	44
Uga, river	B2	70
Ugalla, river	B2	68
Uganda		61
Uíge	C2	70
Uitenhage	C3	71
Ujae, river	B2	16
Ujelang, island	A2	16
Ujjain	C4	20
Ujung Pandang	C2	13
Ukhta	C4	44
Ukmerg>	C2	46
Ukraine		47
Ulaan-Uul	C2	11
Ulaanbaatar, capital	C2	11
Ulaangom	B2	11
Ulan-Ude	D7	44
Ulansuhai, lake	D1	10
Ulchin	C4	9
Ulhas, river	Inset I	20
Uliastay	B2	11
Ulithi, atoll	B1	15
Ull»ng-do, island	D4	9
Ullapool	B1	30
Ulm	B4	40
Ulsan	D4	9
Ulster, province	C1	31
Ulu DaÆ (Mt. Olympus), mt.	B2	27
UlÚa, river	B2	86
Ulubaria	Inset II	20
Uluru (Ayers Rock)	C2	14
Uman	C2	47

	Key	Page
Umbeluzi, river	B2	71
Umboi, island	A2	15
Umbria	C2	38
Umeå	D2	53
Umeälven, river	C2	53
Umm al-Qaywayn	C2	25
Umm Bab	B3	25
Umm Qasr	C2	24
Umm Said (Musayid)	D4	25
Umniati, river	B2	69
Umtata	C3	71
Umuahia	D5	65
Umzingwani, river	B2	69
Una, river	A1	48
Unayzah	B1	24
Ungava, bay	L3	92
Ungheni	A2	50
Unión	C2	76
Union, island	A4	91
United Arab Emirates		25
United States		126
Unity	A8	104
Unst, island	Inset I	30
Upemba, lake	C3	67
Upernavik	B2	106
Upington	B2	71
Upolu, island	C2	18
Upper Arrow, lake	O6	95
Upper Liard	D5	105
Upper Lough Erne, lake	A	30
Upper Musquodoboit	E2	100
Upper Ohio	B4	100
Uppsala	C3	53
Ural, mts.	D4	44
Ural, river	B2	23
Uran	Inset I	20
Uranium City	B1	104
Urawa	C3	8
Urganch	B2	23
Urmia, lake	B2	22
Uro%evac	B3	49
Uruapan	D4	84
Urubamba, river	C3	77
Uruguai, river	C4	81
Uruguay		75
Uruguay, river	D3	74
Urukthapel, island	B3	17
Ürümqi	B1	10
Usak	B2	27
Ushuaia	B7	74
Usk, river	C3	30
Üsküdar	B2	27
Usmas, lake	A1	46
Ussuri, river	E8	44
Ussuriysk	E8	44
Ust-Ilimsk	D7	44
Ust-Kamchatsk	D10	44
Ust-Kut	D7	44
Ust-Ordynskiy Buryat, autonomous okrug	D7	44
Ust-Ordynskiy	D7	44
Ústí nad Labem	B2	42
Ustica, island	C3	38
Ustka	C1	41
Ustyurt, plateau	A2, B2	23
Usulután	B2	86
Usumacinta, river	F4	84
Utah	B2	126
Utah, beach	Inset I	34
Utan	Inset I	20
Utena	C2	46
Utikuma, lake	C3	94
Utila, island	B1	86
Utrecht	C2	32
Utsunomiya	C2	8
Uttaradit	B2	12
Utuado	B2	90
Utupua, island	C2	16
Uummannaq	B2	106
Uvira	B2	67
Uvs, lake	B1	11
Uwajima	B3	8
Uwaynat, al-	B2	56
Uyo	D5	65
Uyuni	A4	77
Uzbekistan		23
Uzhhorod	A2	47
U«ice	A3	49

V

	Key	Page
Vaal, reservoir	C2	71
Vaal, river	C2	71
Vaalserberg, mt.	D4	32
Vaasa	B2	53
Vác	B2	43
Vache, island	B2	89
Vadodara	B4	20
Vados	F1	52
Vaduz, capital	B2	33
Vágar, island	Inset	32
Váh, river	A2	42
Vahsh, river	A1	23
Vaitupu, island	C2	16
Val Comeau	E1	97
Val Marie	C11	104
Val-d'Or	A4	101
Val-des-Bois	A6	103
Valcourt	D6	103
Valdecaño	D2	37
Valdepeñas	E3	37
Valdés, peninsula	C5	74
Valdivia	B6	76
Valemount	N5	95
Valença	A1	36
Valence	D4	34
Valencia	C3	79
Valencia	F3	37
Valencia, gulf	C2	37
Valenciennes	C1	34
Valera	C2	79
Valga	D3	46
Valira d'Orient, river	B2	36
Valira, river	B2	36
Valjevo	A2	49
Valka	C2	46
Valladolid	G3	84

	Key	P
Valladolid		.D2
Valle d'Aosta		.A1
Valledupar		.B2
Vallenar		.B3
Valletta, capital		.A3
Valley, river		.A3
Valmiera		.C2
Valparaíso	B4,	Inset
Van		.E2
Van, lake		.E2
Vancouver		.L6
Vancouver, island		.J6
Vanderhoof		.K4
Vänern, lake		.B3
Vanguard		.C11
Vanier		.H5
Vanier		.L5
Vanikolo, islands		.C2
Vanimo		.A2
Vannes		.B3
Vanrhynsdorp		.A3
Vanscoy		.D8
Vansittart, island		.M3
Vantaa		.B2
Vanua Balavu, island		.B1
Vanua Lava, island		.B1
Vanua Levu, island		.B2
Vanuatu		
Varanasi		.C2
Vara«din		.C2
Vardar, river		.B3
Varde, river		.B3
Vardenis		.C2
Varkaus		.C2
Varna		.F2
Vasai		.Inset I
Vasai, creek		.Inset I
Vaslui		.D2
Vassar		.C3
Västerås		.C3
Vatican City		
Vatnajökull, ice cap		.B2
Vättern, lake		.B3
Vatu Lele, island		.A3
Vaudreuil		.C6
Vaupés, river		.C4
Vava'u, island		.C2
Vavenby		.N5
Vavuniya		.C3
Vawkavysk		.B3
Växjö		.B3
Vega		.C4
Vega Alta		.C1
Vega Baja		.C1
Vegreville		.E4
Veimandu, channel		.A3
Vejle		.B3
Velika Morava, river		.B2
Veliki, canal		.A2
Veliko T»rnovo		.D2
Vélingara		.B2
Vélingara		.B3
Vella Lavella, island		.A1
Vellore		.C6
Veneto		.B1
Venezuela		
Venezuela, gulf		.C1
Venice		.C1
Venice, gulf		.C1
Venlo		.D3
Venta, river		.A2
Ventimiglia		.A2
Ventspils		.A2
Veracruz		.E4
Vercelli		.C3
Verde, river		.C3
Verdun		.D2
Verdun		.J6
Vereeniging		.C2
Verkhoyansk		.C8
Verkhoyansk, range		.C8
Vermillion, river		.C2
Vermont		.F1
Vernal, Utah		.C2
Verner		.E1
Vernon		.N6
Vernon Bridge		.C2
Vernon River		.C2
Véroia		.B1
Verona		.J3
Versailles	C2,	Inset II
Vert, cape		.A2
Verviers		.D2
Vesoul		.D3
Vesterålen, islands		.C1
Vestmanna		.Inset
Vestmannaeyjar		.A3
Vesuvius, volcano		.A2
Veszprém		.A2
Vetauua, island		.C1
Viana do Castelo		.A2
Vibank		.G10
Viborg		.B2
Vicenza		.B1
Vich		.H2
Vichada, river		.C3
Vichy		.C4
Victoria		.D3
Victoria		.B1
Victoria		.A1
Victoria		.C4
Victoria Beach		.C4
Victoria Beach		.C4
Victoria Land, region		.B5
Victoria Nile, river		.B1
Victoria, capital		.Inset
Victoria, capital		.L7
Victoria, falls		.B1
Victoria, island		.F2
Victoria, island	B4,	C4
Victoria, peak		.C1
Victoria, Tex.		.D3
Victoriaville		.E5
Vidin		.A2
Viedma		.C5

Name	Key	Page
...lma, lake	A6	74
...le Case	A1	90
...na, capital	E2	39
...ne, river	C3	34
...atiane, capital	B3	11
...ques	D2	90
...ques	B2	90
...ques, passage	D2	90
...ques, sound	E2	90
...zon	C3	34
...Tri	A2	11
...nam		11
...ax Fort	B3	91
...ma	B2	12
...nemale, mt.	B5	34
	B1	37
...yawada	D5	20
...së, river	A3	49
...do Conde	A2	36
...Nova de Gaia	A2	36
...Real	B2	36
...Real de Santo Antonio	B4	36
... capital	C3	18
...ine, river	B3	34
...nculos	A4	68
...abamba, mts.	C3	77
...andi	C2	46
...avi9ókis	B2	46
...n Ahumada	C1	84
...a Hayes	D4	75
...a María	C3	74
...n Obregón	Inset	84
...ach	C4	39
...hermosa, state capital	F4	84
...alba	C2	90
...rreal de los Infantes	F3	37
...arrica	D4	75
...vicencio	B3	78
...ázón	A4	77
...eneuve-Saint-Georges	Inset II	34
...cennes	Inset II	34
...eroy	E5	103
...ius, capital	C2	46
...uy, river	C7	44
...uysk	C8	44
...a del Mar	B4, Inset	76
...cennes	Inset II	34
...cente de Carvalho	Inset II	81
...delälven, river	C2	53
...dhya, range	C4	20
	A2	11
...nitsa	B2	47
...son Massif, mt.	B10	107
...len	A4	96
...in, river	C3	104
...in, islands		82
...ginia	F2	126
...su	B2	46
...unga, mts.	B1	61
...khapatnam	D5	20
...ayan, islands	B4	12
...ayan, sea	B4	12
	C3	53
...count Melville, sound	F2	99
...eu	B2	36
...a	A4	96
...a Hermosa	B4	78
...ula, river	D2, E3	41
...erbo	C2	38
...Levu, island	A2	17
...oria	E1	37
...oria	D4	81
...oria da Conquista	D3	81
...yebsk	E2	47
	C4	96
...aíno, desert	B2	84
...ardingen	B3	32
...divostok	E8	44
...eland, island	B1	32
...singen	A3	32
...sk	A3	49
...dischе	B3	42
...cklabruck	C2	39
...njama	B1	63
...vodina, province	A2	49
...cano, islands	Inset III	8
...ga, river	E4	44
...gograd	E4	44
...ogda	D3	44
...os	B2	51
...ta Redonda	D4	81
...a, lake	C3	64
...nda	D8	104
...kuta	C5	44
...ronezh	D3	44
...rotan, river	C3	45
...rskla, river	C1	47
...ru Järv, lake	D2	46
...ru	D3	46
...s	D2	34
...stok, island	D3	17
...nje	B3	49
...tsa	B2	50
...as	A2	49
...as, river	B1	48
...bac	B2	49
...burg	D2	48
...kovar	A3	17
...haniu, bay	A3	49
...ng Tau-Con Dao	B4	11
...hisea	B3	17

W

Name	Key	Page
...al, river	A1	64
...al, river	C3	32
...aga	B2	15
...abamun, lake	C4	94
...abe Gestro, river	E5	98
...abasca, river	C2	94
...abe Shebele, river	D3	60
...abowden	B2	96
...abush	D4	98
...aco, Tex.	D2	126
...ad Madani	C2	59

Name	Key	Page
Waddan	C2	56
Waddenzee, sound	C1	32
Waddington, mt.	K5	95
Wadena	G9	104
Wadi al-Malik, river	B2	59
Wadi as-Sirhan, depression	B2	26
Wadi Halfa	C1	59
Wafrah, al-	B3	24
Wagga Wagga, N.S.W.	D3	14
Waigeo, island	E2	13
Waikato, river	C2	15
Waimamaku	B2	15
Waingapu	D2	13
Wairau, river	B3	15
Waitaki, river	B3	15
Wajh, al-	A1	24
Wakasa, bay	B3	8
Wakaw	E8	104
Wakayama	B3	8
Wakefield	C3	30
Wakkanai	Inset I	8
Wakomata, lake	B1	102
Wakrah, al-	D3	25
Walachia, region	B3	43
Wa(brzych	C3	41
Walcheren, island	A3	32
Walden	D1	102
Waldersee	B4	96
Waldheim	D8	104
Walensee, lake	D1	35
Walkerton	D3	102
Wallace	D2	100
Wallaceburg	C5	102
Wallsall	C3	30
Walton	C2	100
Walton	D4	102
Walvis Bay	B2	70
Wami, river	C2	68
Wanaka, lake	A3	15
Wanapitei, lake	E1	102
Wandering River	D3	94
Wando	B5	9
Wanganui	C2	15
Wanham	A3	94
Wapawekka, lake	F5	104
Wapawsik	B1	96
Wapiti, river	A4	94
Warangal	C5	20
Warbah, island	C1	24
Wardlow	E6	94
Ware	K2	95
Warman	D8	104
Warner	D6	94
Warren	C4	96
Warren	E1	102
Warren Landing	C2	96
Warri	C5	65
Warrington	C3	30
Warrnambool, Vic.	D3	14
Warsaw, capital	B2	41
Warta, river	B2, C2	41
Warwick	C3	30
Wasa	P6	95
Wasaga Beach	F3	102
Wasagaming	B4	96
Washago	F3	102
Wash, bay	D3	30
Washington	A1	126
Washington, cape	A3	17
Washington, capital, D.C.	F2	126
Waskada	A4	96
Waskaganish	A3	101
Waskesiu Lake	D7	104
Waspam	C1	87
Water Valley	C5	94
Waterborough	C3	97
Waterbury, lake	F2	104
Waterford	C2	31
Waterhen, lake	B3	96
Waterloo	E4	102
Waterloo	D6	103
Watertown, N.Y.	F1	126
Watford	Inset III	30
Watford	D5	102
Wathaman, lake	G3	104
Watrous	E9	104
Watsa	C1	67
Watson	F8	104
Watson Lake	D5	105
Wau	A2	15
Wavre	C2	33
Waw	B3	59
Wawa	D3	101
Wawa, river	B1	87
Wawanesa	B4	96
Weagamow Lake	B2	101
Webbwood	D1	102
Webequie	C2	101
Webi Shabeelle, river	B3	60
Wedgeport	A4	100
Weert	C3	32
Wei, river	D2	10
Weiden	C4	40
Weifang	E2	10
Weimar	B3	40
Weipa, Qld.	D1	14
Weitzel, lake	D3	104
Wekusko	B2	96
Wekusko, lake	B2	96
Weldiya	C2	71
Welkom	C2	70
Wellington	A2	100
Wellington, capital	B3	15
Wellington, island	A8	76
Wels	C2	39
Welsford	C3	97
Welshpool	B3	30
Welwyn	A4	96
Wembere, river	B1	68
Wenchi	A3	64
Weno	C2	15
Weno, island	C2	15
Wenshan	D2	10
Wentworth	D2	100
Wentzel, lake	C1	94
Wenzhou	F3	10

Name	Key	Page
Werder	D3	60
Werra, river	B3	40
Weser, river	B2	40
Wesley	B2	90
Wesleyville	E4	98
West Antarctica	A8	107
West Devon	A2	100
West Frisian, islands	B1	32
West Ice Shelf, glacier	C1	107
West Palm Beach, Fla.	E3	126
West Point	A2	100
West Road, river	K4	95
West Siberian, plain	C5	44
West St. Modeste	C3	98
West Virginia	E2	126
Westbank	N6	95
Westbourne	B4	96
Western Australia	B2	14
Western Dvina, river	C2	46
Western Ghats, mts.	B5	20
Western Sahara		58
Western, channel	C5	9
Westerschelde, channel	A3	32
Westfield	C3	97
Westlock	D4	94
Westminster	Inset III	30
Weston	J5	102
Westport	B3	15
Westport	B2	31
Westport	J3	102
Westray	A2	96
Westray, island	Inset I	30
Wetar, island	D2	13
Wetaskiwin	D5	94
Wete	C1	68
Wetzlar	B3	40
Wewak	A1	15
Wexford	C2	31
Weyakwin	E6	104
Weyburn	G11	104
Weymouth	A3	100
Whakatane	C2	15
Whale Cove	K4	99
Whaletown	K6	95
Whangarei	B2	15
Wheatland	A4	96
Wheatley	C5	102
Wheeling, W. Va.	E1	126
Whistler	L6	95
Whitbourne	E5	98
Whitby	G4	102
White Fox	F7	104
White Lake	J2	102
White Nile, river	C3	59
White Rock	L6	95
White Sands	C3	100
White Volta, river	B1, D2	64
White, bay	C4	98
White, island	L3	99
White, river	A4	105
Whitecourt	C4	94
Whitefish Falls	D1	102
Whitefish, bay	A1	102
Whitehaven	B2	30
Whitehorse	C5	105
Whitelaw	A3	94
Whiteman, range	A2	15
Whitemouth	D4	96
Whitestone, river	B3	105
Whitewood	H10	104
Whitney	G2	102
Whitney mt., Calif.	B2	126
Wholdaia, lake	H4	99
Whyalla, S.A.	C3	14
Whycocomagh	F2	100
Wiarton	D3	102
Wichita Falls, Tex.	D2	126
Wichita, Kans.	D2	126
Wick	B1	30
Wicklow	C2	31
Wicklow Head, cape	D2	31
Wicklow, mts.	C2	31
Wiener Neustadt	E3	39
Wieprz, river	F3	41
Wiesbaden	B3	40
Wigan	C3	30
Wight, island	C4	30
Wilberforce	G2	102
Wilge, river	C2	71
Wilhelm, mt.	A2	15
Wilhelmina, canal	B3	32
Wilhelmina, mts.	A2	80
Wilhelmshaven	B2	40
Wilkes Land, region	C3	107
Wilkie	B8	104
Williams Harbour	D3	98
Williams Lake	L5	95
Williamsport	C4	98
Williston, lake	K3	95
Willow Bunch	E11	104
Willow Creek	A11	104
Willowbunch, lake	E11	104
Wilmington, Del.	F2	126
Wilmington, N.C.	F2	126
Wilmot	B3	100
Wiltondale	C4	98
Wiltz	A2	33
Winchester	C3	30
Winchester	K2	102
Wind, river	B3	105
Windermere	O6	95
Windermere	F2	102
Windfall	B4	94
Windhoek, capital	B2	70
Windsor	Inset III	30
Windsor	C3	100
Windsor	C5	102
Windsor	D6	103
Windward Group	B2	58
Windward, islands	B4	91
Windward, passage	F3	88
Winefred, river	C3	94
Winfield	N6	95
Wingham	D4	102
Winisk	C1	101
Winisk, lake	C2	101
Winisk, river	C2	101

Name	Key	Page
Winkler	C4	96
Winneba	B4	64
Winnemucca, Nev.	B1	126
Winnipeg	C4, D2	96
Winnipeg Beach	C4	96
Winnipeg, lake	B3, C4, D2	96
Winnipeg, river	D4	96
Winnipegosis	B3	96
Winnipegosis, lake	A3	96
Winslow, Ariz.	B2	126
Winston-Salem, N.C.	E2	126
Winter Harbour	H6	95
Winterthur	C1	35
Wisconsin	D1	126
Wismar	B2	40
Witless Bay	E5	98
Witten	A3	40
Wittenberg	C3	40
Wittenberge	B2	40
Witu, island	A2	15
Wiwili	B2	87
Woburn	F6	103
Wodzis(aw ¿í]ski	D3	41
Woking	A3	94
Wolf, lake	C5	105
Wolfsberg	D4	39
Wolfsburg	B2	40
Wolfville	C2	100
Wollaston Lake	G2	104
Wollaston, lake	H2	104
Wollaston, peninsula	E3	99
Wollongong, N.S.W.	E3	14
Wolseley	G10	104
Wolverhampton	C3	30
Wong, river	A2	19
W(nju	B4	9
Wonowon	M3	95
W(nsan	B3	9
Wood Islands	C3	100
Woodbridge	J5	102
Woodlands	B1	13
Woodlands	C4	96
Woodlark (Muyua), island	B2	15
Woodnorth	A4	96
Woodridge	C4	96
Woods, lake	B3	101
Woodstock	B2	97
Woodstock	A2	100
Woodstock	E4	102
Woody Point	C4	98
Woomera, S.A.	C3	14
Worcester	C3	30
Worcester	A3	71
Worcester, Mass.	F1	126
Worms	B4	40
Wotho, island	B1	16
Wotje, island	C1	16
Wrangel, island	B10	44
Wrath, cape	B1	30
Wreck Cove	D5	98
Wrentham	D6	94
Wrigley	D4	99
Wroc(aw	C3	41
Wuhan	E2	10
Wuhu	E2	10
Wukari	E4	65
Wum	B2	65
Wuppertal	A3	40
Würzburg	B4	40
Wutivi, mt.	B1	63
Wuwei	D2	10
Wuxi	F2	10
Wuzhong	D2	10
Wuzhou	E3	10
Wye, river	C3	30
Wyndham, W.A.	B1	14
Wynyard	F9	104
Wyoming	C1	126

X

Name	Key	Page
Xaçmaz	C2	45
Xai-Xai	B5	68
Xam Nua	C1	11
Xangongo	C5	70
Xankändi	B3	45
Xánthi	C1	51
Xau, lake	B2	69
Xi'an	D2	10
Xiamen	E3	10
Xiangfan	E2	10
Xiangkhoang	B2	11
Xiangtan	E3	10
Xigaze	B3	10
Xingu, river	C3	81
Xining	D2	10
Xinjiang Uygur	B1	10
Xinxiang	E2	10
Xinyang	E2	10
Xochimilco	Inset	84
Xuddur	A3	60
Xuzhou	E2	10

Y

Name	Key	Page
Ya'an	D2	10
Yablonovyy, range	D7	44
Yabucoa	D2	90
Yacuiba	B4	77
Yafran	B1	56
Yaguarí, river	C1	75
Yaguarón, river	D2	75
Yahk	O6	95
Yakima, Wash.	A1	126
Yaku, island	A4	8
Yakutsk	C8	44
Yala	B5	12
Yale	M6	95
Yalinga	C2	66
Yalta	C4	47
Yalu, river	B2	10
Yamagata	D2	8
Yamaguchi	A3	8
Yamal, peninsula	C5	44
Yamalo-Nenesiya, autonomous okrug	C5	44

Name	Key	Page
Yambio	B4	59
Yambol	E3	50
Yamoussoukro, capital	D3	63
Yampi, sound	B1	14
Yamuna, river	C3	20
Yan, river	B3	19
Yanbu al-Bahr	A1	24
Yangambi	C1	67
Yangd!k	B3	9
Yangon (Rangoon), capital	C3	12
Yangquan	E2	10
Yangtze, river	C2, D2	10
Yangzhou	E2	10
Yanji	F1	10
Yantai	F2	10
Yantra, river	D2	50
Yao	B3	8
Yaoundé, capital	B3	65
Yap, islands	A2	15
Yapen, island	E2	13
Yaque del Norte, river	A1	89
Yaque del Sur, river	A2	89
Yaqui, river	C2	84
Yare, river	D3	30
Yaren, capital	B3	16
Yariga, mt.	C2	8
Yarmouth	A4	100
Yaroslavl	D3	44
Yasawa, island group	A2	17
Yasuj	C3	22
Yata, river	A2	77
Yates	B4	94
Yatsushiro	A3	8
Yauco	B2	90
Yavarí, river	C1	77
Yaviza	D2	87
Yazd	C3	22
Yazd, region	C3	22
Ybbs, river	D2	39
Ye	C3	12
Yeboah	C3	30
Yecla	F3	37
Yeguas, point	D2	90
Yekaterinburg	D5	44
Yekepa	B2	63
Yell, island	Inset I	30
Yellow Grass	F11	104
Yellow, sea	F2	10
Yellowknife, capital	F4	99
Yemen		25
Yen Bai	A2	11
Yendi	B2	64
Yenisey, river	C6	44
Yeovil	C4	30
Yerevan, capital	B2	45
Yesilhrmak, river	D2	27
Yeu, island	B3	34
Yevlax	B2	45
Yevpatoriya	C3	47
Yevrey, autonomous oblast	E8	44
Yi, river	C2	75
Yialousa	C1	27
Yibin	D3	10
Yichang	E2	10
Yichun	F1	10
Yin Shan, mts.	E1	10
Yinchuan	D2	10
Yingkou	F1	10
Yining	B1	10
Ylikitka, lake	C1	53
Ylivieska	B2	53
Yoboki	B2	60
Yogyakarta	C2	13
Yojoa, lake	B2	86
Yokkaichi	C3	8
Yokohama	C3	8
Yokosuka	C3	8
Yola	G3	65
Yom, river	B2	12
Yomou	D4	62
Yonago	B3	8
Yonaguni, island	Inset II	8
Yonne, river	C2	34
Yopal	B3	78
York	C3	30
York	B2	100
York	K5	102
York Factory	E1	96
York, cape	D1	14
Yorkton	H9	104
Yoro	B2	86
Yoron, island	Inset II	8
Yoshino, river	B3	8
Yoshkar-Ola	D4	44
Yİsu	B5	9
Yotvata	B3	26
Youghal	C3	31
Young	E9	104
Youngs Cove	C2	97
Ypané, river	D3	75
Ypoá, lake	D4	75
Ypres	A2	33
Ysyk-Köl, lake	E1	23
Yú Shan, mt.	B2	10
Yuan, river	D3	10
Yubari	Inset I	8
Yucatán, channel	A2	88
Yucatán, peninsula	G4	84
Yuen Long	Inset	10
Yueyang	E3	10
Yugoslavia		49
Yukon, river	D2	92
Yuma, Ariz.	B2	126
Yumen	C2	10
Yuna, river	B2	89
Yundum	A3	72
Yungas, region	A3	77
Yungho	B1	9
Yunnan	D2	10
Yurimaguas	B3	77
Yuscarán	B3	86
Yushu	C2	10
Yuzhno-Sakhalinsk	E9	44
Yverdon	A2	35

Z

Name	Key	Page
Zabbar	C2	36
Zabid	A2	25
Zabol	E3	22
Zabrze	D3	41
Zacapa	D5	85
Zacatecas, state capital	D3	84
Zacatecoluca	B2	86
Zadar	B3	48
Zafra	B3	37
Zagazig	B1	56
Zaghouan	C1	57
Zagreb, capital	B2	48
Zagros, mts.	C3	22
Zahedan	E4	22
Zahlah	A2	26
Zaječar	C3	49
Zákinthos, island	B3	51
Zakopane	D4	41
Zalaegerszeg	A2	43
ZalŒu	B2	43
Zambales, mts.	B3	12
Zambezi	A2	67
Zambezi, river	A3, B3	67
Zambia		67
Zamboanga	B5	12
Zamboanga, peninsula	B5	12
Zamora	D2	37
Zamora	B5	79
Zamora	B4	79
Zamoj~	F3	41
Zanderij	B2	80
Zanjan	B2	22
Zanzibar	C2	68
Zao, mt.	D2	8
Zapadna Morava, river	B3	49
Zapatera, island	B2	87
Zaporizhzhia	D2	47
Zaqatala	B2	45
Zarafobod	A1	23
Zarafshon	B2	23
Zaragoza	F2	37
Zaranj	A2	22
Zareh Sharan	B2	22
Zaria	D2	65
Zarqa, az-	B2	26
Zarzis	C3	57
Zavidovi-i	B1	48
Zaysan	E2	23
Zaysan, lake	E2	23
Zebbug	B1	36
Zeebrugge	B1	33
Zefat	B1	48
Zenica	B1	48
Zeravshan, river	B2	23
Zeravshan, river	A1, B2	23
Zermatt	B2	35
Zestaponi	B3	45
Zeta, river	A3	49
Zêzere, river	A3	36
Zhambyl (Dzhambul)	D2	23
Zhangjiakou	E1	10
Zhangye	D2	10
Zhanjiang	E3	10
Zhejiang	E3	10
Zhelaniya, cape	B5	44
Zhengzhou	E2	10
Zhenjiang	E2	10
Zhezqazghan	C2	23
Zhitomir	B1	47
Zhlobin	B2	47
Zhob, river	C3	21
Zhoda	C4	96
Zhu, river	E3	10
Zhuzhou	E3	10
Zibo	E2	10
Zielona Góra	B3	41
Zigong	D3	10
Ziguinchor	A3	62
Zile	D2	27
Zillah	C2	56
Žilina	B2	42
Zima, lake	A2	94
Zimbabwe		69
Zinder	B3	59
Zion	C3	99
Zittau	C3	40
Ziway, lake	C3	60
Zlatibor, mts.	A3	49
Zlín	C3	42
Znojmo	C4	42
Zomba	C3	68
Zonguldak	B2	27
Zorzor	B2	63
Zouar	B2	59
Zouîrât	B2	58
Zrenjanin	B2	49
Zug	C1	35
Zugdidi	A3	45
Zugspitze, mt.	B5	40
Zuid-Willemsvaart, canal	C3	32
Zújar, reservoir	B3	37
Zululand, region	D2	71
Zunyi	D3	10
Zürich	C1	35
Zürichsee, lake	C1	35
Zurrieq	B2	36
Zuwarah	B1	56
Zvishavane	B2	69
Zvolen	B2	42
Zvornik	B2	48
Zwedru	B2	63
Zwickau	C3	40
Zwolle	D2	32
Zyryanka	C9	44

Z

Name	Key	Page
Zaanstad	B2	32

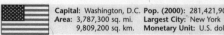

Capital: Washington, D.C. **Pop. (2000):** 281,421,90•
Area: 3,787,300 sq. mi. **Largest City:** New York
9,809,200 sq. km. **Monetary Unit:** U.S. dollar

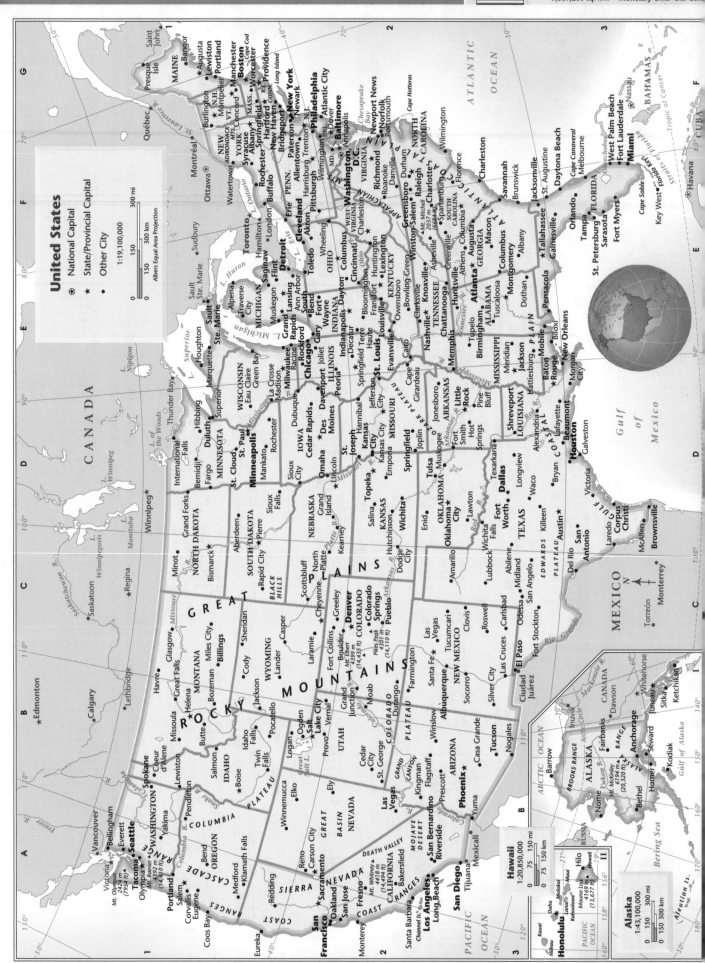

United States

⊕ National Capital
★ State/Provincial Capital
• Other City

1:19,100,000

	150	300 mi
0 150 300 km
Albers Equal Area Projection

Hawaii 1:20,850,000
0 75 150 mi
0 75 150 km

Alaska 1:43,100,000
0 150 300 mi
0 150 300 km

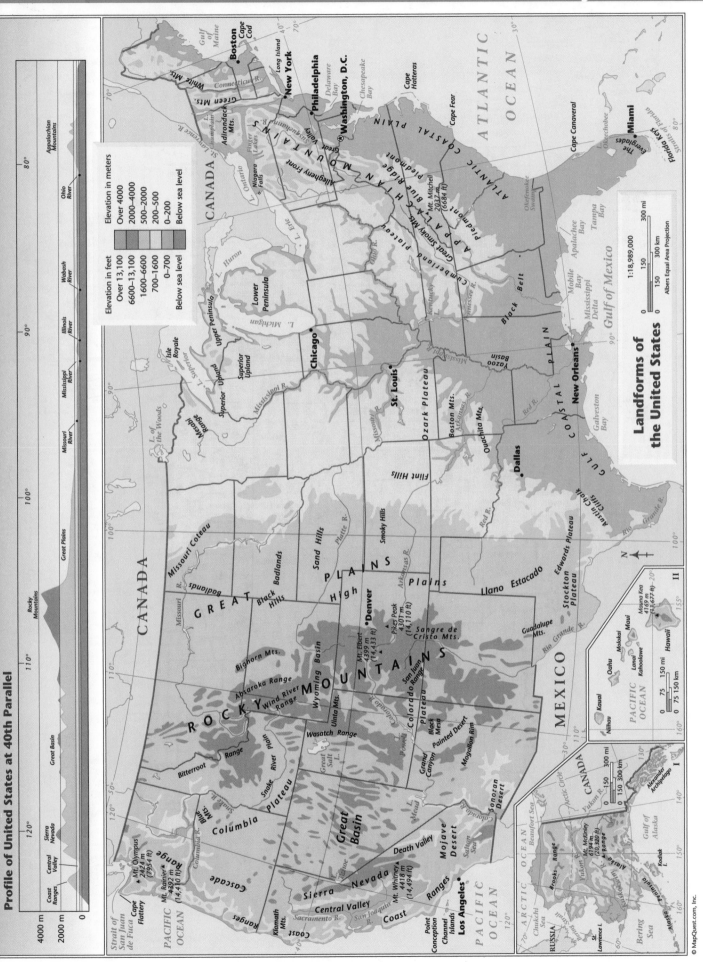

Profile of United States at 40th Parallel

Elevation in feet
Over 13,100
6600–13,100
1600–6600
0–700
Below sea level

Elevation in meters
Over 4000
2000–4000
500–2000
200–500
0–200
Below sea level

Landforms of the United States

1:18,989,000

Albers Equal Area Projection

© MapQuest.com, Inc.

Capital: Montgomery   **Pop. (2000):** 4,447,100
Area: 52,400 sq. mi.   **Largest City:** Birmingham,
135,800 sq. km.   242,820

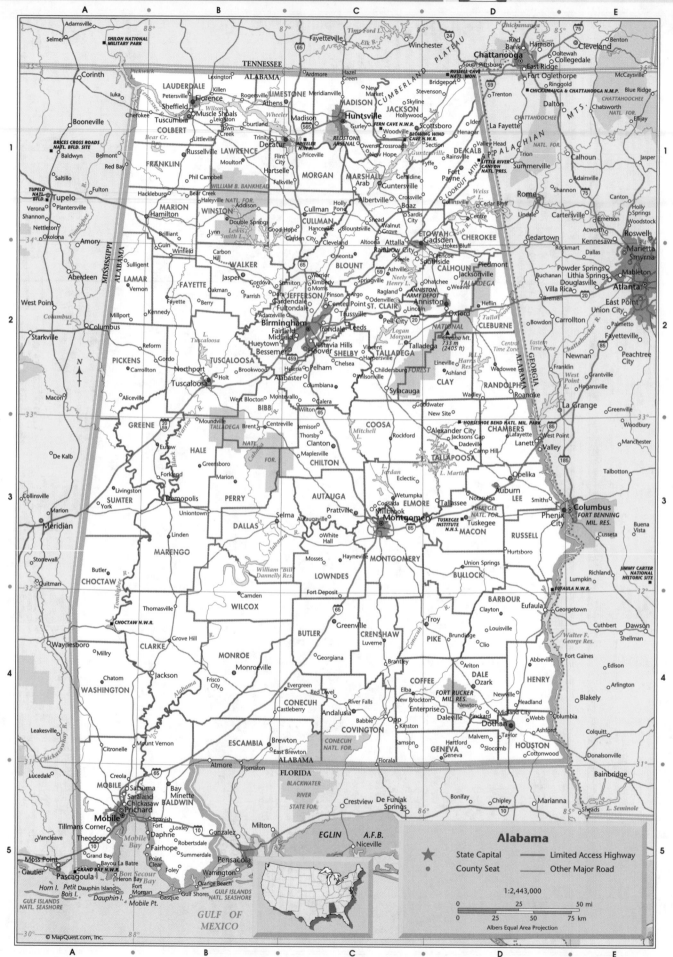

Alabama

★ State Capital   —— Limited Access Highway
● County Seat   —— Other Major Road

1:2,443,000

0   25   50 mi
0   25   50   75 km

Albers Equal Area Projection

© MapQuest.com, Inc.

Capital: Juneau
Area: 656,400 sq. mi.
1,700,000 sq. km.
Pop. (2000): 626,932
Largest City: Anchorage
260,283

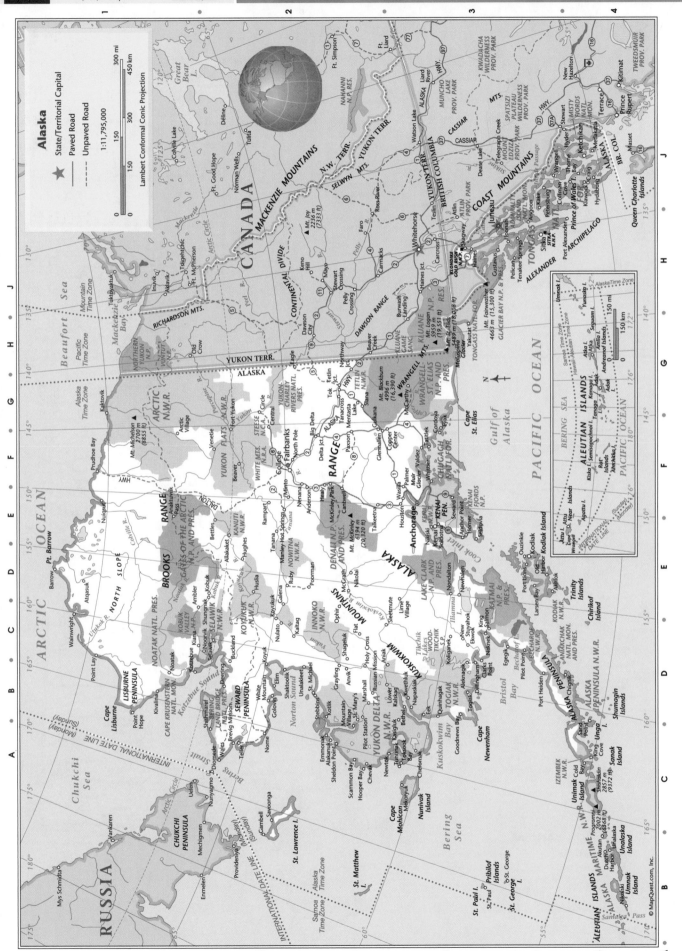

Alaska
★ State/Territorial Capital
— Paved Road
--- Unpaved Road

1:11,795,000
Lambert Conformal Conic Projection

© MapQuest.com, Inc.

Capital: Phoenix
Area: 114,000 sq. mi.
295,300 sq. km.
Pop. (2000): 5,130,632
Largest City: Phoenix 1,321,045

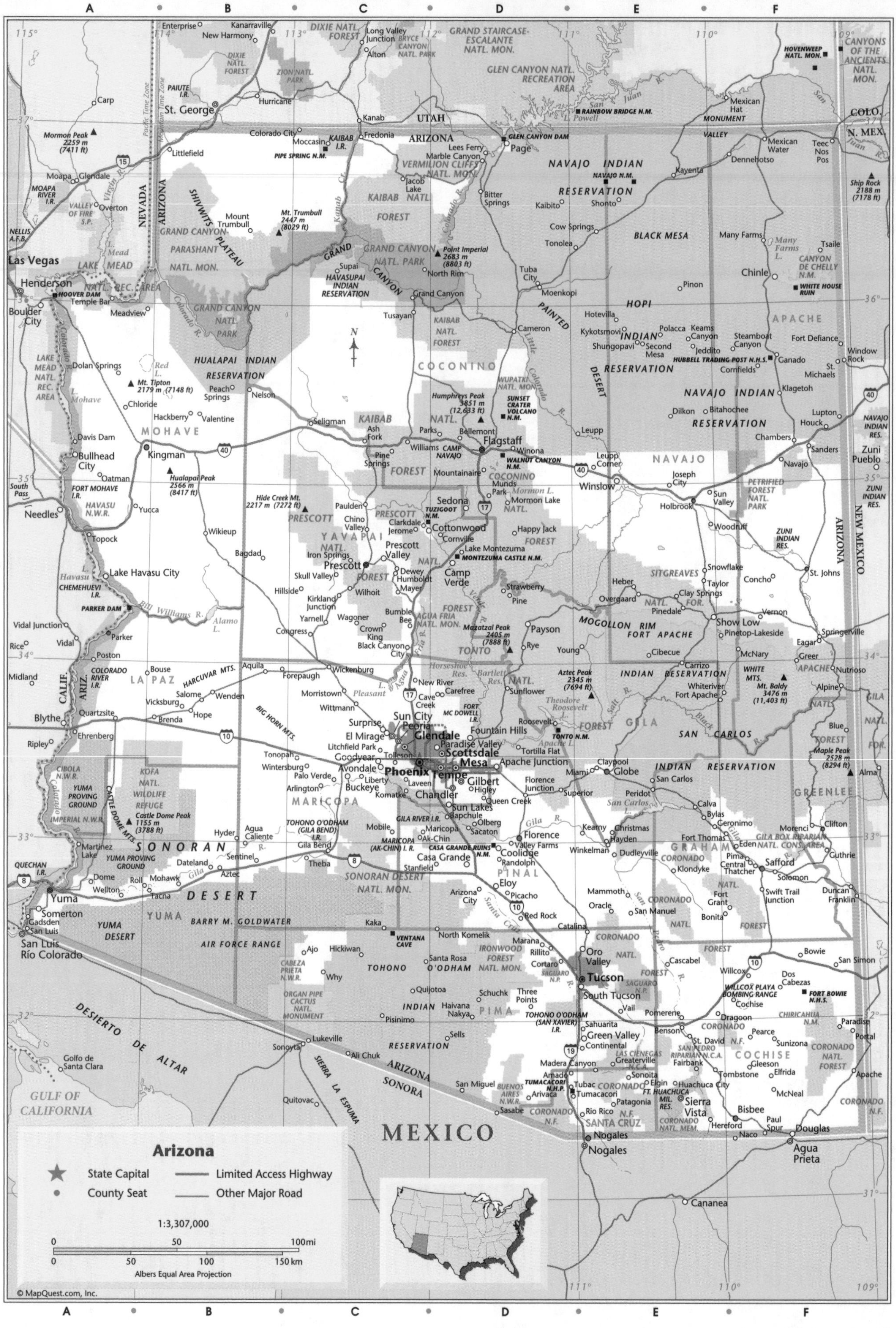

UTAH

ARIZONA

NEVADA

CALIFORNIA

NEW MEXICO

COLO.

N. MEX.

MEXICO

SONORA

GULF OF CALIFORNIA

DESIERTO DE ALTAR

Las Vegas · Henderson · Boulder City

GRAND CANYON NATL. PARK

NAVAJO INDIAN RESERVATION

HOPI INDIAN RESERVATION

APACHE

COCONINO

MOHAVE

YAVAPAI

LA PAZ

MARICOPA

YUMA

PIMA

PINAL

GILA

GRAHAM

GREENLEE

COCHISE

SANTA CRUZ

SONORAN DESERT

Phoenix · Scottsdale · Mesa · Tempe · Gilbert · Chandler · Glendale · Peoria · Sun City

Flagstaff · Sedona · Prescott · Payson · Winslow · Holbrook · Show Low

Kingman · Bullhead City · Lake Havasu City · Parker

Yuma · San Luis · Somerton · Gadsden

Tucson · South Tucson · Oro Valley · Green Valley · Sierra Vista · Nogales · Douglas · Bisbee · Willcox

Casa Grande · Florence · Coolidge · Eloy

Safford · Clifton · Morenci

Arizona

★ State Capital — Limited Access Highway
• County Seat — Other Major Road

1:3,307,000

0   50   100 mi
0   50   100   150 km

Albers Equal Area Projection

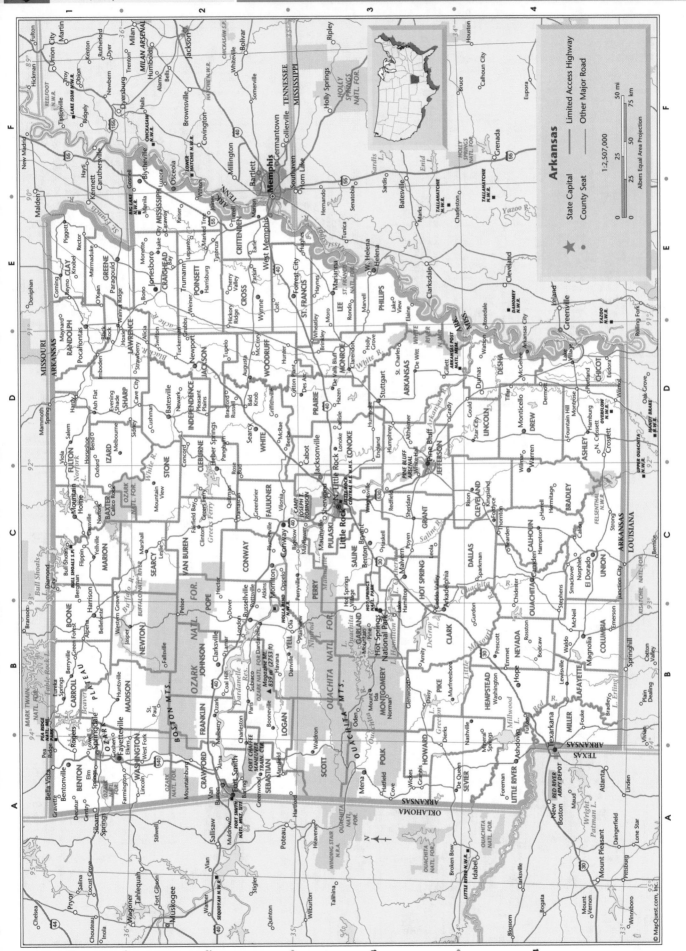

Capital: Sacramento
Area: 163,700 sq. mi.
424,000 sq. km.
Pop. (2000): 33,871,64[8]
Largest City: Los Angele[s]
3,694,820

CALIFORNIA REPUBLIC

California

★ State Capital
• County Seat
— Limited Access Highway
— Other Major Road

1:5,273,000

0 — 50 — 100 mi
0 — 50 — 100 — 150 km

Albers Equal Area Projection

© MapQuest.com, Inc.

PACIFIC OCEAN

OREGON

NEVADA

ARIZONA

MEXICO

Capital: Denver
Area: 104,100 sq. mi.
269,600 sq. km.
Pop. (2000): 4,301,261
Largest City: Denver
554,636

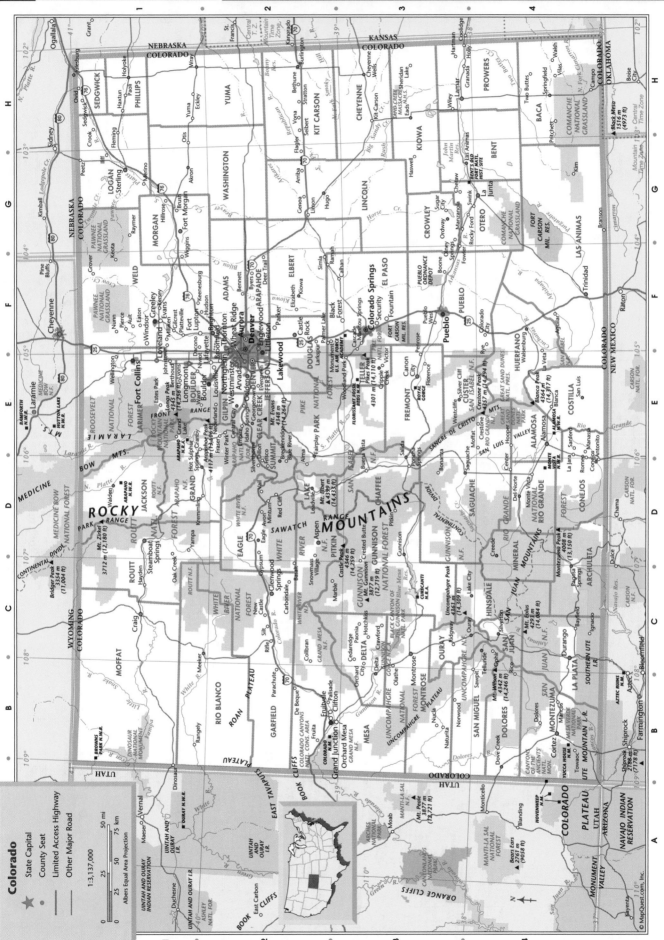

Colorado

★ State Capital
• County Seat
— Limited Access Highway
— Other Major Road

1:3,137,000

Albers Equal Area Projection

©MapQuest.com, Inc.

Capital: Hartford
Area: 5,500 sq. mi.
14,400 sq. km.
Pop. (2000): 3,405,565
Largest City: Bridgeport
139,529

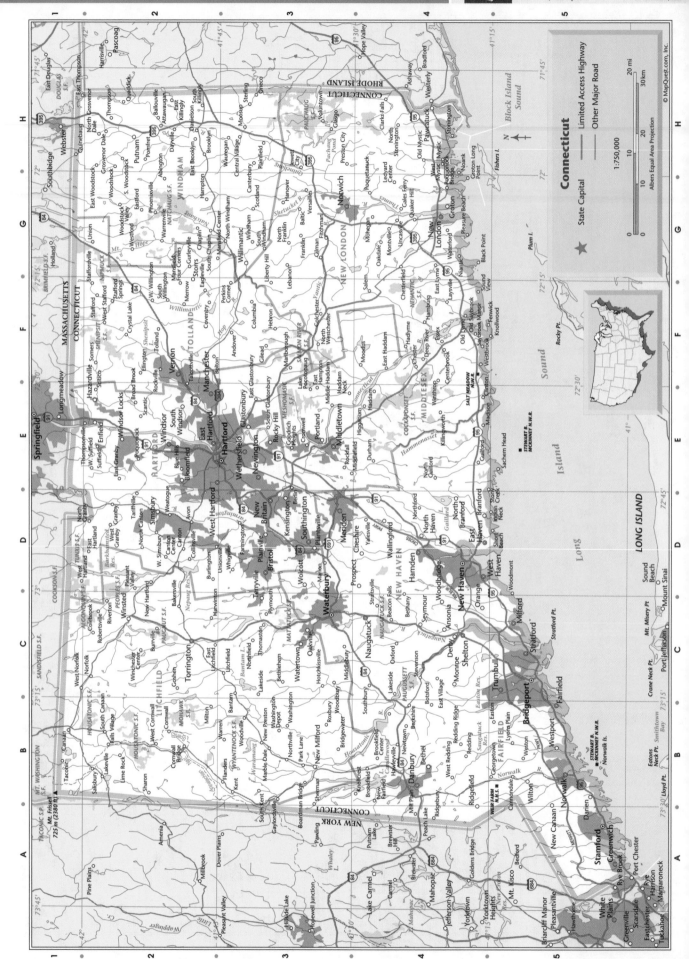

Connecticut

★ State Capital

— Limited Access Highway
— Other Major Road

1:750,000
Albers Equal Area Projection

Capital:	Dover	Pop. (2000):	783,600
Area:	2,500 sq. mi.	Largest City:	Wilmington
	6,400 sq. km.		72,664

DELAWARE 135

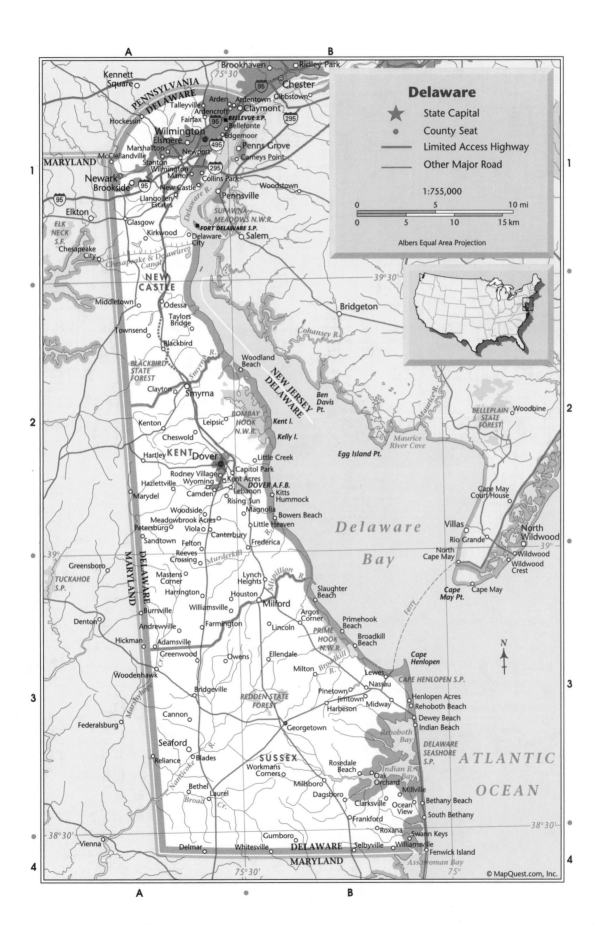

Capital: Tallahassee   **Pop. (2000):** 15,982,37
Area: 65,800 sq. mi.   **Largest City:** Jacksonvill
170,300 sq. km.   735,617

Florida

★ State Capital
• County Seat
━━ Limited Access Highway
━━ Other Major Road

1:3,135,000

0   25   50 mi
0   25   50   75 km
Albers Equal Area Projection

© MapQuest.com, Inc.

Capital: Atlanta
Area: 59,400 sq. mi.
153,900 sq. km.
Pop. (2000): 8,186,453
Largest City: Atlanta
416,474

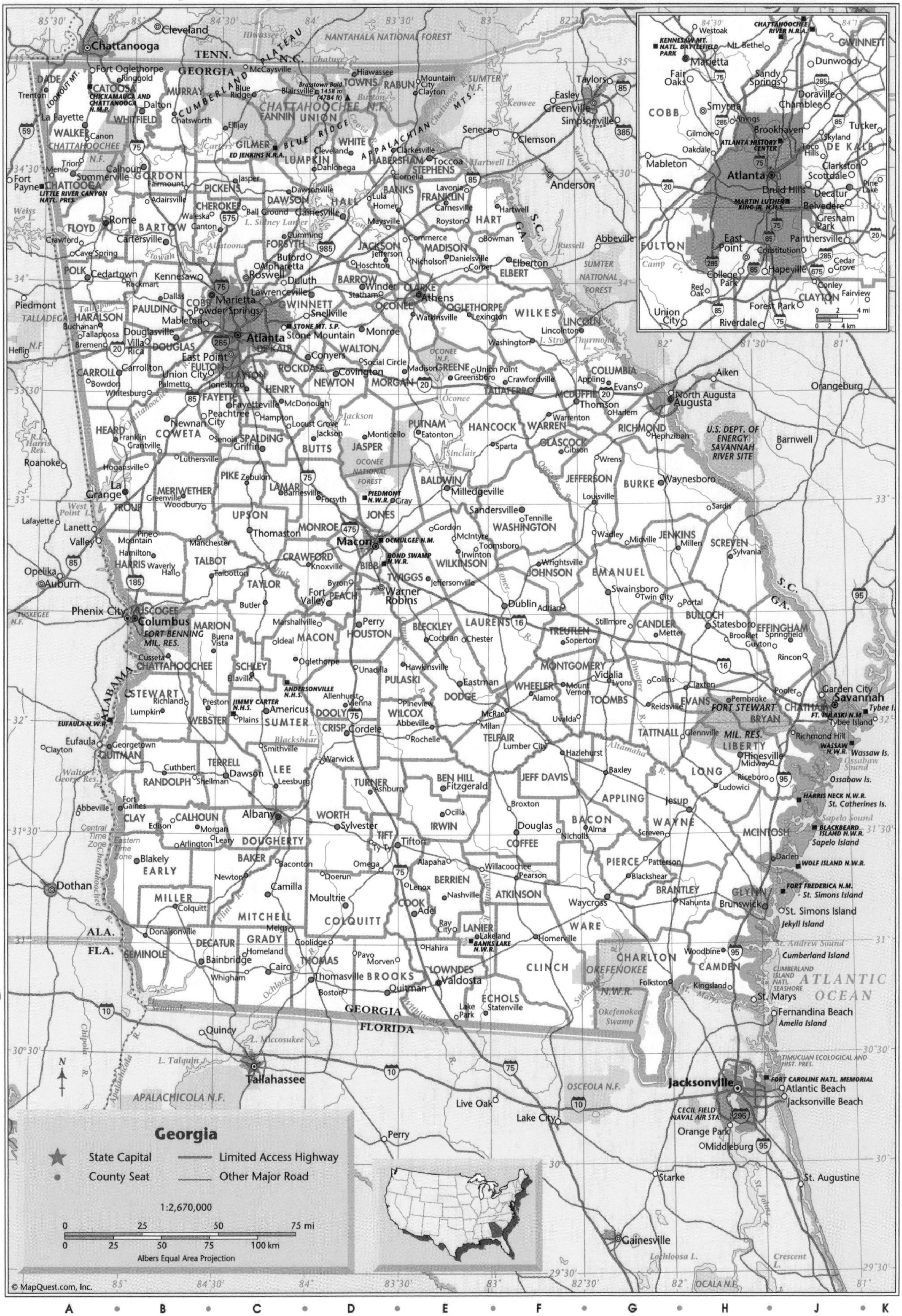

Georgia

★ State Capital
• County Seat
— Limited Access Highway
— Other Major Road

1:2,670,000

0 25 50 75 mi
0 25 50 75 100 km
Albers Equal Area Projection

© MapQuest.com, Inc.

Capital: Honolulu   Pop. (2000): 1,211,53
Area: 10,900 sq. mi.   Largest City: Honolulu
28,300 sq. km.   371,657

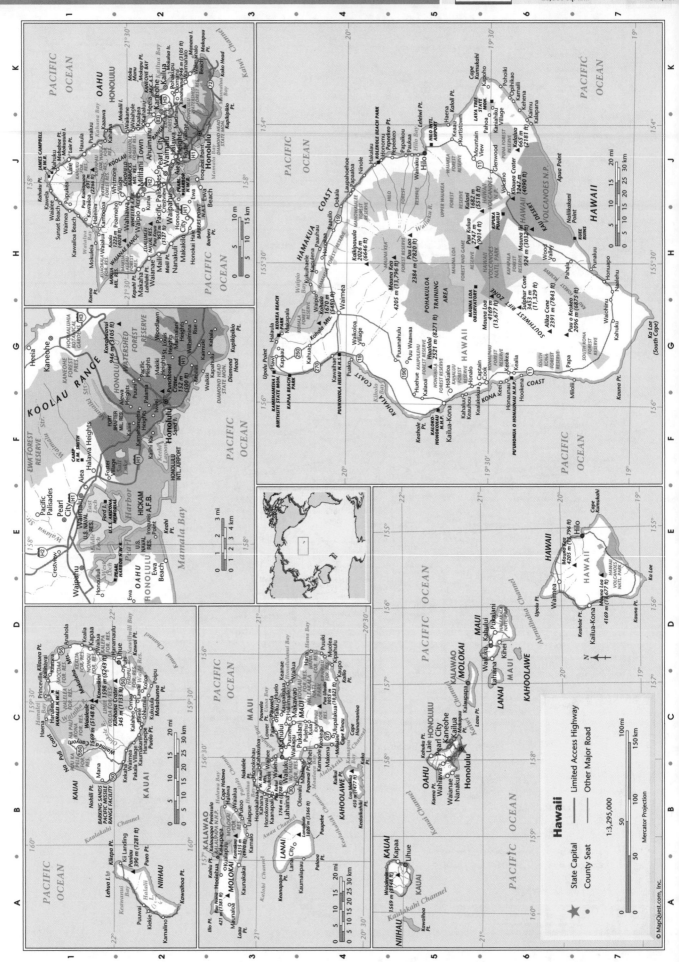

© MapQuest.com, Inc.

Capital: Boise
Area: 83,600 sq. mi.
216,500 sq. km.
Pop. (2000): 1,293,953
Largest City: Boise
185,787

Idaho

★ State Capital — Limited Access Highway
○ County Seat — Other Major Road

1:3,295,000

0   50   100mi
0   50   100   150 km

Albers Equal Area Projection

© MapQuest.com, Inc.

UPPER MISSOURI RIVER BREAKS NATIONAL MONUMENT

CAN.
U.S.

B.C.
MONTANA

WATERTON LAKES N.P.
Waterton

Mt. Cleveland 3190 m (10,466 ft)
GLACIER NATIONAL PARK
BLACKFEET I.R.

Trail
Porthill
Eastport
Moyie Springs
Bonners Ferry
Naples
Kootenai
Elmira
Priest River
Oldtown
Laclede
Sandpoint
Dover
Sagle
Hope
Clark Fork
Cocolalla
Blanchard
Careywood
Lakeview
Athol
Spirit Lake
Rathdrum
Hayden
Coeur d'Alene
Post Falls
Spokane
Country Homes
Opportunity
Cheney

COLVILLE NATL. FOREST
LITTLE PEND ORIELLE N.W.R.
SELKIRK
KANIKSU NATL. FOREST
KALISPEL I.R.
KANIKSU N.F.
BONNER
KOOTENAI N.W.R.
KOOTENAI NATL. FOREST
BOUNDARY
COEUR D'ALENE NATIONAL FOREST
TURNBULL N.W.R.

WASH.
IDAHO

Coolin
Samuels
Nordman
Kootenai

Whitefish
Kalispell
FLATHEAD NATIONAL FOREST
Hungry Horse Res.
Flathead L.
SWAN RIVER N.W.R.
FLATHEAD IND. RES.
PABLO N.W.R.
NINEPIPE N.W.R.
NATIONAL BISON RANGE

Coolin
Murray
Kingston
Pinehurst
Kellogg
Osburn
Wallace
Mullan
Burke
Rose Lake
Harrison
Worley
Plummer
Maries
St. Joe
Calder
Avery

SHOSHONE
LOLO NATIONAL FOREST
BENEWAH
COEUR D'ALENE I.R.
St. Joe R.

LEWIS AND CLARK NATL. FOREST
CONTINENTAL DIVIDE
HELENA
HELENA NATIONAL FOREST
Helena
LEWIS AND CLARK N.F.
HIGHWOOD MTS. LEWIS AND CLARK NATL. FOR.
LITTLE BELT MTS.
BIG BELT MTS.
HELENA CANYON FERRY FOREST

Potlatch
Viola
Harvard
Bovill
Moscow
Deary
Helmer
Elk River
Troy
Kendrick
Genesee
Southwick
Ahsahka
Lenore
Peck
Gifford
Greer
Weippe
Pierce
Headquarters
Grangemont
Orofino

LATAH
CLEARWATER
CLEARWATER NATIONAL FOREST
Dworshak Res.
ST. JOE NATIONAL FOREST
Clarkia
Fernwood
Santa
Emida
Bovill

Missoula
Lolo Peak 2786 m (9139 ft)
LEE METCALF N.W.R.
RATTLESNAKE NATL. REC. AREA
LOLO NATIONAL FOREST
GRANT-KOHRS RANCH N.H.S.
BITTERROOT N.F.
BEAVERHEAD-DEERLODGE NATIONAL FOREST
Anaconda
Butte
BEAVERHEAD-DEERLODGE N.F.

Pullman
Clarkston
Lewiston
Winchester
Waha
Craigmont
Nezperce
Ferdinand
Cottonwood
Fenn
Grangeville
Harpster
Kamiah
Kooskia
Lowell
Stites
Golden

NEZ PERCE N.H.P. (SPALDING AREA)
NEZ PERCE I.R.
NEZ PERCE
LEWIS
NEZ PERCE N.H.P. (EAST KAMIAH SITE)
CLEARWATER N.F.
IDAHO
RANGE
BITTERROOT R.

UMATILLA NATIONAL FOREST
WASH.
ORE.
WALLOWA-WHITMAN NATIONAL FOREST

White Bird
Orogrande
Dixie
Lucile
Riggins
Pollock
Burgdorf
Warren
Shoup
Carmen
Salmon
Baker
Tendoy
Gibbonsville
North Fork
Cobalt
Leadore
Lemhi

NEZ PERCE NATIONAL FOREST
Elk City
Red River Hot Springs
HELLS CANYON NATL. REC. AREA
Sacajawea Peak 2998 m (9839 ft)
PAYETTE NATIONAL FOREST
SALMON-CHALLIS NATIONAL FOREST
LEMHI
SALMON RIVER MOUNTAINS
BIG HOLE N.B.
Warren Peak 3189 m (10,464 ft)
ANACONDA RANGE
BEAVERHEAD-DEERLODGE NATL. FOR.
BEAVERHEAD-DEERLODGE NATIONAL FOREST
Granite Peak 3228 m (10,590 ft)
Livingston
Bozeman
GALLATIN NATIONAL FOREST
GALLATIN N.F.
MONTANA
WYOMING

New Meadows
Yellow Pine
Big Creek
McCall
Fruitvale
Council
Mesa
Cambridge
Indian Valley
Midvale
Lake Fork
Donnelly
Cascade
Warm Lake
Smiths Ferry
Garden Valley
Banks
Gardena
Placerville
Horseshoe Bend

ADAMS
VALLEY
Cascade Res.
Payette L.
BOISE NATIONAL FOREST
SAWTOOTH RANGE

Ellis
May
Patterson
Challis
Clayton
Stanley
Sunbeam
Lowman

CUSTER
SALMON-CHALLIS NATIONAL FOREST
Borah Peak 3859 m (12,662 ft)
SALMON-CHALLIS N.F.
Castle Peak 3601 m (11,815 ft)
Scott Peak 3473 m (11,393 ft)
CONTINENTAL DIVIDE
TARGHEE N.F.
Humphrey
Kilgore
Spencer
Dubois
Island Park
TARGHEE NATIONAL FOREST
RED ROCK LAKES N.W.R.
YELLOWSTONE NATIONAL PARK
Yellowstone L.
J.D. ROCKEFELLER JR. MEM. PKWY.

Weiser
Ontario
Payette
Fruitland
New Plymouth
Letha
Sweet
Emmett
Parma
Notus
Middleton
Caldwell
Nampa
Star
Eagle
Garden City
Boise
Kuna
Melba
Marsing
Bowmont
Murphy
Oreana
Silver City
Reynolds
Grand View
Bruneau

WASHINGTON
PAYETTE
GEM
ADA
CANYON
DEER FLAT N.W.R.
OWYHEE
SNAKE RIVER BIRDS OF PREY NATL. CONS. AREA
ELMORE
Idaho City
Atlanta
Rocky Bar
Featherville
Prairie
Pine
Mayfield
Orchard
Mountain Home
Hammett
Glenns Ferry
King Hill
Bliss
Hot Spring
Hagerman

Ryan Peak 3595 m (11,795 ft)
Hyndman Peak 3660 m (12,009 ft)
Sun Valley
Ketchum
Mackay
Leslie
Darlington
Moore
Arco
Howe
Atomic City
Bellevue
Hailey
Gannett
Corral
Fairfield
Hill City
Picabo
Carey

CAMAS
BLAINE
BUTTE
CLARK
FREMONT
JEFFERSON
MADISON
TETON
BONNEVILLE

SAWTOOTH NATL. REC. AREA
CAMAS N.W.R.
Monteview
Terreton
Mud Lake
Roberts
Menan
Rigby
Ririe
Monteview
St. Anthony
Sugar City
Rexburg
Thornton
Newdale
Teton
Tetonia
Driggs
Victor
Felt
Ashton
Chester
Warm River
Hamer
Lewisville
Ammon
Idaho Falls
Iona
Ucon
Shelley
Swan Valley
Irwin

Grand Teton 4280 m (13,770 ft)
GRAND TETON NATIONAL PARK
NATL. ELK REFUGE
Jackson
BRIDGER-TETON N.F.
TETON RANGE
TARGHEE NATIONAL FOREST
BRIDGER-TETON NATIONAL FOREST

IDAHO NATIONAL ENGINEERING AND ENVIRONMENTAL LAB
Lost River
Big Lost R.
Little Lost R.
CRATERS OF THE MOON NATL. MON.
LINCOLN
Shoshone
Dietrich
Richfield
Gooding
Wendell
Hagerman
Jerome
Eden
Hazelton
Paul
Acequia
Rupert
Minidoka
Burley
Declo
Albion

GOODING
JEROME
MINIDOKA
MINIDOKA N.W.R.
MINIDOKA INTERNMENT NATL. MON.
HAGERMAN FOSSIL BEDS N.M.
SNAKE RIVER
SAWTOOTH NATIONAL FOREST

Springfield
Sterling
Aberdeen
American Falls
Rockford
Pingree
Fort Hall
Blackfoot
Chubbuck
Pocatello
Rockland
Pauline
Arbon
Holbrook

POWER
BINGHAM
FORT HALL I.R.
CARIBOU
FORT HALL
American Falls Res.
Blackfoot Res.
Grays L.
Palisades Res.
CARIBOU NATIONAL FOREST
CARIBOU N.F.
Wayan
Henry
Conda
Soda Springs
Bancroft
Grace
Lava Hot Springs
McCammon
Arimo
Robin
Virginia
Downey
Swanlake
Thatcher

BANNOCK
CARIBOU
BRIDGER-TETON NATIONAL FOREST
IDAHO
WYOMING
WASATCH
BEAR LAKE
CARIBOU-TARGHEE N.F.
Georgetown
Bennington
Montpelier
Ovid
Paris
Bloomington
St. Charles
Fish Haven
BEAR LAKE N.W.R.

Buhl
Castleford
Filer
Twin Falls
Kimberly
Hansen
Murtaugh
Roseworth
Hollister
Rogerson
Three Creek
Grasmere
Riddle

TWIN FALLS
CASSIA
ONEIDA
FRANKLIN
Oakley
Malta
Sublett
Almo
Bridge
Stone
Woodruff
Dayton
Weston
Preston
Clifton
Oxford
Malad City
CURLEW NATL. GRASSLAND
Cache Peak 3151 m (10,339 ft)
CITY OF ROCKS NATL. RESERVE
CACHE N.F.
JUNIPER

OWYHEE
DUCK VALLEY I.R.

NEVADA
UTAH
HUMBOLDT-TOIYABE NATIONAL FOREST
SAWTOOTH N.F.
Bear L.

Pacific Time Zone
Mountain Time Zone

OREGON
IDAHO MTS.
HELLS CANYON NATL. REC. AREA

Capital: Springfield
Area: 57,900 sq. mi.
150,000 sq. km.
Pop. (2000): 12,419,293
Largest City: Chicago
2,896,016

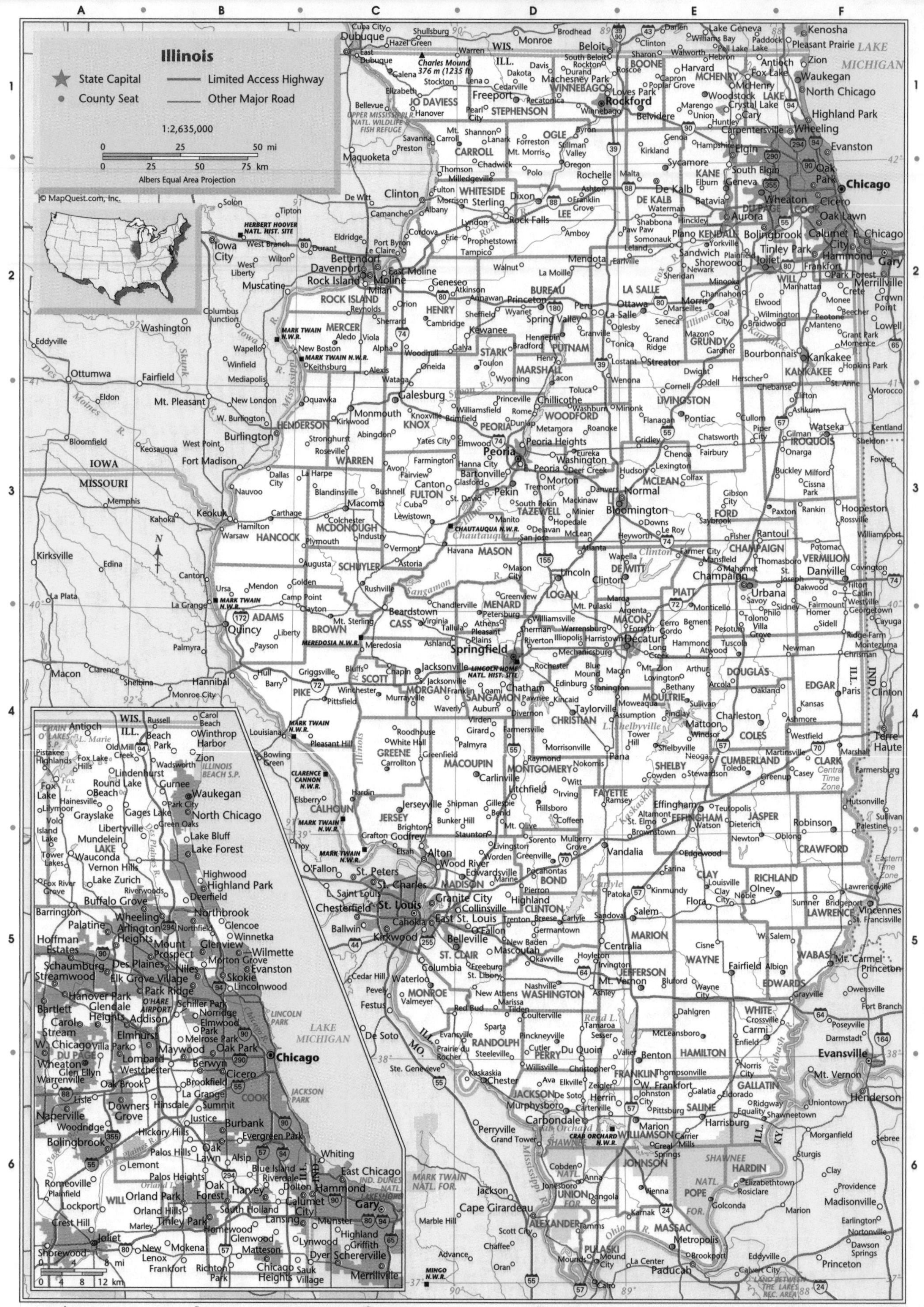

Illinois

★ State Capital
• County Seat

— Limited Access Highway
— Other Major Road

1:2,635,000

0   25   50 mi
0   25   50   75 km

Albers Equal Area Projection

© MapQuest.com, Inc.

Capital: Indianapolis	Pop. (2000): 6,080,485
Area: 36,400 sq. mi.	Largest City: Indianapolis
94,300 sq. km.	791,926

Lake Michigan

Chicago

South Bend

Fort Wayne

Indianapolis

Terre Haute

Bloomington

Columbus

Cincinnati

Evansville

Louisville

Owensboro

Indiana

★ State Capital — Limited Access Highway
● County Seat — Other Major Road

1:2,099,000

0   25   50 mi
0   25   50   75 km
Albers Equal Area Projection

© MapQuest.com, Inc.

SHAWNEE NATIONAL FOREST

HOOSIER N.F.

MUSCATATUCK N.W.R.

NAVAL SURFACE WARFARE CENTER CRANE DIV.

GEORGE ROGERS CLARK N.H.P.

LINCOLN BOYHOOD NATL. MEMORIAL

WYANDOTTE CAVE

FORT KNOX MIL. RES.

Central Time Zone
Eastern Time Zone

MICH.
IND.
OHIO
ILLINOIS
INDIANA
IND.
KY.

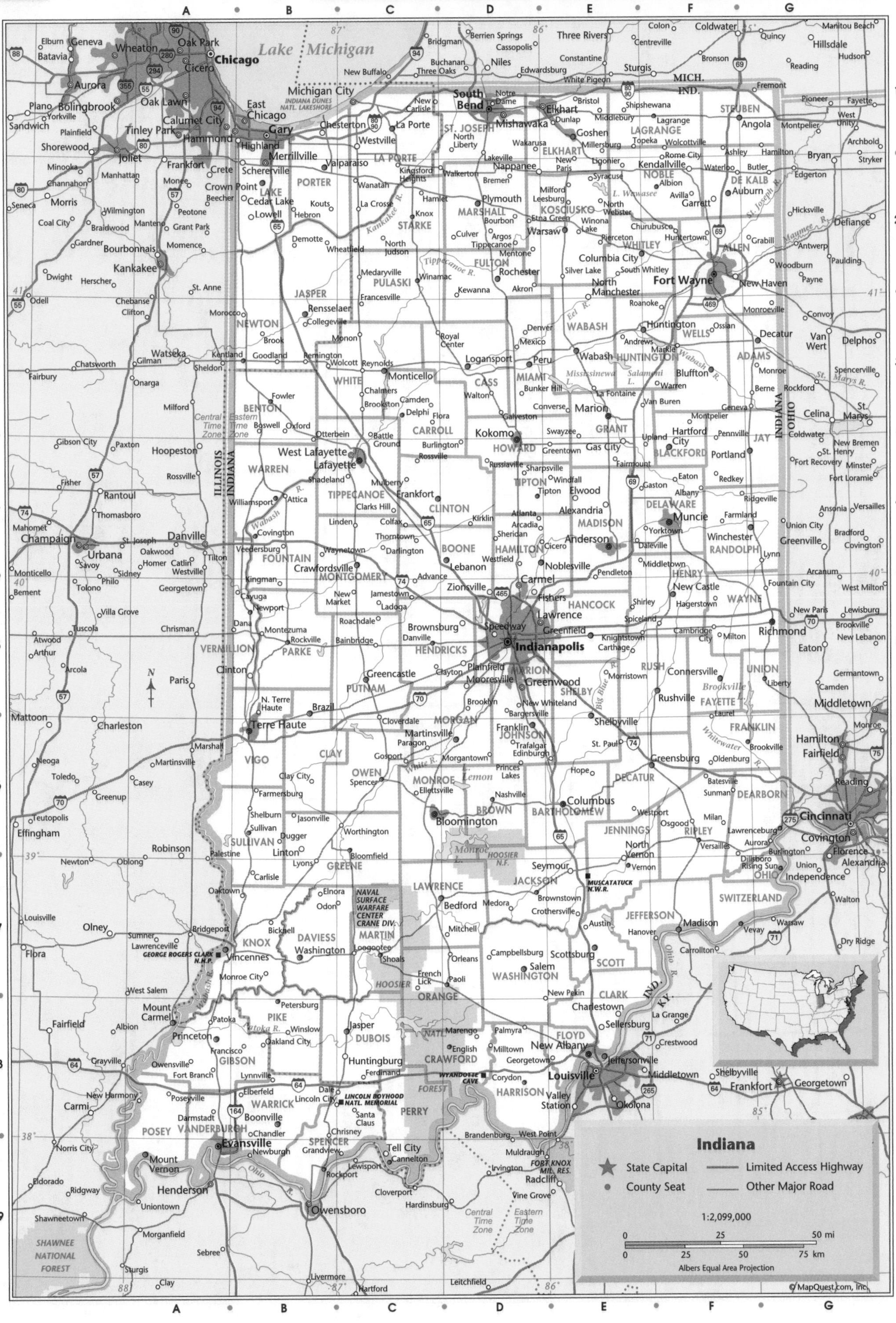

Capital: Des Moines
Area: 56,300 sq. mi.
145,800 sq. km.

Pop. (2000): 2,926,32
Largest City: Des Moin
198,682

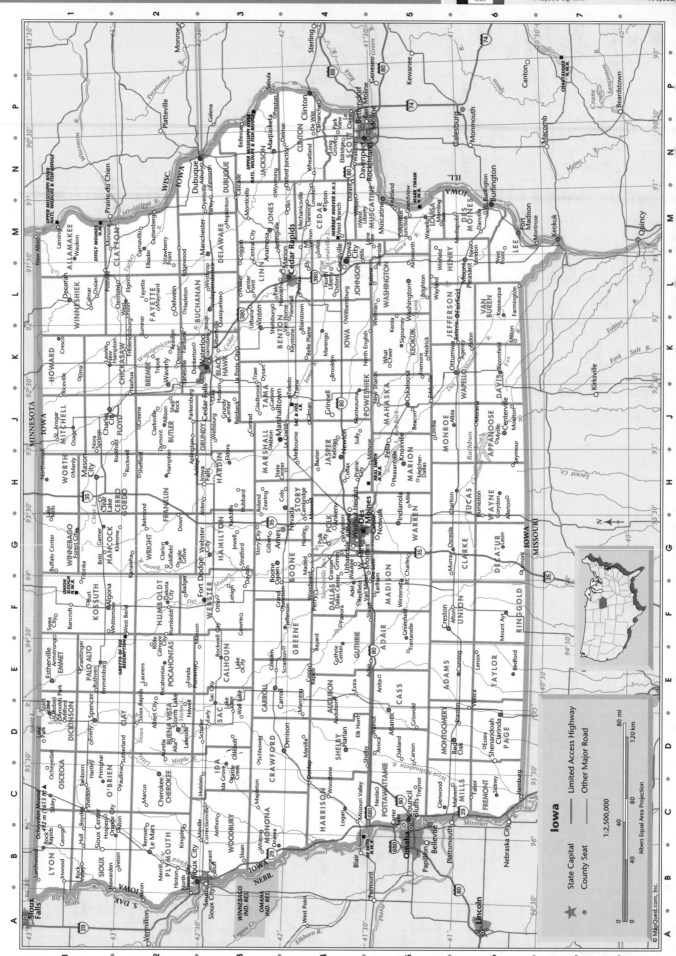

Iowa

— Limited Access Highway
— Other Major Road

★ State Capital
◉ County Seat

1:2,500,000

Albers Equal Area Projection

© MapQuest.com, Inc.

Capital: Topeka
Area: 82,300 sq. mi.
213,100 sq. km.
Pop. (2000): 2,688,418
Largest City: Wichita
344,284

KANSAS

Kansas

★ State Capital
• County Seat

— Limited Access Highway
— Other Major Road

1:2,841,000
Albers Equal Area Projection

100 mi
150 km

Central Time Zone
Mountain Time Zone

Mt. Sunflower
1231 m
(4039 ft)

Surrounding states/regions: IOWA, MISSOURI, NEBRASKA, OKLAHOMA, COLORADO

Selected counties: CHEYENNE, RAWLINS, DECATUR, NORTON, PHILLIPS, SMITH, JEWELL, REPUBLIC, WASHINGTON, MARSHALL, NEMAHA, BROWN, DONIPHAN, ATCHISON, JACKSON, POTTAWATOMIE, RILEY, CLAY, CLOUD, MITCHELL, OSBORNE, ROOKS, GRAHAM, SHERIDAN, THOMAS, SHERMAN, WALLACE, LOGAN, GOVE, TREGO, ELLIS, RUSSELL, LINCOLN, OTTAWA, SALINE, DICKINSON, GEARY, WABAUNSEE, SHAWNEE, JEFFERSON, LEAVENWORTH, WYANDOTTE, JOHNSON, DOUGLAS, OSAGE, MORRIS, CHASE, MARION, McPHERSON, ELLSWORTH, RICE, BARTON, RUSH, NESS, LANE, SCOTT, WICHITA, GREELEY, HAMILTON, KEARNY, FINNEY, HODGEMAN, PAWNEE, STAFFORD, RENO, HARVEY, SEDGWICK, BUTLER, GREENWOOD, LYON, COFFEY, FRANKLIN, MIAMI, LINN, ANDERSON, ALLEN, WOODSON, WILSON, NEOSHO, BOURBON, CRAWFORD, CHEROKEE, LABETTE, MONTGOMERY, CHAUTAUQUA, ELK, COWLEY, SUMNER, KINGMAN, PRATT, EDWARDS, KIOWA, FORD, GRAY, HASKELL, GRANT, STANTON, MORTON, STEVENS, SEWARD, MEADE, CLARK, COMANCHE, BARBER, HARPER

State capital: ★ Topeka

Largest city: Wichita

Selected cities/towns: Kansas City, Overland Park, Olathe, Lawrence, Leavenworth, Manhattan, Salina, Hutchinson, Dodge City, Garden City, Liberal, Emporia, El Dorado, Winfield, Arkansas City, Pittsburg, Coffeyville, Independence, Parsons, Chanute, Iola, Fort Scott, Ottawa, Abilene, Junction City, Hays, Great Bend, Newton, Wellington, Goodland, Colby

OSAGE INDIAN RESERVATION

© MapQuest.com, Inc.

Capital: Frankfort
Area: 40,400 sq. mi.
104,700 sq. km.
Pop. (2000): 4,041,76●
Largest City: Lexingto●
260,512

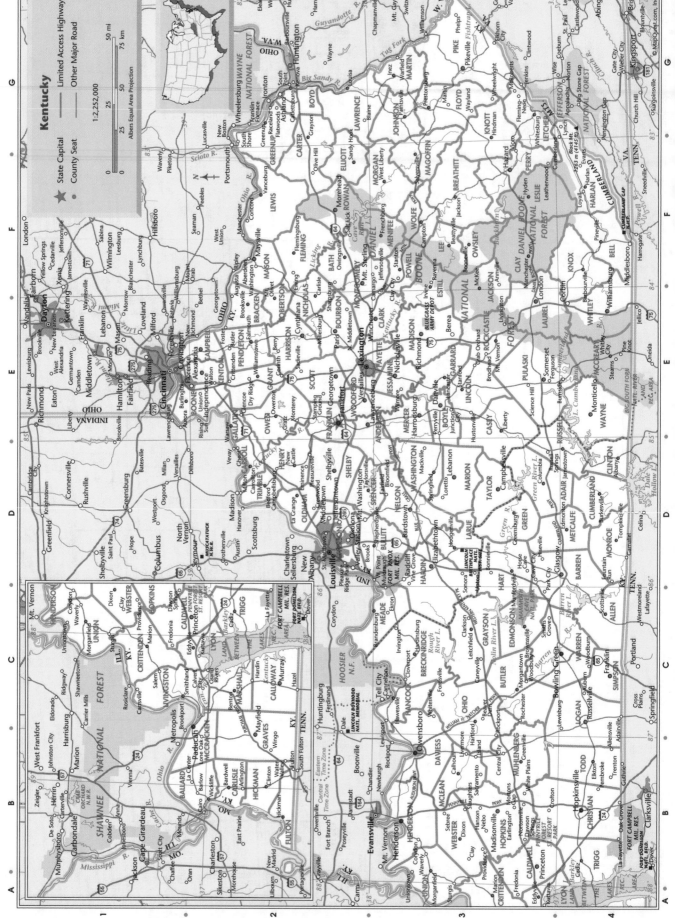

Capital: Baton Rouge
Area: 51,800 sq. mi.
134,300 sq. km.
Pop. (2000): 4,468,976
Largest City: New Orleans
484,674

Louisiana

★ State Capital
• Parish Seat

—— Limited Access Highway
—— Other Major Road

1:2,750,000

Albers Equal Area Projection

© MapQuest.com, Inc.

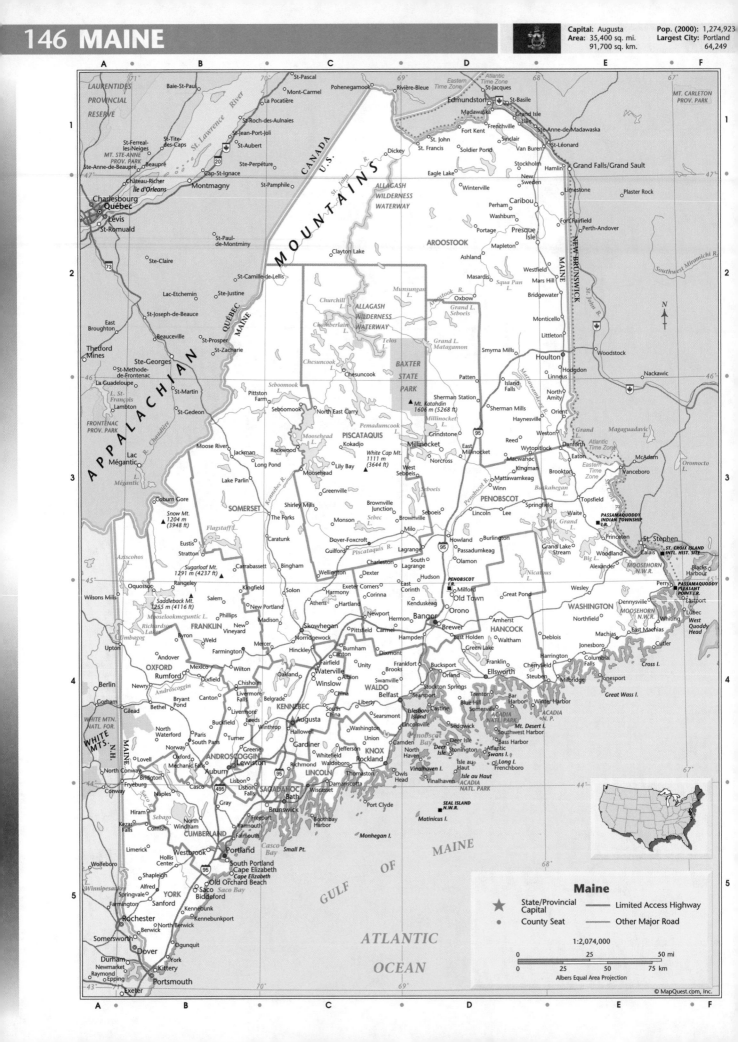

Capital: Augusta
Area: 35,400 sq. mi.
91,700 sq. km.
Pop. (2000): 1,274,923
Largest City: Portland
64,249

Maine

★ State/Provincial Capital
• County Seat
━━ Limited Access Highway
── Other Major Road

1:2,074,000

0   25   50 mi
0 25 50 75 km
Albers Equal Area Projection

© MapQuest.com, Inc.

Capital: Annapolis	Pop. (2000): 5,296,486
Area: 12,400 sq. mi. 32,100 sq. km.	Largest City: Baltimore 651,154

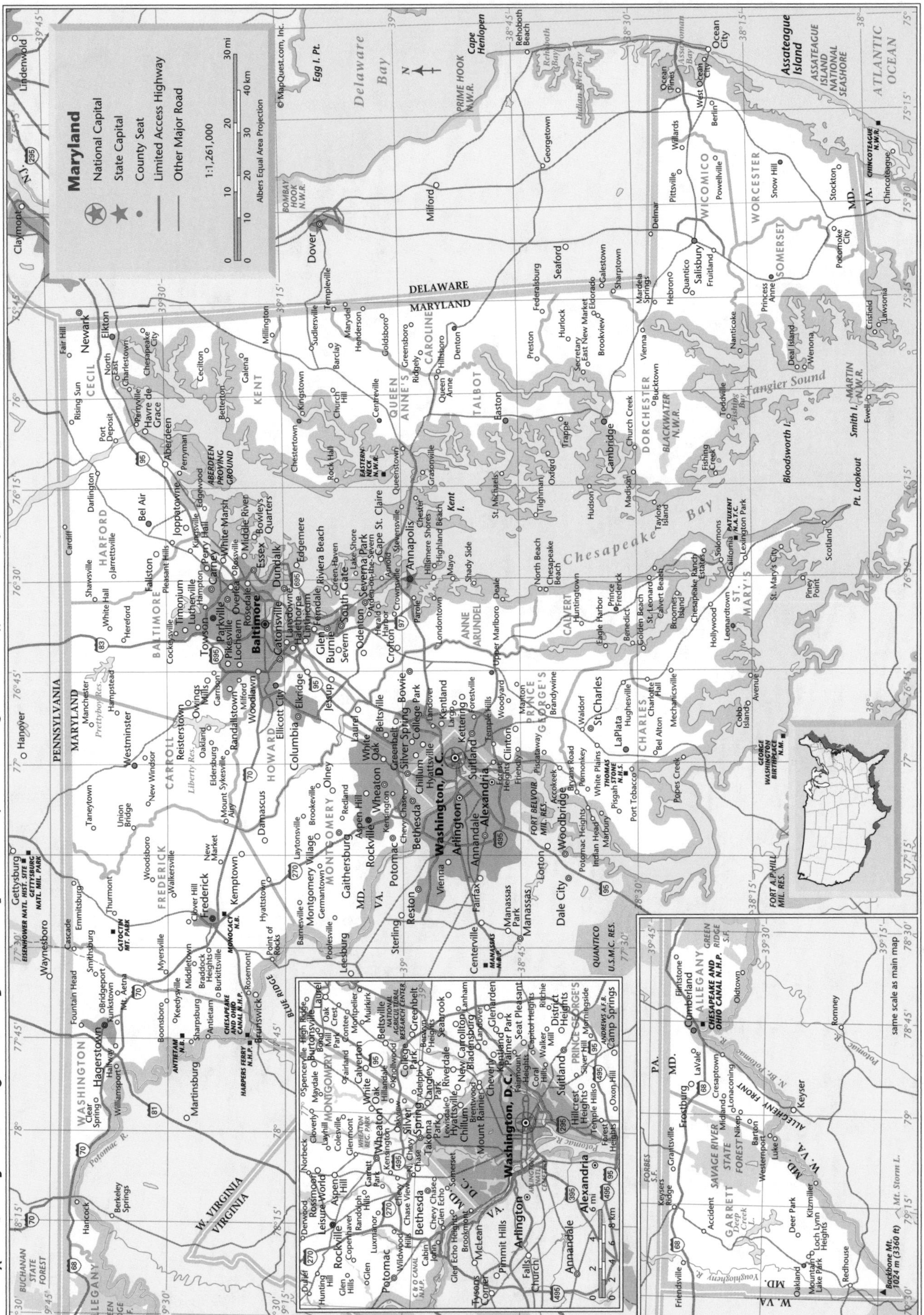

Maryland

- National Capital ★
- State Capital ★
- County Seat •
- Limited Access Highway
- Other Major Road

1:1,261,000

30 mi

40 km

Albers Equal Area Projection

©MapQuest.com, Inc.

Capital: Boston
Area: 10,600 sq. mi.
27,300 sq. km.
Pop. (2000): 6,349,09[7]
Largest City: Boston
589,141

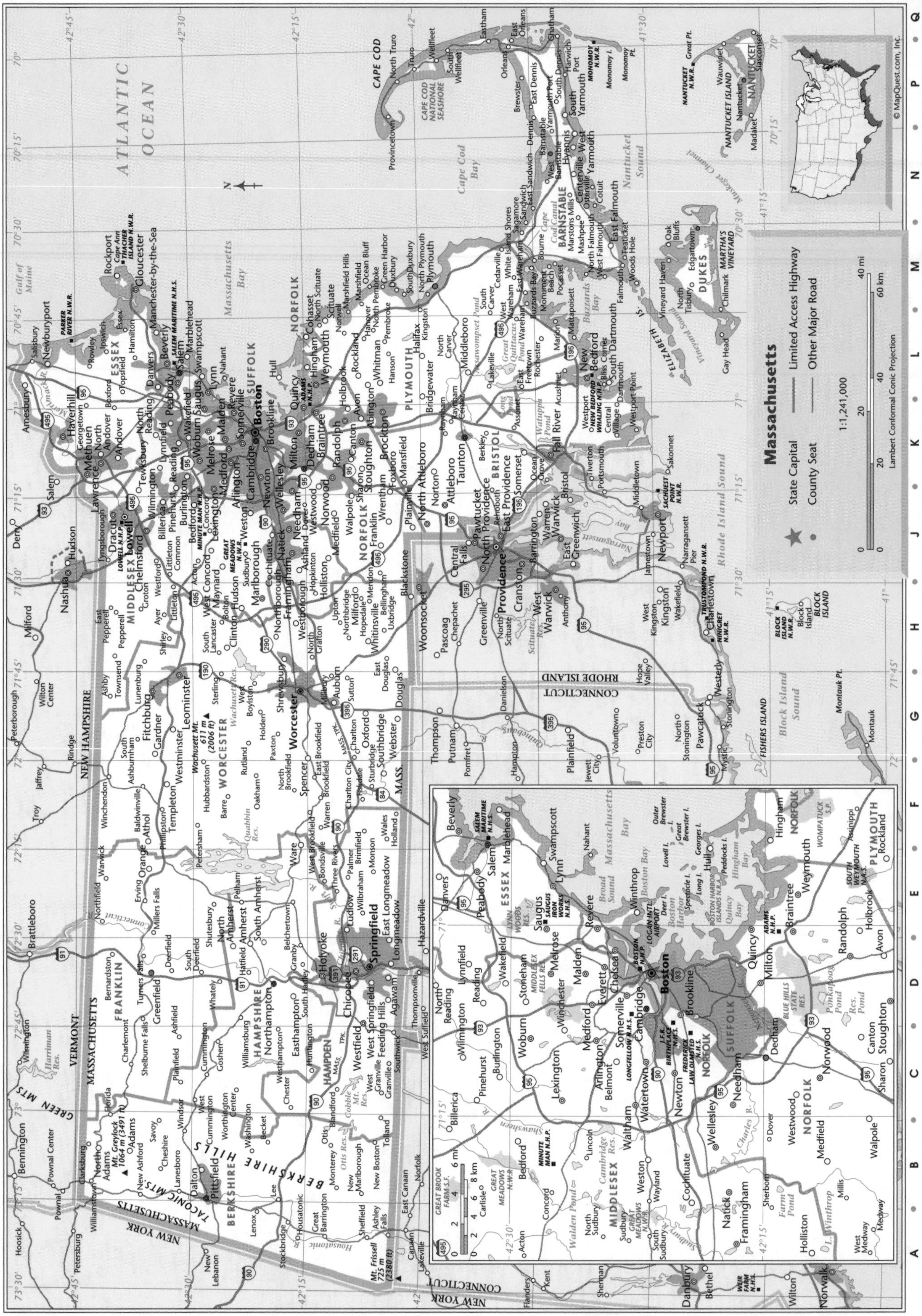

Massachusetts

State Capital
County Seat

Limited Access Highway
Other Major Road

1:1,241,000

Lambert Conformal Conic Projection

0   20   40 mi
0   20   40   60 km

ATLANTIC OCEAN

NEW HAMPSHIRE

VERMONT

NEW YORK

CONNECTICUT

RHODE ISLAND

Cape Cod Bay

Massachusetts Bay

Gulf of Maine

Nantucket Sound

CAPE COD

CAPE COD NATIONAL SEASHORE

NANTUCKET ISLAND

MARTHA'S VINEYARD

BLOCK ISLAND

BERKSHIRE HILLS

TACONIC MTS.

GREEN MTS.

Mt. Greylock 1064 m (3491 ft)

Wachusett 611 m (2006 ft)

Mt. Frissell 725 m (2380 ft)

Counties: FRANKLIN, HAMPSHIRE, HAMPDEN, BERKSHIRE, WORCESTER, MIDDLESEX, ESSEX, SUFFOLK, NORFOLK, PLYMOUTH, BRISTOL, BARNSTABLE, DUKES, NANTUCKET

Boston

© MapQuest.com, Inc.

Capital: Lansing
Area: 96,700 sq. mi. / 250,500 sq. km.
Pop. (2000): 9,938,444
Largest City: Detroit / 951,270

Michigan

★ State Capital
• County Seat
— Limited Access Highway
— Other Major Road

1:3,205,000

0 — 50 — 100 mi
0 — 50 — 100 — 150 km
Albers Equal Area Projection

© MapQuest.com, Inc.

same scale as main map
Central Time Zone / Eastern Time Zone

Inset (Upper Peninsula west)
Apostle Islands Natl. Lakeshore
APOSTLE ISLANDS
Outer I.
Madeline I.
LAKE SUPERIOR
Silver City
Ontonagon
Government Peak 564 m (1850 ft)
PORCUPINE MTS. WILDERNESS S.P.
White Pine
ONTONAGON
OTTAWA N.F.
Ewen
Birch
Connorville
Merriweather
Bessemer
Wakefield
BAD RIVER I.R.
Hurley
Montreal
Ironwood
MICH.
WIS.
GOGEBIC
Lake Gogebic
Marenisco
Turtle Flambeau Flowage
Presque Isle
Manitowish Waters
NORTHERN HIGHLAND AMERICAN LEGION S.F.
Butternut
Lac du Flambeau
LAC DU FLAMBEAU I.R.
Park Falls
CHEQUAMEGON N.F.
Eagle River
Minocqua

Main Map

LAKE SUPERIOR
CANADA
U.S.
ONT. MICH.
Thunder Bay
Thunder Cape
Pie I.
Edward I.
Sibley Prov. Park
ISLE ROYALE
ISLE ROYALE NATL. PARK
Sugar Mt. 415 m (1362 ft)
Eagle River
Manitou I.
Keweenaw Pt.
Traverse Pt.
KEWEENAW
KEWEENAW PENINSULA
KEWEENAW N.H.P.
Fourteen Mile Pt.
Hancock
Houghton
HURON N.W.R.
HOUGHTON
BARAGA
L'Anse
L'Anse I.R.
HURON MTS.
Mt. Arvon 603 m (1979 ft)
OTTAWA N.F.
Ishpeming
Negaunee
Marquette
MARQUETTE
IRON
Crystal Falls
Eastern Time Zone / Central Time Zone
OTTAWA NATIONAL FOREST
MICHIGAMME RES.
NICOLET NATIONAL FOREST
DICKINSON
Kingsford
Iron Mountain
Norway
Niagara
Crandon
SOKAOGON CHIPPEWA POTAWATOMI I.R.
MENOMINEE INDIAN RES.
STOCKBRIDGE MUNSEE IND. COMM.
Shawano
MENOMINEE
Peshtigo
Marinette
Menominee
CHAMBERS I.
Howard
ONEIDA I.R.
Green Bay
De Pere
New London
Appleton
Kaukauna
Neenah
Omro
Oshkosh
Chilton
Berlin
Ripon
L. Poygan
L. Winnebago
DOOR PENINSULA
Sturgeon Bay
Two Rivers
Manitowoc
GREEN BAY N.W.R.
GRAVEL ISLAND N.W.R.
GREEN BAY
LAKE MICHIGAN
Central Time Zone / Eastern Time Zone

Laughing Fish Pt.
Au Sable Pt.
GRAND ISLAND NATL. REC. AREA
Grand I.
Munising
PICTURED ROCKS NATL. LAKESHORE
TAHQUAMENON FALLS S.P.
Whitefish Bay
HIAWATHA NATIONAL FOREST
ALGER
SCHOOLCRAFT
SENEY N.W.R.
LUCE
Newberry
Manistique
Seul Choix Pt.
Scott Pt.
DELTA
NATIONAL FOREST
Indian L.
Gladstone
Escanaba
Big Bay De Noc
Summer I.
Pt. aux Barques
Garden I.
High I.
MICHIGAN ISLANDS N.W.R.
Hog I.
Beaver I.
St. Martin I.
Pt. Detour
South Fox I.
North Fox I.
Charlevoix
N. Manitou I.
S. Manitou I.
Cathead Pt.
Leland
Glen L.
SLEEPING BEAR DUNES NATL. LAKESHORE
Pt. Betsie
Crystal L.
Beulah
Pt. aux Barques
CHIPPEWA
Sault Ste. Marie
Sault Ste. Marie
BAY MILLS I.R.
ST. JOSEPH I.
Thessalon
Blind River
Massey
Elliot Lake
Quirke L.
MACKINAC
Les Cheneaux Is.
St. Ignace
Mackinac Island
Straits of Mackinac
DRUMMOND I.
North Channel
Clapperton I.
Barrie
COCKBURN I.
ONTARIO
MICHIGAN
CANADA
U.S.
MANITOULIN ISLAND
Great Duck I.
BOIS BLANC I.
Cheboygan
Sturgeon Bay
Ranger L.
EMMET
Petoskey
Boyne City
Rogers City
Adams Pt.
Hammond Bay
CHEBOYGAN
PRESQUE ISLE
Gaylord
MONTMORENCY
Atlanta
ALPENA
Alpena
North Pt.
Thunder Bay
MICHIGAN ISLANDS N.W.R.
South Pt.
LAKE HURON
Grand Traverse Bay
CHARLEVOIX
ANTRIM
Bellaire
OTSEGO
LEELANAU
Traverse City
GRAND TRAVERSE
KALKASKA
Kalkaska
CAMP GRAYLING MIL. RES.
OSCODA
Mio
ALCONA
Harrisville
Sturgeon Pt.
HURON N.F.
Grayling
CRAWFORD
BENZIE
WEXFORD
MISSAUKEE
Lake City
ROSCOMMON
Houghton Lake
Higgins L.
Roscommon
OGEMAW
West Branch
IOSCO
East Tawas
Tawas City
Au Sable Pt.
Manistee R.
Skidway Lake
Cadillac
MANISTEE
Manistee
LAKE
OSCEOLA
CLARE
GLADWIN
Harrison
Gladwin
ARENAC
Standish
ISABELLA I.R.
Pt. Lookout
Pt. Au Gres
Sand Pt.
Big Sable Pt.
Ludington
MANISTEE NATIONAL FOREST
MASON
Baldwin
Reed City
Clare
Saginaw Bay
Fish Pt.
HURON
Bad Axe
Little Sable Pt.
OCEANA
Hart
NEWAYGO
White Cloud
MECOSTA
Big Rapids
ISABELLA I.R.
MIDLAND
Midland
BAY
Essexville
Bay City
Caro
Sandusky
TUSCOLA
SANILAC
Carrollton
Shields
Saginaw
Bridgeport
Frankenmuth
Vassar
Fremont
MUSKEGON
North Muskegon
Wolf Lake
Whitehall
Muskegon
Muskegon Hts.
Norton Shores
Spring Lake
Grand Haven
MONTCALM
Stanton
Cedar Springs
Sparta
Rockford
Greenville
Belding
GRATIOT
Ithaca
Alma
St. Louis
SAGINAW
Chesaning
Owosso
GENESEE
Flushing
Flint
Mt. Morris
Mt. Clemens
Burton
Grand Blanc
LAPEER
Lapeer
Imlay City
Davison
ST. CLAIR
Port Huron
Marysville
Sarnia
OTTAWA
Allendale
Walker
Jenison
Hudsonville
Zeeland
Holland
Grand Rapids
Wyoming
Kentwood
Cutlerville
KENT
Lowell
IONIA
Ionia
Portland
CLINTON
De Witt
St. Johns
SHIAWASSEE
Durand
Fowlerville
LIVINGSTON
Howell
Brighton
OAKLAND
Milford
Holly
Fenton
Pontiac
New Baltimore
MACOMB
Sterling Heights
Warren
Livonia
Detroit
Windsor
St. Clair
Algonac
Marine City
Wallaceburg
LANSING
Lansing
E. Lansing
Okemos
Williamston
INGHAM
Mason
Holt
Eaton Rapids
EATON
Charlotte
Grand Ledge
BARRY
Hastings
ALLEGAN
Allegan
Wayland
Otsego
Plainwell
South Haven
VAN BUREN
Paw Paw Lake
Paw Paw
KALAMAZOO
Kalamazoo
Portage
CALHOUN
Battle Creek
Marshall
Albion
JACKSON
Jackson
Michigan Center
Chelsea
WASHTENAW
Ann Arbor
Ypsilanti
Saline
Whitmore Lake
S. Lyon
Milan
Dundee
Carleton
Flat Rock
Rockwood
MONROE
Monroe
Temperance
Lambertville
Toledo
Oregon
Port Clinton
PT. PELEE
Pelee I.
Kelleys I.
PERRYS VICTORY AND INT. PEACE MEM.
OTTAWA N.W.R.
Maumee
Perrysburg
Wauseon
LAKE ERIE
CAN.
U.S.
Leamington
Kingsville
Essex
Amherstburg
Tecumseh
LENAWEE
Adrian
Blissfield
Hudson
Hillsdale
HILLSDALE
Coldwater
BRANCH
Sturgis
ST. JOSEPH
Centreville
Three Rivers
CASS
Dowagiac
Cassopolis
BERRIEN
Benton Harbor
St. Joseph
Niles
Buchanan
Michigan City
INDIANA
Elkhart
South Bend
Mishawaka
Goshen
Lagrange
Angola
Montpelier
Sylvania
MICHIGAN
INDIANA
OHIO

Detroit Metro Inset
Huron Heights
Union Lake
West Acres
Bingham Farms
Pontiac
Rochester Hills
Troy
Utica
Sterling Heights
Chesterfield
Waldenburg
Mount Clemens
MACOMB
Fraser
Warren
Van Dyke
Keego Harbor
Orchard Lake
Bloomfield Hills
Clawson
Birmingham
OAKLAND
Franklin
Beverly Hills
Royal Oak
Berkley
Huntington Woods
Madison Hts.
Center Line
Roseville
St. Clair Shores
Eastpointe
Harper Woods
Grosse Pte.
Grosse Pointe Woods
Grosse Pointe Shores
Farmington Hills
Farmington
Southfield
Oak Park
Ferndale
Hazel Park
Hamtramck
Highland Park
Grosse Pointe Farms
Grosse Pointe
Grosse Pointe Park
Livonia
WAYNE
MIDDLE ROUGE PARKWAY
LOWER ROUGE PARKWAY
Dearborn Hts.
Dearborn
Detroit
Windsor
CAN. U.S.
River Rouge
Ecorse
Wyandotte
Westland
Garden City
Inkster
Melvindale
Wayne
Taylor
Allen Park
Lincoln Park
Romulus
Southgate
La Salle
Oliver
St. Clair Beach
Tecumseh
Elmstead
Lake St. Clair

0 — 3 — 6 mi
0 — 3 — 6 — 9 km

Chicago area
Lake Zurich
Carpentersville
Wheeling
Elgin
Evanston
De Kalb
Wheaton
Oak Park
Highland Park
Batavia
Cicero
Chicago
Aurora
Sandwich
Bolingbrook
Joliet
Calumet City
Hammond
Gary
East Chicago
La Porte
Westville

Capital: St. Paul
Area: 86,900 sq. mi.
225,200 sq. km.
Pop. (2000): 4,919,479
Largest City: Minneapo®
382,618

Minnesota

★ State Capital — Limited Access Highway
• County Seat — Other Major Road

1:2,773,000

0   40   80 mi
0   40   80   120 km

Albers Equal Area Projection

MANITOBA
MINNESOTA
Whitemouth L.
Red Lake I.R.
Lake of the Woods
Warroad
Roseau
Greenbush
Baudette
Hallock
Karlstad
KITTSON
ROSEAU
Stephen
Argyle
Warren
MARSHALL
Thief River Falls
PENNINGTON
East Grand Forks
Grand Forks
Crookston
RED LAKE
LAKE OF THE WOODS
RED LAKE INDIAN RES.
BELTRAMI
Mud L.
AGASSIZ N.W.R.
Upper Red L.
Ponemah
Lower Red L.
Red Lake
Redby
Blackduck
CHIPPEWA NATIONAL FOREST
ITASCA
KOOCHICHING
Fort Frances
International Falls
Littlefork
NETT LAKE IND. RES.
DEER CREEK I.R.
ST. LOUIS
SUPERIOR
Cook
VERMILION LAKE I.R.
Ely
Tower
Babbitt
VERMILION RANGE
MESABI RANGE
Mountain Iron
Buhl
Virginia
Keewatin
Nashwauk
Chisholm
Eveleth
Hibbing
Aurora
COOK
LAKE
NATIONAL FOREST
SUPERIOR NATIONAL FOREST
Silver Bay
Two Harbors
Lake Superior

POLK
McIntosh
Fertile
Fosston
NORMAN
Halstad
Ada
Twin Valley
Mahnomen
Ulen
CLAY
Moorhead
Fargo
West Fargo
Glyndon
Dilworth
Hawley
Barnesville
WHITE EARTH I.R.
MAHNOMEN
ITASCA S.P.
BECKER
Lake Park
Detroit Lakes
Frazee
Pelican Rapids
Perham
New York Mills
HUBBARD
Park Rapids
Menahga
Sebeka
Wadena
Verndale
Staples
WADENA
Clearbrook
Bagley
Bemidji
LEECH LAKE
Cass Lake
IND. RES.
Walker
Pine River
Emily
Cross Lake
Nisswa
Crosby
Deerwood
Aitkin
CASS
Lower Whitefish
Pequot Lakes
Lake Shore
East Gull Lake
Baxter
Brainerd
CROW WING
Bertha
Eagle Bend
Clarissa
Browerville
TODD
Randall
Pierz
MORRISON
Little Falls
MILLE LACS I.R.
Onamia
Isle
Mille Lacs L.
AITKIN
Grand Rapids
Deer River
Marble
Bovey
Pokegama L.
CHIPPEWA NATIONAL FOREST
Floodwood
Hermantown
Proctor
Cloquet
Carlton
Duluth
Superior
CARLTON
FOND DU LAC I.R.
Moose Lake
RICE LAKE N.W.R.
Sandstone
Hinckley
PINE
Rock Creek
ST. CROIX STATE PARK
KANABEC
Mora
Ogilvie
Pine City
MILLE LACS

WILKIN
Breckenridge
Wahpeton
OTTER TAIL
Fergus Falls
Battle Lake
Henning
Parkers Prairie
Evansville
Elbow Lake
GRANT
Hoffman
Alexandria
Osakis
Long Prairie
DOUGLAS
Glenwood
POPE
Starbuck
Brooten
Belgrade
Sauk Centre
Melrose
Freeport
Albany
Avon
St. Joseph
Waite Park
St. Cloud
STEARNS
Richmond
Cold Spring
Paynesville
Rockville
SHERBURNE
SHERBURNE N.W.R.
Becker
Big Lake
Zimmerman
Princeton
Foley
BENTON
Sauk Rapids
Sartell
Stephen
Milaca
Braham
ISANTI
Cambridge
Isanti
North Branch
CHISAGO
Stacy
Wyoming
Forest Lake
E. Bethel

TRAVERSE
LAKE TRAVERSE (SISSETON) INDIAN RES.
N.DAK
S.DAK
Wheaton
Browns Valley
Graceville
BIG STONE
Clinton
Ortonville
BIG STONE N.W.R.
Milbank
Beardsley
STEVENS
Morris
Chokio
Hancock
Benson
SWIFT
Appleton
Kerkhoven
Spicer
New London
Atwater
KANDIYOHI
Willmar
Kandiyohi
MEEKER
Litchfield
Dassel
Cokato
WRIGHT
Buffalo
Monticello
Albertville
Elk River
Annandale
Maple Lake
St. Michael
Ramsey
Coon Rapids
ANOKA
Anoka

STEVENS
Madison
Montevideo
Clara City
CHIPPEWA
LAC QUI PARLE
Dawson
Granite Falls
Clarkfield
YELLOW MEDICINE
Canby
Hendricks
Ivanhoe
LINCOLN
Tyler
Lake Benton
Cottonwood
Minneota
Marshall
LYON
Tracy
Walnut Grove
Balaton
PIPESTONE
PIPESTONE N.M.
Pipestone
Jasper
Edgerton
MURRAY
Slayton
Westbrook
Mountain Lake
ROCK
Luverne
Hills
Adrian
NOBLES
Worthington
Rushmore
JACKSON
Lakefield
Jackson
Heron Lake
Brewster
Fulda
Windom
COTTONWOOD
Butterfield
St. James
Madelia
WATONWAN
Truman
Trimont
Fairmont
MARTIN
Sherburn
Welcome
Blue Earth
FARIBAULT
Wells
Kiester
Elmore

RENVILLE
Olivia
Bird Island
Hector
Buffalo Lake
Danube
Renville
Sacred Heart
Granite Falls
Clara City
Prinsburg
Hutchinson
MCLEOD
Glencoe
Brownton
Stewart
Young America
Norwood
Winsted
Lester Prairie
Mound
Chanhassen
Chaska
Shakopee
Prior Lake
SCOTT
Belle Plaine
Jordan
New Prague
Henderson
SIBLEY
Gibbon
Winthrop
Arlington
Gaylord
Morgan
Wabasso
REDWOOD
Redwood Falls
Lamberton
Springfield
Sleepy Eye
New Ulm
BROWN
North Mankato
Mankato
NICOLLET
Le Sueur
St. Peter
LE SUEUR
Montgomery
Le Center
Cleveland
Kasota
Eagle Lake
Lake Crystal
Good Thunder
Amboy
BLUE EARTH
Mapleton
Vernon Center
Winnebago

HENNEPIN
Maple Grove
Plymouth
Minneapolis
Orono
Edina
Bloomington
Burnsville
Corcoran
WASHINGTON
Stillwater
Bayport
St. Paul
DAKOTA
Hastings
Farmington
Lakeville
Rosemount
Apple Valley
PRAIRIE ISLAND I.R.
Red Wing
GOODHUE
Cannon Falls
Northfield
Lonsdale
RICE
Faribault
Morristown
Medford
WASECA
Waseca
Janesville
Waterville
STEELE
Owatonna
Blooming Prairie
New Richland
DODGE
Hayfield
Dodge Center
Kasson
Mantorville
Zumbrota
Wanamingo
Kenyon
Pine Island
Oronoco
Goodhue
WABASHA
Wabasha
Plainview
Elgin
Mazeppa
OLMSTED
Rochester
Eyota
Byron
St. Charles
Stewartville
Chatfield
Spring Valley
MOWER
Austin
Brownsdale
Grand Meadow
Dexter
Lyle
Adams
FREEBORN
Albert Lea
Glenville
Clarks Grove
FILLMORE
Preston
Harmony
Canton
Mabel
Spring Grove
Caledonia
HOUSTON
Houston
Hokah
La Crescent
Rushford
Lanesboro
Peterson
WINONA
Winona
Goodview
La Crosse
Onalaska
Whitehall
Osseo
WISCONSIN

MANITOBA
MINNESOTA
IOWA
SOUTH DAKOTA
NORTH DAKOTA
ONTARIO
CANADA
U.S.
Lake of the Woods
Rainy L.
Namakan L.
Kawnipi L.
Agnes L.
QUETICO PROV. PARK
VOYAGEURS NATL. PARK
Pickerel L.

Inset (lower right, Twin Cities):
Fridley
North Oaks
White Bear Lake
Brooklyn Center
Columbia Hts.
Maplewood
New Hope
Robbinsdale
Golden Valley
HENNEPIN
Medicine L.
St. Louis Park
Hopkins
Minnetonka
Edina
Richfield
Bloomington
MALL OF AMERICA
FT. SNELLING S.P.
MINNEAPOLIS ST. PAUL INTL. AIRPORT
Minneapolis
St. Paul
RAMSEY
Roseville
Falcon Heights
Little Canada
St. Anthony
Maplewood
Lilydale
Mendota
South St. Paul
Newport
DAKOTA
Eagan

Inset (upper right, Grand Portage):
ONTARIO
MINNESOTA
COOK
Eagle Mt. 701 m (2301 ft)
Brule L.
Pigeon River
GRAND PORTAGE I.R.
GRAND PORTAGE N.M.
Grand Portage
GRAND PORTAGE ST. FOR.
Hovland
Grand Marais
Lutsen
Lake Superior
Central Time Zone / Eastern Time Zone
same scale as main map

© MapQuest.com, Inc.

Capital: Jackson
Area: 48,400 sq. mi.
125,400 sq. km.
Pop. (2000): 2,844,658
Largest City: Jackson
184,256

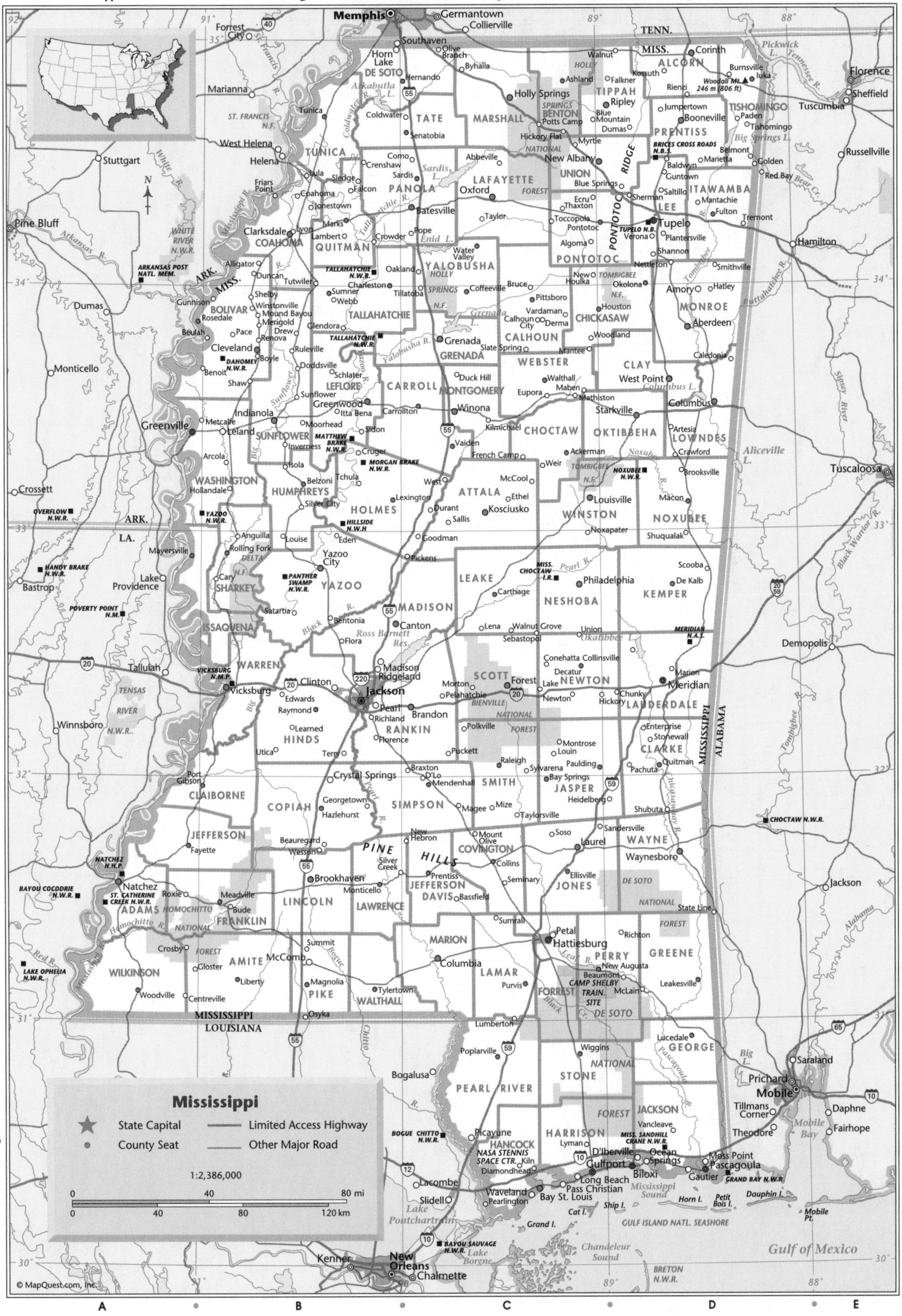

Mississippi

★ State Capital
• County Seat
— Limited Access Highway
— Other Major Road

1:2,386,000

0 — 40 — 80 mi
0 — 40 — 80 — 120 km

© MapQuest.com, Inc.

Capital: Jefferson City
Area: 69,700 sq. mi.
180,500 sq. km.
Pop. (2000): 5,595,211
Largest City: Kansas City
441,545

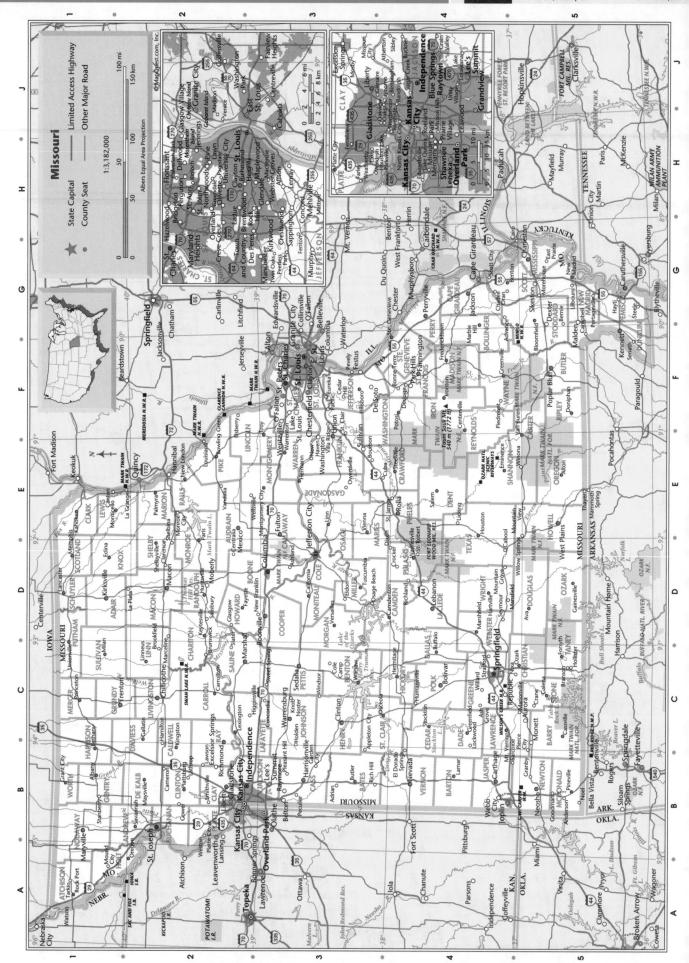

Capital:	Helena	Pop. (2000):	902,195
Area:	147,000 sq. mi.	Largest City:	Billings
	380,800 sq. km.		89,847

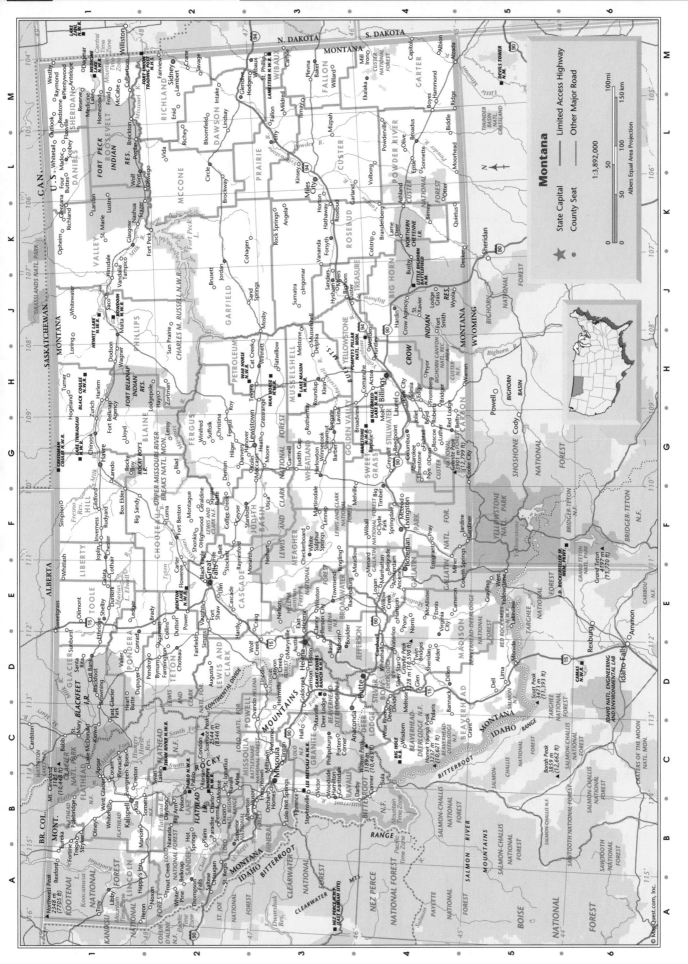

Montana

1:3,892,000

Albers Equal Area Projection

- ★ State Capital
- ● County Seat
- — Limited Access Highway
- — Other Major Road

Capital: Lincoln
Area: 77,400 sq. mi.
200,300 sq. km.
Pop. (2000): 1,711,263
Largest City: Omaha
390,007

Nebraska

Limited Access Highway
Other Major Road

★ State Capital
• County Seat

1:3,068,000

Albers Equal Area Projection

100 mi
150 km

© MapQuest.com, Inc.

Capital: Carson City	**Pop. (2000):** 1,998,257
Area: 110,600 sq. mi.	**Largest City:** Las Vegas
286,400 sq. km.	478,434

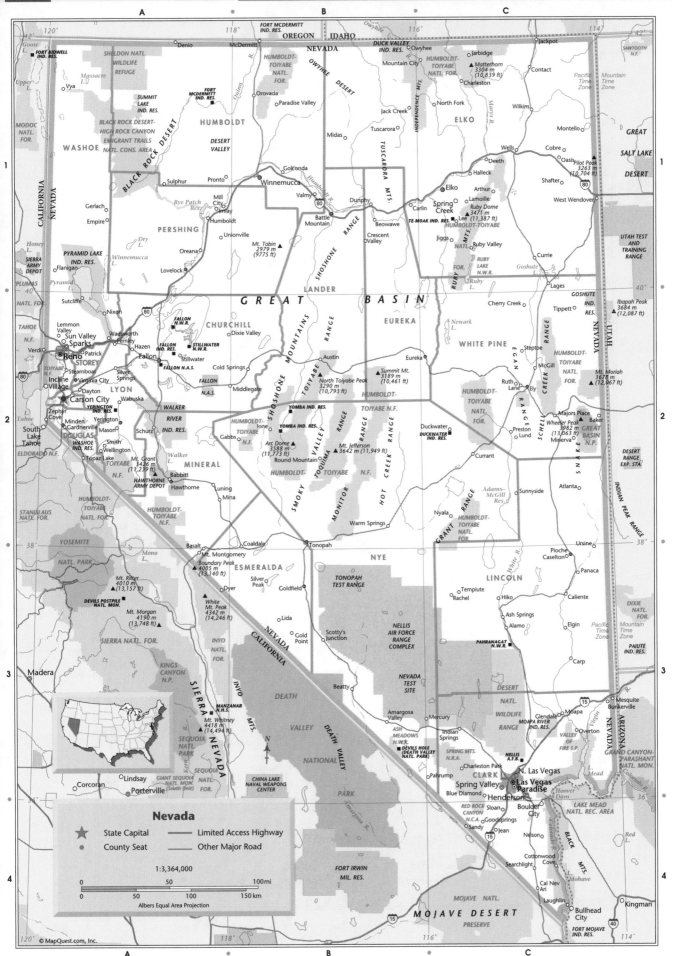

Nevada

★ State Capital   — Limited Access Highway

● County Seat   — Other Major Road

1:3,364,000

0   50   100mi

0   50   100   150 km

Albers Equal Area Projection

© MapQuest.com, Inc.

Capital: Concord
Area: 9,400 sq. mi.
24,200 sq. km.
Pop. (2000): 1,235,786
Largest City: Manchester
107,006

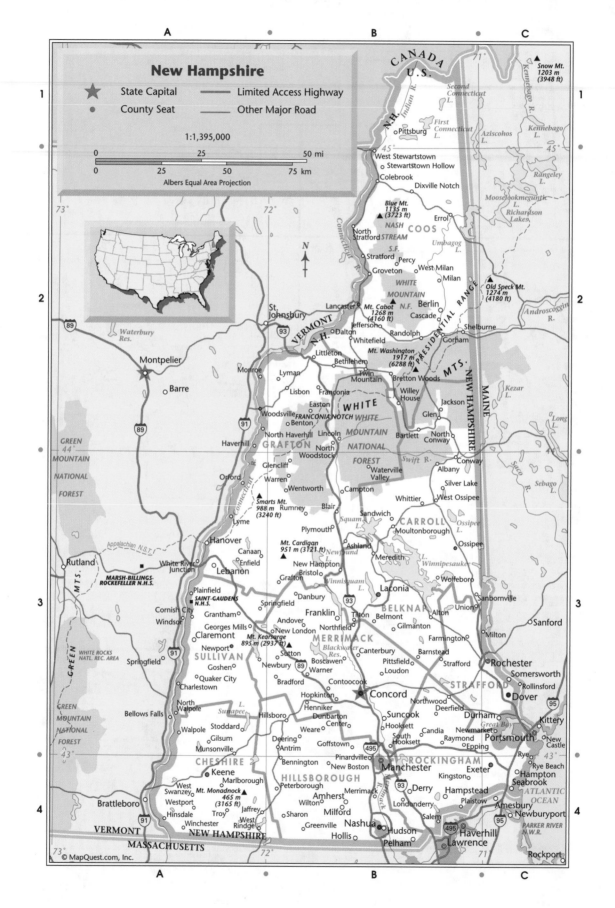

New Hampshire

★ State Capital   ⎯⎯ Limited Access Highway
• County Seat   ⎯⎯ Other Major Road

1:1,395,000

0   25   50 mi
0   25   50   75 km

Albers Equal Area Projection

© MapQuest.com, Inc.

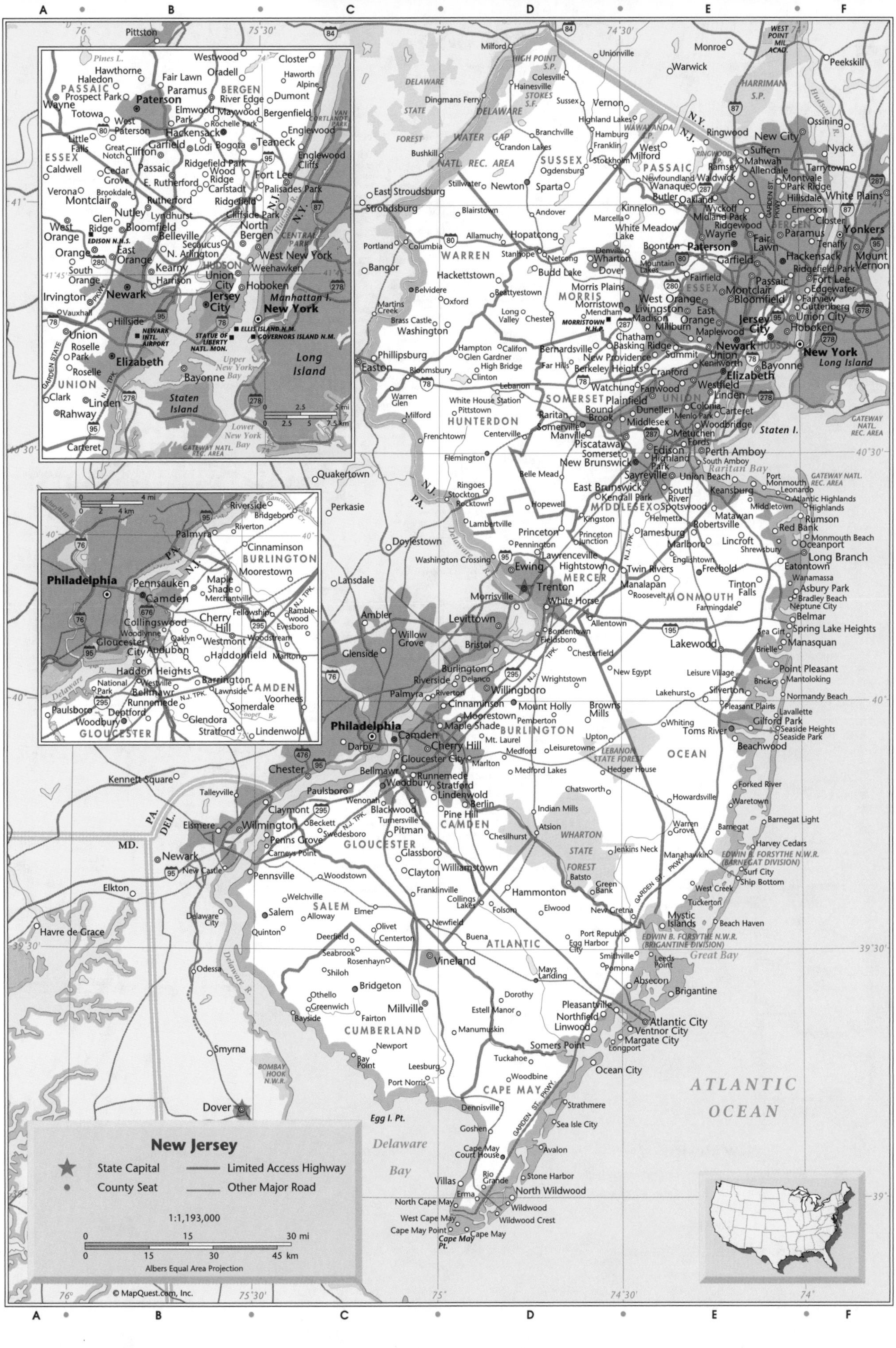

Capital: Trenton
Area: 8,700 sq. mi.
22,600 sq. km.
Pop. (2000): 8,414,350
Largest City: Newark
273,546

New Jersey

★ State Capital
• County Seat
— Limited Access Highway
— Other Major Road

1:1,193,000

0 15 30 mi
0 15 30 45 km

Albers Equal Area Projection

© MapQuest.com, Inc.

ATLANTIC OCEAN

Delaware Bay

Counties: PASSAIC, BERGEN, ESSEX, UNION, HUDSON, SUSSEX, WARREN, MORRIS, HUNTERDON, SOMERSET, MIDDLESEX, MERCER, MONMOUTH, OCEAN, BURLINGTON, CAMDEN, GLOUCESTER, SALEM, CUMBERLAND, ATLANTIC, CAPE MAY

Inset cities: Philadelphia, Camden, Cherry Hill, Gloucester City, Haddonfield, Collingswood, Pennsauken, Moorestown, Cinnaminson, Riverton, Palmyra, Maple Shade, Merchantville, Voorhees, Somerdale, Stratford, Lindenwold, Glendora, Barrington, Lawnside, Runnemede, Bellmawr, Westville, Woodbury, Deptford, Paulsboro, Woodbury Heights

NY metro inset: Paterson, Hackensack, Newark, Jersey City, New York, Elizabeth, Bayonne, Clifton, Passaic, Paramus, Fair Lawn, Englewood, Fort Lee, Teaneck, Union City, Hoboken, Weehawken, West New York, North Bergen, Kearny, Harrison, Bloomfield, Belleville, Nutley, Montclair, Orange, East Orange, West Orange, Irvington, Hillside, Roselle, Linden, Rahway, Carteret, Staten Island, Long Island, Manhattan I.

Capital: Santa Fe
Area: 121,600 sq. mi.
314,900 sq. km.
Pop. (2000): 1,819,046
Largest City: Albuquerque
448,607

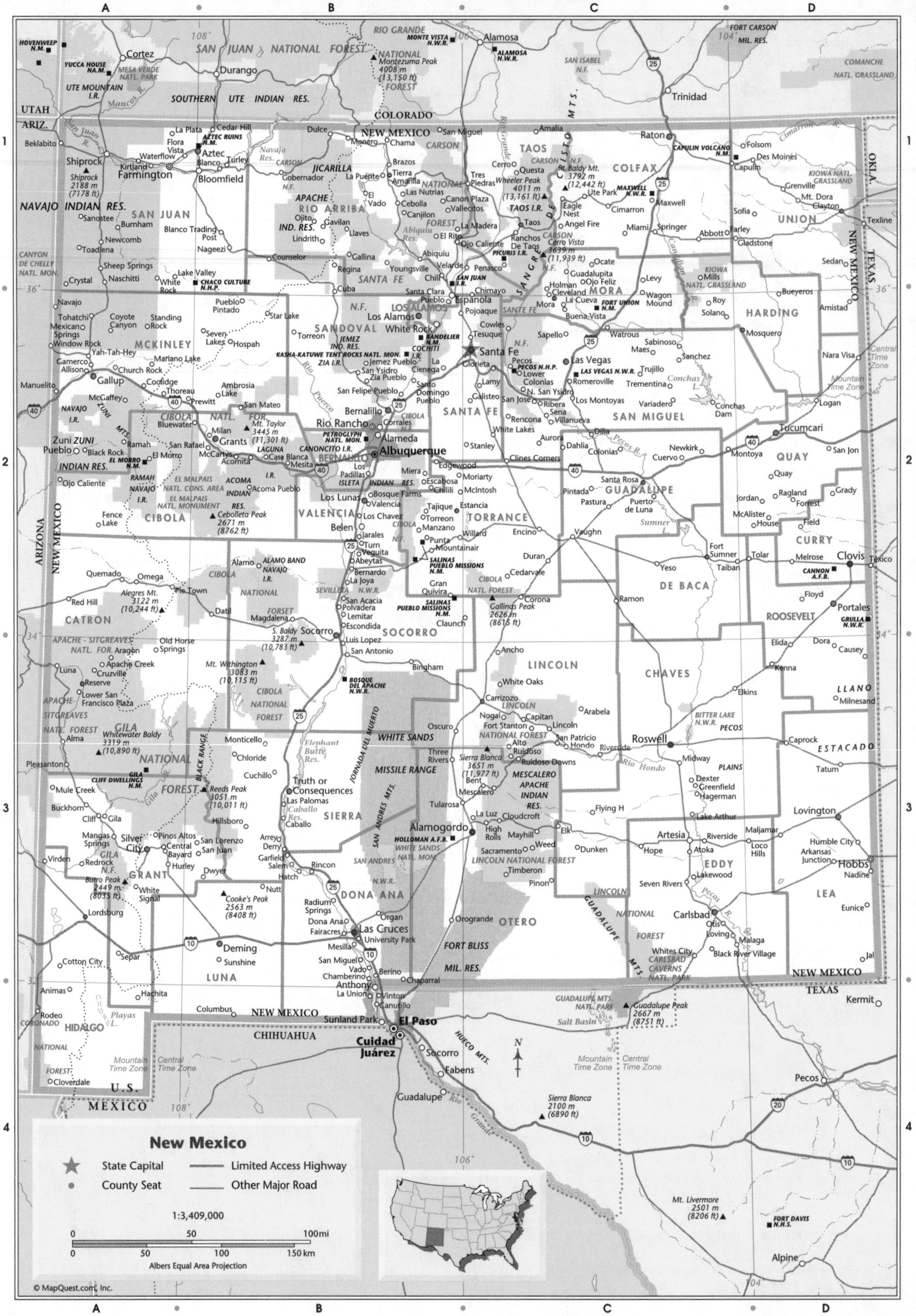

New Mexico

★ State Capital
● County Seat

⎯⎯ Limited Access Highway
⎯ Other Major Road

1:3,409,000

0   50   100mi
0   50   100   150 km

Albers Equal Area Projection

© MapQuest.com, Inc.

Capital: Albany
Area: 54,700 sq. mi.
141,100 sq. km.
Pop. (2000): 18,976,457
Largest City: New York
8,008,278

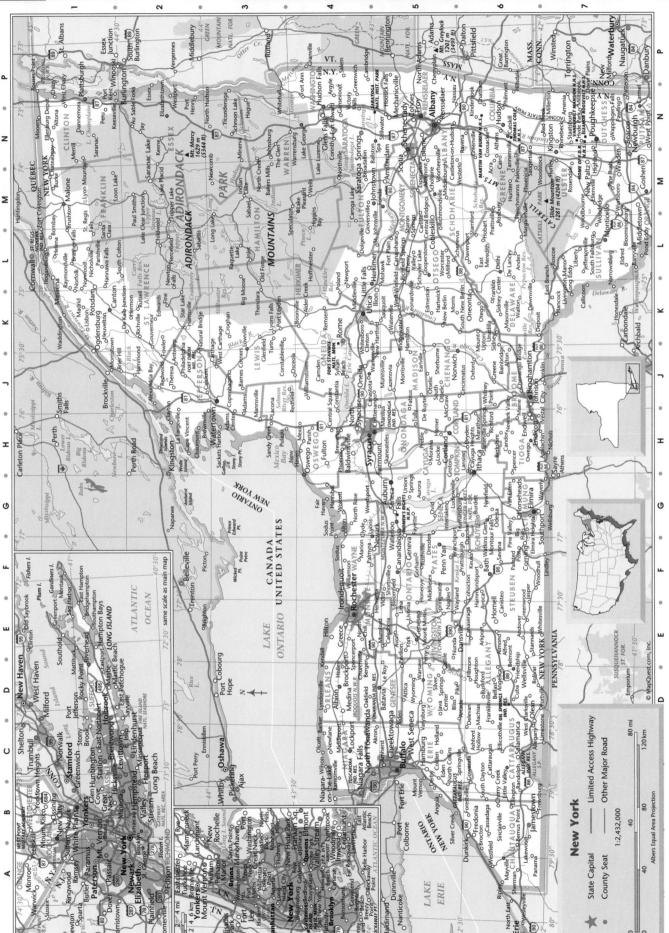

New York

★ State Capital
• County Seat

— Limited Access Highway
— Other Major Road

1:2,432,000

Albers Equal Area Projection

© MapQuest.com, Inc.

Capital: Raleigh
Area: 53,800 sq. mi.
139,400 sq. km.
Pop. (2000): 8,049,313
Largest City: Charlotte
540,828

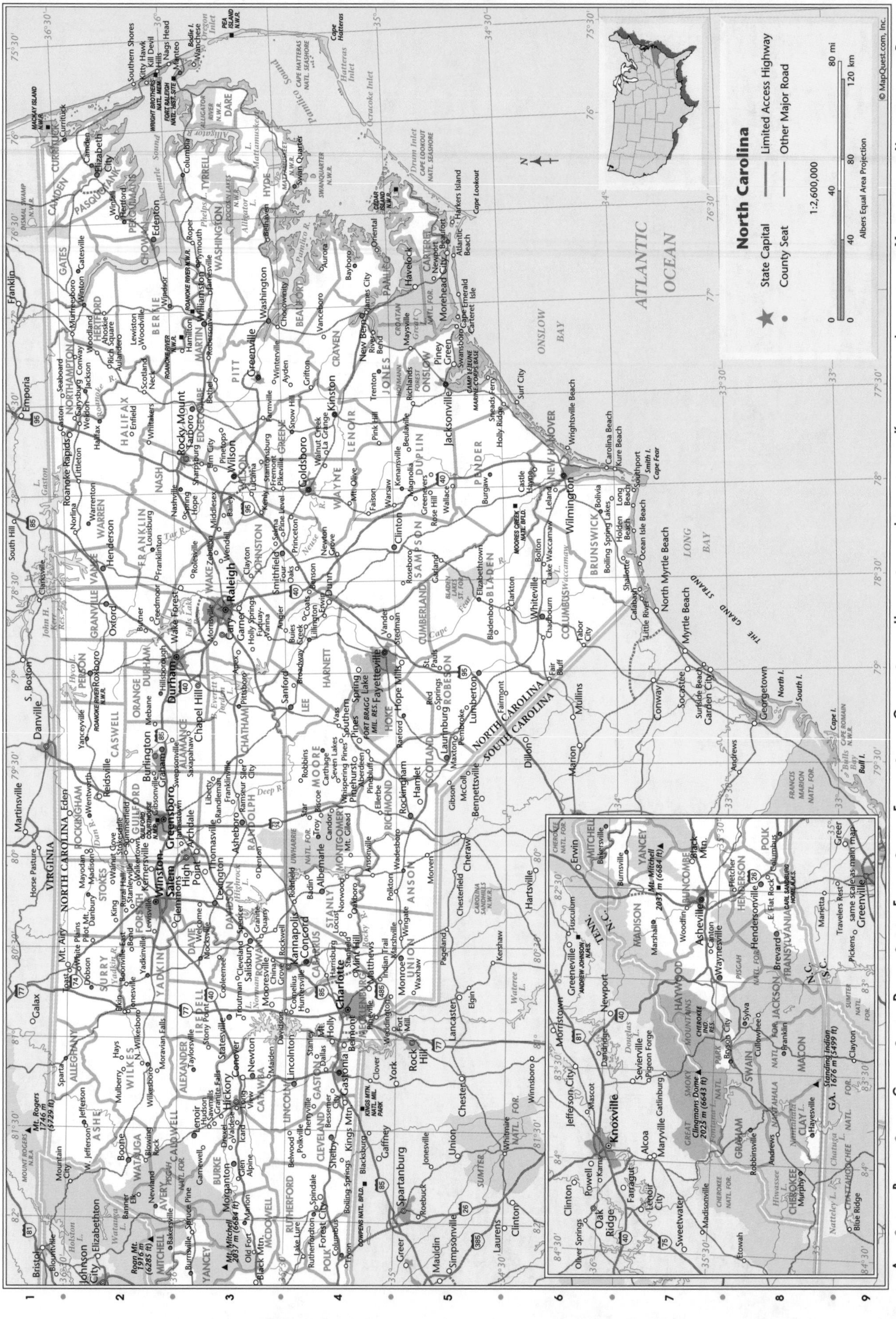

North Carolina

★ State Capital
● County Seat

— Limited Access Highway
— Other Major Road

1:2,600,000

Albers Equal Area Projection

80 mi
120 km

© MapQuest.com, Inc.

ATLANTIC OCEAN

VIRGINIA

NORTH CAROLINA

SOUTH CAROLINA

TENN.

GA.

N.C.

S.C.

ONSLOW BAY

LONG BAY

THE GRAND STRAND

PAMLICO SOUND

Raleigh

Charlotte

Greensboro

Winston-Salem

Durham

Fayetteville

Wilmington

Asheville

Mt. Mitchell (6684 ft)
Clingmans Dome 2025 m (6643 ft)
Mt. Rogers (5729 ft)
Regal Mt. (6285 ft)
Standing Indian 1676 m (5499 ft)

Capital: **Bismarck** Pop. (2000): 642,200
Area: 70,700 sq. mi. Largest City: Fargo
183,100 sq. km. 90,599

NORTH DAKOTA 161

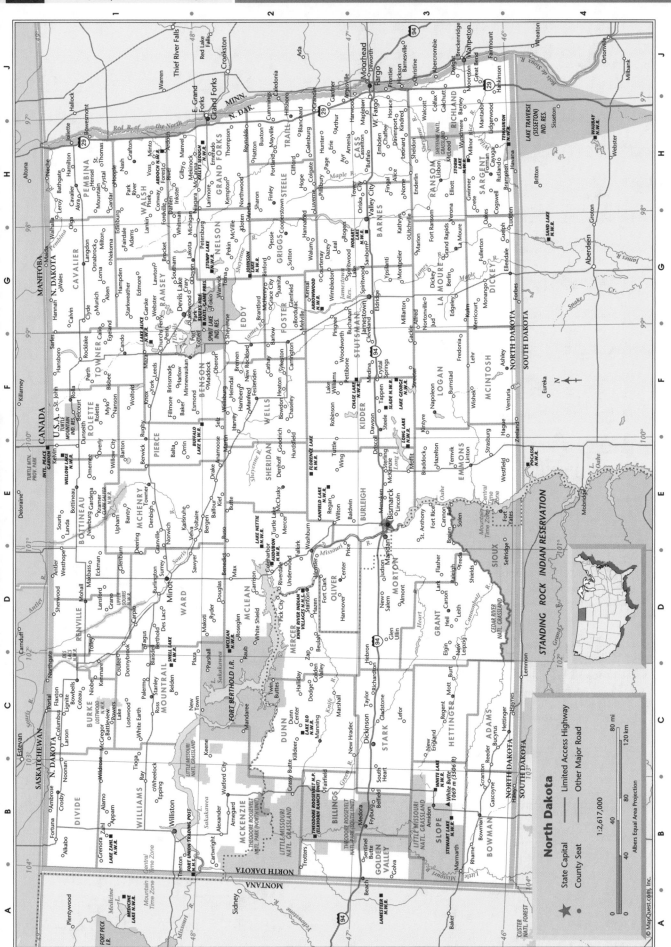

North Dakota

State Capital ★
County Seat •
— Limited Access Highway
— Other Major Road

1:2,617,000

0 40 80 mi
0 40 80 120 km

Albers Equal Area Projection

STANDING ROCK INDIAN RESERVATION

© MapQuest.com, Inc.

Capital: Columbus
Area: 44,800 sq. mi.
116,100 sq. km.
Pop. (2000): 11,353,1...
Largest City: Columbu...
711,470

Capital: Oklahoma City   **Pop. (2000):** 3,450,654
Area: 69,900 sq. mi.   **Largest City:** Oklahoma City
181,000 sq. km.   506,132

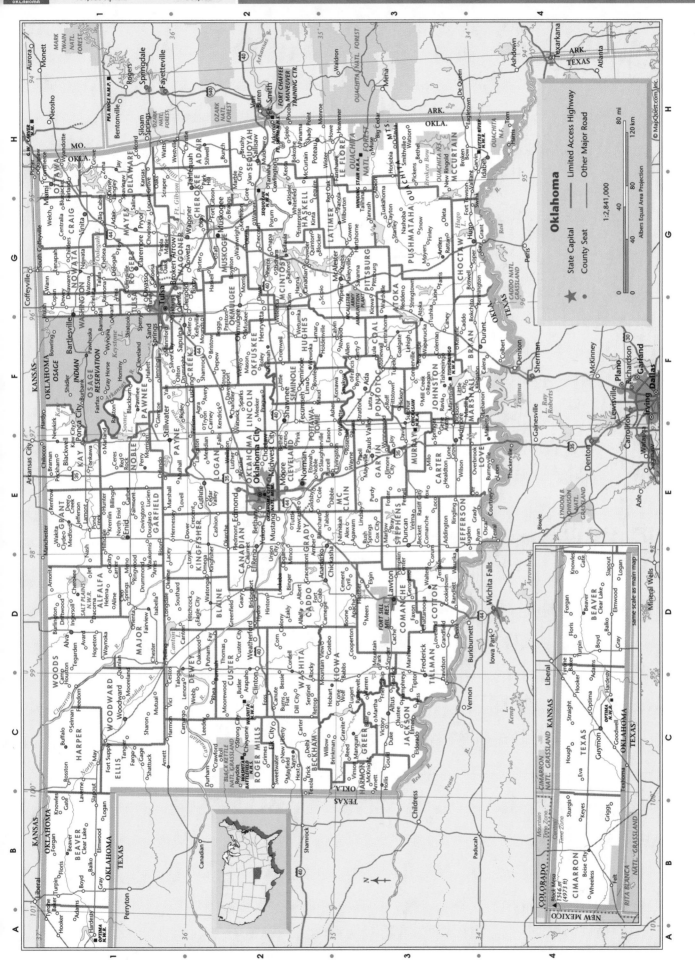

Capital: Salem
Area: 98,400 sq. mi.
254,800 sq. km.
Pop. (2000): 3,421,399
Largest City: Portland
529,121

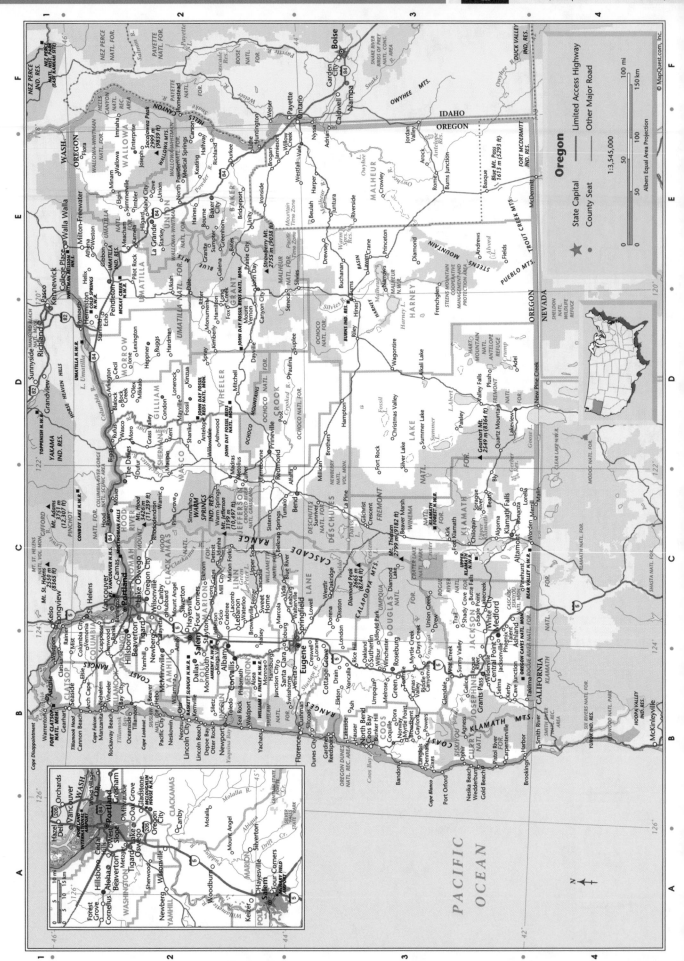

Capital: Harrisburg	Pop. (2000): 12,281,054
Area: 45,300 sq. mi.	Largest City: Philadelphia
117,300 sq. km.	1,517,550

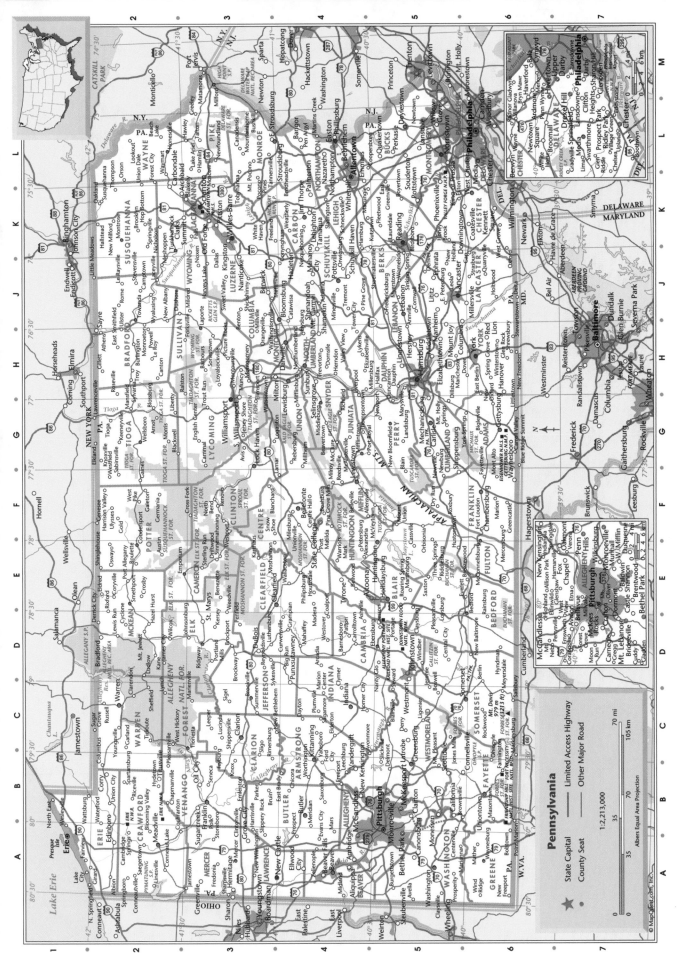

Pennsylvania

State Capital ★
County Seat •

Limited Access Highway
Other Major Road

1:2,213,000

Albers Equal Area Projection

© MapQuest.com, Inc.

Capital: Providence	Pop. (2000): 1,048,319
Area: 1,500 sq. mi.	Largest City: Providence
4,000 sq. km.	173,618

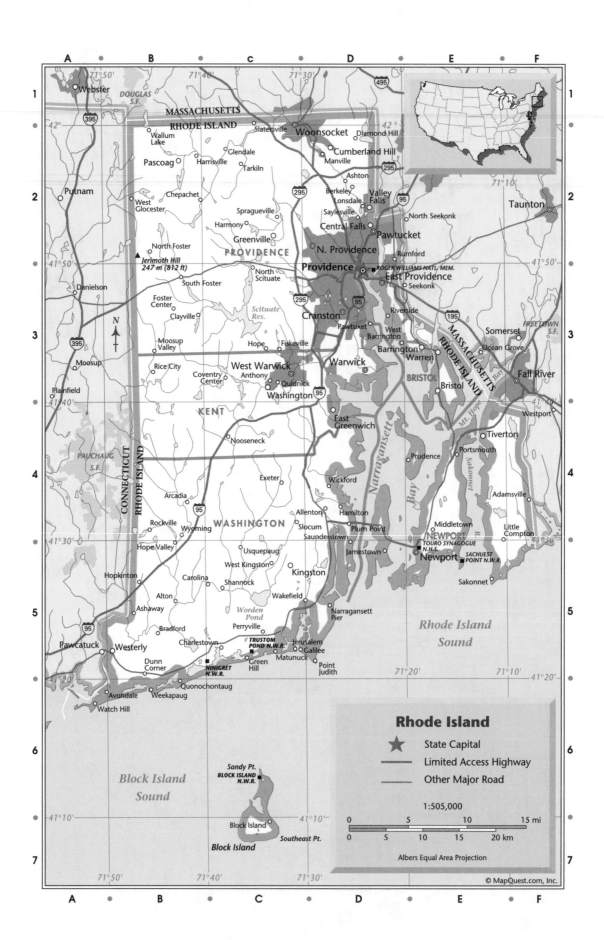

Rhode Island

★ State Capital
▬▬ Limited Access Highway
── Other Major Road

1:505,000

0   5   10   15 mi
0 5 10 15 20 km

Albers Equal Area Projection

© MapQuest.com, Inc.

Capital: Columbia
Area: 32,000 sq. mi.
82,900 sq. km.
Pop. (2000): 4,012,012
Largest City: Columbia
116,278

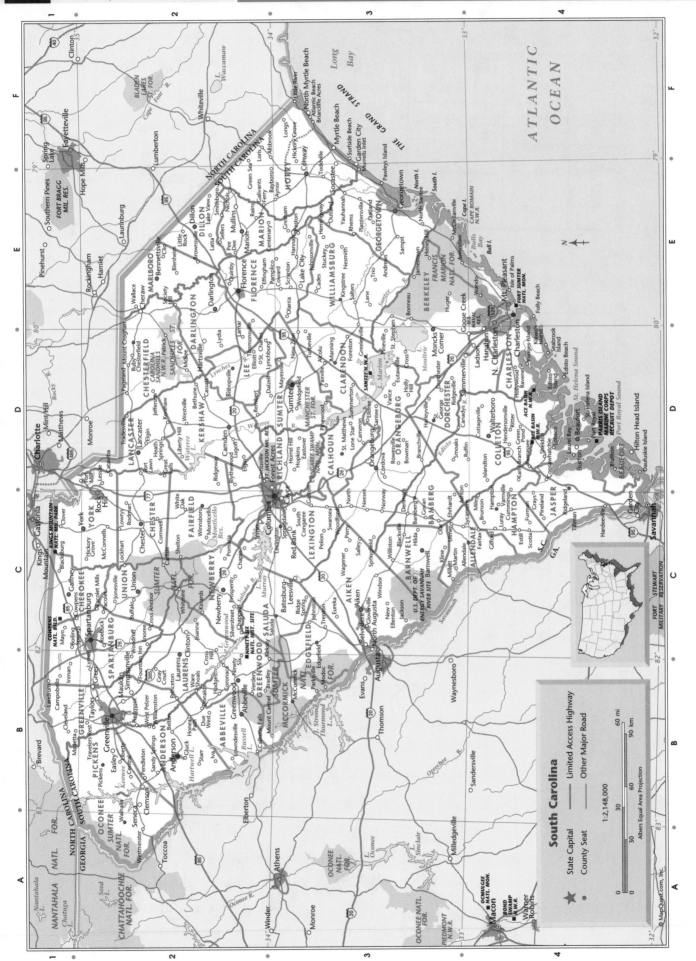

South Carolina

★ State Capital
• County Seat

— Limited Access Highway
— Other Major Road

1:2,148,000
Albers Equal Area Projection

0   30   60   60 mi
0   30   60   90 km

© MapQuest.com, Inc.

Capital: Pierre	Pop. (2000): 754,844
Area: 77,100 sq. mi.	Largest City: Sioux Falls
199,700 sq. km.	123,975

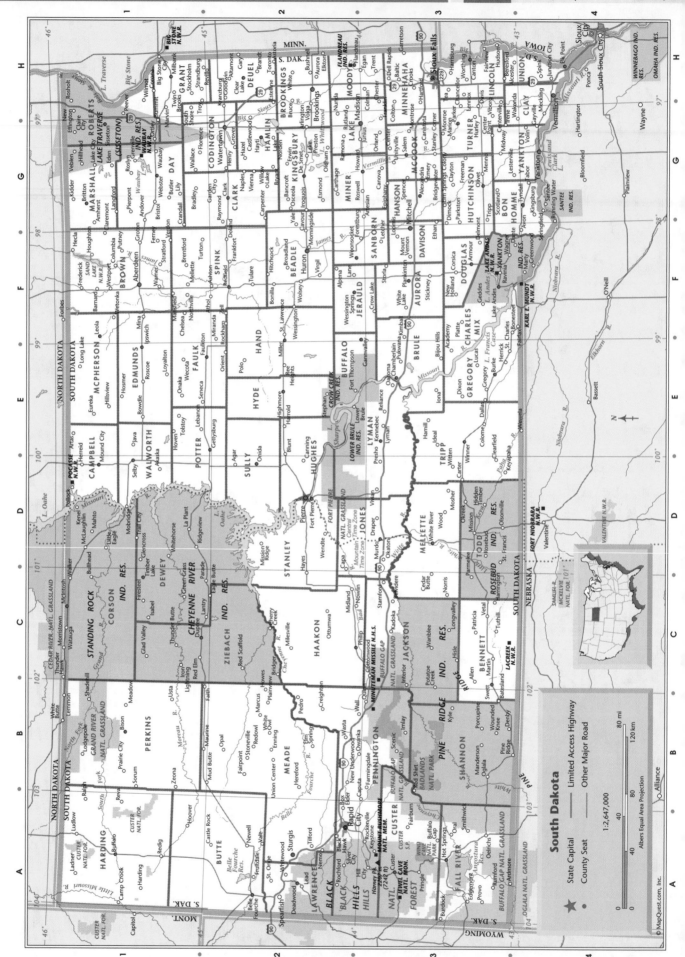

South Dakota

★ State Capital
• County Seat
—— Limited Access Highway
—— Other Major Road

1:2,647,000

0   40   80 mi
0   40 80 120 km

Albers Equal Area Projection

©MapQuest.com, Inc.

Capital:	Nashville	Pop. (2000):	5,689,283
Area:	42,100 sq. mi.	Largest City:	Memphis
	109,200 sq. km.		650,100

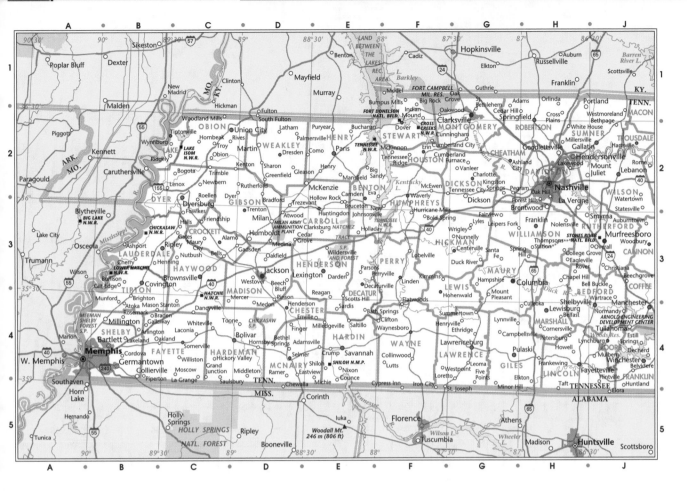

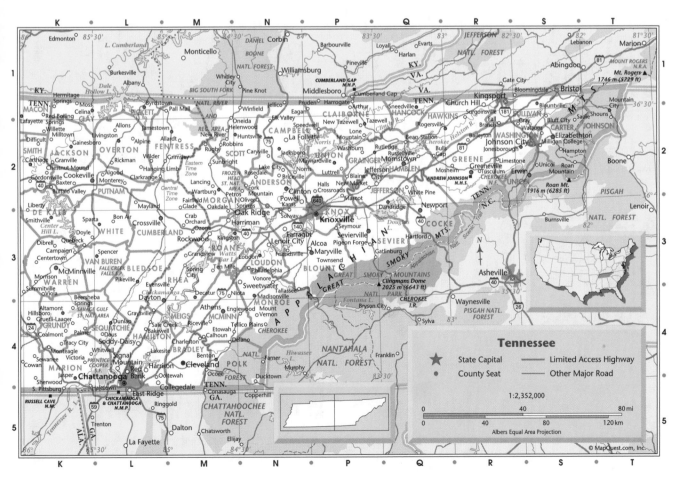

Tennessee

★ State Capital ── Limited Access Highway
• County Seat ── Other Major Road

1:2,352,000

0 — 40 — 80 mi
0 — 40 — 80 — 120 km

Albers Equal Area Projection

© MapQuest.com, Inc.

Capital: Austin
Area: 268,600 sq. mi.
695,700 sq. km.
Pop. (2000): 20,851,82[...]
Largest City: Houston
1,953,63[...]

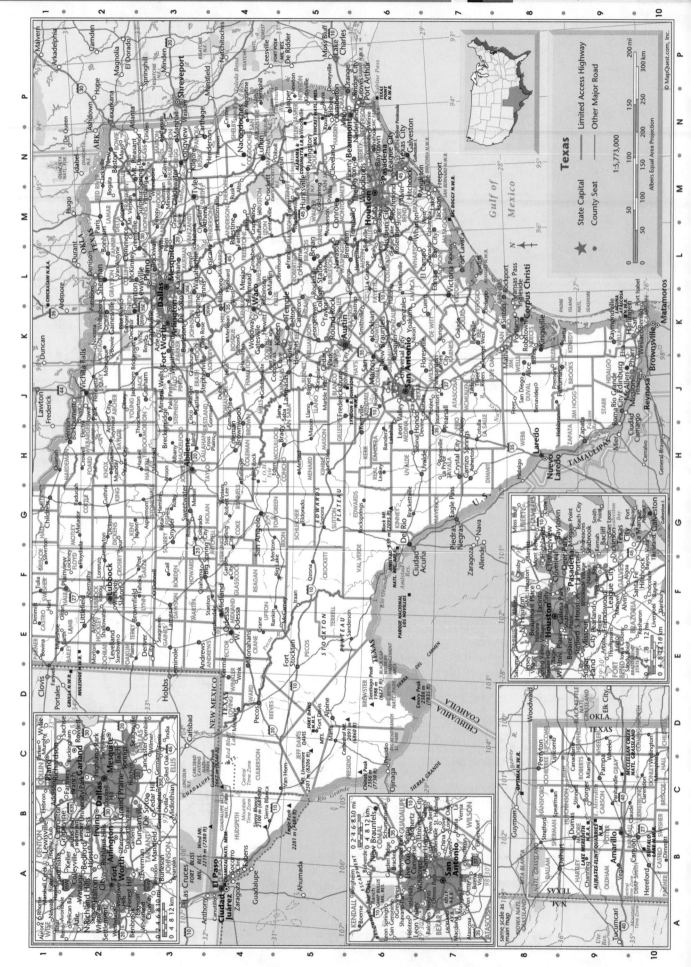

Capital: Salt Lake City
Area: 84,900 sq. mi.
219,900 sq. km.
Pop. (2000): 2,233,169
Largest City: Salt Lake City
181,743

Utah

★ State Capital
• County Seat
— Limited Access Highway
— Other Major Road

1:2,830,000

0   40   80 mi
0   40   80   120 km
Albers Equal Area Projection

CRATERS OF THE MOON N.M.
SHOSHONE NATL. FOREST
FORT HALL I.R.
CARIBOU NATL. FOREST
MINIDOKA N.W.R.
Rupert
Burley
SAWTOOTH NATL. FOREST
SAWTOOTH NATL. FOREST
Cache Peak 3151 m (10,339 ft)
CITY OF ROCKS NATL. RES.
CURLEW NATL. GRASSLAND
CARIBOU NATL. FOREST
Garden City
Bear L.
IDAHO
UTAH
Yost
Standrod
Snowville
Portage
Lewiston
Clarkston
Richmond
Newton
Laketown
BEAR LAKE N.W.R.
Lynn
Rosette
Park Valley
Plymouth
Howell
Smithfield
Logan
Sage Creek Junction
Grouse Creek
Kelton
Bothwell
Tremonton
Garland
CACHE
CACHE
NATL.
RICH
Randolph
GOLDEN SPIKE N.H.S.
Promontory
Honeyville
Corinne
Hyrum
Paradise
Woodruff
Pacific Time Zone
Mountain Time Zone
BOX ELDER
Penrose
Brigham City
Mantua
Willard
WYOMING
Lucin
GREAT
SALT
LAKE
Lakeside
Plain City
North Ogden
Huntsville
Evanston
Rock Springs
Pilot Peak 3263 m (10,704 ft)
NEVADA
UTAH
Bonneville Salt Flats
Promontory Point
Roy
Ogden
WEBER
FOR.
MORGAN
Devils Slide
Castle Rock
Manila
Dutch John
FLAMING GORGE N.R.A.
BROWNS PARK N.W.R.
Wendover
Clearfield
Layton
Farmington
Henefer
Echo
WASATCH - CACHE NATL. FOREST
Flaming Gorge Res.
DAGGETT
UTAH TEST AND TRAINING RANGE
DAVIS
N. Salt Lake
Centerville
Bountiful
Coalville
SUMMIT
UINTA
MOUNTAINS
ASHLEY NATL. FOREST
Kings Peak 4123 m (13,528 ft)
Marsh Peak 3731 m (12,240 ft)
DINOSAUR NATL. MON.
SALT LAKE
SALT LAKE CITY
Magna
W. Valley City
Murray
Peoa
Oakley
Kamas
DUCHESNE
Hanna
Mountain Home
Neola
Maeser
Vernal
Burmester
Cottonwood Heights
Heber City
Tabiona
Altamont
Lapoint
Jensen
COLORADO
Grantsville
W. Jordan
S. Jordan
Sandy
Draper
WASATCH
Talmage
Roosevelt
Upalco
Ballard
TOOELE
WASATCH-CACHE NATL. FOREST
Tooele
Stockton
Riverton
Bluffdale
Lehi
TIMPANOGOS CAVE N.M.
American Fork
Pleasant Grove
Orem
Provo
UINTAH AND OURAY INDIAN RESERVATION
Fruitland
Bridgeland
Duchesne
Myton
Fort Duchesne
Randlett
OURAY N.W.R.
UINTAH
Deseret Peak 3362 m (11,031 ft)
SKULL VALLEY I.R.
Cedar Fort
Fairfield
Spanish Fork
Springville
Mapleton
UINTA
Strawberry R.
Ouray
Bonanza
Dugway
Rush Valley
Faust
Salem
NATL.
FOR.
ASHLEY NATL. FOREST
White R.
UINTAH AND OURAY I.R.
DUGWAY PROVING GROUND
Vernon
Utah L.
Santaquin
Payson
WASATCH-CACHE NATL. FOREST
Goshen
Thistle
Soldier Summit
Ibapah
Eureka
Silver City
Elberta
Birdseye
Colton
CARBON
GOSHUTE I.R.
Callao
Mt. Nebo 3636 m (11,929 ft)
Indianola
Helper
Spring Glen
Bruin Pt. 3135 m (10,285 ft)
UINTAH AND OURAY I.R.
Ibapah Peak 3684 m (12,087 ft)
Trout Creek
GREAT
JUAB
Mona
Nephi
UINTA
MANTI
Fairview
Scofield
Clear Creek
Price
Wellington
East Carbon
Sunnyside
FISH SPRINGS N.W.R.
LITTLE SAHARA REC. AREA
Levan
Fountain Green
LA SAL
Mount Pleasant
Spring City
Hiawatha
Elmo
BOOK
CLIFFS
Mt. Moriah 3678 m (12,067 ft)
Lynndyl
Learmington
Mills
Moroni
NATL.
Cleveland
Huntington
GRAND
COLORADO CANYONS NATL. CONS. AREA
Gandy
Salt Marsh L.
Swasey Peak 2947 m (9669 ft)
Sugarville
Delta
Hinckley
Deseret
Oak City
Scipio
Fayette
Sterling
FOR.
Orangeville
Castle Dale
Ferron
BOOK
CLIFFS
UNCOMPAHGRE NATL. FOREST
CONFUSION
BASIN
MILLARD
Clear Lake
Holden
SANPETE
Manti
Mayfield
Clawson
San Rafael Desert
ARCHES NATL. PARK
Castle Valley
HUMBOLDT-TOIYABE NATL. FOREST
RANGE
SEVIER
Centerfield
Gunnison
Axtell
Heliotrope Mt. 3392 m (11,130 ft)
Moore
EMERY
Green River
Crescent Junction
Thompson Springs
Cisco
GREAT BASIN NATL. PARK
Flowell
Redmond
Aurora
Salina
Emery
Moab
FISHLAKE NATL. FOREST
Meadow
Sigurd
Richfield
Glenwood
FISHLAKE
NATL.
FOREST
MANTI - LA SAL NATL. FOREST
HUMBOLDT-TOIYABE NATL. FOREST
DESERT RANGE EXPERIMENTAL STATION
Fillmore
PAVANT
Black Rock
Cove Fort
Joseph
Elsinore
Monroe
Sevier
Burrville
SEVIER
Fremont Junction
Mt. Marvine 3539 m (11,610 ft)
San Rafael R.
Mt. Peale 3877 m (12,721 ft)
Frisco Peak 2944 m (9660 ft)
Frisco
Milford
Koosharem
La Sal Junction
La Sal
Marysvale
Greenwich
Fremont
Loa
WAYNE
Hanksville
CANYONLANDS NATL. PARK
BEAVER
Delano Peak 3709 m (12,169 ft)
Manderfield
Lyman
Bicknell
Torrey
Caineville
GLEN CANYON NATL. REC. AREA
Adamsville
Greenville
Beaver
Junction
Kingston
Circleville
Angle
Teasdale
Grover
Fruita
CAPITOL REEF
HENRY
Summit Point
Minersville
Antimony
NATL.
Lund
Mt. Dutton 3365 m (11,040 ft)
Spry
Boulder
Mt. Pennell 3466 m (11,371 ft)
PARK
CIRCLE CLIFFS
Monticello
Abajo Peak 3463 m (11,360 ft)
Beryl
Modena
IRON
Paragonah
Parowan
Panguitch
Escalante
Ticaboo
Fry Canyon
MANTI-LA SAL NATL. FOREST
Iron Springs
Enoch
GARFIELD
Escalante R.
NATURAL BRIDGES N.M.
Blanding
Uvada
Newcastle
Hamilton Fort
Brian Head
DIXIE NATL. FOREST
CEDAR BREAKS N.M.
Rubys Inn
Bryce Canyon
Hatch
Tropic
Cannonville
Henrieville
KAIPAROWITS PLATEAU
GLEN CANYON N.R.A.
SAN JUAN
CANYONS OF THE ANCIENTS NATL. MON.
HOVENWEEP N.M.
Enterprise
Cedar City
Kanarraville
BRYCE CANYON NATL. PARK
Long Valley Junction
Alton
KANE
Montezuma Creek
Bluff
Aneth
New Harmony
Central
Pine Valley
Pintura
Glendale
GRAND STAIRCASE-ESCALANTE NATL. MON.
Paria R.
L. Powell
San Juan R.
UTE MTN. I.R.
DIXIE NATL. FOREST
ZION NATL. PARK
Orderville
Mount Carmel
Mount Carmel Junction
GLEN CANYON NATL. RECREATION AREA
WASHINGTON
Veyo
Gunlock
Toquerville
Leeds
Virgin
Springdale
Rockville
RAINBOW BRIDGE N.M.
Navajo Mt. 3166 m (10,388 ft)
NAVAJO INDIAN RESERVATION
MONUMENT VALLEY
PAIUTE I.R.
Ivins
St. George
Santa Clara
Hurricane
Washington
Kanab
Big Water
Mexican Hat
ARIZONA
UTAH
Hildale
Fredonia
Page
UTAH
ARIZONA
N. MEX.
VERMILION CLIFFS NATL. MON.
KAIBAB I.R.
PIPE SPRING N.M.
KAIBAB NATL. FOREST
GRAND CANYON NATL. PARK
NAVAJO IND. RES.
NAVAJO N.M.
GRAND CANYON-PARASHANT NATL. MON.

© MapQuest.com, Inc.

Capital: Montpelier	**Pop. (2000):** 608,827
Area: 9,600 sq. mi.	**Largest City:** Burlington
24,900 sq. km.	38,889

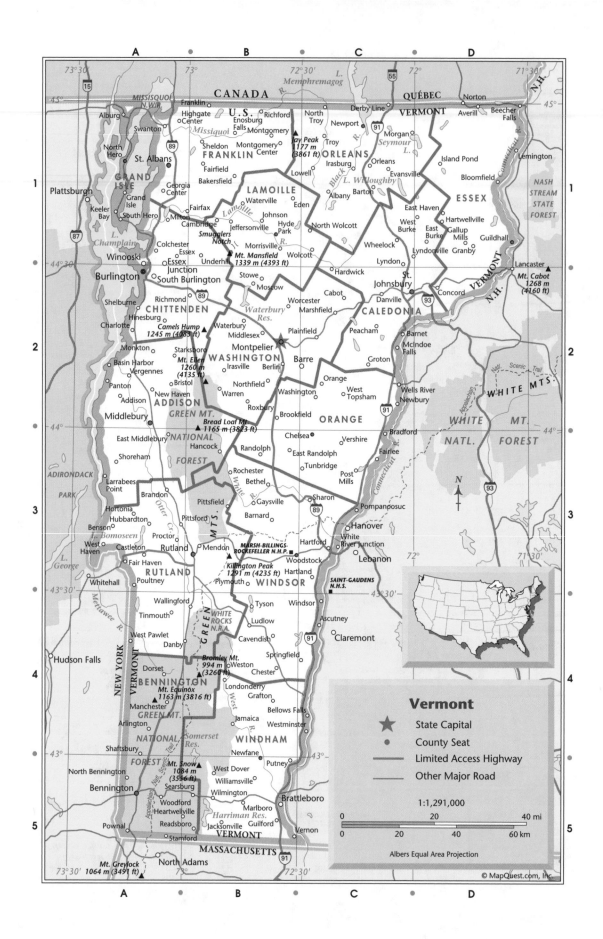

Vermont

★ State Capital
• County Seat
— Limited Access Highway
— Other Major Road

1:1,291,000

0   20   40 mi
0   20   40   60 km

Albers Equal Area Projection

© MapQuest.com, Inc.

Capital: Richmond
Area: 42,800 sq. mi.
110,800 sq. km.
Pop. (2000): 7,078,515
Largest City: Virginia Beach
425,257

VIRGINIA 173

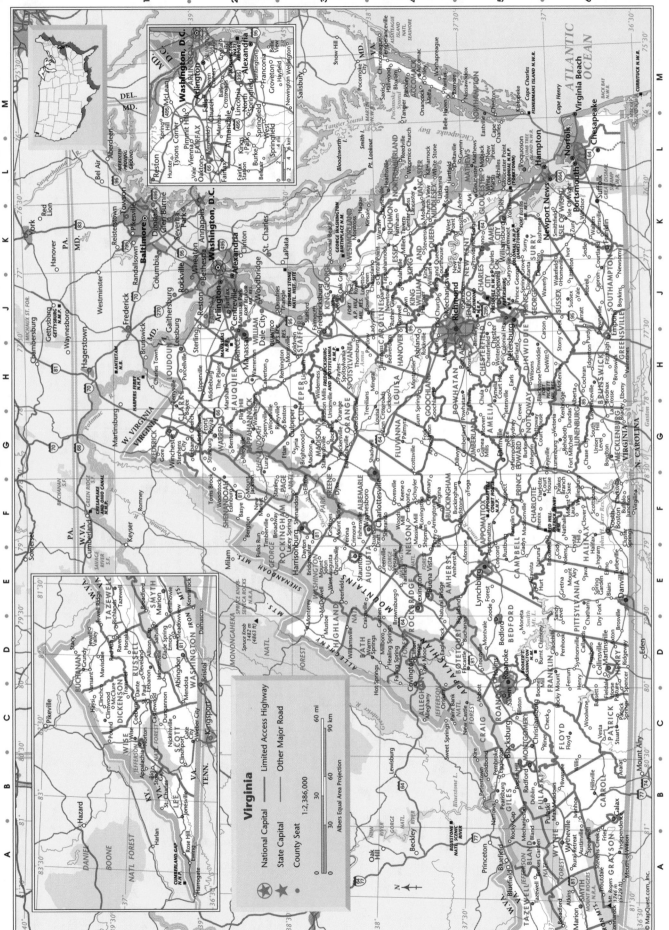

Capital: Olympia
Area: 71,300 sq. mi.
184,700 sq. km.
Pop. (2000): 5,894,121
Largest City: Seattle
563,374

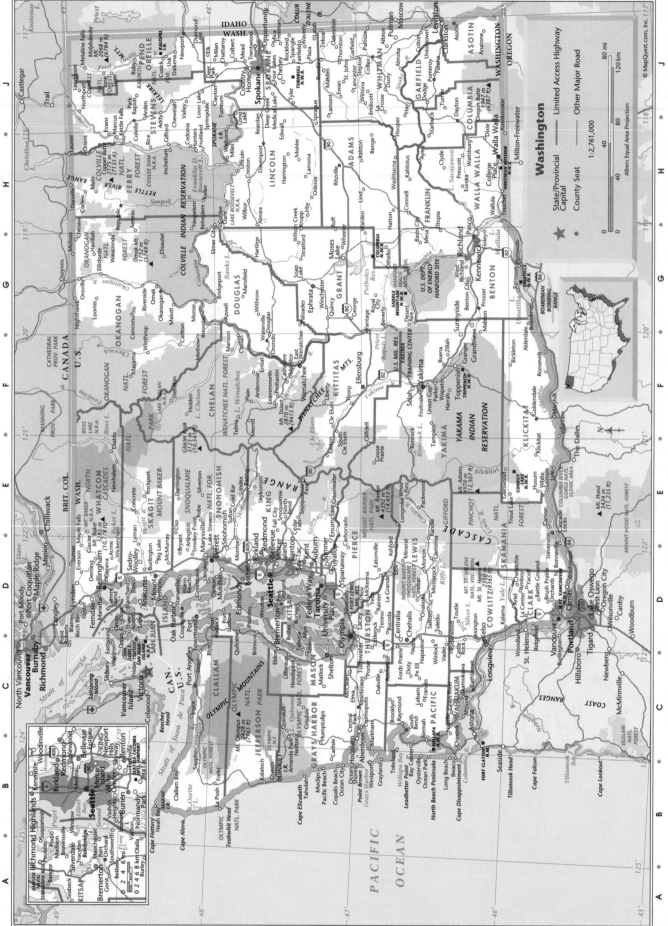

Capital: Charleston	**Pop. (2000):** 1,808,344	
Area: 24,200 sq. mi.	**Largest City:** Charleston	
62,800 sq. km.	53,421	

West Virginia

- ★ State Capital
- • County Seat

— Limited Access Highway
— Other Major Road

1:1,830,000

Albers Equal Area Projection

0 30 60 mi
0 30 60 90 km

© MapQuest.com, Inc.

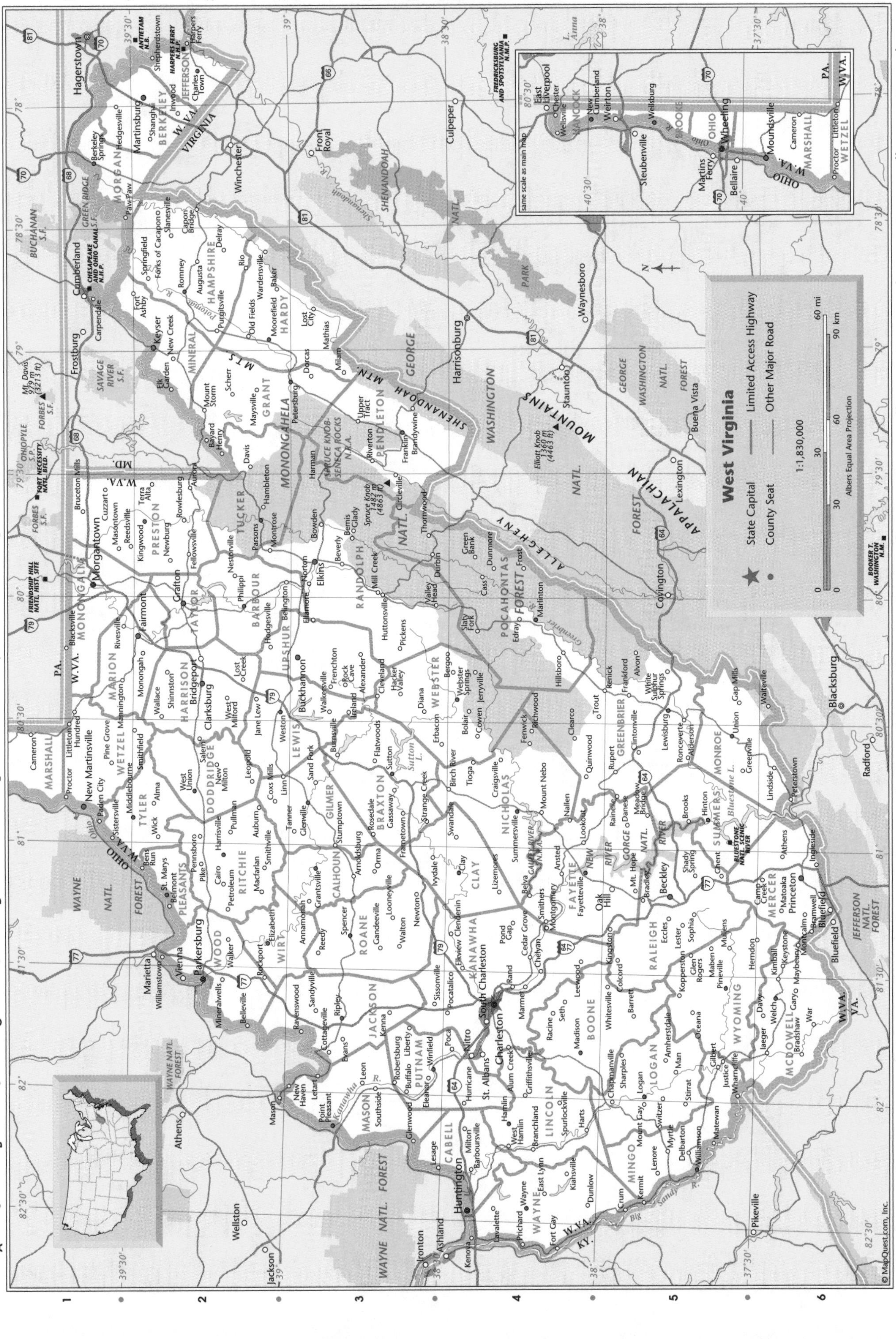

WISCONSIN 1848

Capital: Madison
Area: 65,500 sq. mi.
169,600 sq. km.

Pop. (2000): 5,363,675
Largest City: Milwaukee
596,974

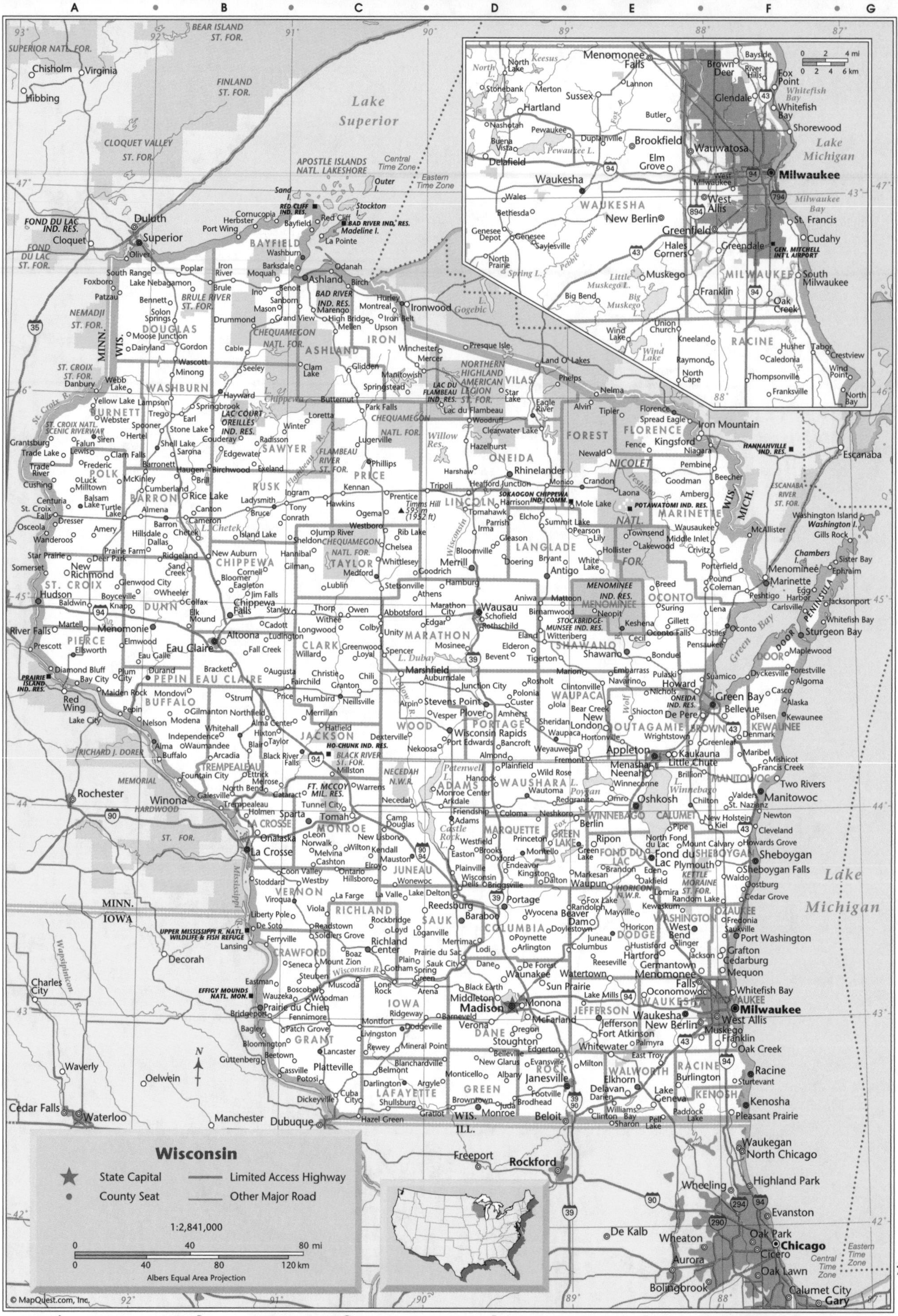

Wisconsin

★ State Capital
• County Seat
— Limited Access Highway
— Other Major Road

1:2,841,000

0   40   80 mi
0   40   80   120 km

Albers Equal Area Projection

© MapQuest.com, Inc.

Capital: Cheyenne
Area: 97,800 sq. mi.
253,300 sq. km.
Pop. (2000): 493,782
Largest City: Cheyenne
53,011

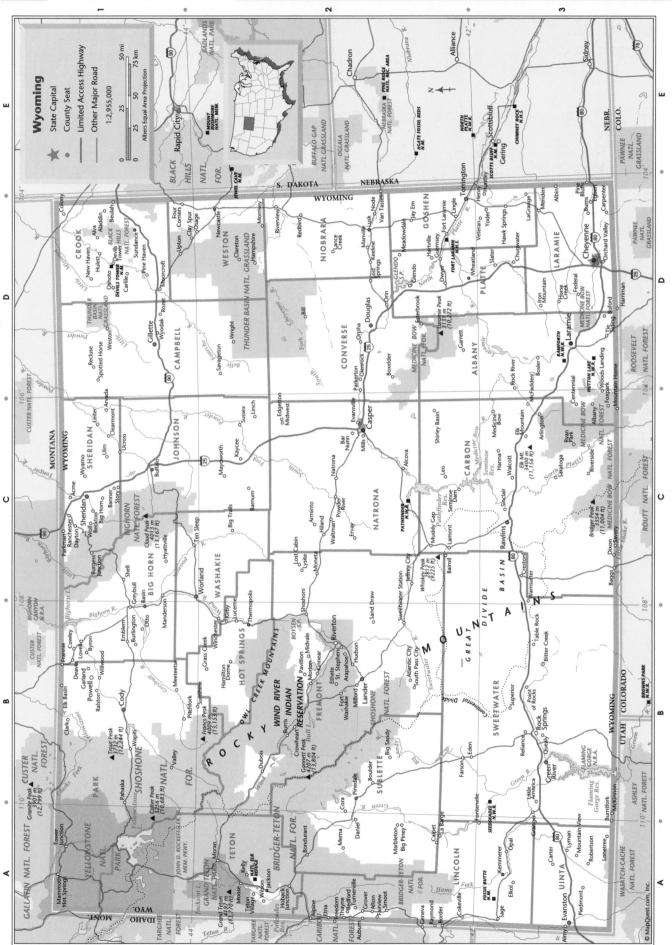

Wyoming

★ State Capital
● County Seat
— Limited Access Highway
— Other Major Road

1:2,955,000

Albers Equal Area Projection

178 ALABAMA–CALIFORNIA

Abbreviations
N.H.P. .... National Historical Park
N.H.S. .... National Historic Site
N.M. .... National Monument
N.P. .... National Park
N.R.A. .... National Recreation Area

Alabama .... page 128

Cities and Towns
Abbeville D4
Adamsville C2
Alabaster C2
Albertville C1
Alexander City D3
Aliceville A2
Andalusia C4
Anniston D2
Arab C1
Ashford D4
Ashland D2
Ashville C2
Athens C1
Atmore B4
Attalla C1
Auburn D3
Bay Minette B5
Bayou La Batre A5
Bessemer C2
Birmingham C2
Blountsville C1
Boaz C1
Brent B3
Brewton B4
Bridgeport D1
Brundidge D4
Butler A3
Calera C2
Camden B4
Camp Hill D3
Carbon Hill B2
Carrollton A2
Center Point C2
Centre D1
Centreville B3
Chatom A4
Chelsea C2
Cherokee B1
Chickasaw A5
Childersburg C2
Citronelle A4
Clanton C3
Clayton D4
Clio D4
Collinsville D1
Columbiana C2
Cordova B2
Cottonwood D4
Creola A5
Crossville D1
Cullman C1
Dadeville D3
Daleville D4
Daphne B5
Decatur C1
Demopolis B3
Dora B2
Dothan D4
Double Springs B1
East Brewton B4
Elba C4
Enterprise D4
Eufaula D4
Eutaw B3
Evergreen C4
Fairfield C2
Fairhope B5
Falkville C1
Fayette B2
Flomaton B4
Florala C4
Florence B1
Foley B5
Fort Morgan A5
Fort Payne D1
Frisco City B4
Fultondale C2
Gadsden C1
Gardendale C2
Gasque B5
Geneva D4
Georgiana C4
Glencoe D2
Good Hope C1
Goodwater C2
Gordo B2
Grand Bay A5
Greensboro B3
Greenville C4
Grove Hill B4
Guin B2
Gulf Shores B5
Guntersville C1
Haleyville B1
Hamilton B1
Hanceville C1
Hartford D4
Hartselle C1
Hayneville C3
Hazel Green C1
Headland D4
Heflin D2
Helena C2
Henagar D1
Heron Bay A5
Hokes Bluff D2
Holt B2
Hoover C2
Hueytown B2
Huntsville C1
Irondale C2
Jackson B4
Jacksonville D2
Jasper B2
Jemison C3
Lafayette D3
Lanett D3
Leeds C2
Lincoln C2
Linden B3
Lineville D2
Livingston A3
Luverne C4
Madison C1
Marion B3
Meridianville C1
Midfield C2
Midland City D4
Millbrook C3
Mobile A5
Monroeville B4
Montevallo C2
Montgomery, *capital* C3
Moulton B1
Moundville B3
Muscle Shoals B1
New Hope C1
Newton D4
Northport B2
Oneonta C2
Opelika D3
Opp C4
Orange Beach B5
Oxford D2
Ozark D4
Parrish B2
Pelham C2
Pell City C2
Petersville B1
Phenix City D3
Phil Campbell B1
Piedmont D2
Pinson C2
Point Clear B5
Prattville C3
Priceville C1
Prichard A5
Ragland C2
Rainbow City C2
Rainsville D1
Reform A2
Roanoke D2
Robertsdale B5
Rockford C3
Russellville B1
Samson C4
Saraland A5
Sardis City C2
Satsuma A5
Scottsboro C1
Selma B3
Sheffield B1
Slocomb D4
Smiths D3
Southside C2
Spanish Fort B5
Springville C2
Stevenson D1
Sulligent A2
Sumiton B2
Sylacauga C2
Talladega C2
Tallassee D3
Taylor D4
Theodore A5
Thomasville B4
Thorsby C3
Tillmans Corner A5
Town Creek B1
Trinity B1
Troy D4
Trussville C2
Tuscaloosa B2
Tuscumbia B1
Tuskegee D3
Union Springs D3
Uniontown B3
Valley D3
Vernon A2
Vestavia Hills C2
Vincent C2
Warrior C2
Weaver D2
Wedowee D2
West Blocton B2
Wetumpka C3
Winfield B2
York A3

Other Features
Alabama, *river* B4
Appalachian, *mts.* D1
Bear Creek, *reservoir* B1
Black Warrior, *river* B3
Bon Secour, *bay* B5
Cahaba, *river* B3
Cheaha, *mt.* D2
Conecuh, *river* C4
Coosa, *river* D1
Dauphin, *island* A5
Guntersville, *lake* C1
Jordan, *lake* C3
Lewis Smith, *lake* B1
Logan Morgan, *lake* C2
Lookout, *mt.* D1
Martin, *lake* D3
Mitchell, *lake* C3
Mobile, *bay* A5
Neely Henry, *lake* C2
Pickwick, *lake* A1
R.L. Harris, *reservoir* D2
Russell Cave Natl. Monument D1
Tallapoosa, *river* D2
Tennessee, *river* A1
Tombigbee, *river* A4
Tuscaloosa, *lake* B2
Tuskegee Institute Natl. Hist. Site D3
Weiss, *lake* D1
Wheeler, *lake* B1
William "Bill" Dannelly, *reservoir* B3
Wilson, *lake* B1

Alaska .... page 129

Cities and Towns
Adak Inset
Anchorage F2
Barrow D1
Bethel C2
Big Delta F2
College F2
Cordova F2
Craig J3
Delta Jct. F2
Dillingham D3
Fairbanks F2
Haines H3
Homer E3
Juneau, *capital* J3
Kenai E2
Ketchikan J3
Kodiak E3
Kotzebue C1
McKinley Park F2
Metlakatla J3
Nikiski E2
Nome B2
North Pole F2
Palmer F2
Petersburg J3
Prudhoe Bay F1
Seward F2
Sitka H3
Skagway H3
Soldotna E2
Talkeetna E2
Tok G2
Unalaska B4
Valdez F2
Wasilla F2
Whittier F2
Wrangell J3

Other Features
Adak, *island* Inset
Admiralty Island Natl. Monument J3
Agattu, *island* Inset
Alaska, *gulf* F3
Alaska, *peninsula* C3
Alaska, *range* E2
Aleutian, *islands* A4, Inset
Alexander, *archipelago* H3
Amchitka, *island* Inset
Amlia, *island* Inset
Andreanof, *islands* Inset
Aniakchak N.M. and Preserve D3
Atka, *island* Inset
Attu, *island* Inset
Barrow, *point* D1
Beaufort, *sea* H1
Becharof, *lake* D3
Bering, *sea* B3
Bering, *strait* B2
Blackburn, *mt.* G2
Bristol, *bay* C3
Brooks, *range* D1
Cape Krusenstern N.M. C1
Chirikof, *island* D3
Chukchi, *sea* A1
Colville, *river* E1
Cook, *inlet* E3
Copper, *river* G2
Denali Natl. Park and Preserve E2
Fairweather, *mt.* H3
Gates of the Arctic N.P.
and Preserve E1
Glacier Bay N.P. and Preserve H3
Iliamna, *lake* D3
Inside Passage, *waterway* J3
Kanaga, *island* Inset
Katmai Natl. Park and Preserve D3
Kenai, *peninsula* E2
Kenai Fjords Natl. Park F3
Kiska, *island* Inset
Klondike Gold Rush N.H.P H3
Kobuk, *river* D1
Kobuk Valley Natl. Park D1
Kodiak, *island* E3
Kotzebue, *sound* C1
Koyukuk, *river* D1
Kuskokwim, *bay* C3
Kuskokwim, *mts.* D2
Kuskokwim, *river* D2
Lake Clark Natl. Park and Preserve E2
Lisburne, *cape* B1
Lisburne, *peninsula* C1
Logan, *mt.* G2
Lynn, *canal* J3
McKinley, *mt.* E2
Malaspina, *glacier* G3
Michelson, *mt.* G1
Mohican, *cape* B2
Muir, *glacier* F2
Near, *islands* Inset
Noatak, *river* D1
Norton, *sound* C2
Nunivak, *island* B3
Porcupine, *river* G1
Pribilof, *islands* B3
Prince of Wales, *island* J3
Progromni, *volcano* C4
Rat, *islands* Inset
St. Elias, *mt.* G2
St. George, *island* B3
St. Lawrence, *island* A2
St. Matthew, *island* A2
St. Paul, *island* A3
Samalga, *pass* B4
Sanak, *island* C4
Seguam, *island* Inset
Semisopochnoi, *island* Inset
Seward, *peninsula* C1
Shishaldin, *volcano* C4
Shumagin, *islands* D4
Sitka N.H.P. H3
Stikine, *river* J3
Tanaga, *island* F3
Tanana, *river* E2
Tikchik, *lakes* D2
Trinity, *islands* E3
Umnak, *island* Inset
Unalaska, *island* B4
Unga, *island* C3
Unimak, *island* C4
Utukok, *river* C1
White Mts. Natl. Rec. Area F1
Wrangell, *mts.* G2
Wrangell-St. Elias N.P.
and Preserve G2
Yukon, *river* D2
Yukon-Charley Rivers
Natl. Preserve G2
Yunaska, *island* Inset

Arizona .... page 130

Cities and Towns
Ajo C5
Apache Junction D4
Avondale C4
Bagdad B3
Benson E6
Bisbee F6
Bitahochee E2
Buckeye C4
Bullhead City A2
Camp Verde D3
Carefree D4
Casa Grande D5
Catalina E5
Cave Creek D4
Chandler D4
Chinle F1
Chino Valley C3
Cibecue E3
Clarkdale C3
Claypool E4
Clifton F4
Colorado City C1
Coolidge D5
Cornville D3
Cow Springs E1
Crown King C3
Douglas F6
Dudleyville E5
Eagar F3
El Mirage C4
Eloy D5
Flagstaff D2
Florence D4
Fort Defiance F2
Fountain Hills D4
Ganado F2
Geronimo E4
Gila Bend C5
Gilbert D4
Globe E4
Goodyear C4
Grand Canyon C1
Greaterville E6
Green Valley E6
Guthrie F5
Happy Jack D3
Holbrook E3
Huachuca City E6
Kayenta E1
Kearny E4
Kingman A2
Kirkland Junction C3
Lake Havasu City A3
Lake Montezuma D3
Litchfield Park C4
Mammoth E5
Many Farms F1
Marana D5
Mesa D4
Miami E4
Nogales E6
Oracle E5
Oro Valley E5
Page D1
Paradise Valley D4
Parker A3
Payson D3
Peoria C4
Phoenix, *capital* C4
Pima F5
Pinetop-Lakeside F3
Prescott C3
Prescott Valley C3
Quartzsite A4
Queen Creek D4
Randolph D5
Sacaton D4
Safford F5
Sahuarita E6
St. David E6
St. Johns F3
San Carlos E4
Sanders F2
San Manuel E5
Scottsdale D4
Sedona D3
Sells D6
Show Low E3
Sierra Vista E6
Snowflake E3
Somerton A5
South Tucson E5
Springerville F3
Sun City C4
Sun Lakes D4
Superior D4
Surprise C4
Taylor E3
Tempe D4
Thatcher F5
Three Points D5
Tolleson C4
Tombstone E6
Tuba City D1
Tucson E5
Whiteriver F4
Wickenburg C4
Willcox F5
Williams C2
Window Rock F2
Winslow E2
Yuma A5

Other Features
Agua Fria, *river* C4
Alamo, *lake* B3
Apache, *lake* E4
Aztec Peak, *mt.* E4
Baldy, *mt.* F4
Bartlett, *reservoir* D4
Big Horn, *mts.* B4
Bill Williams, *river* A3
Black, *mesa* E1
Black, *river* E4
Canyon De Chelly N.M. F1
Casa Grande Ruins N.M. D5
Castle Dome, *mts.* A4
Castle Dome Peak, *mt.* A4
Chiricahua Natl. Monument F6
Colorado, *river* B2, D1
Coronado Natl. Mem. E6
Gila, *river* B5, D4, F4
Glen Canyon, *dam* D1
Glen Canyon Natl. Rec. Area D1
Grand, *canyon* C1
Grand Canyon Natl. Park B2, C1
Grand Canyon-Parashant N.M. B1
Harcuvar, *mts.* B4
Havasu, *lake* A3
Hide Creek, *mt.* C3
Hoover, *dam* A1
Hopi Indian Res. E2
Horseshoe, *reservoir* D4
Hualapai, *mt.* B2
Hubbell Trading Post N.H.S. F2
Humphreys Peak, *mt.* D2
Lake Mead Natl. Rec. Area B1
Little Colorado, *river* D2
Many Farms, *lake* F1
Maple Peak, *mt.* F4
Mazatzal Peak, *mt.* D3
Mohave, *lake* A2
Montezuma Castle N.M. D3
Monument, *valley* F1
Mormon, *lake* D3
Navajo Indian Res. E1, E2
Navajo Natl. Monument E1
Organ Pipe Cactus N.M. C5
Painted, *desert* D2
Parker, *dam* A3
Petrified Forest Natl. Park F3
Pipe Spring Natl. Monument C1
Pleasant, *lake* C4
Point Imperial, *mt.* D1
Powell, *lake* D1
Red, *lake* B2
Saguaro Natl. Monument E5
Salt, *river* E4
San Carlos, *lake* E4
San Pedro, *river* E5
Santa Cruz, *river* D5
Sonoran, *desert* B5
Sunset Crater Volcano N.M. D2
Theodore Roosevelt, *lake* D4
Tipton, *mt.* A2
Tonto Natl. Monument D4
Trumbull, *mt.* B1
Tumacacori Natl Hist. Park D6
Tuzigoot Natl. Monument C3
Ventana, *cave* C5
Verde, *river* D3
Virgin, *river* A1
Walnut Canyon Natl. Monument D2
White, *mts.* F4
White House, *ruin* F1
Wupatki Natl. Monument D2
Yuma, *desert* A5

Arkansas .... page 131

Cities and Towns
Alicia D2
Alma A2
Arkadelphia B3
Arkansas City D4
Ashdown A4
Ash Flat D1
Atkins C2
Augusta D2
Bald Knob D2
Barling A2
Batesville D2
Bay E2
Beebe D2
Bella Vista A1
Benton C3
Bentonville A1
Berryville B1
Blytheville F2
Bodcaw B4
Booneville B2
Brinkley D3
Bryant C3
Bull Shoals C1
Cabot D3
Camden C4
Caraway E2
Carlisle D3
Cave City D2
Charleston A2
Clarendon D3
Clarksville B2
Clinton C2
Conway C2
Corning E1
Crossett D4
Daisy B3
Damascus C2
Danville B2
Dardanelle B2
De Queen A3
Dermott D4
Des Arc D3
De Valls Bluff D3
De Witt D3
Dierks A3
Dumas D4
Earle E2
El Dorado C4
England D3
Eudora D4
Eureka Springs B1
Fairfield Bay C2
Fallsville B2
Farmington A1
Fayetteville A1
Fordyce C4
Foreman A4
Forrest City E2
Fort Smith A2
Fountain Hill D4
Gentry A1
Glenwood B3
Gosnell F2
Gould D4
Gravette A1
Greenbrier C2
Green Forest B1
Greenwood A2
Griffithville D2
Gurdon B4
Hamburg D4
Hampton C4
Harrisburg E2
Harrison B1
Haskell C3
Hatfield A3
Hazen D3
Heber Springs C2
Helena E3
Hope B4
Horseshoe Bend D1
Hot Springs National Park B3
Hot Springs Village B3
Hoxie E1
Hughes E3
Hunter D2
Huntsville B1
Jacksonville C3
Jasper B1
Jonesboro E2
Lake City E2
Lake Hamilton B3
Lake Village D4
Lepanto E2
Lewisville B4
Lincoln A2
Little Rock, *capital* C3
Lonoke D3
Luxora F2
McCrory D2
McGehee D4
McNeil B4
McRae D2
Magnolia B4
Malvern C3
Manila E2
Marianna E3
Marion E2
Marked Tree E2
Marshall C2
Marvell E3
Maumelle C3
Mayflower C3
Melbourne D1
Mena A3
Monticello D4
Morrilton C2
Mountain Home C1
Mountain View
Mount Ida
Mulberry
Murfreesboro
Nashville
Newport
North Crossett
North Little Rock
Oden
Osceola
Ozark
Paragould
Paris
Parkin
Pea Ridge
Pelsor
Perryville
Piggott
Pine Bluff
Pocahontas
Prescott
Rector
Rison
Rogers
Rose Bud
Russell
Russellville
St. Charles
St. Paul
Salem
Searcy
Sheridan
Sherwood
Siloam Springs
Smackover
Springdale
Springhill
Star City
Stuttgart
Texarkana
Tillar
Trumann
Tuckerman
Tupelo
Van Buren
Waldo
Waldron
Walnut Ridge
Warren
Washington
West Fork
West Helena
West Memphis
White Hall
Wynne
Yellville

Other Features
Arkansas, *river*
Arkansas Post Natl. Mem.
Beaver, *lake*
Black, *river*
Boston, *mts.*
Buffalo, *river*
Buffalo Natl. River
Bull Shoals, *lake*
Cache, *river*
Catherine, *lake*
Dardanelle, *reservoir*
DeGray, *lake*
Erling, *lake*
Fort Smith Natl. Hist Site
Greers Ferry, *lake*
Greeson, *lake*
Hamilton, *lake*
Hot Springs Natl. Park
Little Missouri, *river*
Little Rock Central H.S N.H.S.
Magazine, *mt.*
Maumelle, *lake*
Millwood, *lake*
Mississippi, *river*
Nimrod, *lake*
Norfork, *lake*
Ouachita, *lake*
Ouachita, *mts.*
Ouachita, *river* B3
Ozark, *plateau*
Pea Ridge Natl. Mil. Park
Red, *river*
St. Francis, *river*
Saline, *river*
Table Rock, *lake*
White, *river* C2

California .... page

Cities and Towns
Adelanto
Alameda
Alamo
Albany
Alhambra
Alpine
Altadena
Alturas
Anaheim E1
Anderson
Antioch D
Apple Valley
Aptos
Arcadia
Arcata
Arnold
Arroyo Grande
Arvin
Ashland
Atascadero
Atherton
Atwater
Auberry
Auburn
Avalon
Avenal
Azusa
Bakersfield
Baldwin Park
Barstow
Bell
Bellflower
Belmont
Belvedere
Benicia
Berkeley C
Beverly Hills
Big Bear Lake
Bishop
Black Point
Blythe
Bonita
Boron

	Key
ego Springs	J9
ley	K10
...leport	E11
	F4
...ane	J2
...admoor	J2
...lton	E8
...a Park	E11
...ngame	C10
...bank	J3
...ey	D2
...onwillow	F7
...basas	B10
...exico	K10
...fornia City	H7
...patria	K9
...toga	C4
...abria	D7
...pbell	L4
...on	K2
...sbad	H9
...nel Valley	D6
...interra	F8
...on	D11
...roville	D6
...hedral City	J9
...ucos	E7
...ral Valley	C2
...ister	E5
...o	D2
...o	D3
...owchilla	E5
...la Vista	C9, H10
...lemont	F10
...ton	L1
...arlake	C4
...erdale	B4
...vis	F6
...chella	L1
...ninga	B2
...o	C4
...lax	E3
...usa	D3
...pton	D11
...cord	L1
...coran	F6
...ning	C3
...ona	F11
...onado	B8
...e Madera	J1
...a Mesa	E11
...onwood	C2
...na	E10
...van Heights	E11
...cent City	A1
...stline	K8
...er City	C10
...pertino	L4
...ress	D11
...City	J2
...ville	J2
...s	D4
...no	F7
...Mar	H10
...ert Hot Springs	J9
...lo	L2
...mond Bar	E10
...e Palos	E6
...mey	D11
...nieville	E3
...lin	L2
...smuir	C1
...mart	F7
...Los Angeles	D10
...an	F6
...Palo Alto	K3
...ajon	C8, J10
...entro	K10
...errito	K1
...anada	J3
...Grove	D4
...onte	D10
...egundo	C11
...brante	K1
...ryville	K2
...nitas	H9
...ndido	H9
...ka	A2
...er	F6
...fax	H1
...field	D4
...brook	H9
...dale	A2
...baugh	E6
...ence	D11
...d	D4
...Bragg	B3
...una	A2
...er City	K3
...ntain Valley	E11
...mont	D5, L3
...er Park	G8
...no	F6
...erton	E11
	D4
...den Grove	E11
...oy	D5
...ndale	D10, G8
...ndora	E10
...rview	B10
...fork	B2
...azales	D6
...ss Valley	D3
...enacres	F6
...enbrae	J1
...enfield	D6
...enville	E2
...dley	D3
...veland	E5
...dalupe	E8
...Moon Bay	J3
...sford	F6
...thorne	C11
...fork	B2
...ward	C5, L2
...dsburg	D3
...net	J9
...cules	K1
...mosa Beach	C11
...eria	H8
...den Hills	B10
...borough	J3
...ington Beach	E11, G9
...acio	E6
...erial Beach	B9, H10

	Key
Independence	G6
Indio	J9
Inglewood	C11, G8
Ingot	C2
Inyokern	H7
Ione	D4
Irvine	E11, H9
Isla Vista	F8
Jackson	E4
Joshua Tree	J8
Julian	J9
Kelseyville	C4
Kensington	K1
Kentfield	J1
Kerman	E6
Kernville	G7
Kettleman City	F6
King City	D6
La Canada-Flintridge	D10
La Crescenta	D10
Lafayette	K1
La Habra	E11
La Honda	K4
Lake Isabella	G7
Lakeport	C3
Lakeside	J10
Lakewood	D11
La Mesa	C8
La Mirada	D11
Lamont	G7
Lancaster	G8
La Puente	E10
Larkspur	J1
Laton	F6
Lawndale	C11
Lee Vining	F5
Lemon Grove	C8
Lemoore	F6
Lincoln	D4
Lindsay	F6
Littlerock	H8
Livermore	D4
Livingston	E5
Lockeford	D4
Lodi	D4
Loma Mar	K4
Lomita	C11
Lompoc	E8
Lone Pine	G6
Long Beach	D11, G9
Los Altos	K3
Los Altos Hills	K4
Los Angeles	D10, G8
Los Banos	E5
Los Molinos	C2
Los Osos	E7
Lynwood	D11
McCloud	C1
McFarland	G7
McKinleyville	A2
Madera	E6
Malibu	B10
Mammoth Lakes	G5
Manhattan Beach	C11
Manteca	D5
Marina	D6
Marina del Rey	C11
Marin City	J1
Marinwood	J1
Mariposa	F5
Markleeville	F4
Martinez	C4, K1
Marysville	D3
Maywood	D10
Mecca	J9
Mendota	E6
Menlo Park	K3
Merced	E5
Midway City	E11
Millbrae	J2
Mill Valley	J1
Milpitas	L3
Miranda	B2
Modesto	D5
Mojave	G7
Monrovia	E10
Montara	J3
Montclair	F10
Montebello	D10
Monte Nido	B10
Monterey	D6
Monterey Park	D10
Monte Sereno	L4
Moraga	K2
Moreno Valley	H9
Morgan Hill	D5
Morongo Valley	J8
Morro Bay	E7
Moss Beach	J3
Mountain View	K3
Mount Shasta	C1
Muir Beach	H1
Napa	C4
National City	C9
Needles	L8
Nevada City	D3
Newark	L3
Newberry Springs	J9
Newport Beach	H9
Nicasio	H1
Nice	C3
Nipomo	E7
Nipton	K7
Norco	F11
North Edwards	H7
North Fair Oaks	K3
Novato	H1
Oakdale	E5
Oakhurst	F5
Oakland	K2, C5
Oceanside	H9
Oildale	F7
Ojai	F8
Olema	H1
Olivehurst	D3
Ontario	F10, H8
Orange	E11
Orinda	K1
Orland	C3
Oroville	D3
Otay	C9
Oxnard	F8
Pacheco	L1
Pacifica	J2
Palermo	D3
Palmdale	G8
Palm Desert	J9
Palm Springs	J9
Palo Alto	K3
Palos Verdes Estates	C11
Paradise	D3
Pasadena	D10, G8

	Key
Patterson	D5
Petaluma	C4
Pico Rivera	D10
Piedmont	K2
Pine Valley	J10
Pinole	K1
Pismo Beach	E7
Pittsburg	L1
Placentia	E11
Placerville	E4
Pleasant Hill	L1
Pleasanton	L2
Pomona	E10, H8
Port Costa	K1
Porterville	G6
Portola	E3
Poway	H10
Prunedale	D6
Quartz Hill	G8
Quincy	D3
Ramona	J9
Rancho Cucamonga	F10
Rancho Palos Verdes	C11
Rancho Rinconada	L4
Rancho Santa Margarita	F11
Red Bluff	C2
Redding	C2
Redlands	H8
Redondo Beach	C11
Redwood City	C5, K3
Reedley	F6
Richgrove	F7
Richmond	J1
Ridgecrest	H7
Rio Dell	A2
Riverside	H9
Rodeo	K1
Rolling Hills	C11
Rolling Hills Estates	C11
Rosamond	G8
Roseville	D4
Sacramento, capital	D4
Salinas	D6
San Andreas	E4
San Anselmo	H1
San Bernardino	H8
San Bruno	J2
San Carlos	K3
San Clemente	H9
San Diego	B8, H10
San Francisco	C5, J2
San Gabriel	D10
Sanger	F6
San Gregorio	K4
San Jose	D5, L4
San Juan Bautista	D6
San Juan Capistrano	H9
San Leandro	K2
San Lorenzo	K2
San Luis Obispo	E7
San Mateo	C5, K3
San Pablo	J1
San Quentin	J1
San Rafael	C5, J1
San Ramon	L2
Santa Ana	E11, H9
Santa Barbara	F8
Santa Clara	L4
Santa Clarita	G8
Santa Cruz	C6
Santa Maria	E8
Santa Monica	C10
Santa Paula	F8
Santa Rosa	C4
Santa Venetia	J1
Santa Ynez	E8
Saratoga	L4
Sausalito	J2
Scotts Valley	C5
Seal Beach	D11
Sebastopol	C4
Selma	F6
Shafter	F7
Shingletown	D2
Shoshone	J7
Simi Valley	G8
Soledad	D6
Solvang	E8
Sonoma	C4
Sonora	E5
South Lake Tahoe	F4
South San Francisco	J2
Spring Valley	C8
Squaw Valley	F6
Stanford	K3
Stinson Beach	H1
Stockton	D5
Sunnyvale	C5, L4
Sunol	L3
Sunset Beach	D11
Susanville	E2
Taft	F7
Tamalpais Valley	J1
Tehachapi	G7
Temecula	H9
Templeton	E7
Terra Bella	F7
Thermalito	D3
Thousand Oaks	G8
Tiburon	J1
Tipton	F6
Topanga	B10
Torrance	C11, G9
Tracy	D5
Truckee	E3
Tulare	F6
Turlock	E5
Tustin	E11
Twain Harte	E4
Twentynine Palms	J8
Ukiah	C3
Union City	L3
Upland	F10
Vacaville	D4
Vallejo	C4, K1
Vandenberg Village	E8
Ventucopa	F8
Ventura	F8
Victorville	H8
Villa Park	E11
Vine Hill	L1
Visalia	F6
Vista	H9
Walnut	L1
Walnut Creek	L1
Wasco	F7
Watsonville	D6
Weaverville	C2
Weed	C1
West Covina	E10
West Hollywood	C10

	Key
Westminster	E11
Westmorland	K9
West Pittsburg	L1
Westwood	E2
Wheatland	D3
Whittier	D10
Willits	B3
Willow Creek	B2
Willows	C3
Windsor	C4
Wofford Heights	G7
Woodlake	F6
Woodland	D4
Woodside	K3
Wrightwood	H8
Yorba Linda	E11
Yosemite Village	F5
Yreka	C1
Yuba City	D3
Yucaipa	H8
Yucca Valley	J8
Zenia	B2

Other Features

	Key
Alameda, river	L3
Alcatraz, island	J2
Allison, mt.	L3
Almanor, lake	D2
Amargosa, range	J6
Amargosa, river	J7
Angel, island	J1
Balboa, park	B8
Berryessa, lake	C4
Boundary, peak	G5
Bullion, mts.	J8
Cascade, range	D1
Central, valley	K2
Chabot, lake	K2
Channel, islands	F9
Channel Islands Natl. Park	E9, F9
Chatsworth, reservoir	B10
Chino, river	F10
Chocolate, mts.	K9
Clair Engle, lake	C1
Clear, river	C3
Clear Lake, reservoir	D1
Coast, ranges	C2, D6
Colorado, desert	J9
Colorado, river	L9
Cucamonga, river	F11
Death, valley	H6
Death Valley Natl. Park	H6
Devils Postpile Natl. Monument	F5
Diablo, mt.	L1
Eagle, lake	E2
Eagle, peak	D2
Eel, river	B2
Eugene O'Neill Natl. Hist. Site	K2
Farallon, islands	B5
Farallones, gulf	B5
Giant Sequoia Natl. Mon.	F6, G6
Golden Gate Natl. Rec. Area	C5, J2
Goose, lake	E1
Grizzly, bay	L1
Half Moon, bay	J3
Honey, lake	E2
Humboldt, bay	A2
Imperial, valley	K9
Inyo, mts.	H6
Irvine, lake	F11
Joshua Tree Natl. Park	K8
Kern, river	G6
Kings, river	F6
Kings Canyon Natl. Park	G5
Klamath, mts.	B1
Klamath, river	B1
Lanfair, valley	K7
Lassen, peak	D2
Lassen Volcanic Natl. Park	D2
Lava Beds Natl. Monument	D1
McCoy, mts.	L9
Mad, river	B2
Manzanar Natl. Hist. Site	G6
Merced, river	E5
Middle Alkali, lake	F1
Mission, bay	B8
Mission Bay, park	B8
Mojave, desert	H7
Mojave, river	J8
Mono, lake	G4
Monterey, bay	D6
Morgan, mt.	G5
Morris, reservoir	E10
Muir Woods Natl. Monument	H1
Nacimiento, reservoir	D7
Napa, river	K1
Nicasio, reservoir	H1
Old Woman, mts.	K8
Oroville, reservoir	D3
Otay, river	C9
Panamint, range	H6
Panamint, valley	H6
Pescadero, river	J4
Pinnacles Natl. Monument	D6
Point Reyes Natl. Seashore	B4
Redwood Natl. Park	A1
Ritter, mt.	F5
Sacramento, river	C3
Salton, sea	K9
San Antonio, reservoir	D7
San Bernardino, mts.	J8
San Clemente, island	G10
San Diego, bay	B9
San Diego, river	B8
San Fernando, valley	B10
San Francisco, bay	J2
San Gabriel, mts.	H8
San Gabriel, reservoir	E10
San Joaquin, river	E5
San Luis Obispo, bay	E7
San Miguel, island	E8
San Nicolas, island	F9
San Pablo, bay	J1
San Rafael, mts.	F8
Santa Ana, river	F11
Santa Barbara, channel	E8
Santa Barbara, island	F9
Santa Catalina, island	G9
Santa Cruz, island	F8
Santa Cruz, mts.	J3
Santa Lucia, range	D6
Santa Monica, bay	B11
Santa Monica, mts.	B10
Santa Monica Mts. N.R.A.	B10
Santa Rosa, island	E9
Santa Rosa and San Jacinto Mountains N.M.	J9
Santiago, river	F11
Sequoia Natl. Park	G6
Shasta, lake	C2
Shasta, mt.	C1

	Key
Sierra, peak	F11
Sierra Nevada, range	D3, G5
Siskiyou, mts.	B1
Smith River N.R.A.	B1
Tahoe, lake	E3
Tehachapi, mts.	G8
Telescope, peak	H6
Trinity, river	B2
Tule, river	F6
Turtle, mts.	L8
Upper, lake	F3
Upper San Leandro, reservoir	L2
Vizcaino, cape	B3
Whiskeytown-Shasta-Trinity N.R.A.	D1
White, mts.	G5
Whitney, mt.	G6
Wilson, mt.	D10
Yosemite Natl. Park	F5

Colorado ....page 133

Cities and Towns

	Key
Akron	G1
Alamosa	E4
Arvada	D2
Aspen	D2
Aurora	E2
Avon	D2
Bennett	F2
Berthoud	E1
Black Forest	F3
Boulder	E1
Breckenridge	D2
Brighton	E2
Broomfield	E2
Brush	G1
Buena Vista	D3
Burlington	H2
Canon City	E3
Carbondale	C2
Castle Rock	F2
Cedaredge	C3
Center	D4
Central City	E2
Cheyenne Wells	H3
Clifton	B2
Colorado Springs	F3
Conejos	D4
Cortez	B4
Craig	C1
Crawford	C3
Creede	D4
Cripple Creek	E3
Dacono	F1
Del Norte	D4
Delta	B3
Denver, capital	F2
Dinosaur	A1
Dove Creek	B4
Durango	C4
Eads	H3
Eagle	D2
Eaton	F1
Elizabeth	F2
Englewood	F2
Estes Park	E1
Evans	F1
Evergreen	E2
Fairplay	E2
Florence	E3
Fort Collins	E1
Fort Lupton	F2
Fort Morgan	F1
Fountain	F3
Frisco	D2
Fruita	B2
Fruitvale	B2
Georgetown	E2
Glenwood Springs	C2
Golden	E2
Grand Junction	B2
Greeley	F1
Gunnison	C3
Gypsum	D2
Haswell	G3
Hayden	C1
Holyoke	H1
Hot Sulphur Springs	D1
Hugo	G2
Idaho Springs	E2
Johnstown	F1
Julesburg	H1
Keota	F1
Kiowa	F2
Kit Carson	H3
Lafayette	E2
La Junta	G4
Lake City	C3
Lakewood	E2
Lamar	G3
Las Animas	G3
Leadville	D2
Limon	G2
Littleton	F2
Longmont	E1
Louisville	E2
Loveland	E1
Manitou Springs	F3
Meeker	C1
Milliken	F1
Monte Vista	D4
Montrose	C3
Niwot	E1
Northglenn	F2
Olathe	C3
Orchard City	C3
Orchard Mesa	B2
Ordway	G3
Ouray	C3
Pagosa Springs	C4
Palisade	B2
Palmer Lake	F2
Paonia	C3
Parker	F2
Platteville	F1
Pritchett	H4
Pueblo	F3
Pueblo West	E3
Rangely	B1
Rifle	C2
Rocky Ford	G3
Saguache	D3
Salida	D3
San Luis	E4
Security	F3
Silverthorne	D2
Silverton	C4
Snowmass Village	D2
Springfield	H4
Steamboat Springs	D1
Sterling	G1
Telluride	C4

	Key
Thornton	F2
Trinidad	F4
Vail	D2
Vilas	H4
Walden	D1
Walsenburg	E4
Wellington	E1
Westcliffe	E3
Westminster	E2
Wheat Ridge	E2
Wiley	H3
Windsor	F1
Woodland Park	E3
Yuma	H1

Other Features

	Key
Animas, river	C4
Apishapa, river	F4
Arapaho, peak	E1
Arapaho Natl. Rec. Area	E1
Arikaree, river	H2
Arkansas, river	F4
Bent's Old Fort Natl. Hist. Site	G3
Black Canyon of the Gunnison Natl. Park	C3
Blanca, peak	E4
Blue Mesa, reservoir	C3
Bonny, reservoir	H2
Canyons of the Ancients N.M.	B4
Castle, peak	D2
Colorado, plateau	A4
Colorado, river	C2
Colorado Natl. Monument	B2
Crestone, peak	E4
Cucharas, river	F4
Curecanti Natl. Rec. Area	C3
Dinosaur Natl. Monument	B1
Dolores, river	B2
Elbert, mt.	D2
Eolus, mt.	C4
Evans, mt.	E2
Florissant Fossil Beds N.M.	E3
Front, range	E2
Great Sand Dunes N.P.	E4
Green, river	A1
Gunnison, mt.	C3
Hovenweep Natl. Monument	B4
John Martin, reservoir	G3
Laramie, mts.	E1
Laramie, river	E1
Little Snake, river	B1
Longs, peak	E1
Mancos, river	B4
Medicine Bow, mts.	D1
Mesa Verde Natl. Park	B4
Montezuma, peak	D4
North Fork Cimarron, river	H4
North Fork Smoky Hill, river	H2
North Platte, river	D1
Park, range	D1
Pikes, peak	E3
Purgatoire, river	G4
Rio Grande, river	D4
Roan, plateau	B2
Rocky, mts.	E1
Rocky Mt. Natl. Park	E1
Royal Gorge, canyon	E3
Sand Creek Massacre N.H.S.	H3
Sangre de Cristo, mts.	E4
San Juan, mts.	C4
San Luis, valley	E4
Sawatch, range	D2
South Fork Republican, river	E2, G1
South Platte, river	E2, G1
Uncompahgre, river	C3
U.S. Air Force Academy	F3
White, river	B1
Wilson, mt.	B1
Yampa, river	B1
Yucca House Natl. Monument	B4
Zirkel, mt.	D1

Connecticut ....page 134

Cities and Towns

	Key
Abington	G2
Andover	F3
Ansonia	C4
Attawaugan	H2
Avon	D2
Bakersville	C2
Ballouville	H2
Baltic	G3
Beacon Falls	C4
Berkshire	B4
Berlin	E3
Bethany	C4
Bethel	B4
Bethlehem	C3
Black Point	F4
Bloomfield	E2
Blue Hills	E2
Boardman Bridge	B3
Bolton	F2
Botsford	B4
Branford	D4
Bridgeport	C5
Bridgewater	B3
Bristol	D3
Broad Brook	E2
Brookfield	B4
Brookfield Center	B4
Brooklyn	H2
Burlington	D2
Burrville	C2
Cannondale	B5
Canterbury	H3
Canton	D2
Canton Center	D2
Centerbrook	F4
Central Village	H3
Chaplin	G2
Cheshire	D3
Chester	F4
Chesterfield	G3
Clarks Falls	H4
Clinton	E4
Colchester	F3
Colebrook	C2
Collinsville	D2
Columbia	F3
Cornwall	B2
Cornwall Bridge	B2
Coventry	F2
Cromwell	E3
Danbury	B4
Danielson	H2
Darien	B5
Dayville	H2

	Key
Deep River	F4
Derby	C4
Durham	E4
Eagleville	F2
East Brooklyn	H2
Eastford	G2
East Glastonbury	E3
East Granby	E2
East Haddam	F4
East Hampton	E3
East Hartford	E2
East Hartland	D2
East Haven	D4
East Killingly	H2
East Litchfield	C2
East Lyme	G4
Easton	B5
East Thompson	H1
East Village	C4
East Woodstock	H2
Ellington	F2
Enfield	E2
Essex	E4
Fairfield	B5
Falls Village	B2
Farmington	D3
Fitchman	G3
Flanders	B3
Franklin	G3
Gales Ferry	G4
Gaylordsville	B3
Georgetown	B5
Gilead	F3
Gilman	G3
Glasgo	H3
Glastonbury	E3
Goodrich Heights	E3
Goshen	C2
Granby	D2
Greenwich	A5
Grosvenor Dale	H2
Groton	G4
Groton Long Point	G4
Guilford	E4
Gurleyville	G2
Haddam	E4
Haddam Neck	E3
Hadlyme	F4
Hamburg	F4
Hamden	D4
Hampton	G2
Hanover	G3
Hartford, capital	E3
Harwinton	C2
Hawleyville	B4
Hazardville	E2
Hebron	F3
Higganum	E4
Hotchkissville	C3
Indian Neck	D5
Jewett City	H3
Kensington	D3
Killingworth	E4
Knollcrest	B4
Knollwood	D2
Lake Pocotopaug	E3
Lakeside	C3
Lakeside	C4
Laysville	F4
Lebanon	G3
Ledyard Center	G4
Liberty Hill	F3
Lime Rock	B2
Litchfield	C3
Lyons Plain	B5
Madison	E4
Manchester	E2
Mansfield Center	G3
Mansfield Four Corners	F2
Marble Dale	B3
Marion	D3
Meriden	D3
Merrow	F2
Middlebury	C3
Middlefield	E3
Middle Haddam	E3
Middletown	E3
Milford	C5
Mill Plain	A4
Milton	B2
Mohegan	G4
Monroe	C4
Montville	G4
Moosup	H3
Mystic	H4
Naugatuck	C4
New Britain	D3
New Canaan	B5
New Fairfield	B4
New Hartford	D2
New Haven	D4
Newington	E3
New London	G4
New Milford	B3
Newtown	B4
Niantic	G4
Noank	H4
Norfolk	C2
North Branford	D4
North Canton	D2
Northfield	C3
Northford	D4
North Franklin	G3
North Grosvenor Dale	H2
North Guilford	E4
North Haven	D4
North Stonington	H4
Northville	B3
North Westchester	F3
North Windham	G3
Norwalk	B5
Norwich	G4
Oakdale	G4
Oakville	C3
Old Lyme	F4
Old Mystic	H4
Old Saybrook	F4
Oneco	H3
Orange	C4
Oxford	C4
Park Lane	B3
Pawcatuck	H4
Perkins Corner	F3
Phoenixville	H3
Plainfield	H3
Plainville	D3
Plantsville	D3
Pleasant Valley	D2
Pleasure Beach	G4
Plymouth	C3
Pomfret	H2
Poquetanuck	G4

	Key
Poquonock	E2
Poquonock Bridge	G4
Portland	E3
Preston City	H3
Prospect	D4
Putnam	H2
Quaddick	H2
Quaker Hill	G4
Redding	B4
Redding Ridge	B4
Ridgebury	B4
Ridgefield	B4
Riverton	C2
Robertsville	C2
Rockfall	E3
Rockville	F2
Rocky Hill	E3
Roxbury	B3
Sachem Head	E5
Salem	F4
Salisbury	B2
Scantic	E2
Scitico	E2
Scotland	G3
Seymour	C4
Sharon	B2
Shelton	C4
Sherman	B3
Short Beach	D5
Simsbury	D2
Somers	F2
Sound View	F4
Southbury	C4
South Canaan	B2
South Chaplin	G2
South Glastonbury	E3
Southington	D3
South Kent	B3
South Killingly	H2
South Willington	F2
South Windham	G3
South Windsor	E2
Stafford	F2
Stafford Springs	F2
Staffordville	F2
Stamford	A5
Sterling	H3
Stevenson	C4
Stony Creek	E5
Storrs	G2
Straitsville	C4
Stratford	C5
Suffield	E2
Taconic	B1
Talcottville	F2
Tariffville	D2
Terryville	C3
Thompson	H2
Thompsonville	E2
Tolland	F2
Torrington	C2
Trumbull	C5
Uncasville	G4
Union	G2
Unionville	D2
Vernon	F2
Versailles	G3
Voluntown	H3
Wallingford	D4
Warren	B3
Warrenville	G2
Washington	B3
Washington Depot	B3
Waterbury	C3
Waterford	G4
Watertown	C3
Weatogue	D2
Westbrook	F4
West Cornwall	B2
Westford	G2
West Granby	D2
West Hartford	E2
West Hartland	D1
West Haven	D4
West Mystic	H4
West Norfolk	C1
Weston	B5
Westport	B5
West Redding	B4
West Simsbury	D2
West Stafford	F2
West Suffield	E2
West Willington	F2
Wethersfield	E3
Whigville	D3
Willimantic	G3
Wilton	B5
Winchester Center	C2
Windham	G3
Windsor	E2
Windsor Locks	E2
Winsted	D2
Winthrop	E4
Wolcott	D3
Woodbridge	C4
Woodmont	D5
Woodstock	H2
Woodstock Valley	G2
Woodville	B3
Yalesville	D4

Other Features

	Key
Appalachian Natl. Scenic Trail	B2
Bantam, lake	C3
Barkhamsted, reservoir	D2
Candlewood, lake	B3
Connecticut, river	E4
Easton, reservoir	B4
Farmington, river	D3
Frissell, mt.	B1
Gaillard, lake	D4
Hammonasset, river	E4
Hop, river	F3
Housatonic, river	C4
Long Island, sound	D5
Mt. Hope, river	G2
Natchaug, river	G2
Naugatuck, river	C4
Nepaug, reservoir	D2
Norwalk, islands	B5
Norwalk, river	B4
Saugatuck, reservoir	B4
Shenipsit, lake	F2
Shetucket, river	G3
Thames, river	G4
Waramaug, lake	B3
Weir Farm Natl. Hist. Site	B5
Willimantic, river	F2
Yantic, river	F3

Delaware .... page 135

Cities and Towns

	Key
Adamsville	A3
Andrewville	A3
Argos Corner	B3
Blackbird	A2
Broadkill Beach	B3
Brookside	A1
Burrsville	A3
Camden	A2
Cannon	A3
Canterbury	A2
Capitol Park	A1
Clarksville	B3
Claymont	B1
Collins Park	A1
Delaware City	A1
Dover, capital	A2
Edgemoor	A1
Elsmere	A1
Fairfax	A1
Georgetown	B3
Glasgow	A1
Gumboro	B4
Harbeson	B3
Harrington	A2
Hartley	A2
Hazlettville	A2
Hickman	A3
Hockessin	A1
Indian Beach	B3
Jimtown	A2
Kirkwood	A1
Kitts Hummock	A2
Laurel	A3
Lewes	B3
Lincoln	B3
Little Heaven	A2
Llangollen Estates	A1
Lynch Heights	A2
McClellandville	A1
Marshallton	A1
Marydel	A2
Mastens Corner	A2
Middletown	A2
Midway	B3
Milford	A2
Millsboro	B3
Milton	B3
Nassau	B3
Newark	A1
New Castle	A1
Oak Orchard	B3
Owens	A3
Petersburg	A2
Pinetown	B3
Primehook Beach	B3
Reeves Crossing	A3
Rehoboth Beach	B3
Reliance	A3
Rosedale Beach	B3
Roxana	B3
Sandtown	A2
Seaford	A3
Selbyville	B4
Smyrna	A2
Stanton	A1
Swann Keys	B4
Talleyville	A1
Taylors Bridge	A2
Whitesville	B4
Williamsville	B4
Wilmington	A1
Wilmington Manor	A1
Woodenhawk	A3
Woodland Beach	B2
Workmans Corners	B3

Other Features

	Key
Broadkill, river	B3
Chesapeake & Delaware, canal	A1
Delaware, bay	B2
Delaware, river	A1
Henlopen, cape	B3
Indian River, bay	B3
Mispillion, river	A3
Murderkill, river	A3
Nanticoke, river	A3
Rehoboth, bay	B3
Smyrna, river	A2

Florida .... page 136

Cities and Towns

	Key
Alachua	C2
Altamonte Springs	D3
Anna Maria	C4
Apalachicola	A2
Apollo Beach	C4
Apopka	D3
Arcadia	D4
Archer	C2
Astor	D2
Atlantic Beach	D1
Auburndale	D3
Aventura	E6
Avon Park	D4
Baldwin	C1
Bal Harbour	B3
Bartow	D4
Bay Harbor Islands	B3
Bayonet Point	C3
Bee Ridge	C4
Belle Glade	E5
Belleview	C2
Beverly Hills	C3
Big Pine Key	D7
Biscayne Park	A3
Blountstown	A1
Boca Raton	E5
Bonifay	C6
Bonita Springs	D5
Boynton Beach	E5
Bradenton	C4
Brandon	C4
Bristol	A1
Bronson	C2
Brooksville	C3
Buckhead Ridge	D4
Bunnell	D2
Bushnell	C3
Callaway	C6
Cape Canaveral	E3
Cape Coral	D5
Carol City	A3, E6
Chattahoochee	A1
Chiefland	C2
Chipley	C6
Clearwater	C4

	Key
Clermont	D3
Clewiston	E5
Cocoa	E3
Cocoa Beach	E3
Coconut Grove	A3
Cooper City	A3
Coral Gables	A3, E6
Coral Springs	E5
Crawfordville	A1
Crescent City	D2
Crestview	B6
Cross City	B2
Crystal River	C3
Dade City	C3
Dania	B2
Davie	A2, E5
Daytona Beach	D2
De Bary	D3
Deerfield Beach	E5
De Funiak Springs	B6
De Land	D2
Delray Beach	E5
Deltona	D3
Destin	B6
Dunedin	C4
Dunnellon	C2
East Naples	D5
Eastpoint	A2
Edgewater	E3
El Portal	A3
Elfers	C3
Englewood	C5
Eustis	D3
Fellsmere	E4
Fernandina Beach	D1
Flagler Beach	D2
Florida City	E6
Fort Lauderdale	B2, E5
Fort Meade	D4
Fort Myers	D5
Fort Myers Beach	D5
Fort Myers Villas	D5
Fort Pierce	E4
Fort Walton Beach	B6
Frostproof	D4
Gainesville	C2
Gifford	E4
Golden Gate	D5
Gonzalez	A6
Goulds	E6
Greenacres City	E5
Green Cove Springs	D2
Gretna	A1
Gulf Breeze	A6
Haines City	D3
Hallandale	B3, E6
Havana	A1
Hawthorne	C2
Hialeah	A3, E6
Hialeah Gardens	A3
High Springs	C2
Hilliard	D1
Holiday	C3
Holly Hill	D2
Hollywood	A3, E6
Holmes Beach	C4
Homestead	E6
Homosassa Springs	C3
Hudson	C3
Immokalee	D5
Indian Harbour Beach	E3
Indian Rocks Beach	C4
Indiantown	E4
Inverness	C3
Jacksonville	D1
Jacksonville Beach	D1
Jasper	C1
Jensen Beach	E4
Jupiter	E5
Kendall	A4, E6
Key Biscayne	B4
Key Largo	E6
Keystone Heights	C2
Key West	D7
Kissimmee	D3
La Belle	D5
La Crosse	C2
Lady Lake	D3
Lake Buena Vista	D3
Lake Butler	C1
Lake City	C1
Lakeland	D3
Lake Mary	D3
Lake Panasoffkee	C3
Lake Wales	D4
Lake Worth	E5
Land O' Lakes	C3
Lantana	E5
Largo	C4
Lauderdale Lakes	A2
Lauderdale-by-the-Sea	B2
Lauderhill	C1
Lawtey	C1
Layton	E7
Leesburg	D3
Live Oak	C1
Longboat Key	C4
Lutz	C3
Lynn Haven	C6
Macclenny	C1
Madison	B1
Marathon	D7
Marco	D6
Margate	E5
Marianna	C6
Marineland	D2
Mayo	B1
Merritt Island	E3
Miami	A3, E6
Miami Beach	B3, E6
Miami Lakes	A3, A5
Miami Shores	A3, A5
Miami Springs	A3, A5
Middleburg	D1
Milton	A6
Mims	E3
Miramar	A3, E6
Monticello	B1
Moore Haven	D5
Mount Dora	D3
Naples	D5
Naples Manor	D5
Naples Park	D5
Naranja	E6
New Port Richey	C3
New Smyrna Beach	E2
Niceville	B6
Noma	B6
North Bay Village	A3
North Fort Myers	D5
North Miami	A3, E6
North Miami Beach	A3

	Key
North Naples	D5
North Port	C4
Oakland Park	B2, E5
Ocala	C2
Ocoee	D3
Okeechobee	C4
Oldsmar	C3
Olympia Hts.	A3
Opa-Locka	A3
Orange City	D3
Orange Park	D1
Orlando	D3
Ormond Beach	D2
Ormond-by-the-Sea	D2
Otter Creek	C2
Oviedo	D3
Pace	A6
Pahokee	E5
Palatka	D2
Palm Bay	E3
Palm Beach	E5
Palm Beach Gardens	E5
Palm Coast	D2
Palmetto	C4
Palm Harbor	C3
Panama City	C6
Pembroke Park	A3
Pembroke Pines	A3
Pennsuco	A3
Pensacola	A6
Perrine	E6
Perry	B1
Pierson	D2
Pine Castle	D3
Plantation	A2, E5
Plant City	D3
Polk City	D3
Pomona Park	D2
Port Charlotte	C5
Port Orange	E2
Port St. Joe	C7
Port St. Lucie	E4
Port Salerno	E4
Punta Gorda	C5
Quincy	A1
Raiford	C1
Ridge Manor	C3
Riverview	C4
Riviera Beach	E5
Rockledge	E3
Royal Palm Beach	E5
St. Augustine	D2
St. Augustine Shores	D2
St. Cloud	D3
St. Pete Beach	C4
St. Petersburg	C4
San Carlos Park	D5
Sanford	D3
Sanibel	C5
Sarasota	C4
Satellite Beach	E3
Sebastian	E4
Sebring	D4
Silver Springs	C2
Sneads	A1
South Miami	A3
South Venice	C4
Springfield	C6
Spring Hill	C3
Starke	C2
Stuart	E4
Sunrise	A2
Surfside	B3
Sweetwater	A3, E6
Tallahassee, capital	A1
Tamarac	A2, E5
Tampa	C4
Tarpon Springs	C3
Tavares	D3
Tavernier	E6
Temple Terrace	C4
Titusville	E3
Treasure Island	C4
Trenton	C2
Umatilla	D3
Venice	C4
Vero Beach	E4
Vilano Beach	D2
Virginia Gardens	A3
Warrington	A6
Wauchula	D4
Webster	C3
Weeki Wachee	C3
Welaka	D2
West Melbourne	E3
West Miami	A3
Weston	A2
West Palm Beach	E5
West Pensacola	A6
Westwood Lakes	A3
Wildwood	C3
Williston	C2
Wilton Manors	B2
Winter Garden	D3
Winter Haven	D3
Winter Park	D3
Woodville	A1
Yulee	D1
Zephyrhills	C3

Other Features

	Key
Amelia, island	D1
Apalachee, bay	A2
Apalachicola, bay	A1
Apalachicola, river	A1
Aucilla, river	B1
Big Cypress, swamp	D5
Biscayne, bay	B3, E6
Biscayne Natl. Park	E6
Boca Chica Key, island	D7
Caloosahatchee, river	D5
Canaveral, cape	E3
Canaveral Natl. Seashore	E3
Castillo de San Marcos N.M.	D2
Cedar Keys, islands	B2
Charlotte, harbor	C5
Chattahoochee, river	A1
Choctawhatchee, bay	B6
Crooked, island	C7
De Soto Natl. Memorial	C4
Deadman, bay	B2
Dog, island	A2
Dry Tortugas Natl. Park	C7
Elliott Key, island	E6
Escambia, river	A5
Everglades, swamp	A5, E6
Everglades Natl. Park	E6
Fisher, island	E6
Florida, bay	E6
Florida, straits	D7
Florida Keys, islands	D7
Fort Caroline Natl. Memorial	D1

	Key
Fort Matanzas Natl. Monument	
Gasparilla, island	
George, lake	
Gulf Islands Natl. Seashore	
Homosassa, bay	
Indian, river	
Iron, mt.	
Istokpoga, lake	
John F. Kennedy Space Center	
Key Biscayne, island	
Key Largo, island	
Kissimmee, lake	
Lochloosa, lake	
Marquesas Keys, islands	
Mexico, gulf	B5
Ochlockonee, river	
Okeechobee, lake	
Okefenokee, swamp	
Peace, river	
Pensacola, bay	
Ponce de Leon, bay	
Romano, cape	
Sable, cape	
St. Andrews, bay	
St. George, island	
St. Johns, river	
St. Joseph, bay	
St. Marys, river	
St. Vincent, island	
San Blas, cape	
Sands Key, island	
Sanibel, island	
Santa Rosa, island	
Seminole, lake	
Sugarloaf Key, island	
Suwannee, river	C1
Talquin, lake	
Tamiami, canal	
Tampa, bay	
Virginia Key, island	
Waccasassa, bay	
Withlacoochee, river	
Yellow, river	

Georgia .... page 1

Cities and Towns

Abbeville	
Adairsville	
Adel	
Alamo	
Albany	
Alma	
Alpharetta	
Americus	
Appling	
Arlington	
Ashburn	
Athens	
Atlanta, capital	C4
Augusta	
Bainbridge	
Barnesville	
Baxley	
Belvedere	
Blackshear	
Blairsville	
Blakely	
Blue Ridge	
Boston	
Bremen	
Brookhaven	
Brunswick	
Buchanan	
Buena Vista	
Buford	
Butler	
Byron	
Cairo	
Calhoun	
Camilla	
Canton	
Carnesville	
Carrollton	
Cartersville	
Cedar Grove	
Cedartown	
Chamblee	
Chatsworth	
Clarkesville	
Clarkston	
Claxton	
Cleveland	
Cochran	
College Park	
Colquitt	
Columbus	
Commerce	
Conley	
Constitution	
Conyers	
Cordele	
Cornelia	
Covington	
Crawfordville	
Cumming	
Cusseta	
Cuthbert	
Dahlonega	
Dallas	
Dalton	
Danielsville	
Darien	
Dawson	
Dawsonville	
Decatur	
Donalsonville	
Doraville	
Douglas	
Douglasville	
Druid Hills	
Dublin	
Dunwoody	
Eastman	
East Point	C4
Eatonton	
Elberton	
Ellaville	
Ellijay	
Evans	
Fair Oaks	
Fairview	
Fitzgerald	
Folkston	
Forest Park	
Forsyth	
Fort Gaines	
Fort Oglethorpe	
Fort Valley	

	Key
...klin	A5
...esville	D3
...en City	J7
...getown	A8
...on	F5
...ore	H2
...ville	H8
	E6
	D5
...ensboro	E4
...enville	B5
...sham Park	J3
...in	C5
...ra	E10
...ilton	B6
...pton	C5
...eville	J3
...well	F3
...kinsville	F8
...churst	F8
...nzibah	G5
...vassee	D2
...esville	H8
...er	D3
...herville	F9
...nton	E6
...son	D5
	C3
...rson	E3
...rsonville	A6
	H8
...boro	C4
...hesaw	B3
... Island	H10
...kville	D6
...ayette	A2
...range	A5
...land	E9
...ania	E3
...renceville	D4
...burg	C8
...ngton	D4
...pinton	G4
...conia	C5
...ville	F6
...ogville	C5
...wici	H8
...ber City	F8
...pkin	B7
	C7
...leton	B4, G2
...onough	C5
...ntyre	E6
...on	D6
...ae	F7
...ison	A4
...chester	C3
...shallville	B4, H1
...etta	C3
...edgeville	E5
...ter	D4
...roe	D4
...nticello	D5
...gan	B8
...ltrie	D9
...nt Vernon	F7
...Bethel	E9
...nville	E9
...man	A4
...dale	C9
... Hills	H2
...thorpe	C7
...dersville	K3
...htree City	B5
...son	F9
...broke	H7
	D7
...er	J7
...der Springs	B4
...on	B7
...man	E10
...ville	H4
...Oak	A4
...and	B7
...mond Hill	J8
...on	J7
...gold	A2
...rdale	J4
...elle	E8
...mart	A3
...e	A3
...ton	E3
...well	C3
...on City	B4, H4
...on Point	E10
...osta	G7
...alia	D7
...na	A2
... Rica	B4
...dley	G6
...ner Robins	D6
...kinsville	E4
...ycross	G9
...ynesboro	G5

	Key
Westoak	H1
Winder	D4
Woodbine	H10
Wrens	G5
Wrightsville	F6
Zebulon	C5

Other Features

	Key
Alapaha, *river*	E9
Allatoona, *lake*	B3
Altamaha, *river*	G8
Andersonville Natl. Hist. Site	C7
Appalachian, *mts.*	D2
Blackshear, *lake*	D8
Blue, *ridge*	C2
Brasstown Bald, *mt.*	D2
Burton, *lake*	D2
Carters, *lake*	B2
Chattahoochee, *river*	A5, A9, G3
Chattahoochee River N.R.A.	J1
Chattooga, *river*	E2
Chatuge, *lake*	D1
Chickamauga and Chattanooga Natl. Military Park	A2
Coosa, *river*	D2
Cumberland, *island*	J10
Cumberland Island Natl. Seashore	J10
Ed Jenkins Natl. Rec. Area	C2
Etowah, *river*	B3
Flint, *river*	C9
Fort Frederica Natl. Monument	J9
Fort Pulaski Natl. Monument	K7
Hartwell, *lake*	F2
Jackson, *lake*	D5
Jekyll, *island*	J9
Jimmy Carter Natl. Hist. Site	C7
J. Strom Thurmond, *lake*	G4
Lookout Mt., *ridge*	A2
Martin Luther King Jr. N.H.S.	J3
Ocmulgee Natl. Monument	D6
Ochlockonee, *river*	C10
Ocmulgee, *river*	E7
Oconee, *lake*	E5
Oconee, *river*	F6
Ogeechee, *river*	F5
Ohoopee, *river*	G7
Okefenokee, *swamp*	G10
Ossabaw, *island*	J8
Russell, *lake*	F3
St. Catherines, *island*	J8
St. Marys, *river*	H10
St. Simons, *island*	J9
Sapelo, *island*	J9
Savannah, *river*	H5
Seminole, *lake*	B10
Sidney Lanier, *lake*	C3
Sinclair, *lake*	E5
Stone Mt. State Park	C3
Suwannee, *river*	F10
Tallapoosa, *river*	A4
Tybee, *island*	K7
Walter F. George, *reservoir*	A8
Wassaw, *island*	J8
Weiss, *lake*	A3
West Point, *lake*	A6
Withlacoochee, *river*	E10

Hawaii .....page 138

Cities and Towns

	Key
Ahuimanu	J2
Aiea	F1, J2
Captain Cook	G6
Crestview	E1, J2
Eleele	C2
Ewa	D2, J2
Ewa Beach	E2, J3
Foster Village	F1, J2
Haena	C1, J5
Halawa	B3
Halawa Heights	F1, J2
Haleiwa	H1
Hana	D4
Hanamaulu	D1
Hanapepe	C2
Hauula	J1
Heeia	G1, K2
Hilo	E7, J5
Holualoa	G5
Honalo	G5
Honokaa	H4
Honolulu, *capital*	C5, F2, J2
Iroquois Point	E2, J2
Kaanapali	B3
Kahana	B3, J1
Kahului	C3, D6
Kailua	C5, K2
Kailua-Kona	D7, F5
Kalaheo	C2
Kalaoa	F5
Kalaupapa	B3
Kaneohe	C5, G1, K2
Kapaa	A5, D1
Kaunakakai	A3
Keaau	J5
Kealakekua	G5
Kealia	D1, G6
Kekaha	B2
Kihei	C4, D6
Kilauea	C1
Koloa	C2
Kualapuu	A3
Kula	C4
Lahaina	B3, C5
Laie	C5, J1
Lanai City	B3
Lawai	C2
Lihue	A5, D2
Maili	H2
Makaha	H2
Makakilo City	H2
Makawao	C3
Maunawili	K2
Mililani Town	J2
Mokuleia	H1
Mountain View	J5
Nanakuli	B5, H2
Pacific Palisades	E1, J2
Pahala	H6
Papaikou	J5
Pearl City	C5, E1, J2
Pepeekeo	K2
Pohakupu	C3, D6
Pukalani	C3
Pupukea	J1
Volcano	J6
Waialua	B3, H1
Waianae	B5, H2
Waihee	C3
Waikiki	G3
Waikoloa Village	G4

	Key
Wailua	C3, D1
Wailuku	C3, D6
Waimalu	E1, J2
Waimanalo	K2
Waimanalo Beach	K2
Waimea	C2, D6, H1
Waipahu	E1, J2
Waipio	H4
Waipio Acres	J2
Whitmore Village	J2

Other Features

	Key
Alenuihaha, *channel*	D6
Alika Cone, *mt.*	G6
Diamond Head, *point*	G3
Ford, *island*	E1
Haleakala Natl. Park	C4, D6
Hamakua, *coast*	H4
Hawaii, *island*	E6, G5
Hawaii Volcanoes Natl. Park	E7, H6
Hilo, *bay*	J5
Hualalai, *mt.*	G5
Kaala, *mt.*	H1
Kaena, *point*	B5, H1
Kahoolawe, *island*	B4, D6
Kahului, *bay*	C3
Kaikipauula, *mt.*	H4
Kailua, *bay*	K2
Kaiwi, *channel*	C5, K3
Ka Lae (South Cape), *cape*	D7, G7
Kalalua, *mt.*	H4
Kalaupapa, *peninsula*	B3
Kalaupapa Natl. Hist. Park	B3
Kaloko-Honokohau Natl. Hist. Park	F5
Kamakou, *mt.*	B3
Kau, *desert*	H6
Kauai, *channel*	B5, D2
Kauai, *island*	A5, B1
Kaulakahi, *channel*	A5, B1
Kawaikini, *mt.*	C1
Kiholo, *bay*	G4
Kilauea, *crater*	J6
Kilohana, *crater*	C2
Kinau, *cape*	C4
Kipuka Puaulu, *mt.*	H6
Kohala, *coast*	F5
Kohala, *mt.*	G4
Kohala, *mts.*	G4
Kona, *coast*	F6
Konahuanui, *mt.*	G2, K2
Koolau Range, *mts.*	F1, J1
Kulani, *mt.*	H5
Kumukahi, *cape*	E7, K5
Lanai, *island*	B3, C6
Lehua, *island*	A1
Lua Makika, *mt.*	B4
Maalaea, *bay*	C4
Makaleha, *mts.*	C1
Makapuu, *point*	C5, K2
Mamala, *bay*	E2, J3
Maui, *island*	C3, D6
Mauna Iki, *mt.*	H6
Mauna Kea, *mt.*	E6, H5
Mauna Loa, *mt.*	D7, H6
Maunalua, *bay*	K3
Mokolii, *island*	J2
Mokuauia, *island*	J1
Mokulua, *island*	K2
Moku Manu, *island*	H1
Molokai, *island*	A3, C5
Molokini, *island*	C4
Na Pali, *coast*	B1
Niihau, *island*	A2, A5
Oahu, *island*	B5, D2, K1
Pearl, *harbor*	J2
Punchbowl, *crater*	E1
Pu'uhonua O Honaunau N.H.P.	G6
Puu Kainapuaa, *mt.*	J1
Puu Kaua, *mt.*	H2
Puukohola Heiau Natl. Hist. Site	G4
Puu Kukui, *mt.*	B3
Puu Kulua, *mt.*	H5
Puu Loa, *mt.*	H5
Puu O Keokeo, *mt.*	G6
Puu Ulaula, *mt.*	C4
Sand, *island*	F2
Sulphur Cone, *mt.*	G6
U.S.S. Arizona Memorial	E1
Upolu, *point*	D6, G3
Waialeale, *mt.*	A5, C1
Waianae Range, *mts.*	H1
Wailuku, *river*	H5
Waimea, *canyon*	C2
West Maui, *mts.*	B3

Idaho .....page 139

Cities and Towns

	Key
Aberdeen	E7
American Falls	E7
Ammon	F6
Arco	D6
Banks	A5
Bellevue	C6
Bennington	F7
Blackfoot	E6
Boise, *capital*	A6
Bonners Ferry	A1
Buhl	C7
Burley	D7
Caldwell	A6
Cascade	A5
Challis	C5
Chubbuck	E7
Coeur d'Alene	A2
Council	A5
Driggs	F6
Dubois	E5
Eagle	A6
Emmett	A6
Fairfield	C6
Filer	C7
Fish Haven	F7
Fruitland	A6
Fruitvale	A5
Garden City	A6
Garden Valley	B5
Glenns Ferry	B7
Gooding	C7
Grangeville	A4
Hailey	C6
Hayden	A2
Idaho City	B6
Idaho Falls	E6
Jerome	C7
Kamiah	B4
Kellogg	A2
Ketchum	C6
Kuna	A6
Laclede	A1
Lewiston	A3

	Key
McCall	A5
Malad City	E7
May	D5
Middleton	A6
Montpelier	F7
Moscow	A3
Mountain Home	B6
Murphy	A6
Nampa	A6
New Plymouth	A6
Nezperce	A3
Orofino	A3
Osburn	A2
Paris	F7
Parma	A6
Patterson	D5
Pauline	A6
Payette	A5
Pinehurst	A2
Pocatello	E7
Post Falls	A2
Preston	F7
Priest River	A1
Rathdrum	A2
Rexburg	F6
Rigby	F6
Rupert	D7
St. Anthony	F6
St. Maries	A2
Salmon	D4
Sandpoint	A1
Shelley	E6
Shoshone	C7
Soda Springs	F7
Sugar City	F6
Sun Valley	C6
Thatcher	F7
Twin Falls	C7
Wallace	B2
Weiser	A5
Wendell	C7

Other Features

	Key
American Falls, *reservoir*	E7
Bear, *lake*	F7
Bear, *river*	F7
Big Lost, *river*	D6
Bitterroot, *range*	B3, D4
Blackfoot, *reservoir*	F6
Blackfoot, *river*	F6
Bruneau, *river*	B7
Cache, *mt.*	D7
Caribou, *range*	F6
Cascade, *reservoir*	A5
Castle, *mt.*	C4
Clearwater, *mts.*	B3
Clearwater, *river*	B4
Craters of the Moon N.M.	D6
Dworshak, *reservoir*	A3
Grays, *lake*	F6
Hagerman Fossil Beds N.M.	C7
Hells, *canyon*	A5
Hells Canyon Natl. Recreation Area	A4
Kootenai, *river*	A1
Lemhi, *river*	D5
Lochsa, *river*	B3
Middle Fork Salmon, *river*	B5
Minidoka Internment Natl. Mon.	C7
Nez Perce N.H.P.	A3, B3
North Fork Clearwater, *river*	B3
Owyhee, *mts.*	A6
Owyhee, *river*	A6
Palisades, *reservoir*	F6
Payette, *lake*	A5
Payette, *river*	A5
Pend Oreille, *lake*	A1
Pend Oreille, *river*	A1
Priest, *lake*	A1
Ryan, *mt.*	C6
St. Joe, *river*	B4
Salmon, *river*	C5
Salmon River, *mts.*	C5
Sawtooth, *range*	B5
Sawtooth Natl. Recreation Area	C5
Scott, *mt.*	E5
Snake, *river*	A4
South Fork Selway, *river*	B3
Teton, *river*	F6
Weiser, *river*	A5
Yellowstone Natl. Park	F5

Illinois .....page 140

Cities and Towns

	Key
Abingdon	C3
Addison	B5
Albion	E5
Aledo	C2
Alsip	B6
Altamont	E4
Alton	C5
Amboy	D2
Anna	D6
Antioch	A4, E1
Arcola	E4
Arlington Heights	A5
Arthur	E4
Ashland	C4
Athens	D3
Atlanta	D3
Atwood	E4
Auburn	D4
Aurora	E2
Barrington	A5
Barry	B4
Bartlett	A5
Bartonville	D3
Batavia	E2
Beach Park	B4
Beardstown	C3
Beecher	F2
Belleville	D5
Belvidere	E1
Bement	E4
Benld	D4
Benton	E6
Berwyn	B6
Bethany	E4
Bloomington	D3
Blue Island	B6
Bolingbrook	A6, E2
Bourbonnais	F2
Braceville	E2
Braidwood	E2
Breese	D5
Bridgeport	F5
Brighton	C4
Brookfield	B6
Buffalo Grove	B5
Bunker Hill	D4
Burbank	B6
Bushnell	C3

	Key
Byron	D1
Cahokia	C5
Cairo	D6
Calumet City	C6, F2
Cambridge	C2
Canton	C3
Capron	E1
Carbondale	D6
Carlinville	D4
Carlyle	D5
Carmi	E5
Carol Stream	A5
Carpentersville	E1
Carrier Mills	E6
Carrollton	C4
Carterville	D6
Carthage	B3
Cary	E1
Casey	F4
Catlin	F3
Centralia	D5
Cerro Gordo	E3
Champaign	E3
Channahon	E2
Charleston	E4
Chatham	D4
Chenoa	E3
Chester	D6
Chicago	B5, F2
Chicago Heights	B6
Chillicothe	D3
Christopher	D6
Cicero	B6, F2
Clifton	F3
Clinton	E3
Coal City	E2
Colchester	C3
Collinsville	D5
Columbia	C5
Crest Hill	A6
Crete	F2
Crystal Lake	E1
Cuba	C3
Danville	F3
Decatur	E4
Deerfield	B5
De Kalb	D1
Delavan	D3
De Soto	D6
Des Plaines	B5
Dixon	D1
Dolton	B6
Downers Grove	B6
Du Quoin	D6
Dwight	E2
Earlville	D2
East Dubuque	C1
East Moline	C2
East Peoria	D3
East St. Louis	D5
Edwardsville	D5
Effingham	E4
Elburn	E2
Eldorado	E6
Elgin	E1
Elizabethtown	E6
Elk Grove Village	B5
Elmhurst	B5
Elmwood	D3
Elmwood Park	B5
Erie	C2
Eureka	D3
Evanston	B5, F1
Evergreen Park	B6
Fairbury	E3
Fairfield	E5
Farmer City	E3
Farmington	C3
Fisher	E3
Flora	E5
Forrest	E3
Forsyth	E4
Fox Lake	A4, E1
Fox Lake Hills	A4
Fox River Grove	A5
Frankfort	B6, F2
Freeburg	D5
Freeport	D1
Fulton	C2
Gages Lake	B4
Galena	C1
Galesburg	C3
Galva	C2
Geneseo	C2
Geneva	E2
Genoa	E1
Georgetown	F4
Gibson City	E3
Gillespie	D4
Gilman	F3
Girard	D4
Glen Ellyn	A5
Glencoe	B5
Glendale Heights	A5
Glenview	B5
Glenwood	B6
Godfrey	C4
Golconda	E6
Granite City	D5
Granville	D2
Grayslake	A4
Grayville	E5
Green Oaks	B4
Greenup	E4
Greenville	D5
Gridley	E3
Gurnee	B4
Hainesville	A4
Hamilton	B3
Hampshire	E1
Hanover Park	A5
Hardin	C4
Harrisburg	E6
Harristown	D4
Harvard	D1
Harvey	B6
Havana	C3
Hennepin	D2
Henry	D2
Herrin	E6
Herscher	E2
Heyworth	D3
Hickory Hills	B6
Highland	D5
Highland Park	B5, F1
Highwood	B5
Hillsboro	D4
Hinckley	E2
Hinsdale	B6
Hoffman Estates	A5
Homer	F3
Homewood	F2

	Key
Hoopeston	F3
Huntley	E1
Island Lake	A5
Jacksonville	C4
Jerseyville	C4
Johnston City	D6
Joliet	A6, E2
Jonesboro	D6
Justice	B6
Kankakee	F2
Kaskaskia	D6
Kewanee	C2
Kincaid	D4
Knoxville	C3
Lacon	D2
La Grange	B6
La Harpe	C3
Lake Bluff	B4
Lake Forest	B4
Lake Zurich	A5
Lanark	C1
La Salle	D2
Lansing	F2
Lawrenceville	F5
Lemont	B6
Lena	D1
Le Roy	E3
Lewistown	C3
Lexington	E3
Libertyville	B5
Lilymoor	A4
Lincoln	D3
Lincolnwood	B5
Lindenhurst	A4
Lisle	B6
Litchfield	D4
Lockport	A6
Lombard	B6
Louisville	E5
Loves Park	E1
Lynwood	C6
McHenry	E1
Machesney Park	D1
Mackinaw	D3
McLeansboro	E5
Macomb	C3
Macon	E4
Mahomet	E3
Manhattan	F2
Manito	D3
Manteno	F2
Marengo	E1
Marion	E6
Marissa	D5
Marley	B6
Maroa	E3
Marseilles	E2
Marshall	F4
Mascoutah	D5
Mason City	D3
Matteson	B6
Mattoon	E4
Maywood	B5
Melrose Park	B5
Mendota	D2
Metamora	D3
Metropolis	E6
Milan	C2
Milford	F3
Minonk	D3
Minooka	E2
Mokena	B6
Moline	C2
Momence	F2
Monmouth	C3
Monticello	E3
Morris	E2
Morrison	C2
Morton	D3
Morton Grove	B5
Mound City	D6
Mounds	D6
Mount Carmel	F5
Mount Carroll	C1
Mount Morris	D1
Mount Olive	D4
Mount Prospect	B5
Mount Pulaski	D3
Mount Sterling	C4
Mount Vernon	E5
Mount Zion	E4
Moweaqua	D4
Mundelein	A5
Murphysboro	D6
Naperville	A6
Nashville	D5
Neoga	E4
New Athens	D5
New Baden	D5
New Lenox	B6
Newton	E5
Niles	B5
Nokomis	D4
Normal	E3
Norridge	B5
Northbrook	B5
North Chicago	B4, F1
Northfield	B5
Oak Brook	B6
Oak Forest	B6
Oak Lawn	B6, F2
Oak Park	B5, F2
Oakwood	F3
Oblong	F4
O'Fallon	D5
Oglesby	D2
Okawville	D5
Old Mill Creek	B4
Olney	E5
Onarga	F3
Oquawka	C3
Oregon	D1
Orion	C2
Orland Hills	B6
Orland Park	B6
Ottawa	D2
Palatine	A5
Palestine	F4
Palos Heights	B6
Palos Hills	B6
Pana	D4
Paris	F4
Park City	B4
Park Forest	B6
Park Ridge	B5
Pawnee	D4
Paxton	E3
Pecatonica	D1
Pekin	D3
Peoria	D3
Peoria Heights	D3
Peotone	F2

Key
Peru D2
Petersburg D4
Pinckneyville D5
Pittsfield C4
Plainfield A6, E2
Plano E2
Polo D2
Pontiac E3
Princeton D2
Princeville D3
Prophetstown D2
Quincy B4
Rantoul E3
Red Bud D5
Richton Park B6
Riverdale B6
Riverton D4
Riverwoods B5
Roanoke D3
Robinson F4
Rochelle D2
Rochester D4
Rock Falls D2
Rock Island C2
Rockford D1
Rockton D1
Rome D3
Romeoville A6
Roodhouse C4
Roscoe D1
Rosiclare E6
Rossville F3
Round Lake Beach A4
Rushville C3
Russell B4
St. David C3
St. Elmo E4
St. Joseph E3
St. Libory D5
Salem E5
Sandoval D5
Sandwich E2
Sauk Village C6
Savanna C1
Savoy E3
Schaumburg A5
Schiller Park B5
Seneca E2
Sesser D5
Shawneetown E6
Shelbyville E4
Sheridan E2
Sherman D4
Shorewood A6, E2
Skokie B5
Somonauk E2
South Beloit D1
South Elgin E2
South Holland B6
South Jacksonville C4
Sparta D5
Spring Valley D2
Springfield, *capital* D4
Staunton D4
Steeleville D5
Sterling D2
Stockland F3
Stockton C1
Streamwood A5
Streator E2
Sullivan E4
Summit B6
Sycamore E2
Taylorville D4
Teutopolis E4
Tilton F3
Tinley Park B6, F2
Toledo E4
Tolono E4
Toluca D3
Toulon D2
Tower Lakes A5
Tremont D3
Trenton D5
Tuscola E4
Urbana E3
Vandalia D5
Vernon Hills B5
Vienna E6
Villa Grove E4
Villa Park B5
Virden D4
Virginia C4
Volo A4
Wadsworth B4
Walnut D2
Wapella E3
Warren D1
Warrensburg D4
Warrenville A6
Warsaw B3
Washington D3
Waterloo C5
Watseka F3
Wauconda A5
Waukegan B4, F1
Waverly D4
Westchester B6
West Chicago A5
West Frankfort E6
Westville F3
Wheaton A6, E2
Wheeling B5, F1
White Hall C4
Wilmette B5
Wilmington E2
Winchester C4
Winnebago D1
Winnetka B5
Winthrop Harbor B4
Woodridge A6
Wood River C5
Woodstock E1
Wyoming D2
Yorkville E2
Zeigler D6
Zion B4, F1

Other Features
Carlyle, *lake* D5
Chautauqua, *lake* C3
Chicago, *river* B5
Clinton, *lake* E3
Crab Orchard, *lake* D6
Des Plaines, *river* A6, B4
Du Page, *river* A6
Fox, *lake* A4
Fox, *river* E2
Illinois, *river* D3
Ind. Dunes Natl. Lakeshore C6
Kankakee, *river* E2
Kaskaskia, *river* E4
Lincoln Home Natl. Hist. Site D4
Marie, *lake* A4
Michigan, *lake* F1
O'Hare, *airport* B5
Ohio, *river* D6
Orland, *lake* B6
Rend, *lake* D5
Rock, *river* D2
Sangamon, *river* C3
Shelbyville, *lake* E4
Spoon, *river* C3
Wabash, *river* E6

Indiana ....page 141

Cities and Towns
Albany F4
Albion E2
Alexandria E4
Anderson E4
Angola G1
Arcadia D4
Argos D2
Atlanta D4
Attica B4
Auburn F2
Aurora G6
Austin E7
Avilla F2
Bargersville D5
Batesville F6
Bedford D7
Berne G3
Bicknell B7
Bloomfield C6
Bloomington C6
Bluffton F3
Boonville B8
Bourbon D2
Brazil B5
Bremen D2
Brookston C3
Brookville F6
Brownsburg D5
Brownstown D7
Butler G2
Cambridge City F5
Cannelton C9
Carmel D5
Chandler B8
Charlestown E8
Chesterton B1
Churubusco F2
Cicero D4
Clayton C5
Clinton B5
Cloverdale C5
Columbia City E2
Columbus E6
Connersville F5
Corydon D8
Covington B4
Crawfordsville C4
Crothersville E7
Crown Point B2
Culver D2
Dale C8
Daleville E4
Danville C5
Darmstadt A8
Decatur G3
Delphi C3
Demotte B2
Dunlap E1
East Chicago B1
Eaton F4
Edinburgh E6
Elkhart E1
Ellettsville C6
Elwood E4
English D8
Evansville A9
Fairmount E4
Farmland F4
Ferdinand C8
Fishers D5
Flora C3
Fort Branch A8
Fort Wayne F2
Fowler B3
Frankfort C4
Franklin D6
Fremont G1
French Lick C7
Galveston D3
Garrett F2
Gary B1
Gas City E4
Geneva G3
Georgetown E8
Goshen E1
Greencastle C5
Greenfield E5
Greensburg F6
Greentown E4
Greenwood D5
Hagerstown F5
Hammond A1
Hanover F7
Hartford City F4
Hebron B2
Highland B1
Hope E6
Huntertown F2
Huntingburg C8
Huntington F3
Indianapolis, *capital* D5
Jasonville B6
Jasper C8
Jeffersonville E8
Kendallville F2
Kentland B3
Kingsford Heights C2
Knox C2
Kokomo D3
Kouts B2
Lafayette C4
Lagrange F1
Lakeville D1
La Porte C1
Lawrence D5
Lawrenceburg G6
Lebanon D4
Liberty G5
Ligonier E1
Lincoln City B8
Linton B6
Logansport D3
Loogootee C7
Lowell B2
Madison F7
Marion E3
Martinsville D6
Merrillville B2
Michigan City C1
Middlebury E1
Milan F6
Milford E2
Mishawaka D1
Mitchell D7
Monon C3
Monticello C3
Montpelier F3
Mooresville D5
Mount Vernon A9
Mulberry C4
Muncie F4
Nappanee D2
Nashville D6
New Albany E8
Newburgh B9
New Carlisle C1
New Castle F5
New Haven F2
Newport B5
New Whiteland D5
Noblesville D4
North Judson C2
North Liberty D1
North Manchester E2
North Terre Haute B5
North Vernon E6
Notre Dame D1
Oakland City B8
Odon C7
Orleans D7
Osgood F6
Ossian F3
Otterbein B3
Oxford B3
Paoli D7
Pendleton E4
Peru D3
Petersburg B8
Plainfield D5
Plymouth D2
Portland G4
Princeton A8
Redkey F4
Rensselaer B3
Richmond G5
Rising Sun G7
Rochester D2
Rockport B9
Rockville B5
Rushville F5
Salem D7
Schererville B2
Scottsburg E7
Sellersburg E8
Seymour E7
Shadeland C4
Shelbyville E5
Sheridan D4
Shoals C7
South Bend D1
South Whitley E2
Speedway D5
Spencer C6
Sullivan B6
Syracuse E2
Tell City C9
Terre Haute B6
Thorntown C4
Tippecanoe D2
Tipton D4
Union City G4
Upland F4
Valparaiso B2
Veedersburg B4
Vernon E7
Versailles F6
Vevay F7
Vincennes A7
Wabash E3
Wakarusa E1
Walkerton D2
Warsaw E2
Washington B7
Waterloo F2
Westfield D4
West Lafayette C4
Westport E6
Westville C1
Williamsport B4
Winamac C2
Winchester G4
Winona Lake E2
Woodburn G2
Worthington C6
Yorktown F4
Zionsville D5

Other Features
Big Blue, *river* E5
Brookville, *lake* F5
Eel, *river* E3
George Rogers Clark N.H.P. A7
Indiana Dunes Natl. Lakeshore B1
Kankakee, *river* C2
Lemon, *lake* D6
Lincoln Boyhood Natl. Memorial C8
Maumee, *river* G2
Michigan, *lake* B1
Mississinewa, *lake* E3
Monroe, *lake* D6
Ohio, *river* A9
Patoka, *river* B8
St. Joseph, *river* G2
Salamonie, *lake* E3
Tippecanoe, *river* C2
Wabash, *river* A8
Wawasee, *lake* E2
White, *river* C6
Whitewater, *river* F6

Iowa ....page 142

Cities and Towns
Ackley H2
Adel F4
Akron A2
Albia J5
Algona F1
Allison J2
Alta D2
Altoona H4
Ames G3
Anamosa M3
Ankeny G4
Asbury N3
Atlantic D5
Audubon E4
Avoca D5
Batavia K5
Bayard E4
Bedford E6
Belle Plaine K4
Bellevue P3
Belmond G2
Bettendorf P4
Bloomfield K6
Boone G3
Brighton L5
Britt G1
Brooklyn K4
Burlington M6
Camanche P4
Carlisle G5
Carroll E3
Carter Lake C5
Cascade N3
Cedar Falls K3
Cedar Rapids L4
Center Point L3
Centerville J6
Chariton H5
Charles City J1
Cherokee C2
Clarinda D6
Clarion G2
Clarksville J2
Clear Lake H1
Clinton P4
Colfax H4
Columbus Junction M5
Coon Rapids E4
Coralville L4
Corning E6
Corydon H6
Council Bluffs C5
Cresco K1
Creston F5
Dakota City F2
Dallas Center G4
Davenport N4
Decorah L1
Denison D4
Denver K2
Des Moines, *captial* G4
De Witt N4
Dubuque N2
Dunlap C4
Durant N4
Dyersville M3
Eagle Grove G2
Eldora H3
Eldridge N4
Elgin L2
Elkader M2
Emmetsburg E1
Epworth N3
Estherville E1
Evansdale K3
Fairfield L6
Farley M3
Fayette L2
Forest City G1
Fort Dodge F2
Fort Madison M6
Garner G1
Gilmore City F2
Glenwood C5
Greenfield F5
Grimes G4
Grinnell J4
Grundy Center J3
Guthrie Center E4
Guttenberg M2
Hampton H2
Harlan D4
Hartley D1
Hawarden B1
Hiawatha L3
Holstein C3
Hudson K3
Hull B1
Humboldt F2
Huxley G4
Ida Grove C3
Independence L3
Indianola G5
Iowa City L4
Iowa Falls H3
Jefferson F4
Jesup K3
Johnston G4
Kalona L5
Keokuk M7
Keosauqua L6
Knoxville H5
Lake City E3
Lake Mills G1
Lake View D3
Lamoni G6
La Porte City K3
Laurens E2
Le Claire P4
Le Mars B2
Lenox E6
Leon G6
Logan C4
Lovilia J5
Madrid G4
Manchester M3
Manly H1
Manning D4
Manson E2
Mapleton C3
Maquoketa N3
Marengo K4
Marion L4
Marshalltown J3
Mason City H1
Mediapolis M5
Melcher-Dallas H5
Milford D1
Missouri Valley C4
Monona M1
Monroe H4
Montezuma J4
Monticello M3
Mount Ayr F6
Mount Pleasant L6
Mount Vernon M4
Moville B3
Muscatine M5
Nashua J2
Nevada H3
New Hampton K1
New London M6
Newton H4
Nora Springs J1
North Liberty L4
Northwood H1
Norwalk G5
Oakland D5
Oelwein L2
Ogden F3
Onawa B3
Orange City B1
Osage J1
Osceola G5
Oskaloosa J5
Ottumwa K5
Park View N4
Parkersburg J2
Pella J5
Perry F4
Pleasantville H5
Pocahontas E2
Polk City G4
Postville L1
Prairie City H4
Primghar C1
Red Oak D5
Reinbeck J3
Remsen C2
Rock Rapids B1
Rock Valley B1
Rockwell City E3
Sac City E3
Sanborn C1
Sergeant Bluff B3
Sheldon C1
Shell Rock J2
Shenandoah D6
Sibley C1
Sidney C6
Sigourney K5
Sioux Center B1
Sioux City B2
Spencer D1
Spirit Lake D1
Storm Lake D2
Story City G3
Strawberry Point L2
Stuart F4
Sumner K2
Tama J4
Tipton M4
Toledo J4
Traer K3
Urbandale E4
Villisca E6
Vinton K3
Walcott N4
Wapello M5
Washington L5
Waterloo K3
Waukee G4
Waukon M1
Waverly K2
Webster City G2
West Branch M4
West Burlington M6
West Des Moines G4
West Liberty M4
West Union L2
Williamsburg L4
Wilton M4
Windsor Heights G4
Winterset F5
Woodbine C4

Other Features
Big Sioux, *river* A1
Boone, *river* G2
Cedar, *river* K3
Chariton, *river* H6
Clear, *lake* H1
Coralville, *lake* L4
Des Moines, *river* F3
Effigy Mounds Natl. Monument M1
Floyd, *river* B2
Fox, *river* K6
Herbert Hoover Natl. Hist. Site M4
Iowa, *river* K4
Little Sioux, *river* D2
Maple, *river* D2
Mississippi, *river* M2
Missouri, *river* B4
Rathbun, *lake* J6
Red Rock, *lake* J5
Saylorville, *reservoir* G4
Skunk, *river* L5
Spirit, *lake* D1
Storm, *lake* D2
Turkey, *river* L2
Wapsipinicon, *river* K2
West Nishnabota, *river* K2

Kansas ....page 143

Cities and Towns
Abilene E3
Adrian G3
Alma F3
Andover E4
Anthony D4
Arkansas City E4
Arma H4
Ashland C4
Atchison G2
Atwood A2
Augusta F4
Baldwin City G3
Baxter Springs H4
Belle Plaine E4
Belleville E2
Beloit D2
Bonner Springs H2
Buhler E3
Burlington G3
Butler G3
Caldwell E4
Caney G4
Carbondale G3
Chanute G4
Chapman E3
Cheney E4
Cherryvale G4
Chetopa G4
Cimarron B4
Clay Center E2
Clearwater E4
Clifton E2
Coffeyville G4
Colby A2
Coldwater C4
Columbus H4
Concordia E2
Conway Springs E4
Coolidge A3
Cottonwood Falls F3
Council Grove
Derby
De Soto
Dighton
Dodge City
Douglass
El Dorado
Elkhart
Ellinwood
Ellis
Ellsworth
Emporia
Erie
Eudora
Eureka
Florence
Fort Scott
Fredonia
Frontenac
Galena
Garden City
Gardner
Garnett
Girard
Goddard
Goodland
Gove
Great Bend
Greensburg
Halstead
Harper
Hays
Haysville
Herington
Hesston
Hiawatha
Hill City
Hillsboro
Hoisington
Holcomb
Holton
Horton
Howard
Hoxie
Hugoton
Humboldt
Hutchinson
Independence
Iola
Iuka
Jetmore
Johnson
Junction City
Kansas City
Kansas City
Kingman
Kinsley
La Crosse
Lakin
Lansing
Larned
Lawrence
Leavenworth
Leoti
Liberal
Lincoln
Lindsborg
Lorraine
Louisburg
Lyndon
Lyons
McPherson
Maize
Manhattan
Mankato
Marion
Marysville
Meade
Medicine Lodge
Minneapolis
Mound City
Moundridge
Mulvane
Neodesha
Ness City
Newton
North Newton
Norton
Oakley
Oberlin
Ogden
Olathe
Osage City
Osawatomie
Osborne
Oskaloosa
Oswego
Ottawa
Overland Park
Paola
Park
Park City
Parsons
Peabody
Phillipsburg
Pittsburg
Plainville
Pratt
Rich Hill
Rose Hill
Rose Hill
Russell
Sabetha
St. Francis
St. John
St. Marys
Salina
Scott City
Sedan
Sedgwick
Seneca
Sharon Springs
Silver Lake
Smith Center
South Hutchinson
Spring Hill
Stafford
Sterling
Stockton
Sublette
Syracuse
Tecumseh
Tonganoxie
Topeka, *capital*
Towanda
Tribune
Troy
Ulysses
Valley Center
Valley Falls
Wakeeney
Wamego

KANSAS–MARYLAND 183

Key
hington E2
erville E2
lington E4
lsville G3
stmoreland F2
hita E4
field F4
s Center G4

er Features
nsas, *river* A4, D3
Blue, *river* F2
ar Bluff, *reservoir* C3
ney, *reservoir* E4
kaskia, *river* D4
arron, *river* A4
ton, *lake* G3
river F4
Hills F4
Larned Natl. Hist. Site C3
Scott Natl. Hist. Site H4
apolis, *lake* E3
sas, *river* F2
vin, *reservoir* C2
e Blue, *river* E1
rion, *lake* E3
dicine Lodge, *river* C4
vern, *lake* G3
ord, *lake* F2
souri, *river* G2
osho, *river* G3
odemus Natl. Hist. Site C2
th Fork Solomon, *river* B2
publican, *river* D1
ne, *river* C2
oky Hill, *river* B3
omon, *river* D2
th Fork Republican, *river* A2
flower, *mt.* A2
le Creek, *lake* F2
digris, *river* F3
conda, *lake* D2
son, *lake* D3

ntucky .... page 144

es and Towns
erdeen F2
any D4
xandria E2
nsville B4
land G2
burn C4
gusta E2
bourville F4
dstown D3
dwell B2
attyville F3
ver Dam C3
lford D2
ton C2
ea E3
ry E2
oneville F3
wling Green C4
andenburg C3
oks D2
oksville E2
wnsville C3
kesville D4
lington E1
ler E2
diz B4, C2
houn B3
vert City C2
mpbellsville D3
mpton F3
lisle E2
rollton D2
rsville C1
ettsburg G2
e City D3
ntral City B3
y City F3
ton B2
umbia D3
ncord F2
bin E4
rinth E2
vington E1
stwood D2
mberland G4
nthiana E2
nville E3
wson Springs B3, C1
on B3, C1
Ridge E2
lington B3
dyville A3, C2
monton D4
on C3
abethtown D3
ton B4
inence D2
field D3
mouth E2
twoods G2
mingsburg F2
rence E2
ster E2
nkfort, *capital* E2
nklin C4
nchburg F3
ton B2
orgetown E2
asgow D3
atz E2
ayson G2
eensburg D3
eenup G2
eenville B3
thrie B4
rdinsburg C3
rlan F4
rrodsburg E3
rtford C3
wesville C3
zard F3
nderson B3
ckman B2
ndman G3
seville D3
bson D3
dgenville D3
pkinsville B4
rse Cave D3
den F3
dependence E2
ez G3
ine F3
kson F3

Key
Jamestown D4
Jeffersontown D2
Jeffersonville F3
Jenkins G3
Junction City E3
La Fayette B4, C2
La Grange D2
Lancaster E3
Lawrenceburg E2
Leatherwood F3
Lebanon D3
Leitchfield C3
Lewisport C3
Lexington E2
Liberty E3
Livermore B3
Livingston E3
London E3
Louisa G2
Louisville D2
McKee F3
Mackville D3
Madisonville B3
Manchester F3
Marion A3, C1
Mayfield B2
Maysville F2
Middlesboro F4
Middletown D2
Monterey E2
Monticello E4
Morehead F2
Morganfield B3, C1
Morgantown C3
Mt. Olivet E2
Mt. Sterling F2
Mt. Vernon E3
Mt. Washington D2
Muldraugh C3
Munfordville D3
Murray C2
Nebo B3
New Castle D2
Nicholasville E3
Oak Grove B4
Okolona D2
Olive Hill F2
Owensboro B3
Owenton E2
Owingsville F2
Paducah C2
Paris E2
Patesville C3
Phelps G3
Pikeville G3
Pine Knot E4
Pineville F4
Pleasure Ridge Park D2
Prestonsburg G3
Princeton B3, C2
Providence B3, C1
Raceland G2
Radcliff D3
Richmond E3
Rochester C3
Russell Springs D3
Russellville C4
St. Matthews D2
Salyersville F3
Sandy Hook F2
Scottsville C4
Sebree B3
Shelbyville D2
Shepherdsville D3
Slaughters B3
Smithland C1
Somerset E3
South Shore G2
Springfield D3
Stanford E3
Stanton F3
Sturgis A3, C1
Taylorsville D2
Tompkinsville D4
Valley Station D2
Vanceburg F2
Versailles E2
Vicco F3
Vine Grove D3
Walton E2
Warsaw E2
West Liberty F3
Wheelwright G3
Whitesburg G3
Whitley City E4
Wickliffe B2
Williamsburg E4
Williamstown E2
Wilmore E3
Winchester E3
Woodbury C3
Zion B3

Other Features
Barkley, *lake* B4, C2
Barren, *river* C3
Barren River, *lake* C4
Big Sandy, *river* G2
Big South Fork Natl. River and Rec. Area F3
Buckhorn, *lake* F3
Cave Run, *lake* F2
Cumberland, *lake* E4
Cumberland, *river* C4
Cumberland Gap Natl. Hist. Park F4
Dale Hollow, *lake* D4
Fish Trap, *river* G3
Green, *river* B3, D3
Green River, *lake* D3
Kentucky, *lake* C2
Kentucky, *river* D2, E3
Licking, *river* F2
Lincoln Birthplace Natl. Hist. Site D3
Mammoth Cave Natl. Park C3
Nolin River, *lake* C3
Ohio, *river* F2
Rough, *river* C3
Rough River, *lake* C3
Tennessee, *river* C2
Tug Fork, *river* G3

Louisiana .... page 145

Cities and Towns
Abbeville E7
Abita Springs J6
Alexandria E4
Ama Inset
Amelia G7
Amite J5
Arabi Inset

Key
Arcadia D1
Arnaudville F6
Avondale Inset
Baker G5
Baldwin F7
Ball E4
Basile D6
Bastrop F1
Baton Rouge, *captial* G6
Bayou Cane H7
Bayou Vista G7
Belle Chasse Inset
Bentley E3
Bernice D1
Bertrandville Inset
Bogalusa K5
Bossier City B1
Boyce D4
Braithwaite Inset
Breaux Bridge F6
Bridge City Inset
Broussard F6
Bunkie E5
Buras K8
Caernarvon Inset
Cameron C7
Carencro E6
Carville G6
Cecilia F6
Chalmette Inset, K7
Charenton F7
Chauvin H8
Church Point E6
Clinton G5
Colfax D3
Columbia E2
Cottonport E5
Coushatta C2
Covington J6
Crowley E6
Crown Point Inset
Cullen C1
Cut Off J7
Dalcour Inset
Delcambre F7
Delhi G2
Denham Springs H5
De Quincy C6
De Ridder C5
Des Allemands J7
Destrehan Inset
Donaldsonville H6
Edgard H6
Elton D6
English Turn Inset
Erath E7
Estelle Inset
Eunice E6
Farmerville E1
Ferriday F3
Franklin F7
Franklinton J5
Frenier Inset
Galliano J8
Garyville H6
Glenmora D5
Golden Meadow J8
Gonzales H6
Grambling D1
Grand Isle K8
Gray H7
Greensburg H5
Greenwood B2
Gretna Inset, J7
Gueydan E6
Hackberry C6
Hahnville Inset, J7
Hammond J5
Harahan Inset
Harrisonburg E2
Harvey Inset
Haughton C1
Haynesville C1
Henderson F6
Homer C1
Houma H7
Independence J5
Inniswold G6
Iota D6
Iowa C6
Jackson G5
Jeanerette F7
Jean Lafitte J7
Jefferson Inset
Jena E3
Jennings D6
Jesuit Bend Inset
Jonesboro D2
Jonesville F3
Kaplan E6
Kenilworth Inset
Kenner Inset, J7
Kentwood J5
Killona Inset
Kinder D6
Krotz Springs F5
Labadieville H7
Lacombe K6
Lafayette E6
Lafitte J7
Lake Arthur D6
Lake Charles C6
Lake Providence G1
Laplace Inset, J6
Larose J7
Lecompte E4
Leesville C4
Livingston H5
Lockport H7
Logansport B3
Luling Inset
Mamou E5
Mandeville J6
Mansfield B3
Mansura E4
Many C3
Marion E1
Marksville E4
Marrero Inset, J7
Melder D4
Melville F5
Meraux Inset
Metairie Inset, J7
Mimosa Park Inset
Minden C1
Monroe E1
Montegut H8
Montz Inset
Morgan City G7
Moss Bluff C6
Napoleonville G7
Natalbany J5

Key
Natchitoches C3
Newellton G2
New Iberia F6
New Llano C4
New Orleans Inset, J7
New Roads G5
New Sarpy Inset
Norco Inset
Oakdale D5
Oak Grove G1
Oakville Inset
Oberlin D5
Oil City B1
Olla E3
Opelousas E5
Paincourtville G6
Paradis Inset
Patterson G7
Plaquemine G6
Point a la Hache K7
Ponchatoula J6
Port Allen G5
Port Barre F5
Port Sulphur K8
Poydras Inset
Raceland H7
Rayne E6
Rayville F2
Reserve H6
Richwood E2
Ringgold C2
River Ridge Inset
Ruston D1
St. Bernard Inset
St. Francisville G5
St. Joseph G3
St. Martinville F6
St. Rose Inset
Scarsdale Inset
Schriever H7
Scott E6
Shreveport B2
Simmesport F5
Slidell K6
Springhill C1
Stonewall B2
Sulphur C6
Sunset E6
Swartz F1
Taft Inset
Tallulah G2
Terrytown Inset
Thibodaux H7
Toca Inset
Vidalia G3
Ville Platte E5
Vinton B6
Violet Inset, K7
Vivian B1
Waggaman Inset
Walker H6
Washington E5
Welsh D6
Westlake C6
West Monroe E1
Westwego Inset, J7
White Castle G6
Winnfield D3
Winnsboro F2
Zachary G5
Zwolle B3

Other Features
Atchafalaya, *bay* G8
Atchafalaya, *river* F5
Barataria, *bay* K8
Bistineau, *lake* C2
Black, *river* F4
Borgne, *lake* Inset, K6
Breton, *islands* L8
Caddo, *lake* A1
Caillou, *bay* G8
Calcasieu, *lake* C7
Caney, *lake* E2
Cane River Creole Natl. Hist. Park D3
Catahoula, *lake* E3
Chandeleur, *islands* M7
Driskill, *mt.* C2
Grand, *lake* D7
Jean Lafitte N.H.P. and Preserve J7
Little, *river* D2
Marsh, *island* F7
Mississippi, *river* G3
Ouachita, *river* E2
Pearl, *river* K5
Pontchartrain, *lake* Inset, J6
Red, *river* C3
Sabine, *lake* B7
Sabine, *river* B5
Terrebonne, *bay* H8
Timbalier, *bay* J8
Toledo Bend, *reservoir* B4
Vermilion, *bay* F7
West Cote Blanche, *bay* F7
White, *lake* E7

Maine .... page 146

Cities and Towns
Alfred B5
Amherst D4
Athens C4
Auburn B4
Augusta, *capital* C4
Bangor D4
Bar Harbor D4
Bass Harbor D4
Bath C4
Belfast C4
Berwick B5
Biddeford B5
Boothbay Harbor C4
Brewer D4
Bridgton B4
Brunswick C4
Bucksport D4
Calais E3
Camden C4
Cape Elizabeth B5
Caribou D2
Chisholm B4
Clinton C4
Conway A4
Damariscotta C4
Dexter C3
Dixfield B4
Dover-Foxcroft C3
East Millinocket D3
Eastport F4
Ellsworth D4
Fairfield C4

Key
Falmouth B5
Farmington B4
Fort Fairfield E2
Fort Kent D1
Frankfort D4
Franklin D4
Freeport B5
Frenchboro D4
Frenchville D1
Fryeburg B4
Gardiner C4
Greene B4
Hallowell C4
Hampden D4
Houlton E2
Howland D3
Kennebunk B5
Kittery B5
Lewiston B4
Lincoln D3
Lisbon Falls B4
Livermore Falls B4
Machias E4
Madawaska D1
Madison C4
Mars Hill E2
Mechanic Falls B4
Mexico B4
Milbridge E4
Milford D4
Millinocket D3
Milo D3
Norridgewock C4
North Amity E3
North Berwick B5
North Conway A4
North East Carry C3
North Windham B5
Norway B4
Oakland C4
Old Orchard Beach B5
Old Town D4
Orono D4
Oxford B4
Patten D3
Portland B5
Presque Isle D2
Richmond C4
Rockland C4
Rumford B4
Saco B5
Sanford B5
Skowhegan C4
South Paris B4
South Portland B5
Springvale B5
Thomaston C4
Van Buren E1
Waldoboro C4
Waterville C4
Westbrook B5
Westfield E2
Wilsons Mills A4
Wilton B4
Winslow C4
Winthrop C4
Wiscasset C4
Woodland E3
Yarmouth B5
York B5

Other Features
Acadia Natl. Park D4
Androscoggin, *river* B4
Appalachian, *mts.* A3
Aroostook, *river* D2
au Haut, *island* D4
Aziscohos, *lake* A3
Baskahegan, *lake* E3
Baxter State Park D2
Big, *lake* E3
Casco, *bay* C4
Chamberlain, *lake* C2
Chesuncook, *lake* C2
Churchill, *lake* C2
Cross, *island* E4
Deer, *island* D4
Elizabeth, *cape* B4
Flagstaff, *lake* B3
Grand, *lake* E3
Grand Matagamon, *lake* D2
Grand Seboeis, *lake* D2
Great Wass, *island* E4
Islesboro, *island* D4
Katahdin, *mt.* D3
Kennebec, *river* C3
Long, *island* D4
Maine, *gulf* C4
Matinicus, *island* D4
Mattawamkeag, *river* D2
Millinocket, *lake* D3
Monhegan, *island* C4
Moosehead, *lake* C3
Mooselookmeguntic, *lake* B4
Mt. Desert, *island* D4
Munsungan, *lake* D2
Nicatous, *lake* D3
Pemadumcook, *lake* C3
Penobscot, *bay* D4
Penobscot, *river* D3
Piscataquis, *river* C3
Richardson, *lakes* B4
Saco, *bay* B5
Saco, *river* B5
Saddleback, *mt.* B4
St. Croix, *river* E3
St. John, *river* C2
Sebago, *lake* B5
Sebec, *lake* C3
Seboeis, *lake* D3
Seboomook, *lake* C3
Snow, *mt.* B3
Sugarloaf, *mt.* B3
Swans, *island* D4
Telos, *lake* C2
Umbagog, *lake* A4
Vinalhaven, *island* D4
West Grand, *lake* E3
West Quoddy Head, *peninsula* F4
White Cap, *mt.* C3

Maryland .... page 147

Cities and Towns
Aberdeen K2
Accident A6
Accokeek F5
Adelphi C4
Annapolis, *capital* J4
Arden-on-the-Severn H3
Arnold J3

Key
Aspen Hill B3, F3
Avenue G7
Baltimore H2
Bel Air J1
Beltsville C3, G3
Berlin P6
Berwyn Heights C4
Bethesda B4, F4
Bladensburg C4
Boonsboro D1
Bowie G4
Bowleys Quarters J2
Braddock Heights D2
Brandywine G5
Brentwood C4
Brunswick D2
Bucktown K6
Burtonsville C3
Cabin John A4
California J6
Calverton C3
Cambridge K5
Cape St. Claire J3
Camp Springs C5
Carney H2
Cascade D1
Catonsville H2
Centreville K3
Chesapeake Beach H5
Chesapeake Ranch Estates J6
Chestertown K3
Cheverly C4
Chillum C4, G4
Clinton G4
Clover Hill E2
Cloverly C3
Cockeysville H2
Colesville C3
College Park C4, G4
Columbia G3
Contee D3
Copenhaver A3
Coral Hills C5
Cresaptown C6
Crisfield L7
Crofton H3
Crownsville H3
Cumberland D6
Damascus F2
Deale H4
Delmar M6
Denton L4
Derwood A3
District Heights D5
Dufief A3
Dundalk H2
Easton K4
Edgemere J3
Edgewood J2
Eldersburg G2
Elkridge G3
Elkton L1
Ellicott City G2
Emmitsburg E1
Essex J2
Fair Hill L1
Fallston J1
Federalsburg L5
Ferndale H3
Forest Heights B5, G4
Forestville G4
Fountain Head D1
Frederick E2
Friendsville A6
Frostburg C6
Fruitland M6
Gaithersburg F3
Garrison G2
Germantown E3
Glen A3
Glenarden D4
Glen Burnie H3
Glen Echo Heights B4
Glen Hills A3
Glenmont B3
Golden Beach H6
Grantsville B6
Grasonville K4
Green Haven H3
Greenbelt D4, G3
Greensboro L4
Hagerstown D1
Halfway C1
Hampstead G1
Hampton H2
Hancock B1
Havre de Grace K1
Herald Harbor H3
High Ridge D3
Hillandale C3
Hillcrest Heights C5
Hillsmere Shores J4
Hughesville G5
Hunting Hill A3
Hurlock L5
Hyattstown E2
Hyattsville C4, G4
Indian Head F5
Jarrettsville J1
Jessup G3
Joppatowne J2
Kemptown E2
Kensington B3, F3
Kentland D4, G4
Kettering G4
Keysers Ridge B6
Kingstown K3
Kingsville J2
Knollwood C3
Lake Shore J3
Landover C4, G4
Langley Park C4
Lanham D4
Lansdowne H3
LaPlata G5
Largo G4
Laurel D3, G3
LaVale C6
Lawsonia L7
Layhill B3
Leonardtown H6
Lewisdale C4
Lexington Park J6
Linthicum H3
Lochearn H2
Londontown H4
Lutherville H2
Luxmanor B3
Manchester G1
Marlton G4
Maydale C3
Middle River J2

Key

Middletown ... D2
Milford ... G2
Montgomery Village ... F3
Montpelier ... D3
Mount Aetna ... D1
Mountain Lake Park ... A7
Mount Airy ... F2
Mount Rainier ... C4
Muirkirk ... D3
New Carrollton ... D4
Norbeck ... B3
North Chevy Chase ... B4
North East ... L1
Oak Crest ... D3
Oakland ... A7
Oakland ... G2
Oakview ... C3
Ocean City ... P6
Ocean Pines ... P6
Odenton ... H3
Olney ... F3
Overlea ... H2
Owings Mills ... G2
Oxon Hill ... C5
Palmer Park ... D4
Parkville ... H2
Parole ... H4
Perry Hall ... J2
Perryman ... K2
Perryville ... K1
Pikesville ... H2
Pleasant Hills ... H2
Pocomoke City ... M7
Poolesville ... E3
Potomac ... A3, F3
Potomac Heights ... F5
Preston ... L5
Prince Frederick ... H5
Princess Anne ... M7
Randallstown ... G2
Randolph Hills ... B3
Redhouse ... A7
Reisterstown ... G2
Rising Sun ... K1
Ritchie ... D5
Riverdale ... C4
Riviera Beach ... H3
Rock Hall ... K3
Rockville ... A3, F3
Rosedale ... H2
Rossmoor Leisure World ... B3
Rossville ... J2
St. Charles ... G5
St. Michaels ... M6
Salisbury ... M6
Seabrook ... D4
Seat Pleasant ... D5
Severn ... H3
Severna Park ... H3
Shady Side ... H4
Shawsville ... H1
Silver Hill ... C5
Silver Spring ... B4, F4
Snow Hill ... N7
South Gate ... H3
Spencerville ... C3
Stevensville ... J3
Suitland ... C5, G4
Sykesville ... G2
Takoma Park ... C4
Taneytown ... F1
Temple Hills ... C5, G4
Thurmont ... E1
Timonium ... H2
Towson ... H2
Upper Marlboro ... H4
Waldorf ... G5
Walker Mill ... D5
Walkersville ... E2
Westernport ... B7
Westminster ... F1
West Ocean City ... P6
Wheaton ... B3, F3
White Marsh ... J2
White Oak ... C3, G3
White Plains ... G5
Wildwood Hills ... A3
Williamsport ... C1
Woodlawn ... G2
Woodyard ... G4

Other Features
Allegheny Front, mt. ridge ... C7
Antietam Natl. Battlefield ... D2
Appalachian Natl. Scenic Trail ... D2
Assateague Island Natl. Seashore ... P7
Assawoman, bay ... P6
Backbone, mt. ... A7
Chesapeake, bay ... J5
Chesapeake and Ohio Canal N.H.P. ... A4, D2
Chester, river ... K3
Chincoteague, bay ... N7
Choptank, river ... K5
Deep Creek, lake ... A6
Liberty, reservoir ... G2
North Branch Potomac, river ... C7
Nanticoke, river ... L6
Patapsco, river ... H3
Patuxent, river ... H4
Potomac, river ... A4
Susquehanna, river ... J1
Thomas Stone Natl. Hist. Site ... F5
Wicomico, river ... L6
Youghiogheny, river ... A6

Massachusetts ... page 148

Cities and Towns
Abington ... L4
Acton ... A5, J3
Acushnet ... L6
Adams ... B2
Amesbury ... L1
Amherst ... D3
Andover ... K2
Arlington ... C6, K3
Ashby ... J3
Ashfield ... C2
Ashland ... J3
Assinippi ... J8
Assonet ... K5
Athol ... F2
Attleboro ... G4
Auburn ... G4
Avon ... D8, K4
Ayer ... H2
Baldwinville ... F2
Barnstable ... N6
Becket ... B3
Bedford ... B5, J3

Belchertown ... E3
Bellingham ... J4
Belmont ... C6
Berkley ... K5
Bernardston ... D2
Beverly ... F5, L2
Billerica ... B5, J2
Blackstone ... H4
Blandford ... C4
Bliss Corner ... L6
Bolton ... H3
Bondsville ... E4
Boston, capital ... D6, K3
Boxford ... L2
Braintree ... E8, K4
Brewster ... P5
Bridgewater ... L5
Brimfield ... F4
Brockton ... L4
Brookfield ... F4
Brookline ... C7, K3
Brookville ... F4
Burlington ... C5, K2
Buzzards Bay ... M5
Cambridge ... D6, K3
Canton ... C8, K4
Carlisle ... B5
Cedarville ... M5
Centerville ... N6
Central Village ... K6
Charlton ... G4
Charlton City ... G4
Chatham ... Q6
Chelmsford ... J2
Chelsea ... D6
Cheshire ... B2
Chester ... C3
Chicopee ... D4
Chilmark ... M7
Clarksburg ... B2
Clinton ... G3
Cochituate ... B7, J3
Cohasset ... L4
Concord ... B6, J3
Cotuit ... N6
Dalton ... B3
Danvers ... E5, L2
Dartmouth ... K6
Dedham ... C7, K4
Dennis ... P6
Douglas ... H4
Dover ... B8, J4
Dracut ... J2
Duxbury ... M4
East Brookfield ... F4
East Dennis ... P6
East Douglas ... H4
East Falmouth ... M6
East Freetown ... L5
East Longmeadow ... D4
Eastham ... Q5
Easthampton ... D3
East Orleans ... Q5
East Pepperell ... H2
East Wareham ... M5
Edgartown ... M7
Erving ... E2
Essex ... L2
Everett ... D6
Fall River ... K6
Falmouth ... M6
Feeding Hills ... D4
Fiskdale ... F4
Fitchburg ... G2
Florida ... B2
Foxboro ... K4
Framingham ... A7, J3
Franklin ... J4
Gardner ... G2
Gay Head ... L7
Georgetown ... L2
Gloucester ... M2
Granby ... D3
Granville ... C4
Great Barrington ... A4
Greenfield ... D2
Green Harbor ... M4
Halifax ... L5
Hamilton ... L2
Hanover ... L4
Hanson ... L4
Haverhill ... H3
Hingham ... F8, L4
Holbrook ... E8, K4
Holland ... F4
Holliston ... A8, J4
Holyoke ... D4
Hopedale ... H4
Hopkinton ... H4
Hubbardston ... G3
Hudson ... H3
Hull ... F7, L3
Huntington ... N6
Hyannis ... N6
Ipswich ... L2
Kingston ... M5
Lakeville ... L5
Lawrence ... K2
Lee ... A3
Lenox ... A3
Leominster ... G2
Lexington ... C6, K3
Lincoln ... B6
Littleton ... H2
Littleton Common ... J2
Longmeadow ... D4
Lowell ... J2
Ludlow ... E4
Lunenburg ... G2
Lynn ... E6, L3
Lynnfield ... D5, L2
Madaket ... P7
Malden ... D6, K3
Manchester-by-the-Sea ... L2
Mansfield ... K4
Marblehead ... F5, L3
Marion ... L6
Marlborough ... H3
Marshfield ... M4
Marshfield Hills ... M4
Mashpee ... N6
Mattapoisett ... L6
Maynard ... J3
Medfield ... B8, J4
Medford ... D6, K3
Medway ... J4
Melrose ... D6, K3
Mendon ... H4
Methuen ... K2
Middleboro ... L5
Milford ... H4
Millis ... J4
Milton ... D7, K3

Monson ... E4
Monterey ... B4
Monument Beach ... M6
Nahant ... E6, L3
Nantucket ... P7
Natick ... B7, J3
Needham ... C7, K3
New Ashford ... B2
New Bedford ... L6
New Boston ... B4
Newburyport ... L1
New Marlborough ... B4
Newton ... C7, K3
North Adams ... B2
North Amherst ... D3
Northampton ... D3
North Andover ... K2
North Attleboro ... J5
Northborough ... H3
Northbridge ... H4
North Brookfield ... F3
North Carver ... L5
North Falmouth ... M6
Northfield ... E2
North Grafton ... H4
North Pembroke ... L4
North Plymouth ... M5
North Reading ... D5, K2
North Scituate ... L4
North Sudbury ... A6
North Tisbury ... M7
Norton ... K5
Norwell ... L4
Norwood ... C8, K4
Oakham ... F3
Ocean Bluff ... M4
Ocean Grove ... K6
Orange ... E2
Orleans ... Q5
Osterville ... N6
Otis ... B4
Oxford ... G4
Palmer ... E4
Paxton ... G3
Peabody ... E5, L2
Pelham ... E3
Pembroke ... L4
Pepperell ... H2
Petersham ... F2
Phillipston ... F2
Pinehurst ... C5, K2
Pittsfield ... B3
Plainfield ... C2
Plainville ... J4
Plymouth ... M5
Pocasset ... M6
Provincetown ... P4
Quincy ... E7, K3
Randolph ... D8, K4
Raynham ... K5
Raynham Center ... K5
Reading ... D5, K2
Rehoboth ... K5
Revere ... E6, K3
Rochester ... L6
Rockland ... E8, L4
Rockport ... M2
Rutland ... G3
Sagamore ... M5
Salem ... F5, L2
Salisbury ... L1
Sandwich ... N5
Saugus ... E6, K3
Savoy ... B2
Scituate ... L4
Sharon ... C8, K4
Sheffield ... A4
Shelburne Falls ... D2
Sherborn ... B8
Shirley ... H2
Shrewsbury ... H3
Shutesbury ... E3
Somerset ... K5
Somerville ... D6, K3
South Amherst ... D3
Southbridge ... F4
South Carver ... M5
South Deerfield ... D3
South Dennis ... P6
South Duxbury ... M4
South Lancaster ... H3
South Sudbury ... A7
South Wellfleet ... P5
South Yarmouth ... P6
Spencer ... G4
Springfield ... D4
Sterling ... G3
Stoneham ... D5
Stoughton ... D8, K4
Sturbridge ... F4
Sudbury ... A6, J3
Sutton ... G4
Swampscott ... E6, L3
Taunton ... K5
Teaticket ... M6
Templeton ... F2
Tewksbury ... K2
Three Rivers ... E4
Tolland ... B4
Topsfield ... L2
Truro ... P5
Turners Falls ... D2
Tyngsborough ... J2
Upton ... H4
Uxbridge ... H4
Vineyard Haven ... M7
Wakefield ... D5, K2
Wales ... F4
Walpole ... C8, J4
Waltham ... C6, B6
Ware ... F3
Wareham ... M5
Warren ... F4
Warwick ... E2
Washington ... B3
Watertown ... C6
Wauwinet ... P7
Wayland ... B7
Webster ... G4
Wellesley ... B7, J3
West Barnstable ... N6
Westborough ... H3
West Boylston ... G3
West Brookfield ... F4
West Concord ... J3
West Cummington ... C3
West Falmouth ... M6
Westfield ... D4
Westford ... J2
West Granville ... C4
Westhampton ... C3
West Medway ... A8

Westminster ... G2
Weston ... B6, J3
Westport ... K6
Westport Point ... K6
West Springfield ... D4
West Wareham ... P6
Westwood ... C8, K4
West Yarmouth ... P6
Weymouth ... E8, L4
Whately ... D3
White Island Shores ... M5
Whitinsville ... H4
Whitman ... L4
Wilbraham ... E4
Williamstown ... B2
Wilmington ... C5, K2
Winchendon ... F2
Winchester ... C6
Windsor ... B2
Winthrop ... E6
Woburn ... C5, K3
Worcester ... G3
Worthington Center ... C3
Wrentham ... J4
Yarmouth Port ... P6

Other Features
Adams Natl. Hist. Park ... E8, L4
Ann, cape ... M2
Berkshire, hills ... B4
Boston, bay ... E6
Boston, harbor ... E6
Boston Harbor Islands N.R.A. ... E7
Boston Natl. Hist. Park ... D6
Buzzards, bay ... M6
Cape Cod, bay ... N5
Cape Cod, canal ... M5
Cape Cod Natl. Seashore ... P5
Charles, river ... B7
Chicopee, river ... D4
Cobble Mt., reservoir ... C4
Cod, cape ... P4
Connecticut, river ... E2
Deer, island ... E7
Elizabeth, islands ... L7
Frederick Law Olmsted N.H.S. ... C7
Georges, island ... E7
Greylock, mt. ... B2
Hingham, bay ... E7
Housatonic, river ... A4
J.F.K. Birthplace Natl. Hist. Site ... D7
Long, island ... E7
Longfellow Natl. Hist. Site ... D6
Lowell Natl. Hist. Park ... J2
Maine, (state) ... M1
Martha's Vineyard, island ... M7
Massachusetts, bay ... F6, M3
Merrimack, river ... K1
Minute Man Natl. Hist. Park ... B6, J3
Monomoy, island ... P6
Muskeget, channel ... N7
Nantucket, island ... P7
New Bedford Whaling N.H.P. ... L6
Neponset, river ... C7
Otis, reservoir ... B4
Peddocks, island ... E7
Quabbin, reservoir ... F3
Quincy, bay ... E7
Salem Maritime N.H.S. ... F5, L2
Saugus Iron Works N.H.S. ... E6
Shawsheen, river ... B6
Spectacle, island ... E7
Swift, river ... E3
Taconic, mts. ... A2
Wachusett, reservoir ... G3
Wachusett, mt. ... G3
Walden, pond ... B6

Michigan ... page 149

Cities and Towns
Adrian ... E8
Albion ... E7
Algonac ... G7
Allegan ... D7
Allen Park ... A7
Alma ... E6
Alpena ... F4
Ann Arbor ... F7
Atlanta ... E5
Bad Axe ... G6
Baldwin ... D6
Battle Creek ... D7
Bay City ... F6
Belding ... D6
Bellaire ... D5
Belleville ... F7
Benton Harbor ... C7
Berkley ... A6
Bessemer ... C2
Beulah ... C5
Beverly Hills ... A6
Big Rapids ... D6
Birmingham ... A6
Blissfield ... F8
Bloomfield Hills ... A6
Boyne City ... D4
Bridgeport ... F6
Brighton ... F7
Buchanan ... C8
Burton ... F6
Cadillac ... D5
Carleton ... F7
Caro ... F6
Carrollton ... F6
Cassopolis ... C8
Cedar Springs ... D6
Center Line ... B6
Centreville ... D8
Charlevoix ... D4
Charlotte ... E7
Cheboygan ... E4
Chelsea ... E7
Chesaning ... E6
Chesterfield ... C3
Christmas ... C3
Clare ... E6
Clawson ... A6
Clio ... F6
Coldwater ... E8
Connorville ... C2
Coopersville ... D7
Crystal Falls ... A3
Cutlerville ... D7
Davison ... F6
Dearborn ... A7, F7
Dearborn Hts. ... A7
Detroit ... B7, F7
De Witt ... E7
Dowagiac ... C8

Dundee ... F8
Durand ... F7
Eagle River ... A2
East Lansing ... E7
Eastpointe ... B6
East Tawas ... F5
Eaton Rapids ... E7
Ecorse ... B7
Escanaba ... B4
Essexville ... F6
Farmington ... A6
Farmington Hills ... A6
Fenton ... F7
Ferndale ... B6
Ferrysburg ... C6
Flat Rock ... F7
Flint ... F6
Flushing ... F6
Fowlerville ... E7
Frankenmuth ... F6
Franklin ... A6
Fraser ... D6
Fremont ... D6
Garden City ... A7
Gaylord ... E4
Gladstone ... B4
Gladwin ... E6
Grand Blanc ... F7
Grand Haven ... C6
Grand Ledge ... E7
Grand Rapids ... D6
Grayling ... E5
Greenville ... D6
Grosse Pointe ... B7
Grosse Pointe Farms ... B7
Grosse Pointe Park ... B7
Grosse Pointe Shores ... B6
Grosse Pointe Woods ... B6
Hamtramck ... B7
Hancock ... A2
Harper Woods ... B6
Harrison ... E5
Harrisville ... F5
Hart ... C6
Hastings ... D7
Hazel Park ... B6
Highland Park ... B7
Hillsdale ... E8
Holland ... C7
Holly ... F7
Holt ... E7
Houghton ... A2
Houghton Lake ... E5
Howell ... E7
Hudson ... E8
Hudsonville ... D7
Huntington Woods ... A6
Huron Heights ... A6
Imlay City ... F6
Inkster ... A7
Ionia ... D6
Iron Mountain ... A4
Ironwood ... C2
Ishpeming ... B3
Ithaca ... E6
Jackson ... E7
Jenison ... D7
Kalamazoo ... D7
Kalkaska ... D5
Keego Harbor ... A6
Kentwood ... D7
Kingsford ... A4
Lake City ... D5
Lake Orion ... F7
Lambertville ... F8
L'Anse ... A3
Lansing, capital ... E7
Lapeer ... F6
Lincoln Park ... A7
Livonia ... A7, F7
Lowell ... D7
Ludington ... C6

Madison Hts. ... B6
Manistee ... C5
Manistique ... C4
Marenisco ... D2
Marine City ... G7
Marquette ... B3
Marshall ... E7
Marysville ... G7
Melvindale ... A7
Menominee ... B4
Merriweather ... D2
Michigan Center ... E7
Midland ... E6
Milan ... F7
Milford ... E6
Mio ... E5
Monroe ... F8
Mount Clemens ... B6
Mount Morris ... F6
Mount Pleasant ... E6
Munising ... C3
Muskegon ... C6
Muskegon Hts. ... C6
Negaunee ... B3
New Baltimore ... D3
Newberry ... D3
Niles ... C8
North Muskegon ... C6
Norton Shores ... C6
Norway ... B4
Oak Park ... A6
Okemos ... E7
Ontonagon ... D1
Orchard Lake ... A6
Otsego ... D7
Owosso ... E6
Oxford ... F7
Paw Paw ... D7
Paw Paw Lake ... C7
Petoskey ... E4
Plainwell ... D7
Pontiac ... A6, F7
Portage ... D7
Port Huron ... G7
Portland ... E7
Rapid River ... C4
Reed City ... D6
River Rouge ... B7
Rochester Hills ... B6
Rockford ... D6
Rogers City ... F4
Romeo ... F7
Romulus ... F7
Roscommon ... E5
Roseville ... B6
Royal Oak ... B6
Saginaw ... F6

St. Clair ... G7
St. Clair Shores ... B6
St. Ignace ... E4
St. Johns ... E7
St. Joseph ... C7
St. Louis ... E6
Saline ... F7
Sandusky ... G6
Sault Ste. Marie ... D3
Shields ... F6
Silver City ... D1
Skidway Lake ... F5
Southfield ... A6
Southgate ... A7
South Haven ... C7
South Lyon ... F7
Sparta ... D6
Spring Lake ... C6
Standish ... F6
Stanton ... D6
Sterling Heights ... B6
Sturgis ... D8
Sylvan Lake ... A6
Tawas City ... F5
Taylor ... A7
Tecumseh ... F8
Temperance ... F8
Three Rivers ... D8
Traverse City ... D5
Troy ... B6
Union Lake ... A6
Utica ... B6
Vassar ... F6
Wakefield ... C2
Waldenburg ... B6
Walker ... D6
Warren ... B6
Wayland ... D7
Wayne ... A7
West Acres ... E5
West Branch ... E5
Westland ... A7
White Cloud ... D6
Whitehall ... C6
White Pine ... D1
Whitmore Lake ... E7
Williamston ... E7
Wixom ... A6
Wolf Lake ... D7
Wyandotte ... B7
Wyoming ... D7
Ypsilanti ... F7
Zeeland ... C7

Other Features
Arvon, mt. ... A3
Au Sable, river ... E5
Beaver, island ... D4
Big Bay De Noc, bay ... B4
Big Sable, point ... C5
Bois Blanc, island ... E4
Cass, river ... F6
Chambers, island ... C2
Detroit, river ... B7
Drummond, island ... F3
Erie, lake ... F8
Escanaba, river ... B4
Glen, lake ... C5
Gogebic, lake ... C2
Government Peak, mt. ... C2
Grand, island ... C3
Grand Island Natl. Rec. Area ... C3
Grand Traverse, bay ... D4
Green, bay ... B4
Hamlin, lake ... C6
Hammond, bay ... E4
Higgins, lake ... E5
High, island ... D4
Hog, island ... D4
Houghton, lake ... E5
Hubbard, lake ... F5
Huron, bay ... A3
Huron, lake ... G5
Huron, mts. ... B3
Indian, lake ... C4
Isle Royale, island ... A1
Isle Royale Natl. Park ... A1
Keweenaw, bay ... A3
Keweenaw, peninsula ... A2
Keweenaw, point ... B2
Keweenaw Natl. Hist. Park ... A2
Lookout, point ... F5
Manistee, river ... D5
Manitou, island ... B2
Menominee, river ... A4
Michigamme, reservoir ... A3
Michigan, lake ... C5
North Manitou, island ... C4
Paint, river ... A3
Pictured Rocks Natl. Lakeshore ... C3
Porcupine, mts. ... C2
Saginaw, bay ... F5
St. Clair, lake ... B6
St. Martin, island ... B4
Sleeping Bear Dunes Natl. Lakeshore ... C5
South Fox, island ... D4
South Manitou, island ... C4
Straits of Mackinac ... E4
Sturgeon, bay ... B4
Superior, lake ... B2
Thunder, bay ... F4
Whitefish, bay ... C3
Wixom, lake ... E6

Minnesota ... page 15[0]

Cities and Towns
Ada
Aitkin
Albany
Albert Lea
Albertville
Alexandria
Annandale
Anoka
Appleton
Arlington
Aurora
Austin
Babbitt
Bagley
Barnesville
Baudette
Baxter
Bayport
Belle Plaine
Bemidji
Benson
Big Lake
Bird Island

Minnesota (continued)

	Key
...ming Prairie	D7
...mington	D6
...Earth	C7
...herd	C4
...ckenridge	A4
...oklyn Center	E5
...alo	D5
...esville	D6
...donia	F7
...by	A6
...on Falls	E6
...ter City	E5
...hassen	D6
...ska	C4
...field	E7
...holm	E3
...City	B6
...ks Grove	D7
...rwater	C5
...to	C5
...l Spring	C5
...mbia Hts	F5
...n Rapids	D5
...coran	D4
...okston	A3
...sby	D4
...son	A6
...oit Lakes	B4
...orth	A4
...ge Center	E4
...th	A3
...e Lake	D6
...Bethel	D5
...Grand Forks	A3
...w Lake	B5
...River	F3
...sville	B4
...eth	A4
...ta	E7
...mont	C7
...on Heights	F5
...ault	D6
...ington	D6
...us Falls	A4
...y	D5
...st Lake	E5
...ton	B3
...ey	F5
...lord	C6
...ncoe	C6
...nwood	B5
...den Valley	E5
...dview	F6
...d Forks	A3
...d Marais	F5
...d Portage	F4
...d Rapids	D3
...ite Falls	B6
...ock	A2
...tings	E6
...vley	A4
...field	E7
...mantown	E4
...bing	E3
...ah	F7
...kins	E5
...land	C5
...ard Lake	C5
...tchinson	C6
...national Falls	D2
...hoe	A6
...son	B7
...sville	D6
...an	D6
...on	C4
...yon	E6
...rescent	C6
...Crystal	C6
...field	B7
...ville	D6
...enter	D6
...seur	D6
...iston	F7
...field	C5
...e Canada	F5
...e Falls	C5
...g Prairie	C5
...sdale	D6
...en	E5
...erne	A7
...ntosh	B3
...delia	C6
...dison	A5
...nmen	B3
...nkato	D6
...ntorville	E6
...ole Grove	D5
...ole Lake	D6
...pleton	D7
...elewood	F5
...shall	B6
...rose	C5
...dota	F6
...aca	E5
...neapolis	D6
...nneota	B6
...ntevideo	B6
...ntgomery	D6
...nticello	D5
...orhead	A4
...und	D5
...rris	B5
...und	D6
...untain Iron	E3
...untain Lake	C7
...w Hope	E5
...wport	F6
...w Prague	D6
...w Ulm	C6
...sswa	C4
...rth Branch	E5
...rthfield	D6
...rth Mankato	C6
...rth Oaks	F5
...via	C6
...ono	D6
...onoco	E6
...ctonville	A5
...akis	B5
...vatonna	D6
...rk Rapids	B4
...ynesville	C5
...lican Rapids	B4
...rham	B4
...geon River	F4
...ne City	E5

	Key
Pine Island	E6
Pipestone	A7
Plainview	E6
Plymouth	D5
Preston	E7
Princeton	D5
Prinsburg	B6
Prior Lake	D6
Proctor	E4
Ramsey	F5
Red Lake Falls	A2
Red Wing	E6
Redwood Falls	B6
Renville	B6
Richfield	F6
Robbinsdale	E5
Rochester	E6
Roseau	B2
Roseville	F7
Rushford	F7
St. Anthony	F5
St. Charles	E7
St. Cloud	C5
St. Francis	D5
St. James	C7
St. Joseph	C5
St. Louis Park	E5
St. Michael	D5
St. Paul, *capital*	D6
St. Peter	D6
Sandstone	E4
Sartell	C5
Sauk Centre	C5
Sauk Rapids	C5
Shakopee	D6
Silver Bay	F3
Slayton	B7
Sleepy Eye	C6
South St. Paul	F5
Spring Valley	E7
Springfield	C6
Staples	C4
Stewartville	E7
Stillwater	E5
Thief River Falls	A2
Tracy	C7
Truman	C7
Two Harbors	F3
Tyler	A6
Virginia	E3
Wabasha	E6
Wadena	B4
Waite Park	C5
Walker	C3
Warren	A2
Warroad	B2
Waseca	D6
Waterville	D6
Wells	D7
Wheaton	A5
White Bear Lake	F5
Willmar	B5
Windom	B7
Winnebago	C7
Winona	F6
Winsted	C6
Winthrop	C6
Worthington	B7
Wyoming	E5
Young America	D5
Zimmerman	D5
Zumbrota	E6

Other Features

	Key
Big Fork, *river*	D2
Brule, *lake*	E4
Buffalo, *lake*	A4
Chippewa, *river*	B5
Clearwater, *river*	B3
Cloquet, *river*	F3
Des Moines, *river*	B6
Eagle, *mt.*	F4
Grand Portage Natl. Monument	F4
Gull, *lake*	C4
Lake of the Woods, *lake*	C1
Leech, *lake*	C3
Little Fork, *river*	D2
Lower Red, *lake*	B3
Lower Whitefish, *lake*	C4
Mall of America	F6
Mesabi, *range*	D3
Mille Lacs, *lake*	D4
Minnesota, *river*	B6
Mississippi, *river*	C3
Mud, *lake*	B2
Namakan, *lake*	E2
Pipestone Natl. Monument	A6
Pokegama, *lake*	D3
Rainy, *river*	C2
Red River of the North, *river*	A3
Root, *river*	D5
Rum, *river*	D5
St. Croix, *river*	E5
St. Louis, *river*	E3
Superior, *lake*	F3
Upper Red, *lake*	B3
Vermilion, *range*	E3
Voyageurs Natl. Park	D2
Winnibigoshish, *lake*	D3

Mississippi .... page 151

Cities and Towns

	Key
Aberdeen	D2
Ackerman	C2
Alligator	B1
Amory	D2
Ashland	C1
Baldwyn	D1
Bassfield	C4
Batesville	C1
Bay St. Louis	C5
Bay Springs	C4
Beauregard	B4
Belmont	D1
Belzoni	B2
Biloxi	D5
Blue Springs	D1
Booneville	D1
Brandon	C3
Braxton	C3
Brookhaven	B4
Bruce	C2
Calhoun City	C2
Canton	C3
Carrollton	C2
Carthage	C3
Centreville	A4
Charleston	C1
Clarksdale	B1
Cleveland	B2
Clinton	B3
Coahoma	B1
Coffeeville	C2
Coldwater	C1
Collins	C4
Collinsville	D3
Columbia	C4
Columbus	D2
Como	C1
Corinth	D1
Crystal Springs	B4
Decatur	C3
De Kalb	D3
Diamondhead	C5
D'Iberville	D5
Doddsville	B2
Drew	B2
Durant	C2
Eden	B3
Edwards	B3
Ellisville	C4
Eupora	C2
Falcon	B1
Falkner	D1
Fayette	A4
Flora	B3
Florence	C3
Forest	C3
Friars Point	B1
Fulton	D1
Gautier	D5
Glendora	B2
Gloster	A4
Golden	D1
Goodman	C3
Greenville	A2
Greenwood	C2
Grenada	C2
Gulfport	C5
Hattiesburg	C4
Hazlehurst	B4
Hernando	C1
Hollandale	B2
Holly Springs	C1
Horn Lake	B1
Houston	D2
Indianola	B2
Itta Bena	B2
Iuka	D1
Jackson, *capital*	B3
Jonestown	B1
Kiln	C5
Kosciusko	C2
Kossuth	D1
Laurel	C4
Leakesville	D4
Learned	B3
Leland	B2
Lena	C3
Lexington	B2
Liberty	B4
Long Beach	C5
Louisville	C2
Lucedale	D5
Lula	B1
Lumberton	C4
Lyman	C5
McComb	B4
McCool	C2
Macon	D2
Madison	B3
Magee	C4
Magnolia	B4
Mantee	C2
Marion	D3
Marks	B1
Marysville	A3
Meadville	B4
Mendenhall	C4
Meridian	D3
Monticello	B4
Montrose	C3
Moorhead	B2
Morton	C3
Moss Point	D5
Mound Bayou	B2
Natchez	A4
Nettleton	D1
New Albany	D1
New Augusta	C4
Newton	C3
Ocean Springs	D5
Okolona	D1
Olive Branch	C1
Oxford	C1
Paden	D1
Pascagoula	D5
Pass Christian	C5
Paulding	C3
Pearl	B3
Pearlington	C5
Pelahatchie	C3
Petal	C4
Philadelphia	C3
Picayune	C5
Pickens	C3
Pittsboro	C2
Polkville	C3
Pontotoc	C1
Pope	C1
Poplarville	C4
Port Gibson	B4
Prentiss	C4
Purvis	C4
Quitman	D3
Raleigh	C3
Raymond	B3
Richland	B3
Ridgeland	B3
Ripley	D1
Rolling Fork	B3
Rosedale	B2
Ruleville	B2
Sallis	C2
Saltillo	D1
Sardis	C1
Satartia	B3
Seminary	C4
Senatobia	C1
Shannon	D1
Shaw	B2
Shelby	B2
Shubuta	D4
Silver Creek	B4
Slate Spring	C2
Southaven	B1
Starkville	D2
Summit	B4
Sumner	B2
Sylvarena	C3
Taylorsville	C4
Tchula	B2
Tillatoba	C2
Toccopola	C1
Tunica	B1
Tupelo	D1
Tutwiler	B1
Tylertown	B4
Union	C3
Vaiden	C2
Vancleave	D5
Verona	D1
Vicksburg	B3
Walthall	C2
Water Valley	C1
Waveland	C5
Waynesboro	D4
Wesson	B4
West	C2
West Point	D2
Wiggins	C5
Winona	C2
Woodland	C2
Woodville	A4
Yazoo City	B3

Other Features

	Key
Arkabatula, *lake*	B1
Big Black, *river*	B3
Big Springs, *lake*	D1
Big Sunflower, *river*	B2
Bogue Chitto, *river*	B4
Buttahatchee, *river*	D2
Cat, *island*	C5
Chickasawhay, *river*	D4
Coldwater, *river*	B1
Columbus, *lake*	D2
Enid, *lake*	C1
Grenada, *lake*	C2
Gulf Island Natl. Seashore	D5
Homochitto, *river*	A4
Horn, *island*	D5
Leaf, *river*	C4
Mississippi, *river*	B1
Mississppi, *sound*	D5
Natchez Natl. Hist. Park	A4
Noxubee, *river*	D3
Okatibbee, *lake*	D5
Pascagoula, *river*	C3
Pearl, *river*	C3
Petit Bois, *island*	D5
Pickwick, *lake*	D1
Pontotoc, *mt. ridge*	D1
Ross Barnett, *reservoir*	C3
Sardis, *lake*	C1
Ship, *island*	D5
Tallahatchie, *river*	B1
Tombigbee, *river*	D1
Tupelo Natl. Battlefield	D1
Vicksburg Natl. Mil. Park	B3
Woodall, *mt*	D1
Yazoo, *river*	B2

Missouri .... page 152

Cities and Towns

	Key
Adrian	B3
Affton	H3
Albany	B1
Alton	E5
Anderson	B5
Appleton City	B3
Ashland	D3
Atherton	J4
Aurora	C5
Ava	D5
Barnett	D3
Belton	B3
Benton	G4
Bernie	G5
Bethany	B1
Birmingham	J4
Bloomfield	G5
Blue Springs	J4
Bolivar	C4
Bonne Terre	F4
Boonville	D3
Bowling Green	E2
Branson	C5
Brentwood	H2
Bridgeton	H2
Brookfield	C2
Buckner	J4
Buffalo	C4
Butler	B3
Cabool	D4
California	D3
Calverton Park	H2
Camdenton	D4
Cameron	B2
Campbell	G5
Canton	E1
Cape Girardeau	G4
Carrollton	C2
Carthage	B4
Caruthersville	G5
Cassville	C5
Cedar Hill	F3
Centerville	F4
Centralia	D2
Chaffee	G4
Charleston	G5
Chesterfield	F3
Chillicothe	C2
Claycomo	J4
Clayton	F3, H2
Clinton	C3
Columbia	D3
Concord	H3
Concordia	C3
Crestwood	H3
Creve Coeur	H2
Crocker	D4
Dellwood	H2
De Soto	F3
Des Peres	H2
Dexter	G5
Dixon	D3
Doniphan	F5
East Prairie	G5
Edina	D1
Eldon	D3
El Dorado Springs	B4
Elsberry	E2
Eminence	E4
Eureka	F3
Excelsior Springs	B2, J3
Farley	J4
Farmington	F4
Fayette	D2
Fenton	G3
Ferguson	H2
Festus	F3
Florissant	H2
Forsyth	C5
Fredericktown	F4
Fulton	D3
Gainesville	D5
Galena	C5
Gallatin	C2
Gladstone	B2, J3
Glasgow	D2
Glasgow Village	H2
Glendale	H3
Grain Valley	J4
Granby	B5
Grandview	J4
Grant City	B1
Greenfield	C4
Greenville	F4
Hamilton	C2
Hannibal	E2
Harrisonville	B3
Hartville	D4
Hayti	G5
Hazelwood	H2
Hermann	E3
Hermitage	C4
Higginsville	C2
Hillsboro	F3
Holden	C3
Hollister	C5
Houston	E4
Huntsville	D2
Independence	B2, J4
Ironton	F4
Jackson	G4
Jefferson City, *capital*	D3
Jennings	H2
Joplin	B4
Kahoka	E1
Kansas City	B2, H4
Kennett	F5
Keytesville	D2
Kingston	B2
Kinloch	H2
Kirksville	D1
Kirkwood	H3
Knob Noster	C3
Ladue	H2
Lake Lotawana	J4
Lake St. Louis	F3
Lamar	B4
Lancaster	D1
La Plata	D1
Lathrop	B2
Lawson	B2
Lebanon	D4
Lee's Summit	B3, J4
Lemay	H3
Lexington	C2
Liberty	B2, J3
Licking	E4
Lilbourn	G5
Linn Creek	D3
Linneus	C2
Louisiana	E2
Mackenzie	H3
Macon	D2
Malden	G5
Manchester	G3
Mansfield	D4
Maplewood	H3
Marble Hill	G4
Marceline	D2
Marionville	C5
Marshall	C2
Marshfield	D4
Maryland Heights	H2
Maryville	B1
Mattese	H3
Maysville	B2
Mehlville	H3
Memphis	D1
Mexico	D2
Milan	C1
Millard	D1
Moberly	D2
Monett	C5
Monroe City	E2
Montgomery City	E3
Monticello	E1
Mosby	J3
Mound City	A1
Mountain Grove	D4
Mountain View	E4
Mt. Vernon	C5
Murphy	G3
Neosho	B4
Nevada	B4
New Haven	E3
New London	E2
New Madrid	G5
Nixa	C5
North Kansas City	H4
Northwoods	H2
Oaks	J4
O'Fallon	F3
Olivette	H2
Oregon	A2
Osage Beach	D3
Osceola	C3
Overland	H2
Owensville	E3
Ozark	C4
Pacific	F3
Pagedale	H2
Palmyra	E2
Paris	D2
Park Hills	F4
Parkville	H4
Peculiar	B3
Peerless Park	G3
Perryville	G4
Pevely	F3
Piedmont	F4
Pierce City	C5
Pine Lawn	H2
Pineville	B5
Platte City	B2, H3
Plattsburg	B2
Pleasant Hill	B3
Poplar Bluff	F5
Portageville	G5
Potosi	F4
Princeton	C1
Randolph	J4
Raymore	J4
Raytown	J4
Republic	C4
Rich Hill	B3
Richland	D4
Richmond	C2
Richmond Heights	H2
Riverside	H4
Rock Hill	H2
Rock Port	A1
Rolla	E4
St. Ann	H2
St. Charles	F3, G2
St. Clair	F4
Ste. Genevieve	F4
St. James	E4
St. John	H2
St. Joseph	B2
St. Louis	F3, H2
St. Peters	F3
St. Robert	D4
Salem	E4
Salisbury	D2
Sappington	H3
Sarcoxie	B4
Savannah	B2
Scott City	G4
Sedalia	C3
Senath	F5
Seymour	D4
Shelbina	D2
Shelbyville	D2
Shirley	F4
Sikeston	G5
Slater	C2
Smithville	B2
Springfield	C4
Stanberry	B1
Steele	G5
Steelville	E4
Stockton	C4
Stoutsville	D2
Sugar Creek	J4
Sullivan	E3
Sweet Springs	C3
Tarkio	A1
Thayer	E5
Town and Country	G2
Trenton	C1
Troy	F3
Tuscumbia	D3
Union	E3
Unionville	C1
Unity Village	J4
University City	H2
Van Buren	E5
Vandalia	D2
Versailles	D3
Vienna	D3
Villa Ridge	F3
Waldron	H3
Warrensburg	C3
Warrenton	E3
Warsaw	C3
Washington	E3
Watson	A1
Waynesville	D4
Weatherby Lake	H3
Webb City	B4
Webster Groves	H2
Wellsville	E2
Wentzville	F3
West Plains	E5
Weston	B2
Willard	C4
Willow Springs	E4
Windsor	C3

Other Features

	Key
Bull Shoals, *lake*	D5
Eleven Point, *river*	E5
Fox, *river*	E1
G.W. Carver Natl. Monument	B5
Grand, *river*	B1
Harry S. Truman, *reservoir*	C3
Lake of the Ozarks, *lake*	D3
Mark Twain, *lake*	E2
Meramec, *river*	E4
Mississippi, *river*	G4
Missouri, *river*	D2
Osage, *river*	B4, D3
Ozark Natl. Scenic Riverways	E4
Platte, *river*	B2
St. Francis, *river*	F4
Stockton, *lake*	C4
Table Rock, *lake*	C5
Taum Sauk, *mt.*	F4
Thomas Hill, *reservoir*	D2
Weldon, *river*	C2

Montana .... page 153

Cities and Towns

	Key
Anaconda	D3
Baker	M3
Belgrade	E4
Big Timber	F4
Billings	H4
Boulder	D3
Bozeman	E4
Bridger	G4
Broadus	L4
Butte	D3
Chester	F1
Chinook	G2
Choteau	D2
Circle	L2
Columbus	G4
Conrad	E1
Crow Agency	J4
Cut Bank	D1
Deer Lodge	D3
Dell	D4
Dillon	D4
East Helena	E3
Ekalaka	M4
Evergreen	B1
Forsyth	K3
Fort Benton	F2
Gardiner	E4
Glasgow	K1
Glendive	M2
Great Falls	E2
Hamilton	C3
Hardin	J4
Harlowton	G3
Hathaway	K3
Havre	F1
Helena, *capital*	D3
Kalispell	B1
Lame Deer	K4
Laurel	G4
Lewistown	G2
Libby	A1
Lincoln	D2
Livingston	F4
Lolo Hot Springs	B3
Malta	J1
Miles City	L3

Key

Missoula C3
Orchard Homes B3
Philipsburg C3
Plentywood M1
Polson B2
Pony E4
Red Lodge G4
Ronan B2
Roundup H3
Rudyard F1
St. Regis A2
Scobey L1
Shelby E1
Sidney M2
Somers B1
Stanford F2
Superior B2
Terry L3
Thompson Falls A2
Townsend E3
West Yellowstone E5
Whitefish B1
Wibaux M3
Wolf Point L1

Other Features

Bighorn, river J4
Bighorn Canyon Natl. Rec. Area ...H4
Bitterroot, river B3
Bull, mts. H3
Canyon Ferry lake E3
Clark Fork, river D3
Cleveland, mt. C1
Custer Battlefield Natl. Monument ..J4
Elwell, lake E1
Flathead, lake B2
Flathead river B1
Fort Peck, lake K2
Fresno, reservoir F1
Glacier Natl. Park C1
Granite Peak, mt. D4
Granite Peak, mt. G4
Grant-Kohrs Ranch N.H.S. D3
Homer Youngs Peak, mt. ...C4
Hungry Horse, reservoir ...C1
Koocanusa, lake A1
Kootenai, river A1
Little Missouri, river M5
Madison, river E4
Marias, river E1
Middle Fork, river C1
Milk, river D1
Missouri, river G2
Musselshell, river H3
Northwest Peak, mt. A1
Pompeys Pillar Natl. Mon. ...H3
Powder, river L3
Rocky, mts. C2
St. Mary, river C1
St. Regis, river B2
Scarface Peak, mt. C2
South Fork, river C2
Swan, river C2
Teton, river E2
Tongue, river K4
Upper Missouri River Breaks N.M. ..G2
Warren Peak, mt. C4
Yellowstone, river L3
Yellowstone Natl. Park F5

Nebraska ....page 154

Cities and Towns

Ainsworth E2
Albion G3
Alliance B2
Alma E4
Ashland H3
Atkinson F2
Auburn J4
Aurora F4
Bartlett F3
Bassett E2
Beatrice H4
Beaver City E4
Bellevue J3
Benkelman C4
Blair H3
Brewster E3
Bridgeport A3
Broken Bow E3
Burwell E3
Butte G2
Center G2
Central City F3
Chadron B2
Chapman F3
Chappell B3
Clay Center F4
Columbus G3
Cozad D4
Crete H4
Dakota City H2
David City G3
Elkhorn H3
Elwood E4
Exeter G4
Fairbury G4
Falls City J4
Franklin F4
Fremont H3
Fullerton G3
Geneva G4
Gering A3
Gibbon F4
Gordon B2
Gothenburg D4
Grand Island F4
Grant C4
Greeley F3
Gretna H3
Guide Rock F4
Harrisburg A3
Harrison A2
Hartington G2
Hastings F4
Hayes Center C4
Hebron G4
Holdrege E4
Hyannis C3
Imperial C4
Kearney E4
Kimball A3
La Vista H3
Leigh G3
Lexington E4
Lincoln, capital H4
Loomis E4
Loup City F3
McCook D4
Madison G3

Milford G4
Minden F4
Mitchell A3
Mullen C2
Nebraska City J4
Neligh F2
Nelson F4
Norfolk G2
North Platte D3
Oakland H3
Ogallala C3
Omaha J3
O'Neill F2
Ord F3
Osceola G3
Oshkosh B3
Papillion H3
Pawnee City H4
Paxton C3
Pender H2
Pierce G2
Plainview G2
Plattsmouth J3
Plymouth H4
Ponca H2
Prague H3
Ravenna F3
Red Cloud F4
Rushville B2
St. Paul F3
Schuyler G3
Scottsbluff A3
Seward G4
Sidney B3
South Sioux City H2
Springfield H3
Springview E2
Stanton G3
Stapleton D3
Stockville D4
Superior F4
Sutton G4
Syracuse H4
Taylor E3
Tecumseh H4
Tekamah H3
Thedford D3
Trenton D3
Tryon D3
Valentine D2
Valley H3
Wahoo H3
Waverly H4
Wayne G2
West Point H3
Wilber H4
Wisner H3
Wymore H4
York G4

Other Features

Agate Fossil Beds N.M. A2
Arikee, river B5
Big Blue, river C3
C.W. McConaughy, lake ...C3
Calamus, reservoir E3
Calamus, river E2
Cedar, river E2
Chimney Rock Natl. Hist. Site ..A3
Elkhorn, river E2, G3
Harlan Co., lake E4
Homestead Natl. Monument ...H4
Lewis and Clark, lake G2
Little Blue, river G4
Loup, river F3
Middle Loup, river D3
Missouri, river J4
Niobrara, river B2, E2
North Loup, river C2, E3
North Platte, river B3
Pine, mt. ridge A2
Pine Ridge Natl. Rec. Area ...A2
Platte, river D4, G3
Republican, river D4
Sand, hills C3
Scotts Bluff Natl. Monument ...A3
South Fork Republican, river ...B5
South Loup, river E3

Nevada ....page 155

Cities and Towns

Alamo C3
Battle Mountain B1
Beatty B3
Boulder City C4
Carlin B1
Carson City, capital A2
Elko C1
Ely C2
Eureka C2
Fallon A2
Fernley A2
Gardnerville A2
Goldfield B3
Hawthorne A2
Henderson C4
Incline Village A2
Las Vegas C4
Laughlin C4
Lovelock A1
McGill C2
Mesquite C3
Minden A2
North Fork C1
North Las Vegas C3
Pahrump C3
Paradise C4
Pioche C3
Reno A2
Silver Peak B3
Sparks A2
Spring Creek C1
Spring Valley C3
Sun Valley A2
Tonopah B2
Virginia City A2
Wells C1
West Wendover C1
Winnemucca B1
Yerington A2
Zephyr Cove A2

Other Features

Arc Dome, mt. B2
Black Rock, desert A1
Boundary Peak, mt. A3
Colorado, river C4
Desert, valley C2
Egan, range C1
Goshute, lake C1

Grant, mts. C2
Grant, mts. A2
Great Basin B2
Great Basin Natl. Park C2
Hoover Dam C3
Hot Creek, range B2
Humboldt, river C1
Independence, mts. C1
Jefferson, mt. C1
Lake Mead Natl. Rec. Area ...C3
Marys, river C1
Matterhorn, mt. C1
Mead, lake C3
Mohave, lake C4
Monitor, range C2
Moriah, mt. C2
North Toiyabe Peak, mt. B2
Owyhee, desert B1
Owyhee, river B1
Pilot Peak, mt. C1
Pyramid, lake A1
Quinn, river B1
Ruby, mts. C1
Ruby Dome, mt. C1
Rye Patch, reservoir A1
Schell Creek, range C2
Shoshone, mts. B2
Shoshone, range B1
Smoky, valley B2
Snake, range C2
Summit, mt. B2
Tahoe, lake A2
Tobin, mt. B1
Toiyabe, range B2
Toquima, range B2
Tuscarora, mts. B1
Virgin, river C3
Walker, river A2
Wheeler Peak, mt. C2
White, river C3

New Hampshire ....page 156

Cities and Towns

Albany B3
Amherst B4
Antrim B3
Barnstead B3
Bartlett B2
Benton B2
Berlin B2
Blair B3
Bradford B3
Bretton Woods B2
Bristol B3
Candia B3
Cascade B2
Claremont A3
Concord, capital B3
Contoocook B3
Conway B2
Cornish City A3
Dalton B2
Deerfield B3
Deering B3
Derry B4
Dixville Notch B1
Dover C3
Dunbarton Center B3
Durham C3
Easton B2
Enfield A3
Epping B3
Exeter C4
Farmington B3
Franklin B3
Gilmanton B3
Glencliff B2
Gorham B2
Groveton B2
Hampstead B4
Hampton C4
Hanover A3
Haverhill A2
Henniker B3
Hillsboro B3
Hinsdale A4
Hollis B4
Hooksett B3
Hudson B4
Jackson B2
Jaffrey A4
Jefferson B2
Keene A4
Laconia B3
Lancaster B2
Lebanon A3
Littleton B2
Loudon B3
Lyman B2
Manchester B4
Meredith B3
Merrimack B4
Milan B2
Milford B4
Monroe A2
Munsonville A3
Nashua B4
Newbury A3
New Castle C3
New London B3
Newmarket C3
Newport A3
North Conway B2
Northfield B3
North Haverhill A2
North Walpole A3
North Woodstock B2
Orford A3
Ossipee B3
Pelham B4
Percy B2
Peterborough B4
Pinardville B3
Pittsfield B3
Plymouth B2
Portsmouth C3
Quaker City A3
Randolph B2
Raymond B3
Rochester C3
Rumney B3
Rye C4
Sandwich B3
Sharon A4
Shelburne B2
Silver Lake B3
Somersworth C3
South Hooksett B3
Springfield A3
Stewartstown Hollow B2

Strafford B3
Stratford B2
Suncook B3
Sutton B3
Tilton B3
Warner B3
Waterville Valley B2
Westport A4
West Rindge A4
West Stewardstown B2
Whittier B3
Willey House B2
Winchester A4
Wolfeboro B3
Woodsville A2

Other Features

Appalachian Natl. Scenic Trail A3
Blackwater, reservoir B3
Blue, mt. B2
Cabot, mt. B2
Cardigan, mt. B3
Connecticut, river A3
First Connecticut, lake B1
Franconia, notch B2
Great, bay C3
Indian, river B1
Kearsarge, mt. B3
Merrimack, river B4
Monadnock, mt. A4
Newfound, lake B3
Ossipee, lake B3
Presidential, mt. range B2
Saint-Gaudens Natl. Hist. Site ...A3
Second Connecticut, lake ...B1
Smarts, mt. A3
Squam, lake B3
Sunapee, lake A3
Swift, river B2
Umbagog, lake B2
Washington, mt. B2
White, mt. B2
Winnipesaukee, lake B3
Winnisquam, lake B3

New Jersey ....page 157

Cities and Towns

Absecon E5
Allendale E1
Allentown D3
Alloway C4
Alpine C1
Asbury Park E3
Atlantic City E5
Atlantic Highlands E3
Atsion D4
Avalon D5
Barrington B3
Basking Ridge D2
Batsto D5
Bay Point C5
Bayonne E2
Bayside C5
Beachwood E4
Beattystown D2
Beckett C4
Belle Mead D3
Belleville E2
Bellmawr B3, C4
Belmar E3
Belvidere C2
Bergenfield B1
Berkeley Heights E2
Berlin D4
Bernardsville D2
Blackwood C4
Blairstown D2
Bloomfield E2
Bogota B1
Boonton E2
Bordentown D3
Bound Brook D2
Bradley Beach E2
Brass Castle C2
Brick E3
Bridgeboro C3
Bridgeton C5
Brielle E3
Brigantine E5
Brookdale B1
Browns Mills D4
Budd Lake D2
Buena D4
Burlington D3
Butler E1
Caldwell A1
Camden B3, C4
Cape May D6
Cape May Court House D5
Carlstadt B1
Carneys Point C4
Carteret E2
Carteret B2
Cedar Grove B1
Centerton C4
Centerville D2
Chatham E2
Cherry Hill B3, C4
Chesilhurst D4
Chesterfield D3
Cinnaminson B3, C4
Clark A2
Clayton C4
Cliffside Park B1
Clifton B1
Clinton D2
Closter F2
Colesville D1
Collings Lakes D4
Collingswood B3
Colonia E2
Cranford E2
Deerfield C4
Delanco D3
Denville D2
Deptford B4
Dover D2
Dumont B1
Dunellen E2
East Brunswick E3
East Orange E2
East Rutherford B1
Eatontown E3
Edgewater F2
Edison E2
Egg Harbor City D4
Elizabeth E2
Elmer C4
Elmwood Park B1
Elwood D4

Emerson E2
Englewood C1
Englewood Cliffs C1
Englishtown E3
Erma D6
Estell Manor D5
Evesboro C3
Ewing D3
Fair Lawn B1, E2
Fairfield E2
Fairton C5
Fairview F2
Fanwood E2
Farmingdale E3
Fellowship C3
Fieldsboro D3
Flemington D3
Folsom D4
Fords E2
Forked River E4
Fort Lee F2
Franklin D1
Franklinville C4
Freehold E3
Frenchtown C2
Garfield B1
Gilford Park E4
Glassboro C4
Glen Gardner D2
Glen Ridge B2
Glendora B4
Gloucester City B3, C4
Goshen D5
Great Notch B1
Green Bank D4
Greenwich C5
Guttenberg C1
Hackensack E2
Hackettstown D2
Haddon Heights B3
Haddonfield B3
Hainesville D1
Haledon B1
Hamburg D1
Hammonton D4
Hampton D2
Harrison B2
Haworth C1
Hawthorne B1
Hedger House D2
High Bridge D2
Highland Lakes E1
Highland Park E3
Highlands F3
Hightstown D3
Hillsdale E1
Hillside B2
Hoboken E2
Hopatcong D2
Hopewell D3
Howardsville E4
Indian Mills D4
Irvington E2
Jamesburg E3
Jenkins Neck D5
Jersey City E2
Keansburg E3
Kearny B2
Kendall Park D3
Kenilworth E2
Kinnelon E2
Lakehurst E3
Lakewood E3
Lambertville D3
Lavallette E4
Lawnside B3
Lawrenceville D3
Leeds Point E5
Leisure Village E4
Leisuretowne D4
Leonardo E2
Lincroft E3
Linden E2
Lindenwold B4, C4
Linwood D5
Little Falls B1
Livingston E2
Lodi B1
Long Branch E3
Long Valley D2
Lyndhurst B2
Madison E2
Mahwah E1
Manahawkin E4
Manalapan E3
Manasquan E3
Manumuskin C5
Manville D2
Maple Shade B3, D4
Maplewood E2
Marcella D2
Margate City E5
Marlboro E3
Marlton C3, D4
Matawan E3
Mays Landing D5
Maywood B1
Medford Lakes D4
Mendham D2
Menlo Park E2
Merchantville B3
Metuchen E2
Middlesex E2
Middletown E3
Midland Park B1
Milford C2
Millburn E2
Millstone D3
Millville C5
Monmouth Beach F3
Montclair E2
Montvale E1
Moorestown C3, D4
Morris Plains E2
Morristown E2
Mountain Lakes E2
Mount Holly D4
Mount Laurel D4
Mystic Islands E4
National Park B3
Neptune City E3
Netcong D2
Newark E2
New Brunswick E3
New Egypt D3
Newfield C4
New Gretna E4
Newfoundland E1
New Providence E2
Newton D1
Normandy Beach E3
North Arlington B2
North Bergen B2

North Cape May D6
Northfield D5
North Wildwood D6
Nutley E2
Oakland E1
Oaklyn B3
Ocean City D5
Oceanport E3
Ogdensburg D1
Olivet C5
Oradell E2
Orange E2
Othello B3
Oxford C2
Palisades Park C1
Palmyra B3, C3
Paramus B1, E2
Park Ridge E1
Passaic E2
Paterson E2
Paulsboro A4, C4
Pemberton D4
Pennington D3
Penns Grove C4
Pennsauken C3
Pennsville C4
Perth Amboy E2
Phillipsburg C2
Piscataway E2
Pine Hill C4
Pitman C4
Pittstown D2
Plainfield E2
Pleasant Plains E3
Pleasantville D5
Point Pleasant E3
Pomona D5
Port Monmouth E3
Port Norris C5
Princeton D3
Princeton Junction D3
Prospect Park B1
Quinton C5
Rahway E2
Ramblewood C3
Ramsey E1
Raritan D2
Red Bank E3
Ridgefield B1
Ridgefield Park B1
Ridgewood E1
Ringoes D3
Ringwood E1
Rio Grande D6
River Edge E2
Riverside C3, D3
Riverton B3, D3
Robertsville E3
Rochelle Park B1
Rocktown D3
Roselle E2
Roselle Park E2
Rumson E3
Runnemede B4, C4
Rutherford B2
Salem C4
Sayreville E3
Seabrook C5
Sea Girt E3
Sea Isle City D5
Seaside Heights E4
Seaside Park E4
Secaucus B2
Ship Bottom E4
Shrewsbury E3
Silverton E3
Smithville D5
Somerdale C4
Somers Point D5
Somerset E2
Somerville D2
South Amboy E3
South Orange E2
South River E3
Sparta D1
Spotswood E3
Spring Lake Heights E3
Stanhope D2
Stillwater D2
Stockholm E1
Stratford B4, C4
Strathmere D5
Summit E2
Surf City E4
Sussex D1
Swedesboro C4
Teaneck B1
Tenafly C1
Tinton Falls E3
Toms River E4
Totowa B1
Trenton, capital D3
Tuckahoe D5
Tuckerton E4
Turnersville C4
Twin Rivers D3
Union E2
Union Beach E3
Union City B2
Upton E2
Vauxhall E2
Ventnor City E5
Vernon D1
Verona E2
Villas D6
Vineland C5
Voorhees C4
Waldwick E1
Wanamassa E3
Wanaque E1
Waretown E4
Warren Glen C2
Warren Grove E4
Washington D2
Washington Crossing D3
Watchung E2
Wayne A1, E2
Weehawken B2
Welchville D4
Wenonah C4
Westfield E2
West Milford E1
Westmont B3
West New York B2
West Orange E2
West Paterson B1
Westville B3
Westwood E2
Wharton D2
White Horse D3
White House Station D2
White Meadow Lake E2

NEW JERSEY–NORTH CAROLINA 187

Key
ing ... E4
wood ... D6
wood Crest ... D6
amstown ... D4
ngboro ... D3
dbine ... D5
dbridge ... E2
dbury ... B4, C4
dlynne ... B3
d Ridge ... B1
dstown ... C4
dstream ... C3
htstown ... D3
koff ... E1

er Features
e May, *point* ... D6
per, *river* ... B4
ware, *bay* ... C5
ware, *river* ... D3
ware Water Gap N.R.A. ... D1
on Natl. Hist. Site ... B2
way Natl. Rec. Area ... F3
t, *bay* ... E5
son, *river* ... C3
ristown Nat. Hist. Park ... D2
s, *lake* ... B1
an, *bay* ... E3
ue of Liberty N.M. ... B2

w Mexico ... page 158

es and Towns
ma Pueblo ... B2
mita ... B2
neda ... B2
nogordo ... C3
querque ... B2
hony ... B4
sia ... C3
ec ... B1
ard ... A3
en ... B2
nalillo ... B2
omfield ... B1
que Farms ... B2
sbad ... C3
rizozo ... C3
tral ... A3
parral ... B3
mayo ... C1
ton ... D1
vis ... D2
rales ... B2
ning ... B3
ce ... B1
a ... D3
... D3
ns ... C3
nola ... B2
ncia ... B2
ice ... D3
acres ... B3
nington ... A1
d ... D2
Sumner ... C2
up ... A2
nts ... B2
enfield ... C3
bs ... D3
ley ... A3
... D3
ez Pueblo ... B2
land ... A1
uz ... C3
Cruces ... B3
Vegas ... C2
dsburg ... A3
Alamos ... B2
Chavez ... B2
Lunas ... B2
Padillas ... B2
ington ... D3
ver Colonias ... C2
ver San Francisco Plaza ... A3
well ... C1
hill ... C3
silla ... B3
an ... B2
ra ... C2
riarty ... B2
squero ... D2
vajo ... A2
vadera ... B2
tales ... D2
esta ... C1
chos De Taos ... C1
on ... C1
erve ... A3
Rancho ... B2
well ... C3
doso ... C3
inoso ... C2
Felipe Pueblo ... B2
Miguel ... B1
Miguel ... B3
nta Fe, *capital* ... C2
nta Rosa ... C2
nto Domingo Pueblo ... B2
prock ... A1
ver City ... A3
corro ... B2
inger ... C1
nland Park ... B4
s ... C1
suque ... C2
rra Amarilla ... B1
th or Consequences ... B3
cumcari ... D2
arosa ... B3
versity Park ... B3
e Park ... C1
lencia ... B2
terflow ... A1
ni Pueblo ... A2

her Features
iquiu, *reservoir* ... B1
gres, *mt.* ... A2
tec Ruins Natl. Monument ... B1
dy, *mt.* ... C1
ndelier Natl. Monument ... B2
ack, *mt. range* ... B3
rro, *mt.* ... A3
ballo, *reservoir* ... B3
nadian, *river* ... C1
pulin Volcano N.M. ... D1
rlsbad Caverns Natl. Park ... C3
bolleta, *mt.* ... B2
erro Vista, *mt.* ... C1
aco Culture Natl. Hist. Park ... B1

Key
Cimarron, *river* ... D1
Conchas, *lake* ... C2
Contintal Divide, *mt. ridge* ... B2
Cooke's, *mt.* ... B3
Elephant Butte, *res.* ... B3
El Malpais Natl. Monument ... B2
El Morro Natl. Monument ... A2
Fort Union Natl. Monument ... C2
Gallinas, *mt.* ... C2
Gila, *river* ... A3
Gila Cliff Dwellings N.M. ... A3
Guadalupe, *mts.* ... C3
Jornada Del Muerto ... B3
Kasha-Katuwe Tent Rocks N.M. ... B2
Llano Estacado, *plateau* ... D3
Navajo, *reservoir* ... B1
Navajo Indian Res. ... A1
Pecos, *river* ... C2, C3
Pecos, *plains* ... C3
Pecos N.H.P. ... C2
Petroglyph Natl. Monument ... B2
Playas, *lake* ... A4
Reeds, *mt.* ... B3
Rio Grande, *river* ... C1
Rio Hondo, *river* ... C3
Rio Puerco, *river* ... B2
Salinas Pueblo Missions N.M. ... B2
San Andres, *mts.* ... B3
San Juan, *river* ... A1
Sangre De Cristo, *mts.* ... C1
Shiprock, *mt.* ... A1
Sierra Blanca, *mt.* ... C3
South Baldy, *mt.* ... B3
Sumner, *lake* ... C2
Taylor, *mt.* ... B2
Wheeler, *mt.* ... C1
White Sands Natl. Monument ... B3
Whitewater Baldy, *mt.* ... A3
Withington, *mt.* ... B3
Zuni, *mts.* ... A2

New York ... page 159

Cities and Towns
Adams ... H3
Adams Center ... H3
Akron ... C4
Albany, *capital* ... N5
Albion ... D4
Alden ... D5
Alfred ... E6
Allegany ... D6
Altamont ... M5
Amsterdam ... M5
Angola ... B5
Arcade ... D5
Astoria ... A3
Athens ... N6
Attica ... D5
Auburn ... G5
Avon ... E5
Bainbridge ... J6
Baldwinsville ... H4
Ballston Spa ... N4
Batavia ... D4
Bath ... F6
Beacon ... N7
Bedford-Stuyvesant ... A4
Belle Harbor ... B6
Belmont ... D6
Bensonhurst ... A4
Big Flats ... G6
Binghamton ... J6
Bloomfield ... F5
Bolivar ... D6
Boonville ... K4
Breezy Point ... A4
Brentwood ... C1
Brewerton ... H4
Bridgehampton ... E1
Brighton Beach ... A4
Broadalbin ... M4
Brockport ... E4
Brocton ... B6
Bronx ... A3, B1
Bronxville ... A2
Brooklyn ... A4, B2
Buffalo ... C5
Cairo ... M6
Calcium ... J2
Caledonia ... E5
Cambridge ... P4
Camden ... J4
Canajoharie ... L5
Canandaigua ... F5
Canarsie ... A4
Canastota ... J4
Canisteo ... E6
Canton ... K1
Carmel ... N7
Carthage ... J3
Castleton-on-Hudson ... N5
Catskill ... N6
Cayuga Heights ... H6
Cazenovia ... J5
Cedarhurst ... B4
Central Square ... H4
Chatham ... N6
Cheektowaga ... C5
Chittenango ... J4
Churchville ... E4
Clayton ... H2
Clinton ... K4
Clyde ... G4
Cobleskill ... L5
Cohoes ... N5
College Point ... D4
Colonie ... N5
Coney Island ... A4
Cooperstown ... L5
Corinth ... N4
Corning ... F6
Cortland ... H6
Coxsackie ... N6
Cuba ... D6
Dannemora ... J3
Dansville ... E5
Delhi ... L6
De Ruyter ... J5
Deposit ... K6
Dolgeville ... L4
Dover Plains ... N7
Dryden ... H6
Dundee ... G6
Dunkirk ... B6
East Atlantic Beach ... A4
Eastchester ... A2
East Hampton ... E1
East Islip ... C2
East New York ... A4
East Northport ... C1

Key
East Patchogue ... D1
Eden ... C5
Elizabethtown ... N2
Ellenville ... M7
Elmira ... G6
Elmira Heights ... G6
Elmont ... B4
Endicott ... H6
Endwell ... H6
Fairmount ... H4
Far Rockaway ... B4
Fayette ... G5
Fine ... K2
Flatbush ... A4
Flushing ... A3
Fonda ... M5
Fort Edward ... N4
Fort Plain ... L5
Franklin Sq. ... B4
Franklinville ... D6
Fredonia ... B6
Freeport ... C2
Frewsburg ... B6
Friendship ... D6
Fulton ... H4
Geneseo ... E5
Geneva ... G5
Glen Cove ... B1
Glens Falls ... N4
Gloversville ... M4
Goshen ... M7
Gouverneur ... K2
Gowanda ... C6
Granville ... P4
Gravesend ... A4
Great Neck ... B1
Greece ... E4
Greene ... J6
Greenport ... E1
Greenwich ... P4
Groton ... H5
Hamburg ... C5
Hamilton ... J5
Hampton Bays ... E1
Hancock ... K7
Harlem ... A3
Hempstead ... B2
Herkimer ... L4
Hicksville ... C1
Highland ... N7
Hilton ... E4
Holbrook ... C1
Holland ... C5
Holley ... D4
Homer ... H5
Hoosick Falls ... P5
Hornell ... E6
Horseheads ... G6
Houghton ... D6
Howard Beach ... A4
Hudson ... N6
Hudson Falls ... N4
Huntington Station ... C1
Hurley ... M7
Ilion ... K4
Inwood ... B4
Irondequoit ... E4
Ithaca ... H6
Jamaica ... B2
Jamestown ... B6
Johnson City ... J6
Johnstown ... M4
Keeseville ... P1
Kew Gardens ... A4
Kinderhook ... N6
Kingston ... N7
Lake George ... N4
Lake Placid ... M2
Lake Pleasant ... M4
Lakewood ... B6
Lansing ... H5
Larchmont ... B2
Lawrence ... B4
Le Roy ... D5
Levittown ... C1
Liberty ... L7
Lima ... E5
Lindenhurst ... C2
Little Falls ... L4
Little Valley ... C6
Livingston Manor ... L7
Livonia ... E5
Lockport ... C4
Long Beach ... B2
Long Eddy ... K7
Long Island City ... A3
Long Lake ... M3
Loon Lake ... M1
Lowville ... K3
Lynbrook ... B4
Lyons ... G4
Malone ... M1
Mamaroneck ... B2
Manhasset Hills ... B3
Manhattan ... A3
Manlius ... J4
Manorhaven ... B3
Massapequa ... C2
Massena ... L1
Mastic ... D1
Mastic Beach ... D1
Mattituck ... E4
Mayville ... A6
Mechanicville ... N5
Medina ... D4
Mexico ... H4
Middleburgh ... M5
Middleport ... D4
Middletown ... M7
Millbrook ... N7
Mineola ... B1
Mohawk ... K5
Monroe ... A1
Montauk ... F1
Monticello ... L7
Montour Falls ... G6
Moravia ... H5
Mount Kisco ... B1
Mount Morris ... E5
Mount Vernon ... B1, C5
Munnsville ... J5
Nassau ... N5
Newark ... F4
Newburgh ... M7
New City ... B1
Newfane ... C4
New Hartford ... K4
New Hyde Park ... B3
New Paltz ... M7
New Rochelle ... B3
New York ... B2
Niagara Falls ... B4

Key
Norfolk ... L1
North Collins ... C5
North Hills ... B3
North Syracuse ... H4
North Tonawanda ... C4
Norwich ... J5
Norwood ... L1
Nunda ... E5
Nyack ... B1
Oakfield ... D4
Ogdensburg ... K1
Olcott ... C4
Olean ... D6
Oneida ... J4
Oneonta ... K6
Ossining ... B1
Oswego ... H4
Owego ... H6
Oxford ... J6
Ozone Park ... A4
Painted Post ... F6
Palmyra ... F4
Pawling ... N7
Peekskill ... B1
Pelham ... A3
Pelham Manor ... A3
Penn Yan ... F5
Perry ... D5
Peru ... N1
Philadelphia ... J2
Philmont ... N6
Phoenix ... H4
Pine Bush ... M7
Plattsburgh ... P1
Port Henry ... P2
Port Jefferson ... D1
Port Morris ... A3
Port Washington ... B3
Potsdam ... L1
Poughkeepsie ... N7
Pulaski ... H3
Queens ... B4
Randolph ... C6
Ransomville ... C4
Ravena ... N6
Red Hook ... N7
Rensselaer ... N5
Rhinebeck ... N7
Richfield Springs ... L5
Riverhead ... D1
Rochester ... E4
Rockaway Point ... A4
Rocky Point ... D1
Rome ... K4
Rosendale ... M7
Rouses Point ... P1
Rye ... B2
Sackets Harbor ... H3
Sag Harbor ... E1
St. George ... A2
St. Johnsville ... L4
Salamanca ... C6
Sands Point ... B3
Saranac Lake ... M2
Saratoga Springs ... N4
Saugerties ... N6
Sayville ... D2
Schenectady ... N5
Schoharie ... M5
Scotia ... N5
Seneca Falls ... G5
Sherburne ... K5
Shortsville ... F5
Sidney ... K6
Silver Creek ... B5
Skaneateles ... H5
Sodus ... F4
Southampton ... E1
South Fallsburg ... L7
Southold ... E1
Southport ... G6
Spencerport ... E4
Springville ... C5
Stillwater ... N5
Stony Brook ... C1
Suffern ... A1
Syracuse ... H4
Throgs Neck ... A3
Ticonderoga ... P3
Troy ... N5
Trumansburg ... G5
Tupper Lake ... M2
Unadilla ... K6
Utica ... K4
Valley Stream ... B2
Victory Mills ... N4
Voorheesville ... M5
Walden ... M7
Walton ... K6
Wampsville ... J4
Wappingers Falls ... N7
Warrensburg ... N4
Warsaw ... D5
Warwick ... A1
Waterloo ... G5
Watertown ... J3
Waterville ... K5
Watkins Glen ... G6
Waverly ... G6
Wayland ... E5
Weedsport ... G4
Wellsville ... E6
West Carthage ... J3
Westfield ... A6
West Point ... N7
West Seneca ... C5
Whitehall ... P3
White Plains ... B1
Whitesboro ... K4
Whitestone ... A3
Williamsburg ... A4
Wilson ... C4
Wolcott ... G4
Woodmere ... B4
Woodstock ... M6
Yonkers ... B1
Yorktown Heights ... B1

Other Features
Adirondack, *mts.* ... L2
Adirondack Park ... M2
Appalachian Natl. Scenic Trail ... A1
Black, *lake* ... J2
Black, *river* ... K3
Cannonsville, *reservoir* ... K6
Catskill, *mts.* ... L7
Catskill Park ... L6
Cayuga, *lake* ... G5
Champlain, *lake* ... P1
Chenango, *river* ... J6
Cranberry, *lake* ... L2
Delaware, *river* ... K7

Key
Eleanor Roosevelt N.H.S. ... N7
Erie, *canal* ... J4
Erie, *lake* ... A5
Fire Island Natl. Seashore ... D2
Fishers, *island* ... F1
Fort Stanwix Natl. Monument ... K4
Galloo, *island* ... H3
Gardiners, *island* ... F1
Gateway Natl. Rec. Area ... B2
Genesee, *river* ... D6
George, *lake* ... N3
Governors Island Natl. Mon. ... A4
Great Sacandaga, *lake* ... M4
Hinckley, *reservoir* ... K4
Home of F.D.R. Natl. Hist Site ... N7
Hudson, *river* ... M3
Indian, *lake* ... M3
J.F.K. Int'l Airport ... A4
Keuka, *lake* ... F5
Long, *island* ... E1
Long, *lake* ... M3
Long Island, *sound* ... C1
Marcy, *mt.* ... N2
Martin Van Buren Natl. Hist. Site ... N6
Mettawee, *river* ... P3
Mohawk, *river* ... L5
Oneida, *lake* ... J4
Ontario, *lake* ... E3
Pepacton, *reservoir* ... L6
Piseco, *lake* ... L4
St. Lawrence, *river* ... K1
Salmon River, *reservoir* ... J3
Saratoga, *lake* ... N4
Saratoga Natl. Hist. Park ... N4
Schoharie, *reservoir* ... M6
Schroon, *lake* ... N3
Slide, *mt.* ... M7
Staten, *island* ... A2
Stony, *island* ... H3
Susquehanna, *river* ... J6
Thomas Cole Natl. Hist. Site ... N6
Thousand, *islands* ... H2
Tupper, *lake* ... L2
Unadilla, *river* ... K5
Upper Saranac, *lake* ... M2
Vanderbilt Mansion N.H.S. ... N7
West Point Military Academy ... A1
Women's Rights N.H.P. ... G5

North Carolina ... page 160

Cities and Towns
Aberdeen ... G4
Ahoskie ... L2
Albemarle ... E4
Andrews ... C8
Angier ... H3
Apex ... H3
Archdale ... F3
Asheboro ... F3
Asheville ... E7
Atlantic Beach ... M5
Ayden ... L4
Badin ... E4
Bakersville ... A2
Bayboro ... M4
Beaufort ... M5
Belhaven ... M3
Belmont ... C4
Benson ... H4
Bessemer City ... C4
Bethel ... L3
Biscoe ... F4
Black Mt. ... A3
Bladenboro ... H5
Blowing Rock ... B2
Boiling Spring Lakes ... J6
Boiling Springs ... B4
Bolivia ... J6
Boone ... B2
Brevard ... E8
Bryson City ... C8
Buies Creek ... H4
Burgaw ... K5
Burlington ... G2
Burnsville ... A3
Butner ... H2
Camden ... N2
Canton ... E7
Carolina Beach ... K6
Carthage ... G4
Cary ... H3
Chadbourn ... H6
Chapel Hill ... G3
Charlotte ... D4
Cherryville ... C4
China Grove ... D3
Clayton ... J3
Clemmons ... E3
Clinton ... J5
Coats ... H4
Columbia ... N3
Columbus ... A4
Concord ... D4
Conover ... C3
Cornelius ... D4
Creedmoor ... H2
Cullowhee ... D8
Currituck ... N2
Dallas ... C4
Danbury ... E2
Davidson ... D3
Denton ... E3
Dobson ... D2
Drexel ... B3
Dunn ... H4
Durham ... H2
E. Flat Rock ... E8
Eden ... F2
Edenton ... M2
Elizabeth City ... N2
Elizabethtown ... H5
Elkin ... D2
Elm City ... K3
Emerald Isle ... M5
Enfield ... K2
Erwin ... H4
Fairmont ... G5
Farmville ... K3
Fayetteville ... H4
Fletcher ... E8
Forest City ... B4
Four Oaks ... J4
Franklin ... C8
Franklinton ... J2
Fremont ... K3
Fuquay-Varina ... H3
Gamewell ... B3
Garner ... H3
Gastonia ... C4
Gatesville ... M2

Key
Gibsonville ... F2
Goldsboro ... K4
Graham ... G2
Granite Falls ... C3
Granite Quarry ... E3
Greensboro ... F2
Greenville ... L3
Grifton ... L4
Halifax ... K2
Hamlet ... F5
Harkers Island ... M5
Harrisburg ... D4
Havelock ... M5
Hayesville ... C8
Hays ... C2
Henderson ... J2
Hendersonville ... E8
Hertford ... N2
Hickory ... C3
High Point ... E3
Hillsborough ... G2
Hope Mills ... H5
Hudson ... C3
Huntersville ... D4
Icard ... C3
Indian Trail ... D4
Jackson ... L2
Jacksonville ... L5
Jamestown ... F3
Jefferson ... C2
Jonesville ... D2
Kannapolis ... D4
Kenansville ... K5
Kenly ... J3
Kernersville ... E2
Kill Devil Hills ... P2
King ... E2
Kings Mt. ... C4
Kinston ... K4
Kitty Hawk ... P2
La Grange ... K4
Laurinburg ... G5
Leland ... J6
Lenoir ... B3
Lewisville ... E2
Lexington ... E3
Liberty ... F3
Lillington ... H4
Lincolnton ... C4
Locust ... E4
Long Beach ... J7
Long View ... C3
Louisburg ... J2
Lumberton ... G5
Madison ... F2
Maiden ... C3
Manteo ... P3
Marion ... A3
Marshall ... E7
Marshville ... E5
Matthews ... D4
Maxton ... G5
Mayodan ... F2
Mebane ... G2
Mint Hill ... D4
Mocksville ... D3
Monroe ... D5
Mooresville ... D3
Moravian Falls ... C2
Morehead City ... M5
Morganton ... B3
Mt. Airy ... D2
Mt. Gilead ... F4
Mt. Holly ... D4
Mt. Olive ... J4
Mulberry ... C2
Murfreesboro ... L2
Murphy ... B8
Nags Head ... P3
Nashville ... K3
New Bern ... L4
Newland ... B2
Newport ... M5
Newton ... C3
Norwood ... E4
North Wilkesboro ... C2
Oxford ... H2
Pembroke ... G5
Pinehurst ... G4
Pinetops ... K3
Pineville ... D4
Piney Green ... L5
Pittsboro ... G3
Plymouth ... M3
Polkville ... B4
Raeford ... G5
Raleigh, *capital* ... H3
Randleman ... F3
Red Springs ... G5
Reidsville ... F2
River Bend ... L4
Roanoke Rapids ... K2
Robbinsville ... C8
Robersonville ... L3
Rockingham ... F5
Rockwell ... E3
Rocky Mount ... K3
Rolesville ... J3
Rose Hill ... J5
Roseboro ... H5
Roxboro ... H2
Rural Hall ... E2
Rutherfordton ... B4
Salisbury ... E3
Sanford ... G4
Sawmills ... C3
Scotland Neck ... L2
Selma ... J3
Seven Lakes ... F4
Sharpsburg ... K3
Shelby ... B4
Siler City ... G3
Smithfield ... J3
Sneads Ferry ... L5
Snow Hill ... K4
Southern Pines ... G4
Southern Shores ... P2
Southport ... J7
Sparta ... C1
Spencer ... E3
Spindale ... B4
Spring Lake ... H4
Spruce Pine ... A3
St. Pauls ... H5
Stanley ... C4
Stanleyville ... E2
Statesville ... D3
Stokesdale ... F2
Stony Point ... C3
Summerfield ... F2
Swan Quarter ... N4
Sylva ... D8

Tabor City H6
Tarboro K3
Taylorsville C3
Thomasville E3
Toast D2
Trenton L4
Troutman D3
Troy F4
Valdese B3
Wadesboro E5
Wake Forest H3
Wallace K5
Wanchese P3
Warrenton J2
Warsaw J5
Washington L3
Waxhaw D5
Waynesville D7
Weddington D4
Welcome E3
Weldon K2
Wendell J3
Wentworth F2
W. Jefferson C2
Whiteville H6
Wilkesboro C2
Williamston L3
Wilmington K6
Wilson K3
Windsor M2
Winfall N2
Wingate E5
Winston-Salem E2
Winterville L3
Winton M2
Woodfin E7
Wrightsville Beach K6
Yadkinville D2
Yanceyville G2
Zebulon J3

Other Features

Albemarle, sound N3
Alligator, lake N3
Alligator, river N3
B. Everett Jordan, lake G3
Bodie, island P3
Cape Fear, river H5
Cape Hatteras Natl. Seashore P4
Cape Lookout Natl. Seashore N5
Chatuga, river C8
Clingmans Dome, mt. C7
Dan, river F2
Deep, river F3
Falls Lake, reservoir H3
Fear, cape K7
Fontana, lake C7
Fort Raleigh Natl. Hist. Site P3
Gaston, lake K1
Great, lake L5
Great Smoky Mts. Natl. Park C7
Hatteras, cape P4
Hatteras, inlet P4
Highrock, lake E3
Hiwassee, lake B8
Hyco, lake G2
John H. Kerr, reservoir H1
Lookout, cape M5
Mattamuskeet, lake N3
Mitchell, mt. A3
Nantahala, lake C8
Neuse, river J4
Norman, lake D3
Ocracoke, inlet N4
Oregon, inlet P3
Pamlico, river M4
Pamlico, sound N3
Phelps, lake N3
Roan, mt. A2
Roanoke, river K2
Rocky, river E4
Smith, island K7
Standing Indian, mt. C8
Tar, river J2
Waccamaw, lake J6
Wright Brothers Natl. Memorial P2
Yadkin, river D2

North Dakota ....page 161

Cities and Towns

Ashley F3
Beach A3
Belcourt F1
Beulah D2
Bismarck, capital E3
Bowman B3
Cando F1
Carrington F2
Casselton H3
Cavalier H1
Center D2
Cooperstown G2
Crosby B1
Devils Lake G1
Dickinson C3
Ellendale G3
Fargo J3
Fessenden F2
Finley H2
Forman H3
Fort Yates E3
Garrison D2
Grafton H1
Grand Forks H2
Harvey F2
Hazen D2
Hettinger C3
Hillsboro H2
Jamestown G3
Lakota G1
La Moure G3
Langdon G1
Larimore H2
Linton E3
Lisbon H3
McClusky E2
Mandan E3
Mayville H2
Mohall D1
Mott C3
Napoleon F3
New Rockford F2
New Town C2
Oakes G3
Park River H1
Rolla F1
Rugby F1
Stanley C1
Stanton D2
Steele F3

Tioga C1
Towner E1
Valley City H3
Wahpeton J3
Washburn D2
Watford City B2
West Fargo J3
Williston B1

Other Features

Cannonball, river D3
Devils, lake G1
Fort Union Trading Post N.H.S. A1
Green, river B2
Heart, river C3
Intl. Peace Garden E1
James, river F2
Jamestown, reservoir G2
Knife, river C2
Knife River Indian Villages N.H.S. D2
Little Missouri, river B3
Long, lake E3
Maple, river G3, H2
Missouri, river B2
Oahe, lake E3
Pembina, river G1
Sakakawea, lake C2
Sheyenne, river E2, G2, H3
Souris, river D1
Theodore Roosevelt N.P. B2, B3
White Butte, mt. B3
Wild Rice, river H3

Ohio ....page 162

Cities and Towns

Aberdeen C8
Ada C4
Akron G3
Alliance H4
Ansonia A5
Antrim H5
Antwerp A3
Arabia F8
Arcanum A6
Archbold B2
Arlington C4
Ashland F4
Ashtabula J2
Athens F7
Aurora H3
Avon Lake F2
Baltimore E6
Barberton G3
Barnesville H6
Batavia B7
Beachwood J9
Bedford J9
Bedford Heights J9
Bellaire J5
Bellefontaine C5
Bellevue E3
Bellville E4
Berea G9
Berlin Heights F3
Bethel B8
Beverly G6
Blanchester C7
Blissfield C1
Blue Ash B9
Bluffton C4
Boardman J3
Bowling Green C3
Bradford B5
Bremen F6
Brewster G4
Bridgetown B9
Broadview Heights H10
Brook Park G9
Brooklyn H9
Brookville B6
Brunswick G3
Bryan A3
Bucyrus E4
Burton H3
Cadiz J5
Caldwell G6
Cambridge G5
Camden A6
Canal Fulton G4
Canal Winchester E6
Canfield J3
Canton G4
Cardington E5
Carey D4
Carrollton H4
Cedarville C6
Celina A4
Centerburg E5
Chagrin Falls H3
Chardon H2
Chesterhill G7
Cheviot B9
Chillicothe E7
Cincinnati A7
Circleville E6
Cleveland G2
Cleveland Heights H3
Cleves A9
Clyde E3
Coldwater A5
Columbiana J4
Columbus, capital D6
Columbus Grove B4
Congress F4
Conneaut J2
Cortland J3
Coshocton G5
Covington B5
Crestline E4
Creston G4
Crooksville F6
Cuyahoga Falls H3
Dalton G4
Dayton B6
De Graff C5
Deer Park C9
Defiance B3
Delaware D5
Delhi Hills B9
Delphos B4
Delta C2
Deshler C3
Dover H4
Dresden F5
Dublin D5
Dunkinsville D8
E. Cleveland H8
East Liverpool J4
East Palestine J4

Eaton A6
Edgerton A3
Elida B4
Elyria F3
Euclid G2
Fairborn C6
Fairfield A7
Fairport Harbor H2
Fairview Park G9
Findlay C3
Fitchville F3
Forest C4
Forest Park B8
Forestville B7
Fort Recovery A5
Fort Shawnee B4
Fostoria D3
Franklin B6
Fredericktown E5
Fremont D3
Fresno G5
Gahanna E5
Galion E4
Gallipolis F8
Gambier F5
Garfield Hts. H9
Geneva J2
Genoa D2
Georgetown C8
Germantown B6
Gibsonburg D3
Grafton F3
Granville E5
Green G4
Green Springs D3
Greenfield D7
Greenville A5
Greenwich E3
Grove City D6
Hamilton A7
Hannibal J6
Harrisburg D6
Harrison A9
Heath F5
Hebron F6
Hicksville A3
Hillsboro C7
Hiram H3
Holgate B3
Hubbard J3
Huron E3
Independence H9
Jackson F7
Jackson Center B5
Jefferson J2
Jeffersonville C6
Johnstown E5
Keene G5
Kent H3
Kenton C4
Kettering B6
Kimbolton G5
Kirtland H2
Lakewood G9
Lancaster E6
Lebanon B7
Leipsic C3
Lewisburg A6
Lexington E4
Lima B4
Lisbon J4
Lodi G3
Logan F6
London D6
Lorain F3
Loudonville F4
Louisville H4
Loveland B7
Lucasville E8
Lyndhurst J8
McArthur F7
McConnelsville G6
Macedonia J10
Macksburg H6
Madeira C9
Manchester C8
Mansfield E4
Maple Hts. J9
Marietta H7
Marion E4
Martins Ferry J5
Marysville D5
Mason B7
Massillon G4
Maumee C2
Mayfield Hts. J9
Mechanicsburg C5
Medina G3
Mentor H2
Miamitown B9
Middleburg Heights G9
Middlefield H3
Middletown B6
Milan E3
Milford B7
Millersburg G4
Minerva H4
Minster B5
Monfort Heights B9
Monroe B7
Montgomery C9
Montpelier A2
Mount Gilead E4
Mount Healthy B9
Mount Orab C7
Mount Sterling D6
Mount Vernon E5
Napoleon B3
Nelsonville F7
Newark F5
New Baltimore B9
New Boston E8
New Bremen B5
New Carlisle B6
Newcomerstown G5
New Concord G6
New Lebanon B6
New Lexington F6
New London E3
New Paris A6
New Philadelphia H5
New Richmond B8
Newtown C9
Niles J3
North Baltimore C3
North Canton H4
North College Hill B9
North Kingsville J2
North Olmsted E2
North Royalton H10
Northfield H3
Northridge C6

Norwalk E3
Norwood C9
Oak Harbor D2
Oak Hill E8
Oberlin F3
Olmsted Falls G9
Oregon D2
Orrville G4
Orwell J2
Otsego G5
Ottawa B3
Painesville H2
Parma G3
Parma Heights H9
Pataskala E6
Paulding B3
Peebles D8
Pepper Pike J9
Perrysburg C2
Pickerington E6
Piketon E7
Pioneer A2
Piqua B5
Plain City D5
Plymouth E4
Pomeroy F7
Port Clinton E2
Portsmouth E8
Powhatan Point J6
Ravenna H3
Reading B7
Reynoldsburg E6
Richmond Heights J8
Richwood D5
Ripley C8
Rittman G4
Roseville F6
Russells Point C5
Sabina C7
Sagamore Hills J9
St. Bernard C9
St. Clairsville J5
St. Henry A5
St. Louisville F5
St. Marys B4
St. Paris C5
Salem J4
Salineville J4
Sandusky E3
Selma C6
Seven Hills H9
Shadyside J6
Shaker Hts. J9
Sharonville C9
Shelby E4
Shreve F4
Sidney B5
Silverton C9
Smithville G4
Solon J9
Somerset F6
South Charleston C6
South Euclid J8
South Point E9
Springdale C9
Springfield C6
Steubenville J5
Strasburg G4
Streetsboro H3
Strongsville G3
Stryker B3
Sugarcreek G5
Sunbury E5
Sylvania C2
The Village of Indian Hill C9
Tiffin D3
Tipp City B6
Toledo C2
Troy B5
Twinsburg J10
Uhrichsville H5
University Hts. J9
Upper Sandusky D4
Urbana C5
Utica F5
Van Wert A4
Vandalia B6
Venedocia B4
Vermilion F3
Versailles B5
Wapakoneta B4
Warren J3
Warrensville Heights J9
Warsaw G5
Washington Court House D6
Waterville C2
Wauseon B2
Waverly E7
Waynesville B6
Wellington F3
Wellston E7
Wellsville J4
West Alexandria A6
West Jefferson D6
West Lafayette G5
West Liberty C5
West Milton B6
West Salem F4
West Union C8
West Unity B2
Westerville E5
Westlake G9
Weston C3
Wheelersburg E8
Wickliffe J8
Wilkesville F7
Willard E3
Williamsburg B7
Williamsport D6
Williamsport E4
Wilmington C7
Woodsfield H6
Woodville D3
Wooster G4
Wyoming C9
Xenia C6
Yellow Springs C6
Youngstown J3

Other Features

Clendening, lake H5
Cuyahoga Valley N.P. G3, H9
Dayton Aviation N.H.P. B6
Erie, lake F1
First Ladies Natl. Hist. Site H4
Hocking, river F7
Hopewell Culture N.H.P. E7
James A. Garfield N.H.P. H2
Kelleys, island E2
Mohican, river F4
Muskingum, river G6
Ohio, river J6

Salt Fork, lake H5
Sandusky, river D3
Scioto, river D4
Senecaville, lake H6
William H. Taft Natl. Hist. Site C9

Oklahoma ....page 163

Cities and Towns

Ada F3
Agawam E3
Altus C3
Alva D1
Anadarko D2
Antlers G3
Apache D3
Arapaho D2
Ardmore F3
Arkoma H2
Atoka F3
Barnsdall F1
Bartlesville F1
Beaver B1
Bethel Acres E2
Bixby G2
Blackwell E1
Blanchard E2
Boise City B4
Bristow F2
Broken Arrow G1
Broken Bow H3
Buffalo C1
Cache D3
Calera F4
Carnegie D2
Catoosa G1
Chandler F2
Checotah G2
Chelsea G1
Cherokee D1
Cheyenne C2
Chickasha E2
Choctaw E2
Chouteau G1
Claremore G1
Cleveland F1
Clinton D2
Coalgate F3
Collinsville G1
Comanche E3
Commerce H1
Cordell D2
Corum G2
Coweta G2
Cushing E2
Davis E3
Dewey F1
Drumright F2
Durant F4
Eagletown H3
Edmond E2
Elk City C2
Enid E1
Eufaula G2
Fairfax F1
Fairview D1
Farris F3
Fittstown F3
Floris B1
Forgan B1
Fort Gibson G2
Frederick D3
Geary D2
Glenpool G2
Granite C3
Grove H1
Guthrie E2
Guymon A1
Harmon C2
Hartshorne G3
Haskell G2
Healdton E3
Heavener H3
Hennessey E1
Henryetta F2
Hobart C2
Holdenville F2
Hollis B3
Hominy F1
Hooker A1
Hugo G3
Idabel H4
Inola G1
Jay H1
Jenks G1
Joy E3
Kingfisher E2
Konawa F3
Krebs G3
Laverne C1
Lawton D3
Lenora C1
Lindsay E3
Locust Grove G1
Lone Grove E3
Loveland D3
Lovell E1
McAlester G3
McCurtain H2
McKnight C2
Madill F3
Mangum C3
Manford F1
Marietta E3
Marlow E3
Medford E1
Midwest City E2
Minco E2
Moore E2
Muldrow G2
Muskogee G2
Mustang E2
Newcastle E2
Newkirk E1
Norman E2
Nowata G1
Oakhurst F1
Okeene D1
Okemah F2
Oklahoma City, capital E2
Okmulgee G2
Owasso G1
Panama H2
Pawhuska F1
Pawnee F1
Perkins E2
Perry E1
Picher H1
Piedmont E2
Ponca City E1
Poteau H2
Prague F2

Pryor Creek
Purcell
Roll
Sallisaw
Sand Springs
Sapulpa
Sayre
Seminole
Shattuck
Shawnee
Skiatook
Slaughterville
Snyder
Sparks
Spiro
Stanley
Stigler
Stillwater
Stilwell
Stratford
Stroud
Sulphur
Tahlequah
Talihina
Tecumseh G2
Tishomingo
Tonkawa
Tulsa
Turley F2
Tuttle
Vian
Vinita
Wagoner
Walters
Warner
Warren
Watonga
Watova
Waukomis
Waurika
Weatherford
Westville
Wetumka
Wewoka
Wilburton
Wilson
Woodward
Wynnewood
Yale
Yukon

Other Features

Arkansas, river
Black Mesa, mt.
Broken Bow, lake
Canadian, river
Canton, lake
Chickasaw Natl. Rec. Area
Cimarron, river
Fort Gibson, lake
Hugo, lake
Illinois, river
Kaw, lake
Keystone, lake
North Canadian, river
Oklahoma City Natl. Memorial
Oologah, lake
Ouachita, mts.
Red, river
Sooner, lake
Texoma, lake
Washita Battlefield N.H.S.
Winding Stair Natl. Rec. Area

Oregon ....page 1

Cities and Towns

Albany
Aloha
Altamont
Ashland
Astoria
Baker City
Bandon
Beaverton ....A2, C
Bend
Brookings
Brownsville
Burns
Canby ....A2, C
Canyon City
Cedar Hills
Central Point
Clatskanie
Condon
Coos Bay
Coquille
Cornelius
Corvallis
Cottage Grove
Creswell
Crowley
Dallas
Eagle Point
Elgin
Enterprise
Eugene
Florence
Forest Grove
Fossil
Four Corners ....A2, C
Glendale
Gold Beach
Grants Pass
Green ....A2, C
Gresham
Harbor
Harrisburg
Hayesville ....A2, C
Heppner
Hermiston
Hillsboro ....A2, C
Hines
Homestead
Hood River
Hubbard
Jacksonville
Jefferson
John Day
Junction City
Juntura
Keizer
Klamath Falls
Lafayette
La Grande
Lakecreek
Lake Oswego
Lakeside
Lakeview
Lebanon C

	Key
...gton	D2
...n Beach	B2
...ln City	B2
...nville	C2
...ham	E2
...ford	C3
...City	C2
...n-Freewater	E2
...aukie	A2
...alla	A2
...ument	D2
...D2	D2
...nt Angel	A2, C2
...nt Vernon	D2
...e Creek	B3
...e Point	B3
...berg	A2, C2
...port	B2
...h Bend	B3
...E3	E3
...Grove	A2
...idge	C3
...rio	F2
...gon City	A2, C2
...leton	E2
...nix	E2
...Rock	E2
...and	A2, C2
...D2	D2
...ville	D2
...er	C1
...mond	C2
...sport	B3
...D3	D3
...e River	B3
...burg	B3
...s	B3
...elens	C2
...field	D2
...n, capital	A2, B2
...a Clara	B2
...apoose	A2
...de	A2
...ca	E2
...y Cove	C3
...wood	A2
...rton	A2, C2
...igfield	D2
...ton	C3
...iver	C3
...er	B3
...erlin	C2
...et Home	C2
...nt	C2
...Dalles	C2
...A2, C2	A2, C2
...rd	A2
...mook	B2
...edo	B3
...qua	B3
...E3	E3
...ta	B2
...onia	B2
...sport	B2
...m Springs	C2
...renton	B1
...erloo	C2
...t Slope	A2
...e City	C3
...amina	B2
...onville	A2, C2
...dburn	A2
...d Village	B2

...er Features

	Key
...t, lake	D3
..., mts.	E2
...pooya, mts.	C3
...ade, range	C3
...ade-Siskiyou Natl. Mon.	C3
...kamas, river	C2
...st, mt. ranges	B2
...mbia, river	C2
...s, bay	B3
...er, lake	C3
...er Lake Natl. Park	C3
...cent, lake	C3
...ooked, river	D2
...s, lake	C3
...chutes, river	C2
...mond Peak, mt.	C3
...rhart Mtn., mt.	D3
...en Peter, lake	C3
...ney, basin	D3
...ney, lake	D3
...s, canyon	F2
...s Canyon Natl. Rec. Area	F2
...ding, river	A2
...olo, mts.	E3
...ue, river	E3
...ajawea Peak, mt.	F2
...law, river	C3
...ke, river	F2
...th Umpqua, river	B3
...ens, mts.	E3
...wberry Mt., mt.	E3
...elsen, mt.	C3
...nook, bay	C3
...mook, bay	B2
...t Creek, mts.	F3
...atilla, river	D2
...er Klamath, lake	C3
...do, river	C3
...amette, river	A2

...nnsylvania ....page 165

...es and Towns

	Key
...ion	A2
...quippa	A4

	Key
Allensville	F4
Allentown	L4
Allison Park	E6
Altoona	E4
Ambridge	A4
Annville	H5
Archbald	K2
Ardmore	M6
Arnot	G2
Ashland	J4
Athens	H2
Austin	E2
Avalon	D7
Avis	G3
Bala Cynwyd	M6
Baldwin	E7
Bangor	L4
Barnesboro	D4
Beaver	A4
Beaver Falls	A4
Beavertown	G4
Bedford	E5
Bellefonte	F4
Belleville	F4
Bellevue	D7
Bellwood	E4
Berlin	D6
Berwick	J6
Berwyn	L6
Bethel Park	A5, D7
Bethlehem	L4
Birdsboro	K5
Blairsville	C5
Blakely	K3
Bloomsburg	J4
Blossburg	G2
Boalsburg	F4
Boothwyn	L7
Boswell	C5
Boyertown	K5
Bradford	D2
Brentwood	E7
Bridgeville	D7
Brockport	D3
Brockway	D3
Brodheadsville	L4
Brooklyn	K2
Brookville	C3
Broomall	L6
Brownsville	B5
Bryn Mawr	L6
Burgettstown	A5
Butler	B4
California	B5
Cambridge Springs	A2
Canonsburg	A5
Canton	H2
Carbondale	K2
Carlisle	G5
Carnegie	D7
Carroll Valley	G6
Carrolltown	D4
Castle Shannon	E7
Catawissa	J4
Chambersburg	F6
Chelsea	L7
Chester	L6, L7
Clairton	B5
Clarion	C3
Clarks Summit	K2
Claysburg	E5
Clearfield	E3
Clifton Heights	L7
Clymer	C4
Coatesville	K6
Columbia	G5
Connellsville	B6
Conyngham	J4
Coopersburg	L5
Coraopolis	D7
Cornwall	J5
Corry	B2
Coudersport	E2
Crafton	D7
Cresson	D5
Crosby	E2
Cuddy	D7
Curwensville	D4
Dallas	K3
Danville	H4
Darby	M7
Delmont	B5
Denver	J5
Derry	C5
Dillsburg	G5
Dormont	E7
Dover	H5
Downingtown	K6
Doylestown	L5
Drexel Hill	M7
DuBois	D3
Duncannon	G5
Duquesne	E7
Dushore	J2
East Greenville	K5
East Lansdowne	M7
East Petersburg	J5
East Stroudsburg	L3
Ebensburg	D4
Eddystone	L7
Edinboro	A2
Effinwild	E6
Elizabethtown	H5
Elizabethville	H4
Elkland	F2
Ellwood City	A4
Elysburg	H4
Emlenton	B3
Emmaus	L4
Emporium	E2
Emsworth	D7
Ephrata	J5
Erie	A1
Etna	E7
Evans City	A4
Everett	E5
Exton	K5
Fayetteville	F6
Fleetwood	K5
Ford City	B4
Forest City	L2
Forest Grove	D7
Forksville	H2
Fox Chapel	E7
Freeland	K3
Freeport	B4
Galeton	F2
Gettysburg	G6
Girard	A2
Gladden	D7
Gladwyne	M6

	Key
Glenolden	M7
Glen Riddle	L7
Glen Rock	H6
Gradyville	L7
Greencastle	F6
Greensburg	B5
Greenville	A3
Gregg	D7
Grove City	A3
Hallstead	K2
Hamburg	K4
Hanover	H6
Harmarville	E6
Harrisburg, capital	H5
Harrisville	A3
Harveys Lake	J3
Haverford	M6
Havertown	M6
Hazel Hurst	D2
Hazleton	K4
Hermitage	A3
Herndon	H4
Hershey	H5
Highland	D6
Hollidaysburg	E5
Homer City	C4
Honesdale	L2
Huntingdon	E5
Hyndman	D6
Indiana	C4
Indianola	E6
Jersey Shore	G3
Jim Thorpe	K4
Johnsonburg	D3
Johnstown	D5
Kane	D2
Kennett Square	K6
King of Prussia	L6
Kingston	K3
Kittanning	B4
Kutztown	K5
Lake City	A1
Lancaster	J5
Lansdale	L5
Lansdowne	M7
Laporte	J3
Latrobe	C5
Lebanon	J5
Leechburg	B4
Lehighton	K4
Levittown	M5
Lewisburg	H4
Lewistown	F4
Ligonier	C5
Lima	L7
Linglestown	H5
Lititz	J5
Littlestown	G6
Lock Haven	G3
Lykens	H4
McCandless	A4, D6
McConnellsburg	E6
McConnellsburg	D7
McKees Rocks	D7
McKeesport	B5
Macungie	K4
Mahanoy City	J4
Manchester	H5
Manheim	J5
Mansfield	G2
Mars	A4
Martinsburg	E5
Marysville	H5
Masontown	B6
Matamoras	M3
Meadville	A2
Mechanicsburg	L3
Media	L6, L7
Mercer	A3
Mercersburg	F6
Meridian	B4
Merion	M6
Meyersdale	C6
Middleburg	G4
Middletown	H5
Midland	A4
Mifflinburg	G4
Mifflintown	G4
Mifflinville	J3
Milford	M3
Millersburg	H4
Millersville	J6
Millheim	G4
Millvale	E7
Milroy	F4
Milton	H3
Minersville	J4
Monessen	B5
Monroeville	B5, F7
Mont Alto	F6
Montgomery	H3
Montoursville	H3
Montrose	K2
Moon Run	D7
Moscow	K3
Mt. Carmel	J4
Mt. Holly Springs	G5
Mount Joy	H5
Mt. Lebanon	D7
Mt. Nebo	D6
Mt. Oliver	E7
Mt. Pleasant	B5
Mt. Pocono	L4
Mount Union	F5
Muncy	H3
Munhall	E7
Myerstown	J5
Nanticoke	J3
Nanty Glo	D5
Nazareth	L4
Nesquehoning	K4
New Bloomfield	G5
New Castle	A4
New Freedom	H6
New Holland	J5
New Kensington	B4, F6
New Oxford	G6
Newport	G5
Newtown	M5
Newtown Square	L6
Newville	G5
New Wilmington	A3
Norristown	L5
North East	A1
Northampton	L4
North Springfield	A1
Northumberland	H4
Oakmont	E7
Oil City	B3
Old Forge	K3
Orwigsburg	J4
Oxford	J7
Palmerton	K4

	Key
Patton	D4
Pen Argyl	L4
Penn Hills	F7
Penn Wynne	M6
Perkasie	L5
Philadelphia	L6, M7
Philipsburg	E4
Phoenixville	K5
Picture Rocks	H3
Pine Grove	J4
Pittsburgh	B5, E7
Pittston	K3
Pleasantville	B2
Pleasantville	D5
Point Marion	B6
Polk	B3
Port Allegany	E2
Port Matilda	E4
Portage	D5
Portland Mills	D3
Pottstown	K5
Pottsville	J4
Powell	H2
Prospect Park	L7
Punxsutawney	D4
Quakertown	L5
Quarryville	J6
Radnor	L6
Rainsburg	D6
Reading	K5
Red Lion	H6
Renovo	F3
Reynoldsville	D3
Ridgway	D3
Ridley Park	L7
Roaring Spring	E5
St. Marys	D2
Saxonburg	B4
Sayre	H2
Schnecksville	K4
Schuylkill Haven	J4
Scottdale	B5
Scranton	K3
Selinsgrove	H4
Shamokin	H4
Sharon	A3
Sharon Hill	M7
Sharpsville	A3
Sheffield	C2
Shenandoah	J4
Shippensburg	F5
Shoemakersville	K5
Shrewsbury	H6
Sinking Spring	J5
Slatington	K4
Slippery Rock	A3
Smethport	E2
Somerset	C5
Souderton	L5
South Williamsport	G3
Spring Grove	H6
Springdale	F6
Springfield	L7
State College	F4
Stewartstown	H6
Strasburg	J6
Stroudsburg	L4
Sugarcreek	B3
Sunbury	H4
Susquehanna	K2
Swarthmore	L7
Sykesville	D3
Tamaqua	K4
Tionesta	C3
Titusville	B2
Tobyhanna	L3
Towanda	J2
Tower City	H4
Tremont	J4
Trevorton	H4
Troy	H2
Tunkhannock	K2
Tyrone	E4
Union City	B2
Uniontown	B6
Upland	L7
Valley View	H4
Vandergrift	B4
Verona	E7
Village Green	L6
Villanova	L6
Warren	C2
Washington	A5
Waterford	B2
Watsontown	H3
Waymart	L2
Wayne	L6
Waynesboro	F6
Waynesburg	A6
Weatherly	K4
Wellsboro	G2
Wesleyville	A1
West Chester	K6
West Grove	K6
West Mifflin	E7
Westmont	D5
West Pike	F2
West View	E7
Whitehall	K4
White Horse	D2
Wilcox	D2
Wilkes-Barre	K3
Wilkinsburg	E7
Williamsport	G3
Willow Grove	L5
Windber	D5
Womelsdorf	J5
York	H6
York Springs	G5
Youngsville	C2
Zelienople	A4

Other Features

	Key
Allegheny, reservoir	D2
Allegheny, river	D3
Allegheny Natl. Rec. Area	D2
Allegheny Portage Railroad N.H.S.	D5
Appalachian, mts.	F5
Clarion, river	C4
Conemaugh, river	C6
Davis, mt.	C6
Delaware, river	L2
Delaware Water Gap N.R.A.	M3
Eisenhower Natl. Hist. Site	G6
Erie, lake	A1
Friendship Hill Natl. Hist. Site	B6
Gettysburg Natl. Mil. Park	G6
Johnstown Flood Natl. Memorial	D5
Juniata, river	F5
Lehigh, river	K3
Ohio, river	A4
Presque Isle, island	A1

	Key
Raystown, lake	E5
Schuylkill, river	K5
Steamtown Natl. Hist. Site	K3
Susquehanna, river	J2
Tioga, river	G2
Valley Forge Natl. Hist. Park	L5

Rhode Island ....page 166

Cities and Towns

	Key
Adamsville	F4
Allenton	D4
Alton	B5
Anthony	C4
Arcadia	B4
Ashaway	B5
Ashton	A6
Avondale	A6
Barrington	E3
Berkeley	A5
Bradford	B5
Bristol	E3
Carolina	C5
Central Falls	C5
Charlestown	C5
Chepachet	B3
Clayville	B3
Coventry Center	C3
Cranston	D3
Cumberland Hill	D2
Diamond Hill	D2
Dunn Corner	B5
East Greenwich	D4
East Providence	C4
Exeter	C4
Fiskeville	C3
Foster Center	B3
Galilee	C5
Glendale	C5
Green Hill	C5
Greenville	C3
Hamilton	D4
Harmony	C3
Harrisville	B2
Hope	C3
Hope Valley	B5
Hopkinton	B5
Jamestown	D5
Jerusalem	C5
Kingston	C5
Little Compton	E4
Lonsdale	D2
Matunuck	C5
Middletown	E4
Moosup Valley	B3
Narragansett Pier	D5
Newport	E5
Nooseneck	C4
North Foster	B2
North Providence	C3
North Scituate	C3
Pascoag	B2
Pawtucket	C5
Pawtuxet	C5
Perryville	C5
Plum Point	D4
Point Judith	D5
Portsmouth	E4
Providence, capital	D3
Prudence	C4
Quidnick	C3
Quonochontaug	B6
Rice City	B3
Riverside	D3
Rockville	B4
Rumford	D3
Sakonnet	E5
Saunderstown	D4
Saylesville	C5
Shannock	C5
Slatersville	C1
Slocum	C4
South Foster	B3
Spragueville	C3
Tarkiln	C3
Tiverton	E4
Usquepaug	C5
Valley Falls	D2
Wakefield	C5
Wallum Lake	B2
Warren	D3
Warwick	C4
Washington	C4
Watch Hill	A6
Weekapaug	B6
West Barrington	D3
Westerly	C5
West Glocester	B2
West Kingston	C5
West Warwick	C4
Woonsocket	C1
Wyoming	B4

Other Features

	Key
Block, island	C7
Block Island, sound	B6
Mt. Hope, bay	E4
Narragansett, bay	D4
Rhode Island, sound	E5
Roger Williams Natl. Mem.	D3
Sakonnet, river	E4
Scituate, reservoir	C3
Touro Synagogue N.H.S.	E5

South Carolina ....page 167

Cities and Towns

	Key
Abbeville	B2
Aiken	C3
Allendale	C3
Anderson	B2
Andrews	E3
Bamberg	C3
Barnwell	C3
Batesburg-Leesville	C3
Beaufort	D4
Belton	B2
Belvedere	C3
Bennettsville	E2
Bishopville	D2
Blacksburg	C1
Blackville	C3
Boiling Springs	C1
Brownsville	C5
Buffalo	C1
Burton	D4
Calhoun Falls	B2
Camden	D2
Cayce	C3
Central	B2

	Key
Charleston	E4
Cheraw	E2
Chester	C2
Chesterfield	D2
Clemson	B2
Clinton	C2
Clover	C1
Columbia, capital	C2
Conway	C1
Cowpens	C1
Darlington	E2
Denmark	C3
Dentsville	D2
Dillon	E2
Easley	B2
Edgefield	C3
Elgin	C2
Enoree	C2
Estill	C4
Fairfax	C4
Florence	E2
Folly Beach	E4
Forest Acres	D2
Foreston	D3
Fort Mill	D1
Fountain Inn	B2
Furman	C4
Gaffney	C1
Garden City	F3
Georgetown	E3
Gifford	C4
Gloverville	C3
Goose Creek	E3
Great Falls	D2
Greeleyville	E3
Greenville	B2
Greenwood	B2
Greer	B2
Hampton	C4
Hanahan	E4
Hardeeville	C4
Harleyville	D3
Hartsville	D2
Hickory Grove	C2
Hickory Grove	F3
Hilda	C3
Hilton Head Island	D4
Holly Hill	D3
Hollywood	D4
Honea Path	B2
Horrel Hill	D1
Inman	C1
Irmo	C2
Isle of Palms	E4
Jackson	C3
Jefferson	D2
Joanna	C2
Johnsonville	E3
Johnston	C3
Kershaw	D2
Kiawah Island	E4
Kingstree	E3
Kline	C3
Ladson	D4
Lake City	E3
Lancaster	D2
Landrum	B1
Lane	E3
Latta	E2
Laurel Bay	D4
Laurens	C2
Lexington	C3
Liberty	B2
Little River	F3
Little Rock	E2
Loris	F2
Lugoff	D2
Lyman	B2
Lynchburg	D2
McBee	D2
McClellanville	E3
McCormick	B3
Manning	D3
Marion	E2
Mauldin	B2
Mayesville	D3
Mayo	C1
Moncks Corner	D3
Mt. Pleasant	E4
Mullins	E2
Murrells Inlet	E3
Myrtle Beach	F3
Neeses	C3
New Ellenton	C3
Newberry	C2
Nichols	E2
Ninety Six	C2
North Augusta	C3
North Charleston	E4
North Myrtle Beach	F3
Norway	C3
Olanta	E3
Olar	C3
Orangeburg	D3
Pacolet	C2
Pacolet Mills	C2
Pageland	D2
Pamplico	E3
Patrick	D2
Pelion	C3
Pendleton	B2
Pickens	B2
Piedmont	B2
Pinewood	D3
Pomaria	C2
Port Royal	D4
Ravenel	D4
Red Bank	C3
Ridgeland	C4
Ridgeville	D3
Ridgeway	D2
Rock Hill	C1
Roebuck	C2
Rowesville	C3
Ruby	D2
St. George	D3
St. Matthews	D3
Salley	C3
Salters	E3
Saluda	C3
Santee	D3
Seneca	B2
Simpsonville	B2
Socastee	F3
Society Hill	E2
South Congaree	C3
Spartanburg	C2
Springfield	C3
Starr	B2
Stuckey	E3

Key

Summerville D3
Sumter D3
Surfside Beach F3
Swansea C3
Sycamore C3
Taylors B2
Timmonsville E2
Travelers Rest B2
Trenton C3
Turbeville D3
Union C2
Varnville C4
Wagener C3
Walhalla A2
Walterboro D4
Ware Shoals B2
Westminster A2
Whitmire C2
Williamston B2
Williston C3
Winnsboro C2
Woodruff B2
Yemassee D4
York C2

Other Features

Bull, island E4
Bulls, bay E4
Cape, island E3
Congaree Swamp N.M. D3
Cowpens Natl. Bfld. C1
Edisto, river D3
Fort Sumter Natl. Monument .. E4
Greenwood, lake C2
Hartwell, lake B2
J. Strom Thurmond, lake B3
Keowee, lake B2
Kings Mt. Natl. Mil. Park C1
Long, bay F3
Lynches, river D2
Marion, lake D3
Monticello, reservoir C2
Moultrie, lake D3
Murray, lake C2
Ninety Six Natl. Hist. Site B2
North, island E3
Port Royal, sound D4
Russell, lake B2
St. Helena, sound D4
Saluda, river C2
Santee, river D2
Savannah, river C3
South, island E3
The Grand Strand F3
Wateree, lake D2
Wateree, river D2

South Dakota .... page 168

Cities and Towns

Aberdeen F1
Alexandria G3
Armour F3
Belle Fourche A2
Beresford H3
Black Hawk A2
Box Elder A2
Britton G1
Brookings H2
Burke E3
Canton H3
Chamberlain E3
Cherry Creek C2
Clark G2
Clear Lake H2
Custer A3
Deadwood A2
Dell Rapids H3
De Smet G2
Dupree C1
Elk Point H4
Faulkton E1
Flandreau H2
Fort Pierre D2
Freeman G3
Gettysburg E1
Hartford H3
Highmore E2
Hot Springs A3
Howard G2
Huron F2
Ipswich E1
Kadoka C3
Lake Andes F3
Lead A2
Lemmon B1
Lennox G3
Leola F1
Madison G2
Martin B3
Milbank H1
Miller E2
Mitchell G3
Mobridge D1
Murdo D3
Onida D2
Parker G3
Parkston G3
Philip C2
Pierre, capital D2
Pine Ridge B3
Plankinton F3
Platte F3
Rapid City A2
Redfield F2
Rosebud D3
Salem G3
Selby D1
Sioux Falls H3
Sisseton G1
Spearfish A2
Sturgis A2
Timber Lake C1
Tyndall G4
Vermillion H4
Volga H2
Wagner F3
Watertown G2
Webster G1
Wessington Springs F2
White River D3
Winner E3
Woonsocket F2
Wounded Knee B3
Yankton G4

Other Features

Andes, lake F3
Angostura, reservoir A3
Bad, river C2
Badlands Natl. Park B3

Key

Belle Fourche, reservoir A2
Belle Fourche, river A2
Big Sioux, river H1
Big Stone, lake H1
Black, hills A2
Bois de Sioux, river H1
Cheyenne, river C2
Francis Case, lake F3
Grand, river C1
Harney Peak, mt. A3
James, river F1
Jewel Cave Natl. Monument A3
Keya Paha, river D3
Lewis and Clark, lake G4
Little Missouri, river A1
Little White, river D3
Minuteman Missile N.H.S. .. B3, C3
Missouri, river E3
Moreau, river B1
Mount Rushmore Natl. Memorial . A3
North Fork Grand, river B1
Oahe, lake D2
Pine, ridge B3
Sharpe, lake E2
South Fork Grand, river A1
Traverse, lake H1
Vermillion, river G3
Waubay, lake G1
White, river D3
Whitewood, river G2
Wind Cave Natl. Park A3

Tennessee .... page 169

Cities and Towns

Adamsville E4
Alamo C3
Alcoa P3
Algood L2
Altamont L4
Arlington B4
Ashland City G2
Athens M4
Bartlett B4
Baxter K2
Bells C3
Benton N4
Bethel Springs D4
Bethpage J2
Blaine P2
Blountville S1
Bluff City S1
Bolivar D4
Brentwood H2
Bristol S1
Brownsville C3
Bruceton E2
Buffalo Valley K2
Byrdstown L1
Camden E2
Campaign K3
Carthage K2
Caryville N2
Celina K1
Centerville G3
Charlotte G2
Chattanooga L4
Church Hill R1
Clarksville G1
Cleveland M4
Clinton N2
Collegedale L4
Collierville B4
Columbia G3
Conasauga M4
Cookeville L2
Covington B3
Cowan J4
Crossville L3
Dandridge Q2
Dayton L4
Decatur M3
Decaturville E3
Dechend J4
Dickson G2
Dover F2
Dresden D2
Dunlap L4
Dyer C2
Dyersburg C2
East Ridge L4
Elizabethton S2
Englewood N4
Erin F2
Erwin S2
Estill Springs J4
Etowah M4
Fairfield Glade M2
Farragut N3
Fayetteville H4
Forest Hills H2
Frankewing H3
Franklin H3
Gainesboro K2
Gallatin J2
Gatlinburg Q3
Germantown B4
Gleason D2
Goodlettsville H2
Granville K2
Graysville L4
Greenbrier H2
Greenfield D2
Grimsley M2
Gruetli-Laager K4
Halls C3
Halls Crossroads P2
Hampshire G3
Harriman M3
Hartsville J2
Henderson D4
Hendersonville H2
Humboldt D3
Huntingdon E3
Huntsville N2
Jacksboro N2
Jackson M2
Jamestown M2
Jasper K4
Jefferson City Q2
Jellico N1
Johnson City S2
Jonesborough S2
Karns N3
Kenton C2
Kingsport R1
Kingston M3
Kingston Springs G2
Knoxville P3
Lafayette J1
La Follette N2

Key

Lake City N2
Lakewood H2
La Vergne H2
Lawrenceburg G4
Lebanon J2
Lenoir City N3
Lewisburg H4
Lexington E3
Linden F3
Livingston L2
Loretto G4
Loudon N3
Lynchburg J4
McEwen F2
McKenzie D2
McKinnon F2
McMinnville K3
Madisonville N3
Manchester J4
Martin D2
Maryville P3
Mascot P2
Maynardville P2
Medon D4
Memphis A4
Middleton D4
Milan D3
Millersville H2
Milligan College S2
Millington B4
Monterey L2
Morristown Q2
Mosheim R2
Mountain City T1
Mount Juliet H2
Mount Pleasant G3
Munford B4
Murfreesboro J3
Nashville, capital H2
Newbern C2
New Johnsonville F2
New Tazewell P2
Nolensville H3
Norris N2
Oak Hill H2
Oak Ridge N2
Oliver Springs N2
Oneida M2
Overall J3
Paris E2
Parsons E3
Pegram G2
Pigeon Forge P3
Pikeville L3
Portland H1
Powell N2
Pulaski G4
Reagan E3
Red Bank L4
Ridgely C2
Ripley B3
Rockwood M3
Rogersville R2
Rutherford D2
Rutledge Q2
Savannah E4
Selmer D4
Sevierville P3
Sewanee K4
Shelbyville J4
Signal Mountain L4
Smithville K3
Smyrna H3
Sneedville Q1
Soddy-Daisy L4
Somerville C4
South Fulton D2
South Pittsburg K4
Sparta L3
Spencer L3
Spring City M3
Spring Hill H3
Springfield H1
Stanton C4
Surgoinsville R2
Sweetwater N3
Taft H4
Tazewell P2
Tellico Plains N4
Tennessee Ridge F2
Tiptonville B1
Tracy City K4
Trenton D3
Trimble C2
Tullahoma J4
Tusculum R2
Union City C2
Wartburg M2
Waverly F2
Waynesboro F4
Westmoreland J1
White House H2
White Pine Q2
Whitwell K4
Winchester J4
Woodbury J3

Other Features

Andrew Johnson Natl. Hist. Site ... R2
Appalachian, mts. N4
Appalachian Natl. Scenic Trail . Q3
Barkley, lake F1
Big South Fork Natl.
 River and Rec. Area M1
Center Hill, lake K3
Cherokee, lake Q2
Chickamauga & Chattanooga
 Natl. Mil. Park L5
Chickamauga, lake M3
Clinch, river N2
Clingmans Dome, mt. Q3
Cumberland, river G2
Dale Hollow, lake L1
Douglas, lake Q3
Duck, river H3
Great Smoky, mts. P3
Great Smoky Mts. Natl. Park Q3
Holston, river R2
Kentucky, lake F2
Mississippi, river B3
Norris, lake P2
Roan, mt. S2
Shiloh Natl. Mil. Park D4
Tennessee, river E5, K5
Watts Bar, lake M3
Woods, reservoir J4

Texas .... page 170

Cities and Towns

Abernathy F2

Key

Abilene H3
Addison C1
Alamo Heights B7
Albany H3
Algoa F9
Alice J8
Alpine D5
Alvin M6
Amarillo B9
Anahuac N6
Anderson M5
Andrews E3
Angleton M6
Anson H3
Anthony A3
Aransas Pass K8
Archer City H2
Arlington L3
Asherton H7
Aspermont G2
Atascosa A7
Athens M3
Atlanta N2
Austin, capital K5
Avondale A1
Azle K3
Bacliff G9
Baird H3
Balch Springs C2
Balcones Heights A7
Ballinger H4
Bandera H6
Barrett F8
Bastrop K5
Batesville H7
Bay City M7
Bayou Vista G10
Baytown N6
Beaumont N5
Beaumont Place F8
Beaver C8
Bedford B2
Beeville K7
Bellaire E8
Bellmead K4
Belton K4
Benavides J8
Benbrook A2
Benjamin H2
Bergheim A6
Big Lake F4
Big Spring F3
Bishop K8
Boerne J6
Bogata M2
Bonham L2
Borger C9
Bovina E1
Bowie K2
Bracken B6
Brackettville G6
Brady H4
Breckenridge J3
Brenham L5
Briar A1
Bridge City P5
Bridgeport K2
Brookshire M6
Brookside Village F9
Brownfield E2
Brownsville K10
Brownwood J4
Bryan L5
Buckingham C1
Buena Vista B7
Buffalo L4
Bulverde A6
Buna P5
Bunker Hill Village E8
Burkburnett J1
Burleson A3
Burleson K3
Burnet J5
Caldwell L5
Cameron L5
Canadian D9
Canton M3
Canutillo A4
Canyon B9
Carrizo Springs H7
Carrollton B1
Carthage N3
Castle Hills A6
Cedar Hill J6
Cedar Park K5
Center N4
Centerville M4
Chandler M3
Channelview F8
Channing B9
Childress G1
Chocolate Bayou F10
Cisco J3
Clarendon C10
Clarksville M2
Claude C9
Cleburne K3
Cleveland M5
Clifton K4
Cloverleaf F8
Clute M6
Cockrell Hill B2
Coldspring M5
Coleman H4
College Station L5
Colleyville A2
Colorado City G3
Columbus L6
Comanche J4
Combine D2
Commerce L2
Conroe M5
Converse B6
Cooper M2
Copperas Cove K4
Corpus Christi K8
Corsicana L4
Crandall H7
Crockett M4
Crosby F8
Crosbyton F2
Crowell H2
Crowley A3
Crystal City H7
Cuero K6
Daingerfield N2
Dalhart B8
Dallas L3
Dalworthington Gardens B2
Danbury F10

Key

Dayton N5
Decatur K2
Deer Park F8
Del Rio G6
Denison L2
Denton K2
Denver City E3
De Soto L3
Devine J6
Diboll N4
Dickens G2
Dickinson F9
Dilley H7
Dimmitt E1
Dublin J3
Dumas B9
Duncanville B2
Eagle Lake L6
Eagle Pass G7
Eastland J3
Eden H4
Edgecliff A3
Edinburg J9
Edna L7
El Campo L6
Eldorado G5
El Paso A4
Electra J1
Elgin K5
Elsa J9
Emory M3
Ennis L3
Euless B2
Everman A3
Fabens A4
Fair Oaks Ranch A6
Fairfield L4
Falfurrias J8
Farmers Branch B1
Farwell D1
Ferris C3
Flatonia K6
Floresville J6
Floydada F2
Forest Hill A2
Fort Davis D5
Fort Stockton E5
Fort Worth K3
Franklin L4
Fredericksburg J5
Freeport M7
Freer J8
Friendswood F9
Gail F3
Gainesville L2
Galena Park F8
Galveston N6
Ganado L6
Garden City F4
Garden Ridge B6
Gardendale B7
Garland C2
Gatesville K4
George West J7
Georgetown K5
Germann C3
Giddings L5
Gilmer N3
Gladewater N3
Glen Rose K3
Glenn Heights B3
Goldthwaite J4
Goliad K7
Gonzales K6
Graham J2
Granbury K3
Grand Prairie B2
Grand Saline M3
Grapeland M4
Grapevine B1
Grapevine K3
Greenville L2
Groesbeck L4
Groves P6
Groveton M4
Guthrie G2
Hallettsville L6
Haltom City A2
Hamilton J4
Hamlin G3
Harker Heights K4
Harlingen K9
Haskell H2
Hearne L5
Hebbronville J8
Helotes A6
Hemphill P4
Hempstead L5
Henderson N3
Henrietta J2
Hereford B10
Hewitt K4
Hico J4
Hidalgo J9
Highland Park C2
Highlands F8
Hillsboro K3
Hitchcock F9
Hitchcock M6
Hollywood Park A6
Hondo H6
Honey Grove M2
Hubbard L4
Huntsville M5
Hurst A2
Hutchins C2
Idalou F2
India C3
Ingleside K8
Iowa Park J2
Irving B2
Jacinto City F8
Jacksboro J2
Jacksonville M4
Jasper P5
Jayton G2
Jefferson N3
Jersey Village E8
Johnson City J5
Jourdanton J7
Juliff F9
Junction H5
Karnes City K7
Katy M6
Kaufman L3
Kermit D4
Kerrick K5
Kerrville H5
Kilgore N3
Killeen K4

Key

Kingsland J5
Kingsville K8
Kirby B7
Kirbyville P4
Knox City H2
Kountze P5
La Grange K6
Lake Jackson M6
Lakehills A6
La Marque F9
Lamesa F2
Lampasas J4
Lancaster C2
La Porte F8
La Pryor H7
Laredo H8
League City F9
Leon Springs A6
Leon Valley A7
Levelland E2
Lewisville B1
Liberty N5
Linden N2
Lipscomb C9
Littlefield E1
Live Oak B6
Livingston N5
Llano J5
Lockhart K6
Lockney F2
Longview N3
Lubbock F2
Lufkin N4
Luling K6
Lumberton P5
Mabank L3
McAllen J9
McCamey F4
Macdona A7
McKinney L2
Madisonville M5
Mangus Corner C3
Mansfield B2
Manvel F10
Marble Falls J5
Marfa C5
Marlin L4
Marshall N3
Mason H5
Matador G2
Mathis K8
Memphis C10
Menard H5
Mentone D4
Meridian K4
Merkel H3
Mertzon G4
Mesquite C2
Mexia L4
Miami C9
Midland F4
Midlothian K3
Mineola M3
Mineral Wells K3
Mission J9
Missouri City E9
Monahans E4
Mont Belvieu N5
Montague K2
Morgans Point F8
Morton E1
Moss Bluff F8
Mt. Houston E8
Mt. Pleasant N2
Mt. Vernon M2
Muleshoe E1
Munday H2
Murphy C1
Nacogdoches N4
Nassau Bay F9
Navasota L5
Nederland P6
New Berlin B6
New Boston N2
New Braunfels J6
Newton P4
Nixon K6
Nocona K2
North Houston E8
North Richland Hills A2
Odessa E4
Olmos Park A7
Olney J2
Olton E1
Orange P5
Ovilla B3
Ozona G5
Paducah G1
Paint Rock H4
Palacios L7
Palestine M4
Palo Pinto K3
Pampa C10
Panhandle C9
Pantego B2
Paris M2
Parita A3
Parker C1
Pasadena F8
Pearland F9
Pearsall H7
Pecos D4
Pelican Bay A1
Perryton C9
Pharr J9
Pilot Point L2
Pittsburg N2
Plains E2
Plainview F2
Plano C1
Pleasanton J7
Port Arthur P6
Port Bolivar N6
Port Isabel K9
Portland K8
Port Lavaca L7
Post F2
Poteet J7
Premont J8
Presidio C6
Quanah H1
Quitman M3
Ranger J3
Rankin F4
Raymondville K9
Red Oak C3
Refugio K7
Reno A1
Richardson C1
Richland Hills A2

Key

...mond M6
...Grande City I9
....A1
...ert Lee G4
...oke K4
...stown K8
....G3
...kdale L5
...ksprings G5
...kwall L3
....H9
...kport K7
...Point E9
...coe M6
...enberg M6
...aron E9
....G3
...an G3
...nd Rock K5
...lett C2
....M4
...al H6
....H6
...se C1
...edwig B7
...Angelo G4
...Antonio J6
...Augustine N4
...Benito K9
...derson E5
...Diego J8
...dy Point E9
...ger K2
...Geronimo A6
...Leon G9
...Marcos K6
...Saba J4
...som Park A2
...ta K8
...uma E8
...erton B7
...ers B6
...umansville C6
...brook F9
...drift L7
...goville E3
...graves E3
...ly L6
...uin K6
...arkana N2
...as City N6
...Woodlands M5
...mpsons E9
...ee Rivers J7
...ockmorton H2
....J7
...mball M5
....M5
...phy Club F1
....F1
...versal City J6
...versity Park C2
...alde H6
....H6
...a Alstyne L2
....C4
...n Horn C4
...ga B9
...a H1
...toria L7
...or N5
...a A7
...n Ormy A7
...co K4
...skom N3
...tauga A2
...xahachie L3
...atherford K3
...bster F9
...llington D10
...slaco K9
...st K4
...st Columbia M6
...st Odessa E4
...stover Hills A2
...st University Place E8
...sworth A2
...arton L6
...eatland A3
...eeler D9
...ite Settlement A2
...itesboro L2
...chita Falls J2
...lis M5
...ls Point L3
....C3
...ndcrest B6
...nie N3
...nsboro M3
...fforth F2
...odville N5
...odway K4
...lie D1
...kum K6
...pata H9
...ehl B7

Key

Other Features

Alibates Flint Quarries N.M. B9
Amistad, *reservoir* F6
Amistad Natl. Rec. Area G6
Balcones, *escarpment* A6
Big Bend Natl. Park D6
Big Thicket Natl. Preserve N5
Black, *mt.* C9
Canadian, *river* C9
Cathedral, *mt.* D5
Chamizal Natl. Mem. A4
Chinati Peak, *mt.* C6
Dallas-Fort Worth Intl. Airport B2
Davis, *mts.* C5
Eagle Peak, *mt.* B5
Edwards, *plateau* G5
Emory Peak, *mt.* D6
Falcon, *reservoir* H9
Fort Davis Natl. Hist. Site D5
Galveston, *bay* O2
Galveston, *island* N6
Guadalupe, *mt.* C4
Guadalupe Mts. Natl. Park C4
Guadalupe Peak, *mt.* C4
Kemp, *lake* H2
Lake Meredith Natl. Rec. Area C9
Livermore, *mt.* C5
Livingston, *lake* M5
Lyndon B. Johnson N.H.P. J5
Meredith, *lake* J7
Nueces, *river* H4
O.H. Ivie, *lake* H4
Padre Island Natl. Seashore K8
Pecos, *river* E4
Pelican, *island* G9
Red, *river* H1
Red Bluff, *lake* D4
Rio Grande, *river* F6
Sabine, *lake* P6
Sabine, *river* P5
Sam Rayburn, *reservoir* N4
Santiago Peak, *mt.* D6
Sierra Del Carmen, *mt.* D6
Stockton, *plateau* E5
Toledo Bend, *reservoir* P4

Utah .....page 171

Cities and Towns

American Fork C3
Beaver B5
Bicknell C5
Blanding E6
Bluffdale C3
Bountiful C3
Brigham City C2
Castle Dale D4
Cedar City A6
Centerville C3
Clearfield B2
Coalville C2
Cottonwood Heights B3
Delta B4
Draper C3
Duchesne D3
East Carbon D4
Enoch A6
Ephraim C4
Ferron C4
Fillmore B5
Garland B2
Grantsville B3
Gunnison C4
Heber City C3
Helper D4
Hildale A6
Huntington D4
Hurricane A6
Hyrum C2
Ivins A6
Junction B5
Kanab B6
Layton C2
Lehi C3
Lewiston C2
Loa C5
Logan C2
Long Valley Junction B6
Maeser E3
Magna B3
Manila E3
Manti C4
Mapleton C3
Moab E5
Monroe C5
Monticello E6
Morgan C2
Mount Pleasant C4
Murray C3
Myton D3
N. Salt Lake C3
Nephi C4
North Ogden C2
Ogden C2
Orangeville C4
Orem C3
Panguitch B6
Parowan B6
Payson C3
Plain City B2
Pleasant Grove C3
Price D4
Provo C3
Randolph C2
Richfield B5
Richmond C2
Riverton C3
Roosevelt D3
Roy B2
St. George A6
Salem C3
Salina C4
Salt Lake City, *capital* C3
Sandy C3
Santa Clara A6
Santaquin C3
Smithfield C2
South Jordan C3
Spanish Fork C3
Springville C3
Sugarville B4
Tooele B3
Tremonton B2
Vernal E3
Washington A6
Wellington D4
West Jordan C3
West Valley City C3
Willard B2

Key

Other Features

Abajo Peak, *mt.* E6
Arches Natl. Park E5
Bear, *lake* C2
Bear, *river* C2
Beaver, *river* B5
Bonneville Salt Flats A3
Bruin Point, *mt.* D4
Bryce Canyon Natl. Park B6
Canyonlands Natl. Park E5
Capitol Reef Natl. Park C5
Cedar Breaks Natl. Monument B6
Colorado, *river* E5
Delano Peak, *mt.* B5
Deseret Peak, *mt.* B3
Dinosaur Natl. Monument E3
Dutton, *mt.* B5
Escalante, *river* C6
Flaming Gorge, *reservoir* E2
Flaming Gorge Natl. Rec. Area E2
Frisco Peak, *mt.* A5
Glen Canyon Natl. Rec. Area D6
Golden Spike Natl. Hist. Site B2
Grand Staircase-Escalante N.M. C6
Great, *basin* A4
Great Salt, *lake* B2
Great Salt Lake, *desert* A3
Green, *river* D4
Heliotrope, *mt.* C4
Henry, *mts.* D6
Ibapah Peak, *mt.* A4
Kings Peak, *mt.* D3
Marsh Peak, *mt.* E3
Marvine, *mt.* C5
Monument, *valley* D6
Natural Bridges Natl. Monument E6
Navajo, *mt.* E6
Navajo Indian Res. E6
Nebo, *mt.* C4
Paria, *river* C6
Pavant, *range* B5
Peale, *mt.* E5
Pennell, *mt.* D6
Powell, *lake* D6
Price, *river* D4
Rainbow Bridge Natl. Monument D6
Salt Marsh, *lake* A4
San Juan, *river* D6
San Rafael, *river* D4
Sevier, *desert* B4
Sevier, *river* A5
Strawberry, *river* D3
Swasey Peak, *mt.* A4
Timpanogos Cave N.M. C3
Uinta, *mts.* D3
Utah, *lake* C3
Wasatch, *plateau* C5
White, *river* E3
Zion Natl. Park A6

Vermont .....page 172

Cities and Towns

Addison A2
Albany C1
Ascutney C4
Averill D1
Bakersfield B1
Barnard B3
Barnet C2
Barre C2
Basin Harbor A2
Beecher Falls D1
Bellows Falls C4
Bennington A5
Benson A3
Berlin B2
Bethel B3
Bloomfield D1
Bradford C3
Brandon A3
Brattleboro B5
Bristol A2
Brookfield B2
Burlington A2
Cabot C2
Cambridge B1
Castleton A3
Cavendish B4
Charlotte A2
Chelsea C3
Colchester A1
Concord D2
Danby B4
Danville C2
Dorset A4
East Burke D1
East Haven D1
East Middlebury A3
East Randolph B3
Eden B1
Enosburg Falls B1
Essex A1
Essex Junction A1
Evansville C1
Fair Haven A3
Fairfax B1
Fairfield B1
Fairlee C3
Franklin B1
Gallup Mills D1
Gaysville B3
Georgia Center A1
Grafton B4
Granby D1
Grand Isle A1
Groton C2
Guildhall D1
Guilford B5
Hancock B3
Hanover C3
Hardwick C2
Hartford C3
Hartland C3
Hartwellville A5
Heartwellville A5
Highgate Center A1
Hinesburg A2
Hortonia A3
Hubbardton A3
Hyde Park B1
Irasburg C1
Irasville B3
Jacksonville B5
Jamaica B4
Jeffersonville B1
Johnson B1
Keeler Bay A1
Larrabees Point A3
Lemington D1

Key

Londonderry B4
Lowell C1
Lyndon C1
Lyndonville C1
McIndoe Falls C2
Marlboro B5
Mendon B3
Middlebury A2
Middlesex B2
Milton A1
Monkton A2
Montgomery B1
Montgomery Center B1
Montpelier, *capital* B2
Morgan B1
Morrisville B1
Moscow B1
Newbury C2
Newfane B4
New Haven A2
Newport C1
North Bennington A5
Northfield B2
North Hero A1
North Wolcott C1
Norton D1
Orange C2
Panton A2
Peacham C2
Pittsfield B3
Pittsford A3
Plainfield C2
Plymouth B3
Pompanoosuc C3
Post Mills C3
Poultney A3
Pownal A5
Proctor A3
Putney B5
Randolph B3
Readsboro B5
Richford B1
Richmond A2
Rochester B3
Roxbury B2
Rutland B3
St. Albans A1
St. Johnsbury C2
Searsburg B5
Shaftsbury A4
Sharon C3
Shelburne A2
Sheldon B1
Shoreham A3
South Burlington A2
South Hero A1
Springfield C4
Stamford A5
Starksboro A2
Swanton A1
Tinmouth A4
Troy C1
Tunbridge C3
Tyson B4
Underhill B1
Vergennes A2
Vernon B5
Vershire C3
Warren B2
Washington C2
Waterbury B2
Waterville B1
Wells River D1
West Burke D1
West Dover B5
West Haven A3
Westminster C4
Weston B4
West Pawlet A4
West Topsham C2
Wheelock C1
White River Junction C3
Williamsville B5
Wilmington B5
Windsor C4
Winooski A1
Wolcott C1
Woodford A5
Woodstock B3
Worcester C2

Other Features

Appalachian Natl. Scenic Trail A5
Black, *river* C1
Bomoseen, *lake* A3
Bread Loaf, *mt.* B2
Bromley, *mt.* B4
Camels Hump, *mt.* B2
Champlain, *lake* A1
Connecticut, *river* C3
Ellen, *mt.* B2
Equinox, *mt.* A4
Green, *mts.* B4
Harriman, *reservoir* B5
Jay Peak, *mt.* B1
Killington Peak, *mt.* B3
Lamoille, *river* B1
Mansfield, *mt.* B1
Marsh-Billings-Rockefeller N.H.P. B3
Mettawee, *river* A4
Missisquoi, *river* B1
Seymour, *lake* C1
Smugglers Notch, *pass* B1
Snow, *mt.* B5
Somerset, *reservoir* B4
Waterbury, *reservoir* B2
West, *river* B4
White, *river* B3
White Rocks N.R.A. B4
Willoughby, *lake* C1

Virginia .....page 173

Cities and Towns

Abingdon D1
Accomac M4
Achilles L5
Alberta H6
Alexandria J2
Allison Gap D1
Altavista E5
Amelia Court House H5
Amherst E4
Annandale M2
Appalachia B1
Appomattox F5
Arlington J2
Ashland H4
Baileys Crossroads M2
Bassett C6
Basye F2

Key

Bedford D5
Belleair L2
Belle Haven M4
Belle View M2
Bensley J5
Berryville H1
Big Stone Gap B1
Blacksburg B5
Blackstone H5
Bland A5
Bloxom M4
Bluefield A5
Bon Air H4
Bowling Green J3
Boyce G6
Boydron G6
Boykins J6
Bridgewater F3
Bristol D2
Brodnax G6
Brookneal F5
Brunswick H6
Buckingham F4
Buena Vista E4
Burke L2
Burkeville G5
Callands D6
Cape Charles L5
Castlewood C1
Centreville J2
Charles City J5
Charlotte Court House F5
Charlottesville G3
Chase City G6
Chatham E6
Cheriton M5
Chesapeake L6
Chester J5
Chesterfield H5
Chilhowie E1
Chincoteague M4
Christiansburg C5
Chula H5
Claremont K5
Clifton Forge D4
Clinchco C1
Clintwood C1
Collinsville D6
Colonial Beach K3
Colonial Hts. J5
Concord E5
Courtland J6
Covington C4
Crewe G5
Crimora F3
Crystal City M2
Crystal Hill F6
Culpeper G3
Cumberland G4
Dale City J2
Danville E6
Dendron K5
Dillwyn G4
Dinwiddie H5
Drakes Branch F6
Dublin B5
Dumfries J2
Dungannon C1
Eastville M5
Elkton G3
Emory D1
Emporia H6
Ewing A1
Fairfax J2
Fairfax Station L2
Falls Church M2
Falmouth J3
Farmville G5
Ferrum D6
Figsboro D6
Fincastle D4
Fishersville F3
Flint Hill G2
Floyd C6
Forest E5
Fort Mitchell G6
Franconia M2
Franklin K6
Fredericksburg J3
Fries B6
Front Royal G2
Galax B6
Gate City C1
Glade Spring D1
Gloucester K5
Gloucester Point L5
Goochland H4
Gordonsville G3
Goshen D4
Gretna E6
Grottoes F3
Groveton M2
Grundy D1
Halifax F6
Hampton L5
Hanover J4
Harrisonburg F3
Harrogate A1
Heathsville L4
Hollins D5
Hopewell J5
Horse Pasture D6
Huntington M2
Hurt E5
Independence A6
Isle of Wight K6
Jetersville G5
Jonesville B1
Kenbridge G6
King and Queen Courthouse K4
King George J3
Kings Park L2
King William K4
Lancaster L4
Lawrenceville H6
Lebanon D1
Leesburg H1
Lexington E4
Lincolnia M2
Louisa G4
Lovingston F4
Lunenburg G6
Luray G2
Lynchburg E5
McLean M1
Madison G3
Manakin H4
Manassas J2
Manassas Park J2
Mantua L2
Marion A6

Key

Martinsville D6
Mathews L5
Mechanicsville A5
Mechanicsburg A5
Meherrin G5
Millboro D3
Monterey D3
Montross K3
Mount Jackson F2
Narrows B5
New Castle K4
New Kent K4
New Market F2
Newport News L6
Newport J6
Norfolk L6
North Springfield M2
Norton C1
Nottoway Court House L2
Oakton L2
Onancock M4
Orange G3
Palmyra G4
Pearisburg B5
Petersburg J5
Peterstown A5
Pimmit Hills M1
Poquoson L5
Portsmouth L6
Powhatan H4
Prince George J5
Pulaski B5
Purcellville H1
Radford B5
Raven D1
Reston J2
Richlands D1
Richmond, *capital* J4
Ridgeway D6
Roanoke D5
Rocky Mount D6
Rustburg E5
Ruther Glen J4
Salem C5
Saltville D1
Saluda K4
Shenandoah F3
Smithfield K6
South Boston F6
South Hill G6
Spotsylvania H3
Springfield M2
Spring Hill M1
Stafford J3
Stanardsville G3
Staunton E3
Sterling J1
Stony Creek J5
Strasburg G2
Stuart D6
Stuarts Draft E3
Suffolk K5
Surry K5
Sussex J6
Tappahannock K4
Tazewell A5
Timberville F2
Triangle J2
Tysons Corner M1
Vale L1
Verona E3
Victoria G6
Vienna L1
Virginia Beach M6
Warm Springs D3
Warrenton H2
Warsaw K4
Washington G2
Waverly J5
Waynesboro F3
Weber City C1
Wellington M3
West Point K4
West Springfield L2
Williamsburg K5
Winchester G1
Wise C1
Woodbridge J2
Woodstock F2
Wytheville A6
Yorktown K5

Other Features

Allegheny, *mts.* D3
Anna, *lake* H3
Appalachian, *mts.* C5
Appomattox Court House N.H.P. F5
Arlington Natl. Cem. M2
Assateague Island Natl. Seashore M4
Booker T. Washington N.M. D5
Charles, *cape* M5
Chesapeake, *bay* L5
Colonial Natl. Hist. Park K5
Fredericksburg & Spotsylvania
  Natl. Mil. Park H3
Gaston, *lake* G6
George Washington Birthplace N.M. K3
Henry, *cape* M6
Iron, *mts.* A6
James, *river* K5
John H. Kerr, *reservoir* F6
Manassas Natl. Battlefield Park H2
Mount Rogers Natl. Rec. Area A6
Petersburg Natl. Battlefield J5
Potomac, *river* J3
Rappahannock, *river* J3
Rogers, *mt.* E3
Shenandoah, *mts.* E3
Shenandoah, *river* F3
Shenandoah Natl. Park G2
Smith Mtn., *lake* D5
York, *river* K5

Washington .....page 174

Cities and Towns

Aberdeen C4
Amboy D5
Anacortes C2
Arlington D2
Asotin J4
Auburn D3
Bangor C3
Battle Ground D5
Bellingham C2
Belvedere H2
Benton City G4
Bethel C3
Birch Bay C2
Blaine C1
Boardman G5

192 WASHINGTON–WYOMING

Key
Bothel D3
Bremerton D3
Brewster G2
Bridgeport G3
Bucoda D4
Burien B2
Burlington D2
Camas D5
Cashmere F3
Castle Rock D4
Cathlamet C4
Central Park C3
Centralia D4
Chehalis D4
Chelan F3
Cheney J3
Chewelah J2
Clarkston J4
Cle Elum F3
Clinton D3
Colfax J4
College Place H4
Colville J2
Connell H4
Cosmopolis C4
Country Homes J3
Coupeville D2
Davenport H3
Dayton J4
Deer Park J3
Dusty J4
Eastgate B2
Easton E3
Eastsound D2
East Wenatchee F3
Eatonville D4
Edmonds D3
Ellensburg F3
Elma C3
Elmer City H3
Enumclaw E3
Ephrata G3
Everett D2
Everson D2
Fall City E3
Federal Way D3
Ferndale D2
Fords Prairie C4
Forks B3
Four Lakes J3
Friday Harbor C2
Fruitvale F4
Goldendale F5
Gorst A2
Grandview G4
Granger F4
Hoquiam C3
Inglewood C2
Kelso D4
Kenmore B1
Kennewick G4
Kent D3
Kettle Falls H2
Kirkland D3
Lacey D3
La Grande D4
Lake Stevens D2
Leavenworth F3
Lexington D4
Longmire E4
Longview D4
Lynden D2
Mabton G4
McKenna D4
McMurray D2
Markham C4
Marysville D2
Medical Lake J3
Medina B2
Mercer Island D3
Merritt F3
Monroe D3
Montesano C4
Moses Lake G3
Mount Vernon D2
Mukilteo D3
Newhalem E2
Newport J2
Newport Hills B2
Normandy Park B2
North Bend E3
Oak Harbor D2
Ocean Park B4
Ocean Shores B3
Okanogan G2
Olalla B2
Olympia, *capital* D3
Omak G2
Opportunity J3
Orchards D5
Oroville G2
Othello G4
Oysterville B4
Pasco G4
Plymouth G5
Pomeroy J4
Port Angeles C2
Porter C4
Port Hadlock D2
Port Ludlow D3
Port Orchard D3
Port Townsend D2
Poulsbo D3
Prosser G4
Pullman J4
Puyallup D3
Quincy G3
Raymond C4
Redmond D3
Renton D3
Republic H2
Richland G4
Richmond Highlands B1
Ridgefield D5
Ritzville H3
St. John J3
Seabeck A2
Sea-Tac D3
Seattle D3
Sedro-Woolley D2
Selah F4
Sequim C2
Shelton C3
Silverton E2
Skyway B2
Smokey Point D2
Snohomish D3
Snoqualmie E3
South Bend C4
Southworth B2
Spanaway D3
Spokane J3

Key
Stanwood D2
Stevenson E5
Sultan E3
Sumas D2
Sumner D3
Sunnyside F4
Suquamish A1
Tacoma D3
Tekoa J3
Tenino D4
Tiger J2
Toppenish F4
Tracyton A2
Trentwood J3
Tukwila B2
Tumwater D4
Union Gap F4
University Place D3
Vancouver D5
Vashon B2
Walla Walla H4
Wapato F4
Warden G4
Washougal D5
Waterville F3
Wenatchee F3
Westport B4
West Richland G4
White Center B2
White Salmon E5
Winslow D3
Woodinville B1
Woodland D5
Yakima F4
Yelm D4
Zillah F4

Other Features

Adams, *mt.* E4
Bainbridge, *island* B2
Baker, *mt.* E2
Banks, *lake* G3
Cascade, *range* E4
Chelan, *lake* F2
Chewuch, *river* F2
Columbia, *river* G2
Copper Butte, *mt.* H2
Cowlitz, *river* E4
Disappointment, *cape* B4
Elliott, *bay* B2
Flattery, *cape* B2
Franklin D. Roosevelt, *lake* H2
Glacier Peak, *mt.* E2
Grays, *harbor* B4
Green, *river* E3
Hanford Reach Natl. Mon. G4
Hood, *canal* C3
Kettle River, *range* H2
Klickitat, *river* E4
Lake Chelan Natl. Rec. Area F2
Lake Roosevelt Natl. Rec. Area H2
Lewis, *river* E4
Mt. Baker Natl. Rec. Area E2
Mount Rainier Natl. Park E4
Mt. St. Helens Natl. Vol. Mon. D4
North Cascades Natl. Park E2
Okanogan, *river* G2
Olympic, *mts.* C3
Olympic Natl. Park C3
Olympus, *mt.* C3
Omak, *mt.* G2
Orcas, *island* D2
Oregon Butte, *mt.* J4
Ozette, *lake* B2
Pasayten, *river* F2
Pend Oreille, *river* J2
Potholes, *reservoir* G3
Priest Rapids, *lake* G4
Puget, *sound* B1, D2
Rainier, *mt.* E4
Riffe, *lake* D4
Rimrock, *lake* E4
Ross, *lake* F2
Ross Lake Natl. Rec. Area F2
Sacajawea, *lake* H4
St. Helens, *mt.* D4
San Juan, *island* C2
Sanpoil, *river* H2
Selkirk, *mts.* J2
Skagit, *river* E2
Skykomish, *river* E3
Snake, *river* J4
Spokane, *river* H3
Strait of Juan de Fuca B2
Stuart, *mt.* F3
Umatilla, *lake* G5
Vashon, *island* B2
Wallula, *lake* H4
Washington, *lake* B1
Wenatchee, *lake* F3
Wenatchee, *mts.* F3
Wenatchee, *river* F3
White, *pass* E4
Whitman Mission Natl. Hist. Site H4
Willapa, *bay* B4
Yakima, *river* F4
Yale, *lake* D4

West Virginia .... page 175

Cities and Towns

Ansted D4
Barboursville B4
Beckley D5
Belington G2
Berkeley Springs K1
Bluefield D6
Bradley D5
Bridgeport F2
Buckhannon F3
Charles Town L2
Charleston, *capital* C4
Chester K4
Circleville G3
Clarksburg F2
Clay D4
Clendenin D4
Craigsville E4
Davis H2
East Liverpool K4
Edray F4
Eleanor C3
Elizabeth D2
Elkins G3
Fairmont F2
Fayetteville D4
Fort Ashby J2
Franklin H3
Gary C6
Glenville E3
Grafton F2

Key
Grantsville D3
Hamlin B4
Harpers Ferry L2
Harrisville D2
Hinton E5
Huntington B4
Hurricane B4
Inwood K2
Kenova A4
Keyser J2
Kingwood G2
Lewisburg F5
Logan C5
Madison C4
Mannington F1
Marlinton F4
Marmet C4
Martinsburg L2
Matewan B5
Middlebourne E2
Milton B4
Montgomery D4
Moorefield J2
Morgantown G1
Moundsville K6
Mt. Hope D5
Mullens D5
Newburg G2
New Cumberland K4
New Haven C3
New Martinsville E1
New Milton E2
Nitro C4
Oak Hill D5
Oceana C5
Orma D3
Paden City E1
Parkersburg C2
Parsons G2
Pennsboro E2
Petersburg H3
Peterstown E6
Philippi F2
Pineville C5
Point Pleasant B3
Princeton D6
Rainelle E5
Ravenswood C3
Reedy D3
Richwood E4
Ripley C3
Romney J2
Ronceverte F5
Rupert E5
St. Albans C4
St. Marys D2
Salem E2
Shady Spring D5
Shepherdstown L2
Shinnston F2
Sistersville E1
Slanesville J2
South Charleston C4
Spencer D3
Summersville E4
Sutton E3
Terra Alta G2
Union E5
Vienna C2
Wayne B4
Webster Springs F4
Weirton K5
Welch C6
Wellsburg K5
Wellsville K4
West Milford F2
Weston F2
West Union E2
Wheeling K5
White Sulphur Springs F5
Whitesville C5
Williamson B5
Williamstown D2
Winfield C3

Other Features

Allegheny, *mts.* G4
Big Sandy, *river* B5
Bluestone, *lake* E5
Bluestone Natl. Scenic River E5
Gauley River Natl. Rec. Area D4
Greenbrier, *river* F4
Harpers Ferry Natl. Hist. Park L2
Kanawha, *river* B3
New River Gorge Natl. River D5
Ohio, *river* E1
Potomac, *river* J2
Shenandoah, *mts.* H4
Spruce Knob, *mt.* G3
Spruce Knob-Seneca Rocks N.R.A. H3
Sutton, *lake* E3

Wisconsin .... page 176

Cities and Towns

Abbotsford C4
Adams D5
Algoma F4
Alma B4
Altoona B4
Amery A3
Antigo D3
Appleton E4
Arcadia B4
Ashland C2
Augusta B4
Baldwin A4
Balsam Lake A3
Baraboo D5
Barronett A3
Bayside F1
Beaver Dam E5
Belleville D6
Bellevue F4
Beloit D6
Bennett B2
Berlin E5
Bethesda D2
Big Bend E2
Black River Falls C4
Bloomer B3
Bloomville D3
Boscobel C5
Breed E3
Brillion E4
Brodhead D6
Brookfield E1
Brown Deer F1
Bryant D3
Buena Vista D1
Burlington E6

Key
Butler E1
Cadott B4
Cameron B3
Canton B3
Carlsville F4
Cedarburg F5
Cedar Grove F5
Chelsea C3
Chetek B3
Chili C4
Chilton E4
Chippewa Falls B4
Cleveland F5
Clinton E6
Clintonville E4
Colby C4
Coloma D5
Columbus D5
Conrath B3
Cornell B3
Cornucopia B2
Crandon E3
Crestview F2
Cuba City C6
Cudahy F2
Cumberland A3
Darlington C6
De Forest D5
De Pere E4
Delafield D1
Delavan E6
Denmark F4
Dodgeville C6
Duplainville E1
Durand B4
Eagle River D3
Easton D5
East Troy E6
Eau Claire B4
Edgar C4
Edgerton D6
Elkhorn E6
Ellsworth A4
Elm Grove E1
Elroy C5
Evansville D6
Fennimore C6
Florence E3
Fond du Lac E5
Forestville F4
Fort Atkinson E6
Fox Lake E5
Fox Point F1
Fredonia F5
Friendship D5
Galesville B4
Genesee D2
Genesee Depot D2
Germantown E5
Gillett E4
Glendale F1
Grafton F5
Green Bay F4
Greendale F2
Greenfield F2
Green Lake E5
Greenleaf E4
Hales Corners E2
Hamburg D3
Harrison D3
Hartford E5
Hartland D1
Hayward B2
Hillsboro C5
Hollister E3
Holmen B5
Horicon E5
Hortonville E4
Howard E4
Howards Grove F5
Hudson A4
Hurley C2
Husher F2
Jackson E5
Janesville D6
Jefferson E6
Juda D6
Jump River C3
Juneau E5
Kaukauna E4
Kenosha F6
Keshena E4
Kewaskum E5
Kewaunee F4
Kiel E5
Kneeland F2
Lac du Flambeau D3
La Crosse B5
Ladysmith B3
Lake Delton D5
Lake Geneva E6
Lake Mills E5
Lampson B3
Lancaster C6
La Pointe C2
Little Chute E4
Lodi D5
Lomira E5
McFarland D6
Madison, *capital* D5
Maiden Rock A4
Manitowish C2
Manitowoc F4
Marathon City D4
Marinette F3
Markesan E5
Marshfield C4
Mason B2
Mattoon D3
Mauston C5
Mayville E5
Medford C3
Menasha E4
Menomonee Falls E5
Menomonie B4
Mequon F5
Merrill D3
Middleton D5
Milton E6
Milwaukee F5
Mineral Point C6
Mishicot F4
Modena B4
Mole Lake E3
Mondovi B4
Monona D5
Monroe D6
Montello D5
Montfort C6
Mosinee D4
Muscoda C5
Muskego E6

Key
Neenah E4
Neillsville C4
Nekoosa D4
New Berlin E6
New Glarus D6
New Holstein E5
New Lisbon C5
New London E4
New Richmond A3
Newton F5
Niagara F3
North Fond du Lac E5
North Lake D1
North Prairie D2
Oak Creek F6
Oconto F4
Oconto Falls E4
Odanah C2
Omro E5
Onalaska B5
Oostburg F5
Oregon D6
Osceola A3
Oshkosh E4
Paddock Lake E6
Palmyra E6
Park Falls C3
Pell Lake E6
Peshtigo F3
Pewaukee E1
Phillips C3
Platteville C6
Pleasant Prairie F6
Plover D4
Plymouth F5
Polonia D4
Portage D5
Port Edwards D4
Porterfield F3
Port Washington F5
Port Wing B2
Poynette D5
Prairie du Chien B5
Prairie du Sac D5
Prescott A4
Princeton D5
Pulaski E4
Racine F6
Randolph E5
Random Lake F5
Raymond F2
Reedsburg D5
Rhinelander D3
Rice Lake B3
Richland Center C5
Ridgeway D5
Ripon E5
River Falls A4
River Hills F1
Rothschild D4
St. Croix Falls A3
St. Francis F2
Sauk City D5
Saukville F5
Saylesville D2
Schofield D4
Shawano E4
Sheboygan F5
Sheboygan Falls F5
Shell Lake B3
Shorewood F1
Slinger E5
South Milwaukee F2
Sparta C5
Spencer C4
Spooner B3
Spread Eagle E3
Spring Green C5
Stanley C4
Stevens Point D4
Stonebank D1
Stoughton D6
Sturgeon Bay F4
Sturtevant F6
Summit Lake D3
Sun Prairie D5
Superior A2
Sussex E1
Tabor F2
Thompsonville F2
Thorp C4
Tomah C5
Tomahawk D3
Tony C3
Two Rivers F4
Verona D6
Viroqua C5
Wales D2
Wanderoos A3
Washburn C2
Watertown E5
Waukesha E6
Waunakee D5
Waupaca D4
Waupun E5
Wausau D4
Wautoma D4
Wauwatosa E1
Wauzeka C5
West Allis F6
West Bend E5
Westby C5
West Milwaukee F1
Weyauwega E4
Whitehall B4
Whitewater E6
Williams Bay E6
Wind Lake E2
Wind Point G2
Winneconne E4
Wisconsin Dells D5
Wisconsin Rapids D4
Wrightstown E4

Other Features

Apostle Islands Natl. Lakeshore C1
Big Muskego, *lake* E2
Castle Rock, *lake* D5
Chetek, *lake* B3
Chippewa, *lake* B3
Door, *peninsula* F4
Dubay, *lake* D4
Flambeau, *river* C3
Green, *bay* F4
Madeline, *island* C2
Michigan, *lake* G5
Mississippi, *river* B5
Outer, *island* C1
Peshtigo, *river* E3
Petenwell, *lake* D4
Pewaukee, *lake* D1
Poygan, *lake* E4
St. Croix Natl. Scenic Riverway
Sand, *island*
Spring, *lake*
Stockton, *island*
Superior, *lake*
Timms Hill, *mt.*
Winnebago, *lake*
Wisconsin, *river*
Wolf, *river*
Yellow, *river*

Wyoming .... page

Cities and Towns

Afton
Basin
Boxelder
Buffalo
Byron
Casper
Cheyenne, *capital*
Cody
Cokeville
Deaver
Douglas
Evanston
Evansville
Gillette
Glenrock
Green River
Greybull
Jackson
Kemmerer
Lander
Laramie
Lovell
Lusk
Lyman
Medicine Bow
Mills
Newcastle
Pinedale
Powell
Rawlins
Reliance
Riverton
Rock Springs
Saratoga
Sheridan
Sundance
Thermopolis
Torrington
Wamsutter
Wheatland
Worland

Other Features

Absaroka, *range*
Belle Fourche, *river*
Big Sandy, *river*
Bighorn, *lake*
Bighorn, *mts.*
Bighorn, *river*
Bighorn Canyon Natl. Rec. Area
Bridger Peak, *mt.*
Clarks Fork Yellowstone, *river*
Cloud Peak, *mt.*
Colter Peak, *mt.*
Continental Divide, *mt. ridge*
Devils Tower Natl. Monument
Elk, *mt.*
Flaming Gorge, *reservoir*
Flaming Gorge Natl. Rec. Area
Fort Laramie Natl. Hist. Site
Fossil Butte Natl. Monument
Francs Peak, *mt.*
Gannett Peak, *mt.*
Grand Teton, *mt.*
Grand Teton Natl. Park
Great Divide, *basin*
Green, *river*
Greybull, *river*
Jackson, *lake*
Laramie, *mts.*
Laramie, *river*
Laramie Peak, *mt.*
Little Bighorn, *river*
Little Missouri, *river*
Little Powder, *river*
Little Snake, *river*
Medicine Bow, *river*
North Platte, *river*
Nowood, *river*
Owl Creek, *mts.*
Pathfinder, *reservoir*
Powder, *river*
Rocky, *mts.*
Seminoe, *reservoir*
South Fork Cheyenne, *river*
South Fork Powder, *river*
Sweetwater, *river*
Teton, *river*
Tongue, *river*
Trout Peak, *mt.*
Whiskey Peak, *mt.*
Wind, *river*
Wind River, *range*
Yellowstone, *lake*
Yellowstone Natl. Park